D0742035

THE REICHSWEHR
AND POLITICS
1918 TO 1933

F. L. CARSTEN

THE REICHSWEHR AND POLITICS

1918 TO 1933

OXFORD
AT THE CLARENDON PRESS
1966

Oxford University Press, Ely House, London W. 1

GLASGOW NEW YORK TORONTO MELBOURNE WELLINGTON
CAPE TOWN SALISBURY IBADAN NAIROBI LUSAKA ADDIS ABABA
BOMBAY CALCUTTA MADRAS KARACHI LAHORE DACCA
KUALA LUMPUR HONG KONG

PREFACE

IN recent years, many books and articles have been published on the subject of 'the Reichswehr and Politics'. Yet, strangely enough, there has been no work that discusses the period of the Weimar Republic as a whole. The book by Harold J. Gordon ends in 1926, the year of Seeckt's dismissal; the book by Thilo Vogelsang begins in 1930, the year of the ascendancy of Schleicher. Both Professor Gordon Craig and Mr. Wheeler-Bennett treat the years 1918 to 1933 rather cursorily; in the latter book they figure as a kind of prelude to the Hitler period. But as little as the rise of Hitler was an inevitable outcome of German history, equally little can the relations between the army and the government in the years before 1933 be considered a prelude to the Third Reich. For the relations between a strong and indispensable army and the weak and changing governments of the Weimar era differed in principle from the relations between the army and a strong and popular government: popular not least with many generals on account of the rapid rearmament of Germany and the loudly proclaimed nationalism.

In addition, the wealth of primary source material in many German archives (in spite of the destruction of the *Heeresarchiv* at Potsdam during an allied air raid in April 1945) sheds much new light even on periods which have already been closely investigated. This applies in particular to the era when General von Seeckt was the undisputed leader of the German army: my interpretation of this period differs strongly from those of Professor Gordon and Mr. Wheeler-Bennett. To enlarge the picture, I have also made use of the German naval archives, which contain detailed evidence on the activities of the navy, and those of the German Foreign Office, which contain a wealth of documents on German-Russian military relations. The last years of the Weimar Republic, on the other hand, have been studied in minute detail, especially by Karl Dietrich Bracher, Wolfgang Sauer, and Thilo Vogelsang, and the present book owes much to their researches.

I am also greatly indebted to all those who have permitted me to use source material hitherto inaccessible, or who have drawn my attention to new sources: above all to Colonel Hermann Teske, the director of the *Militärarchiv* at Koblenz; to Colonel Hans Meier-Welcker, the director of the *Militärgeschichtliches Forschungsamt* at Freiburg im Breisgau; to Commander M. G. Saunders, R.N., of the Historical Section of the Admiralty; to Frau Oberstudienrätin Lotte Reinhardt, the daughter of General Reinhardt, and to the late Professor Fritz Ernst; to Dr. Friedrich Freiherr Hiller von Gaertringen, who permitted me to use the papers of Count Westarp; to Dr. Thilo Vogelsang, and to Dr. Walter Baum. Many former Reichswehr officers have willingly answered my questions, especially Lieutenant-General Paul Mahlmann, Major-General Curt Ulrich von Gersdorff, Colonel Hermann Teske, and Admiral Paul Zieb, and my thanks are due to them too. Dr. Volker Berghahn has made extracts from documents in the *Deutsches Zentralarchiv* at Potsdam and supplied me with valuable details about the papers of Gustav Stresemann from the files of the *Auswärtiges Amt.*

The German Academic Exchange Service and the School of Slavonic and East European Studies of the University of London have supported my researches in German archives by generous grants, without which this work would have been impossible for me. My greatest debt of gratitude, however, is due to my wife who for many years encouraged the progress of my work and helped me with her advice and criticism.

This book was first published, under the title *Reichswehr und Politik*, by Kiepenheuer & Witsch at Cologne. In the present version a certain amount of the documentary detail has been omitted; but some comment and new material (especially from the papers of General Lequis and of Major-General Ferdinand von Bredow) has been added.

F. L. C.

London, March 1965

CONTENTS

PART ONE

REVOLUTION AND COUNTER-REVOLUTION

I. TO WEIMAR AND VERSAILLES   3
    I. *Collapse of a World*   3
    II. *Soviets or National Assembly?*   12
    III. *The High Command and the Minister of War*   24
    IV. *To Sign or not to Sign?*   37

II. THE REICHSWEHR UNDER REINHARDT   49
    I. *New Conflicts about the Army Structure*   49
    II. *The Army and Politics*   58
    III. *With the White or with the Red Russians?*   66
    IV. *Against the Republican Führerbund and the Free
        Corps*   71
    V. *The Kapp Putsch*   78
    VI. *Seeckt's Nomination*   89
    VII. *The Purge*   93

PART TWO

THE SEECKT ERA

III. YEARS OF CONSOLIDATION   103
    I. *Seeckt's Personality*   103
    II. *Seeckt's First Months*   108
    III. *Seeckt and the Institutions of the Republic*   114
    IV. *Politics in Army and Navy*   124
    V. *The Pact with Russia*   135
    VI. *The Frontier Defence and Secret Military Pre-
        parations*   147

IV. YEAR OF CRISIS   153
    I. *Occupation of the Ruhr and Military Counter-
        Measures*   153
    II. *Seeckt and Stresemann*   163

III. *Seeckt and Lossow: the Bavarian Crisis*   173
IV. *Executive Power in the Hands of Seeckt*   186

V. THE END OF THE SEECKT ERA   196
    I. *Termination of the State of Emergency*   196
   II. *The Army and the Great Political Issues*   198
  III. *Seeckt and the Officer Corps*   209
  IV. *New Military Preparations*   220
    V. *Connexions with Russia*   232
  VI. *The Navy*   238
VII. *The Dismissal of Seeckt*   245

PART THREE

FROM THE REPUBLIC TO DICTATORSHIP

VI. MOVING TO THE LEFT?   253
    I. *The New Army Command and the Republic*   253
   II. *Military Measures and the Government*   265
  III. *Closer Relations with Russia*   275
  IV. *The Lohmann Scandal and the New Naval Command*   284
    V. *The Politics of Groener*   290
  VI. *The Rise of Schleicher*   296

VII. THE REICHSWEHR DURING THE CRISIS   309
    I. *Officers and National Socialists*   309
   II. *The Case of Scheringer and Ludin*   315
  III. *The Policy of the Army Command*   325
  IV. *The Fall of Groener*   338
    V. *The Frontier Defence and Reichswehr Expansion*   350

VIII. THE ESTABLISHMENT OF DICTATORSHIP   364
    I. *Schleicher and the Papen Government*   364
   II. *The Fall of Papen*   378
  III. *Schleicher as Chancellor*   384
  IV. *The Reichswehr and the Seizure of Power*   390
    V. *The Reichswehr and Politics*   397

BIBLIOGRAPHY   406

INDEX   413

PART ONE

REVOLUTION AND
COUNTER-REVOLUTION

———

'The officers must learn again to obey and stop
meddling with the confounded politics; politics
must be conducted by a few only—tenaciously
and silently. . . .'

(Lieutenant-General Groener on 9 July 1919)

I

TO WEIMAR AND VERSAILLES

1. *Collapse of a World*

THE kingdom of Prussia was made and formed by its army. From the reign of Frederick William I in the early eighteenth century the nobility of Prussia had its sons educated in the cadet schools where they were trained for their future profession: it was the honour and the duty of a nobleman to serve his king as an officer, a duty that was strictly enforced. During the Wars of Liberation against Napoleon the ranks of the officer corps were indeed opened to commoners, and some commoners rose to leading positions in the army; but the nobility remained the predominant group in the officer corps. Its attitude, code, and way of life were quickly adopted by officers of non-noble origin, many of whom were ennobled in the course of their careers. When Prussia, in the nineteenth century, became an industrial country its officer corps retained the characteristics of a pre-industrial world. The bond which linked the officer to the person of the 'Supreme War Lord' was a modern variant of the nexus between the vassal and his liege lord; the relationship remained the same throughout the great changes of the nineteenth century. Very much as in the British army, the guards and the cavalry regiments remained the *élite* units of the army, and very few commoners were admitted to their officer corps, though they predominated in the infantry regiments, in the artillery and the technical branches, and in the navy.

The bond between the officer corps and the king was forged and riveted by the three wars of unification between 1864 and 1871. It was the Prussian army that united Germany by its victories on the battlefield from Düppel to Sedan, in Denmark, Bohemia, and France—not the German middle class, whose efforts had been defeated by the Prussian army. It was a Prussian Germany that emerged in the Hall of Mirrors at

Versailles on 18 January 1871. By the expulsion of Austria from Germany the balance shifted more strongly still in favour of Prussia and her traditional institutions. The armies of the other German states were incorporated with the Prussian army or reorganized according to its model. In no other European country did the army exercise such a tremendous influence on the whole political and cultural life of the nation as in Prussia and Germany; its prestige cast a shadow over the country. The officers formed the first Estate, protecting the throne against all 'subversive' elements. But the army did not directly intervene in political affairs, the conduct of which was left to the professional politicians. The leaders of the army, the general staff, the officer corps stood outside political developments, which hardly touched them, and in which they showed surprisingly little interest. Politics were considered somewhat dirty, and unworthy of the attention of a gentleman. 'Politics were of equally small importance in the Military Academy and in the regiment, and my north-German comrades were no more political than myself. . . . The officers of the higher ranks had non-political heads too, and not only those who came from the cadet corps. . . .'[1]

This changed radically during the world war of 1914–18. The organization of war production and transport, the scarcity of essential raw materials and food, the mobilization of the masses, the incompetence of many civil authorities, the occupation of large territories in east and west, presented problems which forced the military to intervene in many spheres. The great victories of the German armies surrounded the leaders of the army, especially Hindenburg and Ludendorff, with a halo which even Moltke and Roon did not possess. In political matters too the power of the military High Command increased rapidly. It curtailed the influence of the Imperial government and the civil authorities; Hindenburg and Ludendorff became the *de facto* government of Germany and successfully imposed their will in home as well as in foreign affairs. They aimed at the annexation of wide areas in east and west and forced the defeated Russia to accept the conditions of the Treaty of Brest

[1] Wilhelm Groener, *Lebenserinnerungen*, ed. Friedrich Freiherr Hiller von Gaertringen, Göttingen, 1957, pp. 59–60. General Groener came from Swabia and was the son of a professional N.C.O. of the Württemberg army.

Litovsk. In Germany the military leaders were venerated. But the longer the war lasted the clearer it became that the hopes put in a collapse of the enemy were not going to be realized. The enormous efforts of the German nation to gain victory proved in vain. After the failure of the great offensives in France in the spring of 1918 the signs multiplied that Germany had lost the war. The vast superiority of the Entente powers, the appearance of strong, well-equipped American divisions, the progressive disintegration of the Habsburg Empire, the collapse of Germany's allies Bulgaria and Turkey, who were forced to conclude an armistice with their adversaries, proved that the end was near. In the west the German armies were forced on to the defensive and their enemies seized the initiative; even if Germany could hold out a little longer, this could not change the outcome of the war.

It was therefore entirely justified that the High Command of the army, at the end of September 1918, insisted that an immediate offer of peace be made to the western powers. The only question was why this had not been done much earlier, at a time when the defeat of the central powers was not yet obvious. The High Command was also responsible for the fact that public opinion in Germany was in no way prepared for this blow, because it had been fed for years with the hope of a 'victor's peace'. In view of the lost war as well as the distribution of political power in Germany, it would have been not only logical, but also politically wise, to let the High Command conduct the armistice negotiations. But this did not happen. It was left to the Catholic politician and secretary of state, Matthias Erzberger, who was thus saddled with the responsibility for this step. The successor of Ludendorff as First Quartermaster-General, Lieutenant-General Wilhelm Groener, wrote in his memoirs: 'I could only be pleased if the army and the High Command remained as little burdened as possible with these negotiations from which nothing good was to be expected. Thus Erzberger . . . was entrusted with the conduct of the armistice negotiations. . . .'[1] That the High Command in doing so followed a political plan, that it looked to the future and saw the consequences much more clearly than the badly informed and confused civil authorities, is indicated by another remark

[1] Ibid., p. 449.

of Groener: 'The High Command deliberately adopted the position of refuting the responsibility for the armistice and all later steps. Strictly legally seen, it did so without justification, but to me and my associates it was vital to keep the armour shining (*die Waffe blank*) and the general staff free of burdens for the future. . . .'[1]

Thus General Groener—a Württemberger by birth and not a 'Prussian'—played a decisive political part at the birth of the German Republic, as he was to do several times during the subsequent fourteen years. Again it was Groener, and not a Prussian general, who dared several days later, after the outbreak of revolution in Berlin and elsewhere in Germany, to tell the Emperor William the unvarnished truth—perhaps for the first time during the four years of the war. He intended to bring about the Emperor's abdication, and, what was to remain his principal objective during the following years, to preserve the unity of Germany. During his report to the Emperor on the morning of 9 November another officer, General Count von der Schulenburg, a scion of one of the oldest Brandenburg families, suggested that

the Emperor should abdicate as Emperor, but should remain king of Prussia and stay with the army as the king. The Emperor took up this idea. I was perturbed by this plan which would have meant the break-up of Germany. . . . When Schulenburg clung to the scheme, which also impressed the other officers present, I lost my patience in view of their lack of a sense of reality, and I declared more sharply than I might have done otherwise what I considered my duty to say: 'The army will march home in peace and order under its leaders and commanding generals, but not under the command of Your Majesty, for it stands no longer behind Your Majesty.' . . .[2]

This certainly corresponded with the facts and shows Groener's sober realism, an attitude of mind that had been reinforced by his long service as head of the railway section of the general staff. He also remained loyal to his aim of preserving the unity of Germany. Everything else must be subordinated to it, for no one could know at that moment whether Germany would

---

[1] Groener, *Lebenserinnerungen*, p. 466.
[2] Ibid., p. 460. Groener was unable to foresee that later he was to be bitterly attacked on account of this candid utterance, especially by former officers.

survive the storms of the coming months. German unity had existed for less than half a century: if the crown which had created the state disappeared, would Germany not dissolve into its component parts? Would not the south-German states use the opportunity to rid themselves of Prussian predominance?

There was another question which politically was even more important. At the beginning of November the sailors of Kiel and Wilhelmshaven had mutinied, hoisted the red flag on the battleships, and formed sailors' councils. The authority of the naval officers had gone. From the ports the torch of revolution was carried to western and southern Germany; everywhere workers' and soldiers' councils were formed. It was merely a question of time and the whole of Germany would be submerged by the revolutionary wave. What had happened in Russia in February 1917 occurred now in Germany. Many thousands looked towards Soviet Russia and hoped that it would bring about the realization of the ideals of socialism. Would not—as the Russian October revolution had followed upon the February revolution—the German revolution pass into more and more radical phases? Would not Karl Liebknecht and Rosa Luxemburg, the leaders of the Spartacus League, supplant the moderate socialist leaders, Ebert and Scheidemann? Would not the army follow the example of the navy? In occupied Russia many thousands of German soldiers had come into touch with Bolshevism; since the outbreak of the Russian revolution Bolshevik propagandists tried with all their strength to bring about a fraternization between the German and Russian armies. There was ample evidence that their efforts had not been entirely in vain.

In this situation it became a vital political test, an opportunity to prove the mettle of the officer corps, whether it would succeed in leading back the units from the western front under their old leaders and under the guidance of the general staff. It also became a question which was to decide the political future of Germany. Groener's self-confidence and the pride which animated the officer corps were reflected in his declaration of 9 November that the army would march back in peace and order under its leaders and its generals. A French historian of the German army wrote full of admiration: 'Who, in the Germany of that time, could have accomplished such a magnificent performance, if not the general staff? The central government? The revolutionaries? In view of this triumph of technique and of authority over the spirit of disorder and indiscipline the officer corps regained its old self-confidence. . . . Psychologically the retreat meant a victory for the officer corps. . . .'[1] This resurrection of the old pride and the old *esprit de corps* were absolutely essential, not only because of the revolutionary unrest and the mutinies in the navy. Especially in the officer corps of the navy 'the reproach of having started the revolution of 1918 through the naval mutiny . . . caused a trauma that it never overcame. . . .'[2]

But the abdication of the Emperor was 'not a mere change of the form of government. It was—at least for the Prussian army —the collapse of the world. The army had been "royal", i.e. linked indissolubly with the person of the king. . . . This army was inconceivable without the king. . . .'[3] The Prussian officer was tied by bonds of special loyalty to the monarchy and to the bearer of the crown, to whom alone he was responsible.[4] Under William I this had been a bond of personal trust, made particularly close by the battles of three victorious wars. Under William II every officer remained linked to the person of the 'Supreme War Lord' through his oath, which enforced unconditional obedience to the Emperor.[5] The officers felt they were his loyal paladins; they had a relationship to him that was quite different from that of his other subjects. Thus the officer corps in November 1918 was suddenly deprived of the spiritual and ideological centre on which its whole existence rested.[6] The abdication of the Emperor, even the south-German Groener remarked, 'removed the basis of the existence of the officers, their guiding principle. They had to be shown an aim that was worthy of the effort and gave back to them their inner security. . . .'[7]

The revolutionary upheavals deeply depressed a younger

[1] J. Benoist-Méchin, *Histoire de l'armée allemande*, i, Paris, 1936, pp. 77–78.

[2] Walter Baum, 'Marine, Nationalsozialismus und Widerstand', *Vierteljahrshefte für Zeitgeschichte*, xi, 1963, p. 44. This 'trauma' was to have important results for the political attitude of the navy.

[3] Erich von Manstein, *Aus einem Soldatenleben*, Bonn, 1958, p. 51.

[4] Karl Demeter, *Das deutsche Offizierkorps in Gesellschaft und Staat*, Frankfurt, 1962, p. 171.

[5] Article 64 of the German Constitution of 16 Apr. 1871.

[6] Demeter, op. cit., p. 172.   [7] Groener, op. cit., p. 467.

very gifted officer, Major Ludwig Beck, who one day was to become chief of the general staff and to resign from this post as a protest against Hitler's plans of aggression. 'What we all without exception have lived through during the last weeks', he wrote at the end of November, 'is so enormous that one often believes one is still dreaming. At the most difficult moment of the war the . . . long-prepared revolution has attacked our rear. . . . I do not know of any revolution in history that has been undertaken in so cowardly a manner. . . . It is poisonous if the people in the rear, most of whom never heard a shot, . . . fabricate a contrast between officer and private soldier. And it is the worst thing they can do, to undermine the authority of the officer; it leads directly into anarchy. . . . For an officer like myself and many thousands who live through this, the decline of our army is something dreadful. . . .'[1] The characteristic part of this letter is not so much the conviction that a catastrophe had occurred, as this was also felt by von Manstein and other officers. But subconsciously Beck already used the counter-poison, the idea on the basis of which the officers' destroyed pride was to revive: the 'undefeated army' had been attacked 'from the rear' by the revolutionaries, the revolution had been brought about by 'people in the rear, most of whom never heard a shot' during the war, traitors to their own country. If that was the case, the High Command and the officer corps were indeed free from blame.

The questions asked by Major Beck, above all that of the maintenance of the officers' authority and the decline into 'chaos', were equally put by the High Command and by other officers. As early as 9 November Major Jarosch, who was stationed in Kiev, wrote in his diary that the real problem was 'whether it would be possible to prevent the plunge into anarchy'.[2] On the following day Field-Marshal von Hindenburg himself sent a telegram to all army groups:

Since the movement to form soldiers' councils has already penetrated into the field army and in my opinion can no longer be

[1] Letter of 28 Nov. 1918: Wolfgang Foerster, *Ein General kämpft gegen den Krieg—Aus nachgelassenen Papieren des Generalstabchefs Ludwig Beck*, Munich, 1949, pp. 12–14.

[2] Quoted by Friedrich Freiherr Hiller von Gaertringen, '"Dolchstoß"-Diskussion und "Dolchstoß-Legende" im Wandel von vier Jahrzehnten', *Geschichte und Gegenwartsbewußtsein*, Festschrift Hans Rothfels, Göttingen, 1963, p. 128.

stopped by resistance, it is necessary to get the movement into the officers' hands. For this purpose councils of trusted men (*Vertrauens-räte*) are to be formed in all companies, batteries, squadrons, etc. . . . These councils should be used by the commanding officers for closest co-operation in all economic and social questions, so that order can be preserved within the army. The command over the troops, however, has to remain firmly in the hands of the military authorities. . . . It may be announced that the High Command intends to co-operate with the Chancellor Ebert, hitherto the leader of the moderate Social Democrats, to prevent the expansion of terrorist Bolshevism into Germany. . . .[1]

In the place of the dangerous soldiers' councils, which might try to curtail the officers' authority, innocuous *Vertrauensräte* were to be formed whose competence was to be limited to economic and social questions. In this form the councils would not be an element of decomposition of the military order, but would on the contrary help towards the maintenance of the officers' authority. In contrast with the home army no soldiers' councils were constituted in the field army; it marched back across the Rhine under its old flags and its old officers. Groener was proved right. A mutiny such as had occurred in the navy did not take place in the army.

Meanwhile in Berlin Ebert had not become 'chancellor', but a new, entirely socialist, government was formed, with three moderate and three radical Social Democrats as members;[2] it was confirmed in office by a mass meeting of the Berlin workers' and soldiers' councils on 10 November. It seemed as if the Russian development would be repeated in Germany. A proclamation unanimously adopted by the same meeting declared:

Germany is a republic, a socialist republic. . . . The bearers of political power are the workers' and soldiers' councils. . . . The workers' and soldiers' council is convinced that a similar revolution will occur in the whole world. . . . It remembers with admiration the Russian workers and soldiers who have shown the path to revolution; it is proud that the German workers and soldiers have

[1] Otto-Ernst Schüddekopf, *Das Heer und die Republik*, Hanover and Frankfurt, 1955, no. 1, pp. 19–20.

[2] The radicals during the war had formed their own party, the Independent Social Democrats.

followed them and have thus retained the old glory of being the vanguard of the International. . . . Long live the German Socialist Republic![1]

It was in the evening of the same day, after Ebert's return from the mass meeting, that he and General Groener had a telephone conversation of historic importance:

In the evening I 'phoned the *Reichskanzlei* and told Ebert that the army put itself at the disposal of his government, that in return for this the Field-Marshal and the officer corps expected the support of the government in the maintenance of order and discipline in the army. The officer corps expected the government to fight against Bolshevism and was ready for the struggle. Ebert accepted my offer of an alliance. . . .[2]

The new government was weak and disunited—sharp differences separating the moderate from the radical Social Democrats. It had no instrument of power at its disposal. The Prussian minister of war, General Scheüch, appointed the socialist deputy Otto Wels commandant of Berlin,[3] but no reliable troops were available in the capital. These could only be furnished by the High Command of the army; it was thus able to negotiate with Ebert as an equal and to make its support dependent upon conditions, on the fulfilment of which it insisted later. Even if the word 'alliance' was not used over the telephone during their historic conversation, it nevertheless corresponded with the facts. Groener, in any case, used the expression when he said that Hindenburg had 'allied' himself with Ebert only a few weeks later.[4] On 16 November the High Command issued *Richtlinien* (directives) which expressed similar ideas:

The High Command has . . . put itself at the disposal of the present government led by Ebert without any reservation. The power of this government is not yet fully consolidated. . . . The new government needs an element of power on which it can lean, and which gives it the required prestige against all subversion. Only a field army, which marches back united, can give to the present government

[1] Richard Müller, *Vom Kaiserreich zur Republik*, ii, Vienna, 1925, pp. 40, 234–5.
[2] Groener, *Lebenserinnerungen*, p. 467.
[3] On 10 Nov. 1918: Müller, op. cit. ii. 229.
[4] On 8 Dec. 1918 in a letter to Ebert: see below, p. 13.

the power and the respect that will secure it against *Putsche* of terrorists. . . .[1]

On the following day Groener wrote to his wife:

The Field-Marshal and I intend to support Ebert, whom I estimate as a straightforward, honest and decent character, as long as possible so that the cart does not slide further to the left. But where is the courage of the middle class? That a tiny minority could simply overthrow the whole German Empire together with its member states, is one of the saddest events of the whole history of the German nation. During four years the German people stood unbroken against a world of enemies—now it permits a handful of sailors to knock it down as if it were a dummy. . . .[2]

There was another reason why Groener sought the alliance with the new government. 'He thought he knew that a reconstruction of Germany was impossible without the help of the officer corps, and when on 9 November 1918 he let the monarchy go by default, it was precisely because he feared that it would otherwise drag the officer corps with it. . . .'[3] Groener himself wrote even more outspokenly in his memoirs: 'We hoped to transfer through our activity part of the power in the new state to the army and the officer corps; if we succeeded in this, the best and the strongest element of the old Prussia was saved for the new Germany, in spite of the revolution. . . .'[4] It is remarkable that a non-Prussian expressed this idea so clearly; but there remains some doubt whether Groener saw so clearly as early as November 1918.

II. *Soviets or National Assembly?*

A few weeks later the political balance had shifted so strongly in favour of the High Command that it put forward its programme like an ultimatum to the government. On 8 December Field-Marshal von Hindenburg, from his headquarters now established at Wilhelmshöhe near Cassel, sent a letter to Ebert

[1] Wolfgang Sauer, 'Das Bündnis Ebert-Groener', unpublished Ph.D. thesis, Free University of Berlin, 1956, p. 139.

[2] Dorothea Groener-Geyer, *General Groener, Soldat und Staatsmann*, Frankfurt, 1955, p. 117.

[3] Sauer, op. cit., p. 47.

[4] Groener, *Lebenserinnerungen*, pp. 468–9. But it has to be borne in mind that these were written considerably later. In Groener's diary this idea cannot be found.

which contained important military and political demands, above all the request that a National Assembly should be summoned immediately—to curtail or to eliminate the influence of the workers' and soldiers' councils.

If I address myself to you as follows, I am doing so because I have been told that you too as a loyal German love your fatherland more than anything else. . . .[1] In this sense I have allied myself with you to save the nation from threatening disaster. . . .

If the army is to remain a usable instrument of power in the hands of the government, the authority of the officer has to be restored immediately by every means, and politics have to be eliminated from the army. This requires a decree of the government which stipulates clearly:

1. The right to issue military commands rests solely with the commanding authorities (*Kommandobehörden*).
2. The authority of the officers and the regulations connected with it must be completely restored. In particular I should like to point out the absolute necessity of the duty to salute, which is of decisive importance for the maintenance of discipline. . . .
3. The soldiers' councils must disappear from the units; only *Vertrauensräte* are permissible, which should inform the commanding officers of the mood of the other ranks and transmit their wishes and complaints. A participation of the *Vertrauensräte* in the issuing of military orders is out of the question.

These are the military demands. But I feel also obliged to inform you about the mood which is shown in numerous communications from the field army and all other groups of the population. This amounts above all to the demand that the National Assembly must be summoned *at once*. . . .

I am convinced that only the following measures can help us to overcome the present difficulties:

1. Summoning of the National Assembly in the course of December.
2. Until then, or until the decisions of the National Assembly can be carried out, conduct of the administration solely by the government and the legitimate administrative organs.
3. So as to fulfil the justified wishes of the working class . . . qualified people of working-class origin should be attached to

---

[1] The formula is very cautious. Hindenburg himself was apparently not fully convinced of this fact.

the administrative authorities in an advisory capacity. These should not form an independent 'council', but should work together with the authorities. The need of 'workers' councils' would thus be eliminated.

4. The security service must be solely in the hands of the legal police organs and of the armed forces.

5. Safeguarding of the orders of the government by a reliable police force and, after the restoration of discipline, by the army.

In your hands lies the fate of the German nation. It will depend on your decision whether the German nation will rise once more. I am prepared, and with me the whole army, to support you without any reservation. . . .[1]

The immediate cause of this letter was the outbreak of a conflict in Berlin between General Lequis, commander of units returned from the western front which were to parade through the city, and the so-called Executive Council of the Berlin workers' and soldiers' councils. This had been elected on 10 November in the same meeting as the government and rivalled its influence; it consisted half of workers' and half of soldiers' deputies. The Executive Council feared the outbreak of unrest and demanded the postponement of the military parade, the entry of the divisions without ammunition, their accompaniment by stewards selected by the workers' organizations, and the participation of workers' columns. General Lequis and the High Command were in favour of a trial of strength and the refutation of these demands. If the Executive Council persisted Ebert should leave Berlin and transfer the seat of his government to army headquarters. Lequis was ordered 'to act independently, even against the orders of the government or of military authorities, including the minister of war. . . .'[2] The High Command sent Major von Harbou to Berlin, and he reported that the Prussian minister of war, General Scheüch, 'in his weakness and nervousness went so far as to concede on

---

[1] The letter was certainly written by Groener. Copies in Nachlaß Groener, box 22, no. 241, and Nachlaß Schleicher, no. 9, Bundesarchiv Koblenz; Büro des Reichspräsidenten, vol. 761, pp. 2–7, Deutsches Zentralarchiv Potsdam. Printed with some abbreviations in Groener, *Lebenserinnerungen*, p. 474, and Schüddekopf, *Heer und Republik*, no. 7, pp. 34–36.

[2] 'Tagebuch des Ersten Generalquartiermeisters ab 30. Okt. 1918–19. März 1919', under 9 Dec. 1918: Nachlaß Groener, box 5, no. 16i, Bundesarchiv Koblenz.

9 December the demands of the Executive Council. . . . When I pointed out to him that these demands were unacceptable, he replied that the High Command simply did not know what things were like in Berlin, that in his opinion it was impossible to refuse the demands, and that the whole scheme of staging a military parade was utterly wrong. If he (the war minister) had been informed in time he would have strongly advised against it. . . .' But Major von Harbou, by addressing the government in person, prevailed upon it to decline the demands of the Executive Council.[1] A clash was avoided and the troops could parade on 10 December. Yet this did not bring the desired success, for the soldiers—after their return to barracks—soon demobilized and went home; thus the government was still left without any reliable units. The conflicts between the High Command and the Prussian ministry of war, which was more inclined to make concessions, were soon to break out anew.

In the course of December the attention of the High Command continued to focus on the questions which were decisive for the future of Germany: was Germany to become a Soviet republic? was the future constitution to be decided upon by a national assembly elected by the people? what influence was to be exercised by the workers' and soldiers' councils? should they remain or disappear? how was the authority of the government and of the officers to be restored? It was only natural that the High Command, to secure its own authority, co-operated ever more closely with the moderate section of the government and its leader, Ebert. Groener himself has testified: 'we conferred daily about the necessary measures, over a secret wire between the *Reichskanzlei* and the High Command. . . .'[2] It became more and more obvious that the units which returned from the western front soon disintegrated when they reached their garrisons, that they came there under the influence of the political left and could no longer be used against political disorders emanating from it. Therefore the idea began to emerge, not to keep certain trusted units or classes with the colours—this soon proved an impossibility—but to recruit volunteer units from professional officers and soldiers of the old

[1] 'Notizen des Majors von Harbou über das Zusammenwirken mit dem Kriegsministerium', s.d. Nachlaß von Schleicher, no. 9, ibid.
[2] Groener, *Lebenserinnerungen*, p. 467.

army, to protect the government against the revolutionary left.

On 14 December Groener, in a report to the government, underlined the difficulties of the situation:

Everybody wants to get home. . . . The influence of local workers' and soldiers' councils induces whole units to enforce their departure out of turn. All authority of the officers and non-commissioned officers is being undermined by the propaganda of the Independents [Social Democrats] and the Spartacists. The High Command is powerless as the government does not counteract this. If the authority of the state is not established the army must disintegrate. The soldiers' councils must disappear and be replaced by *Vertrauensleute* elected by the units. The introduction of the right of combination makes the army unusable. The carrying of arms, badges of rank, and the duty to salute must be reintroduced. The position of the professional officers and non-commissioned officers must be secured. If an army on the old basis is impossible for internal political reasons, an army has to be created from volunteers![1]

According to a later testimony, it was one of Groener's closest collaborators, Major Kurt von Schleicher, who was one of the first to recognize the necessity 'to recruit new forces on the basis of voluntary service to protect the government as well as to secure the eastern frontiers'.[2] For the frontiers with the new Polish Republic were undefined; nobody knew where they would finally be established; and Polish and German irregulars were fighting for the possession of certain villages and districts. If the government decided to recruit volunteer units these would not only serve on the eastern frontier, but they could also play a decisive part in internal developments; indeed, they might become the principal source of political power.

To discuss the political situation a conference was held on 16 December in the building of the Great General Staff in Berlin; it was attended by the staff officers of the units which had returned to the area of Berlin, and was conducted by Majors von Harbou and von Schleicher from the High Command. One of them emphasized that the government was lacking all instruments of power: 'the Social Democrats now had to

---

[1] *Die Wirren in der Reichshauptstadt und im nördlichen Deutschland 1918–1920 (Darstellungen aus den Nachkriegskämpfen deutscher Truppen und Freikorps*, vi), Berlin, 1940, p. 11.

[2] Manstein, *Aus einem Soldatenleben*, p. 204.

experience it themselves that only force guarantees power and therewith the law. . . .' Some of the participants advocated leaving the field to the revolutionary forces, expecting a cure from the 'chaos' which in their opinion would inevitably occur. But the Generals Lequis and von Seeckt[1] opposed this violently: the officer corps must under no circumstances abdicate voluntarily—and their view prevailed.[2]

Four days later, on 20 December, another political conference was held in the building of the general staff. Major von Schleicher declared that, as the government was without any means of power, it had to be provided with them; thus volunteer units had to be recruited which would restore law and order. 'If the soldier helped towards this, it could be done relatively quickly. On the basis of the restored order the recovery of the economic life could take place. Only on the foundations of an economy rebuilt out of ruins would it be possible to reconstruct, after long, strenuous years, Germany's external power.' In contrast with this, General von Seeckt emphasized 'that an economy cannot be rebuilt in a country that is politically powerless. A country which at the moment was without the means of power to further its struggle had to mould its remaining military forces in such a way that it became desirable as an ally. As quickly as possible Germany must again become capable of concluding alliances (*bündnisfähig*).'[3] That was the programme which Seeckt realized in the years after 1920. In these conferences active officers for the first time discussed political problems—as they were to do again before the signing of the peace treaty and during the Kapp Putsch; they proved how strongly the officer corps was drawn into politics by the events of 9 November 1918. One of the participants wrote later: 'What began to stir again in the words of Seeckt was the spirit of the army.'[4] Yet it was not the old spirit of unconditional loyalty to the House of Hohenzollern; but a

---

[1] Major-General Hans von Seeckt had just returned to Berlin from Turkey; this was his first appearance after his return.

[2] Friedrich von Rabenau, *Seeckt—Aus seinem Leben*, Leipzig, 1940, p. 117, after his own notes written immediately after the conference; Sauer, *Bündnis Ebert-Groener*, pp. 174–5.

[3] Rabenau, *Seeckt*, p. 118, after his own contemporary notes; Walter Görlitz, *Der deutsche Generalstab, Geschichte und Gestalt*, Frankfurt, 1950, p. 300.

[4] Rabenau, *Seeckt*, pp. 118–19.

new—and much more political—wind was beginning to blow. It was no accident that the two most prominent political heads of the Reichswehr during the years of the Weimar Republic were the intellectual leaders of these officers' meetings.

On the day on which the first conference took place the first congress of the German workers' and soldiers' councils also met in Berlin. With regard to the military problem it brought about an exacerbation of the situation. On the other hand, the congress with an overwhelming majority voted in favour of holding the elections to the National Assembly—not on 16 February, but as early as 19 January 1919. It thus agreed with Hindenburg's chief political demand of 8 December, as the elections could hardly be held sooner, and rejected the Soviet system decisively.[1] The large majority of the delegates belonged to the moderate Social Democrats, while the extreme left—the Spartacists—mustered only a tiny minority and their leaders, Liebknecht and Rosa Luxemburg, were not even admitted to the congress. Yet the anti-militarist mood was not confined to the extreme left, but embraced wide circles. Thus the congress adopted the seven points proposed by a moderate Socialist from Hamburg:

1. The power of command over army and navy rests with the government under the control of the Executive Council. In the garrisons the power of military command is exercised by the local workers' and soldiers' councils in constant co-operation with [those exercising] the highest power of command. . . .

2. As a symbol of the destruction of militarism and the abolition of servile discipline (*Kadavergehorsam*) it is decreed that all badges of rank be removed and no weapons be carried when off duty.

3. The soldiers' councils are responsible for the reliability of the units and for the maintenance of discipline. . . .

4. The removal of the former epaulettes, N.C.O. stripes, etc., cockades, shoulder-straps, and bayonets falls exclusively within the competence of the soldiers' councils and not of individuals. . . . The congress demands the abolition of all decorations and insignia of honour and of the nobility.

5. The soldiers elect their own leaders. Former officers, who enjoy the confidence of the majority of their unit, can be re-elected.

---

[1] Müller, *Vom Kaiserreich zur Republik*, ii. 99–100, 216. The majority was 344 to 98 votes.

6. Officers of the military administration and officials with the rank of officer may remain in their positions, in the interest of demobilization, if they declare that they will not undertake anything against the Revolution.

7. The abolition of the standing army and the formation of a people's militia (*Volkswehr*) are to be speeded up.[1]

These points attacked the roots of the Prussian and German military system. On their basis it might have been possible to build a militia, as it existed in Switzerland, but if the plans were carried out it meant the end of the old army. Furthermore, the vital first point was far from clear. The power of command was to be exercised by the councils 'in constant co-operation with the highest power of command': was that the government, or the Executive Council elected by the congress? Who was to decide if these two organs disagreed? Who was to exercise the power of command over units not stationed in the garrisons, and what was to be the competence of the elected officers?[2]

The 'Hamburg points' were Utopian, the expression of an anti-militarist longing rather than a concrete programme. As was to be expected the reaction of the High Command was extremely sharp: it amounted to a renunciation of the alliance concluded on 10 November. The High Command believed that the moderate Social Democrats had let themselves be intimidated. Its reaction, according to Groener's report, was

a telegram in which Hindenburg threatened his own and my immediate resignations if the government accepted this resolution. In the evening on the telephone I made it clear to Ebert in the strongest terms that the High Command would not budge from this position. Ebert asked me to come to Berlin; I agreed, so as to explore the last possibility of helping the Ebert government. . . . On the 20th I was in Berlin. I walked with Major von Schleicher demonstratively in full uniform, with all decorations, from the General Staff to the *Reichskanzlei*; nobody touched us. I first had a conversation with Ebert and Landsberg, during which I once more explained with absolute frankness the point of view of the officers, and pointed out to Ebert the inadequacy of his government, which depended on our support. After this conversation I went with the ministers to the meeting of the Central Council [elected by the

[1] The text ibid. ii. 211–13, with several amendments carried in the course of the discussions.

[2] Cf. the view of Sauer, *Bündnis Ebert-Groener*, p. 172.

workers' and soldiers' congress] which I equally informed of the views of the High Command. . . .

There Groener was ably supported by Ebert, and the meeting ended inconclusively.[1] That might have been expected in view of the Utopian character of the 'Hamburg points' and of Ebert's political attitude, which was well known to the High Command. The threats of resignation and of ending the alliance of 10 November had been quite unnecessary. But perhaps Groener found it useful to demonstrate to Ebert the weakness of his government 'which depended on our support', and thus to show the government how indispensable the army was.

On 19 December Hindenburg sent an order to the army commands which strongly refuted the 'Hamburg points':

I do not recognize the resolution adopted by the Central Council of the workers' and soldiers' councils on 18 December 1918 in Berlin. . . . I am of the opinion that such a change, vitally affecting the life of the nation and of the army, cannot be made by the representatives of one social group only, but solely by the National Assembly appointed by the entire people. The army nevertheless stands behind the Ebert government and expects this government to honour its promise concerning the existence of the army and the directives on the competences of the *Vertrauensmänner* in the army, so enabling officers and non-commissioned officers to continue to serve. . . .[2]

Under certain conditions, but only if they were met, was the officer corps prepared to lend its support to the government. 'Therewith the High Command had come a step closer to its aim, the foundation of a firm government and the curtailment of the influence of the soldiers' councils', as was emphasized in a later official comment from the military side.[3]

How weak the position of the government was and how unreliable the units of the High Command, was shown only a few days later. The palace of Berlin was occupied by a 'revolutionary' formation of sailors, the *Volksmarinedivision*. Its members were accused of having appropriated stocks of wine and linen in the palace. The government tried in vain to induce the sailors to evacuate the palace; they reacted on 23 December by

---

[1] Groener, *Lebenserinnerungen*, p. 475.

[2] Printed with slight variations ibid., p. 475; Müller, *Vom Kaiserreich zur Republik*, ii. 222; Schüddekopf, *Heer und Republik*, p. 38.

[3] *Die Wirren in der Reichshauptstadt und im nördlichen Deutschland 1918–1920*, p. 24.

demanding their pay and, when this was not forthcoming, by arresting the city commandant, Otto Wels, and taking him with them as a hostage. Ebert demanded help from the High Command, and the latter ordered the regiments of General Lequis to attack the palace. This was unsuccessful, however, as the soldiers showed little zeal for the task and were soon impeded in their movements by masses of workers who were drawn towards the palace by the firing of cannon. The government had to negotiate, pay the sailors their arrears, and promise an amnesty; whereupon the sailors evacuated the palace and released Wels, to take up their new quarters in the royal stables near by. This military and political débâcle deeply depressed the officers of the High Command. The idea of dissolving the High Command and letting things take their course was gaining ground; some officers had already advocated it on 16 December. Groener and Schleicher, however, pleaded strongly for a continuation of the struggle and pointed to the formations of volunteers which were being recruited.[1]

To the High Command, however, the battle for the palace of Berlin brought one great gain. The three members of the government belonging to the Independent Social Democrats resigned in protest and were replaced by members of the moderate wing—among them Gustav Noske. The government became much more unified—all its members now belonged to the same party—and was willing to use, if need be, military force against the wild revolutionaries. Within the new government Noske was entrusted with military affairs. He was one of the military experts of his party and a non-commissioned officer in the *Landwehr*. Sent to Kiel at the outbreak of the naval mutiny there, he had quickly gained the confidence of the sailors and used his influence to quieten them and to gain control of the movement. A few days after his recall to Berlin, and after the outbreak of new unrest, Noske was appointed *Oberbefehlshaber in den Marken* (commander-in-chief in Brandenburg)—as it seems, at the suggestion of the new Prussian minister of war, the Württemberg Colonel Walther Reinhardt.[2]

---

[1] Sauer, *Bündnis Ebert-Groener*, p. 203; in general, Arthur Rosenberg, *Geschichte der Deutschen Republik*, Karlsbad, 1935, pp. 52–56.

[2] Eye-witness account of Hans-Werner von Zengen in *Deutsche Allgemeine Zeitung* of 16 Aug. 1930. Reinhardt was the son of a Württemberg officer and then 46 years old.

According to Noske's own description he accepted his appointment with the words: 'Someone has to become the bloodhound;
I do not fight shy of responsibility!'[1]

Reinhardt from the outset was conscious of the difficulties
which were connected with the fact that he as a Württemberg
colonel was to rank higher than the Prussian generals.[2] It was
a sign of the times that the last Prussian minister of war came
from Württemberg and was, in addition, willing to accept the
new state of affairs. The following fifteen months were characterized by a close—and on the whole successful—co-operation
between Noske, who soon became minister of defence, and
Reinhardt, who became the first chief of the army command of
the Reichswehr. This co-operation made it possible to rebuild
the army and contributed much to a strengthening of the new
republican system. The first step in that direction was that
Noske and Reinhardt persuaded the government to use military
force against further revolutionary upheavals—a decision which
was apparently difficult for Ebert.[3] In Berlin meanwhile the
so-called Spartacus rising had broken out. When the Independent Social Democrats resigned from the government the police
president of Berlin, Eichhorn, declined to do the same and to
accept his dismissal by the Prussian government. To 'defend'
him the radical left organized mass demonstrations; on
5 January 1919 revolutionary shock troops occupied certain
newspaper buildings. A Revolutionary Committee was formed
which summoned the Berlin workers to further demonstrations,
but did nothing to overthrow the government or to conquer
political power. The government, however, was no longer as
helpless as it had been two weeks earlier during the battle for
the palace.

There now existed several volunteer units and free corps
which were prepared to restore law and order, and most of
which obeyed the orders of the High Command. These units,
especially the *Freiwillige Landesjägerkorps* and the *Gardekavallerieschützendivision*, recruited from the guards regiments, received orders to march into Berlin. Highly superior to the
small revolutionary minority in their training, equipment, and

---

[1] Gustav Noske, *Von Kiel bis Kapp*, Berlin, 1920, p. 68.
[2] Eye-witness account of Major Wolfgang Fleck: Fritz Ernst, *Aus dem Nachlaß
des Generals Walther Reinhardt*, Stuttgart, 1958, p. 15.   [3] Zengen, loc. cit.

leadership, they quickly proved their value in bloody street battles, conquered the occupied newspaper buildings, and restored order. They also used the opportunity to kill the leaders of the Spartacus League, Liebknecht and Rosa Luxemburg, who had not participated in the fighting. It was of great political importance that the government did not entrust its defence to the units which were formed in Berlin from Social Democrats (for example, the *Regiment Reichstag*) and fought successfully against the extreme left,[1] but that it used the free corps which were subject to the orders of the High Command. These were commanded by professional officers and were certainly more efficient from a purely military point of view. But most likely, in the political sphere too, Ebert considered the continuation of the alliance of 10 November the only realistic course. The policy followed so consistently by Groener during the past weeks was now consummated.

This decision had far-reaching repercussions because it became the basis of the future policy. The example of Berlin was imitated during the following months in many parts of Germany. Everywhere free corps, which largely consisted of officers, non-commissioned officers, and soldiers of the old army, restored law and order, broke the power of the workers' and soldiers' councils and decisively defeated the extreme left. Several republican or social-democratic free corps also came into being,[2] but they were hardly used for this task. The composition of the free corps, which were formed in the east against Poland and in the Baltic area, or were sent there to fight the Poles and Russians, was politically even more one-sided. Yet the Reichswehr grew out of these free corps, and the old officer corps, above all the general staff, was the principal factor in its formation. It is impossible to answer the question whether there was an alternative way of forming an efficient republican army; but there can be no doubt that there were democratic officers who might have been willing to serve in such an army.[3]

---

[1] According to Rosenberg, *Geschichte der Deutschen Republik*, p. 70, three regiments of socialist volunteers were organized in Berlin and took up the struggle against the Spartacists. One of the leaders was the Social Democratic journalist Erich Kuttner, who has confirmed this to the author.

[2] See the comparatively short list in Harold J. Gordon, *The Reichswehr and the German Republic*, Princeton, 1957, p. 434.

[3] This is also the opinion of Gordon, op. cit., p. 294, who says that several of

It is interesting that several of them transferred to the Prussian police, probably because there was no place for them in the Reichswehr or because they disliked its political atmosphere. No one who in later years had occasion to observe the Prussian police in action against disturbers of the peace can maintain that it was unable to preserve law and order. It was a well-armed and highly efficient military force.[1] But the High Command and the general staff would never have been willing to co-operate in the creation of a democratic and republican army. If co-operation with the High Command and the officer corps was considered essential, then there was no way but that of Ebert and Noske. In the short run they thus strengthened their own position; but it is a different question whether they acted wisely and correctly. Throughout its short history the Weimar Republic was to show the traces of the alliance between the government and the High Command of the army, an alliance in which the army only too often was the stronger partner.

III. *The High Command and the Minister of War*

Colonel Reinhardt made his appointment as Prussian minister of war dependent upon the approval of the High Command, which was readily granted. At the beginning of January 1919 he went to Wilhelmshöhe near Cassel to discuss his views with Hindenburg and Groener and to achieve a uniform approach. 'The new minister of war was particularly anxious to restore to the officers their unlimited power of command and to reduce the soldiers' councils to the position of *Vertrauensleute* attached to the individual commanders. To achieve this it was important that the soldiers' councils should not obtain their own chain of command (*Soldatenrat-Dienstweg*). The situation was such that it was necessary to make concessions on other matters to gain these important points. . . .' The 'other matters' concerned above all the question of the badges of rank which stood in the centre of the discussion at Wilhelmshöhe.[2]

them left the Reichswehr voluntarily. Noske, *Von Kiel bis Kapp*, p. 199, writes: 'There were no *well-known* democratic officers in Germany when I began to form the Reichswehr' (my italics); but that was not the problem.

[1] This is also proved by the fact that under Hitler whole police divisions were incorporated into the army.

[2] Contemporary notes of Major Fleck: Ernst, *Aus dem Nachlaß des Generals Walther Reinhardt*, p. 15.

Only a few days after the defeat of the Spartacus rising, on 19 January—the day of the elections to the National Assembly —three decrees were published in the army gazette. One of them introduced, in the place of the former epaulettes, stripes of various sizes to be worn on the left sleeve, such as were customary in the navy. Another decree defined saluting as a mutual obligation, which had to be performed by the younger and lower-ranking soldier first and to be returned by the older one.[1] The meaning of this was not clear as the younger soldier was by no means always inferior in rank. But both decrees were certainly conceived as concessions to the new order.

This also applied to the most important of the three decrees, the 'preliminary regulation of the power of command and the position of soldiers' councils in the peace-time army'. It achieved Reinhardt's main aims—unlimited power of command for the officers and prevention of a separate chain of command of the soldiers' councils; but it retained this obnoxious institution, and legalized it after a fashion.

The decree stipulated:

1. The highest power of command rests with the government (*Rat der Volksbeauftragten*) elected by the Central Council of the German Socialist Republic.
2. The government (*Rat der Volksbeauftragten*), in so far as it does not itself issue direct orders, transfers the exercise of the power of command to the Prussian minister of war. . . .
3. The minister of war is responsible to the government for the way in which he conducts the command. All military offices of Prussia, as well as those common to Prussia and the Reich, are subordinate to the minister of war. . . .
4. The leaders of higher echelons, of units, and other formations exercise the power of issuing orders (*Befehlsgewalt*). . . .

This clearly meant a great step forward compared with the 'Hamburg points' of December 1918 and went a long way towards restoring the power of the officers. The same applied to the clauses concerning the soldiers' councils:

5. Soldiers' councils have to be elected in the regiments, independent battalions, and similar formations. They supervise the activities of the leaders to ensure that they do not misuse

[1] Ibid., p. 17.

their power to take action against the existing government. The soldiers' councils participate in the promulgation of general and permanent orders relating to the welfare of the troops, to social and economic questions, to leave and disciplinary matters, and append their signatures to them. Purely military orders, relating to training, command, and use of the troops, emanate solely from the leaders, and need not be countersigned by a soldiers' council. . . .

Similar regulations applied to the corps and their districts. In each of them a soldiers' council was to take part in the investigation of complaints of the lower councils; but the decision was left to the *Generalkommando* responsible for the area, and ultimately to the ministry of war and the government. The soldiers' councils were thus assigned advisory and supervisory functions, but only outside the purely military sphere. In addition, the decree clearly stipulated what lay outside their field of competence:

9. The ministry of war is responsible for all appointments. . . . The soldiers' councils are not entitled to remove leaders or to eliminate them, but they can request their dismissal. The decision within the regiment rests as far as possible with the leader, otherwise with the *Generalkommando* or the ministry of war. . . .

11. . . . The soldiers' councils are not entitled to interfere with matters pertaining to other military offices or to the civil authorities, nor to conduct correspondence alone and independently. . . . Directives, orders, etc. issued by them alone have no validity. . . .[1]

This decree caused a wave of indignation in the officer corps as well as among the soldiers' councils, whose whole position it undermined:[2] perhaps a proof that Reinhardt's solution constituted a *via media*. Many officers sharply attacked Reinhardt personally.[3] He was reproached for signing the decree, together with Ebert and Noske, and became the scapegoat of

---

[1] The full text of the decree is printed in Maercker, *Vom Kaiserheer zur Reichswehr — Geschichte des freiwilligen Landesjägerkorps*, Leipzig, 1921, pp. 390–3.

[2] See the quotations in Noske, *Von Kiel bis Kapp*, pp. 95–96.

[3] See the letters of Major Gudowius, Colonel von Thaer, and General von Tschischwitz in Nachlaß Reinhardt, Hauptstaatsarchiv Stuttgart, and Reinhardt himself, in Ernst, op. cit., p. 19.

many an embittered officer.[1] In particular the loss of the epaulettes—symbol of their whole social position—was considered
unbearable by the officer corps and provoked enormous
indignation. As one of the leading generals wrote later, 'this
constituted a particularly marked bow before left radicalism,
which had always looked with jealous eyes at the officers'
epaulettes'.[2] Groener was especially critical of the sanctioning
of the soldiers' councils by Reinhardt, and wrote to Ebert:
'Officers, non-commissioned officers, and a section of the private
soldiers are highly indignant; the malevolent radical elements
among the soldiers' councils, which are pining for power,
render open and passive opposition even to this decree. Men
with experience and proven in war and peace are to receive
certificates from immature and inexperienced boys of 19 to
20 years that they possess the confidence of their unit, and are
to be controlled by them. This is complete nonsense, and in
addition a demand that in the long run cannot be reconciled
with the honour and dignity of an upright man. Apart from
this, the whole army is so enraged against the entire institution
of the soldiers' councils that, but for the recognition they have
now achieved, they would soon have died an inglorious
death. . . .'[3]

During the following weeks too the fight against the soldiers'
councils remained a central issue for Groener—combined with
the creation of a reliable fighting force and the struggle against
the minister of war, who in his opinion was too soft. On 31
January Groener had a conference with Ebert about which he
made this note: 'Break resistance of soldiers' councils to decree
regulating power of command; will not suffer councils' congress
[to take place]; elimination of the radical elements from the
soldiers' councils of East and West Prussia. . . '. On the next
day a meeting took place with the liaison officers, about which
Groener noted: 'firm attitude to the demands of the soldiers'
councils; elimination of the radical soldiers' councils through
elections or by force. . . .' During discussions in Berlin on
10 February the questions of 'army organization, position of

[1] Ibid., p. 17.
[2] Walther Freiherr von Lüttwitz, *Im Kampf gegen die November-Revolution*,
Berlin, 1934, p. 41.
[3] Groener to Ebert, 27 Jan. 1919: Nachlaß Schleicher, no. 9, Bundesarchiv
Koblenz.

the general staff, elimination of the soldiers' councils' were the most important points noted.[1]

On 22 March a conference was held at the High Command, which had meanwhile moved its seat from Wilhelmshöhe to Kolberg in Pomerania to be closer to the threatened eastern frontiers, with the chiefs of all army corps and *Armeeoberkommandos*.[2] To them Groener outlined his ideas on the foreign and domestic situation:

With regard to the council system, he said, two kinds have to be distinguished: soldiers' councils and workers' councils. The soldiers' councils must be classified as entirely bad; they are the worst enemies of quick recuperation because they aim at political power and undermine all discipline. In the form of *Vertrauensräte* one can consent to their co-operation in the social and economic sphere only; all further-reaching demands must be refuted most energetically, especially those touching on politics and discipline. The workers' councils would be equally dangerous only if socialization were extended to all factories. If all factories were to be dominated by workers' councils the grave danger would arise that the initiative of the individual entrepreneur would be stultified and thus the revival of our economic life become impossible. . . . Groener recommended the study of the history of the working-class movement, with a particular view to the means of combating it. . . .

With regard to the *internal consolidation* of the army it was emphasized how important it was to restore discipline. Disobedient councils [are] to be removed, if need be by force of arms. But it was stressed at the same time that conflicts with soldiers' councils should be conducted in such a way that they were put clearly in the wrong. . . . Noske, during a recent visit to the High Command, had put his opinion about the soldiers' councils in the words 'Chuck the fellows out!' The High Command is of the following opinion: 1. Politics do not exist in the army. 2. Soldiers' councils which do not toe the line have to be eliminated. As the ministry of war shows a very conciliatory attitude towards the soldiers' councils, the High Command thinks it highly desirable that the corps stiffen the back of the war minister in this question by requests and protests. . . .

---

[1] 'Tagebuch des Ersten Generalquartiermeisters ab 30. Okt. 1918–19. März 1919', under 31 Jan., 1 Feb., and 10 Feb.: Nachlaß Groener, box 5, no. 16 i, Bundesarchiv Koblenz.

[2] 'Tagebuch des Ersten Generalquartiermeisters ab 20. März 1919 bis 20. Sept. 1919': ibid., no. 16 ii.

With regard to the officer corps of the future army Groener stressed:

Most important for the future organization of the army [is] the position and creation of a healthy and efficient officer corps. To create an efficient officer corps a battle with the government must not be feared. The ministry of war at the moment follows only one line, that of reducing the army. In doing so all the elderly and the younger officers are to be discharged. What remains is a rump without head and limbs, which is not viable. The High Command by contrast desires a severe screening of the officer corps and the retention of officers of all classes. . . . General indignation is caused by a decree of the Personnel Office, which instructs all commanding generals to see to it that the majority of the officers is discharged by 15 April 1919. . . . On the side of the High Command it would be strongly welcomed if from all sides objections were raised against the Personnel Office. . . .[1]

Thus Groener fought the battle not only against the soldiers' councils, but also against the minister of war and the army's Personnel Office, the head of which was General von Braun. Even 'a battle with the government must not be feared' if the existence of the officer corps was at stake. 'Requests and protests' could easily be organized to further the cause.

About Reinhardt, Groener at the same time wrote to his wife: 'at times I fail to understand Reinhardt's behaviour; he talks like a book but remains by nature a teacher, and perhaps he is also a kind of profiteer from revolution (*Revolutionsgewinnler*). I have the impression that he wants above all to remain in the good books of the government. . . . The indignation against Reinhardt is in part so strong that an officer of the general staff in his fury exclaimed he would like to throw a hand-grenade at the feet of the war minister. . . .'[2] The contrast between the two Württemberg officers was not only personal, but it extended to their military views. In a memorandum which must have been written about this time Reinhardt developed ideas about the formation of the Reichswehr, which were quite

[1] 'Besprechung bei der O.H.L. am 22.3.19', signed by Major Freiherr von Fritsch, the later chief of the army command, then the first staff officer with the *Armeeoberkommando Nord*: Nachlaß Seeckt, box 17, no. 125, Militärgeschichtliches Forschungsamt Freiburg. The Personnel Office was a section of the Prussian war ministry.

[2] Groener to his wife, 21 Mar. 1919: Groener-Geyer, *General Groener*, p. 151.

unacceptable to the High Command, but are proof of his political acumen:

In wide circles the old army under its officer corps is looked upon as a 'shield of reaction'. This view cannot be changed within a few days; it is quite understandable if the tradition of Imperial Germany appears dangerous to the republicans. In view of the threatening situation it is therefore better not to provoke such opposition, which is difficult to overcome and would cost valuable time, but to present the young republic with a young republican army, detaching ourselves firmly from our military past. In doing so it is important to preserve so many strong and viable links between the old and the new army that the future peace-time army can receive its life blood from both. . . .

Reinhardt too attached the greatest value 'to strict discipline that alone guarantees the military worth of the army'; but at the same time he advocated that 'antiquated and faulty institutions, which in the present internal situation arouse distrust or dislike, should be courageously thrown overboard. . . '.[1]

Such 'revolutionary' ideas were bound to cause violent opposition in the officer corps. In June 1919 Major von Stülpnagel, chief of the operations section in the High Command, wrote a letter to General von Seeckt which expressed exactly the opposite point of view:

In my opinion it is absolutely essential that an officer corps with monarchical convictions and of the old stamp should be preserved for the miserable creature of the new army. Counter-moves are naturally on the way. I have been informed that *Herr General* [Seeckt] has handed in his resignation. After the decree of the war minister no other step was really feasible. . . . I am hoping that within the foreseeable future the resurrection of the monarchy, a struggle with Poland and perhaps with France too will be possible, and I therefore consider it my duty to ask *Herrn General* to remain in the army for these tasks and for these aims. . . .[2]

[1] 'Denkschrift über Aufstellung einer Reichswehr', s.d.: Nachlaß Reinhardt, no. 18, Heeresarchiv Stuttgart. Many years later Groener mentioned a letter from Reinhardt to Ebert in which the former had made far-reaching promises regarding the democratization of the army, of which the High Command disapproved: Nachlaß Seeckt, box 13, no. 111, Militärgeschichtliches Forschungsamt Feiburg.

[2] Stülpnagel to Seeckt, Kolberg, 28 June 1919: Nachlaß Seeckt, box 17, no. 124, Militärgeschichtliches Forschungsamt Freiburg.

Seeckt himself—at that time chief of the *Armeeoberkommando Nord*—equally disliked the new government. At the beginning of 1919 he wrote to his wife:

I have no intention to slide towards the left, but say openly to everybody that the present developments more easily induce me to make the jump to Social Democracy. With *Herr* Ebert and comrades I can perhaps [work], in spite of our diametrically opposed views on the world and economic matters, because I consider these people relatively (!) honest, although ideologists and weaklings. With *Herr* Th. Wolf of the *Berliner Tageblatt*, Dernburg, Solf, Bernstorff, and similar brethren I cannot, and shall never be able to, because I do not believe them to be true to their convictions. . . .[1]

And a few weeks later he wrote about the new prime minister of Prussia:

The new prime minister Hirsch, I have the honour, is not so bad and is an old parliamentarian. For this post he seems quite unsuitable, especially as a Jew; not only because this is in itself provocative, but because the Jewish talent is purely critical, hence negative, and can never help in the construction of a state. This is no good, for as things are, we should wish this government to last. A bourgeois one is not yet possible. . . .[2]

On the other hand, Seeckt advocated a strengthening of the new government against the left and criticized the violent agitation of the officers against Reinhardt. He wrote to his wife:

Everything depends on our succeeding in making the government firm and keeping it firm; whether it pleases us or not, there is nothing else and whoever can, should help. Who is unable to do so, or cannot bring himself to do it, should at least not disturb. But that is done by stupid newspaper articles which publicize the many weaknesses and ridiculous traits of the republic. That is also done by resolutions and speeches against the military decrees which emanate from the officers' side. It is very easy to say 'This is unheard of', and then to do nothing; it is very difficult to try to find usable timber among the ruins. Politics is the art of what is possible, not

---

[1] Seeckt to his wife, Bartenstein, 6 Feb. 1919: Nachlaß Seeckt, roll 28, microfilm in Institut für Zeitgeschichte, Munich. Clearly, Dernburg, Solf, and Count Bernstorff were particularly obnoxious to Seeckt because they had been high officials before the revolution and now co-operated loyally with the new government: to him, they were mere turncoats.

[2] Seeckt to his wife, Bartenstein, 19 Mar. 1919: ibid.

what is desirable. My world looks different from that of to-day; but I will try and help that the two of us and another few Germans can live in the world of the future. To achieve this will be difficult enough, if it can be achieved. . . .[1]

In contrast with many other officers Seeckt was a political realist; he saw that the past could not be restored and that 'resolutions and speeches' could not alter facts. According to the maxim 'politics is the art of what is possible' he was to act during the following years.

A further step towards the consolidation of the new order and towards the strengthening of the officers' position was marked by the 'law concerning the formation of a provisional Reichswehr' of 6 March 1919. It stipulated: 'The Reichswehr shall be formed on a democratic basis through the co-ordination of existing volunteer units and the recruitment of volunteers. . . .'[2] But the law did not say how this 'democratic basis' was to be erected—only that proven non-commissioned officers could be commissioned. Much more important was the fact that the Reichswehr was to be formed from the existing volunteer units 'and similar formations': the free corps with their one-sided political composition became the basis of the new army.

According to the decree of the same day which implemented the law of 6 March, the supreme command of the Reichswehr was a prerogative of the president of the republic (Ebert), who entrusted its exercise to the minister of defence (Noske) and, within his contingent, to the Prussian minister of war. The minister of defence was competent in all questions of discipline and of complaints against superior officers; he decided what units were to be taken over intact into the Reichswehr. The selection, promotion, and dismissal of general officers rested with the president, who was to be advised by the war ministry (later the Reichswehr ministry); that of all officers below the rank of general remained with the military authorities: the commanding officers of the regiments retained their decisive voice in the selection of the junior officers. The *Generalkommandos* of the old army were responsible for the recruiting of the soldiers who, in the first instance, had to enlist for six months.

---

[1] Seeckt to his wife, Bartenstein, 12 Feb. 1919: Rabenau, *Seeckt*, p. 145.
[2] *Reichsgesetzblatt 1919*, pp. 295–8; Maercker, *Vom Kaiserheer zur Reichswehr*, pp. 395–6.

The soldiers' councils were replaced by *Vertrauensräte*, as Hindenburg had ordered as early as 10 November 1918. They were elected by the soldiers of the unit in question, were to present the soldiers' complaints to the proper authorities, and to be heard in questions of pay, food, clothing, and billeting, but were excluded from all purely military issues.[1] The hated name of the soldiers' councils disappeared for good. The officers regained their full powers of command. The officer corps in its old form and with its old methods of selection had again come into being, or rather it had survived the crisis of the revolution. As a later comment from the military side put it: 'Thus order was restored. . . . The constant admonitions of the High Command to create a serviceable army had been success-ful. . . . The sacrifices which the volunteer units had made so gladly had been recognized.'[2]

A further conference of Groener with the officers of the High Command, the army corps, and *Armeeoberkommandos* took place at Frankfurt-on-Oder on 5 May. Groener thought it 'desirable, just at the beginning of the peace negotiations, to exchange views about the military and internal situation. It is essential that all military authorities have a uniform conception of the situation, it is not permissible that at any place *personal* views should be decisive. . . .' According to Groener, the army had 'three tasks: preservation of law and order, restoration of the authority of the state and of an orderly administration, and measures against the collapse of economic life'.

For the first task the reorganization of the police, especially in Berlin, is being undertaken. . . . Further military support will be given through the reinforcement of the police and the gendarmes by reliable non-commissioned officers, by motorized and railway shock troops, finally by calling up military volunteers in case of imminent danger. . . . It is important too to render harmless agitators and creators of unrest, to prevent the holding of meetings leading to incitement (*Hetzversammlungen*) and to curtail incitement through the press (*Hetzpresse*), if need be to proclaim a state of siege at the psychologically right moment.

As measures to restore the authority of the state and an orderly

---

[1] Gordon, *Reichswehr and the German Republic*, pp. 55–57; *Die Wirren in der Reichshauptstadt und im nördlichen Deutschland, 1918–1920*, p. 121.

[2] Ibid., p. 121. Cf. the critical remarks of Gordon, op. cit., p. 57, especially about the selection of junior officers.

administration, the following measures must be considered: above all the illegal soldiers' councils must be eliminated. But against the workers' councils too measures have to be taken as soon as they claim competences which do not belong to them. . . .

Against the collapse of economic life the same measures have to be taken as for the restoration of state authority: intervention against incitement to strikes (*Streikhetzer*), compulsory labour (*Arbeitszwang*), prohibition of incitement in meetings and of leaflets, if need be a state of siege. . . .[1]

The question of the workers' and soldiers' councils was still of principal importance to the High Command, especially as it overlapped with the general struggle against the revolutionary left and its propaganda and with the measures considered necessary to restore 'the authority of the state'.

The same ideas recurred in the 'directives for our policy', which were drafted by Major von Schleicher and sent to Ebert by Groener at the end of June 1919. They also contained a further, very important point, which was to figure prominently in the policy of the Reichswehr leaders for many years to come:

The creation of a unitary German state. Prussia must become Germany, and this Germany must above all conduct an internal policy, the policy of a modern Frederick William I. . . . With the greatest efforts, and thanks to the unselfish and devoted co-operation of the officer corps, it has been possible to create in the Reichswehr an instrument that the government can use to a certain extent. This instrument must now be employed with the utmost vigour to secure the authority of the state in all fields of public life and to make the law respected. This applies in the first instance to the administration. The nonsense of the workers' councils must disappear from the administration quickly and completely. This counter-government . . . is impossible in an orderly state and unbearable. . . .

The recovery of our economic life, the pre-condition of all reconstruction, depends—apart from questions of raw materials and related issues—above all on two things: order and work. That means in the present situation a state of siege and the prohibition of strikes. . . .

To conduct an active foreign policy is impossible for us, and we

[1] 'Niederschrift über die Besprechung in Frankfurt a./O. am 5. Mai 1919', *streng geheim!*, sent by Colonel von Feldmann to Noske on 20 May: Nachlaß Reinhardt, Hauptstaatsarchiv Stuttgart. It seems that Groener considered the soldiers' councils 'illegal' on the basis of the law on the formation of the provisional Reichswehr.

are lacking the means for it; but two things must be dealt with immediately and with the greatest emphasis: the war guilt question and the organization of a German *irredenta* in the territories to be ceded. . . .[1]

In a lecture to the officers Groener also emphasized that it was the goal 'to weld together the sixty millions of the German nation in one state, if possible a unitary state. . . . The single states must disappear, as soon as this can be achieved either by peaceful or by violent methods. . . .'[2] The unity of the Reich remained his principal aim, and to this unity he was willing to sacrifice the rights of the federal states which made up the German Empire of 1871.

Groener's conference with the leading officers took place on 5 May, a few days after the suppression of the Munich Soviet Republic by the troops of the government. Earlier, a second revolutionary uprising in Berlin had been defeated, Bremen had been conquered, large areas of Central Germany had been occupied by the *Freiwillige Landesjägerkorps* of General Maercker. Everywhere the power of the workers' and soldiers' councils was broken and the old authorities were restored. The tasks which Groener emphasized were to a large extent achieved. The authority of the government was considerably strengthened, and it had behind it a majority in the National Assembly which sat at Weimar. In spite of this, the local military authorities still exercised wide powers. Thus Major Freiherr von Fritsch reported to Seeckt: 'Our area of activity has been . . . considerably extended during the past weeks. . . . With the district of the second army corps we have also taken over the Soviet Republic of Pomerania. The Pomeranian *Oberpräsident* [head of the provincial administration], a Jewish democrat, Herr Lippmann, works entirely in the modern spirit; he lets the workers' councils govern freely, and contributes as best he can towards draining the power of the civil authorities of which they possess only a limited amount. Faced with this the *Generalkommando* is in a difficult position; as all fighting units are employed on the Netze front, it has hardly any troops at

---

[1] Schüddekopf, *Heer und Republik*, no. 33, p. 96; 'Tagebuch des Ersten General-quartiermeisters ab 20. März 1919 bis 20. Sept. 1919', under 27 June: Nachlaß Groener, box 5, no. 16 ii, Bundesarchiv Koblenz.

[2] Groener, *Lebenserinnerungen*, p. 495: lecture of 19–20 May 1919.

its disposal; it also seems that the former chief [of the *General-kommando*'s general staff], Niemann, was from the outset too soft and conciliatory. As he had lived through the days of the revolution in Stettin, he stood . . . under the impression that everything had developed very nicely. . . .' Niemann was replaced by von Falkenhausen, under whom, the writer hoped, things would improve.[1]

Yet the difficulties with the *Oberpräsident* continued. In July a strike of the agricultural workers broke out in Pomerania, and the military authorities wanted to proclaim a state of siege, so as not to endanger the harvest. But after negotiations between the *Oberpräsident*, the *Generalkommando*, and representatives of the striking workers, this measure was rescinded, and it was agreed that in future the state of siege should only be proclaimed with the consent of the representatives of the organized workers. This, General von Kessel declared, was 'out of the question': the *Oberpräsident* was too soft towards the left. Reinhardt addressed a sharp letter to the Prussian government:

> I consider that such a concession is illegal and, on account of its one-sidedness, politically untenable. . . . I request the ministry urgently, in the interest of a fruitful co-operation, to entrust the post of the *Oberpräsident* to a different person. The *Oberpräsident* Löppmann (*sic*) after these events no longer enjoys the confidence of the military authorities, and the way in which he sided against the *Generalkommando* in the presence of the contending parties in the meeting at Stettin on 16 July must, from the point of view of the government too, be called extremely derogatory to the authority of the Prussian state. . . .[2]

For the time being, however, Lippmann remained in his office.

For Groener and the High Command the proclamation of the state of siege, which transferred executive power to the military authorities,[3] was the means by which they hoped to gain their political ends. It is thus not surprising that the agreement reached at Stettin touched them in a very tender spot, for

---

[1] Fritsch to Seeckt, Bartenstein, 18 June 1919: Nachlaß Seeckt, no. 87, fasc. 20, Militärgeschichtliches Forschungsamt Freiburg.

[2] General von Kessel to Reinhardt, Berlin, 22 July, and Reinhardt to the Prussian government, Weimar, 24 July 1919: Nachlaß Schleicher, no. 14, Bundesarchiv Koblenz.

[3] The legal basis was provided by the Prussian law of 4 June 1851, to which the German constitution of 16 Apr. 1871 referred in art. 68.

it threatened to deprive them of an instrument which to them was indispensable. During the early months of 1919 Groener and the High Command had become more and more concerned with political questions. They not only dealt—as was perhaps only natural—with issues of military policy, such as the soldiers' councils, the restoration of the officers' power, and recruitment, but also with the crucial problems of internal policy in general: the preservation of state authority, the workers' councils, strikes, the radicalization of the working class, and economic recovery. In addition, the most prominent politicians of the High Command—Groener as well as Schleicher —were busy with even more general problems: the German constitution, the relationship between Prussia and the Reich, and even foreign policy. It was, indeed, a question of foreign policy which was to cause the most bitter controversy in Germany as well as among the generals: the question whether the peace treaty should be signed or not signed.

iv. *To Sign or Not to Sign?*

At the end of April 1919 the German peace delegation went to Versailles, and with it General von Seeckt as the leading military expert. In a telegram to Groener a few days earlier he insisted on an army of at least 300,000 men and on the preservation of general conscription, as a mercenary army would be too expensive.[1] But a possibility of negotiating did not exist at Versailles. The German chief plenipotentiary, Count Brockdorff-Rantzau, had to accept the demand that the army within a given time be reduced to 200,000, and later to 100,000 men, hoping thus to gain concessions in other fields. Groener thereupon protested in a telegram to Chancellor Scheidemann:

General von Seeckt reports that the military propositions, sanctioned by the cabinet, have been modified by the peace delegation without consulting him, among other points the figure of 100,000 being accepted after a transitional period. The military positions were entirely abandoned to obtain more in other questions. I feel obliged to point out the grave obstacles to this decision. Its execution would result in:

    1. Germany's becoming absolutely powerless abroad, even against aggression by its smallest neighbours;

[1] Rabenau, *Seeckt*, p. 159.

2. the impossibility of maintaining the authority of the government internally. . . .

I have to mention further that it would make a particularly unfavourable impression on the volunteer units if this decision of the
government became known. Officers, non-commissioned officers,
and common soldiers will say with justification: We have created
law and order in the country and made possible the revival of the
economic life, and now the government abandons us without
scruple as an object of compensation and shows us the door. . . .
In addition I should like to say that it must be extremely offensive
to the military experts of the peace delegation . . . if they are not
consulted at all during the discussion of important military issues. . . .
Addendum for General von Seeckt:

I request you to make my opinion clear to Count Rantzau and to
tell him that I have the gravest doubts about the development of our
internal situation and therefore consider such experiments at the
present time as folly and madness. It would amount to the complete
suicide of the German nation. . . .[1]

A few days later there were the first signs that the Bavarian
units might act independently. General von Lüttwitz informed
Groener that 'the Bavarian General Möhl . . . was showing
strong particularist tendencies. Möhl had remarked that
Bavaria would be forced to sign a separate peace if southern
Germany were occupied by the Entente, in case Germany
refused to sign' the peace treaty. Of the Bavarian staff officers
only two were considered reliable in a 'greater German sense'.[2]
The Bavarian problem, and that of the Bavarian Reichswehr,
was to remain acute for many years.

In June 1919 it became obvious that no major concessions
were to be expected from the Entente powers. The question,
whether Germany should accept or refuse the peace terms,
threatened to split the National Assembly and to overthrow the
government; it also provoked the most violent struggles within
the officer corps. The idea of resistance to Poland was above all
propagated in West Prussia, which was to be ceded to Poland,
and in East Prussia, which was to become geographically

[1] Groener to Major von Harbou, 27 May 1919: Nachlaß Seeckt, roll 20, no. 110,
microfilm in Institut für Zeitgeschichte, Munich.
[2] 'Tagebuch des Ersten Generalquartiermeisters ab 20. März 1919 bis 20.
Sept. 1919', under 29 May: Nachlaß Groener, box 5, no. 16 ii, Bundesarchiv
Koblenz.

separated from Germany by the peace treaty. It was widely believed that Germany would be able to defend the east against the Poles and to regain Toruń and Poznań. The plan was accepted by General von Below, the commanding officer of the two eastern provinces, and by the two brothers von Stülpnagel on his staff, who made the necessary preparations. A prominent civil official and leading Social Democrat, Winnig, went to Kolberg to sound the views of the High Command. But he found Groener opposed to the idea of resistance, which he believed hopeless: Germany had no choice but to accept the peace; then the United States would aid Germany with credits and trade facilities and thus bring about Germany's recovery.[1]

It was Groener who during the fateful days emerged as the leader of the party advocating acceptance, while Reinhardt became the spokesman of the opposite side. During a conference in the war ministry on 14 May Reinhardt foresaw difficulties with the troops if the treaty were signed; if not, the east was relatively in the best position, but Reinhardt feared strong internal opposition from below.[2] Groener remembered that during this meeting Reinhardt for the first time clearly stood out for resistance to the enemy in the east and thus giving up German unity for the time being. 'For this plan, which figured in numerous Prussian heads, I had no sympathy. The preservation of the unity of Germany was the *conditio sine qua non* for which I was prepared to make *any* sacrifice. In my conviction, the decisive point was gained if we preserved the political unity of the German tribes. . . .'[3] Four months later Groener informed the president: several weeks before 23 June he was approached by Reinhardt as to whether he was willing to put himself at the head of a military uprising in the east, but he and Hindenburg declined.[4]

During the following weeks Reinhardt's plan won adherents

---

[1] August Winnig, *Heimkehr*, Hamburg, 1935, pp. 195, 215–16. Winnig was 'Reichskommissar für Ost- und Westpreußen' and a member of the National Assembly.
[2] Notes of Major Fleck: Ernst, *Aus dem Nachlaß des Generals Walther Reinhardt*, p. 30.
[3] Groener, *Lebenserinnerungen*, p. 493.
[4] Groener's *Tagebuch* under 11 Sept. 1919: Nachlaß Groener, box 5, no. 16 ii, Bundesarchiv Koblenz.

in the officer corps and among the military leaders; but Groener remained steadfast. At Weimar, where the National Assembly debated the issue hotly, the leading officers assembled to discuss it once more. Reinhardt maintained: 'In the west the peace terms can be carried out. In the east this is in my opinion not feasible. The danger exists that the weakmindedness (*Flaumacherei*) of the west and south will ruin the national feelings of the east and its national strength. A breach between east and west will be inevitable, the gulf will be very deep. But we can manage the breach, give up the west and instead create a strong east, which should perhaps include the lands up to the Elbe. The old Prussia must form the nucleus of the Reich.'[1] On this vital issue the Württemberg colonel, who was so readily considered too 'soft' by his comrades, thought in a more Prussian fashion than the majority of the Prussian officers.

The decisive meeting of the generals—a war council which Groener considered unnecessary and even dangerous[2]—took place at Weimar on 19 June 1919. All the leading officers of the new army were present: General Groener and the Majors von Stülpnagel and von Schleicher from the High Command, the Generals von Below, von Loßberg, von Lüttwitz, von Möhl, and von Seeckt, Colonel Heye, Vice-Admiral von Trotha from the navy—in all more than thirty officers. Major-General von Loßberg reported about the situation in Silesia: the spirit of the soldiers was good, discipline had improved, confidence in the officers was restored; the *Armeeoberkommando Süd* could rely on the troops, but they would not obey an order to evacuate the disputed areas (which were to become Polish). Von Loßberg and von Below both emphasized that the Poles would be defeated if it came to hostilities. From the *Armeeoberkommando Nord* Colonel Heye stated that its forces were strong enough to cope with any internal uprising. The commanding generals of Bavaria, Saxony, and Württemberg feared the outbreak of revolts and severe unrest if the peace treaty were not signed. General von Lüttwitz of *Reichswehrgruppenkommando* 1 declared that the refusal to sign the treaty would be well received by the troops; they would in no circumstances agree to the acceptance of the 'shame paragraphs'—the articles which insisted on

---

[1] Groener, *Lebenserinnerungen*, p. 499, 502.   [2] Ibid., p. 503.

Germany's responsibility for the outbreak of the war, and demanded the trial of the Emperor and the alleged war criminals. General von Below mentioned that not only the troops, but the civilian population of West Prussia too were ready to fight the Poles.[1]

Then Groener spoke:

An offensive in the east is easy, the province of Poznań can be regained without difficulty, and the offensive can be carried as far as Warsaw. But we have to view the situation with the eyes of the statesman and in its wider perspectives. It is certain that forces of the Entente will appear in the east. In the west the Entente has built up a ten-fold superiority. Resistance is at most possible behind the Elbe, which can be reached by the Entente within four weeks. . . . Southern Germany will make itself independent. If the war ministry were able to collect a million men at the Elbe, resistance would not be impossible. . . . Our stocks of coal are very low; they are only sufficient for ten and a half days. After initial successes the military action would finally be condemned to failure. . . .

Groener's own version given a few days later is slightly different:

In the conference at Weimar on 19 June I declared my readiness to resume the struggle if the minister of war were prepared to put a million men at my disposal. This the war minister declared to be impossible and emphasized that the provisioning of such masses would create the greatest difficulties. . . . In view of this situation and of the impossibility of mobilizing our national energy for the struggle, I consider all fine speeches foolish and the resumption of the fight madness. Such a decision would result not only in considerable losses, the destruction of large flourishing districts and industrial centres, the hostile occupation of vital economic areas for many years, but I am firmly convinced would result in a war of annihilation by France against Germany. . . .

Noske by and large supported Groener: if the movement in the east were fired by an enormous enthusiasm, he would put himself at its head 'with fire and sword', but he did not believe this was so.[2]

[1] 'Protokoll der Sitzung in Weimar am 19. Juni 1919', quoted by Ernst, *Aus dem Nachlaß des Generals Walther Reinhardt*, pp. 34–35. The *Schmachparagraphen* are articles 227–31 of the Versailles Treaty.

[2] Ibid., p. 35; Groener's version in 'Vortrag des Ersten Generalquartiermeisters . . . gehalten im Großen Hauptquartier am 23.6.1919': Nachlaß Seeckt, box 13, no. 111, Militärgeschichtliches Forschungsamt Freiburg.

Reinhardt by contrast emphasized that acceptance of the treaty would destroy too many moral values; considerable sections of the army would thus be alienated or even be driven to the Communists; he believed it particularly dangerous to recognize the 'shame paragraphs'.[1] According to Groener, the idea was seriously discussed within the officer corps to make Noske head of the government, with dictatorial powers. Now he declared: 'Above all the disintegration of the Reich must be prevented. The shame paragraphs must of course be eliminated from the peace treaty. I go with Noske through thick and thin.' This declaration of confidence in the minister of defence was joined by the other officers present.[2] On the other hand they informed him that many officers and volunteers would refuse to serve a government that accepted the 'shame paragraphs', and this was repeated to Noske on the following day by Field-Marshal von Hindenburg. He also declared that a favourable course of the military operations was more than doubtful, but said 'as a soldier I must prefer death with honour to [the conclusion of] a shameful peace'.[3]

In this memorable officers' council—a junta such as had never existed in the history of the Prussian army—only the generals commanding in the old Prussian provinces demanded a people's war against Poland, but they were a minority. General von Seeckt was at first uncertain. On the afternoon of the 19th he discussed the situation with Major von Stülpnagel. The latter still believed that Hindenburg would be willing to put himself at the head of a movement of resistance if Seeckt became his chief of staff. Seeckt wanted to think matters over. In the evening the members of the National Assembly who came from the eastern provinces met; they were addressed by General von Loßberg, who developed the military plans but was strongly opposed by other speakers. Seeckt and Stülpnagel, who were present, then came to the conclusion that the resumption of the struggle was hopeless if the representatives of the civilian population so sharply resisted it.[4] There can be no doubt that they were right: a fight of desperation, as it was

[1] Diary of Lieutenant-Colonel van den Bergh, quoted by Ernst, op. cit., p. 33, n. 23.   [2] Ibid., p. 36.

[3] Telegram of Hindenburg to Ebert, Kolberg, 23 June 1919: Reichskanzlei, Akten betr. Oberste Heeresleitung und Heerführer, R 43 I 702, Bundesarchiv Koblenz.

[4] Stülpnagel's diary of 19 June 1919: Rabenau, Seeckt, p. 182, n. 1.

envisaged by some of the generals, was only feasible if it was supported by the civil authorities, and that meant not only by the deputies from the eastern provinces, but above all by the government. Otherwise such a step would have been directed against the government, a revolt of the military, which would have been violently opposed by the war-weary masses and especially by the working class. Even if the government had proclaimed a *levée en masse*, a policy of national resistance, it seems very doubtful whether the masses would have followed suit. The country was exhausted after five years of war and blockade; the people desired peace and order; anything that smelled of 'militarism' was out of favour. In short, any such policy lacked a basis in reality, however justified it might have been from the national point of view.

Yet some generals were still inclined to action, even if it was directed against the government. On 22 June Hindenburg received a letter from General von Below in which he inquired whether Hindenburg was willing to put himself at the head of an uprising in East Prussia; if not, von Below would do so. Hindenburg, however, declined and declared he would not suffer any arbitrary actions of the generals. A few days later Below was dismissed from the army.[1] But this remained an isolated case. Seeckt now fully supported Groener's policy.[2] As during later crises—in the Kapp Putsch as well as in 1923— he was not willing to act openly against the government, however strongly he disliked its policy.

Meanwhile Chancellor Scheidemann had resigned because he was unwilling to sign the peace treaty. On 22 June the new chancellor, Bauer, informed the Entente that he was prepared to sign, but only without the 'shame paragraphs'. This the Entente refused to accept; on 23 June it demanded immediate signature without any reservations. The two strongest parties, Social Democrats and Centre, were now willing to do so, albeit under protest. These events deprived the policy of Groener and the majority of the generals—acceptance, but without the 'shame paragraphs'—of its basis.[3] On 23 June

---

[1] Groener, *Lebenserinnerungen*, p. 510.

[2] Report of Captain Geyer to Colonel von Xylander of 25 June 1919: Nachlaß Seeckt, roll 26, no. 284, microfilm in Institut für Zeitgeschichte, Munich.

[3] Ernst, op. cit., p. 44.

Ebert, who feared the outbreak of military revolts if the treaty was signed as it stood, telephoned Groener at Kolberg and asked his opinion. Groener repeated that he considered a resumption of the fight—after initial successes in the east—hopeless in the long run. He advised the president to appoint Noske head of the government, with dictatorial powers; only thus, he believed, was it possible 'to save the German nation for the time being, because it would provide a goal for the officers and soldiers as well as for the entire nation. . .'. Noske should encourage every officer to remain at his post to save the fatherland and do his duty: then there was a chance of avoiding revolutionary unrest at home and new battles in the east.[1]

Three weeks later, in a lecture to the liaison officers of the High Command, Groener expressed himself much more critically about Noske:

The gist of my advice to Ebert was that we should achieve a government that possesses dictatorial powers for the conduct of internal policy; I am not absolutely certain, however, that Noske is the man to do this, for he too is a party man, gentlemen, he cannot shed his skin, and I fear that we should gain nothing with a party government; we need a government that stands above party and is willing to use strong measures against the left and the right, and in addition a firm, strong army. . . . For the soldier there is only one way: obedience, execution of orders. If we do not achieve that this is once more instilled in the officer corps, we remain stuck in the bog (*dann kommen wir nicht wieder aus der Schweinerei heraus*); politics must disappear from the officer corps. By this wedge, which has been driven into the officer corps and has been strengthened by the pronunciamentos, distrust of the officers has grown again among the people. We must represent the authority of the state, then power will be in our hands. Otherwise you must not be surprised if we slide further and further to the left, instead of pushing slowly towards the right. . . . We must reconstitute the good old officer corps, whether or not the individual remains a monarchist in his heart. . . .

Groener also told his audience that, instead of a dismemberment of Prussia, the other German states must disappear and be combined with Prussia in a unitary German state, for a federal state was out of date. The new Reichswehr ministry should

[1] Groener, op. cit., p. 508; E. O. Volkmann, *Revolution über Deutschland*, Oldenburg, 1930, p. 303.

throughout bear the stamp of the general staff, and its main departments should be transferred to the new ministry.[1]

It still took a considerable time, however, before the rift within the officer corps was closed. Precisely because the government—following Groener's advice—signed the peace treaty, a new storm broke out. On 26 June the officer commanding *Armee-oberkommando Süd*, General von dem Borne, reported to Noske that the officers of his units, especially the general staff officers, 'had lost confidence in General Groener on account of his attitude during the past months, especially in the recent negotiations which led to the signing of the shame paragraphs. . .'.[2] The same general wired to the government: 'The officers preserve their loyalty to the fatherland. They protect it against internal collapse. But the officer corps has lost confidence in a government which has inflicted such a shame on army and nation.'[3] Other generals expressed similar views orally to the minister of war. But in a conference with all the leading generals from Berlin and its environs it proved possible to persuade them not to resign, as they had threatened, and to assuage the conflict. Yet the assembled officers put forward the following political demands: the Kaiser and the 'war criminals' not to be handed over; unpopular members of the government, in particular Erzberger, to resign; the political parties' 'horse-trading' (*Kuhhandel*) to cease; and the attacks on the army to be suppressed.[4]

On 26 July General von Lüttwitz of *Reichswehrgruppenkommando* 1 discussed the political situation with seven other generals. They unanimously adopted the following programme:

1. The alleged war criminals must under no circumstances be handed over.
2. It is not permissible to reduce the army, as long as the Bolshevik danger makes it necessary to maintain the present strength.
3. The re-entry of the Independents [Social Democrats into the government] will not be permitted.
4. More must be done for the welfare of the troops. . . .
5. The unity of the Reich must be preserved.

---

[1] 'Vortrag Groeners am 12. Juli 1919 an die Verbindungsoffiziere der O.H.L.', pp. 19–22: Nachlaß Schleicher, no. 10, Bundesarchiv Koblenz; Groener, *Lebenserinnerungen*, p. 516.   [2] Ernst, op. cit., p. 44.

[3] Volkmann, op. cit., p. 305: telegram of 25 June 1919.

[4] Kurt Caro and Walter Oehme, *Schleichers Aufstieg*, Berlin, 1933, pp. 84–85.

The generals, however, could not agree on the question what they should do if the government did not accept their demands. About half the number present were in favour of demonstrations and the use of force, while the other half advocated at most the use of pressure and close co-operation with Ebert and Noske, without whom these aims could not be achieved.[1]

General von Lüttwitz was equally outspoken about his opposition to the Social Democrats and to the government for which they furnished the chief support. During the same month he addressed a sharp letter to Noske repudiating the attacks made by the party newspaper, the *Vorwärts*, on the attitude of the officer corps: they would only fill it with bitterness against the Social Democrats. 'As I see from numerous utterances of the troops the danger exists that their justified indignation will be directed not only against the party, which stands behind the *Vorwärts*, but also against the government, which in its majority belongs to the Social Democratic party. . . .' Public opinion was identifying the views and judgements of the *Vorwärts* with those of the ministers belonging to the same party, hence the government ought to protect the officer corps against disparaging criticisms.[2]

His own subordinate officers distrusted Lüttwitz's political plans and took precautions against their execution. On 1 August 1919 Major von Hammerstein-Equord informed Groener that Lüttwitz was again very difficult and angry and, if need be, should be removed. Any day it might be necessary for the Majors von Hammerstein and von Stockhausen to resign from their posts, if they were unable to make Lüttwitz give up 'his dark plans'. Ten days later Groener regretfully noted that Hammerstein was taking three months' leave: who was to tame his father-in-law, Lüttwitz, during that time? The two majors had arranged with the commanders of the Reichswehr brigades under Lüttwitz's command that they should not carry out his 'foolish plans'.[3] Yet these plans were carried out seven months later; then too it was Major von Hammerstein who sided

---

[1] Lüttwitz, *Im Kampf gegen die November-Revolution*, pp. 85–86.

[2] Lüttwitz to the minister of defence, Berlin, 11 July 1919: Akten des Gruppenkommandos 4, Bund 7, Akt 1, Bayerisches Kriegsarchiv.

[3] Groener's 'Tagebuch ab 20. März 1919 bis 20. Sept. 1919', under 1 and 11 Aug.: Nachlaß Groener, box 5, no. 16, ii, Bundesarchiv Koblenz. Major von Hammerstein-Equord was the later chief of the army command.

against his father-in-law. But during the intervening period nothing whatsoever was done to remove Lüttwitz from his post or to take effective counter-measures. Was it the instinctive solidarity among the officers which prevented them from warning the government?

Not even Groener hesitated to submit his political demands to the president, demands that had nothing whatever to do with military problems or interests:

The Reichswehr must be employed ruthlessly to secure the authority of the state in all spheres of public life and to guarantee respect for the law. This applies in particular to the administration. What I have seen in this respect during the past weeks is indescribable. The officials—of the old as well as the new régime—show a softness and cowardice which I would have believed impossible. . . . A sense of duty and truthfulness is rare. Instead of combating the wild actions of the workers' councils and their entirely unjustified demands with energy and by using the weight of their whole personalities, they smile and do nothing (*machen sie gute Miene zum bösen Spiel*). Here the cure must begin. All useless and weak personalities must be removed from their posts with an iron broom, and be replaced by men who have to be selected for their efficiency and suitability, not for reasons of party membership and political views. The nonsense of the workers' councils must disappear quickly and completely from the administration. This counter-government by people who to a large extent are entirely incapable and are driven by lust for power, and very often too by the hope of material advantage, remains impossible and unbearable in an orderly state. Their elimination is child's play if their funds are blocked and the government is firm. . . .[1]

Some days later Groener confided to his diary: 'The officers must learn again to obey and stop meddling with the confounded politics; politics must be conducted by a few only—tenaciously and silently—not in the way of William II. . . .'[2] In an address to the liaison officers Groener emphasized again the grave danger that existed if the soldiers continued to conduct politics: if they carried out their orders and abstained from politics, there was no danger whatsoever.[3] He clearly did not realize

[1] Groener to Ebert, Kolberg, 27 June 1919: Nachlaß Groener, box 7, no. 26, Bundesarchiv Koblenz.

[2] Groener's *Tagebuch* under 9 July 1919: ibid., box 5, no. 16, ii.

[3] Groener's address at Kolberg on 18 Aug. 1919: Nachlaß Schleicher, no. 10, ibid.

the danger inherent in his maxim that politics should be conducted by a few officers only. In truth this differentiation
between the mass of the officers, who were to abstain from
politics, and the leaders to whom they were permitted was a
maxim of tremendous importance. It was also novel. While it
corresponded with the practice of Ludendorff during the First
World War, it was far removed from the ideas of the 'good old
officer corps' which Groener strove to revive. According to this
maxim his collaborators and confidants—above all Seeckt and
Schleicher—were to act during the following years. Faced by
a government and a constitution which were alien to the world
of the officer corps, the army as a whole—not the individual
officers—time and again was to play a highly political part.

II

THE REICHSWEHR
UNDER REINHARDT

1. *New Conflicts about the Army Structure*

THE passing of the Treaty of Versailles by the National
Assembly on 16 July and of the Weimar Constitution on
11 August 1919 meant further steps towards political
consolidation. The revolution was over; Germany was a
bourgeois republic. Law and order were restored everywhere,
and the existing military forces were more than sufficient to
maintain them, as was to be shown during all the later *Putsche*
and revolts from the left and the right. According to the new
constitution, the president exercised 'the supreme command
over the entire military forces of the Reich'; but only a few
days later he transferred this function to the Reich minister of
defence, reserving to himself the right of issuing direct commands. At the same time the Reich took over the tasks of
military administration: the individual states ceased to possess
their separate military administrations, powers of command,
and war ministries. For the first time Germany had a uniform
army; the contingents of the states disappeared.[1] The president
further had the right of appointing and dismissing the officers
of army and navy—a function which he could delegate to other
authorities.[2] According to the *Wehrgesetz* of 1921 the president
was the commander-in-chief of all German forces; under him,
the minister of defence exercised the power of command over
them.[3] Thus civilian control of the military forces seemed to be
established.

---

[1] Article 47 of the constitution and decree of 20 Aug. 1919: *Reichsgesetzblatt 1919*,
p. 1475; Benoist-Méchin, *Histoire de l'Armée Allemande*, i. 196; John W. Wheeler-
Bennett, *The Nemesis of Power*, London, 1954, p. 41. Until 1918 Prussia, Bavaria,
Saxony, and Württemberg had their own military contingents.
[2] Article 46 of the constitution.
[3] § 8, ii of the *Wehrgesetz* of 23 Mar. 1921.

Much more important for the development of the Reichswehr were the clauses of the Treaty of Versailles, not the 'shame paragraphs' which had given rise to such bitter controversies, but the military clauses of part v of the treaty. By the enactment of 16 July 1919 it acquired the force of German law and was published in the *Reichsgesetzblatt*.[1] A violation of the provisions of the peace treaty thus became an offence punishable under German law. The military clauses comprised twenty pages of print and stipulated in detail the strength, distribution, period of service, weapons, and equipment of the German army and navy.

According to the treaty, the army was allowed seven infantry and three cavalry divisions, to be grouped under no more than two army corps headquarters. The two headquarters were permitted a maximum of 60 officers and 300 other ranks, an infantry division a maximum of 410 officers and 10,830 other ranks, a cavalry division a maximum of 275 officers and 5,250 other ranks. The total strength of the army was fixed at 100,000, with a maximum of 4,000 officers. The weapons permitted were: 102,000 rifles and carbines, 1,134 light and 792 heavy machine guns, 252 trench mortars, and for the artillery 204 7·7 cm. guns and 84 10·5 cm. howitzers, all with strictly limited stocks of ammunition. The navy was allowed 15,000 men, including a maximum of 1,500 officers and warrant officers. The officers were to serve a minimum of twenty-five years—those already serving at least until their 45th year—and the other ranks a minimum of twelve years. The number of soldiers discharged before that time was not to exceed five per cent. of the total in any one year. This was to prevent a revival of the *Krümper* system of Scharnhorst, who had circumvented the numerical limitation imposed by Napoleon upon the Prussian army through quick training and discharge of those trained, so that new men could be enlisted. The Great General Staff, the military academies, the cadet schools, and all similar institutions were abolished, and only one military school was permitted for the training of the officers of each arm, infantry, cavalry, engineers, and artillery. All measures of mobilization or its preparation were forbidden. Prohibited too were all aeroplanes, submarines, poison gases, their production and import, as well as the import of weapons and war material

[1] *Reichsgesetzblatt 1919*, p. 687.

of any kind. For the fortresses and forts Germany was granted a certain amount of heavy artillery with limited stores of ammunition. The navy was allowed a maximum of six battle-ships, six light cruisers, twelve destroyers and twelve torpedo boats.[1]

Within three months from the coming into force of the peace treaty the German army—which at that time was about half a million strong—was to be reduced to 200,000 men, and by 31 March 1920 to 100,000. Within two months from the coming into force of the treaty all arms, munitions, and war material in excess of the quantities allowed had to be surrendered to the Entente powers. The same applied to eight battleships, eight light cruisers, 42 modern destroyers, 50 modern torpedo boats, all submarines, submarine salvage vessels, and docks, all military aeroplanes and their component parts and appa-ratus. For the supervision of all these clauses Inter-Allied Military Control Commissions were appointed. The German government was obliged to enable them to fulfil their functions, to inform them about stocks of weapons and ammunition, the armament of fortresses and forts, the situation and production of all factories producing war material, and about anything considered necessary by the Control Commissions themselves for the proper fulfilment of their tasks. Their members were entitled to travel throughout Germany and to make inspections of all units and installations. The cost was to be borne by Germany.[2]

Great difficulties were caused during the following months, in particular through the reduction of the army, whose ranks were swollen by the recruitment of the free corps. In addition, there existed from the outset the desire not to surrender weapons and war material to the Entente, but to hide them. During the political unrest of the preceding months many weapons had fallen into private hands, especially those of the extreme left and right. Their collection was impossible, as the existence of the free corps and similar organizations depended on their own stocks of weapons. The activities of the Control Commissions

[1] Articles 160, 164, 167, 170-1, 174-8, 180-1, 183, 191, 194, 198 of the Treaty of Versailles.
[2] Articles 163, 169, 185, 188, 202-10 of the Treaty of Versailles. The time limit or the reduction was later extended to 1 Jan. 1921.

were bound to lead to conflicts with the German military authorities which they were to supervise. There was also the general problem whether it would be possible under these conditions to build up an army that was efficient and could carry out its tasks. Thus from the outset very grave difficulties impeded the implementation of the peace treaty. Even with goodwill on both sides—which hardly existed—constant conflicts could scarcely be avoided.

The immediate result of the signing of the peace treaty was that Field-Marshal von Hindenburg resigned from the High Command and that Groener too announced his impending retirement. At the same time he declared that he was prepared to remain at his post 'in the interest of the cause' until the military affairs were finally settled.[1] This caused a new clash between Groener and Reinhardt. In a telegram of the war ministry to the High Command, of 29 June, it was suggested that the latter should be renamed *Befehlsstelle Kolberg* and that the *Armeeoberkommandos* and *Generalkommandos* in the east, which had been subordinate to the High Command, should be subject to the orders of the minister of defence (Noske) and the Prussian minister of war (Reinhardt). Clearly, both were determined to create a simpler structure of command and to curtail the autonomy of the High Command at Kolberg. This, Groener wrote in his diary, meant 'nothing else but an affront to my person; the *Herr* war minister, the *Schweinehund* [bastard], to whom I am as bothersome as the devil, continues the struggle against me by means that slowly become almost indecent. I would not have expected him to be such a nasty character.— Protest sent to the president, my indignation expressed to the war minister by 'phone.'[2] According to Reinhardt, Groener telephoned and demanded full and unlimited power of command over the *Generalkommandos*; he objected to the name of *Befehlsstelle Kolberg* 'which undermined his authority'. Reinhardt denied any intention of offending Groener and the existence of a personal conflict between Groener and himself: the Prussian minister of war was entitled to issue orders to the units of the Prussian contingent, and it was expedient that the

[1] Ernst, *Aus dem Nachlaß des Generals Walther Reinhardt*, p. 44.
[2] Groener's 'Tagebuch ab 20. März 1919 bis 20. Sept. 1919': Nachlaß Groener, box 5, no. 16 ii, under 29 June 1919, Bundesarchiv Koblenz.

Reich minister of defence should, for certain purposes, be able to issue orders directly without an intermediary; he had therefore been appointed 'commander-in-chief' in wide areas of Prussia by the Prussian and the Reich governments at Reinhardt's suggestion.[1]

Reinhardt made some concessions with regard to the power of issuing orders, so that outwardly a reconciliation with Groener was effected. Several subordinate officers, however, among them Major von Hammerstein-Equord, approached Noske directly. Thus Noske wrote to Reinhardt that the officers had no confidence in the organizational work of the war ministry; therefore General von Seeckt would be entrusted with the task of reorganizing the army. He became chairman of the Organization Committee, with the functions of a peace-time chief of the general staff. On 10 July Noske, Reinhardt, and Seeckt met at Weimar. There Reinhardt accepted Seeckt's proposals, but insisted 'that under the minister of defence there should be a military head to whom all departments . . . would be subordinate, i.e., he himself wants to be that head!!'. But some days later Seeckt fell ill and was incapacitated for some time. Groener strongly regretted this: 'Seeckt had entered the battle with the war minister anew, and it seemed certain that he would gain Noske's confidence—now his illness intervenes. I too am eliminated; thus Reinhardt can triumph and can arrange everything nicely to the advantage of the war minister; he himself is aiming at the long-coveted post in the ministry of defence! . . .'[2]

There were personal as well as objective contrasts between Reinhardt and Seeckt. Reinhardt aimed at the position of chief of the army command (*Chef der Heeresleitung*) with authority in all military matters—to replace the former division into military command, administration, personnel, and general-staff matters.[3] Seeckt was to occupy the post of *Chef des Truppenamtes*, which was to continue the functions of the dissolved Great General Staff; hence he aimed at making this position as strong as possible and at being independent of the chief of

---

[1] Ernst, op. cit., pp. 45–46.

[2] Groener's 'Tagebuch ab 20. März bis 20. Sept. 1919': Nachlaß Groener, box 5, no. 16 ii, under 9, 10, and 19 July 1919, Bundesarchiv Koblenz; Ernst, op. cit., p. 46.

[3] Walther Reinhardt, *Wehrkraft und Wehrwille*, Berlin, 1932, p. 51.

the army command. On 21 July his ideas were put forward in his absence by Lieutenant-Colonel Hasse, who argued that a supreme military authority was not required, for a superior personality would not always be available.[1] Seeckt desired a horizontal top structure under the minister of defence, who was to have no power of command and thus no real influence in military affairs. By contrast, Reinhardt advocated a military head, but was willing to grant Noske powers of command.[2] Again Groener unreservedly took Seeckt's side. He strongly regretted that Seeckt had not succeeded in defeating Reinhardt's views; time alone would show whether he would be able to prevail against the government and against Reinhardt; 'even if Noske has the best will, and undoubtedly he possesses many excellent qualities for the post of minister of defence, he lacks the military knowledge, and in addition he cannot shed his party skin. I would have wished that he had taken Seeckt as his first military adviser. . . . During the past week I was in Schwarzburg at a conference with the president and the minister of defence and could ascertain that both personalities are willing to meet the wishes of the military as much as possible, and in particular to work for the preservation of a firmly welded officer corps. . . .'[3]

During August the conflict continued unabated. Groener almost admitted defeat: 'The war minister has obtained his wish; the old war ministry is recreated unchanged in the Reich ministry of defence; only personal motives have been responsible for the whole scheme. Reinhardt has reserved for himself the nice little post of "chief of the army command".' A few days later, however, Groener made a new attack on Reinhardt, this time directly addressing the president. 'I talk myself into such a rage that I use unparliamentary expressions about Reinhardt. . . . But I have no doubt it is useless; for Reinhardt is not unsympathetic to these people, because he meets their wishes and finds a way out of all difficulties which is not embarrassing to the government. He is a clever fox. . . .' On the next day

[1] Rabenau, *Seeckt*, p. 468.

[2] Hans Meier-Welcker, 'Die Stellung des Chefs der Heeresleitung in den Anfängen der Republik', *Vierteljahrshefte für Zeitgeschichte*, iv, 1956, p. 152; Görlitz, *Der deutsche Generalstab*, p. 316.

[3] Groener to Hindenburg, Kolberg, 7 Aug. 1919: Nachlaß Groener, box 7, no. 28, Bundesarchiv Koblenz.

Groener had a similar conversation with Noske, who promised that in the following spring Seeckt would be given Reinhardt's post; 'Reinhardt is a small man, but very assiduous and hard-working, enough of an intriguer to let no one else rise next to him, and will never become dangerous to Noske and the republic. Thus [he is] the natural military aid of the govern-ment. . . .'[1] In a letter to his wife Groener accused Reinhardt of 'going further in the elimination of the old military achieve-ments than even the Social Democrats would dare to do. . .'.[2] If Groener believed that Reinhardt would 'never become dangerous to . . . the republic', he had apparently a different opinion of Seeckt. In any case, the government was thus fully justified in preferring Reinhardt to Seeckt. It is even more remarkable that Noske's promise that Seeckt would succeed Reinhardt in the following spring was fulfilled in March 1920, although not by Noske.

At the end of August a new difference arose between Reinhardt and Seeckt because the former wanted to allocate training and education to the *Waffenamt*, while Seeckt favoured the *Truppenamt* as he wanted to strengthen his own position. Reinhardt then suggested a compromise according to which the *Truppenamt* remained responsible for education, while training came under the *Waffenamt*.[3] Connected therewith was a more important point. Groener and Seeckt intended to save as much as possible of the traditional weight of the general staff and to take over as many general staff officers as possible into the new army,[4] an endeavour that was not supported by all the leading officers. Therefore Seeckt complained to Rein-hardt:

I have been informed that the Personnel Office opposes the justi-fied attempts to employ as many general staff officers as possible in the new army, with the slogan 'the tried front-line officers have to be considered in the first instance', or with the phrase 'the general staff is at the moment unpopular and carries no weight'. I must resist with all force this tendency to prejudice the general staff officers. I maintain by contrast that the experienced general staff

[1] Groener's 'Tagebuch ab 20. März bis 20. Sept. 1919': ibid., box 5, no. 16 ii, under 15–17, 20 and 21 Aug. 1919.
[2] Groener-Geyer, *General Groener*, p. 169: letter of 24 Aug. 1919.
[3] Groener's *Tagebuch*, under 23 Aug. 1919: Nachlaß Groener, box 5, no. 16 ii.
[4] Meier-Welcker, loc. cit., p. 154; Groener, *Lebenserinnerungen*, p. 516.

officers must be considered in the first place . . . and that the preservation of the general staff means the preservation of the spirit of the army. I further deny that there is an inner conflict between the general staff officer and the front-line officer, and I consider the tendency to construct such a conflict artificially regrettable and reprehensible. . . .

Seeckt considered the formation of the volunteer units and of the Reichswehr to have been due above all to the work of the general staff; its officers had been willing to fulfil any duty, 'be that with the troops or in political work, without sparing themselves'.[1]

Reinhardt as well as the chief of the Personnel Office, General von Braun, repudiated Seeckt's criticisms and emphasized that they agreed with him about the achievements of the general staff. General von Braun added that two leading officers had warned him, independently of each other, not to give preference to the general staff in making appointments in the Reichswehr; the officers were disquieted that front-line officers had to give pride of place to general staff officers as a matter of principle when officers were selected for the Reichswehr. Reinhardt expressly stated 'that we older officers think the same way about the roots of our strength, and work unitedly towards its preservation'.[2] He thus alluded to the fact that the large majority of the Reichswehr generals came from the general staff and identified themselves with its tradition and its principles. As a matter of fact the key positions in the Reichswehr were occupied by general staff officers and former staff officers.[3] This uniform background and mentality of the leading officers was an advantage in building the new army. But it brought with it the danger that new ideas, especially if they came from younger officers, had little chance of being taken into account. It also meant that a strongly conservative spirit permeated the higher ranks of the officer corps.

For the last time Groener attacked Reinhardt sharply, in the presence of Ebert, Noske, Reinhardt himself, and the Majors

---

[1] Seeckt to Reinhardt, 29 Aug. 1919: Ernst, *Aus dem Nachlaß des Generals Walther Reinhardt*, pp. 50–51.

[2] Letter of General von Braun of 2 Sept. 1919 and of Reinhardt, n.d.: ibid., pp. 51–52.

[3] Gordon, *Reichswehr and the German Republic*, p. 191, who states that they 'controlled the army'.

von Gilsa, von Schleicher, and von Stockhausen, on 11
September—a week before he left the army. He declared

without mincing his words, he had wished to see General von Seeckt,
and not Colonel Reinhardt, as the leading military personality in
the ministry of defence. . . . The controversy between Noske and
Reinhardt on the one side and me on the other assumed sharper and
sharper forms. The president tried to smooth the waves; as if a cue
had been given, there appeared first coffee and tea with rolls and
biscuits, later an excellent peach cup, which Schleicher in particular
emptied in deep draughts. Stockhausen correctly enlarged on my
proposal . . . , while Reinhardt stressed that Seeckt as chief of the
Truppenamt could not possess independent powers of command, but
was a part of the defence ministry, and that powers of command
rested with Noske. I got so fed up with the argument that I would
have liked to leave the room. But the first decisive issue for me is the
personal one, Seeckt or Reinhardt. As Noske had long decided in
favour of Reinhardt, the whole palaver was pointless. . . . At the
end, after the majors had left, Reinhardt declared that he must
protest at being told in the presence of his subordinates that he was
unsuitable for his post in the ministry of defence. The president tried
to calm things; I refrained from saying that this is nothing new for
many of his subordinates, in particular for the best and most
intelligent. . . .[1]

Such attacks against their chief in front of junior officers by a
serving general were indeed something new in the history of
the Prussian army.

Seeckt seconded Groener as best he could. In his opinion,
only the ministry of defence was entitled to issue orders to the
leading officers, and within the ministry, the *Truppenamt*;
'all other authorities must be eliminated'.[2] He complained
'about the difficulties of his new position' and about the 'limit-
less insecurity and confusion into which the army had been
thrown by the conduct of the war ministry. . .'.[3] He hesitated for
a while whether to accept the post of chief of the *Truppenamt*,
but at the beginning of October Colonel Heye succeeded in
persuading Seeckt to accept. Heye became his chief of staff,

[1] Groener's *Tagebuch*, under 11 Sept. 1919: Nachlaß Groener, box 5, no. 16
ii, Bundesarchiv Koblenz.
[2] Seeckt to Noske, 16 Sept. 1919, quoted in the notes of General Lieber: Nachlaß
Seeckt, box 19, no. 278, p. 29, Militärgeschichtliches Forschungsamt Freiburg.
[3] Seeckt to Groener, 24 Sept. 1919: ibid., p. 29.

and Lieutenant-Colonel Hasse the head of the first department of the *Truppenamt*, the T 1.[1] Hasse feared that Seeckt would be 'very sovereign and difficult'.[2] Theoretically Seeckt was now subordinate to Reinhardt, but in practice he tried to secure complete autonomy for himself and to expand his sphere of activity. Reinhardt tried to prevent this and his being by-passed as chief of the army command.[3] Early in 1920 an observer found that the relationship between the two leading officers had become very acrimonious.[4] No fruitful co-operation was possible under these conditions.

On 17 September Groener once more addressed himself to the president and developed in detail his ideas about the reorganization of the army and the spirit which should animate the officer corps. Politics, he emphasized, must be eliminated; 'political activities in the army mean the end of all comrade-ship and all discipline. The sooner this undesirable pheno-menon disappears again from the officer corps, the sooner the old rule of comradeship "one for all and all for one" will once more prevail in the officer corps. . . .'[5] What Groener clearly did not ask himself was whether he had not been one of those who had carried politics into the officer corps. On 18 September a farewell dinner was held in Groener's honour at Kolberg, and on the 19th he left. Schleicher had advised him to enter the govern-ment;[6] but—with the exception of a short spell as minister of transport—he did not play any part in politics during the following years. With Groener's departure the High Command of the war years ceased to exist, as did the war ministries of the individual states. An epoch of German military history had come to an end.

11. *The Army and Politics*

After the National Assembly, in August 1919, had accepted the Weimar Constitution and the new colours of black, red,

[1] Nachlaß Seeckt, box 19, no. 278, p. 30; Görlitz, *Der deutsche Generalstab*, p. 317.   [2] Rabenau, *Seeckt*, p. 202.

[3] Ibid.; Gordon, *Reichswehr and the German Republic*, p. 221.

[4] Joachim von Stülpnagel, '75 Jahre meines Lebens', p. 181, Bundesarchiv-Militärarchiv, H 08–5/27.

[5] Groener to Ebert, Kolberg 17 Sept. 1919: Nachlaß Schleicher, no. 10, Bundes-archiv Koblenz.

[6] Groener's *Tagebuch*, under 12 Sept. 1919: Nachlaß Groener, box 5, no. 16 ii, ibid.

and gold, the army had to give up the black, white, and red flag, and the soldiers had to take the oath to the constitution. Even before this the question of the new colours led to protests within the Reichswehr. In July the commander of the Bavarian Infantry Brigade 21, Colonel Franz Ritter von Epp, wrote to the *Gruppenkommando* in Munich: 'Starting from the premiss that in the question of the colours those sections of the population must be heard who are in the first place called upon to wear and to protect the colours of the Reich, i.e. the Reichswehr soldiers, I have held an inquiry in my brigade. The result of this inquiry is the unanimous demand of all troops belonging to the brigade . . . that the old German colours of black, white, and red should be retained. . . .' The Bavarian commander-in-chief, Major-General Ritter von Möhl, supported Epp's demand: 'An inquiry in the other Reichswehr brigades would have the same result as the inquiry of Colonel Epp. The decision of the National Assembly shows a disregard of important emotional values.'[1]

In Berlin the governor, the Social Democratic deputy Schöpflin, approached the *Gruppenkommando* with the request that the Imperial war flag hoisted on the palace by a naval unit should be struck and that the Reichswehr units should not carry so many black, white, and red flags, as this was bound to alienate the population, which was loyal to the government. This request was declined by *Gruppenkommando* 1. 'Numerous manifestations from the ranks of the troops', it replied, 'prove that they want to keep the old colours of black, white, and red, under which they have fought and conquered for four years and a half. The dropping of these colours is considered by the troops, which are once more fighting to preserve the state, as a measure that disregards their feelings. . . .'[2] Before the passing of the new constitution the minister of the interior decreed that all public buildings were to show the new colours on the day after the acceptance of the constitution by the National Assembly. In the war ministry, however, it was suggested 'to do nothing. We have not yet got the new flags and can mention

---

[1] Epp to *Gruppenkommando* 4, Munich, 14 July, and Möhl to the ministry of military affairs, Munich, 18 July 1919: Akten des Gruppenkommandos 4, Bund 7, Akt 1, Bayerisches Kriegsarchiv, Munich.

[2] Schöpflin to *Gruppenkommando* 1, Berlin, 21 July, and reply of the *Gruppenkommando*, Berlin, 22 July 1919: ibid.

this and the impossibility of getting them as reasons. . . .'[1] No reason was given why it was impossible to obtain the new colours during the two weeks between the issue of the decree and the final vote of the National Assembly.

After the promulgation of the constitution the troops had to take the new oath, and this caused more difficulties. The officer commanding the Reichswehr Regiment 29 declared: 'I and my officer corps will take the oath only with the reservation that

1. we shall be permitted to continue to wear the black, white, and red cockades;
2. we shall not be forced to take the oath to the black, red, and gold colours;
3. the black, red, and gold colours shall never be hoisted on our buildings. . . .'

This was supported by Colonel Reinhard, commanding the infantry of Brigade 15, who wrote that he would never wear the black, red, and gold colours. The commanding officer of the Brigade, Lieutenant-General von Oven, was more cautious and sent the declaration to the *Gruppenkommando* 1 with the remark: 'The same opinion is held by many soldiers and also by the Second Naval Brigade.' General von Lüttwitz, the commanding officer of the *Gruppenkommando*, used the opportunity to warn Noske against carrying further inflammable material into the army without a proper reason.[2]

A few days later General von Lüttwitz again addressed the minister of defence to demand sharper measures against the extreme left:

If the government lets the time pass without acting, it will lose its military power through the reduction of the army and will strengthen the power of Bolshevism. But because the government depends upon the energetic co-operation of the troops, everything must be avoided that is likely to influence the temper of the army against the government and the parties supporting it. To this category belong all measures and laws which hurt the military feelings of the troops,

[1] Handwritten note signed 'v.K.' (von Kessel?) of 28 July 1919: Nachlaß Schleicher, no. 13, Bundesarchiv Koblenz.

[2] Lieutenant-Colonel von dem Hagen on 19 Aug., Colonel Reinhard on 20, General von Oven on 21 and General von Lüttwitz on 24 Aug. 1919 to the minister of defence: Nachlaß Reinhardt, Hauptstaatsarchiv Stuttgart.

such as a change in the uniforms, renunciation of the old German Imperial flag, or abolition of the special military courts, even if the government and the parties consider these changes important in their sense. It is more important not to take any measures that create in the army a temper directed against the government and parliament. Today too the army is the foundation of state power. . . .[1]

The last statement of General von Lüttwitz was correct; it indicated the difficulties which the government experienced as a result of the use of the volunteer units and free corps.

The chief of the general staff of *Gruppenkommando* 2, Major-General von Loßberg, also demanded stronger measures against the left, especially preventive steps, so as to make strikes and the outbreak of disorders impossible. President Ebert, however, declined to take the desired steps. In a conference in Berlin on 13 September General von Loßberg emphasized that this attitude of the government was bound to facilitate the organization of the radical elements and 'that the Reichswehr and its leaders do not understand this conduct of the government. He has also stressed that, on the basis of this government decision, the impending struggle of the Reichswehr against Communists and Independents will be rendered much more difficult, and that officers, non-commissioned officers, and other soldiers will most likely have to pay with their blood for the liberty which their enemies now possess to work for the overthrow of the government. . . .' All that Loßberg was able to achieve was Noske's promise that he would take the sharpest measures if law and order were threatened by strikes and revolts.[2] In the autumn of 1919 the Communist Party was still weak and divided, while they and the Independent Social Democrats were by no means united against the government. The sharp course advocated by the *Gruppenkommando* 2—and equally by Lüttwitz's *Gruppenkommando* 1—might easily have driven the Independents into the Communist camp. The officers' vision was a simplified military one, and the government was clearly better qualified to take political decisions.

---

[1] Lüttwitz, *Im Kampf gegen die November-Revolution*, p. 93: letter to Noske of 1 Sept. 1919.
[2] *Reichswehrgruppenkommando* 2, Wilhelmshöhe near Cassel, 16 Sept. 1919: Akten des Gruppenkommandos 4, Bund 7, Akt 1, Bayerisches Kriegsarchiv.

From the generals the tendency to put forward political demands spread to the lower echelons. In July—after the acceptance of the peace treaty—the commanding officer and the *Vertrauensleute* of the Infantry Regiment 39 in East Prussia sent the following wire to Reich president [*sic*] Noske:

> The regiment has heard with indignation that the government has given its consent to a peace which must make the German nation contemptible throughout the world. The government thereby . . . has allocated to Germany the sole responsibility for the world war. It delivers the Kaiser and our leaders . . . to the enemy who, under the semblance of a law court, only wants to satisfy his brutal victor's sentiments, to dishonour Germany and make her contemptible through the treason of her own subjects before all peoples of the world, down to the tribes of savages. The regiment will never bear the shame of seeing the Kaiser and the Field-Marshal, its loved and honoured chief, surrendered to the arbitrary enemy. . . . We can no longer trust a government which has proved that it is unable to guard the nation's honour. We have complete confidence only in the minister of defence, Noske. The main culprit in our opinion is the Reich minister Erzberger. He was one of those who crippled the will of the German nation to triumph, by their frivolous assertions that our enemies were ready for a conciliation. His work is the armistice that has destroyed us. . . . This man has forfeited our respect. We demand that he be removed from the government.

In the Prussian war ministry it was proposed to reprove the senders of the telegram. But General von Kessel considered this 'petty': such utterances caused by patriotic feelings should not be weighed too carefully. Thus no disciplinary measures were taken. Reinhardt merely wrote to the commanding officer that he had full sympathy with the grief and excitement shown in the telegram, but that a demand for the removal of a minister, if expressed in such a way, was not permissible.[1] An answer couched in these terms was bound to create the impression of tacit approval, if not of the form, then at least of the content of the protest.

Later the ministry of defence refused to take action when a Social Democratic deputy complained that a Reichswehr unit

---

[1] Telegram of Reichswehr Regiment 39 of 26 July 1919, proposal by General von Kessel of 1 Aug., and letter of Reinhardt, n.d.: Nachlaß Reinhardt, Hauptstaatsarchiv Stuttgart.

at Frankfurt, commanded by Captain de Neufville, was still carrying black, white, and red ribbons on the right shoulder at the end of 1919. The reply simply said: 'As the chief of the army command, Major-General Reinhardt, could recently and personally convince himself during an official visit to southern Germany, the unit of Captain de Neufville is in an excellent condition and preserves magnificent discipline. As soon as it has received the new insignia, it will naturally wear them; until then it will wear the old ones.' When the same deputy complained again in March 1920, the *Truppenamt* replied that new regulations about the insignia would be promulgated by the ministry of defence in due course: until then the unit was entitled to wear the old ones.[1] At the end of 1919 Rear-Admiral Meurer, the commander of the Baltic station of the navy, published another violent attack against Erzberger:

> Since the negotiator of the German Reich, Erzberger, in November 1918, to the surprise of our enemies, accepted the annihilating armistice stipulations without opposition or conditions, the authority and strength of Germany have declined step by step, via the acceptance of the shameful peace (*Schmachfrieden*) and the disgraceful surrender stipulations (*schandbare Auslieferungsparagraphen*), to complete self-destruction. . . . Let us oppose the united will of our enemies to destroy us by our equally united efforts to recreate a strong Germany; let us oppose the creeping spirit of international decomposition by manly pride in our nationhood and a history glorious during two thousand years: time and again, after periods of peril and disunity, our nation, chastened by misfortune, has risen all the more powerfully. With this vow let us begin the year 1920, then it will bring success! With God for Reich and fatherland! . . .[2]

But in this case action was taken, and Meurer had to resign from the navy, perhaps because his proclamation was too openly anti-republican.[3]

Time and again certain generals approached the leaders of the Reichswehr with political plans, calling for opposition even

---

[1] Deputy Quarck to Chancellor Bauer, Frankfurt, 16 Nov. 1919, and replies of the ministry of defence of 21 Dec. 1919 and 13 Mar. 1920, the latter signed by Hasse: Reichskanzlei, Akten betr. Reichswehr, Volkswehr und Wehrpflicht, vol. 1–2, R 43 I 682–3, Bundesarchiv Koblenz.

[2] Ibid., vol. 1, R 43 I 682.

[3] Erich Raeder, *Mein Leben*, Tübingen, 1956, i. 180.

to the government. This applied in particular to the evacuation of the Baltic states where German volunteers were engaged in bitter fighting against the Red Army, but also against the governments of these new states. Hard-pressed by the Baltic governments and by the Entente powers, the German government attempted to persuade the German units to return home —a course that was sharply repudiated by their leaders. The members of the free corps hoped that they would be able to settle in the Baltic states. Many of them entered the service of the White Russians—under Prince Bermondt—when they received orders to return home. Leading German Social Democrats were suspected of Bolshevik sympathies because they wanted to evacuate the Baltic territories. From this it was only a short step towards making plans to fight 'Marxism' in Germany too.[1] In June 1919 Major Freiherr von Fritsch reported to Seeckt that the situation in the occupied area had deteriorated since Erzberger had given a promise that the German units would be evacuated. 'Apart from the obstacles put in our way by the Entente our shaky position arises from the fact that the Bolshevik heart of Herr Philipp Scheidemann [the German chancellor] beats up there [*sic*] more strongly for our enemies—the Bolsheviks and the Ulmannis people—than for the Germans. . . .' The German commander-in-chief, Count von der Goltz, Fritsch added, was forced to take action against the Latvians under Ulmannis to guarantee the security of the German units, and had thus aroused the distrust of the Social Democrats.[2]

Some months later Major-General Count von der Goltz, in a letter to Seeckt, went even further in attacking leading Social Democrats: 'We will lose our last friends, all the anti-Bolshevik parties of Russia, if we now surpass the Entente demands and completely sabotage the West Russian government, only because it desires to eliminate the friends of Müller [the German foreign minister, and later chancellor]; for they are his friends, especially Lenin, who, he hopes, will move towards the right.' At the same time von der Goltz invited

[1] Rabenau, *Seeckt*, pp. 125, 132, 135–6.

[2] Fritsch to Seeckt, Bartenstein, 18 June 1919: Nachlaß Seeckt, no. 87, fasc. 20, Militärgeschichtliches Forschungsamt Freiburg. Fritsch was the first general staff officer in the *Armeeoberkommando Nord*. Ulmannis was the leader of the new Latvian government.

Seeckt, by reminding him of his victory at Gorlice in Galicia in 1915, to take steps against the German government:

I cannot accept the point of view that one has to carry out the orders of a government which one serves without condition and without will. . . . You have the duty to stick to your opposite point of view to the last consequence. . . . If I may make a personal point, I request you to remember that the whole officer corps puts its hopes in your politically clear-sighted and independent thoughts and actions, and that—forgive me—the fame and the historical name of the victor of Gorlice depend on the position which you take up towards the present government. On this too depends whether the Reichswehr remains, as it has always been, a national and independent instrument under its leaders, standing above party, for the entire fatherland, or whether it deteriorates to the position of a soulless mercenary force in the hands of changing governments, in which no honourable man will be willing to serve. Believe me, innumerable officers think as I do. . . .[1]

To Reinhardt Count von der Goltz wrote in a similar vein: 'The deed which we need is the destruction of the Peace of Versailles, politically and economically, the escape from the blackmailing hands of the Entente, which can use the non-fulfilment of any clause of the treaty to impose upon us anew the blockade. . . . First economic liberation abroad, then political liberation abroad, and in the process it will appear whether our present internal orientation is viable. That I do not believe it is, is obvious. . . .' In his opinion, the officer corps had to choose whether it 'was to carry out the orders of any government, or whether it was to preserve itself as an independent political and national factor which could not be by-passed by the changing party governments. . .'.[2] To this Reinhardt replied at the beginning of 1920: 'Only if all officers in strictest discipline support the responsible leading officers, will it be possible to make sure that the "officer corps" and equally the entire "Reichswehr" find their value as an independent factor in the mechanism of political powers fully considered; unity alone gives strength. But there our comrades, high and low, to

---

[1] Count von der Goltz to Seeckt, Berlin, 2 Nov. 1919: Nachlaß Seeckt, box 10, no. 72, ibid.; partly printed by Rabenau, *Seeckt*, p. 205.

[2] von der Goltz to Reinhardt, Berlin, 4 Nov. 1919: Nachlaß Reinhardt, Hauptstaatsarchiv Stuttgart.

the right and to the left, show the insuperable German spirit of disunity as much as the political parties. . . .'[1]

Reinhardt too desired to make the Reichswehr 'an independent factor' in the political mechanism. But in his opinion this could only be achieved by the elimination of political discussion from the officer corps, by its strict subordination to the 'chief of the army command'.[2] He too wanted to preserve the Reichswehr as 'an independent political and national factor'. But while Count von der Goltz sought to achieve this by constant pressure on the government and, if need be, by resistance to it, Reinhardt was convinced that the aim could only be attained through co-operation, by making the army indispensable and by preserving its internal autonomy. What separated the two sides was not so much a difference of aims as a difference about the means to be used to achieve the aim. Yet this was often not seen in the bitter political struggles of the time. To the officers who believed that they alone were 'national' in their attitude, everybody was suspicious who did not proclaim his views from the roof tops and declare war on the republic and the parties which supported it. But such a policy might easily have resulted in driving the government further to the left and thus have achieved the opposite of what the 'national' side desired. The policy of Reinhardt—and later that of Seeckt—was not only more cautious, but also more intelligent and more successful. As the Kapp Putsch was to show, open resistance to the government would have been met by forces which were stronger than the officer corps.

III. *With the White or with the Red Russians?*

The main aim in the field of foreign policy proclaimed by Count von der Goltz in November 1919 was 'the destruction of the Peace of Versailles', and in this he voiced the opinion of the large majority of the officer corps. The details of this policy he described in a memorandum sent to Reinhardt:

It is necessary time and again to pillory in the neutral and [White] Russian press the British policy, which out of hatred of Germany directly supports Bolshevism and wants to prevent the re-emergence of the old allied Russia stretching to the Baltic. The hatred

---

[1] Reinhardt to von der Goltz, Berlin, 2 Jan. 1920: ibid.
[2] Cf. Reinhardt, *Wehrkraft und Wehrwille*, Berlin, 1932, p. 51.

felt by all anti-Bolshevik Russians against Britain cannot be sufficiently fanned. This, however, entails that all these Russian parties
are shown by deeds that only Germany can be their ally and saviour.
A beginning was made during the evacuation of the Ukraine and in
mobilizing the Corps Bermondt. It is incredibly short-sighted and
illogical if now, out of fear of the Entente, not only are the last
German units withdrawn—that is obvious—but if the Bermondt
enterprise and the West Russian Central Council are directly
sabotaged. Thereby we make the Bolsheviks our friends and the
Russia of the future, which puts its hopes in us, our eternal enemy.
And yet the latter is our only friend, our only hope. . . . The most
important aim for isolated Germany must be to seek a new, strong
friend, and this can only be done by a revival of Bismarck's old
idea of Russo-German friendship. . . . Nothing separates us any
longer. The friendship of the two neighbours threatened by Britain
is simply natural. . . . When we have gained a new friend in Russia
and when we possess a large united East-European economic area,
any new blockade, which Russia [*sic*] would then hardly dare to
impose, would be immaterial to us. . . . Britain has long recognized
this, and hence she wants to block this last hole to us. Only in Germany
do we close our eyes to this last ray of hope, partly out of fear of the
Entente, partly out of ignorance. . . .[1]

What Count von der Goltz wanted was a return to the Bis-
marckian policy of an alliance with Russia, and this policy was
given a burning actuality by the Treaty of Versailles. There
now existed the possibility of a common front against the
victorious powers of the West. General von Seeckt held exactly
the same view; only he—three months later—estimated the
chances of Soviet Russia very much higher than Count von der
Goltz had done. He realized that the Russian civil war was
decided in favour of the Bolsheviks, and he drew the logical
political conclusion from it. At the end of January 1920 he
wrote: 'As I consider a future political and economic agreement
with Great Russia to be the immutable aim of our foreign
policy, we must attempt at least not to make an enemy of
Russia.' Therefore attention should be focused on Red Russia,
victorious over Denikin and Kolchak, and thus Germany must
side against Poland and the Baltic states. 'I refuse to support
Poland, even if that means that Poland will be eaten up. On the

---

[1] Memorandum of Count von der Goltz, 4 Nov. 1919: Nachlaß Reinhardt,
Hauptstaatsarchiv Stuttgart.

contrary, I reckon with this, and if at the moment we cannot help Russia to regain her old Imperial frontiers, we should at least not hinder her from doing so. . . . The same applies to Lithuania and Latvia. . . .'[1]

A few lays later Seeckt in a longer memorandum on 'Germany and Russia' developed the ideas to which he was to remain loyal throughout his career:

Only in firm co-operation with a Great Russia will Germany have the chance of regaining her position as a world power. In place of lengthy proofs in favour of this fundamental thesis of German policy only one will be adduced here: Britain and France fear the combination of the two land powers and try to prevent it with all their means—hence we have to seek it with all our strength. . . . Whether we like or dislike the new Russia and her internal structure is quite immaterial. Our policy would have had to be the same towards a Tsarist Russia or towards a state under Kolchak or Denikin. Now we have to come to terms with Soviet Russia—we have no alternative. One thing this has in common with the old Imperial Russia and with the Russia desired by the generals: the overpowering quest for the unity of the Empire, for Great Russia. This, however, is exactly what we need, a united, strong Empire with a broad frontier at our side. Thereby the always mistaken policy of creating buffer states stands condemned. Even if we do not take into account earlier times . . . everybody's eyes should now be opened to the fact that Poland, Lithuania, Latvia are only to serve as a wall separating Germany from Russia. In Poland France seeks to gain the eastern field of attack against Germany and, together with Britain, has driven the stake which we cannot endure into our flesh, quite close to the heart of our existence as a state. Now France trembles for her Poland which a strengthened Russia threatens with destruction, and now Germany is to save her mortal enemy! Her mortal enemy, for we have none worse at this moment. Never can Prussia–Germany concede that Bromberg, Graudenz, Thorn, (Marienburg), Posen should remain in Polish hands, and now there appears on the horizon, like a divine miracle, help for us in our deep distress. At this moment nobody should ask Germany to lift as much as a finger when disaster engulfs Poland. . . .[2]

[1] Seeckt to General von Massow, 31 Jan. 1920: Nachlaß Seeckt, box 19, no. 278, p. 13, Militärgeschichtliches Forschungsamt Freiburg; partly quoted by Rabenau, *Seeckt*, p. 252.

[2] Manuscript of Seeckt with the date 4/2 (4 Feb. 1920): Nachlaß Seeckt, box 15, no. 212, microfilm in Institut für Zeitgeschichte, Munich. The towns mentioned are: Bydgoszcz, Grudziądz, Toruń, and Poznań.

Here General von Seeckt laid down the basic ideas governing his policy; especially the aim of the common frontier between Germany and Russia, of the regaining of the frontiers of 1914, and of the fourth partition of Poland, runs like a red thread through the involved military relations between the two countries during the Weimar period—to be carried out in 1939. Perhaps the anti-French component was more pronounced with Count von der Goltz, but both generals desired close political and economic relations with Russia. As soon as it became clear that this Russia would be a Soviet Russia, the position of Seeckt was logical and realistic—and in agreement with the principles of Prussian policy since the Seven Years War. It is even possible to go further. If one desired, as Seeckt did, that Germany should regain her position as a world power, this was the only possible way; for where else was Germany to find an ally?

After the outbreak of the Russo-Polish war of 1920 an appreciation of the situation was written in the *Truppenamt*, probably by Colonel Hasse. To a certain extent it went conformably with Seeckt's ideas, but it also differed from them. About Poland the same opinion was expressed:

The present Polish state is a creation of the Entente. It is to replace the pressure formerly exercised by Russia on the eastern frontier of Germany. The fight of Soviet Russia with Poland hits not only the latter, but above all the Entente—France and Britain. If Poland collapses the whole edifice of the Versailles Treaty totters. From this it follows clearly that Germany has no interest in rendering any help to Poland in her struggle with Russia. On the contrary, it can only be agreeable to us if Poland should cease to exist. On the other hand, we must also take the measures necessary to prevent Bolshevism from flooding Germany after the destruction of Poland. In the first place this means disarming the elements hostile to the state and strengthening of the state authority internally. . . . The Entente has not given up its war aim, which it pursues relentlessly, 'the destruction of Germany'. . . . For Germany it is essential to free herself from the chains of the Entente with the help of Soviet Russia, without falling a victim to Bolshevism. . . . Situated between the western powers and Russia, made defenceless by the Treaty of Versailles and the Spa Agreement, Germany will probably be the battlefield for the decisive struggles between the old capitalist and the new Bolshevik ideologies. If we do not want to be ground to pieces between the fighting powers, we must attempt to reconcile the old with the new ideology in our nation and to eliminate the class conflicts. With this we create at the same time the basis for a general uprising of the people, which is to free us from the yoke of the Entente without imposing upon us the yoke of Bolshevism. . . .[1]

The ideas of a reconciliation between the *Weltanschauung* of capitalism and that of Bolshevism, of the elimination of the class conflicts, of a people's war, were alien to Seeckt, who was a staunch protagonist of the conservative Prussian tradition. But they evoke echoes of another Prussian tradition—that of the war of liberation against Napoleon: whoever wrote these lines was more strongly influenced by Scharnhorst than by Moltke. Similar ideas were to exercise a strong influence on some of the younger officers for many years, but the leaders of the Reichswehr remained hostile to them.

As far as Seeckt was concerned, it seems possible that he established contacts with Karl Radek as early as the summer or autumn of 1919, when Radek, while a prisoner in Berlin, had a political 'salon' in his prison cell. It can hardly be doubted that there was at least an indirect contact between the two men, with an old friend and ally of Seeckt, the former Turkish minister of war, Enver Pasha, as the go-between.[2] It is equally likely that Enver Pasha, before he flew to Moscow in October 1919,[3] was instructed by Seeckt to promote if possible German-Russian collaboration. If the first approach came from the Russians, it occurred after the destruction of their hopes of world revolution by their defeat in the Russo-Polish war, by 'the miracle of the Vistula'. A few days after the battle of Warsaw of August 1920 Enver Pasha wrote a curious letter to Seeckt from Moscow, in very bad German:

Dear friend! Yesterday I had a conversation with Sklanski, [Sklyansky, the deputy people's commissar for war] the deputy and right-hand man of Trotsky. . . . A party here, which possesses real power and to which Trotsky also belongs, favours an understanding

---

[1] Memorandum of the T 1 of the *Truppenamt*, Berlin, 26 July 1920: Nachlaß Freiherr von Fritsch, H 08–33/1, Bundesarchiv-Militärarchiv; but it seems unlikely that Fritsch was the author.

[2] O. E. Schüddekopf, 'Radek in Berlin', *Archiv für Sozialgeschichte*, ii, 1962, pp. 97–98. Cf. E. H. Carr, *The Bolshevik Revolution, 1917–1923*, iii, London, 1953, p. 313.

[3] Schüddekopf, loc. cit., pp. 97, 162; Rabenau, *Seeckt*, p. 307, gives a wrong date.

with Germany. Sklanski said his party would be willing to recognize the old German frontier of 1914. And they see only one way
out of the world's chaos: co-operation with Germany and Turkey.
And in order to strengthen this party's position and to win the whole
Soviet government for the cause, [he asked] whether it would not be
possible to render some unofficial help: for example, [to provide]
reports about the Polish army and, if possible, to sell arms and have
them smuggled. . . .

This letter was taken to Berlin by a personal courier who was
empowered to speak to Seeckt or one of his representatives.[1]
Unfortunately, we only know that the letter reached Berlin,
but not whether and when the conversation took place, and
what was discussed. Two years later, however, Count Brockdorff-Rantzau maintained to the Chancellor Josef Wirth that
the military had negotiated directly with Trotsky as early as
1920, and this was not denied by Wirth.[2] It thus seems likely
that Enver Pasha's emissary was received by Seeckt or by one
of his subordinates.

IV. *Against the Republican Führerbund and the Free Corps*

The willingness of Seeckt and other officers to co-operate
with Soviet Russia did not mean that the Reichswehr was
turning towards the left or was prepared to modify its composition and policy in a republican sense. A *rapprochement* with
Russia was, on the contrary, likely to increase friction between
the army and the Social Democrats; for their leaders—men
such as Ebert and Noske—were constantly attacked and
maligned by the extreme left and were sharply opposed to
Bolshevism and the Communist International, an attitude that
was repaid in kind by the Communist leaders. Above all, the
generals were bound to see in any attempt to reform the army
in a democratic and republican sense a serious threat to their
own tradition and position, which were intimately connected
with the structure of the old Imperial army.

---

[1] Enver Pasha to Seeckt, Moscow, 26 Aug. 1920: Nachlaß Seeckt, box 15,
no. 202 f., microfilm in Institut für Zeitgeschichte, Munich. Incorrectly printed by
Rabenau, *Seeckt*, p. 307; and misinterpreted by G. W. F. Hallgarten, 'General
Hans von Seeckt and Russia', *Journal of Modern History*, xxi, 1949, p. 30: it was not
Enver's Turkey which was to be furnished with weapons, but Russia.

[2] Notes of Brockdorff-Rantzau, Berlin, 7 Sept. 1922: Nachlaß Brockdorff-
Rantzau, 9101 H/I, H 223368–69 (microfilm).

This became clear when in 1919 the Republican *Führerbund* was founded by Social Democrats who were critical of the policy of Noske and his close co-operation with the officer corps. The new organization aimed at 'implanting a republican and democratic spirit in the German *Wehrmacht* by gathering all leaders and non-commissioned officers who honestly accept the republic. . . . In the long run the republic is only safe if the powers of command are entrusted to honestly republican officers. The frequent employment of officers who hold monarch-ist views is to be considered a stopgap and must be termi-nated as soon as possible. . . .' The Republican *Führerbund* wanted to create guarantees that the armed forces would become truly reliable supporters of the republic and declined to be misused for political purposes.[1] Its aims were quite unaccep-table to the large majority of the officer corps. The chairman of the *Führerbund* was Hinrich Kopf (after the Second World War the prime minister of Lower Saxony), the deputy chairman was Otto Strasser (at that time like the other leaders a Social Democrat, later a revolutionary National Socialist), and the second deputy was Erich Kuttner (a journalist on the staff of the party paper, the *Vorwärts*, who had been prominent in recruiting republican free corps in Berlin at the time of the Spartacus rising early in 1919).[2] None of them was in any way prominent in the military field.

The generals sharply opposed the new organization, which seemed to threaten their position. General von Lüttwitz wrote to Noske: 'There is certainly no objection to the combination of officers to represent their economic and professional interests; but the "Republikanischer Führerbund", as its name says, is an association with a decidedly political purpose. I cannot warn sufficiently against the carrying of politics into the army. The results of such a mistake would be confusion, division, and finally disintegration of the army. I have informed the officer corps of the units under my command of my opinion concern-ing the "Republikanischer Führerbund".'[3] A few weeks later Groener reported to Hindenburg that the organization so far

---

[1] Schüddekopf, *Heer und Republik*, no. 34, p. 97.

[2] Letter of Otto Strasser in *Frankfurter Allgemeine Zeitung* of 15 Mar. 1961.

[3] Lüttwitz to Noske, Berlin, 11 July 1919: Akten des Gruppenkommandos 4, Bund 7, Akt 1, Bayerisches Kriegsarchiv.

had not gained any importance and consisted mainly of officers on leave of absence and non-commissioned officers.[1] Groener also urged Noske to take action against the *Führerbund*, but the minister declined. Thereupon Groener instructed the liaison officer of the High Command in the ministry to bring the matter frequently to the attention of Noske: a decree should prohibit all active politics in the army.[2] Seeckt also declared that it was necessary to erect a barrier against such organizations.[3] But apparently the *Führerbund* never succeeded in recruiting many members among the officers. The quick reduction of the army offered ample opportunity to get rid of its spokesmen and members: no further barrier was required.

Later Noske wrote that the *Führerbund* was of no help to him in the appointments to officers' posts because it did not contain any able (*brauchbare*) officers.[4] But his party comrade Erich Kuttner attacked Noske because he had permitted the discharge of all republican officers and had let the Republican *Führerbund* go to the wall; wherever a unit was really loyal to the republic, he had let himself be convinced only too easily that it stood under Bolshevik influence and must be dissolved, Kuttner declared in the *Vorwärts*.[5] It was in practice quite impossible for the minister to check in detail on all discharges, and thus 'undesirable elements' could easily be weeded out. The decision whether an officer should be taken over into the Reichswehr or not rested with the local commander who was advised by his personnel officer, usually a captain.[6] In retrospect it is almost impossible to say whether the members of the *Führerbund* could have provided the material for an efficient and loyal officer corps. Probably only a few of them would have been willing to serve for twenty-five years or until they were forty-five years old, as stipulated in the Treaty of Versailles. Its clauses, which imposed upon Germany an army of professional soldiers with long service, in reality made it hopeless to

---

[1] Groener to Hindenburg, Kolberg, 7 Aug. 1919: Nachlaß Groener, box 7, no. 28, Bundesarchiv Koblenz.

[2] 'Protokoll über die Dienstreise des Generalleutnants Groener vom 19.–24. August 19': Nachlaß Schleicher, no. 10, ibid.

[3] Rabenau, *Seeckt*, p. 470.   [4] Noske, *Von Kiel bis Kapp*, p. 199.

[5] Article by Kuttner in *Vorwärts* of 3 Apr. 1920, quoted by Heinrich Stroebel, *Die deutsche Revolution*, Berlin, 1920, p. 220.

[6] Information given by Generalleutnant a.D. Paul Mahlmann.

build up a democratic army. As things were, there could only be a fight to the finish between the old officer corps and the *Führerbund*. As Noske was determined to co-operate with the officer corps, the outcome of the fight was not in doubt.

What Noske was unable to overcome was the deep distrust on both sides. The large majority of the Social Democrats, brought up in an anti-militarist tradition, looked with a barely disguised dislike at the officer corps which re-emerged before their eyes in the old forms. Noske violently complained that the newspapers of his own party day after day attacked the Reichswehr officers and generalized from individual cases. When he published an appeal inviting young people to join the army, none of the more important party papers published it.[1] In 1919–20 it could not be expected that young Social Democrats would enter the Reichswehr in larger numbers, for they had had enough of war and fighting and were not willing to serve under the 'reactionary officers'. The higher-ranking officers who had grown up in a monarchical and sharply anti-socialist tradition could perhaps establish a loyal relationship with individual Social Democrats, such as Noske, or could accept the fact that there was a republic: more could hardly be expected. The Kapp Putsch was to show that even this minimum was only true of a section of the officer corps.

On the other hand, the army command was determined to terminate the period of the free corps and their irregular activities. Many of them, as was indicated by their names, were pledged to loyalty towards a leader and prepared to sacrifice themselves for him. But they kept discipline badly, had little respect for the law, and even less for the republican order. They were in favour of 'action' and of revolt against the government, but their political aims were hazy. As one of their officers wrote, they desired 'the *Wehrmacht*, isolated and strong, to become a state within the state, but so closely linked with the experience of the whole nation that one day it will be called upon to wield, as an arbiter, the dictatorship over the warring political parties and social groups. . .'.[2] Ideas such as these

---

[1] Noske, *Von Kiel bis Kapp*, p. 198, It must also be borne in mind that all the suspicions of the Social Democrats were confirmed by the Kapp Putsch of March 1920 (see below).

[2] Helmut Franke, *Staat im Staate*, Magdeburg, 1924, pp. 244 ff., quoted by

were diametrically opposed to those of Reinhardt and Seeckt. To them, it was necessary to combat the ill-discipline of the free corps and to eliminate it from the Reichswehr. Their political radicalism was a danger to the consolidation desired by the army command. As Seeckt realized, 'it was impossible to take them over into the Reichswehr wholesale and in formations, under their leaders. . . . In the new Reichswehr there had to be a very strict discipline, not resting on the individual alone; the free corps were partly not willing, and partly not capable, of submitting unconditionally to such a discipline. . . .'[1] Seeckt's adjutant, Captain Fischer, also mentions that Seeckt was urging that the free corps should not have the decisive influence on the development of the army: 'thus they had to be dissolved as soon as they had fulfilled their task', but many officers were opposed to Seeckt on this issue.[2] A recent well-informed historian, however, maintains that Seeckt adopted 'a decidedly *attentiste* policy' at the time and remained in touch with the para-military organizations of the right.[3]

New political excitement within the officer corps was caused by the demand of the Entente powers that the 'war criminals' were to be surrendered. Noske feared a revolt of certain units if the government complied with the request, and insisted that it must be refused. Reinhardt thought that it might come to an armed conflict and instructed all commanding officers to bring their units to the maximum degree of readiness for war by any means at their disposal.[4] Finally, however, the Entente accepted a German proposal that the Germans accused of war crimes by their former enemies should be tried by German courts. During the same month the 'restaurative' forces in the officer corps celebrated a triumph of great symbolical significance: the epaulettes were reintroduced.[5] The shame of 9 November 1918

Schüddekopf, *Heer und Republik*, no. 52, p. 129. The book which gives the most accurate impression of the mood and the revolutionary longing of the free corps is Ernst von Salomon's *Die Geächteten*, Berlin, 1930.

[1] Rabenau, *Seeckt*, p. 460, quoting an article of Seeckt's of 1928.

[2] Recollections of Fischer, later Lieutenant-General (of 1937): Nachlaß Seeckt, box 15, no. 202, p. 23; Notes of General Lieber, 'Seeckt als Chef des Truppenamts', p. 13: Nachlaß Seeckt, box 19, no. 278, Militärgeschichtliches Forschungsamt Freiburg. [3] Görlitz, *Der deutsche Generalstab*, p. 320.

[4] Noske, *Von Kiel bis Kapp*, p. 202; Ernst, *Aus dem Nachlaß des Generals Walther Reinhardt*, pp. 57–58.

[5] On 24 Feb. 1920: notes of General Lieber, loc. cit., p. 17.

was wiped off, the revolution was buried. A free corps officer who resigned his commission about this time stated: 'All the evil ghosts of 9 November are laid, the machine functions again to the smallest part, the command presses a button and it runs, there will be no breakdown. We have returned to all the traits of Prussian militarism . . . but also to its mistakes: its spiritual rigidity, its sobriety, its lack of magnanimity, its incapacity to take revolutionary action. . . .'[1]

There was one problem, however, that was not yet solved: the quick reduction in size of the Reichswehr stipulated by the Treaty of Versailles. This was not only a technical, but also a highly political question, especially because General von Lüttwitz, commanding officer of *Gruppenkommando* 1 in Berlin, hotly opposed any reduction and sabotaged the orders in question. Again for political reasons, the government and the army command desired to start the reduction with the disbandment of the two naval brigades of Ehrhardt and von Loewenfeld. This was even more hotly opposed by Lüttwitz because both stood under his command and the Ehrhardt brigade formed his main strength in the area of Berlin. Both naval brigades were known to hold radical views, and the Entente insisted that their strength was to be included in the figure of 15,000 permitted to the navy by the peace treaty, further weighty arguments in favour of their disbandment. A decision to this effect was taken on 29 February 1920 over Lüttwitz's protest. But on the following day he proclaimed at a birthday parade of the Ehrhardt brigade that he would not permit its dissolution, and thus a conflict became inevitable.[2]

On 8 March Seeckt, the chief of the *Truppenamt*, declared that he was not willing to rescind the order of disbandment. On 10 March Noske—probably prompted by Reinhardt— issued an order that the two naval brigades were to be withdrawn from the *Gruppenkommando* 1 and to become subordinate to the naval command. Thereupon Lüttwitz sought an audience with the president which took place the same evening, in the presence of Noske and two generals. Lüttwitz demanded from

[1] Helmut Franke, *Staat im Staate*, pp. 244 ff., quoted by Schüddekopf, *Heer und Republik*, no. 52, p. 129.

[2] Noske, op. cit., p. 203; Gordon, *Reichswehr and the German Republic*, pp. 104–5. For earlier conflicts with Lüttwitz, see above, pp. 45–46.

Ebert not only that the brigades should remain under his orders, but also that Reinhardt should be replaced as chief of the army command by the retired General von Wrisberg. He identified himself with the political programme of the German Nationalist Party by further demanding a general election in the near future, the election of the president by the people,[1] and the appointment of non-political experts as ministers; but Noske should remain the minister of defence. Ebert declined to accept these demands. Noske emphasized that orders had to be carried out, that no general was entitled to put forward demands, and that any *pronunciamiento* would be sharply rejected; Reinhardt would remain at his post; and he assumed (Noske continued) that Lüttwitz would resign on the following morning. He warned Lüttwitz strongly against any attempt at resistance, which would cause the units 'to break like glass'.[2]

On the same day Noske received the first reports about plans for a military revolt. Apparently it was Lüttwitz's son-in-law and subordinate, Major von Hammerstein-Equord, who could claim 'a special merit in the energetic and radical discovering' of these plans.[3] To 'tame' Lüttwitz and to prevent his 'dark plans' from being carried out had been Hammerstein's task already seven months earlier.[4] Probably it was the order for the disbandment of the two naval brigades that resulted in a premature attempt at revolt, before the plans had matured. On 11 March Lüttwitz was relieved of his command, but refused to give it up. The government ordered the arrest of some of his fellow-conspirators—Wolfgang Kapp, Captain Pabst, Colonel Bauer, and others—but they were warned and were able to evade arrest. On 12 March it became known that the Ehrhardt brigade intended to march on Berlin from its camp at Döberitz near the capital.[5] The mutiny had started. The

---

[1] According to article 41 of the constitution; Ebert had been elected by the National Assembly.

[2] Karl Brammer, *Verfassungsgrundlagen und Hochverrat*, Berlin, 1922, pp. 24–25; Rabenau, *Seeckt*, pp. 219–20; Noske, op. cit., p. 207; Gordon, op. cit., pp. 107–8.

[3] Thus expressly the report of Captain Eugen Hahn, from the personal staff of Noske, of 7 Apr. 1920: Nachlaß Hahn, no. 27, Heeresarchiv Stuttgart.

[4] See above, p. 46. Colonel Hasse too remarked as early as Sept. 1919 that is was necessary to 'supervise' Lüttwitz and that he declined to accept orders from Seeckt: Notes of General Lieber: Nachlaß Seeckt, box 19, no. 278, p. 24, Militärgeschichtliches Forschungsamt Freiburg.

[5] Brammer, op. cit., pp. 25–26; Rabenau, op. cit., p. 220; Gordon, op. cit., p. 109.

surprising thing was, not that it broke out in March 1920, but that it had not begun much earlier; and equally that the army command, which had received ample warning, had taken no precautions. For at the decisive moment there were no units in Berlin strong enough to oppose the brigade. It has never been established who was responsible for this omission. Perhaps it was the natural solidarity between the officers, perhaps it was Seeckt's policy of *attentisme* that prevented the taking of any precautionary measures while there was still time.

v. *The Kapp Putsch*

When he received the news that the Ehrhardt brigade intended to march on Berlin, Reinhardt, on the evening of 12 March, went to see the deputy commander of the *Gruppen-kommando* 1, Lieutenant-General von Oven; there he also met the chief of staff of the Berlin militarized police, Colonel Ahrens. Reinhardt told them that the mutineers must be opposed at all costs and that an overthrow of the government, if attempted by the brigade, must be prevented by force of arms. Both officers replied that the officers would do their duty, but that the majority of the other ranks would hardly shoot on other Reichswehr soldiers. Reinhardt declared that their duty demanded fighting in any case. Then he saw Colonel von Thaysen, the commanding officer of Regiment 6, which was guarding the government quarter, to point out his task to him, and found him ready to do his duty. Thereafter Reinhardt went to the chancellor, Gustav Bauer, where he also met Noske. Meanwhile reports came in that soldiers were assembling at Döberitz, that the Potsdam garrison had declared its solidarity with the mutineers, and that an attempt of the Generals von Oven and von Oldershausen to visit Döberitz and to persuade Ehrhardt to desist from his enterprise had failed.[1]

At 1 a.m. on 13 March the leading officers assembled in Noske's room in the defence ministry: the Generals Reinhardt, von Seeckt, von Oven, von Oldershausen, Rear-Admiral von Trotha, the Lieutenant-Colonels Wetzell and Hasse, the

---

[1] Generals Reinhardt and von Oldershausen as witnesses in the Jagow trial in 1921: Brammer, op. cit., pp. 32–34; Ernst, *Aus dem Nachlaß des Generals Walther Reinhardt*, p. 61.

Majors von Bock, von Gilsa, von Hammerstein-Equord and von Stockhausen. The two generals who had been to Döberitz reported their failure and submitted an ultimatum from Ehrhardt: this was identical with the demands of the Nationalist Party—immediate Reichstag elections, election of the president by the people, experts as ministers—and requested an amnesty and the reappointment of General von Lüttwitz to his post. Ehrhardt expected a reply to be handed to him at 7 a.m. at the Siegessäule near the Brandenburg Gate—he was thus determined to continue his march on Berlin and to negotiate, if at all, when he stood outside the government quarter.

Noske declined any negotiation and demanded armed resistance; he was supported by Reinhardt. General von Oven, on the other hand, suggested negotiations on the basis of Ehrhardt's ultimatum—as he was the officer commanding in Berlin, a factor of vital importance. He and General von Oldershausen 'were of the opinion that Reichswehr units would never fire on other Reichswehr units. Although the majority of the officers . . . would doubtless carry out their duty to the utmost, it was almost certain that the troops as a whole would not use their arms. In the militarized police the mood was the same. . . .'[1] General von Seeckt announced in short sentences 'he would never permit Berlin to be presented with the spectacle of their soldiers fighting each other with live ammunition!' According to another participant in the conference he said: 'We cannot conduct a field exercise with live ammunition between Berlin and Potsdam.'[2] Only Reinhardt was of the opposite opinion and advocated the use of artillery against the advancing rebels. Finally Noske asked who was prepared to fight with him and who was not. Of those present only Reinhardt and Major von Gilsa, Noske's adjutant, replied in the affirmative.[3]

The cabinet assembled a few hours later. It was decided, in

[1] Ibid., pp. 61–62; Brammer, op. cit., p. 35; Noske, op. cit., p. 209.

[2] The first quotation from the recollections of Seeckt's adjutant, Captain Fischer: Nachlaß Seeckt, box 15, no. 202, p. 25, microfilm in Institut für Zeitgeschichte, Munich; the second quotation from a marginal note of the later General von Hammerstein-Equord as a correction of the version given by Rabenau, Seeckt, p. 221: Verw. Buch no. 134 in Bundesarchiv-Militärarchiv. Both officers were eye-witnesses.

[3] Valedictory address of General Reinhardt of 29 Mar. 1920: Nachlaß Reinhardt, no. 19, Heeresarchiv Stuttgart.

view of the attitude of the Berlin troops, not to offer battle but to leave the capital. The units were ordered to return to barracks. The Ehrhardt brigade marched into Berlin—their steel helmets decorated with the swastika—and occupied the ministries and other public buildings. A new government, under Wolfgang Kapp, an East Prussian official, and General von Lüttwitz, was proclaimed.[1] Reinhardt demanded to be relieved of his duties, as he considered that his authority was undermined by the countermanding of his orders to offer resistance to the mutineers. On the morning of 13 March he went to Potsdam to try to influence the commanding officer, General von Hülsen, in favour of the government. But Hülsen declared that his final attitude depended on a meeting with General von Lüttwitz.[2] General von Seeckt too offered his resignation; until a decision about it was reached he took leave of absence, divested himself of his uniform, and retired to his flat. His post as chief of the *Truppenamt* was taken over at his instruction by his immediate subordinate, Colonel Heye, with whom he remained in constant touch. Seeckt equally declined to fight against the Ehrhardt brigade and to take any orders from the new government: what he wanted to avoid above all was a battle of Reichswehr against Reichswehr, a battle between German soldiers who had fought side by side against the enemy.[3] In any case, he quietly awaited the further course of events.

General von Lüttwitz in his turn appointed a new chief of the army command and a new chief of the *Truppenamt*, and deprived two officers of the *Gruppenkommando* 1—General von Oldershausen and Major von Hammerstein—of their posts. The other officers of his former staff assured him solemnly of their loyalty to him.[4] Colonel Heye and the officers of the *Truppenamt*, on the other hand, ignored Lüttwitz and the general officers appointed by him. When Lüttwitz visited the *Truppenamt* Heye declared that they received their orders from Seeckt and did not believe in the success of Lüttwitz's

---

[1] Ernst, op. cit., pp. 62–63; Noske, op. cit., p. 209.

[2] Reinhardt's valedictory address of 29 Mar. 1920, loc. cit.; Ernst, op. cit., pp. 63–64.

[3] Thus Seeckt as a witness in the Jagow trial of 1921: Brammer, op. cit., pp. 33–34; Rabenau, *Seeckt*, p. 223.

[4] Lüttwitz, *Im Kampf gegen die November-Revolution*, p. 122; Rabenau, *Seeckt*, p. 223.

enterprise.[1] As Heye wrote later, he found this role 'very disagreeable, for Lüttwitz's final aim was also the wish of my heart.
But I had to carry out my heavy task as was my duty, because
the danger existed that, as the *only* result of the *Putsch*, a "war"
would break out between "Reichswehr East" and "Reichswehr
West", to the joy of the triumphant third party, the Ebert
government. . . .'[2]

Even within the officer corps of the ministry of defence,
however, several groups came into being. In the first place
there was a minority which remained loyal to its oath and was
prepared to obey the orders of the president and the Bauer
government. On 16 March Reinhardt informed the new chief
of the army command, General von Wrisberg, that he refused
to co-operate with men who, contrary to their oath, had used
force against the legitimate government.[3] And as early as
13 March the chief of the Equipment Office (*Ausrüstungsamt*),
Colonel von Feldmann, addressed his officers thus:

Gentlemen, in my opinion nothing more foolish than this affair
could have been undertaken, for it was unnecessary. If one believes
—and that is left to each individual—that the present conditions do
not advance us and ought to be changed, even then the opposition
parties have until now always maintained that the necessary
changes must be brought about by legal means. . . . For the
soldier the question is particularly difficult. He has rendered his oath
to the constitution and sworn to protect the lawful institutions and to
obey the orders of the president. I intend to remain loyal to my
oath and not to look at it as something that I have only taken under
duress. . . . I am of the opinion that, if the officer corps, which during
the last revolution was unable to defend the Supreme War Lord,
now for the second time acts contrary to its oath, it will deprive
itself of the last remnant of respect in which it is held by the people.[4]

With this group of absolutely loyal officers must also be reckoned
some of the younger officers of the personal staff of Noske,

---

[1] Rabenau, op. cit., p. 223.

[2] Wilhelm Heye, 'Mein Lebenslauf', p. 548: Nachlaß Heye, H 08–18/4,
Bundesarchiv-Militärarchiv.

[3] Ernst, op. cit., p. 64.

[4] 'Oberst von Feldmann an die Offiziere des Ausrüstungsamtes den 13.3.1920,
1 Uhr mittags': Nachlaß Mentzel, no. 9, Bundesarchiv Koblenz. This folder,
collected by an officer of the defence ministry, contains highly interesting material
about the situation during the Kapp Putsch.

such as Major von Gilsa and Captain Hahn, who supported him as before.

Apart from this—probably rather small—group there was a second, larger section which hoped for negotiations between the two 'governments' and was willing meanwhile to continue with its duties. On 15 March they accepted the following resolution:

1. The officer corps, the officials and employees of the ministry of defence stand aloof from the events.
2. As they know that negotiations are being conducted between *Generallandschaftsdirektor* Kapp and the old government, they are prepared to continue to serve for the time being for the preservation of law and order. A precondition of this is that the negotiations lead to the formation of a government which enjoys the confidence of a majority of the nation, and that all consideration of the persons who are at the moment in power be disregarded.

This resolution was read to General von Lüttwitz as well as to Kapp. 'Both gentlemen have received it with thanks for the readiness expressed in it to continue to work and have accepted the preconditions stipulated', although Lüttwitz was informed that the officers did not recognize his power of command. This phrase the *Truppenamt*—probably Colonel Heye—thought was not sharp enough and therefore demanded that 'Lüttwitz should resign. This demand was dropped because the influence of the general on the soldiers is at the moment so great that either the army would dissolve or far more radical elements would gain control over it. . .', if the *Truppenamt* had adhered to its demand.[1]

Lieutenant-Colonel Hasse of the *Truppenamt* travelled to Stuttgart, where the president and the government had sought refuge, to inform them of the decisions taken in the defence ministry. But he found the government disinclined to negotiate or to make any concessions; there was a 'belligerent mood' (*Kampfstimmung*). Hence Hasse decided not to submit the resolution of 15 March, but to report orally that 'the officers and officials of the defence ministry had nothing to do with the *Putsch* and continued their work in accordance with their

---

[1] All the documents are to be found ibid., partly also in Nachlaß Reinhardt, Hauptstaatsarchiv Stuttgart.

oath'.[1] This was certainly politically wise as the resolution was more than ambiguous, and as the government was strictly opposed to the negotiations desired by the officers. Unfortunately, nothing is known about the attitude of Seeckt during these days. But it can be surmised that it was identical with that of the *Truppenamt*, in which his influence was paramount.[2] He, too, certainly desired the retirement of Lüttwitz, from whom he was separated by political and personal differences; but he was probably also in favour of negotiations between the government and Kapp, of a compromise between the legitimate authorities and the *Putschists*.

One group within the defence ministry put itself entirely at the disposal of the Kapp–Lüttwitz government: the navy. The chief of the naval command, Rear-Admiral von Trotha, on 13 March communicated this decision to all naval authorities.[3] The naval officers on Noske's personal staff, among them Lieutenant Canaris, decided 'without hesitation' to side with their comrades of the naval brigades, and against Noske and the government.[4] From Silesia the leader of the Third Naval Brigade, Commander von Loewenfeld, sent his most sincere congratulations to Ehrhardt on his success.[5] On the other hand, Trotha's adjutant, the later Admiral Raeder, recounts in his memoirs that General von Lüttwitz on the morrow of the *Putsch* informed Trotha: 'The government has fled to southern Germany, but President Ebert has remained in Berlin and is forming a new government. He, Lüttwitz, was deputizing for the minister of defence. Rear-Admiral von Trotha had no reason to distrust this information. He communicated it to his staff, who unanimously agreed with his decision to support the new government in the maintenance of law and order. . . .'[6]

[1] Hasse's report to the 'versammelten Vertreter der Ämter', 18 Mar. 1920: Nachlaß Mentzel, no. 9, Bundesarchiv Koblenz.

[2] Rabenau, *Seeckt*, pp. 223–4, mentions the constant contacts between Seeckt and Heye.

[3] Bekanntmachung M 1580, Berlin, 13 Mar. 1920: copy in Nachlaß Seeckt, box 17, no. 143, Militärgeschichtliches Forschungsamt.

[4] Karl Heinz Abshagen, *Canaris*, Stuttgart, 1949, p. 74.

[5] Reichskanzlei, Akten betr. Reichsmarine, vol. 1: R 43 I 601, Bundesarchiv Koblenz.

[6] Raeder, *Mein Leben*, i. 181–2. About Raeder's role during the Kapp Putsch, see 'Handakten Raeder', Paket 7813, PG 33951b, Militärgeschichtliches Forschungsamt.

If this version were correct, the question still remains why the naval command did not revoke its decision as soon as it was informed of the true state of affairs, i.e. a day or two later. Thus a marked difference arose between the attitudes of the command of the army and that of the navy. But Captain Hahn, who remained loyal to Noske, also mentions officers of the army who stood in more or less sharp opposition to the minister of defence; thus Hahn found himself 'in the opposite camp'.[1]

Similar groups and differences came into being in the Reichswehr units inside and outside the capital. In Berlin and its environs the troops and the militarized police declared themselves for Lüttwitz, who had been their commanding officer. The same declaration was made by General von Estorff in East Prussia, General Count Schmettow in Breslau, General von Lettow-Vorbeck in Schwerin, Major-General Hagenberg in Weimar, Colonel Freiherr von Wangenheim in Hamburg, and other commanding officers.[2] General von Estorff not only put himself at the disposal of the Kapp government, but issued orders to that effect to the units under his command, which were transmitted by them to the lower echelons. 'The sympathy with the promised national aims' of the new government was general; 'they did not recognize that they had left the basis of the constitution during the Kapp days', Reinhardt reported from his tour of inspection in East Prussia during the following month.[3]

In Silesia too the *Generalkommando* declared itself for Kapp. The Brigade von Loewenfeld marched into Breslau. 'There was no doubt that it could not be considered neutral; it marched into Breslau with the old war flag at the head of the column, convinced that now the new "national state" would be erected and that the revolution of 1918 would be conquered. . . .' But officially it was announced that the brigade would 'preserve law and order in Breslau'.[4] On the evening of 13 March

[1] Report of 7 Apr. 1920 about a conference on 14 Mar.: Nachlaß Hahn, no. 27, Heeresarchiv Stuttgart.

[2] Gordon, *Reichswehr and the German Republic*, pp. 134–6.

[3] Report of Reinhardt to the minister of defence, 19 Apr. 1920: Nachlaß Reinhardt, Hauptstaatsarchiv Stuttgart. About East Prussia cf. Winnig, *Heimkehr*, pp. 299–303.

[4] Recollections of the later Rear-Admiral Siegfried Sorge: Zeugenschrifttum no. 1785, Institut für Zeitgeschichte, Munich.

von Loewenfeld arrested the chief of the staff of the *Befehlsstelle* vi, Major Hesterberg, because he 'had been for a long time politically unreliable'. Apart from this, the brigade was accused of 'violence, assault, and murder'.[1]

General Lequis, who was sent to Breslau to replace Count Schmettow, noted that the brigade and three other free corps had behaved there in such a disgusting fashion that even the former officers were highly indignant, and that the military had conducted intense anti-semitic propaganda. 'There is an indescribable hatred of the military among the large majority of the population.'[2] As he wrote to Noske, the Reichswehr was 'most thoroughly discredited' (*bis auf die Knochen diskreditiert*).[3] Even after the collapse of the Kapp enterprise the units of the Sixth Army Corps only put themselves at the disposal of the government for the fight against Bolshevism, on condition that there would be no further reduction, that the present *Generalkommando* would remain, that there would be a general amnesty, that the right-wing parties would take part in the administration of Silesia and of Breslau, and that the local police president would be removed.[4]

General Maercker, commanding officer of *Wehrkreis* iv at Dresden, decided in favour neither of the government nor of Kapp and Lüttwitz. As the government on the morning of 13 March first fled to Dresden, he was asked by Kapp to arrest the ministers, but declined. 'He declared that he wanted to preserve law and order in Saxony; but he failed to take up a position supporting the old government. . . .'[5] He travelled to Berlin to establish contact with Lüttwitz and apparently aimed at mediation. A few days later he went to Stuttgart, where the government had meanwhile established itself, and tried 'to smooth things over a little, in the interest of Kapp and Lüttwitz'. In this he failed completely: the general strike in favour

---

[1] Reichskanzlei, Akten betr. Reichsmarine, vol. i: R 43 I 601, Bundesarchiv Koblenz.

[2] Lequis's pencil notes, s.d. (written immediately after the Kapp Putsch): Nachlaß Generalleutnant Lequis, no. 39, Bundesarchiv-Militärarchiv.

[3] Lequis to Noske, 22 Apr. 1920, quoted by Noske, *Aufstieg und Niedergang der deutschen Sozialdemokratie*, Zürich, 1947, p. 172.

[4] *Generalkommando VI. A. K.*, Breslau, 18 Mar. 1920; supported by the Reichswehr Brigade viii, Brieg, 18 Mar. 1920: Nachlaß Lequis, no. 39, loc. cit.

[5] Report of Captain Hahn of 7 Apr. 1920: Nachlaß Hahn, no. 27, Heeresarchiv Stuttgart.

of the government was almost universal and crippled the rebel government in Berlin. In Stuttgart nobody was willing to make any concessions or to accept a mediator.[1] Lüttwitz believed that some units under Maercker's command would have refused to carry out his orders if he had declared in favour of Kapp. And Noske reported that as early as 14 March representatives of the regiments in Dresden told him they would kill their officers if they became disloyal to the government.[2] This pressure from below seems to explain in part the vacillating attitude of the general.

An agreement between the government and Kapp–Lüttwitz, mutual concessions, and a reconciliation were equally the aims of the commanding officer of the *Gruppenkommando* 2 at Cassel, General von Schoeler, and his chief of staff, Major-General von Loßberg. They refused to accept any orders from Lüttwitz and tried 'to prevent, in the same spirit as General von Seeckt, an armed clash and a battle of Reichswehr against Reichswehr, and to achieve somehow a peaceful settlement. . .'.[3] They admonished both sides accordingly; but on 16 March it became known in Berlin that they had promised the president that '*Reichswehrgruppenkommando* 2 would fight to the last man for the Ebert government'.[4] The commanding officer of *Wehrkreis* v at Stuttgart, General von Bergmann, assured the government of his loyalty as soon as the first reports of the mutiny were received—as it seems, the first general who did so.[5] The commanding officers of *Wehrkreis* vi at Münster, General Freiherr von Watter, and of *Wehrkreis* vii at Munich, General Ritter von Möhl, were more cautious and at first awaited the further course of events.[6] These were the *Wehrkreise* under the *Gruppenkommando* 2 at Cassel, so that its units were

[1] Hasse's report to the 'versammelten Vertreter der Ämter', 18 Mar. 1920: Nachlaß Mentzel, no. 9, Bundesarchiv Koblenz.

[2] Lüttwitz, *Im Kampf gegen die November-Revolution*, p. 123; Noske as a witness in the Jagow trial of 1921: Brammer, op. cit., p. 52.

[3] Volkmann, *Revolution über Deutschland*, pp. 373–4; Lüttwitz, op. cit., p. 123; Brammer, op. cit., p. 48.

[4] Nachlaß Mentzel, no. 9, Bundesarchiv Koblenz.

[5] Volkmann, op. cit., p. 374.

[6] Carl Severing, *1919/1920 im Wetter und Watterwinkel*, Bielefeld, 1927, p. 133; Maercker as a witness in the Jagow trial: Brammer, op. cit., p. 49; Volkmann, op. cit., p. 374; Waldemar Erfurth, *Geschichte des deutschen Generalstabes von 1918 bis 1945*, Göttingen, 1957, p. 71, with slight discrepancies about the situation in Bavaria.

either neutral or willing to fight for the government. Thus General Maercker was able to inform Kapp as early as the night of 14 to 15 March: 'Germany is at the moment divided into two parts. The one is the whole of western and southern Germany, and the other northern and eastern Germany. If this state of affairs is not terminated soon, a battle between Reichswehr and Reichswehr is inevitable, and that must be prevented at all costs. . . .'[1] Although this was a generalization it more or less corresponded with the facts. In any case, the danger which Seeckt and the other generals tried to avoid with all their strength seemed to be imminent.

We know much less about the attitudes of the junior officers. In the Brigade 16 at Weimar, whose commander declared for Kapp, nearly all the officers were on his side. They deposed the state government and arrested its prime minister, a Social Democrat.[2] The commander of Brigade 4 at Magdeburg was equally for Kapp; but the commanding officer of Regiment 104, which formed part of the brigade, opposed him and finally took over the command of the brigade. About the situation during the days of the *Putsch* he reported to Seeckt:

I have been through terrible conflicts . . .: on the one hand the oath to the president and the constitution, the orders of the superior officers, allied with the small amount of reason and intelligence which I still possess, keeping down the feelings of my heart—on the other the silly decision of Groddeck, my superior officer, and even Maercker and Lüttwitz were still superior officers. From the outset it was a delusion, political stupidity, to believe in the success of this unfortunate enterprise. None of them knew the people, they have their eyes closed and have learnt nothing whatever since November 1918. . . . I do not want to defend the officers; most of them, contrary to their oaths, have orientated themselves sharply towards the right and have attempted to turn their men towards the right too, by more or less clumsy propaganda. . . . I had whole battalions without officers. Gradually it has been possible to reappoint some, and in certain places even all the officers. But we still have units without any officers. But troops which have taken a vote on their officers, as most units in my district did, . . . are no longer capable of fighting, they are mercenaries (*Soldateska*). . . .[3]

[1] Maercker as a witness in the Jagow trial: Brammer, op. cit., p. 49.
[2] Information given by General Paul Mahlmann, then a lieutenant in Brigade 16.
[3] Colonel von Hahnke to Seeckt, Magdeburg, 25 Mar. 1920: Nachlaß Seeckt, roll 19, no. 25, microfilm in Institut für Zeitgeschichte.

More than a year after these events General von Seeckt was heard as a witness in the Jagow trial and maintained:

The mass of the officer corps of the Reichswehr by no means took the side of Herr Kapp and General von Lüttwitz. . . . It did not percolate that General von Lüttwitz had been deposed or sent on leave, so that the commanding officers in the provinces received contradictory orders with which they could not do anything. In their opinion, they were fully covered by the orders of their superior officer. When the first uncertainty, which was also caused by the fact that the government was no longer in Berlin, had disappeared the troops in Bavaria, Hesse, Thuringia, Westphalia, and Hanover declared themselves against the Lüttwitz enterprise. The other troops of *Generalkommando* 1, which hitherto had been under Lüttwitz, could not do so. I knew the mood rather intimately and must emphasize, in opposition to other statements, that only a small section of the officer corps backed the violent enterprise of General von Lüttwitz. . . .[1]

Seeckt's evidence was not in accordance with the facts.

One thing, however, the generals did achieve in March 1920: Reichswehr did not shoot on Reichswehr. There was no civil war, apart from local outbreaks in Saxony and in the Ruhr. But there the Reichswehr and the free corps—once more united—fought against the extreme left, in the Ruhr against a virtual Red Army. Perhaps it was this threat of red revolution which reunited them. Very soon General von Schoeler informed General von Lüttwitz 'that through the *Putsch* a new revolt of the radical circles would be provoked. In some places of the Ruhr the rule of Soviets has been proclaimed. . . .'[2] In the naval bases of Kiel and Wilhelmshaven events occurred which were reminiscent of November 1918. The sailors deposed and arrested numerous officers. New officers were elected on board ship, among them many petty and warrant officers. There were shooting affrays which caused casualties.[3] The general strike had broken out with full force on 14 March, and the Berlin units began to vacillate.[4] A further drift towards the left would have threatened the existence of the officer corps. In this situation their natural solidarity prevailed and the rift was quickly healed.

[1] Brammer, op. cit., pp. 53–54.   [2] Volkmann, op. cit., p. 374.
[3] Report of 25 Mar. 1920: Nachlaß Mentzel, no. 9, Bundesarchiv Koblenz.
[4] Rabenau, *Seeckt*, pp. 224, 226 and n. 5.

VI. *Seeckt's Nomination*

On 17 March it became clear that the *Putsch* had failed. Kapp handed over the 'government' to Lüttwitz and left Berlin. In the *Gruppenkommando* 1 a number of senior officers assembled, adherents as well as opponents of Lüttwitz. They asked Seeckt's confidant, Colonel Heye, to speak in their name. He requested Lüttwitz to finish the affair and transfer the command to Seeckt: Lüttwitz no longer had the confidence of the troops and should resign. But the latter declined and assumed a threatening attitude. Later he declared himself willing to resign if a general election were held and a soldier became minister of defence. An old associate of Seeckt from the war years, Lieutenant-Colonel Wetzell, the chief of staff of the Berlin Brigade, emphasized that it was essential to have a new leader and suggested Seeckt, whose consent he had obtained, provided that he was appointed by the Bauer government. In Berlin the officers of many units were discussing who was to occupy the leading post. In the conference at headquarters Lieutenant-Commander Ehrhardt remarked: 'The meeting here is an officers' council which deposes one leader and appoints a new one.' Wetzell countered this by pointing out: 'It is to General von Seeckt's credit that the Reichswehr has not fired on the naval brigade during the night of the 12th/13th....'[1] What happened was 'a kind of plebiscite by a part of the officer corps, so as to bring Seeckt to the highest military post ... an event such as has hardly ever occurred in the military history of Prussia–Germany...'.[2]

Parallel with this 'election' Dr. Schiffer, the minister of justice, who had remained in Berlin, negotiated with the government at Stuttgart about the person of the new chief of the army command, a post from which Reinhardt had resigned on 13 March. He was given the choice between Seeckt and General von Oven, unless he wanted to reappoint Reinhardt. 'I decided in favour of Seeckt, who refused to co-operate with Reinhardt, while the latter was prepared to accept a post even under Seeckt, who was junior to him. Seeckt's nomination took place in my office, which was filled with deputies and

---

[1] Rabenau, Seeckt, pp. 225–7, and notes; Erfurth, op. cit., p. 71.

[2] Rabenau's comment, op. cit., pp. 227–8.

journalists. . . .'[1] But one of the officers present gives a different account of the event: 'After a brief welcome by Schiffer we three—Reinhardt, Seeckt, and myself—remained alone. The two generals went to a window, while I remained in the middle of the room near a table. General Reinhardt read the telegram to General von Seeckt; I saw clearly the feelings expressed on the faces of both. General Reinhardt then added: "As I believe it necessary that a personality should stand at the head of the army who is less involved in the past than I am, I am using my plenary powers to transfer the command of the army to you, Herr General." Seeckt accepted without a word. . . .'[2] According to this version, Reinhardt had received powers from Stuttgart to nominate a successor and appointed Seeckt; it thus seems as if his nomination took place from three different sides simultaneously. Dr. Schiffer further recounts that Seeckt immediately assumed power 'and used my telephone to issue orders and to remove several senior officers, in the briefest forms and with brusque brutality. . .'.[3]

In these different descriptions one point is controversial: to what post Seeckt was appointed on 17 or 18 March. Although Dr. Schiffer expressly states that he appointed Seeckt chief of the army command, this can hardly be correct. For as late as 22 March Reinhardt signed an order as Major-General and chief of the army command, speaking at the same time of Seeckt as 'deputy commander-in-chief of the Reichswehr *Gruppenkommando* 1'.[4] According to a time-table which Reinhardt wrote soon after the event, he was rung on 18 March by Noske's adjutant, Major von Gilsa, from Stuttgart that he should 'take up his duties again. Conference with Seeckt who receives command. Declaration to Schiffer.'[5] Thus Reinhardt apparently again became chief of the army command, while Seeckt took over the *Gruppenkommando* 1 in place of Lüttwitz, who disappeared.[6] Seeckt's first orders were issued without

[1] Letter of Dr. Schiffer of 1 Nov. 1950: Gordon, op. cit., p. 439.

[2] MS. of Major Fleck, n.d. (without his name): Nachlaß Geßler, no. 46, Bundesarchiv Koblenz.

[3] Gordon, op. cit., p. 439.   [4] Ernst, op. cit., p. 65, n. 43.

[5] Ibid., p. 60.

[6] Rabenau, *Seeckt*, p. 228, especially n. 6. On 23 Mar. 1920 Seeckt signed as *Oberbefehlshaber* of *Gruppenkommando* 1: Nachlaß Generalleutnant Lequis, no. 39, Bundesarchiv-Miltärarchiv.

heading or signature. As early as 19 March, on his own initiative, he removed General von Bernuth from his post at Stettin, and on 21 March he requested General von Estorff at Königsberg 'in the name of the Reich government' to give up his command of *Wehrkreis* i and to transfer it to General von Dassel, the commander of the brigade at Tilsit.[1]

On 18 March Seeckt issued the following decree to the officers under his command: 'We are facing the battle which is to decide whether the German nation is to be or not to be, an attempt of the greatest magnitude to proclaim the Soviet Republic. . . . We shall be victorious if officers and men stand together to preserve order unaffected by political influences; the soldier has to abstain from all politics and fights according to the orders of his military leaders.'[2] But the officers certainly did not yet abstain from politics. Their front was directed against the minister of defence, Noske, who for the time being returned to his post. 'That was an impossible state of affairs. . . . It should have been clear that no member of the government which had supported the general strike could possibly be the minister of defence.'[3] As Captain von Rabenau noted at the time: 'Seeckt must start his activity on 17 March with an order issued on behalf of Noske. That produces the effect almost of an intentional slap in the face. The impression prevails that, if Noske remains, the officer corps may resign collectively. . . .'[4] On 19 March Reinhardt received the generals and asked them 'to oppose the virulent agitation (*Hetze*) and to defend Noske'.[5]

This Fronde against the minister of defence lasted until Noske resigned on 24 March. Through the Kapp Putsch his policy had become discredited. In wide circles of the working class he was considered politically responsible for what had happened. The large majority of the officers whom he had appointed had

<hr />

[1] Notes of General Lieber, 'Seeckt als Chef des Truppenamts', p. 20: Nachlaß Seeckt, box 19, no. 278, Militärgeschichtliches Forschungsamt Freiburg. It seems very doubtful whether Seeckt was also 'deputy chief of the army command', as alleged by Rabenau, op. cit., p. 228, n. 6, and p. 229, n. 1, who refers to Noske, *Von Kiel bis Kapp*; but there is nothing about this in Noske's book. It is possible, however, that Seeckt acted as the deputy to the minister of defence: Rabenau, p. 228, n. 5.

[2] *Die Wirren in der Reichshauptstadt und im nördlichen Deutschland, 1918–1920*, pp. 141–2.

[3] Rabenau, *Seeckt*, pp. 235–6.   [4] Ibid., p. 236, n. 1.

[5] Ernst, op. cit., p. 60.

not sided with the mutineers—but neither were they prepared to
defend the republic and the government. With the exception of
Reinhardt and some younger officers, none were willing to fight
the rebels. Therein lay Noske's historical responsibility, and at
the same time the tragedy of the Weimar Republic.

Noske's resignation had an important sequel within the
army. Reinhardt felt that his position too was untenable. He
had identified himself entirely with Noske and his policy, and
this had failed. He equally realized the strength of the opposition to him inside the officer corps; Seeckt above all refused to
co-operate with Reinhardt. On 25 March he tendered his
resignation to the president, emphasizing once more the continuous and close co-operation between himself and Noske, in
spite of their entirely different political views. With Noske gone,
Reinhardt saw no possibility of remaining chief of the army
command.[1] Ebert did not accept Reinhardt's resignation from
the army. But on the same day Dr. Geßler was appointed
minister of defence, and Seeckt chief of the army command,
superior to the officers commanding the *Gruppenkommandos*.[2]
The Generals von Oven and Reinhardt, who were senior to
Seeckt, voluntarily accepted this. Seeckt thus held a position
much stronger than Reinhardt's had been. There was now a
military commander-in-chief.[3] The Seeckt era had begun.
Noske never forgave Seeckt his refusal to issue an order that
the Ehrhardt brigade should be opposed by force of arms. He
also maintained that Seeckt had reported to him on the
dubious attitude of Lüttwitz only at the last moment, although
Seeckt was well informed about it.[4]

Thus the tenacious struggle, which Groener and Seeckt had
waged against Reinhardt for so long, ended with their victory.
The only general who was prepared to defend the republic by
force of arms resigned his post and was replaced by a general
who had refused to do so. Seeckt's political sympathies were
probably with Kapp and Lüttwitz rather than with the opposite
side. When he was asked in his own house: 'Why on earth did
you not support them?', he replied: 'A general does not break

---

[1] Ernst, op. cit., p. 65; Rabenau, *Seeckt*, p. 229.

[2] Ibid., p. 236. The final nomination dates from 5 June 1920: ibid., p. 247.

[3] The civilian 'commander-in-chief' was the president: see above p. 49.

[4] Noske, *Aufstieg und Niedergang der deutschen Sozialdemokratie*, p. 158.

his oath.'¹ As a conservative German historian wrote: 'A curious utterance and a nice pretext! He had done nothing to carry out his sworn duty! What he desired was only the preservation of the army as a weight in its own right, as his instrument. . . .'² The judgement of Colonel von Thaer was even less friendly. He considered that Seeckt could have obtained the resignation of Lüttwitz in October 1919 and thus have prevented the whole *Putsch*; 'but I believe that from that time until . . . the Kapp Putsch he was throughout fairly well informed, but adopted an attitude that was above all to his own advantage; and I did not like it much. . . .'.³

VII. *The Purge*

Like Seeckt most of the senior Reichswehr officers adopted a waiting attitude during the *Putsch*. But that was not considered a reason to remove them from their posts. Only General Maercker was dismissed on account of his ambiguous actions during the March days, but that was an isolated case. Major von Gilsa, one of the few officers who had been in favour of resistance, soon resigned from the army. As he wrote to Noske a few months later, he would have to resign, otherwise the 'new men' would soon see to it; 'Seeckt has only let those remain who—during the Kapp–Lüttwitz *Putsch*—have at least not given the impression of disturbing him.'⁴ Von Gilsa later became a Reichstag deputy of the German People's Party, and in 1932 went over to the German Nationalists. Like Reinhardt he certainly did not stand on the political left.

In general the army command took the view that officers who had merely handed on the orders of superior officers that the Kapp–Lüttwitz government should be recognized were in no way to blame. Thus Reinhardt reported in April from his journey to East Prussia that General von Dassel had handed on the order of the *Wehrkreiskommando* I to that effect, and was therefore now being attacked by the Social Democrats. In Reinhardt's opinion, however, he had acted correctly as a subordinate military leader, for he had no knowledge of the

¹ Rabenau, *Seeckt*, p. 234.   ² Görlitz, *Der deutsche Generalstab*, p. 322.
³ Colonel von Thaer to Reinhardt, 14 Apr. 1927: Ernst, op. cit., p. 73, n. 47.
⁴ Noske, op. cit., p. 189.

erroneous premisses on the basis of which his superior officer had issued his order.[1] Thus General von Dassel became the successor to the dismissed General von Estorff as commander of East Prussia—a post which he held until 1923. If one remembers Seeckt's evidence in the Jagow case,[2] it was hardly possible to proceed against any officers of the *Gruppenkommando* 1, as they could always plead that Lüttwitz had still been their commanding officer. In the area of *Gruppenkommando* 2 the attitude of the officers had in general been much more loyal; hence the number of those against whom proceedings could be taken was likely to be rather small.

Accordingly, comparatively few officers were dismissed the service. In the defence ministry a committee of investigation was appointed which consisted of deputies and officials, was presided over by a parliamentary under-secretary, and was supported in its work by certain officers. Seeckt was convinced that all those must go who had committed acts of gross indiscipline or any excesses, but also staff officers who had ignored his orders.[3] In a decree of 18 April he declared:

There are numerous indications that many members of the Reichswehr do not see clearly into what a situation we have got through the events of March, and that we must take the consequences for the results of our political short-sightedness. . . . Although it cannot be denied that the majority of misdemeanours can to some extent be excused on grounds of military obedience, we must nevertheless realize and acknowledge that offences have been committed in our ranks which call for punishment. If we do not admit this ourselves, and do not set out on the path of reformation, we must not complain if attempts are made from outside to effect changes. By such offences I not only understand those connected with the political events of the past weeks, but above all the cases of gross indiscipline and brutal behaviour which have occurred in certain units. I do not intend to tolerate or to forget such occurrences. For troops that have tarnished the honour of the soldier there is no room in the Reichswehr. . . . We must use all our efforts to eliminate political activity of any kind from the army. . . . We do not ask what political opinion the individual has; but I must expect from everybody who continues to serve in the Reichswehr that he takes his oath seriously and has,

---

[1] Reinhardt to the defence minister, 19 Apr. 1920: Nachlaß Reinhardt, Hauptstaatsarchiv Stuttgart.

[2] See above, p. 88.   [3] Gordon, op. cit., p. 128.

voluntarily and as an honest soldier, taken his stand on the basis of the constitution. . . .[1]

When the committee of investigation completed its work in September 1920 the balance sheet showed that a total of 172 officers were discharged, among them 12 generals—the majority before the committee began its work.[2]

In Seeckt's opinion the activities of the investigating committee were likely to undermine discipline, to punish innocent officers, and above all to interfere with matters which the army must settle itself. He succeeded in winning over Ebert to this view, so that the committee lost the right of dismissing officers. The autonomy of the army command in military questions had to be preserved against any attempt at interference from outside. Seeckt's attitude in the question of discipline also meant that soldiers had to be discharged who during the revolt had opposed their superior officers because the latter sided with Kapp.[3] In May 1920 the under-secretary of state in the defence ministry, Rausch, resigned from his post and declared:

Numerous individual cases have convinced me that, more than ever, republican elements who are loyal to the constitution are being eliminated from the Reichswehr, consistently and tenaciously, in conscious or subconscious solidarity, and that the central authorities are virtually powerless to prevent this. Even now, six weeks after the Kapp Putsch, the non-commissioned officers and men, who have suffered damage or vexation because of their loyalty to the constitution, are sent from one place to another within the ministry because the . . . committee competent to deal with their affairs has not yet been formed. . . .[4]

During the Kapp Putsch the private soldiers of the Infantry Regiment 42 at Augsburg sent a loyalist address to the ministry of defence. Thereupon a roll-call was held and the soldiers who had sent this address were questioned. Soldiers who, when questioned, accused their officers of sympathies with Kapp were

---

[1] Nachlaß Seeckt, box 13, no. 111, Militärgeschichtliches Forschungsamt Freiburg; Rabenau, *Seeckt*, pp. 239–40, with political abbreviations and omissions.

[2] Caro and Oehme, *Schleichers Aufstieg*, p. 122; Gordon, op. cit., p. 128. In the navy 4 officers were discharged, 18 relieved of their duties, and 40 sent on leave, according to a letter of Dr. Geßler of 31 July 1920: Nachlaß Geßler, no. 20, Bundesarchiv Koblenz.

[3] Gordon, op. cit., pp. 129, 277, 306, 340.

[4] Caro and Oehme, op. cit., p. 114; Schüddekopf, *Heer und Republik*, no. 51, p. 114.

dismissed, and the Augsburg battalion was sent to the training grounds of Grafenwöhr to be purged of all suspected Socialists; this was alleged by a Social Democratic deputy. His accusations were answered by Major von Schleicher:

> The judicial inquiry against the officers of the Infantry Regiment 42, because of alleged propaganda among the soldiers in favour of Kapp, has established that the accusations against the officers were unsupported and untrue. On this occasion it was discovered that in the Augsburg battalion there existed a debating circle of non-commissioned officers and other soldiers who reported the measures taken by their military superiors to their political party for an appreciation and further investigation. . . . The responsible commander therefore considered himself entitled to have these soldiers removed from the army. Their membership of a political party has not influenced this decision taken on grounds of principle.[1]

Worse was the fate of a lance-corporal of the Cavalry Regiment 105 in Upper Silesia, which had sided with Kapp and had published a decree of Lüttwitz as a regimental order. Lance-corporal Dorfstecher thereupon intended to approach the commanding officer in the name of the *Vertrauensleute* of his unit to protest against the decree and to declare its loyalty to the constitution. But he was not admitted to the officer's presence. On the next morning he was arrested 'on account of disobedience, threatening behaviour, and attempted incitement to mutiny' and discharged. He was then sentenced by a court martial to eight months' imprisonment, while the officers who had sided with Kapp were not punished.[2] Similar clashes between officers and other ranks occurred elsewhere. From Magdeburg the commander of Regiment 104 reported that the non-commissioned officers and other soldiers were exposed to a vast propaganda campaign to incite them against their officers, while the officers had made propaganda for the political right among the other ranks. They had voted on their officers; some were deposed, and whole battalions were without any; in the writer's opinion, it was 'the battle against the officer' that was taking place.[3] Seeckt too realized what was at stake. His decree of 18 April began with the words: 'The officer corps of

[1] Caro and Oehme, op.cit., pp.116–17; Schüddekopf, op. cit., no. 47, pp. 110–11.

[2] Caro and Oehme, op. cit., pp. 122–3; Schüddekopf, op. cit., p. 110.

[3] Colonel von Hahnke to Seeckt, Magdeburg, 25 Mar. 1920: Nachlaß Seeckt, roll 19, no. 25, microfilm in Institut für Zeitgeschichte.

the Reichswehr passes through a fateful hour. Its attitude during the next days will decide whether it will be able to retain the leadership of the young army. . . .'[1] The decision which of the junior officers were to be taken over into the army of 100,000, however, remained with the commanding officer of the regiment in question. As he was often interested in hushing up disagreeable incidents which had occurred during the *Putsch*, usually nothing happened to junior officers who had actively sided with Kapp. In Munich some officers tried to force the Bavarian commander-in-chief, General Ritter von Möhl, on to Kapp's side. For this attempt one of the ringleaders, Captain Ernst Röhm, was removed from his post as adjutant to Colonel Ritter von Epp and sent as a liaison officer to the Munich police—that was all.[2] An amnesty voted by the Reichstag made it possible to take over officers who had supported Kapp into the army of 100,000; while it was easy to weed out officers with republican or democratic sympathies during the process of reduction which was continuing apace after the events of March.[3] The civil authorities had no say in the matter, and the new minister of defence, Dr. Geßler, was too weak to assert his influence.

On the side of the republican parties the latent distrust of the Reichswehr was enormously increased by the events of the *Putsch*. The activities of the committee of investigation, the resignation of officials concerned with the matter, the negative attitude adopted by Seeckt to all outside interference, the whole political atmosphere of the months following upon the rebellion, made any improvement impossible. Between the largest and most influential republican party, the Social Democrats, and the army there developed a chasm which was never bridged. Noske had succeeded in partly mitigating the contrast between the army and Social Democracy; before the *Putsch* the large majority of the officers were loyal to him and recognized his work.[4] But this relationship too was destroyed by the events of March 1920. Dr. Geßler never commanded the personal authority of his predecessor.

[1] Rabenau, *Seeckt*, p. 239.
[2] Gordon, op. cit., pp. 128–9. Röhm was the later S.A. leader.
[3] Information given by General Paul Mahlmann from his own experience.
[4] Raeder, *Mein Leben*, i. 181.

In the navy, finally, things developed in a grotesque fashion. It is true that Rear-Admiral von Trotha, who had supported Kapp openly, was dismissed the service. But the naval brigades of Ehrhardt and von Loewenfeld, which had been instrumental in bringing about the *Putsch*, were taken over into the navy and became the basis of its internal structure. At least the members of the Loewenfeld brigade were transferred as complete units, so that a battalion was used as the personnel of a flotilla or a man-of-war.[1] Most officer cadets of the navy who were trained at Mürwik came from the two naval brigades. They looked distrustfully at anyone who had entered the service of the republic before the Kapp Putsch, and considered him almost a deserter.[2] When unrest broke out at Kiel in 1920 officer cadets of the navy embellished their steel helmets with the black, white, and red colours and the swastika and developed 'their own style of warfare'. As one of them wrote later, 'the swastika was adopted precisely because when we quickly penetrated demonstrating crowds we apprehended quite a number of Jews, who in contrast with the others showed "intelligence" and therefore seemed to us to be the wire-pullers. . .'.[3] Thus the spirit of the Ehrhardt brigade and of its song—'Swastika on the steel helmet, black, white and red ribbon'—remained alive in the navy of the republic.

The case of Commander von Loewenfeld himself was investigated by a committee. He declared that he did not know who had sent the telegram of congratulation to the Ehrhardt brigade on 13 March, while he had arrested Major Hesterberg on account of his connexions with dubious personalities of the left.[4] The committee concluded: 'Both actions make Commander von Loewenfeld highly suspect of having sympathized with the Kapp Putsch and having acted in favour of the Kapp government. We suggest that his file be transmitted to the public prosecutor and that he be suspended from the service until the judicial procedures are terminated. . . .' But von

---

[1] Account of Rear-Admiral Siegfried Sorge: Zeugenschrifttum no. 1785, Institut für Zeitgeschichte; Walter Baum, 'Marine, Nationalsozialismus und Widerstand', *Vierteljahrshefte für Zeitgeschichte*, xi (1963), p. 42.

[2] Baum, loc. cit., p. 42. Cf. Raeder, *Mein Leben*, i. 190.

[3] Account of a naval officer—at that time 20 years old—lent to the author by Dr. Baum.

[4] See above, pp. 84–85.

Loewenfeld was not discharged: at the end of 1921 he was promoted captain and soon after appointed commander of the cruiser 'Berlin'. In the following year President Ebert once more tried to have the case investigated, but in vain.[1] Later the captain rose to an even more important position and became chief of the *Flottenabteilung* in the naval command in Berlin.[2] His implication in the Kapp Putsch was no obstacle to his career.

The defeat of the Kapp Putsch was a great victory for the republican forces—one of the very few they gained through their own efforts in the history of the Weimar Republic. Yet this victory did not lead to far-reaching reforms in the Reichswehr, not even to a thorough purge of all those who at the decisive moment refused to defend the republic and its constitution against a mutiny. On the contrary, the result was a strengthening of the conservative tendencies in army and navy, a change in the army command that was contrary to the interests of the republic, and an alienation of the Reichswehr from the most important political currents and from the largest political party, the Social Democrats. After March 1920 there was a chance to effect thorough reforms, above all in the army, which for the moment was thrown into disarray; it was a fleeting chance that was never to recur. The real victor of March 1920 was General von Seeckt.

[1] *Gutachten* of the parliamentary committee of investigation in the case against Commander von Loewenfeld of 26 July 1920, and letter of Ebert to Dr. Geßler, Berlin, 3 July 1922: Reichskanzlei, Akten betr. Reichsmarine, vol. i: R 43 I 601, Bundesarchiv Koblenz.

[2] *Rangliste der Deutschen Reichsmarine nach dem Stande vom 1. November 1925*, Berlin, 1926, p. 3. At that time von Loewenfeld had the rank of Kapitän zur See. Dr. Geßler's adjutant wrote later: 'We had our work cut out later to cover his ambiguous attitude with the cloak of love.' MS. of Major Wolfgang Fleck (without date or name), p. 21: Nachlaß Geßler, no. 46, Bundesarchiv Koblenz.

PART TWO

THE SEECKT ERA

———

'The Reichswehr stands behind you if the German Chancellor goes the German way!'

(General von Seeckt to Chancellor Stresemann on 7 September 1923)

III

YEARS OF CONSOLIDATION

1. *Seeckt's Personality*

THE Kapp Putsch marked a turning-point in the history of the Reichswehr, above all in its relations with the Weimar Republic. The openly anti-republican policy of General von Lüttwitz and the free corps had suffered a crushing defeat; the danger from the right was banished for the moment. Defeated too, however, was the attempt of Noske and Reinhardt to effect a conciliation between the army and the republic and to concede to the civil authorities a stronger say in military affairs.[1] During the subsequent thirteen years the two lived next to each other, but not with each other. Seeckt successfully warded off any efforts of civil authorities to intervene in military questions, and 'surrounded the army with a Chinese wall'.[2] It is difficult to say whether Reinhardt would have steered an entirely different course. There is no indication that, during his years as commander of *Wehrkreis* v and as commander-in-chief of *Gruppenkommando* 2, he ever attempted to do so. The personal relationship between Seeckt and Reinhardt may have been cool, but there was no strong political disagreement.

Lord d'Abernon, the British ambassador to Berlin, in 1923 gave this description of Seeckt: 'In appearance he is emaciated and severe. His face reminds one of a death's-head, or, as somebody has said, of "General into Fox"; but he has few of the fox characteristics, being an honourable and even punctilious gentleman. Those who criticise him say that his principal fault is that he is too intelligent to be a general. Some of his subordinates who aim at a military régime complain that he has insufficient political ambition. . . .'[3] But on this point Lord

---

[1] Gordon, *Reichswehr and the German Republic*, p. 143.
[2] Hilmar Ritter von Mittelberger, 'Lebenserinnerungen', p. 241: MS. in Bundesarchiv Koblenz.
[3] Lord d'Abernon, *An Ambassador of Peace*, ii, London, 1929, p. 271.

d'Abernon was misinformed, for Seeckt had a burning political ambition and aimed at playing a prominent political part.

His close collaborator during many years, Colonel Hasse, saw Seeckt much more correctly when he wrote in his diary in 1922: 'Seeckt criticizes again the narrow-mindedness of the Foreign Office which does not want the generals to be active in politics. . . .'[1] In this respect Seeckt agreed with Groener. Like Groener he was disinclined to conduct his policy openly and was always active behind the scenes. He was rightly considered 'the sphinx' who kept his most secret plans and decisions to himself. One of his closest collaborators, Joachim von Stülpnagel, then a major and later a general, wrote of Seeckt: 'His reticence and disinclination to talk made him appear sinister in the eyes of outsiders, president Ebert, defence minister Dr. Geßler, politicians, and foreign diplomats. They never knew what he really thought and distrusted him often, but they respected his personality. He entered office with the clear intention of forming an army, loyal to the constitution, well disciplined, faithful to the Prussian tradition, and devoted to himself. . . .'[2] These three components—Prussian tradition, strict discipline, and loyalty to himself—were indeed the three basic principles of Seeckt's work. A critical British observer stated that Seeckt 'combined the best traditions of the Prussian military caste with a breadth of outlook and a political flair unusual in these circles. . .'.[3]

Hans von Seeckt was born in 1866, the son of a Prussian general, his family belonging to the Pomeranian nobility. But in contrast with Ludendorff, Groener, Reinhardt, and the majority of the other generals, he was not educated in a cadet school, but attended, until his finishing examination in 1885, a secondary school at Strasbourg, and only then became an ensign in the Emperor Alexander Guards Grenadier Regiment. Perhaps the width of his interests and vision was connected with the fact that during his education he got to know a world entirely different from that of Pomerania and the typical officers' mess. Perhaps too his pro-Russian attitude had something to

---

[1] Notes of General Lieber 'aus Tagebuch Hasse': Nachlaß Seeckt, box 19, no. 278, p. 59, Militärgeschichtliches Forschungsamt Freiburg.

[2] Joachim von Stülpnagel, '75 Jahre meines Lebens', p. 189: Bundesarchiv-Militärarchiv, H 08–5/27.

[3] Wheeler-Bennett, *Nemesis of Power*, p. 85.

do with the fact that his regiment was that of a Czar in which any anti-Russian feeling can hardly have existed prior to 1914. In any case, even during the war years, Seeckt was friendlier towards Russia than many other Germans. Thus he wrote in 1915: 'You know that my wishes go in the direction of a conciliation with Russia which opens up further possibilities and prepares them. Only we must not try to make Russia too strong . . . .'[1] And in the same year—while the most far-reaching plans of annexation were discussed in Germany—he wrote to his wife: 'It seems that in Berlin very many people are busy with conditions of peace, including some who should not do so. There is evidence of an enormous lack of knowledge and responsibility. To us . . . it seems a little stupid and frivolous to act as if we had the choice between annexing half of France or half of Russia. . . .'[2] Even after the outbreak of the Russian revolution and the clear military defeat of Russia Seeckt retained this sober approach: 'The difficulty lies in our wish to retain Courland and Lithuania. I have never been convinced of this necessity; on the contrary I consider it a worsening of our geographical position. . . .'[3]

In the field of home policy, on the other hand, Seeckt sharply opposed any concessions to democracy, any reform of the Prussian three-class franchise. In 1916 he wrote about the plan of such a reform: 'The Prussian diet has not an ideal composition . . . but has done useful work; in spite of this it will be necessary to preserve the [general] franchise for the *Reichstag* and to change the franchise for the diet. I most sincerely regret the announcement of such a change. It is merely a concession to the supposed popular will. . . .'[4] Only two months before the military collapse Seeckt wrote in good Prussian manner to his wife: 'You recently mentioned a speech of [Chancellor] Hertling to the students. Quite nice, but the one in the *Herrenhaus* [House of Lords] is very, very bad. This is the worst we have ever heard. So the dynasty is in danger if we do not introduce the idiotic equal franchise, against better conviction? And no Prussian gives him a reply? That is worse than the

[1] Seeckt to von Winterfeldt-Menkin, 19 July 1915: Hans von Seeckt, *Aus meinem Leben, 1866–1917*, Leipzig, 1938, p. 174.
[2] Letter of Feb. 1915: ibid., p. 97.
[3] Letter of May 1917: ibid., p. 562.
[4] Letter of 4 Feb. 1916: ibid., p. 323.

whole Bethmann and much worse than anything that happens or can happen at the front. . . .'[1] An open mind in questions of foreign policy and a negative attitude towards democracy and the republic at home remained characteristic of Seeckt throughout his life. He was and remained a Prussian aristocrat, and had no understanding of the time of the masses and of mass movements.

His officers found Seeckt 'unapproachable, but his whole demeanour strongly impressed all soldiers. He talked little, his words were highly polished; he used short sentences to laud and to reprove. His criticisms showed an excellent military vision and always included great ideas. . . .'[2] In all military questions there existed only one opinion, his own. When the commanding officer of the Second Cavalry Division added a mounted battery to each cavalry brigade, Seeckt refused his consent. Even Hasse had to state that in questions of troop formation there was for Seeckt 'only his own view; everything else he declines harshly. . .'. When another division desired more fire power, Seeckt refused brusquely, and Hasse noted: 'In such a situation Seeckt has a frightfully wounding manner which he [Hasse] himself also has to experience frequently. . . .'[3] The same is reported by the chief of the training department (*Heeresausbildungsabteilung*) of the *Truppenamt*, Colonel von Blomberg. When he suggested to Seeckt that he should abolish the lances of the cavalry so as to give it greater fire power, the latter replied: 'For the same reason I proposed the removal of the lances during the war. This was refused. Now the cavalry can retain the lances as far as I am concerned.' When the same officer wanted to equip the companies of bicyclists with motor cycles, Seeckt answered: 'Dear Blomberg, if we want to remain friends, then you must refrain from such proposals.'[4]

Entirely unacceptable to Seeckt was anything that smacked of criticism of his own measures. When the *Wehrkeiskommando* v,

[1] Letter of 9 Sept. 1918: Rabenau, *Seeckt*, p. 85. Count Hertling became chancellor in Nov. 1917 as a successor of Michaelis, who a few months earlier had succeeded Bethmann-Hollweg.

[2] Hilmar Ritter von Mittelberger, 'Lebenserinnerungen', p. 242: MS. in Bundesarchiv Koblenz.

[3] Notes of General Lieber 'aus Tagebuch Hasse', under 8 Aug. and 18 Oct. 1922: Nachlaß Seeckt, box 19, no. 278, pp. 66, 75, loc. cit.

[4] Werner von Blomberg, 'Erinnerungen bis 1933', iii. 95: Bundesarchiv-Militärarchiv. Cp. below, p. 213, for more details.

which was under Reinhardt's command, wrote to the army's administrative office that too many telegrams were sent, even for the merest trifles, above all by the defence ministry and the *Gruppenkommando* at Cassel, Seeckt wrote in the margin: 'a threatening, inadmissible criticism which I cannot tolerate. This is to be communicated to the *Wehrkreiskommando*.' And a letter was sent to Lieutenant-General Reinhardt which pronounced the criticism 'inadmissible in form and content'.[1] Twelve months later Colonel Hasse wrote in his diary: 'S. difficult as a leader, creates easily the impression of being ill-tempered, and lets one know, each time he is listening to a suggestion, however cautiously it is made, that he is not willing to take any advice. It is rather difficult to get along. I am doing my best to overlook every whim and touchiness. . . .'[2]

It is perhaps strange that Seeckt, in spite of these traits, was able to gain the confidence and the veneration of so many subordinate officers—although there were many officers who remained critical of him. The cause seems to have been his great military knowledge, the width of his vision, his striking personality, and, last not least, his emphasis on Prussian traditions, which influenced the north-German officers. What they had so often criticized in Reinhardt now worked in favour of Seeckt. Many hoped that—after the failure of the Kapp Putsch— he would find a way to promote the conservative cause, to terminate political unrest and strikes, and to secure to the traditional forces in Germany their proper place. After all the insecurity brought about by the revolution and the reduction of the army, the officer corps again had a 'head' in which it could put its complete trust. Thus Seeckt, in the opinion of a junior officer of the time, became 'a substitute for the monarch' who filled 'the void' created by the abdication of the Emperor.[3] Soon the officers recognized him as their political head, as a substitute for the 'royal shield' which they had lost on 9 November 1918.[4]

[1] Letter of chief of staff of *Wehrkreiskommando* v, Stuttgart, 12 Oct. 1920, and letter of Seeckt to Reinhardt, 24 Oct. 1920: Nachlaß Seeckt, roll 21, no. 129, microfilm in Institut für Zeitgeschichte.

[2] Notes of General Lieber to 8 Oct. 1921: loc. cit., p. 39.

[3] Opinion of Major-General Curt Ulrich von Gersdorff expressed to the author.

[4] Wolfgang Sauer, 'Die Reichswehr', in Bracher, *Die Auflösung der Weimarer Republik*, Stuttgart and Düsseldorf, 1955, p. 256.

11. *Seeckt's First Months*

One thing Seeckt achieved only a short time after his appointment as chief of the army command: a definition of his powers and an extension of his sphere of competence. Provisionally this was done on 22 June, and finally on 11 August 1920.[1] The Personnel Office, which Seeckt had criticized so sharply during the preceding months, was made subordinate to him. Under his orders also came the *Truppenamt*, which remained of decisive importance, the *Wehramt*, and the Inspectors of Weapons and of Education. Above all, the commanders-in-chief of the two Reichswehr corps and of the *Wehrkreise*, the divisional commanders, became Seeckt's subordinates, as was apparently promised to him as early as 25 March 1920: hitherto they had stood directly under the minister of defence. This was of fundamental importance, and equally the stipulation that the chief of the army command was to deputize for the minister of defence in the exercise of the power of command. It was less important that, directly under the minister of defence, the post of quartermaster-general was created, responsible for the military administration and the supply of weapons, the *Waffenamt*.[2] But this was soon recognized as a 'faulty construction' and this office also was put under the chief of the army command, who was now in charge of all the central offices of the army.[3] His powers were thus greater than those of any military commander of an earlier period, be he chief of the general staff or Prussian minister of war. Only the navy remained separate.

At first, however, Seeckt had to act cautiously, for the prestige of the army and its leading officers had suffered badly during the Kapp Putsch. Yet even then his letters showed self-confidence and optimism. To Colonel von Thaer he wrote in June: 'I do not think that the general situation is too bad. The Kapp Putsch, much damage as it has done, has also, I hope, opened the eyes of many. You will see from yesterday's speeches that I have tried above all to issue *everywhere* the slogan "protection of the constitution". At the moment this is the only bond. ...'[4] The

---

[1] *Heeres-Verordnungsblatt* of 21 Sept. 1920; Rabenau, *Seeckt*, p. 479.

[2] Ibid.; Meier-Welcker, in *Vierteljahrshefte für Zeitgeschichte*, iv (1956), pp. 158–9.

[3] Rabenau, *Seeckt*, p. 479; Reinhardt, *Wehrkraft und Wehrwille*, p. 51.

[4] Seeckt to Colonel von Thaer, 4 June 1920: Nachlaß Seeckt, box 10, no. 72, Militärgeschichtliches Forschungsamt Freiburg.

Reichswehr had to defend itself against sharp attacks after the Kapp Putsch, and Seeckt's position was still weak: this was not the time to make far-reaching plans. How weak Seeckt's position was also emerged from a correspondence between him and the Bavarian commander-in-chief, Major-General Ritter von Möhl, of April 1920. Möhl wrote to Seeckt because rumours had appeared in the press that Bavarian officers with pacifist views would obtain posts in the defence ministry. This, Möhl declared, was 'impossible', and simultaneously attacked the new minister, Dr. Geßler:

> That such rumours could develop at all is a significant sign of the total lack of confidence which the Bavarian Reichswehr has in the new minister of defence. His attitude in the question of the revolt in the Ruhr,[1] as well as his participation in negotiations with the trade unions, have brought it about that here we expect anything from this man, or—if you wish—nothing. The call for Noske is general; *in any case he would be far better*, if a general cannot be appointed—that seems to be a matter of course for reasonable people, hence at the moment is out of the question for the German nation. Would it not be possible to approach Noske with the request that he should resume his place—why should this be impossible or inadvisable? Finally, I must warn you against holding an inquisition in the Bavarian Reichswehr on account of its attitude in the *affaire* Kapp. The Bavarian Reichswehr did remain loyal to the 'old government' under my orders. What difficulties and friction had to be overcome in doing so, is an internal matter. . . .

Möhl concluded by pointing out how serious the situation was, and how strongly the Bavarians felt against the central government.[2]

In later years Seeckt would have reacted strongly to a letter which attacked the minister of defence, and indirectly Seeckt himself. But he merely replied: 'I do not share your opinion about the new minister of defence. I do not think that a return of Noske is at the moment possible, apart from the question whether he is willing. No one dreams of an inquisition in the

---

[1] After the Kapp Putsch a left-wing revolt broke out in the Ruhr which was suppressed by the Reichswehr and the free corps. Cf. Rabenau, *Seeckt*, p. 242, for the conflict which occurred on this occasion between Geßler and General Freiherr von Watter.

[2] Möhl to Seeckt, Munich, 11 Apr. 1920: Nachlaß Seeckt, box 17, no. 129, Militärgeschichtliches Forschungsamt Freiburg.

Bavarian Reichswehr. . . . I do not deny that many grievances
of the Reichswehr are justified, but should like to point out
that if the government often does not redress them, it does not
refrain out of bad will or weakness, but because the difficulties
are connected with our general situation. . .'; those of the
Reichswehr had considerably increased through the events of
the Kapp Putsch, and they must be overcome by a common
effort on all sides.[1] This sounded almost apologetic and showed
no trace of refuting Möhl's attacks. What Seeckt did not mention was that he wanted to avoid a return of Noske to his post
in the defence ministry at all costs. When Reinhardt in September 1920 suggested a closer collaboration with certain
associations of ex-servicemen and other leagues, which politically stood on the right, Seeckt did not react sharply to an idea
which was contrary to his own. 'The disadvantages of the
Bünde', he wrote,

far outweigh their advantages; those *Verbände* are the most dangerous
which combine political and professional interests with economic
ones, like the R.d.B. (*Reichsverband deutscher Berufssoldaten*) and the
D.O.B. (*Deutscher Offiziersbund*). Even if outwardly they confine
themselves to economic affairs, they form trade unions, with which
their members in course of time feel more strongly linked than with
their superior officers. At times of political crisis the *Bünde* follow
their political and sectional interests and deprive the army of its
leadership. The R.d.B. has tried to do this during the Kapp
Putsch. . . . The minister of defence and I intend to prohibit
membership of the purely political *Bünde* as well as of the R.d.B.
and the D.O.B., so as to keep the army free of them. . . .[2]

For these reasons Seeckt opposed any closer links with the
Bünde.

Seeckt's aim of prohibiting membership in all parties,
Bünde, and similar organizations was largely achieved by the
Wehrgesetz of 1921. Soldiers were forbidden to engage in any
political activity; the membership of political associations and
clubs and the participation in political meetings were prohibited; even membership of non-political clubs could be
barred for reasons of military discipline.[3] Nevertheless, this did

[1] Draft of Seeckt's reply, n.d.: ibid.
[2] Seeckt to Reinhardt, Berlin, 14 Oct. 1920: Nachlaß Reinhardt, Hauptstaatsarchiv Stuttgart.
[3] §§ 36–37 of the *Wehrgesetz* of 23 Mar. 1921.

not solve the problem of the R.d.B. and of similar professional organizations. This question appeared time and again during the following months in Hasse's diary. Finally, a decree of 24 May declared all military associations within the Reichswehr dissolved, and on 12 July soldiers on the active list were forbidden to belong to any officers' league. A few days later Seeckt signed a list of those associations which were declared political.[1] He thus erected a barrier against their exercising any influence on the army. Yet—as we shall see—there were other *Verbände* with which the Reichswehr continued to co-operate; the issue was to occupy the attention of the army command for many years to come.

The *Wehrgesetz* repeated the stipulations of the Treaty of Versailles about the maximum strength of the army and navy and their officer corps, as well as about the number of divisions, corps, and men-of-war permitted; it thus gave to these clauses renewed legal backing.[2] About the power of command the *Wehrgesetz* said: 'The president of the Reich is the commander-in-chief of the entire *Wehrmacht*. Under him the minister of defence exercises the power of issuing orders (*Befehlsgewalt*) to the entire *Wehrmacht*. At the head of the army stands a general as chief of the army command, at the head of the navy an admiral as chief of the naval command.'[3] This was—probably on purpose—phrased in such a way that the power of command of the chief of the army command was not mentioned at all: a 'concession' to the suspicious powers of the Entente. But the decree of 11 August 1920, which stipulated that the chief of the army command was the deputy of the defence minister in the exercise of the power of command, was not invalidated and remained in force. This seems to have meant that the chief of the army command possessed the *Kommandogewalt* and the minister of defence the *Befehlsgewalt*:[4] he had the right to issue decrees and orders, but—as it seems—not the right of issuing commands to the troops. The latter became a prerogative of the chief of the army command, to whom the commanding officers of the corps and the divisions remained subordinate.

---

[1] Notes of General Lieber 'Seeckt als Chef der Heeresleitung', p. 23: Nachlaß Seeckt, box 19, no. 278, Militärgeschichtliches Forschungsamt Freiburg.
[2] §§ 2–6 of the *Wehrgesetz*.   [3] § 8, II, *Wehrgesetz*.
[4] Rabenau, *Seeckt*, p. 473, n. 3. See above, p. 108, for the decree of 11 Aug. 1920.

Seeckt's rights and position were fairly clearly circumscribed, but those of the minister of defence much less so. To avoid confusion their rights were once more 'finally' defined by a decree of June 1923; but this merely repeated the provisions of 11 August 1920, and did not make the position any clearer than it was.[1] In this situation, only a very strong personality could have asserted itself as minister of defence against the ambitious Seeckt.

It is not known whether Seeckt criticized any of the stipulations of the *Wehrgesetz*. But he was dissatisfied that it gave legal sanction to the institution of a *Heereskammer* (army chamber), which was to have advisory functions and to be elected by a ballot of the units.[2] The *Heereskammer* was created by Reinhardt and was considered a concession to the parliamentary system by the conservative officers. In 1920 its plenary meeting was attended by 69 members—14 officers, 13 non-commissioned officers, and 29 other soldiers; while the main committee had 36 members—14 officers, 7 non-commissioned officers, and 10 other soldiers (the remainder being officials, medical, veterinary, and arsenal officers).[3] Thus the officers were much more strongly represented on the main committee than in the plenary meeting, but even in this the lower ranks only had a majority together with the non-commissioned officers. Dr. Geßler believed that Seeckt had agreed to the formation of the *Heereskammer*; but Seeckt was convinced that his temporary absence from Berlin had been used to insert it into the *Wehrgesetz*. All he was willing to concede was a 'personal council' of senior officers, while the *Heereskammer* should disappear.[4] It does not seem to have existed for long. Its constitution and competence were to be defined by a special law, but this was never promulgated. In Rabenau's opinion it was Seeckt who prevented the *Heereskammer* from developing any real activity. 'He hardly allowed it the function of a superior kitchen committee. . . .'[5]

---

[1] Rabenau, *Seeckt*, p. 473, gives the text.

[2] § 10 of the *Wehrgesetz*; there was to be a parallel chamber for the navy.

[3] These figures are given in a letter of Major-General von Lossow, Munich, 18 Nov. 1920: Akten des Gruppenkommandos 4, Bund 1, Akt 6, Bayerisches Kriegsarchiv, Munich.

[4] Notes of General Lieber, 'Seeckt als Chef der Heeresleitung', p. 17: Nachlaß Seeckt, box 19, no. 278, Militärgeschichtliches Forschungsamt.

[5] Rabenau, *Seeckt*, p. 257.

The *Wehrgesetz* also envisaged the continuation of the institution of the *Vertrauensräte* in all units, as they had existed in the provisional Reichswehr.[1] These spokesmen of the other ranks, however, were too reminiscent of the hated soldiers' councils of the revolution and never assumed any importance; they were only allowed to deal with personal complaints or grievances.

Soon Seeckt felt very much the master in the ministry of defence and in army matters in general. In the negotiations at Spa in the summer of 1920 Germany tried in vain to obtain alleviations of the conditions of Versailles from the Entente powers. In the military field they merely conceded an extension of the time limit, stipulated for the reduction of the army to 100,000, to 1 January 1921: more it proved impossible to achieve, in spite of 'the utmost military tenacity'.[2] The German government had to give an undertaking that the citizens' defence corps (*Einwohnerwehren*) and other paramilitary formations would be disarmed and dissolved. Seeckt issued a proclamation to the Reichswehr:

The negotiations at Spa have not brought the desired result. The struggle for the preservation of a stronger *Wehrmacht* has been in vain. . . . Threatened by the enemy, but also convinced that the army must make this last sacrifice for the common good, I have given my consent to the acceptance of the Convention and bear the responsibility for it. At this moment I am addressing myself to the Reichswehr and asking it to help me—bitter as it is—to fulfil the given promise, and to work, each at his place, so that we can bring the sacrifice demanded of us in complete order and quiet devotion: we must render to the state its strongest support in the small Reichswehr, and thus prepare the ground for better times. . . .[3]

As at Weimar twelve months before, Seeckt had chosen the more cautious and the more realistic course. But the time of the officers' councils which discussed and decided controversial issues was past: the army now had a chief who decided on his own responsibility.

---

[1] § 9 of the *Wehrgesetz*. For the *Vertrauensräte*, see above, pp. 10, 24, 33.
[2] Rabenau, *Seeckt*, pp. 282–3; ibid., pp. 280–7, details about the Spa negotiations.
[3] Chef der Heeresleitung, Berlin, 10 July 1920: Nachlaß Seeckt, box 13, no. 118, Militärgeschichtliches Forschungsamt Freiburg.

At the end of 1920 Seeckt could look back with pride on the achievements of the past nine months. He announced:

The army is finally formed. A new chapter in the history of the German army begins. In the place of all good wishes for the coming year and the future, we vow to stand together in devotion to our profession. We want to keep the sword sharp and the shield shining. . . . Called upon to protect the fatherland, the army and every soldier must be filled with a burning love of the fatherland, willing to sacrifice his life, loyal to his oath and in the fulfilment of his duty. The army is the first instrument of the power of the Reich. Each member must be conscious of the fact that, on and off duty, he is the representative and supporter of the power of the Reich. . . .

The regimental commander (independent staff officer), is in the first place responsible for the education of the officer corps and the commander of the company for the education of the non-commissioned officers and other soldiers, etc. Under the supervision of their senior officers the regimental commanders are to retain their position, as it has historically developed and been proved. . . . The regimental commander has to see to it that a true sense of honour, genuine comradeship, selfless devotion to duty, and dignified conduct prevail in the officer corps. . . . He is the adviser and oldest friend of his officers and, in differences of opinion and doubts, the natural first judge. . . . The commander of the company etc. has the same task towards his non-commissioned officers and other soldiers. . . . The officers of all ranks must always remain conscious of their duty to be teachers and examples in all fields of the service, whether intellectual or physical. . . .[1]

Instead of the words 'republic' and 'constitution', which Seeckt had used some months earlier, there now appeared the 'Reich' and the 'fatherland'. Seeckt's position was no longer weak; his tone was far more self-confident; the army was formed, and it obeyed him.

III. Seeckt and the Institutions of the Republic

Seeckt was a convinced monarchist and Prussian. But this did not mean that he worked for the restoration of the monarchy or even desired the return of William II from Holland. He was too intelligent to consider this a realistic possibility—and probably also too critical of the person of William II. On the

[1] *Heeres-Verordnungsblatt*, no. 79, 30 Dec. 1920.

other hand, Seeckt never attained a positive relationship to the republic and its institutions, nor to a leading politician or a member of the government. He was a true aristocrat of the old school, too proud and conceited to befriend the new masters whom he considered upstarts. This also applied to Ebert and Noske, whose views were acceptable to many officers, and who tried everything to establish good relations with the leading officers. The British ambassador, Lord d'Abernon, wrote 'von Seeckt is intimate with Ebert, the two being close friends';[1] but this was an error. In any case, Seeckt prevented the participation of the president in manœuvres and ordered that guards of honour were not to march past the president:[2] both at a time—September 1922—when the difficulties created by the Kapp Putsch had been overcome, and before the beginning of the crisis of 1923, which caused new friction between the army and the government. There was no reason to snub the commander-in-chief of the army in this way. While Groener, for example, throughout his life preserved great regard for the first president,[3] who had done so much to re-establish law and order in Germany, Seeckt lacked even this feeling of respect.

Seeckt was indifferent to politicians, deputies, and ministers, and rather contemptuous of their feverish activities. In his opinion, the leading men of the new republic did not possess the authority and the stature required by their offices.[4] But this criticism—comprehensible as it was—included prominent politicians and statesmen who were as conservative in their views as Seeckt himself: for example Stresemann, whom he disliked intensely. Exactly as he several times expressed his lack of confidence in Stresemann as chancellor and as foreign minister, he disagreed with the appointment of Rathenau as foreign minister in 1922 and recommended (to the chancellor?) 'that he should not be appointed'.[5] Soon a serious conflict

---

[1] Lord d'Abernon, *An Ambassador of Peace*, ii. 271.

[2] Notes of General Lieber, p. 65, under 8 and 11 Sept. 1922: Nachlaß Seeckt, box 19, no. 278, Militärgeschichtliches Forschungsamt Freiburg; Rabenau, *Seeckt*, p. 275.

[3] Groener to Oberstaatsanwalt Ernst, Potsdam, 5 Feb. 1936: 'Ebert was a patriotic man, he hated the revolution. . . . The officers can be grateful to Ebert, for he did everything to strengthen the position of the officers against many attempts at undermining it. . . .' (Nachlaß Groener, box 8, no. 37, Bundesarchiv Koblenz).

[4] Gordon, *Reichswehr and the German Republic*, p. 307.

[5] Notes of General Lieber, p. 49, under 1 Feb. 1922: loc. cit.

occurred between Seeckt and Rathenau, because the latter in a reply to the Entente powers—which had complained about the military organization of the police—intended to mention the functions of the Reichswehr. This was opposed by Seeckt: in his opinion, the reply must not mention the army at all.[1] Yet Seeckt had noted with approval some months before that Rathenau, in a conference with the chancellor, sided with the army: 'Germany must become stronger internally and await a suitable moment for military action. . . .'[2] Stresemann as well as Rathenau had strong national convictions and they were not opposed to an understanding with Russia—as both proved by their actions. On this basis it should have been possible to co-operate with the chief of the army command, provided he showed his good will.

Particularly obnoxious to Seeckt were those noblemen who genuinely accepted the new order and honestly worked for the republic, such as Count Bernstorff and Count Brockdorff-Rantzau. As he wrote early in 1919: 'I have become accustomed to much and have become silent; but the speech of the shame-faced Count Brockdorff has succeeded in infuriating me. I thought that greater depths and more political dishonesty were impossible to reach, but he has proved otherwise. . . . Much better to have a firm socialist at the head than these propaganda counts and weak-kneed democrats who hide their deadly fear under a diplomatic cloak. . . .'[3] Although in later years Brockdorff-Rantzau, as German ambassador to Moscow, was a protagonist of a *rapprochement* with Russia and supported it with all his strength, the gulf between him and Seeckt could not be bridged. It was in vain that the president of the highest German court, the *Reichsgericht*, wrote to Seeckt and pointed out that Germany could no longer afford that her two most capable political heads should work against each other. Seeckt adhered to his view 'that Count Brockdorff-Rantzau in his personality did not offer the necessary guarantees of patriotic convictions. . . .'[4] Above all, Seeckt was determined to keep the

---

[1] Notes of General Lieber, p. 50, under 24 Feb. and 21 Mar. 1922.

[2] Ibid., p. 40, under 28 Dec. 1921.

[3] Seeckt to von Winterfeldt-Menkin, Bartenstein, 19 Feb. 1919: Nachlaß Seeckt, box 15, no. 90/72, Militärgeschichtliches Forschungsamt Freiburg. Cp. Seeckt's letter to his wife of 6 Feb. 1919, above, p. 31.

[4] Dr. Walter Simons (the *Reichsgerichtspräsident*) to Seeckt, Berlin, 14 Oct. 1922:

threads of his Russian policy securely in his own hands—hence a fruitful co-operation with the foreign minister or the ambassador to Moscow was impossible.

Seeckt was highly critical of the Weimar Constitution and the parties which created and supported it, and perhaps this was the root of his enmity to many leading politicians. At the beginning of November 1923, at the height of the Bavarian crisis, Seeckt wrote to the Bavarian *Generalstaatskommissar* von Kahr:

> The Weimar Constitution is for me not a *noli me tangere*; I did not participate in its creation, and it is in its basic principles contrary to my political thinking. I therefore understand entirely your determination to fight it. . . . I believed that a change of the constitution was approaching, and that I could help towards this by methods which were not unnecessarily to lead through civil war. So far as concerns my attitude towards the international Social Democracy, I have to confess that at the outset I believed in the possibility of winning over part of it to national co-operation; but I have revised this opinion long ago, a long time before our conversation, in so far as the Social Democratic Party is concerned, not the German working class as such. . . . I see clearly that a collaboration with the Social Democratic Party is impossible because it repudiates the idea of military preparedness (*Wehrhaftigkeit*). . . . I do not consider a Stresemann cabinet viable, not even after its transformation. This lack of confidence I have expressed to the chancellor himself as well as to the president, and I have told them that in the long run I could not guarantee the attitude of the Reichswehr to a government in which it had no confidence. . . . A Stresemann government cannot last without the support of the Reichswehr and of the forces standing behind it. . . .[1]

This was an attitude quite different from that taken by Seeckt after the Kapp Putsch; then his slogan had been 'protection of the constitution', and he had emphasized his willingness to serve it.[2] That he had rendered an oath to defend the constitution was not mentioned in the letter to von Kahr.

Nachlaß Seeckt, box 15, no. 214, Militärgeschichtliches Forschungsamt Freiburg. In this letter too is Seeckt's remark against Brockdorff-Rantzau, which he did not deny. For a very positive opinion of Brockdorff-Rantzau, see Theodor Schieder, *Die Probleme des Rapallo-Vertrags*, Cologne and Opladen, 1956, pp. 55–56.

[1] Seeckt to von Kahr, Berlin, 2 Nov. 1923: Schüddekopf, *Heer und Republik*, no. 79, pp. 187–9; Rabenau, *Seeckt*, pp. 369–70.

[2] See above, pp. 95, 108.

The conflicts between Seeckt and Social Democratic ministers were closely connected with the fact that the latter worked hard for a disarmament of the many para-military associations and defence units, which had come into being during the period of the free corps and the frontier struggles in the east. The ministers rightly believed them to be a permanent threat to internal security and used the Prussian police to confiscate the arms caches of the para-military organizations. After the battles in Upper Silesia in 1921, in which the free corps were clandestinely supported by the Reichswehr against the Poles, clashes occurred with the minister of the interior, Köster, who wanted to disarm the irregular formations; this Seeckt tried to prevent by influencing the Chancellor, Wirth, and the minister of defence.[1] Early in 1922 new friction developed between the army command and the ministry of the interior for the same reason; 'the danger exists that this will impede the preparations for the defence of the frontiers. . .'. Again Seeckt intervened personally against Köster with the chancellor. Other officers, especially Major von Schleicher, tried to avoid an exacerbation of the conflict. Senior officers of the Prussian police came on several occasions to Seeckt because 'under the influence of Köster and other Social Democratic ministers, the police moves strongly towards the left. . .'. Seeckt promised that he would influence the chancellor in favour of 'the preservation of the military spirit of the police', and this was done. A colonel of the police was taken to Wirth to report to him.[2]

A new clash occurred in June 1922 when the Prussian government proposed that Reichswehr units should be employed as a frontier police, which would have made them subordinate to the Prussian authorities. Seeckt protested in strong terms to the chancellor:

The purpose of this proposal is to allocate to the army a permanent police function that is contrary to its essence and its tasks. . . . Using this case as a precedent the Reichswehr could be employed for any other police task. That is the end of the Reichswehr. Therewith the only reliable instrument of power of the state would be broken and

[1] Rabenau, *Seeckt*, p. 303; Notes of General Lieber, p. 36, under 17 and 19 Dec. 1921: Nachlaß Seeckt, box 19, no. 278, Militärgeschichtliches Forschungsamt Freiburg.
[2] Ibid., p. 49, under 19 Jan., 18 and 22 Feb. 1922; Rabenau, *Seeckt*, p. 266.

thus the aim of those people who urge this step would be achieved: the Reich would finally be made defenceless abroad, and be delivered to party rule at home. The soldiers are ruined by frontier service and withdrawn from the influence of their leaders. . . . Such an employment of the Reichswehr as a police force is entirely contrary to the principles according to which I have trained and educated it; it would only be possible against my express veto. Thus it is impossible for me to carry out such an order, and I should be forced to resign. . . . For me the question is whether the army will be employed according to the wishes of the French and the ministers Braun and Severing, or according to the principles which I represent and which hitherto have received your consent on the political side. . . .[1]

What is remarkable in this letter is not so much the threat of resignation and of not executing an order, but the frankness with which Seeckt accused the Social Democrats of desiring to make Germany 'defenceless abroad' and of following the same line as the French government. This was the party to which the president and important ministers belonged. If Seeckt really believed this, it would have been more honest to resign.

Two weeks later, the foreign minister, Rathenau, was murdered by members of the *Organisation Consul* which was commanded by Ehrhardt; this caused a 'new wave of distrust against the *Wehrmacht*',[2] which by the left was always suspected of connexions with the extreme right. The Social Democrats, however, did not demand the retirement of Seeckt, but that of the minister of defence, Dr. Geßler, who was responsible in a parliamentary sense. Seeckt, however, declined to issue, on behalf of the commanding officers, a declaration in defence of the attacked minister. Instead Seeckt and the chief of the naval command, Admiral Behncke, issued an order which pointed to the oath the soldiers had rendered to the constitution and repudiated any doubt that it was not binding. The order equally repudiated any attempt to connect the army and navy with movements which used political murder as a weapon, and strongly condemned the murder of Rathenau.[3] Colonel Hasse,

---

[1] Seeckt to Dr. Wirth, Bad Elster, 10 June 1922: copy in Nachlaß Geßler, no. 55, Bundesarchiv Koblenz. The Prussian proposal was based on article 160 of the Treaty of Versailles.   [2] Rabenau, *Seeckt*, p. 272.

[3] Text of the decree in 'Büro des Reichspräsidenten', Deutsches Zentralarchiv Potsdam, vol. 762, p. 13.

however, did not agree with this step because 'the army would not understand this unnecessary apology'; Hasse and Schleicher expressed to Seeckt their objections against the decree, 'whereupon he was offended'.[1]

Probably it was this renewed distrust of the Reichswehr which caused Seeckt to issue—only a few weeks later—an order that official army buildings were to be decorated with flags on 11 August (the day on which the Weimar Constitution had become law) and that troops were to participate in the celebrations, at least in Berlin.[2] Seeckt himself attended the ceremony in the Reichstag, but left immediately after the musical opening. In all the other years Seeckt was prevented from attending the celebrations on 11 August by 'official tours' which took him away from Berlin and were planned well in advance in his annual programme. His adjutant remembered that it was the participation of Social Democratic mass organizations which irritated Seeckt particularly, as the ceremony thus became a popular festival.[3] Seeckt lacked the political sense to realize that in the weak republic support of the state and official meetings by the people was absolutely essential: the absence of such backing was one of the great weaknesses of the republic.

Seeckt also had a strong antipathy to parliament and the parliamentary system, although he became a member of the Reichstag after his dismissal. To his adjutant he described parliament as 'the cancer of our time', and 'often used rude language against parliament. . .'.[4] In spite of admonitions by the minister of defence, Seeckt never appeared in the Reichstag: he left it to the minister to defend the army and its interests there. But this did not prevent Seeckt from negotiating intensively with the parties behind the scenes. At the beginning of 1922 he took great pains to persuade the moderate right to enter the government so that a further development towards the left would be avoided. He saw a leading deputy of the German People's Party to 'advise' him on the attitude of his party. During the following weeks 'the question of a participation

---

[1] Rabenau, *Seeckt*, pp. 272–3; Notes of General Lieber, p. 63, under 24 June 1922: Nachlaß Seeckt, box 19, no. 278, Militärgeschichtliches Forschungsamt.

[2] Ibid., p. 68, under 1 Aug. 1922.

[3] Rabenau, *Seeckt*, p. 199, n. 1; recollections of Seeckt's adjutant von Selchow, p. 7: Nachlaß Seeckt, roll 26, no. 289, microfilm in Institut für Zeitgeschichte.

[4] von Selchow's diary, p. 2: ibid.

of the German People's Party in the government, which the army command tries to bring about by all means, plays an important part'. When the party on 16 February declined to give Chancellor Wirth a vote of confidence, Seeckt considered this a 'disgrace' and declared that he would waste no further efforts on the German People's Party, while Hasse tried to talk him out of it.[1]

As the German People's Party refused to support the Wirth government, the chancellor was forced to seek support further to the left, from the Independent Social Democrats. As the Independents two months later, in September 1922, reunited with the Social Democrats, this was merely a difference of degree; without the Independents' support the government did not possess a parliamentary majority as long as the German People's Party remained in opposition. Yet in the opinion of the army command it meant 'an orientation of the Reich government further to the left' if Independents joined the Wirth government. In July the right-wing extremist deputy Count Reventlow asked Seeckt what his attitude in such a case would be. Seeckt replied that he would 'not quit without further ado', and that it was 'his duty to struggle for the preservation of a usable army'. This could be interpreted in many ways; but unfortunately Seeckt's letter fell into the hands of the police—and thus of the Prussian government—when Count Reventlow was arrested soon after.[2] Further friction between the Reichswehr and the political left was caused in the summer of 1922 by the participation of Reichswehr units in the production of nationalist films glorifying the deeds of *Fridericus Rex*, and by mutinies which occurred in units stationed at Lötzen and Lankwitz.[3]

According to the recollections of his adjutant, it was Seeckt, who in these as well as other cases 'laid down the general political lines, while Schleicher was responsible for the attainment of the aim by complicated manœuvres behind the scenes...'. Apart from him, important parts were played by Colonel Hasse, the chief of the *Truppenamt*, and Lieutenant-

---

[1] Notes of General Lieber, p. 49, under 30 Jan. and 16 Feb. 1922: Nachlaß Seeckt, box 19, no. 278, Militärgeschichtliches Forschungsamt.

[2] Ibid., p. 64, under 6 July 1922.

[3] Ibid., p. 64; Rabenau, *Seeckt*, pp. 273-4.

Colonel von Stülpnagel. 'Every day a large part of the morning was occupied by them: no wonder, for something did always happen in internal politics between 1922 and 1925. . . .'[1] Schleicher's political influence was growing. At the end of 1921 he was busy, at the instruction of Dr. Geßler, in persuading Stresemann that the German People's Party should enter the government; Seeckt was 'agreeably surprised'.[2] Towards the Social Democratic Party Schleicher was more open-minded than Seeckt. When, at the end of 1922, new conflicts broke out with the Prussian minister of the interior, Severing, on account of the frontier defence units and their armament, Seeckt opposed any further collaboration with the Social Democrats; 'while Schleicher was of the opinion that without Social Democracy it would be impossible to gain the support of the working class in case of war. . .'.[3] About this time, when the government was reformed, Geßler was made to declare that he would only continue to serve 'if the question of the weapons of the frontier defence units and the whole frontier defence issue were regulated according to the wishes of the soldiers'.[4] Seeckt again left the conduct of the negotiations with Severing to Geßler, and forbade all officers to participate; but finally he allowed Schleicher to accompany the minister.[3]

In all these questions Geßler did not act as a minister, who himself decided on political issues and tried to realize his aims; but he seconded Seeckt as best he could and shielded him and the Reichswehr in public. According to Stülpnagel's testimony, Seeckt would never have achieved his aims without Geßler's loyal co-operation; 'in purely military questions he only intervened in the field of the personalia of senior officers and of the officers of the ministry. . .'.[5] This was a change of decisive importance since the days of Noske who reserved to himself the vital political influence and had close contacts with the leading officers. It began with a handwritten order of Seeckt to all

[1] Recollections of von Selchow, p. 4: Nachlaß Seeckt, roll 26, no. 289, microfilm in Institut für Zeitgeschichte.

[2] Notes of General Lieber, p. 36, under 19 and 24 Dec. 1921: Nachlaß Seeckt, box 19, no. 278, Militärgeschichtliches Forschungsamt.

[3] Notes of General Lieber on the Bavarian crisis of 1923, p. 4: Nachlaß Seeckt, box 19, no. 281, ibid.

[4] Rabenau, *Seeckt*, p. 266.

[5] Joachim von Stülpnagel to Professor H. J. Gordon, 9 Nov. 1959: copy in Bundesarchiv-Militärarchiv, H 08–5/25.

departments of the defence ministry—issued even before he was finally appointed chief of the army command: 'The offices and departments are forbidden to announce or to give reports to the minister without my *prior* agreement. Reports are first rendered to me, I shall make further decisions. Only T 1 is exempt from this order.'[1] Only ten days prior to this order Geßler had announced in the National Assembly: 'We must start immediately to rebuild the Reichswehr on a democratic basis. . . . I must demand that all members of the Reichswehr declare themselves supporters of the republic and work in this spirit. . . . I shall see to it that the replacements of leaders are in the first instance taken from the circles which have stood up for the republic and democracy, if they have the required military qualifications. . . .'[2] That was only a few days after the collapse of the Kapp Putsch: the Reichswehr was weak and compromised. Perhaps Seeck's order was an indirect reply to Geßler's profession of faith.

It is difficult to say why Geßler consented to the weakening of his whole position; for example, why he did not object to Seeckt's order which forbade the officers to report directly to the minister. Perhaps it was a feeling of inferiority to Seeckt's domineering personality, perhaps a misconceived patriotism, perhaps mere personal weakness. Even in his memoirs many years after these events Geßler wrote: 'I had in any case no illusions about my "power of command". . . . I had no need to bother much about the internal conditions in the army at the beginning of my ministerial career. The responsible man was there: General von Seeckt. . . .'[3] Thus it came to pass that the minister of defence became a 'marginal figure' in his own house, whose main task it was to represent the interests of the Reichswehr in parliament and in public; while the key position in the ministry, in the military and in the political sense, was occupied by the chief of the army command, who was the real

[1] Copy of Seeckt's order of 9 Apr. 1920 in Nachlaß Geßler, no. 17, Bundesarchiv Koblenz; Rabenau, *Seeckt*, p. 245, with the wrong date of 4 Sept. 1920. The T 1— at that time under Hasse—was responsible for military guidance and frontier defence.

[2] Geßler in the National Assembly on 29 March 1920, quoted by Ludwig Haas, 'Der Kampf um die Reichswehr', *Deutsche Republik*, i, 1926–7, p. 15.

[3] Otto Geßler, *Reichswehrpolitik in der Weimarer Zeit*, Stuttgart, 1958, pp. 137, 145.

commander-in-chief of the army.[1] The weakening of the position and influence of the minister of defence had another result. 'It opened for the chief of the army command the way into the meetings of the cabinet and above all to the president. . . .' A special, so-called 'direct military chain of report' was instituted, which connected the president with the chief of the army command and by-passed the minister of defence and the chancellor. The minister perhaps, but not always, received copies 'for his information'.[2] This was a new development which began after the Kapp Putsch.[3] It was an achievement of Seeckt; his success was due to the weakness of changing governments and the political inexperience of the leaders of the republican parties. The documents indicate that Seeckt soon exercised a strong influence on Chancellor Wirth, who belonged to the left wing of the Catholic Centre Party; this predominant influence greatly facilitated the ascendancy of Seeckt, in home as well as in foreign affairs.

IV. *Politics in Army and Navy*

According to the Weimar Constitution the German colours were black, red, and gold, but these were not accepted by the large majority of the officer corps. Only a few weeks after the Kapp Putsch the commander-in-chief of Bavaria, Major-General Ritter von Möhl, wrote to Seeckt:

The abolition of the old colours, as could have been foreseen and as was predicted, has been a serious mistake. . . . The Reichswehr inwardly adheres to black, white and red; that cannot be changed and must neither be overlooked nor underestimated. When the 'Kapp-Lüttwitz government' recognized black, white and red, it gained by this act alone the sympathy of large parts of the Reichswehr. . . . The volunteer units which were mobilized against Bolshevism adorned themselves with the old colours; it would be hopeless to try to prevent this, and yet they acted against the orders of the state, for the preservation of which they went to fight full of national enthusiasm. . . . I have no mandate from the good units of the Bavarian Reichswehr, but I speak in their name when I

[1] Sauer, 'Die Reichswehr', in Bracher, *Die Auflösung der Weimarer Republik*, p. 251.
[2] Ibid., p. 250.
[3] But this was not a 'Geburtsfehler' of the republic, as asserted by Geßler's biographer, Kurt Sendtner, in Geßler, *Reichswehrpolitik in der Weimarer Zeit*, p. 71. It was a later development for which Geßler was responsible.

urgently request the ministry of defence to give back to the army, on whose support the government depends, the colours under which it has accomplished during the world war the greatest deeds of all times.[1]

This was without doubt the opinion of the whole officer corps. Its opposition to black, red, and gold was largely successful. For the Reichswehr a special *Reichskriegsflagge* (war flag) was created; like the flag of the merchantmen, it was black, white, and red with a minute black, red, and gold inset in the upper corner near the flag staff. According to Rabenau, this was Seeckt's achievement.[2]

The government, however, decreed that the soldiers—so as to assimilate their emblems to some extent to the official German colours—should wear on their service caps a new cockade showing the coat of arms of the Reich: a black eagle with red beak and claws on a gold field. The quartermaster-general ordered that all units should send in official reports about the wearing of the new cockade by 1 September 1920. Again General von Möhl protested:

The black, red and gold flag is esteemed as little, or even less, by the Reichswehr as by the majority of the national-minded population. The abolition of the black, white and red colours by the National Assembly was the last echo of the denigration of the German cockade at the collapse of November 1918. This decision of the German people's representatives showed a lack of national tact, not to say of patriotic feeling in general, that will later, even in German history, be regarded as surprising and incomprehensible. Now that this unpardonable step has been taken, there are in my opinion only two ways of making good the mistake to some extent: either the old German colours are reintroduced, . . . or the whole issue is shelved and the continued wearing of the black, white and red cockade is conceded, until there is—for example through the *Anschluß* of Austria—an understandable reason to change the colours. I personally am in favour of the first course. . . . If they cannot take this decision, they should at least abstain from inflaming the army's feelings further by the forcible removal of the glorious old German colours, and that on the fiftieth anniversary of the battle of Sedan. . . .[3]

[1] Möhl to the army command in the defence ministry, Munich, 30 Mar. 1920: Akten des Gruppenkommandos 4, Bund 16, Akt 2, Bayerisches Kriegsarchiv, Munich. [2] Rabenau, *Seeckt*, p. 262.

[3] Möhl to army command, Munich, 9 Aug. 1920: Akten des Gruppenkommandos 4, Bund 16, Akt 2, Bayerisches Kriegsarchiv.

During the following months there arose in the units of the Bavarian Reichswehr a veritable storm of protest against the introduction of the new cockade, a storm which can hardly have developed spontaneously. In the Cavalry Regiment 17 the other ranks of all escadrons were asked 'whether they wanted to retain the black, white and red cockade or favoured the introduction of the black, red and yellow (!) one'; they decided unanimously for black, white and red, while 'drastic voices were raised against the introduction of the black, red and yellow (!) cockade. . .'.[1] In Brigade 24 'all officers, non-commissioned officers, and other soldiers (the latter with very few exceptions) . . . opted for the retention of the black, white, and red cockade'. The commanding officer, Colonel Ritter von Danner, added: 'The abolition of the old colours, under which Germany was united, esteemed, and feared by the whole world, for which it bled for four years, is considered a shameful lack of dignity and patriotic feeling.'[2] The Brigade 23 fully agreed with the views of the *Wehrkreiskommando* and in its overwhelming majority declared for the retention of the old cockade. Infantry Regiment 42 and other units even reported unanimous decisions in the same sense.[3]

Yet all that General von Möhl was able to achieve was a delay in the introduction of the new cockade: it was postponed to 1 February 1921. In his opinion this reverse was above all due to a vote in the *Heereskammer*, where nearly all the other ranks voted against the retention of the old cockade, even the Bavarian representatives. He therefore suggested that the members of the *Heereskammer*, before voting on controversial issues, should consult their electors: otherwise the *Heereskammer* would, 'under the influence of a few gifted orators and agitators, take decisions and make proposals which the Reichswehr will repudiate. . .'.[4] It thus seems that there were considerable differences of opinion on this question between the officers—who identified themselves with 'the Reichswehr'—and the other ranks, who were less attached to the traditions of the German Empire. It is not known whether similar protests also

---

[1] Major Zürn to *Wehrkreiskommando* vii, Bamberg, 14 Sept. 1920: ibid.

[2] Colonel Ritter von Danner to *Wehrkreiskommando* vii, Nuremberg, 22 Sept. 1920: ibid.

[3] Numerous declarations of Sept. 1920 in this sense: ibid.

[4] Möhl to all commanding officers, Munich, 30 Oct. 1920: ibid., Bund 1, Akt 6.

came from units outside Bavaria. Rabenau reports that Seeckt considered the introduction of the new cockade 'a personal defeat'.[1] But he was hardly a friend of such 'spontaneous' demonstrations. In any case, in December 1920 the *Wehrkreiskommando* iii in Berlin ordered the Bavarian company, which was at that time part of the Berlin guard regiment, to wear the new cockade by 19 January 1921. The company, however, maintained that it was entitled to postpone the step until 1 February. 'It was feared that the authority of the officers would suffer if the *Pleitegeier* [vulture of bankruptcy] had to be worn nevertheless. . . .' Perhaps even General von Möhl was not convinced that the authority of the officers would suffer if the *Pleitegeier* was worn two weeks earlier than he had stipulated. He decided that the Bavarian company in Berlin must carry out the orders issued there, although the date of 19 January coincided with the fiftieth anniversary of the foundation of the German Empire.[2]

In Bavaria the issue continued to arouse controversies even after 1 February. In the Artillery Regiment 7 the *Vertrauensleute* and the non-commissioned officers petitioned their officers to be permitted to wear the old cockade, because the new ones 'discoloured when worn for some time in the rain and then had the effect of a yellow spot'.[3] On 9 February General von Möhl announced that the majority of the units of his command had reported they were wearing the new cockade, but that in other reports there appeared a tendency to avoid doing this; those units which had not yet sent in their reports had to furnish them as ordered by 15 February.[4] It seems that after this categorical order only one regimental commander, Lieutenant-Colonel Leupold of the Infantry Regiment 20, was still holding out. He declined on 14 February to send in the desired report: 'The new cockade created by the revolution cannot become a substitute for the outward demonstration of the ideals of the soldier. . . .' He also suggested that his regiment would like to see the senior Bavarian officers wear the new cockade.[5] Möhl

---

[1] Rabenau, *Seeckt*, p. 262, n. 1.
[2] 'Vortragsnotiz' of 27 Dec. 1920: Akten des Gruppenkommandos 4, Bund 1, Akt 6, Bayerisches Kriegsarchiv, Munich.
[3] Letters of 2 and 8 Feb. 1921: ibid.
[4] Lieutenant-General Möhl on 9 Feb. 1921: ibid.
[5] Lieutenant-Colonel Leupold to *Wehrkreiskommando* vii, Regensburg, 14 Feb. 1921: ibid.

replied: 'I not only know and understand the loathing of this emblem which you are expressing, but I would even regret it if it were *not* alive in the heart of *every* German soldier. But the repugnance must be overcome by the members of I.R. 20 exactly as by all the other soldiers of the new army. It is out of the question that parts of the Bavarian Reichswehr should claim for themselves alone the right not to carry out orders. . . .' He requested Colonel Leupold once more to see to it that the order was carried out and to report that he had done so.[1] On 8 March Möhl reported to Berlin that all units of the Bavarian division were wearing the new cockades, and enclosed the reports of the individual units.[2] Yet twelve months later a Bavarian company, transferred to Berlin to join the guard regiment, still refused to wear the new cockades, and Seeckt demanded a report from Munich about it.[3]

The amazing side of these events is not only that orders were simply not carried out by certain units, and that a report was sent to Berlin which was not entirely in accordance with the facts: both were serious enough in an army. It is even more surprising that in official reports the German colours were described as 'black, red and yellow' and the official coat of arms as *Pleitegeier*; in another report, the Bavarian commander-in-chief denied 'national tact' and 'patriotic feeling' to the majority of the National Assembly, while he considered that only those showed national sentiments who were against black, red, and gold. Even in later years the Bavarian soldiers avoided the wearing of the new cockade—which, together with a cockade in the local colours of white and blue, was affixed to their service caps—by wearing forage caps which had only a white and blue cockade.[4] The writ of the central government was not running in Bavaria.

Similar occurrences took place in North Germany. In the Infantry Regiment 18 at Paderborn many soldiers wore the black, white, and red cockades as late as 1922. Flags in the old colours and pictures of the former Emperor were displayed in

---

[1] Lieutenant-General Möhl to Lieutenant-Colonel Leupold, Munich, 16 Feb. 1921: ibid.

[2] Colonel von Ruith to ministry of defence, Munich, 8 Mar. 1921: ibid.

[3] Notes of General Lieber, p. 48, under 8 Mar. 1922: Nachlaß Seeckt, box 19, no. 278.

[4] Information given by Archivdirektor Dr. Böhm, Munich.

barrack rooms of the regiment as well as in the non-commissioned officers' mess. The explanation given was that the barrack rooms were decorated by the soldiers with their own means 'and not in a demonstrative way', while the mess was private, so that it was difficult to effect a change. It was also established that in the regiment two political groups existed, one of them to the right, the other to the left. In the eyes of the minister of defence the commanding officer was responsible for these incidents, and he was asked to hand in his resignation.[1] In the same year the birthday of William II, 27 January, was kept free of parades for a battalion at Göttingen; later an order was issued to attend a lecture on life in Doorn House, where the Emperor was living. When the commanding officer was asked to report on this, he offered his resignation, which was accepted.[2] The officer appointed adjutant to the new minister of defence, Dr. Geßler, candidly informed him 'that he was a convinced monarchist and according to origin, education, and conviction a servant of the House of Hohenzollern. I further told him that I would hardly be able to serve him in political matters, as I was a mere soldier, and felt physically uncomfortable if associating with some of those now in power. . . .'[3] Not even this last remark was sufficient reason to remove the officer from his post; he remained for many years the adjutant of the minister.

About the political mood among the other ranks of the Reichswehr there are a number of reports from Bavaria dating from 1920 to 1922. According to the summary made by General von Möhl they showed fairly generally that there was little interest in day-to-day politics:

Political indifference in units, which are firmly in the hands of their officers, must in general be considered desirable. I have the impression, however, that not all leaders are sufficiently informed about the real political mood of the other ranks and that some do not pay enough attention to it. In our times it is vital that there should not be too much discrepancy between the political views of

[1] 'Bericht des 40. Ausschusses (des Reichstags) zur Prüfung der Vorwürfe gegen die Reichswehr', p. 6: Reichskanzlei, Akten betr. Reichswehr, Volkswehr und Wehrpflicht, vol. iv, R 43 I 685, Bundesarchiv Koblenz.

[2] Ibid., p. 5.

[3] MS. of Major Wolfgang Fleck (without date or name), p. 6: Nachlaß Geßler, no. 46, Bundesarchiv Koblenz.

officers and subordinates. . . . The leader must know how to awaken in his unit a national determination, with a corresponding emphasis on the importance of our closer fatherland [i.e. Bavaria].[1]

The reports sent during the following months by many commanding officers repeated time and again that the large majority of the other ranks were not interested in politics.[2] In the slowly mounting conflict between Bavaria and the Reich the soldiers' sympathies were—as was only natural in Bavaria— on the side of their own government. The Reich government was often criticized because it was too meek in questions of foreign policy—disarmament, Upper Silesia, and its policy towards the Entente; but the efforts of the Bavarian government to preserve order were recognized.[3]

Yet nationalist enthusiasm or political radicalism among the Bavarian troops were rarely mentioned. Only Colonel Ritter von Epp reported that patriotic and *völkisch* feeling was steadily increasing among his infantry units;[4] but perhaps this was more true of himself than of the soldiers under his command. The events in Upper Silesia, the result of the plebiscite, and the fighting between German and Polish irregulars, had a certain echo in Bavaria. The Bavarian artillery regiment reported: 'The favourable result of the vote in Upper Silesia was heartily welcomed. . .'; and a few months later: 'There is general indignation about the treatment of the Upper Silesians. . . .'[5] The commanding officer of an infantry regiment gave more details:

Although in general the soldiers are politically rather indifferent, as they are interested in other matters, they gradually realize the complete impotence of the German Reich. This knowledge is brought home to them by the concessions of the government in the disarmament question, but especially by the events in Upper

---

[1] *Wehrkreiskommando* vii, Munich, 14 June 1920: Akten des Gruppenkommandos 4, Bund 11, Akt 5, Bayerisches Kriegsarchiv, Munich.

[2] Thus 15 reports to *Wehrkreiskommando* vii, between 5 Jan. 1921 and 24 Mar. 1922: ibid.

[3] Thus 8 reports, between 2 Apr. 1921 and 21 Mar. 1922: ibid.

[4] Colonel Ritter von Epp to *Wehrkreiskommando* vii, Munich, 5 Apr. 1921: ibid. Epp soon became a convinced National Socialist and in 1933 Hitler's *Reichskommissar* for Bavaria.

[5] Colonel Freiherr Loeffelholz von Colberg to Seventh Division, Nuremberg, 1 Apr. and 8 July 1921: ibid.

Silesia. The soldiers consider it a shame that defence organizations have to defend the soil of Upper Silesia, while it is not permitted to employ Reichswehr soldiers, whose vocation it is in the first place to defend the German homeland. The soldiers would gladly have gone into battle against the Polish bands. . . .[1]

But this was the only report of its kind. Apparently political indifference was far more prevalent than national enthusiasm or willingness to fight the enemies of Germany.

We know very little about the mood in the Reichswehr in other parts of Germany during these years. When Reinhardt, after his resignation as chief of the army command, formed a mixed brigade for training purposes at Döberitz near Berlin, serious clashes occurred there between Prussian and Bavarian soldiers. The situation became threatening, and Reinhardt himself had to intervene. At the tattoo bawling and screaming crowds assembled at the gate, and the guard which was reinforced was ordered out with loaded rifles and fixed bayonets. Then the order was given to return to barracks immediately and without any noise, and that was done.[2] The political mood existing in this brigade can be deduced from Reinhardt's valedictory address of Easter 1921. According to this, many soldiers

threw all the blame on 'the government' or the people in power and believed themselves to be grand, in the childish superstition that everything would have been all right if only this or that man had had no say. . . . Thus the bad habit must be fought of denying all national and German convictions to those who are not members of clubs or associations which adorn themselves with that epithet. It would be better if 'German' or 'national' were too sacred and too matter-of-course to denote separate groups.

I also want to define openly my position regarding the Jewish question, in the interest of internal peace. Whoever among them does damage to the German fatherland, or is merely indifferent towards it, must be fought in the sharpest manner; but whoever as a German Jew honestly feels and fights with us must be welcomed and respected. The spirit of mammon and of greed is contemptible; we must refute it in Jews and in Christians; but above all we must

[1] The commanding officer of Infantry Regiment 19 to Seventh Division, Munich, 21 June 1921: ibid.
[2] Werner von Blomberg, 'Erinnerungen bis 1933', iii. 66: Bundesarchiv-Militärarchiv.

not, through love of pleasure or carelessness, become the slaves of money and thus often the slaves of Jews. This defensive kind of anti-Semitism is praiseworthy, it operates not in malicious actions against Jews, but through self-restraint. . . .

Let us brand ruthlessly, in all our actions and speeches, the adoration of money and the lack of patriotism; then the bad Jews and their arrogance will be hit more severely than by spiteful attacks; they are incompatible with genuine Christianity, and their ultimate aims are nebulous and unobtainable. For such aims we must not let ourselves be used and our strength be frittered away. Let us rather keep in mind what is truly essential and urgent: *liberation from the chains of the Treaty of Versailles. . . .*[1]

Thus attacks on 'the government', 'the Jews', and all who were considered not to be 'national-minded', seem to have been prominent in the brigade.

About the same time Seeckt believed that a new *Putsch* from the right was imminent and had the troops instructed in this sense: as Germany was facing grave decisions in east and west, the government had to rely on the united support of the people and of all the instruments of power; whoever tried to impose his will upon the government and left the path of legality, would ruin Germany utterly; the duty of the soldiers was to fight any revolt ruthlessly, from whichever direction it might come.[2] Some months later Seeckt—in addressing the officer corps of the Third Cavalry and the Second Infantry Divisions —again pronounced against 'national chauvinism' and admonished them to 'quieter activity'.[3] His fears were thus similar to those of Reinhardt. In March 1921, however, there took place, not another *Putsch* of the right, but a Communist coup in central Germany, an attempt to seize power by armed insurrection. Reichswehr units were mobilized. But it became clear how efficient a force had been created in the Prussian police. Its units—supported only by Reichswehr artillery— stormed the Leuna works, and the revolt soon collapsed. 'The other units did not see why they were not used', Rabenau writes.[4] But it was undoubtedly preferable to use the police,

---

[1] 'An meine Kameraden von der Lehrbrigade!', pp. 2, 5: Nachlaß Reinhardt, Hauptstaatsarchiv Stuttgart.

[2] Notes of General Lieber, p. 15, under 26 Feb. 1921: Nachlaß Seeckt, box 19, no. 278, Militärgeschichtliches Forschungsamt Freiburg.

[3] Ibid., p. 28, under 24 and 29 Aug. 1921.   [4] Rabenau, *Seeckt*, pp. 257–8.

and not the army, to fight internal unrest and revolt: an opinion that was strongly upheld by Seeckt.[1]

Much more radical was the mood in the navy. That was only natural, as it was largely composed of members of the free corps. In addition, the naval officers were in general more loyal to the House of Hohenzollern than those of the army. According to the description of a former officer of the von Loewenfeld brigade, they had to render their oath to the Weimar Constitution in front of a picture of William II adorned with white asters.[2] In 1921 the prime minister of the state of Oldenburg complained to the minister of defence about the attitude of the navy, in particular their monarchist proclivities. Many events proved, he wrote, how strong the political influence of Ehrhardt still was in the navy; this was shown when naval units marched into Cuxhaven, Emden, and Borkum; serious clashes between sailors and the population occurred, in particular on the island of Borkum, caused by anti-republican demonstrations on the part of the troops, such as the hoisting of the flag on the Emperor's birthday, celebrations on that day, setting the flag on half-mast on the 9th of November. During clashes with the local population the sailors used arms, two people were seriously wounded, and one of them died.[3] Naval units continued to sing the Ehrhardt song and the Loewenfeld song, and their officers did not intervene.[4]

The criticisms applied in particular to the naval school at Mürwik, where the officer cadets were educated. The cadets came largely from the two naval brigades. Some openly admitted that they only intended to remain in the navy for a short time, until there was a new chance and Ehrhardt called them again. When Ehrhardt had written to them, one could 'not do anything with them' for some time. They were proud of the fact that 'they represented the harsher and more uncompromising views in a national sense'. Soon, however,

---

[1] Seeckt to Chancellor Wirth, Bad Elster, 10 June 1922: Nachlaß Geßler, no. 55, Bundesarchiv Koblenz. See above, p. 119.

[2] Information given by Admiral Paul Zieb to the author.

[3] Prime Minister Tantzen to Dr. Geßler, Oldenburg, 29 Aug. 1921: Nachlaß Geßler, no. 18, Bundesarchiv Koblenz.

[4] 'Bericht des 40. Ausschusses (des Reichstags) zur Prüfung der Vorwürfe gegen die Reichswehr', pp. 10–11: Reichskanzlei, Akten betr. Reichswehr etc., vol. iv, R 43 I 685, ibid.

differences of degree developed between the cadets from the Ehrhardt and those from the Loewenfeld brigade, the latter becoming more moderate, especially after the entry of their former commander into the navy at the end of 1920. 'With his great personal authority he remained naturally the centre of the old Loewenfelders', exactly as was Ehrhardt for his men. Thus the personal ties of loyalty were transferred from the free corps to the navy. As Ehrhardt continued his anti-republican activities in the sharpest forms, this was reflected at Mürwik. To break the ban exercised by him the commanding officer, Captain Werner Tillessen, addressed the school and emphasized the differences between soldiers and mercenaries; at the end he demanded a promise that the cadets in future would be 'soldiers', and this was given.[1]

Yet that was not the end of the troubles at Mürwik. When the minister Erzberger was murdered in August 1921 by members of the *Organisation Consul*—the head of which was Ehrhardt—open satisfaction with the deed was expressed at Mürwik.[2] When the minister Rathenau was murdered in June 1922 by members of the same organization, celebrations were held at Mürwik at which large quantities of wine were drunk. A pupil who was an ordinary rating was to be returned to his unit, because his eating manners were considered bad and 'his views made him unsuitable to become an officer'; but this request was turned down by the ministry of defence. Finally, the commanding officer was instructed to establish 'to what extent the young people coming from the free corps could be educated at all' and to remove those he considered unsuitable. 27 out of a total of 178 cadets were then discharged.[3] On the other hand, the officers of the cruiser 'Medusa' all condemned the murder of Rathenau, as one of them remembered. Even Captain von Loewenfeld tried to use his moderating influence on young extremist officers, and to convince them that it was

---

[1] Zeugenschrifttum nos. 1481, 1785 in Institut für Zeitgeschichte, Munich; Baum, in *Vierteljahrshefte für Zeitgeschichte*, xi, 1963, p. 42; recollections of a high naval officer lent to the author by Dr. Baum.

[2] Zeugenschrifttum no. 1785 (Rear-Admiral Siegfried Sorge), p. 10: Institut für Zeitgeschichte. The murderer was a former naval officer, Heinrich Tillessen, a brother of Werner Tillessen, and this fact probably influenced the cadets.

[3] 'Bericht des 40. Ausschusses zur Prüfung der Vorwürfe gegen die Reichswehr', p. 10, loc. cit.

necessary to adopt a more positive attitude towards the state, like a *mariage de convenance*.[1]

Thus in the navy too there existed several different shades of opinion, from the extremism of the Ehrhardt followers and the ensigns to the conservatism of senior officers. The latter was later defined by Admiral Raeder as 'a total abstention from all party politics and an unconditional loyalty towards the state and its government...'.[2] This probably applied more to the older and more senior officers who had not served in the free corps and who tried to draw the proper conclusions from the failure of the Kapp Putsch: a repetition of these events must be avoided at all costs.[3] On this point the army command and the naval command agreed.

v. *The Pact with Russia*

Although the first tentative moves between Berlin and Moscow were made as early as 1920,[4] it does not seem that any direct negotiations between the German and Russian military authorities took place in that year; or, if they took place, they had no immediate result. From the end of 1919 an old friend and collaborator of Trotsky, Victor Kopp, was in Berlin as a semi-official diplomatic representative of the Soviet government; he first established contacts with German armament firms and tried to interest them in the production of weapons in Russia. At the beginning of 1921 he was in Moscow on leave and discussed the question with Trotsky, the People's Commissar for War and Chairman of the Revolutionary War Council. Then he returned to Berlin, probably with the instruction to continue the negotiations. From Berlin he reported to Trotsky on 7 April that the Albatros works were prepared to build aeroplanes in Russia under German supervision, Blohm & Voss to construct submarines, and Krupp's to produce ammunition and cannon; a group of German technicians, under 'Neumann, who is known to you', should visit Russia to discuss details. Lenin expressed his consent, and in the early summer of 1921 a group of German experts went to Russia to inspect armament works and to continue the negotiations.

---

[1] Zeugenschrifttum no. 1785, pp. 9–10: Institut für Zeitgeschichte. At that time Captain von Loewenfeld was commander of the cruiser 'Berlin'.
[2] Raeder, *Mein Leben*, i. 185.   [3] Ibid.   [4] See above, pp. 70–71.

It was led by Major Dr. Oskar Ritter von Niedermayer, the 'Neumann' of Kopp's report. He was educated in Russia and spoke Russian fluently. His exploits in Persia and Afghanistan during the world war had given him the name of 'the German Lawrence'. With him came several other officers who were to figure prominently in German-Russian military relations. But it seems that the report made by the group on the Russian armament works was not very favourable, and that the visit had few practical results.[1]

Real progress was only made when the negotiations were resumed in Berlin at the end of September 1921—at a time when the attitude of the Entente in the Upper Silesian question increased anti-western feelings in Germany. On the German side the chief negotiator was Colonel Otto Hasse of the *Truppenamt*, on the Russian side were Leonid Krasin, the Chairman of the Council for Foreign Trade, and Kopp. The negotiations took place in a private apartment, usually that of Major von Schleicher, which was conveniently situated close to the defence ministry in the Bendlerstraße. The Russians declared that they did not want to co-operate in economic matters with the Entente powers, least of all with Britain; first the construction of aeroplanes should be started in Russia, but contact with Krupp should also be established. Seeckt himself did not appear. When Hasse reported to him on 2 October at Kissingen, where he spent his leave, he showed himself rather reluctant. But two weeks later he allowed some more officers of the defence ministry to be informed. The officers concerned frequently conferred with Seeckt, and two more industrial enterprises, Junkers and Stinnes, were approached. Seeckt also informed the chancellor, Wirth, who was at the same time the minister of finance, and whose support was therefore essential. But from the outset the financing proved difficult, as German industry showed little inclination to make large investments in Russia. Wirth agreed that Seeckt 'should participate in the negotiations not as chief of the army command, but only personally'. The Russians refused to conclude without having spoken to Seeckt;

[1] E. H. Carr, *The Bolshevik Revolution*, iii, London, 1953, pp. 317, 362–3; *German-Soviet Relations between the two World Wars*, London, 1952, p. 57; Major Fritz Tschunke to Rabenau, 13 Feb. 1939, published by J. Epstein in *Der Monat*, no. 2, Nov. 1948, p. 48. Kopp's letter, with Lenin's approving remarks, is in the Trotsky archives at Harvard.

this conference took place on 8 December, but Seeckt was unable to provide the financial guarantees desired by the Russians. In addition, they wanted German military support in case of a renewed attack on Poland. But Seeckt was convinced that France and Czechoslovakia would immediately intervene against Germany and therefore 'recommended to the chancellor benevolent neutrality'.[1]

In July 1921 Major von Niedermayer had already inquired at Junkers whether the firm was willing to co-operate with the defence ministry in Russia: these military plans, he claimed, were supported by a political undercurrent and financed by the government. In November General Wurtzbacher and Colonel Hasse visited the Junkers works at Dessau, and an oral agreement was reached that Junkers should build an aeroplane and engine factory in Russia for which the defence ministry would provide the means.[2] In December a mixed committee, which included representatives of Junkers and several officers, among them Hasse, went to Moscow. They had conferences with Trotsky and the Russian chief of staff Lebedev, during which the question of common action in case of a new Russo-Polish war was also discussed; von Niedermayer offered German capital to Trotsky.[3] It seems that in general Niedermayer was very free with his promises, for some months later Chicherin, the People's Commissar for Foreign Affairs, complained to Wirth about far-reaching pledges which Niedermayer had given to him in Wirth's name—and the embarrassed Wirth had to put matters right. In 1923 Chicherin told the German

---

[1] Notes of General Lieber 'Seeckt als Chef der Heeresleitung', p. 38, with extracts from Hasse's diary, under 24, 26, 29 Sept., 2, 18 Oct., 3 and 8 Dec. 1921: Nachlaß Seeckt, box 19, no. 278, Militärgeschichtliches Forschungsamt Freiburg. Gordon, *Reichswehr and the German Republic*, p. 344, overlooks the decisive role of Hasse when he writes that 'Schleicher, Fischer and Ritter von Niedermayer represented the Reichswehr' in the first conversations with the Russians: all three were only majors at the time. Even more inaccurate is the statement of Wheeler-Bennett, *Nemesis of Power*, p. 127, that 'within this group the moving spirit was Kurt von Schleicher, and with him were associated von Hammerstein and Ludwig Haase...'. [sic].

[2] Seeckt to Professor Junkers, 18 Aug. 1924: memorandum of Dr. Schreiber in the case of Junkers versus Deutsches Reich of 12 Jan. 1926, pp. 3, 7–10: Nachlaß Mentzel, no. 5, Bundesarchiv Koblenz.

[3] Tschunke to Rabenau, 13 Feb. 1939, in *Der Monat*, no. 2, Nov. 1948, p. 49; Carr, *Bolshevik Revolution*, iii. 364; Anlage 12 to letter of Hermann Müller and Otto Wels to Geßler, 6 Dec. 1926: Reichskanzlei, Akten betr. Reichswehr etc., vol. v, R 43 I 686, Bundesarchiv.

ambassador, Count Brockdorff-Rantzau, the story of 'Neumann's coal': Russia at that time suffered badly from lack of fuel, and Niedermayer promised that Germany would deliver immediately all the coal required; 'he departed—and of the famous coal we never heard another word, let alone received a single gramme...'.[1]

At the beginning of 1922, however, the financial difficulties were partly overcome. Through Wirth's services the army command received 150 million marks, which were paid out to Hasse. In the *Truppenamt*, a *Sondergruppe R*(ussia) was formed under Seeckt's former adjutant, Major Fischer, which was responsible for all Russian contacts with the defence ministry. About the middle of January Radek reappeared in Berlin—'brought with him by Niedermayer from Moscow'—and demanded to see Seeckt. But the latter detailed Fischer to conduct the negotiations and received Radek only on 10 February. Radek suggested that the two general staffs should discuss possible military situations, and that German military literature and orders should be used in the education of the Russian officer corps; he also complained that Germany 'was siding too much with Britain'. Seeckt replied that 'at the moment and in the immediate future Germany was forced to side with Britain who alone could curb France'. According to Radek, Russia intended in the spring to attack Poland again and needed above all aeroplanes.[2] On 15 March 1922 a preliminary contract was signed between the *Sondergruppe* and Junkers, according to which Junkers was to start immediately with the construction of aeroplanes, and the *Sondergruppe* was to pay Junkers forty million marks and put at its disposal another 100 millions as a capital sum, without any obligation of repayment.[3] At the end of April Junkers was ready to start production in Russia, and the Albatros works were prepared to do the same.[4]

---

[1] Brockdorff-Rantzau to Staatssekretär von Maltzan, Moscow, 13 Apr. 1923, and memorandum of Maltzan, Berlin, 18 Mar. 1924: Nachlaß Brockdorff-Rantzau, 9101 H/VIII, H 224853, 9101 H/XII, H 226818 (microfilm).

[2] Notes of General Lieber 'Seeckt als Chef der Heeresleitung', pp. 50–51, loc. cit.; Tschunke to Rabenau, 13 Feb. 1939, in *Der Monat*, Nov. 1948, p. 48.

[3] Copy of the contract, signed for the *Sondergruppe* by 'Neumann', in Nachlaß Mentzel, no. 5, pp. 63 ff., Bundesarchiv Koblenz.

[4] Notes of General Lieber, p. 51, loc. cit.

At the beginning of April 1922 Chicherin visited Berlin on his way to the conference at Genoa and spoke to Wirth 'about the work of German officers in Russia'. Wirth left it to Seeckt to decide 'whether this activity should be denied by Germany'. Colonel Hasse was a member of the German delegation sent to Genoa and was informed there by Wirth about the course the negotiations were taking, above all about the conclusion of the Treaty of Rapallo between Germany and Russia. Wirth was pleased with the treaty, but feared the opposition of the right-wing parties: Seeckt should try to use his influence so that the press abstained from sharp attacks. Seeckt fully agreed with the conclusion of the treaty, 'above all because it is the first attempt to conduct an active foreign policy. . .'. He desired a further treaty which assured Germany of quick help, and demanded from Wirth 'a military *rapprochement* with Russia'. He also expressed to Wirth his agreement with Germany's eastern policy: for Wirth and Chicherin had discussed the possibility of restoring the frontiers of 1914—an idea that Seeckt always had at heart. The two ministers had also agreed that all Communist agitation in Germany should be curtailed, as only a strong Germany would be of use to Russia.[1]

That Wirth saw eye to eye with Seeckt on the Polish issue and with regard to the Treaty of Rapallo, he confirmed soon after to Count Brockdorff-Rantzau:

As you know, the treaty has met with strong resistance in Germany, and especially—I do not want to hide it—from the socialist parties and, above all, from the president. But what can you do with parties which profess the slogan 'No more war'? This opinion I do not share, and one thing I tell you frankly: Poland must be eliminated. . . . I do not conclude any treaty which might strengthen Poland; but with my consent various things have been done with regard to the eastern frontier which are known only to a few. On this point I am in full agreement with the military, especially with General von Seeckt. . . .

And some days later Wirth mentioned 'that the Treaty of Rapallo should be supplemented . . . as military problems too ought to be settled with special reference to Poland. . .'. When the surprised Brockdorff-Rantzau asked whether the president

[1] Ibid., pp. 51–53, 59.

was informed, Wirth replied in the negative: there were
sharp differences between him and Ebert on this issue.[1] Brockdorff-Rantzau, who was to go to Moscow as German ambassador, then laid down his ideas on German foreign policy in a
long memorandum:

> Our impotence is well known in east and west. We are no longer
> the small weight which might tip the scales; but the least imprudence
> on our side is sufficient to kindle a flame which will destroy the
> Reich and may annihilate the German people. . . . A German policy
> orientated exclusively towards the east would at the present time
> not only be premature and dangerous, but hopeless and therefore
> mistaken. It is premature, because neither we nor Russia are
> economically able to start such an experiment. It is dangerous,
> because we deliver ourselves into the hands of the completely
> unscrupulous Soviet government by agreements which tie us in the
> military field. . . . The policy is hopeless, because in case of a Russian
> attack on Poland . . . we should have to face almost defenceless a
> French attack from the west. . . .[2]

To this Seeckt replied with a memorandum of his own,
which repeated his ideas of 1920 and made them more precise:

> Poland's existence is intolerable, incompatible with the survival
> of Germany. It must disappear, and it will disappear through its
> own internal weakness and through Russia—with our assistance.
> For Russia Poland is even more intolerable than for us; no Russia
> can allow Poland to exist. With Poland falls one of the strongest
> pillars of the Treaty of Versailles, the preponderance of France. . . .
> Poland can never offer any advantage to Germany, either economic-
> ally, because it is incapable of any development, or politically,
> because it is France's vassal. The re-establishment of the broad
> common frontier between Russia and Germany is the precondition
> for the regaining of strength of both countries. 'Russia and Germany
> within the frontiers of 1914!' should be the basis of reaching an
> understanding between the two. . . .
> We aim at two things: first, a strengthening of Russia in the
> economic and the political, thus also in the military field, and so
> indirectly a strengthening of ourselves, by strengthening a possible
> ally of the future; we further desire, at first cautiously and experi-

---

[1] Herbert Helbig, *Die Träger der Rapallo-Politik*, Göttingen, 1958, pp. 119–20:
notes about conversations with Wirth on 24 July and 1 Aug. 1922.

[2] Memorandum of 15 Aug. 1922: Schüddekopf, *Heer und Republik*, no. 68,
pp. 156–8.

mentally, a direct strengthening of ourselves, by helping to create in Russia an armaments industry which in case of need will serve us. . . .

In all these enterprises, which to a large extent are only beginning, the participation and even the official knowledge of the German government must be entirely excluded. The details of the negotiations must remain in the hands of the military authorities. . . .

In case of a war—which seemed imminent to Seeckt—Germany, he concluded, must not remain neutral, but must with all her strength support the right side.[1]

These strong words were not sufficient. Seeckt urgently warned Wirth not to send Brockdorff-Rantzau to Moscow: according to the latter's version, because he had no use for a pacifist in Russia, and according to Seeckt's own version, because he did not believe that the count was willing to support Seeckt's plans in the east, which aimed at a military strengthening of Germany.[2] Brockdorff-Rantzau reacted sharply. He refused to collaborate with Seeckt if the latter adhered to his statement that the count, during the negotiations at Versailles, had sacrificed the honour of the German nation. He then went over to the counter-attack and proved how well informed he was about the secret negotiations with the Russians: those with Trotsky, with Kopp, with Krupp's, the promises of Niedermayer, the intended production of aeroplanes and weapons in Russia, &c. He asked Wirth whether he knew and approved of these steps, and whether the president and the government were informed. Wirth became very excited and replied: 'the president need not be informed'; Seeckt's moves were known to him 'in general but not in particular'.[3]

In his conversation with the chancellor Brockdorff-Rantzau emphasized that his friendly relationship with the president did not permit him to conduct a policy behind the president's

[1] 'Deutschlands Stellung zum russischen Problem', 11 Sept. 1922: Nachlaß Seeckt, box 15, no. 213; printed with minor inaccuracies by Rabenau, *Seeckt*, pp. 316–18, and Epstein, in *Der Monat*, Nov. 1948, pp. 46–47.
[2] Brockdorff-Rantzau's version in his conversation with Wirth on 7 Sept. 1922: Helbig, op. cit., p. 120; Seeckt's version in his letter to the Reichsgerichtspräsident Dr. Simons, ? Oct. 1922: Nachlaß Seeckt, box 15, no. 214, Militärgeschichtliches Forschungsamt Freiburg.
[3] Notes of Brockdorff-Rantzau about his conversation with Wirth on 7 Sept. 1922: Helbig, op. cit., pp. 123–4; Nachlaß Brockdorff-Rantzau: 9101 H/I, H 223367-72 (microfilm).

back. But when he saw Ebert some days later he did not divulge his knowledge of the military negotiations, but only mentioned that he must be prepared as ambassador to discuss military questions with the Russians. But Ebert had meanwhile read Brockdorff-Rantzau's memorandum and expressed his agreement: 'I can only say that I fully agree with the ideas expressed in your memorandum; a different opinion would be madness. About six months ago, when Radek was in Berlin, I saw signs that there were certain currents in the direction you indicate; I immediately opposed these tendencies in the strongest terms and strictly forbade any such attempt, even before Genoa. According to the constitution I am entitled to do so. I appoint the minister of defence and I am chief of the army. Since then I have not heard anything about it. . . .' He added that he would ask the chancellor to resign if any such enterprise were started behind his back.[1] Wirth's remark that he had not informed the president was thus entirely correct. That, according to the constitution, the president was the commander-in-chief of the Reichswehr meant very little in practice.

Meanwhile the negotiations were continued. In May 1922 Colonel Hasse met Krestinsky, the Soviet diplomatic representative in Berlin. The Ruhr industry offered money to finance the Russian enterprises. In July a new Russian negotiator, Rosenblatt, came to Berlin and was received by Seeckt. The questions discussed by them included Russian deliveries of war materials to Germany and the keeping of German aeroplanes in Russia. At the end of July Seeckt empowered Hasse to work out the details of the agreement with Rosenblatt, and a preliminary treaty was signed during the night of the 29th.[2] Two weeks later Major Fischer went to Russia to conclude the military convention. In Berlin the negotiations about the building up of an armaments industry in Russia were continued, usually by Hasse in Schleicher's flat, and with Seeckt's consent. On the German side, the tendency to co-operate with Russia was once more strengthened by French unwillingness to meet Germany's demands at the London conference, while the Russians still

[1] Notes of Brockdorff-Rantzau about his conversation with Ebert on 13 Sept. 1922: ibid., 9101 H/I, H 223412-13.

[2] Notes of General Lieber, pp. 59–60, loc. cit. But this was not a 'preliminary commercial agreement' as asserted by Hallgarten in *Journal of Modern History*, xxi, 1949, p. 32, and Carr, *German-Soviet Relations between the two World Wars*, p. 60.

intended to attack Poland. On 19 December Hasse again met Radek, who developed far-reaching plans in the field of foreign policy.[1] During 1922 the first Reichswehr officers were sent to Russia for training purposes; Russian officers were permitted to visit the German infantry school, and Russian men-of-war German Baltic ports. In September Krasin wrote to his wife from Smolensk that the local aerodrome was crowded with German pilots.[2]

A further result was the foundation of the *Gesellschaft zur Förderung gewerblicher Unternehmungen*, for short *Gefu*, with its seat in Berlin and Moscow, and a considerable capital furnished by the German government. The *Gefu* was the head organization of the German industrial enterprises in Russia: the production of aeroplanes and engines by Junkers at Fili near Moscow, the making of shells at Petrograd, Schlüsselburg, Tula, and Slatust, and the production of poison gas at Trotsk near Samara. For the last purpose, a Russo-German limited company, *Bersol*, was founded, and a German technical director was sent to Trotsk. Soon, however, difficulties developed, caused by the economic conditions in Russia, the disappointing conduct of the German industrialists concerned, the unsolved financial problems, and the rapid devaluation of the German mark.[3]

At the end of 1922 the position of Seeckt and Hasse with regard to relations with Russia was further strengthened. The minister of defence decreed that all issues of 'our military policy *vis-à-vis* Russia' had to be brought under uniform direction and were therefore put under the chief of the *Truppenamt*, including naval matters, for 'the interests of the army deserve precedence. . .'.[4] About this time Hasse succeeded Heye as chief of the *Truppenamt* and thus occupied the key position in the defence ministry. In February 1923 he headed a military mission which went to Russia and negotiated with

[1] Notes of General Lieber, pp. 60, 71, loc. cit.

[2] Ibid., p. 71; Carr, op. cit., pp. 60–61; Görlitz, *Der deutsche Generalstab*, pp. 339–40.

[3] Hilger and Meyer, *The Incompatible Allies*, New York, 1953, p. 194; Tschunke to Rabenau, 13 Feb. 1939, in *Der Monat*, Nov. 1948, p. 49; Notes of General Lieber on the year 1923, pp. 33, 53: Nachlaß Seeckt, box 19, no. 281, Militärgeschichtliches Forschungsamt Freiburg.

[4] Geßler's decree of 23 Nov. 1922: Admiralität, Marine-Kommando-Amt, Flottenabteilung, Organisatorische Fragen, PG 34057 A I a-V, ibid.

the chief of staff Lebedev, his successor Shaposhnikov, and Arkadi Rosengolts of the Red Air Force. The Russians, however, declined to make any binding promises, and Lebedev declared quite openly that Germany was too weak to merit a closer military co-operation. Only certain agreements about the German industrial enterprises were reached: otherwise there was no result, so that Chicherin complained to Brockdorff-Rantzau in strong terms.[1] Another mission under Lieutenant-Colonel Mentzel was therefore sent to Moscow in April 1923. Brockdorff-Rantzau told them in no uncertain terms that he desired to be regularly informed about the course of the negotiations, but again this did not happen. As he later informed the chancellor: 'Neither Lieutenant-Colonel Mentzel not General Hasse informed me sufficiently about the negotiations. . . . In spite of my objections, Lieutenant-Colonel Mentzel concluded an agreement with the Russians about the production of war material for thirty-five million gold marks, without sufficient security about deliveries. . . .' Furthermore, in the meantime Hasse had written a very compromising letter to Rosengolts, which Mentzel too considered so dangerous that he intended to extract it from the Russians; but this was prevented by the ambassador.[2]

During the following months the negotiations continued. The German officers urged that another military mission be sent to Moscow, but this was opposed by Brockdorff-Rantzau. He insisted that the Russians should send a representative to Berlin, who should negotiate there with the civil authorities—the best way to by-pass the army command. Under-secretary of state von Maltzan supported the policy of the ambassador and succeeded in convincing the new chancellor, Wilhelm Cuno, that he must take the matter in hand himself. Brockdorff-Rantzau also overcame the opposition of the Russian military authorities in lengthy discussions, and on 22 July Rosengolts, a brother-in-law of Trotsky and chief of the Supreme

[1] Mentzel's diary 'Die Reise nach Rußland 1923', p. 20: Nachlaß Mentzel, no. 3, Bundesarchiv Koblenz. Brockdorff-Rantzau to Maltzan, Moscow, 16 May 1923: Nachlaß Brockdorff-Rantzau, 9101 H/VIII, H 225607.

[2] Brockdorff-Rantzau to Maltzan, Moscow, 16 May 1923, and to Stresemann, Berlin, 10 Sept. 1923: Nachlaß Brockdorff-Rantzau, 9101 H/VIII, H 225606-07, 9101 H/XII, H 226782-4; Gatzke, 'Russo-German military collaboration during the Weimar Republic', *American Historical Review*, lxiii, 1958, p. 571.

Council of the Red Air Force, arrived in Berlin. Some days later he met the chancellor. Cuno mentioned that he considered, 'next to France, Poland the most dangerous disturber of the peace, not only in Europe, but in the whole world'. Rosengolts agreed, but was in favour of waiting and, meanwhile, for intensive co-operation between Russia and Germany; in the long run war was inevitable, and therefore measures of defence must be taken; the danger existed that the Entente would try first to destroy Germany, and then Russia. Several conferences were held with Rosengolts; it was envisaged to increase the sum of 35 million marks promised by Mentzel to 75 millions (50 in gold and 25 in paper marks); an agreement was signed about the production of war material for Germany in Russia and German help in the reconstruction of the Russian war industries, and it was made dependent upon the fulfilment of certain political conditions by Russia—a result which Brockdorff-Rantzau considered very satisfactory.[1]

On 12 August the Cuno government fell, and on the following day Stresemann became chancellor. At a reception given by the president in September he as well as the chancellor declared their opposition to the negotiations of the military with Moscow; German assistance to the Russian armament industry should be curtailed and be transferred to the purely economic field. Yet during the autumn further German military missions went to Russia and negotiated there with Russian generals.[2] On 20 September a leading German air force officer, Colonel Thomsen, was appointed to go to Russia as the leader of the German flying personnel there; he left for Russia on 13 November. General Hasse also intended to send Major von Niedermayer again to Moscow, in spite of urgent warnings from under-secretary of state von Maltzan. Niedermayer nevertheless appeared in Moscow before the end of the year. When Maltzan demanded an explanation Hasse declared that Niedermayer had long been discharged from the army

---

[1] Notes of Brockdorff-Rantzau about the conference Cuno–Rosengolts on 30 July 1923: Büro von Staatssekretär von Schubert, Akten betr. Militärische Angelegenheiten mit Rußland, 4564/1, E 162550–53; the same to Stresemann, Berlin, 10 Sept. 1923: Nachlaß Brockdorff-Rantzau, 9101 H/XII, H 226784–8.

[2] Helbig, op. cit., pp. 156–7; Mentzel's diary: Nachlaß Mentzel, no. 3, Bundesarchiv Koblenz; Brockdorff-Rantzau to Maltzan, Moscow, 29 Nov. 1923: Nachlaß Brockdorff-Rantzau, 9101 H/VIII, H 225273–4.

and had gone to Moscow as an expert of the Deutsche Werke, which frequently sent their experts to Moscow without informing the defence ministry.[1] 'The situation was baffling: in spite of all the reservations of the president and of Stresemann and their agreement with the German ambassador to Moscow, the co-operation between the Reichswehr and the Red Army continued without any political safeguards. . . .'[2]

At the beginning of 1923 the German naval command too was informed that the Russians were interested in closer connexions, and thereupon established contact with the Russian military attaché in Berlin, Petrov. A conference with him and another Russian took place on 20 March. Petrov informed the German naval officers of the Russian wishes, which were very numerous, and included nearly everything required for the rebuilding of the Russian navy. The German officers declared that they could only entertain these wishes if they could participate in the development of their 'ideas and plans'; for example, if the Russians constructed submarines, aeroplanes, and mines, which were forbidden to Germany by the Treaty of Versailles, then Germany too might derive certain advantages from it. The naval officer concerned even considered it necessary 'to act independently of the army command (General Hasse) if it made any difficulties or showed lack of interest . . .'. A further conference with Petrov some days later was also attended by Major von Niedermayer; the question of submarine construction was once more discussed, but nothing further seems to have happened. Three months later another high naval officer merely noted on the document: 'Further steps omitted by agreement with army.'[3]

But the affair was not quite finished. In the autumn of 1923 Petrov bought weapons from a German firm, allegedly for Russia; payment was made in the Russian embassy in Berlin. The arms were not sent to Russia, but handed over to the

[1] Notes of General Lieber on the year 1923, pp. 33, 53: Nachlaß Seeckt, box 19, no. 281, Militärgeschichtliches Forschungsamt. Notes of Maltzan of 18 Mar. 1924: Nachlaß Brockdorff-Rantzau, 9101 H/XII, H 226819–20.

[2] Helbig, op. cit., p. 159.

[3] 'Niederschrift betr. Besprechung des Kapitäns Steffan mit Herrn Petroff von der russischen Botschaft am 20. III.' 1923, with notes by other naval officers: Admiralität, Marine-Kommando-Amt, Flotten-Abteilung, Marinepolitische Angelegenheiten, 7897 A Ic 1–1, Militärgeschichtliches Forschungsamt Freiburg.

German Communists. Furthermore, rumours began to spread that Petrov was in reality a French naval officer, for he spoke fluent French but bad Russian. Krestinsky, the Russian ambassador, tried to explain this curious fact by Petrov's prolonged stay in France and Switzerland as a political exile before 1917; he indicated that Petrov enjoyed the special confidence of the Executive Committee and was a sort of supervisor of the Committee in the embassy, as Maltzan informed Brockdorff-Rantzau. The Germans were now determined to get rid of Petrov and indicated this wish to Krestinsky 'who understood the hint'.[1] Yet Brockdorff-Rantzau was not yet satisfied and reported several years later that Petrov's real name was Geoumé or Gomenet.[2] He thus seems to have been a Frenchman, probably not—as the Germans feared—a French agent, but an official of the Communist International.

VI. *The Frontier Defence and Secret Military Preparations*

From 1919 onwards the question how to defend the eastern frontier—at first still undefined—against Poland was crucial for the army command. In Germany as well as in Poland free corps and irregular formations were recruited, which tried to conquer disputed areas and places and to drive out the enemy. Farther north, at the Baltic coast, German and Russian, White and Red units were fighting each other and the forces of the new Baltic governments: there the situation was even more confused. In January 1919 Seeckt was sent to Königsberg to organize the retreat of the German armies from the east and the defence of East Prussia, in close collaboration with the High Command under Hindenburg and Groener, which transferred its seat eastwards to Kolberg in Pomerania. To strengthen the resistance to Poland among the civilian population the *Armee-oberkommando Nord*, whose chief of staff Seeckt was, ordered that officers should be appointed as 'mobile *Kreis* commissars'. Usually these were majors or captains who were attached not

---

[1] Maltzan to Brockdorff-Rantzau, Berlin, 28 Sept. and 6 Dec. 1923: Nachlaß Brockdorff-Rantzau, 9101 H/VIII, H 225259–60, 225428–9.

[2] Letter of Brockdorff-Rantzau of 21 Jan. 1926: Büro von Staatssekretär von Schubert, Akten betr. militärische Angelegenheiten mit Rußland, 4564/1, E 162674. Cf. Helbig, op. cit., pp. 160–1.

to the army, but to the civil administration and occupied independent positions within it. They were a kind of 'area commanders' for the civilian population and had the task of keeping alive the military spirit, especially among the young, and of providing suitable outlets for it. Frequently general staff officers were employed in this capacity so as 'to make them useful for the army'. Probably it was intended from the outset to make this into a permanent institution. In any case, 'it continued to exist under different names for years and later enabled Seeckt to take the first military measures outside the army. . .'.[1]

As the Treaty of Versailles prohibited all measures of mobilization and its preparation, and as all weapons beyond the quantities permitted had to be handed over to the Entente, the *Kreis* commissars soon acquired new important functions: the compilation of lists of the men qualified to serve in case of mobilization and the supervision of the storing of secret stocks of weapons and equipment. If the original functions of the *Kreis* commissars were connected with the anarchic conditions at the frontiers, the peace treaty added permanent tasks, as the army command was resolved to disregard the military stipulations on important issues. The secret arms depots had to be guarded and cared for; they were not to fall into the hands of the Interallied Control Commissions, nor into those of the Prussian police or the political left. These duties were undertaken by so-called *Arbeitsgemeinschaften* (work groups) which consisted of members of the dissolved free corps or paramilitary organizations.[2] As the Reichswehr was forbidden to possess any aeroplanes and flying installations, a *Fliegerzentrale* (flying centre) was formed in the defence ministry; at first it consisted of three officers and was a section of the *Truppenamt*. Seeckt—against objections of the Personnel Office—also ordered that 180 experienced flying officers were to be taken over into the Reichswehr. In each *Wehrkreis*—corresponding to the district of a division—an officer was made responsible for all air-force matters, and air-force cells were formed in the different offices, all subordinate to the *Fliegerzentrale* in Berlin. Thus 'a skeleton

---

[1] Rabenau, *Seeckt*, pp. 121–2; Groener, *Lebenserinnerungen*, p. 516.

[2] Görlitz, *Der deutsche Generalstab*, p. 360; Richard Scheringer, *Das große Los unter Soldaten, Bauern und Rebellen*, Hamburg, 1959, pp. 123–4.

came into being which was highly centralized and tightly knit, but not visible from outside'.[1]

Furthermore, the struggles with the Poles dragged on until 1921, above all in Upper Silesia. While it was Seeckt's policy, especially after the Kapp Putsch, to dissolve the free corps which threatened the army's monopoly, the same free corps were needed for the fighting in the east. This was recognized in the *Truppenamt* as early as the time of the Russo-Polish war of 1920. A memorandum of the T 1, probably written by Colonel Hasse, recommended that Germany should keep strict neutrality as long as possible. But, as the existing units were insufficient to maintain neutrality, not to speak of repulsing an enemy attack, volunteer forces had to be mobilized. Preparations for calling volunteers to the colours were in train in East Prussia; for the other eastern provinces the question was less acute, as the Russians were still more than 300 miles from the frontiers of Pomerania and Silesia and could not reach them before the end of September. The remaining time should be used to prepare the mobilization of volunteer units, with a twofold aim: to organize the defence of the frontiers, and to raise units which in case of need could be used against the Entente. 'If the Entente sends its forces to Poland they will come between two fires, between Germany and Russia. From this a situation favourable to us may develop. . . .'[2] Soon after units of the Red Army crossed the East Prussian frontier, but their defeat before Warsaw in August forced them to withdraw hastily. Probably the preparations for mobilization were seriously begun only in East Prussia.

In the following year, however, heavy fighting broke out again in Upper Silesia between Polish insurgents and German defence units. Members of the officially dissolved free corps flocked together from the whole of Germany to fight the Poles. On 23 May they stormed the Annaberg. For reasons of foreign policy it was impossible to employ Reichswehr units in Upper Silesia; but Seeckt ordered that officers of the general staff in mufti were to be available and that weapons and ammunition

---

[1] Rabenau, *Seeckt*, p. 528; Hilmar Ritter von Mittelberger, 'Lebenserinnerungen', p. 254, MS. in Bundesarchiv Koblenz.

[2] Memorandum of the T 1 of the *Allgemeine Truppenamt* of 26 July 1920: Nachlaß Freiherr von Fritsch, H 08–33/1, Bundesarchiv-Militärarchiv. At that time Hasse was the head of the T 1.

were to be supplied. Without this help, the achievements of the German units would not have been possible. 'Seeckt thus came into a situation in which he disapproved of the formation of free corps, but nevertheless had to welcome them in the peril of Silesia, and he felt it his duty to support and help them. That he did. . . .'[1] One of the Reichswehr officers, who organized the supply of the fighting free corps, was Major Buchrucker at Cottbus, with his adjutant First Lieutenant Paul Schulz. They thus acquired a net of connexions which later proved extremely useful to them when they recruited their *Arbeitskommandos* (labour units).[2] When the fighting in Upper Silesia came to an end the free corps had to be dissolved once more, or rather the Prussian authorities urged that this should be done; but it was only partly carried out. Several free corps transformed themselves into *Arbeitsgemeinschaften* (work groups) which hid their weapons for a better day.[3] Such groups were then billeted by *Kreis* commissars or leaders of the *Landbund* (agrarian league) on the estates to the east of the Elbe and Oder. There they led a semi-military existence and hoped for the war of liberation —against Versailles, or against the 'marxist' government, or against both.[4] They were convinced that one day they would again be called upon; but it was another question whether they were willing to obey the army command, which they deeply distrusted.

In eastern Pomerania and Lower Lusatia the local *Landbund* leaders were responsible for the defence measures and the protection of the frontier; they also saw to the storing of the weapons. In the district of Küstrin and Frankfurt-on-Oder First Lieutenant Paul Schulz formed a secret military organization, *Fridericus Rex*, which trained recruits and was financed by the *Landbund*.[5] In several Pomeranian districts on the right

---

[1] Rabenau, *Seeckt*, p. 300; Joachim von Stülpnagel to Rabenau, 16 Apr. 1940, p. 6: Nachlaß Seeckt, no. 287, Militärgeschichtliches Forschungsamt Freiburg.

[2] Scheringer, op. cit., p. 123; Thilo Vogelsang, *Reichswehr, Staat und NSDAP*, Stuttgart, 1962, p. 28, who maintains that Buchrucker was at that time still an officer on the active list.

[3] Rabenau, *Seeckt*, p. 305.

[4] 'Urteil des Schwurgerichts in Landsberg an der Warthe vom 3. November 1926 in der Strafsache gegen Schiburr und Gen. wegen Mordes', p. 9: Reichskanzlei, Akten betr. Rechtsverbände und Rechtsbewegung, vol. iii, 2733, Bundesarchiv Koblenz.

[5] Ibid., pp. 4, 9; Der Reichskommissar für die Überwachung der öffentlichen

bank of the Oder units of the former free corps Roßbach were billeted. The Reichswehr *Wehrkreis* ii at Stettin entrusted them with the storing and care of its arms depots: they were to keep and preserve the weapons for use in the frontier defence. The Roßbach members were convinced that they were still 'soldiers' and that their units were the framework of a later expansion. In Silesia the garrison command of Breslau organized an *Oderschutz* (Oder protection); here too the *Landbund* was prominent in the military preparations. Soon there was in each *Kreis* of the province a *Kreis* officer who was responsible for the training of volunteers.[1] The frontier defence units were recruited from extreme right-wing circles, partly because the local units were often formed by the dissolved free corps, and partly because those willing to undergo secret military training usually belonged to the right. The circles of the left were instinctively opposed to any military training, especially if this was in the hands of former officers. The men were members of the *Heimatverbände*, the *Landbund*, the *Jungdeutscher Orden*, the *Wiking*, or the *Stahlhelm*, and most of them were as hostile to the republic as the soldiers of the free corps.

No wonder that all these preparations met with the resistance of the Prussian government, and especially of the Prussian minister of the interior, Severing. By October 1922 friction had increased to such an extent that the conflict was submitted to the president; he was asked 'whether further preparations for frontier defence should be made or not; in the first case, the counter-measures of Prussian ministers must stop . . .'. Two months later a new conflict broke out, 'caused by the question of [the recruitment of] the frontier defence units from the local population and their weapons. Prussia fears a latent arming of the right-wing parties and opposes it . . .'. Again the army command succeeded in winning over Ebert to its side, and Seeckt demanded that this policy should be pushed through against Prussia as a matter pertaining to the Reich.[2] After

Ordnung to the Minister of the Interior, Berlin, 20 Feb. 1926: Reichskanzlei, Akten betr. Rechtsverbände und Rechtsbewegung, vol. ii, 2732, ibid.

[1] Vogelsang, op. cit., pp. 27–28; Anlage 6 of letter of Müller and Wels to Dr. Geßler, 6 Dec. 1926: Reichskanzlei, Akten betr. Reichswehr, vol. v, R 43 I 686, ibid.

[2] Notes of General Lieber 'Seeckt als Chef der Heeresleitung', pp. 73–74, under 18 Oct. and 28 Dec. 1922: Nachlaß Seeckt, box 19, no. 278, Militärgeschichtliches Forschungsamt Freiburg.

lengthy negotiations an agreement between the army command and the Prussian government was concluded on 7 February 1923, in which the former undertook to terminate its links with private organizations.[1] But this was quite impossible if it did not want to liquidate all the earlier work. In addition, the agreement was soon after published in the Communist paper *Rote Fahne*, under the headline: 'Does the Reichswehr arm for civil war?' In different parts of Germany more arms caches were found, and Severing again took measures against the frontier defence units in Upper Silesia,[2] where their links with the free corps were particularly close.

Friction had again increased sharply. Each side was able to accuse the other of breaking the agreement of February 1923. If the army command was determined to organize a secret frontier defence, it was in practice forced to co-operate with the para-military organizations of the right. Equally, if it wanted to increase the size of the Reichswehr units quickly at times of threatening conflict at home or abroad, only these organizations had men with some military training who were ready to serve in the Reichswehr. Such an increase became necessary in the course of 1923 on a large scale. These activities, however, were bound to increase the suspicion and the dislike of the army felt by the republicans and by the Prussian authorities. It was a problem for which no solution existed, as long as there were no large associations of the republican parties willing to support the army in these matters. And even if such associations came into being, would the army be willing to co-operate with them? The year 1923, the year of the great crisis of the Weimar Republic, began under auspices which were far from favourable.

[1] Vogelsang, op. cit., pp. 33–34.
[2] Notes of General Lieber for the year 1923, p. 4: Nachlaß Seeckt, box 19, no. 281, Militärgeschichtliches Forschungsamt.

IV

YEAR OF CRISIS

1. *Occupation of the Ruhr and Military Counter-Measures*

THE year 1923 was a year of great upheavals in the history of the Weimar Republic. The rapid inflation of the mark caused a tremendous political crisis and a social revolution, such as had not taken place in Germany for centuries. The occupation of the Ruhr by the French and the passive resistance proclaimed by the German government paralysed Germany's most important industrial area. The activities of the separatists in the Rhineland as well as in Bavaria threatened to destroy the unity of Germany, which had been achieved under great difficulties fifty years earlier. The government, which enjoyed but limited support in parliament and in the country, seemed unable to halt the spreading chaos and to stem the tide of economic and political disintegration. For the first time the extremist parties and associations of the right and left, which proclaimed the struggle against the 'system' of Weimar and furthered revolution with all the means at their disposal, became veritable mass organizations. They attracted above all the victims of the economic crisis, the unemployed, the disinherited, and the young. While socialist governments which had Communist support were formed in the two central German states of Saxony and Thuringia, in Bavaria there was a right-wing government which ruled with dictatorial powers. Under its protection the extremist para-military organizations of the right flourished and could prepare for the march on Berlin to overthrow the despised central government; political criminals sought by the police for murder and other crimes found protection in Bavaria. In this desperate situation the Reichswehr became the hope of all who were 'nationally minded', and the 'bracket' that held together the Reich and the warring factions.[1] General von Seeckt was the most powerful

[1] The expression *Klammer des Reiches* was used by Major-General Curt Ulrich von Gersdorff in a personal conversation with the author.

man in Germany. He had the power to decide whether, and in what form, the republic should survive, whether a presidential régime or a military dictatorship should be established, whether the forces of the Reich should be used against the left-wing governments in central Germany or against the right-wing government of Bavaria. All his political dreams seemed to come true. Never again was a German general to wield such far-reaching powers as Seeckt did at the end of 1923.[1]

At the end of 1922 Chancellor Wirth, who had governed with a coalition of the 'Weimar' parties—from the Social Democrats to the Centre—had to resign, as he failed to form a government of the 'Great Coalition'—from the Social Democrats to the German People's Party on the moderate right. The efforts of the army command to try and persuade the German People's Party to enter the government were in vain. The new chancellor was Wilhelm Cuno, a director-general of the Hamburg–America shipping line, and a friend of Seeckt. Cuno governed with the support of the moderate right; for the first time since the revolution there were only parties in the government which wholeheartedly supported the Reichswehr, and the co-operation between government and army command became much closer than it had ever been. Only a few weeks after the formation of the Cuno government the French and Belgians marched into the Ruhr. A close relationship between the government and the army became a necessity for reasons of foreign policy. The government forbade the officials to co-operate in any form with the occupying powers, prohibited any payments or deliveries to them, and proclaimed a policy of 'passive resistance'. As Germany's military forces were too weak to fight the French in the Ruhr an 'active resistance' was out of the question.

Seeckt, who continuously participated in the cabinet meetings, agreed with the policy of the government and was opposed to any active resistance. Yet members of the government as well as officers of the army command were in favour of a more forceful policy. Thus Lieutenant-Colonel von Stülpnagel 'from the national and soldierly point of view of the time' held that it was the duty of the soldier to act. This opinion

---

[1] The power of General von Schleicher nine years later was short-lived and rested on much weaker foundations. Only Ludendorff during the First World War wielded considerably greater power than Seeckt and for a longer time.

he put to Seeckt in many reports, but the latter's 'attitude throughout remained very cautious'—exactly as it did during the Versailles crisis of 1919 and during the Kapp Putsch. But Seeckt consented that large sums should be paid to Stülpnagel to organize the sabotage of the French in the Ruhr. The carrying out of the sabotage plans he entrusted to a man named Jahnke, who 'created an organization which, in agreement with me, executed sabotage actions, which were to hinder the advance of the French and to undermine the morale of the French troops. . . . The aims were: . . . to hinder the advancing French by sabotage actions, . . . to develop the passive resistance of the population into an active one (St. Bartholomew's night), and the state to organize it as far as possible. . . .'[1]

As there was the possibility of an armed clash with France—for example, if the French advanced further into Germany—measures of mobilization were taken, formations of the second and third lines were organized, volunteers—*Zeitfreiwillige*—were enlisted beyond the strength permitted to the army by the Treaty of Versailles, and weapons were bought in neutral countries. All these measures were approved and financed by the government.[2] Thus Major-General Hasse bought 100 Fokker fighter planes in Holland; they were later used to equip the German aerodrome at Lipetsk. The navy had ten fighter seaplanes built at the Heinkel works at Warnemünde, which were assembled and tried out in Stockholm.[3] Within the frontier defence formations a secret organization, the *Feldjäger*, was formed, and its members were trained for guerrilla fighting behind the enemy lines. Lieutenant-General von Loßberg, the commander of *Wehrkreis* vi (which included the Ruhr area), especially, was active in the western provinces in assembling the formations destined to swell the ranks of the army in case of an emergency.[4] His liaison officer to the para-military organizations was General von Oven, who was

---

[1] Stülpnagel to Rabenau, 16 Apr. 1940: Nachlaß Seeckt, no. 287, pp. 7–8, Militärgeschichtliches Forschungsamt Freiburg.

[2] Gordon, op. cit., p. 349; Vogelsang, op. cit., pp. 35–36.

[3] Speidel, 'Reichswehr und Rote Armee', *Vierteljahrshefte für Zeitgeschichte*, i, 1953, p. 23; Völker, 'Die Entwicklung der militärischen Luftfahrt in Deutschland 1920–1933', *Beiträge zur Militär- und Kriegsgeschichte*, iii, Stuttgart, 1962, pp. 133–6.

[4] Vogelsang, op. cit., p. 57; Stülpnagel's letter to Rabenau of 16 Apr. 1940, p. 7, loc. cit.

discharged from the army after the Kapp Putsch on account of his dubious attitude and was now the leader of the *Stahlhelm* at Goslar. According to his own testimony, he was to prepare in the district of Hanover, through his personal contacts, 'the envisaged incorporation of the patriotic associations (*vaterländische Verbände*) into the Reichswehr for its reinforcement'. The practical details were in the hands of a lieutenant-colonel who was on the active list. The associations with which General von Oven had contacts for this purpose were: the *Turnerschaften* of the *Deutschvölkische Freiheitspartei*, the *Stahlhelm*, the *Jungdeutsche Orden*, the Battalion Hindenburg, the Students' Corporations, the National Socialists, and some smaller local organizations.[1]

All these organizations were politically on the right, some of them—the *Deutschvölkische Freiheitspartei* and the National Socialists—on the extreme right, working for the overthrow of the hated republic. But the list did not mirror only the personal sympathies of General von Oven; it reflected the situation which the army command had to face. Where was it to find the men needed urgently to replenish the ranks? in the trade unions and the mass organizations of the republican left? Neither they nor the army command would have been willing to take such a course, although the Social Democrats supported Cuno's policy in the Ruhr. It was obvious that the army and the volunteers might also be used for internal political purposes, as actually happened in Saxony and Thuringia in the autumn of 1923. Thus Seeckt, as early as 15 February, had a 'long and detailed conference' with the leaders of the right-wing organizations about their 'incorporation . . . into the Reichswehr in an emergency'; among the participants were Escherich, the leader of the well-known *Orgesch* (Organisation Escherich), and the Counts von der Schulenburg and Yorck. Already this first conversation revealed that everyone put forward 'claims and rights': the participants clearly hesitated to put themselves under the orders of the army command. In spite of this, Seeckt's adjutant noted in his diary that 'it was gratifying to have them for once together'.[2] During the following months,

---

[1] Testimony of General von Oven in the Roßbach trial: Caro and Oehme, *Schleichers Aufstieg*, p. 159.

[2] Diary of von Selchow: Nachlaß Seeckt, no. 289, pp. 5, 7, Militärgeschichtliches Forschungsamt.

there followed conference upon conference; but it proved impossible to solve the basic problem of the subordination of the 'patriotic associations' to the army command. The question what attitude should be taken towards the formations recruited by the Reichswehr was at the same time discussed by the local right-wing organizations. They were prepared to organize acts of sabotage in the Ruhr and to be armed and trained by the Reichswehr, but their political ambitions went much further. One of the most radical free corps leaders and an active fighter during the Kapp Putsch, indefatigable in the struggle against the hated republic, the former Lieutenant Gerhard Roßbach, later declared: 'At a conference held in Berlin in February, in which His Excellency Ludendorff, Herr von Graefe, and I participated, it was decided to ask His Excellency Ludendorff to get in touch with General von Seeckt . . . and to inform him of our willingness to put the *völkische* fighting corps at the disposal of the Reich— under the condition that the formations remained under their leaders when used in a military capacity. . . .'[1] That the leaders of the right-wing organizations should put forward this demand was natural from their point of view: they were above all interested in not being merged in the Reichswehr, which they distrusted, but to retain their organizational unity and their political force. It is more difficult to understand why the army command, which could not possibly accept such a demand, continued the negotiations. General von Oven later confirmed as a witness in the Roßbach trial that 'General Ludendorff had discussions with responsible government quarters, probably with the chancellor and General von Seeckt, to the effect that the entire *vaterländische Verbände* were to be put at the disposal of the Reichswehr as a defence against attacks of foreign enemies. . . . It is a fact that the associations with which I had contacts co-operated with the Reichswehr on the friendly terms desired by General Ludendorff. . . .'[2]

Exactly as in the province of Hanover a local agreement between the army and the *vaterländische Verbände* operated in the province of Schleswig-Holstein. There the former Major-

---

[1] Testimony of Roßbach in his trial: Carlo and Oehme, op. cit., p. 153.
[2] Testimony of General von Oven in the Roßbach trial: ibid., p. 158. The meeting of Ludendorff and Seeckt took place on 20 Feb. 1923.

General Helfritz functioned as a provincial leader and co-operated closely with the *Stahlhelm*, the *Niederdeutscher Heimatbund*, and other 'national' associations. At a conference held in April the representatives of these organizations met two active Reichswehr officers who were informed that the agreements also covered the contingency of 'internal unrest'.[1] In May, at the instruction of the police president of Altona, the police searched the office of the local officer responsible for liaison between the Reichswehr and the nationalist organizations and threatened him with arrest. Thus a new conflict broke out between the army command and the Prussian government, which considered these illegal preparations a breach of the agreement of 7 February 1923. Seeckt was so indignant that he went to the chancellor and demanded a decision by the president. Geßler, the minister of defence, had to send to Severing, the Prussian minister of the interior, a very sharp letter composed by Schleicher, and Schleicher drew the attention of the chancellor to the possible use of article 48 of the constitution against Prussia (which permitted the central government to use force against a German state that neglected its legal obligations). Thus as early as May plans were discussed in the defence ministry which were to be carried out at the end of the year. Hasse even wrote that 'it was the task of the *Wehrmacht* to fight a system which brought unsuitable personalities into leading positions . . .'.[2]

Considerably larger were the military preparations in the province of Brandenburg, where it was possible to fall back upon the labour units and defence organizations of the former free corps.[3] Responsible for the recruitment of the formations were Major Buchrucker and Lieutenant Paul Schulz, who had meanwhile left the army, but continued to be employed by it. Schulz was responsible for the affairs of the labour units in the offices of *Wehrkreiskommando* iii in Berlin. His superior officer was Lieutenant-Colonel Fedor von Bock, the chief of staff of the *Wehrkreiskommando*.[4] Within a few months Buchrucker and

[1] Vogelsang, op. cit., p. 38.

[2] Notes of General Lieber on the Bavarian crisis of 1923, p. 13, with quotations from Hasse's diary: Nachlaß Seeckt, box 19, no. 281, Militärgeschichtliches Forschungsamt; Rabenau, *Seeckt*, p. 329; Vogelsang, op. cit., p. 38.

[3] See above, pp. 150–1.

[4] The later field-marshal.

Schulz succeeded in assembling from the labour units and former free corps some 18,000 to 20,000 men. They were quartered in small garrison towns of Brandenburg—Döberitz, Spandau, Rathenow, Brandenburg, Fürstenwalde, Beeskow, Lübben, Frankfurt-on-Oder, Küstrin—in disused fortifications and camps, always connected with local Reichswehr units, which were responsible for the provision of uniforms, food, and pay. Letters were sent to the

leaders of the former free corps, and they either came themselves and brought a number of their men along, or they sent the men with letters of recommendation to the 'division', i.e. the office . . . of Schulz in the house of the *Wehrkreiskommando* iii in Berlin, Kurfürstenstraße. Only men who were hostile to the existing form of government, in any case not in favour of it, were considered 'nationally reliable' and suitable for the labour units. If individual leaders, because of lack of candidates or out of kindness, accepted other people . . . it was considered a grave mistake. . . .[1]

The well-known free corps of the years 1919–20—the Ehrhardt brigade, the Loewenfeld brigade, the free corps Roßbach—were strongly represented and formed their own units, as they had demanded.[2] In the Berlin *Wehrkreiskommando* the dangers connected with this policy were apparently not seen—or they were deliberately overlooked. Its attitude can 'after an initial strong interest, be characterized later in 1923, when the organization grew extremely rapidly, as letting things take their course with its benevolent approval . . .'.[3] Similar preparations on a smaller scale were made in other parts of Germany. Even General Reinhardt, the commanding officer of *Wehrkreis* v at Stuttgart, permitted 150 students from Tübingen to be trained by the Infantry Regiment 13 at Gmünd. Further

---

[1] 'Urteil des Schwurgerichts in Landsberg an der Warthe vom 3. November 1926. . .', p. 10: Reichskanzlei, Akten betr. Rechtsverbände und Rechtsbewegung, vol. iii, 2733, Bundesarchiv Koblenz; Der Reichskommissar für die Überwachung der öffentlichen Ordung to the Minister of the Interior, Berlin, 20 Feb. 1926: ibid., vol. ii, 2732. In general, Scheringer, op. cit., p. 123; Vogelsang, op. cit., p. 36; Wheeler-Bennett, op. cit., p. 92.

[2] 'Bericht über Döberitz', Berlin, 3 Oct. 1923: Reichskanzlei, Akten betr. Organisation Escherich (Orgesch), vol. i, 2731; Der Reichskommissar für die Überwachung der öffentlichen Ordnung to the Minister of the Interior, Berlin, 20 Feb. 1926, loc. cit.

[3] Vogelsang, op. cit., p. 36.

training courses followed, but there was apparently no direct co-operation with the *vaterländische Verbände.*[1]

The co-operation between Reichswehr and *vaterländische Verbände* was all the more close in the neighbouring *Wehrkreis* vii, in Bavaria. There the state government and the leading officers were not only strongly pro-Bavarian and 'anti-Berlin' in their political orientation, but some senior and many junior officers sympathized openly with Hitler's National Socialists.[2] The commanding officer of the Bavarian infantry, General Franz Ritter von Epp, allowed the *Heimatbriefe,* which contained massive attacks on the central government, to be distributed to lower echelons. When asked to account for this, he attributed it 'to a technical error in his office'.[3] Like Epp, the Colonels Hierl and Leupold and Captain Röhm, well known for their sympathies with Hitler, remained on the active list (they were only discharged after the events of 1923). As early as 1921 officials of the National Socialist and other extremist organizations were enlisted for a short period and participated in army manœuvres and training courses.[4] In Berlin the army command was above all alarmed about the anti-Prussian and Bavarian separatist mood in Munich, which naturally aroused strong feelings in the defence ministry.[5] It was therefore decided at the end of 1922 to remove the Bavarian commander-in-chief, General Ritter von Möhl, who had strong pro-Bavarian leanings, from his post and to replace him by another Bavarian officer, Lieutenant-General von Lossow. He was an old associate of Seeckt and enjoyed his confidence, although Lossow's political views were as conservative and Bavarian particularist as those of Möhl.[6] But the Bavarian government immediately protested against Lossow's appointment because its views had

[1] Walter Bauer to Dr. Geßler, Tübingen, 1 May 1924: Nachlaß Geßler, no. 55, Bundesarchiv Koblenz.

[2] Gordon, op. cit., p. 445: according to him, this was only the case in Bavaria.

[3] 'Bericht des 40. Ausschusses (des Reichstags) zur Prüfung der Vorwürfe gegen die Reichswehr', Berlin, 15 Feb. 1923, p. 11: Reichskanzlei, Akten betr. Reichswehr, vol. iv, R 43 I 685, Bundesarchiv Koblenz.

[4] The social democratic deputy Alwin Saenger to Dr. Geßler, Munich, 31 July 1921: Nachlaß Geßler, no. 17, ibid.

[5] Hasse in 1922 considered the Bavarian troops at Grafenwöhr *reichstreu* but opposed to any further development to the left: Notes of General Lieber, p. 65: Nachlaß Seeckt, box 19, no. 278, Militärgeschichtliches Forschungsamt Freiburg.

[6] Gordon, op. cit., p. 233.

not been heard; for §12 of the *Wehrgesetz* of 1921 stipulated that the state government had the right of making proposals for the post in question. The minister of defence had to apologize to the prime minister of Bavaria, in writing as well as orally, and only then did the Bavarian government consent to the appointment of Lossow.[1]

Yet the change did not result in a modification of the political line. Lossow was at first believed to represent Seeckt's ideas, which amounted to subordination to Berlin: for this reason several of the Bavarian para-military organizations declined to have their members put under Reichswehr orders.[2] But, even if he had wanted to, Lossow would have been unable to loosen the connexions between the Bavarian Reichswehr and the *vaterländische Verbände*. In April 1923 it was established in Berlin, during a conference with Lossow, 'that in Bavaria one could not do without the rather too numerous patriotic organizations because they possessed at least 51 per cent. of the weapons . . .'.[3] In May Hasse remarked about the situation: 'in this respect Geßler and Seeckt had bad consciences, as they had always given way in Bavaria and had not energetically opposed the tendencies there which were directed against the authority of the state. . . .' Seeckt even thought of resignation, and Hasse had to pacify him. A few weeks later Hasse again reported to Seeckt about the situation in *Wehrkreis* vii, where some were for, and others against, Hitler.[4]

Right-wing extremism also existed in non-Bavarian units. In March 1923 several officers and men took part in a forbidden meeting held by the former Lieutenant Roßbach near Berlin and were punished because of their connexions with him. At Magdeburg an ensign and several other ranks were discharged because it was established that they were closely associated with Roßbach.[5] In July a well-informed conservative politician,

---

[1] The Bavarian foreign minister, Dr. von Knilling, to the defence ministry, Munich, 24 Dec. 1922; General Heye, chief of the Army Personnel Office, to the Reichskanzlei, Berlin, 6 Jan. 1923: Reichskanzlei, Akten betr. Wehrgesetz, R 43 I 609, Bundesarchiv Koblenz.

[2] Hanns Hubert Hofmann, *Der Hitlerputsch*, Munich, 1961, p. 94.

[3] Thus Rabenau, *Seeckt*, p. 348.

[4] Notes of General Lieber on the Bavarian crisis, pp. 13, 17, under 2 and 18 May 1923: Nachlaß Seeckt, box 19, no. 281, loc. cit.

[5] Seeckt to Stresemann, Berlin, 11 Febr. 1925: Nachlaß Schleicher, no. 32, Bundesarchiv Koblenz.

the later Chancellor Gustav Stresemann, wrote very sceptically about the political attitude of the Reichswehr: 'Part of the Reichswehr is supposed to intend to combine with the right-wing extremists. I believe that Geßler's conviction of the absolute reliability of the Reichswehr towards the state of today is unduly optimistic, in view of the mood of the Reichswehr officers and men. Presumably only the potential socialist hundreds and the militarized police of Prussia will be safe partisans of the government and the constitution. . . .'[1] That Seeckt had similar fears was shown by a warning against right- and left-wing extremist views which he issued at the same time.[2] Geßler, the minister of defence, even promulgated a decree against the co-operation between the Reichswehr and the *vaterländische Verbände*;[3] thus measures could be taken against individual soldiers who acted contrary to it. But the generals, who were the commanders of a *Wehrkreis*, were apparently free to disregard the decree and to continue their co-operation. It is obvious that the army command knew of it, and Seeckt himself conducted similar negotiations with the leaders of the right-wing organizations.[4] It was a curious system of book-keeping with double entries that Seeckt adopted, which confused many of his subordinates. Many years later General Groener rightly stated: 'he has set riddles to his subordinates about his own conviction, and many will have thought that a little right-wing extremism may be suitable to get into the good books of the supreme commander, in spite of all the sharp orders to the contrary, which he did issue, but which nobody took seriously. . . .'[5] Perhaps Seeckt really believed that he could separate from the *Verbände* by no longer co-operating with them and denying them the right to carry arms; but he too—especially during the crisis of 1923—wanted to be able to make use of their reserves of manpower.[6] The two courses were

[1] Stresemann to Crown Prince Wilhelm, Bad Homburg, 23 July 1923: Gustav Stresemann, *Vermächtnis*, i, Berlin, 1932, p. 218.

[2] Notes of General Lieber on the Bavarian crisis, p. 21, under 24 July 1923: Nachlaß Seeckt, box 19, no. 281, loc. cit.

[3] Decree of Geßler of 22 Febr. 1923: quoted by Seeckt in his letter to Stresemann of 11 Feb. 1925: Nachlaß Schleicher, no. 32, Bundesarchiv Koblenz.

[4] See above, pp. 156–7.

[5] Groener to Major-General Gerold von Gleich, Berlin, 26 Apr. 1931: Groener-Geyer, *General Groener*, pp. 279–80.

[6] Vogelsang, op. cit., p. 35.

incompatible with each other. Nor could it be assumed that the leaders of the *Verbände*, with their great political ambitions, would be content with the modest role assigned to them by Seeckt.

11. *Seeckt and Stresemann*

On 12 August 1923 Chancellor Cuno resigned. The rapid inflation of the mark, the difficult food situation, the suffering of broad sections of the people, and the outbreak of strikes on a large scale made the position of the Cuno government untenable and required a government that was less clearly to the right. The Social Democrats again entered the government and took over important ministries. Gustav Stresemann, the leader of the German People's Party, became chancellor and foreign minister. The Social Democrats also desired a change in the ministry of defence, but this demand was refused by Ebert; Dr. Geßler remained in office, under this and following governments. Seeckt fully approved of this, as he was certain of Geßler's support on all important issues. He was less satisfied with the new chancellor, as he explained to his sister: 'At this moment a change is not justified, for it would bring a new policy with new methods and new men. It thus remains a victory of fear, on the one hand of the French, on the other of the Communists. . . . Stresemann was on the cards. He certainly is a very clever and even a good politician. I have no close contacts with him and will not seek them. . . .'[1] Between Seeckt and Cuno there had existed 'a closer understanding' on questions of the army, military policy, and general political issues.[2] This Stresemann sought to maintain on his side. Immediately before and after his appointment as chancellor he had several long conferences with Seeckt, during which he developed the lines of his policy and promised his unconditional 'support for the national interests of the Reichswehr', even its secret relations with the Russians.[3]

[1] Letter of Aug. 1923: Rabenau, *Seeckt*, p. 350.
[2] Seeckt to von Kahr, 5 Nov. 1923: ibid., p. 368; Schüddekopf, *Heer und Republik*, no. 79, p. 186.
[3] Notes of Seeckt's adjutant von Selchow: Nachlaß Seeckt, roll 26, no. 289, microfilm in Institut für Zeitgeschichte; G. Freund, *Unholy Alliance*, London, 1957, p. 167, quoting from von Selchow's diary and Nachlaß Stresemann.

This attempt of the new chancellor to establish good relations with Seeckt and the army command met with little success. The officers feared that a government in which the Social Democrats were strongly represented would weaken the German will of resistance to the French and the Poles, and would attempt to curtail the rearmament projects of the army command. It was also believed in the Benlerstraße that Stresemann intended to replace Seeckt by another general, for example, Reinhardt.[1] Only eight days after Stresemann had taken office Hasse wrote that it would be difficult to avoid Reinhardt's succeeding Seeckt if he left; 'but Reinhardt's political activity as a minister has cost him the confidence of the north-German soldiers; for most of them he was too democratic . . .'.[2] At the end of September the Social Democratic minister of finance, Rudolf Hilferding, did indeed demand that the payments for the Russian enterprises of the Reichswehr be suspended.[3] On the same day the passive resistance to the French was broken off: it had not achieved its aim—to paralyse the French in the Ruhr—and it imposed financial burdens on the German people which they could no longer bear. To Lieutenant-Colonel von Stülpnagel the end of passive resistance was 'a new lost war'. How many officers felt at the time becomes clear from his simultaneous remark that they had to carry out two duties: 'protection of the constitution, of a diseased system, and preparation of the war of liberation, which is prevented by the system. . . .'[4] In reality, however, the war of liberation was not prevented by 'the system', but by Germany's weakness after a lost war. Stresemann recognized that this weakness could not be overcome by military measures, but only through negotiations which would take time. Only if Germany again became strong in the economic field would she 'become capable of concluding alliances';[5] and the pre-condition of an economic recovery was the termination of passive resistance and the stabilization of the mark: one was impossible without the other.

[1] Gordon, op. cit., p. 351.

[2] Notes of General Lieber on the Bavarian crisis, p. 18, under 21 Aug. 1923: Nachlaß Seeckt, box 19, no. 281, Militärgeschichtliches Forschungsamt Freiburg.

[3] Ibid., p. 33, under 25 Sept. 1923.

[4] Diary of Joachim von Stülpnagel under 25 Sept. 1923: Nachlaß Seeckt, no. 287, p. 10, ibid.

[5] See above, p. 17.

Stresemann attempted to overcome the distrust of the officer corps, which was well known to him, and to meet it on a friendly basis. On 7 September he and Geßler visited the military camp at Döberitz near Berlin, addressed the assembled officers in the presence of Seeckt, and gave high praise to the troops in well-chosen words.[1] There followed an extended evening in the officers' mess. Stresemann addressed Seeckt in the correct old form as 'Your Excellency', while Seeckt confined himself to 'Herr Reichskanzler'. In the eyes of the officers Seeckt's authority grew: he was the great man, the ministers mere civilians.[2] Turning to Stresemann Seeckt declared: 'Herr Reichskanzler, the Reichswehr will march with you, if you will go the *German* way!'; or, according to the diary of another officer present: 'The Reichswehr stands behind you if the German chancellor goes the German way!'[3] This included a tacit threat that the Reichswehr would refuse to obey the government if the chancellor did not go the German way. Apparently Seeckt reserved to himself the decision what were, and what were not, German ways. None of the witnesses reports a reply from Stresemann: he had been put in his place like a schoolboy; his attempt at a *rapprochement* had failed.

During the same month Seeckt engaged in ceaseless political activity behind the government's back. 'Conference after conference takes place with the right-wing circles. Seeckt is strongly driven, but he retains a cool head', noted his adjutant.[4] On 23 September Seeckt received the deputies Hergt and Count Westarp of the German Nationalist Party and afterwards representatives of the German Nationalist workers. They asked him to become chancellor as they had no confidence in Stresemann. Seeckt replied he would not refuse a loyal offer. Colonel Hasse regretted that Seeckt let himself be influenced in this way. He realized that what mattered was 'the reasonable part of

[1] Wilhelm Heye, 'Mein Lebenslauf', p. 562: Bundesarchiv-Militärarchiv, H 08–18/4.
[2] Description of General Paul Mahlmann who was present at Döberitz as a young lieutenant.
[3] The first quotation in Heye, 'Mein Lebenslauf', p. 562, loc. cit.; the second in the diary of Joachim von Stülpnagel: Nachlaß Seeckt, no. 287, p. 10, Militärgeschichtliches Forschungsamt Freiburg. Hasse only noted: 'Deutsche Wege, Angriffe auf Reichswehr', ibid., no. 281, p. 34.
[4] Diary of von Selchow, under 26 Sept. 1923, p. 7: Nachlaß Seeckt, roll 26, no. 289, microfilm in Institut für Zeitgeschichte.

the working class' rather than the German Nationalists, that
the policy canvassed would only drive the Social Democrats
into opposition, and that Seeckt as a 'dictatorial chancellor'
could not lean only on one party.[1] On the 25th his three most
important political advisers—Hasse, Schleicher, and Stülpnagel
—warned Seeckt of this, 'whereupon he was a little offended,
but it nevertheless has an effect . . .'. Some days later Hasse
noted: 'Today Seeckt is more reasonable, he gradually gets
fed up with his right-wing friends.'[2] When Claß, the leader of
the Pan-Germans, wrote to Seeckt and invited him to seize
power by force, he replied that he would fight to the last bullet
against the revolutionaries of the right and of the left; 'it is the
task of the Reichswehr to preserve the unity of the Reich, and
those who endanger it are my enemies, to whatever side they
may belong!'[3]

On 26 September the government of Bavaria proclaimed a
state of emergency and appointed the former prime minister von
Kahr *Generalstaatskommissar*, with dictatorial powers in Bavaria.
In reply Chancellor Stresemann, with the approval of President
Ebert, decided to entrust the minister of defence, Geßler, with
executive powers, on the basis of article 48 of the constitution,
which gave far-reaching powers to the president in case of an
emergency. As Rabenau remarks, 'but everybody knew that
behind him there stood General von Seeckt as the real holder
of power'. On the morning of the 27th his adjutant found him
seated behind his desk beaming with joy. In reply to the adjutant's puzzled question, Seeckt expressed his satisfaction that
'now the conflict between the Reichswehr and the right-wing
organizations could be avoided'; he had told the cabinet often
enough that a dictatorial power was necessary, and he was
glad that it existed now.[4] On the 29th Hasse had a long
confidential talk with Seeckt and advised him to take the
executive powers into his own hands and to dissolve parliament; 'the cabinet will then either disappear or become the
executive organ for Seeckt's orders'. Simultaneously Hasse

---

[1] Notes of General Lieber on the Bavarian crisis, p. 24, under 23 Sept. 1923:
Nachlaß Seeckt, box 19, no. 281, Militärgeschichtliches Forschungsamt Freiburg.
[2] Ibid., under 25 Sept. 1923.
[3] Seeckt to Claß, 24 Sept. 1923: Benoist-Méchin, *Histoire de l'Armée Allemande*,
ii, Paris, 1938, p. 260; Rabenau, *Seeckt*, p. 387, n. 2.
[4] Ibid., p. 352.

noted: 'Seeckt is reasonable again, he gets on quite well with Stresemann.'[1]

That Seeckt himself was occupied with the idea of becoming chancellor emerges from a 'government programme' he drafted in October, in which he developed his political plans, in home as well as in foreign affairs:

In its essence the cabinet is a government of transition during a state of emergency. The special situation of the Reich, internally and externally, demands special methods. . . . Refusal of entry into the League of Nations. Refusal of any new obligation, beyond the stipulations of the Treaty of Versailles, also with regard to the Rhineland. . . . Intensification of the economic and military-political relations with Russia. Refusal of any, even an economic, *rapprochement* with Poland. To extend the economic *rapprochement* with Russia will be an endeavour of the government because it is convinced that both powers depend upon each other. . . . Suppression of all tendencies directed against the existence of the Reich and against the legitimate authority of the Reich and the state, through the use of the means of power of the Reich. Change of the constitution in a federal sense. Formation of a chamber of Estates, with elected representatives of the professions and occupations. . . . Combination of the offices of chancellor and prime minister of Prussia. . . . Prohibition of cartels and trusts. Cancellation of collective labour agreements. The trade unions to be replaced by occupational chambers. . . .[2]

A very large programme, with far-reaching changes in the constitutional and economic fields, was envisaged by Seeckt. Plans such as the dissolution of the trade unions and the abolition of collective agreements would have been extremely difficult to realize. Once more Seeckt emphasized the idea of a reform of the structure of the Reich 'in a federal sense': the dualism of the Reich and Prussia was to be eliminated by the fusion of the two leading political offices in Germany. This would have brought to an end the interminable squabbles with the Prussian government; but it could hardly be called 'federal', as it would have been a step towards centralization. The largest German

[1] Notes of General Lieber on the Bavarian crisis, p. 25, under 29 Sept. 1923: loc. cit.

[2] Rabenau, *Seeckt*, pp. 359–61; Schüddekopf, *Heer und Republik*, no. 76a, pp. 179–81. Some additional points in Nachlaß Seeckt, box 16, no. 220, Militärgeschichtliches Forschungsamt Freiburg.

state would have lost its autonomy and would have become subordinate to the central government. Until Papen's *coup d'état* of July 1932 this plan was to recur time and again in the political programmes of the generals, and Seeckt himself was to develop it further in 1924.[1]

The same month, October 1923, saw—if not the feared clash between the Reichswehr and the right-wing organizations— an attempt at a *Putsch* by the 'Black Reichswehr' against the government and the republic. It was apparently sparked off by the decision of the government to terminate the passive resistance campaign in the Ruhr, which aroused the fury of the extreme right. The leader of the *Putsch* was the former Major Buchrucker, the commander of the labour units in the *Wehrkreis* iii. After an unsuccessful attempt to occupy the government buildings in Berlin, the units of the 'Black Reichswehr' tried on 1 October to take the fortresses of Küstrin and Spandau near Berlin. But the commander of Küstrin, Colonel Gudowius, kept his nerve and defended himself so that the attempt miscarried. In Spandau the free corps were more successful and occupied the citadel for a time. Seeckt took immediate action and mobilized the neighbouring garrisons. The ringleaders were arrested; their men were disarmed and detained.[2] The battalion of Captain Stennes in Fort Hahnenberg near Spandau only capitulated when Lieutenant-Colonel von Bock promised them an amnesty. The free corps officers declined his word of honour as a Reichswehr officer and demanded instead his word of honour as a royal Prussian officer.[3] In the camp at Döberitz a unit of the 'Black Reichswehr' was disarmed by cavalry from Potsdam; but the men were offered a transfer to the Reichswehr provided they accepted its conditions. They were leaderless and embittered against their officers, who had left them in the lurch.[4] Buchrucker was sentenced by a special court at Cottbus to a term of honourable imprisonment.

The *Putsch* proved how justified was Seeckt's distrust of 'the

[1] See below, pp. 190–1.

[2] Rabenau, *Seeckt*, p. 354; Gordon, *Reichswehr and the German Republic*, p. 234; Scheringer, *Das große Los. . .*, pp. 124 ff. with a detailed description of the events at Küstrin.

[3] Hofmann, *Hitlerputsch*, p. 103.

[4] 'Bericht über Döberitz', Berlin, 3 Oct. 1923: Reichskanzlei, Akten betr. Organisation Escherich (Orgesch), 2731, Bundesarchiv Koblenz.

revolutionaries of the right'. Ehrhardt, Roßbach, and the other free corps leaders had aims which were utterly different from his own; a co-operation was out of the question. Yet nothing happened to the officers who were responsible for the existence of the 'Black Reichswehr', such as Lieutenant-Colonel von Bock, or his chief, General von Horn. The army command, on the other hand, became more determined than ever to draw a definite line between the army and the irregular formations and former free corps.[1] This aversion was increased by the events in Munich four weeks later. A gulf now existed between the officers of the Reichswehr and those of the right-wing extremist organizations who were pledged to revolution and violence—men such as the Captains Göring, Röhm, Stennes, and Pfeffer von Salomon, who became the leaders of Hitler's stormtroopers, or the leaders of the former free corps. They despised all who served 'the system' and considered them *bourgeois* careerists. To the Reichswehr officers, on the other hand, the free corps men were political adventurers and semi-Bolsheviks, who had no existence and no future. There remained the question, however, how the officers who wanted to prepare for the 'war of liberation' could do so without using the manpower of the para-military organizations of the right. Only four weeks after the *Putsch* Lieutenant-Colonel von Bock declared that everything was 'more or less all right again' and that these organizations were 'again in co-operation with the Reichswehr'.[2] In the *Wehrkreis* iii no dividing line had yet been drawn.

The *Putsch* of the 'Black Reichswehr' and the threatening developments in Bavaria did not result in a reconciliation between Seeckt and Stresemann. On the contrary, in the defence ministry fears were expressed that a revolution from the right would attack the Reichswehr too if it was linked too closely with the 'system'. On 26 October Lieutenant-Colonel von Stülpnagel reported to Seeckt and pressed him to seize the initiative in forming a government: 'otherwise a revolution from the right will submerge us.' On the 30th General Hasse too wrote 'that Stresemann must go, otherwise the

[1] Benoist-Méchin, op. cit., ii. 278, who believes that the Küstrin Putsch marked a turning-point in the history of the Reichswehr.
[2] See below, p. 172.

Reichswehr would be caught between two revolutions . . .'.[1]
At the beginning of November Stülpnagel again demanded
from Seeckt that he should seize power.[2] Rabenau further
reports that 'a leading officer of the defence ministry' exclaimed
in great excitement: 'If he does not seize power now he must
be removed!'[3] Seeckt had to reckon with a Fronde of his most
loyal supporters if he did not act. For the morning of 3 November
he invited the commander-in-chief of *Gruppenkommando* i,
General von Berendt, and the commanders of *Wehrkreise* ii and
iii, Generals von Tschischwitz and von Horn, to a conference.
The waiting generals discussed the political situation: Seeckt
was holding all the trumps in his hand and must use them;
they thought that he would now proclaim a military dictatorship.[4]

Meanwhile, Seeckt had gone to the president to report to
him in the presence of Dr. Geßler. When Ebert inquired what
was needed, Seeckt replied: 'An understanding with the right
because otherwise the army will come between two fires.'
Ebert answered: 'An understanding with the right means that
I have to accept the conditions put forward by the right. I
decline to do that. If you are of the opinion that the Reichswehr is unable to protect constitutional conditions in the Reich,
that it cannot do so or does not want to do so, you have to say
so. Then I will leave this house.' Thereupon Seeckt hesitated
and said that this could not be achieved with Stresemann, who
enjoyed no confidence. Ebert suggested that Seeckt should tell
this to the chancellor himself; Seeckt and Geßler went to the
Reichskanzlei, where Seeckt declared: 'Herr Reichskanzler, it
is impossible to fight under you. You do not possess the confidence of the army.' When Stresemann inquired whether the
Reichswehr renounced its obedience to him, Seeckt remained
silent.[5] He returned to the ministry of defence where the
generals awaited him. In a grim mood he described the

---

[1] Notes of General Lieber on the Bavarian crisis, p. 31, under 26 and 28 Oct.
1923: Nachlaß Seeckt, box 19, no. 281, Militärgeschichtliches Forschungsamt
Freiburg.

[2] Rabenau, *Seeckt*, p. 353.

[3] Ibid., p. 364. The conversation took place on 3 Nov.

[4] Ibid., p. 366, after a description by General von Tschischwitz.

[5] Otto Geßler, *Reichswehrpolitik in der Weimarer Zeit*, p. 299; Gordon, op. cit.,
p. 354.

situation to them. 'That was the end of the conference. All were dumbfounded. Nobody had been consulted. The generals left convinced that this was a totally unsatisfactory solution. They believed that Seeckt had made the wrong decision. . . .'[1] But it rather seems that Seeckt had taken no decision.

In his dislike of Stresemann Seeckt went still further. Two days later, in a new conference with the chancellor, he told him that it was the first task to render harmless the extremism of the right; this could only be achieved without the shedding of blood if a cabinet were formed on a different basis. Geßler was forced to declare 'that the political opinion of the chief of the army command had nothing to do with the position of the Reichswehr', and Seeckt confirmed this. In spite of this, Stresemann considered the incident so serious that he reported to Ebert and offered his resignation. But Ebert urged him to stay in office. To mobilize further forces against the chancellor, on 6 November Seeckt informed the deputy Freiherr von Lersner, a personal enemy of Stresemann within the German People's Party, that he (Seeckt) had told Stresemann, 'that in his opinion the Herr Reichskanzler was no longer capable of leading the government'. He expressly permitted Lersner to make use of this communication, and he did so in a meeting of the party's deputies. Another deputy of the German People's Party then interjected the word 'Praetorians!', which certainly seemed justified. Lersner, however, replied: 'No, Seeckt is not a Praetorian. . . .'[2] Lersner also attempted to see the president to inform him of the mood in the Reichswehr and of the grave dangers which had arisen through the 'cleavage' between Stresemann 'and the largest and most important part of the Reichswehr and the so-called *vaterländische Verbände*'.[3] Seeckt was again unsuccessful: for the time being Stresemann remained chancellor. But on 23 November he was forced to resign, when parliament refused to grant him a vote of confidence.

What Seeckt did not know was that the leaders of the *vaterländische Verbände* were at the same time busily intriguing

---

[1] Rabenau, *Seeckt*, p. 366.

[2] Meeting of the German People's Party 'fraction' on 6 Nov. 1923: Stresemann, *Vermächtnis*, i. 198–200. Even Gordon, op. cit., p. 355, remarks that Seeckt's action 'was scarcely in accord with Seeckt's own non-political code'. The question is whether he had such a code.

[3] Stresemann, *Vermächtnis*, i. 232–3.

against himself. In a conference of the leaders of the *Landbund* (Agrarian League) on 3 November with the Colonel of the Munich police, von Seisser, they not only declared that they remained bitterly hostile to the Stresemann government, which they would deprive of food supplies; they also stated that they had

... no confidence in Seeckt, who does not find the strength to break with Ebert and Stresemann; forcible solution only possible with Reichswehr. In the first instance [we must] try once more to bring Seeckt to a decision by strong pressure; if this does not work, change in the leadership of the Reichswehr. Berendt in place of Seeckt; Berendt and Möhl agree; no difficulties if another general leads the Reichswehr. *Vaterländische Kampfverbände* too weak in the north to gain success on their own. ... In general there is distrust of Seeckt, but the view is expressed that one should side with Seeckt if he decides on action (*wenn er den Absprung findet*). ... The *Landbund* will try once more to bring Seeckt to a decision, but simultaneously make preparations with Berendt in case Seeckt refuses. ... [1]

The two commanders-in-chief of the Reichswehr *Gruppenkommandos*, the Generals von Berendt and von Möhl, were intriguing with outsiders against the chief of the army command, with the aim of replacing him by another general, who would side with the conspiracy. But in the conference with Seeckt on 3 November General von Berendt apparently remained silent and did not indicate his opposition to Seeckt.

Lieutenant-Colonel von Bock informed Seisser that the consequences of the *Putsch* at Küstrin had been overcome and that the *Verbände* again co-operated with the Reichswehr. In von Bock's opinion, 'Seeckt was determined to break with Stresemann. Bock goes with Seeckt and believes that he is indispensable.' That the co-operation between the Reichswehr and the *Verbände* was again functioning also emerged from the report of Colonel Friedrichs, 'leader of the *Kampfbünde* in Berlin', that in Berlin there existed five irregular battalions, one of them consisting of National Socialists.[2] Probably Seeckt had not been informed of the renewed close connexions between the *Wehrkreiskommando* iii and the *Verbände*. But that this could happen in Berlin, directly under his nose, shows the different

---

[1] Ernst Deuerlein, *Der Hitler-Putsch*, Stuttgart, 1962, no. 79, pp. 302–4.
[2] Ibid., pp. 302–3.

tendencies existing within the army. It also shows how little his own subordinates took account of his orders if they disagreed with them for political reasons. The same tendency became evident during the conflict between Seeckt and General von Lossow.

III. *Seeckt and Lossow: the Bavarian Crisis*

On 27 September—the day after the transfer of executive powers to the minister of defence—the Munich *Völkischer Beobachter* (the organ of Hitler) published an article, under the heading 'The Dictators Stresemann and Seeckt', containing sharp personal and political attacks on Seeckt. He was accused of planning to eliminate his partner in the near future and to make himself dictator with the help of his friends—plans which certainly were not completely invented. Thereupon Geßler prohibited the printing and sale of the *Völkischer Beobachter* until further notice and ordered General von Lossow to carry out this order. Lossow informed *Generalstaatskommissar* von Kahr, who declined to comply with the order. A Bavarian staff officer was dispatched to Berlin to inform Seeckt of the political objections of Kahr and the fear of Lossow that he might get involved in a conflict with Kahr if he carried out Geßler's order. Geßler refuted these arguments and ordered that the prohibition be enforced, if need be, by force of arms. This, too, Lossow communicated to Kahr, who objected on the grounds that law and order were most seriously endangered. 'General von Lossow now had to choose between obedience to an express order and compliance with the wishes of the Bavarian *Generalstaatskommissar*. He renounced the use of his powers as the possessor of executive authority, and reported that, as he wanted to avoid a conflict with the *Generalstaatskommissar* under any circumstances, the order could not be carried out. . . .'[1]

Seeckt reacted sharply. He wrote to Lossow:

I have raised no objection to the right claimed by Your Excellency to examine an order, to consider whether it can be carried out

---

[1] Letter of Seeckt of 20 Oct. 1923—Heeresleitung, T 1 III: Admiralität, Marine-Kommando-Amt, Flotten-Abteilung, 7896 A IIa 236, Militärgeschichtliches Forschungsamt Freiburg; Deuerlein, *Hitler-Putsch*, nos. 14–15, pp. 185–6; Rabenau, *Seeckt*, pp. 355–6. Extracts from the article in the *Völkischer Beobachter* in Gordon, op. cit., p. 236.

with regard to local political opinion, and to mention any doubts. . . .
The new order, however, given after the examination of these doubts,
had to be carried out immediately. The responsibility for the
carrying out rested solely with Your Excellency as the possessor of
executive authority, and could not be shifted by informing the
Generalstaatskommissar of the order. . . . The refusal to obey the order
of the minister of defence therefore amounts to an offence against
military discipline and deliberate disobedience. . . . I am not
confident that Your Excellency is willing and able to maintain the
interests of the Reichswehr and the authority of the Reich against
local political opposition. The execution of orders for the employment of the Reichswehr, which may become necessary at any
moment in the area of the Reich, is thus jeopardized in a way which
I cannot tolerate. I therefore request Your Excellency to draw
your own conclusions concerning your position from what I have
said. . . .[1]

The officer corps was informed by Seeckt that no commanding
officer would be willing 'to hold a command whose power is
limited by the political approval of his subordinates and the
opinions of civil authorities outside the army . . .'.[2]

On 18 October Geßler met at Augsburg the commanding
officer of the artillery of the Bavarian Reichswehr, Major-
General Freiherr Kreß von Kressenstein; the minister wanted
to settle the conflict peacefully and to persuade Lossow to
resign voluntarily. He explained to General von Kreß that
Seeckt felt himself responsible for the discipline of the army; if
he condoned the disobedience of Lossow, the basis of the army's
discipline would be undermined; his behaviour was, in Seeckt's
opinion, incompatible with the rules of honour of the officer
corps; Lossow's conduct did damage to the confidence in the
reliability of the Reichswehr; his refusal to obey orders had been
compared in Berlin with the Kapp Putsch.[3] Lossow reported
these remarks to the Bavarian government, which drew the
conclusion that there existed a conflict between Bavaria and
the central government. Lossow was suspended from his duties

---

[1] Seeckt to Lossow, Berlin, 9 Oct. 1923: Deuerlein, op. cit., no. 31, p. 205.

[2] Seeckt's letter of 20 Oct. 1923—Heeresleitung, T 1 III: loc. cit. The T 1 III
was the political section of the *Truppenamt* and was under Major von Schleicher.

[3] Freiherr Kreß von Kressenstein to Lossow, Munich, 20 Oct. 1923: Deuerlein,
op. cit., no. 54, p. 244. The 'Berlin envoy' was Geßler, not Freiherr von Kreß, as
assumed by Gordon, op. cit., p. 238.

by Geßler; his discharge from the army was to be the next step. Kahr, in the name of the Bavarian government, declared that he could not accept this, and that Lossow remained the Bavarian commander-in-chief. Bavaria also refused to accept any further orders from the ministry of defence, and the government assumed command of the Seventh (Bavarian) Division. On 22 October the division had to take a new oath to the Bavarian state.[1] There was no longer one German army, under a unified command.

The commanding officers of the other six infantry divisions and of the three cavalry divisions assured Seeckt, through the mouth of General von Berendt, commander-in-chief of *Gruppen-kommando* 1, of their absolute loyalty and obedience. The commander-in-chief of *Gruppenkommando* 2, General von Möhl, was naturally in sympathy with Munich.[2] Seeckt immediately published an order to the army: 'Anyone who follows the example of the Bavarian government is breaking the oath he has rendered to the Reich and is guilty of military disobedience. I solemnly call upon the Seventh (Bavarian) Division of the German army to remain faithful to the oath it has rendered to the Reich and to carry out unconditionally the orders of its highest military commander. . . .' Lossow protested against this edict, which in effect amounted to an invitation to the Bavarian division to disobey Lossow's orders. Seeckt further decreed that the infantry school in Munich, where the officer cadets of the army were trained, should be dissolved and that the Bavarian company, which formed part of the Berlin guard regiment, should be sent back to Bavaria.[3]

The scene in the infantry school on 22 October is described in the letter of a young lieutenant to his battalion commander, Lieutenant-Colonel Freiherr von Hammerstein-Equord. When Seeckt's edict was read out, the commanding officer of the school, General von Tieschowitz, declared

that he had given leave of absence until further notice to all Bavarian citizens in the school, who without exception had taken an oath to

[1] Seeckt's letter of 20 Oct. 1923—Heeresleitung, T 1 III, loc. cit.; Rabenau, *Seeckt*, pp. 357–8.

[2] Hofmann, *Hitlerputsch*, p. 111.

[3] Rabenau, *Seeckt*, pp. 357–9; Gordon, op. cit., p. 239. For the Bavarian company in the Berlin guard regiment, cf. above, pp. 127–8.

the Bavarian government an hour before, as he could not possibly co-operate any longer with these gentlemen. For all non-Bavarians, of course, only the opinion of the army command was valid. . . . Already lively, and partly unnecessarily heated, discussions had taken place among the cadets, especially among the officers: now the speeches became violent. From the outset I had strongly upheld the view that for us the only thing that mattered was the question of discipline or indiscipline in the army, and that the prestige of the officer corps would be at stake if we lightheartedly disregarded our oath to the Reich government. Unfortunately only a few followed me, while most showed a childish enthusiasm for Bavaria and the *völkische* movement, sang the Ehrhardt song all the time, and adorned themselves with black, white and red cockades. I and a few who sided with me were called (behind our backs) Red dogs who sympathized with the Jewish government. . . . During lunch the (Bavarian) Colonel Leupold, commanding officer of our course, appeared, although he was on leave, and in a long speech made propaganda for the Bavarian point of view, which was dominated by the slogan 'Nationalism against Marxism'. At the end he invited those gentlemen who would obey the Bavarian government's orders to enter their names in a list. . . . In fact afterwards several Prussian officers too declared that they would 'of course' follow the Bavarian government. In the afternoon the duty officer, Lieutenant Teichmann of Infantry Regiment 13, informed us that he had reported to Colonel Leupold that the inspection officers stood behind him, with the exception of a few gentlemen only, and not behind General von Tychowitz [*sic*]. . . . In the course of the events I have got into an entirely false position. The large majority of the men, whom I still look upon as my comrades, consider me a traitor to the national cause, especially as I pass for the spokesman of our small party. In my opinion the *völkische* movement—which alone can save the Reich if it proceeds reasonably—must be fought absolutely if it is linked with mutiny and perjury. I consider myself in honour bound to defend a government by all means, the policy and the members of which I desire to go to hell. . . . All ensigns and cadets of the Infantry Regiment 12 unitedly support me, so that the regiment has already got the name of being completely under Jewish influence, Red and Spartacist (*den Ruf eines völlig verjudeten roten Spartakistenregiments erhalten hat*). I for my part would never have thought that I could ever get such a name.[1]

[1] Lieutenant Hansjochen Leist to Lieutenant-Colonel von Hammerstein, Munich, 22 Oct. 1923: Nachlaß Schleicher, no. 17 I, Bundesarchiv Koblenz; printed in *Vierteljahrshefte für Zeitgeschichte*, v, 1957, pp. 95–6. The Infantry Regi-

This was the political mood among the young officers, even among those who remained loyal to their oath. For all of them, it was not the conflict between Bavaria and the Reich government that was the central issue, but the struggle against a government which they fervently 'desired to go to hell'. In their hearts they all enthusiastically supported the *völkische* movement.

The officers of the Seventh Division decided to support General von Lossow. Ritter von Mittelberger, at that time commander of a battalion at Bayreuth, recounts in his memoirs that the commanding officers of the Bavarian units conferred in Lossow's presence about the attitude to be taken towards the Bavarian government. Their views differed, but they all realized that the decision of the Bavarian government endangered the unity of Germany. If, on the other hand, the Bavarian Reichswehr developed internal quarrels, the situation would become still more confused and chaos might result; then power would fall into the hands of the more or less illegal *Kampfverbände* and there would be civil war. In that case, too, the unity of Germany would in all probability be destroyed. For this reason all the officers present, with the sole exception of General Freiherr Kreß von Kressenstein, considered it most important that the Bavarian division remained united. They put themselves under Lossow's orders. 'A whole division refused to obey, urged on by patriotic motives. . . .'[1]

On 24 October—in a conference with the leaders of the *vaterländische Verbände* and the Bavarian police—General von Lossow developed his own ideas and aims. He declared:

There are three possibilities:

1. A march on Berlin and a proclamation of the national dictatorship.
2. To muddle through, Bavaria remaining loyal.
3. Separation of Bavaria from Berlin.

For us Bavarians only the first course can be considered. Little time remains to us; as soon as everything is prepared the first course will

ment 12 was the regiment in which von Hammerstein commanded a battalion at Magdeburg, and in which Leist was a lieutenant.

[1] *Vierteljahrshefte für Zeitgeschichte*, v. 97–98. The MS. of Mittelberger's memoirs is in the Bundesarchiv Koblenz. The opinion of Gordon, *Reichswehr and the German Republic*, p. 242, that Lossow 'was also undoubtedly aware of the fact that the 7. Division did not stand united behind him', seems to be questionable.

be taken. . . . I have called you here to ask you how you envisage the build-up and further developments if your *Verbände* take part in the advance. In my opinion the only possibility is that all the *vaterländische Verbände* should be incorporated into the Reichswehr or the police as a reserve of manpower. . . . You will thus see that we stand on the same ground as you, as leaders of the *vaterländische Verbände*, and that we too are working with these aims: we all have one goal, to liberate Germany from Marxism, under the banner of the black, white and red flag. . . .

Then a Bavarian major explained the deployment of the Seventh Division in case of an advance: each battalion was to be supplemented by two battalions of untrained men who were to be recruited from the *Verbände*. General von Lossow asked their leaders which *Verbände* were in favour of incorporation into the Reichswehr, and which desired to remain independent and to equip their own men. Of those present, only *Bayern und Reich*, *Oberland*, and *Hermannsbund* declared in favour of incorporation; the others—*Blücher, Frankenland, Reichsflagge, Stahlhelm*, and *Wiking*—did not want to give up their independence. Hitler's National Socialists were not present. General von Lossow emphasized that the Seventh Division had exposed itself morally: 'if it remains alone it will be finished; but then the *Verbände* will have their necks wrung too. We sit in the same boat. . . .'[1] But his exhortations did not induce the majority of the *Verbände* to subordinate themselves to the Bavarian Reichswehr. Even those that opted in favour of incorporation did so on the condition that they would be taken over in complete formations, e.g. battalions or companies, to preserve their coherence. The others were only willing to serve under their own leaders, or were aiming at the creation of free corps as in 1919.[2] This problem, of first importance, even General von Lossow was unable to solve, not even after his breach with Berlin, and in spite of his repudiation of Bavarian particularism and his emphasis on the common black, white, and red aims of the movement.

Two days later, on 26 October, *Wehrkeiskommando* vii issued orders for the 'autumn manœuvres', which envisaged a rein-

---

[1] 'Niederschrift über die Besprechung im W.K.K. VII', Munich, 24 Oct. 1923: Deuerlein, *Hitler-Putsch*, no. 61, pp. 257–8.

[2] Order of the *Wehrkreiskommando* vii of 26 Oct. 1923: ibid., no. 68, p. 279.

forcement of the division in 'the case of internal unrest': the infantry battalions were to be trebled and many new units were to be formed. In these orders the question whether whole formations of the *Verbände* were to be taken over into the Reichswehr was also of vital importance. General von Lossow was forced to meet the wishes of the *Verbände* to a large extent.

The question whether whole formations (companies, battalions) of the *Verbände* can be taken over depends upon the military coherence and the discipline of the units offered. The *Wehrkreiskommando* therefore abstains from issuing binding instructions on this issue and leaves it to the commanding officers to decide on the methods of forming the new units. . . . Only as an exception can whole battalions of volunteers be incorporated, and only if there is a guarantee that the unit is organized entirely in military fashion and is disciplined. . . . No free corps traits! The formation of free corps must be opposed. . . .

Reinforcements should in the first instance be taken from the *vaterländische Verbände*; their local groups should immediately get in touch with the local Reichswehr commanders and inform them how many recruits they could offer.[1] These rather ambiguous instructions, which left it to the local commanders to reach an agreement with the leaders of the *vaterländische Verbände*, show the difficulties which Lossow had to face. Even in Bavaria the aims of the two sides were by no means identical.

On 30 October the Bavarian government finally refused to cancel the oath to Bavaria which the Seventh Division had taken. Yet the ministry of defence and the army command adhered to the fiction that only the divisional commander was suspended from his duties, and did not stop the money transfers to *Wehrkreis* vii, so that the 'autumn manœuvres' were largely financed by contributions from Berlin.[2] The commanding officer of the infantry school, General von Tieschowitz, explained to the cadets, after his return from an official report to Berlin, that General von Seeckt undoubtedly (!) had the same aims as General Ludendorff (who closely co-operated with Hitler), that neither was a friend of the existing state. Hitler too addressed the cadets, who applauded him enthusiastically. One of his sentences ran: 'The first obligation of your oath,

---

[1] Ibid., no. 68, pp. 277–80.   [2] Hofmann, *Hitlerputsch*, p. 123.

gentlemen, is to break it!' None of the officers in charge of the course objected to this invitation to perjury.[1] In a further conference with the leaders of the *vaterländische Verbände* on 31 October Lossow declared that what was required in the Reich was a dictatorship of Lossow, Seisser, and Hitler, which in Bavaria would be supported by Kahr and Pöhner; but that it was necessary to delay the attack until the situation in central Germany was clear. He obviously expected that Berlin would take strong measures against the governments of Saxony and Thuringia; there the Communists had joined the Social Democrats in forming 'red' governments which organized armed proletarian hundreds. Already Reichswehr units commanded by Lieutenant-General Müller had marched into Saxony and dissolved the proletarian units.[2] As a precautionary measure—to separate Saxony from the Bavarian nationalists—Berlin also ordered units of the Fifth Division to the northern frontier of Bavaria; but these enthusiastically fraternized with the Bavarian nationalists at a *Deutscher Tag* held at Hof. From other quarters too Lossow received favourable reports about the mood of the non-Bavarian Reichswehr units.[3]

Yet the chances of success for the Munich enterprise did depend less upon the attitude of certain Reichswehr units than on that of the chief of the army command. That Seeckt too aimed at a dictatorship and the elimination of parliament was well known in Munich. Hence Colonel von Seisser was sent to Berlin to establish political contacts and to win Seeckt over to the Bavarian side. On his conversation with Seeckt on 3 November Seisser reported: 'I briefly described opinion in Bavaria and Kahr's greater-German objective: creation of a national dictatorship, freed from parliament, able to take ruthless measures against the socialist mess (*Unrat*). Seeckt: "This is my aim too, but for me things are much more difficult than for you in Bavaria." Doubts about Stresemann. Difference in speed, but not in goal. The legal way must be followed. . . .' Seisser also emphasized that 'all patriotic forces in Bavaria'

[1] Hofmann, *Hitlerputsch*, pp. 118, 143.

[2] For details see: H. J. Gordon, 'Die Reichswehr und Sachsen 1923', *Wehrwissenschaftliche Rundschau*, xi, 1961, pp. 677–92; Rosenberg, *Geschichte der Deutschen Republik*, pp. 168–70; W. T. Angress, *Stillborn Revolution*, Princeton, 1963, pp. 429–35, 438–40.

[3] Hofmann, op. cit., pp. 115, 122.

strongly pressed Kahr to march on Berlin, but that Seeckt was distrusted, and a quick solution was essential. When he asked Seeckt whether he intended to advance against Bavaria, he answered: 'I do not repeat the war of 1866, that is out of the question. I shall in no circumstances let myself be used to attack Bavaria with Reichswehr and proletarian hundreds; I had a sharp conflict with Ebert on this issue and told him clearly that I am leader of the Reichswehr, but not of proletarian hundreds, and that I would never let myself be used for such things. The Reichswehr will shortly take measures against Thuringia. . . .'[1] Thus Seeckt refused to leave the path of legality, but at the same time declined to take measures against Bavaria and to obey the titular 'commander-in-chief' of the army. *Vis-à-vis* Saxony and Thuringia he had no such qualms.

At the same time Seeckt wrote to Kahr and explained to him his political principles, his criticisms of the Weimar constitution and the Stresemann government, but also the necessity of following a legal way: in his opinion a departure from this way was fraught with grave dangers and could only be condoned 'in the case of extreme need'. He informed Kahr that he had no confidence in the Stresemann government, that he did not consider it viable, and that he could not guarantee the attitude of the Reichswehr towards it. 'The Reichswehr must not be brought into a position in which it has to fight, for a government which is alien to it, against people who have the same convictions as the army. On the other hand, it cannot permit irresponsible and unauthorized circles to try and bring about a change by force. If the army has to defend the authority of the state on two fronts it will break up. Then we have played the game of France and have offered the last chance of success to Moscovite Communism. . . .'[2] Seeckt's main endeavour was to avoid a military clash in which the Reichswehr might be forced to shoot on men who held the same convictions, in the defence

---

[1] Notes of Colonel von Seisser about his discussions in Berlin on 3 Nov. 1923: Deuerlein, op. cit., no. 79, p. 303. Seisser was a colonel of the Munich police and one of the leading conspirators. The operations of the Reichswehr against Thuringia began on 6 Nov.: Nachlaß Seeckt, no. 281, p. 45, Militärgeschichtliches Forschungsamt.

[2] Seeckt to von Kahr, Berlin, 2 Nov. 1923 (dispatched on 5 Nov.): Nachlaß Seeckt, box 14, no. 154, ibid.; Schüddekopf, *Heer und Republik*, no. 79, pp. 186–9. Cf. above, p. 117.

of a government which in his opinion was alien (*wesensfremd*) to the soldiers. His ideas had not changed since the days of the Kapp Putsch.

Simultaneously Seeckt issued a new warning to the Reichswehr against distrusting its superior officers and disunity in its own ranks. 'A Reichswehr that is united and obedient is invincible and the strongest factor in the state. A Reichswehr split by political cleavages will break in the hour of danger. . . .'[1] But there were deep political cleavages within the Reichswehr, and the generals at least were politically extremely active. In Munich General von Lossow declared on 6 November that the Bavarian division would support any dictatorship of the right if the affair had a reasonable chance of success. 'I ask for confidence. I will not take part in an adventure, but in any enterprise that will bring the desired success, even if the success can only be achieved by a *coup d'état*. . . .'[2] The question arises which of the two generals at that moment more truly represented the mood prevailing in the Reichswehr.

The fight of the Reichswehr 'on two fronts', which Seeckt feared above all, did not take place. No clash occurred between Reichswehr units and the Bavarian nationalists. The energetic measures taken against Saxony and Thuringia deprived the irregular forces, which were assembled on the northern frontier of Bavaria, of the opportunity to march north into Saxony, and from there to Berlin. Ironically enough, it was Hitler who helped to heal the breach between Munich and Berlin by his premature action on 8 November 1923, by his blackmailing tactics towards Kahr, Lossow, and Seisser at the meeting in the Bürgerbräukeller, and by his wild *Putsch*. He aimed at forcing the hesitating Bavarian government into open rebellion against Berlin—and achieved exactly the opposite. It is true that Lossow wavered to the last moment and even accepted the post of minister of defence under the supreme command of Ludendorff. It was not due to him, but to three Bavarian officers who were opposed to his vacillating course, that the forces of the Seventh Division sided against Hitler's *Putsch* and helped to suppress it:

[1] Seeckt's decree to the Reichswehr, Berlin, 4 Nov. 1923: Schüddekopf, op. cit., no. 78, pp. 185–6; Rabenau, *Seeckt*, p. 371.

[2] Lossow at a conference in the Generalstaastskommissariat on 6 Nov. 1923: Hofmann, op. cit., p. 136.

at this critical moment the Major-Generals Ritter von Danner, the commandant of Munich, Freiherr Kreß von Kressenstein, and Ritter von Ruith sided with Seeckt and against Lossow.[1] Within the Seventh Division, however, considerable resistance to this course developed. The fourth company of the Infantry Regiment 19, which had in October been recruited from volunteers, disbanded on its own account on the morning of 9 November, so as not to have to shoot 'on their brothers and friends'. The units sent from Augsburg to help in the suppression of the revolt were only told at Munich station that they had not come to join the 'national revolution and the march on Berlin'. The commandant of the fortress of Ingolstadt, Lieutenant-Colonel Hofmann, even declined to send his battalion to Munich to fight the rebels. As the chief of *Unterland* he was at the same time leader of a *Kampfbund*; his was an interesting case of the complete overlapping between the Reichswehr and the *Verbände*.[2] His refusal to obey orders did not prevent him from remaining the commandant of Ingolstadt until 1925—then apparently he was retired.[3] Other Bavarian units used the opportunity to tear at least the hated black, red, and gold cockades off their caps. The cadets of the infantry school stood completely on Hitler's side. On the evening of 8 November— at the time of the meeting in the Bürgerbräukeller—four cadets reported to General von Tieschowitz that a national government had been formed, with Ludendorff as the supreme commander, and that the school, under the command of Lieutenant Roßbach, was Ludendorff's storm battalion. Reinforced by Roßbach's men they then marched with full equipment and under the swastika flag to the Bürgerbräukeller.[4] *En route* they met General von Lossow, in his car on his way home, who did not attempt to stop them. On the morning of the 9th Hitler spoke to them in stirring terms and exclaimed that it was their patriotic duty to serve under Ludendorff: whoever doubted this should leave the hall, the others should swear

[1] Ibid., p. 175.   [2] Ibid., pp. 191–2, 195.
[3] *Rangliste des Deutschen Reichsheeres nach dem Stande vom 1. Mai 1925*, Berlin, 1925, p. 22. The later *Ranglisten* do not mention Hofmann.
[4] Hofmann, op. cit., p. 171; 'Der Putsch am 8. November 1923, Vorgeschichte und Verlauf', p. 8: Akten der Bayerischen Landespolizei Bamberg, Bund 12, Akt 3, Bayerisches Kriegsarchiv, Munich. The information about the black, red, and gold cockades was given by Archivdirektor Dr. Böhm in Munich.

loyalty to him. Without exception those present took the oath to Ludendorff.[1]

After the defeat of the Hitler Putsch the mantle of Christian charity was put upon the events in Munich, especially the close connexions of the Reichswehr with the para-military organizations. But the happenings in the infantry school were criticized by Seeckt in the sharpest forms. 'He boiled with rage.' The current courses were interrupted, and the whole school was moved from Munich to Dresden.[2] The commanding officer, General von Tieschowitz, was discharged from the army. Seeckt decreed that the cadets, who were sent back to their units, were to undergo there such a rigid training

that they become fully conscious of the stain caused by the failure of an institution of the army, which ought to inculcate a *particularly* strict discipline and a *particularly* strong devotion to duty, if it should not entirely fail to achieve its object. . . . The undoubted commands of duty and the unconditional obedience without which the army becomes an armed band, have succumbed through a weakness of willpower to illegal influences, and disobedience has been suffered with a resignation that evokes echoes of March 1920. The chief pillars of the movement were some lieutenants, that is, soldiers with a service experience of several years. These years have thus not led to the necessary disciplinary stiffening of their immature heads; I must therefore repeat that the educational guidance of young officers and cadets has to be directed much more strongly towards the duty of unconditional obedience than seems to have been the case, at least partly. . . .[3]

Four weeks later Seeckt's indignation burst forth again in a second decree:

The incredible occurrence unfortunately gives a bad testimonial to the internal value of school discipline. It forces me to employ the entire officer personnel of the school in a different capacity, if the behaviour of the individual officer permits it to retain him in the service. . . . We have not understood yet how to instruct our young officers and our cadets in the most elementary principles of true

[1] Hofmann, op. cit., pp. 171, 195.

[2] Rabenau, *Seeckt*, pp. 378–9.

[3] Reichswehrministerium, Heeresleitung, Berlin, 15 Nov. 1923: Wehrmachtabteilung, Nachrichtenstelle, Geheim-Akten betr. Verschiedenes: microfilm, roll 52, in Institut für Zeitgeschichte.

discipline; but in the older officers too the old tradition of duty has been shaken. Without any resistance the mass of the cadets follows an adventurer . . . and almost without resistance the superior officers allow the command to be taken from their hands. Like a rock the 7th Division stands behind its leaders; it does not waver, although it was exposed to the same blandishments, and like straw in the wind the loyalty of the infantry school is blown away. . . . The behaviour of the infantry school on 8 and 9 November 1923 is a stain on the honour of the young army.[1]

Remarkable in the decree is the warmth with which Seeckt defended the Seventh Division—the same division which he had virtually encouraged to mutiny against General von Lossow.

Seeckt was even prepared to submit to the president Lossow's proposal for the settlement of the conflict between Bavaria and the Reich. According to this, Munich would declare the oath of loyalty, which the Seventh Division had rendered to the Bavarian state, expired, provided that 'the Lossow case' was tacitly settled. To this, however, Seeckt added a characteristic marginal note: 'Tacitly?—Impossible!' In Seeckt's opinion, Ebert had issued a binding order by which Lossow was deprived of his command. This order could not be 'tacitly' disregarded, but had to be revoked. Seeckt was willing to desist from his intention that Lossow should be discharged on 31 January 1924. But he considered it inevitable that Lossow should leave the service: in fact he remained at his post for another few months and was then retired.[2] The new commanding officer of the Seventh Division and commander-in-chief in Bavaria was Freiherr Kreß von Kressenstein, who was promoted lieutenant-general—the only Bavarian general who throughout the Bavarian crisis had always sided with Seeckt. Never again was the Bavarian Reichswehr to follow a policy of its own, directed against Berlin. The Bavarian officers, who later rose to the highest ranks in the German army, held views which were virtually identical with those of their Prussian counterparts.

[1] Reichswehrministerium, Heeresleitung, Berlin, 12 Dec. 1923: ibid. Printed very incompletely by Rabenau, *Seeckt*, p. 379, with the footnote to the word 'adventurer': 'This means Roßbach.' (!).

[2] Ibid., pp. 380–1; Gordon, *Reichswehr and the German Republic*, p. 249.

IV. *Executive Power in the Hands of Seeckt*

The outbreak of the Hitler Putsch in Munich had a decisive influence on Seeckt's whole position. As early as the night of 8 to 9 November Stresemann called a meeting of the cabinet in which Seeckt took part. In Berlin it was believed, when the first news of the revolt arrived from Munich, that the long-announced march on the capital had begun, that Bavaria was separating from Germany, and that the Bavarian Reichswehr sided with the rebels. In the car which took him to the Wilhelmstraße Seeckt told his adjutant: 'Curious things are happening in Munich. I am no longer the chief of the army command; that is Lossow. Ludendorff is minister of defence. . . .'[1] When a Bavarian officer at Bayreuth succeeded in establishing telephonic contact with the ministry of defence in Berlin, the officer to whom he spoke, Lieutenant-Colonel von Stülpnagel, at first refused to believe that Lossow and the Bavarian Reichswehr declined to participate in the *Putsch*. 'Stülpnagel told me that the ministry of defence had reliable reports about the fraternization of the Bavarian Reichswehr with Hitler. Finally I succeeded in convincing him that Berlin was wrongly informed. . . .' Stülpnagel went immediately to Seeckt and told him the news. 'About an hour later Seeckt sent his thanks to me. My report had been of great importance to the Reich government and to him. . . .' Later Schleicher told the same officer that his report took an enormous weight off Seeckt's shoulders; he could now point to the fact that the Bavarian troops stood behind him. 'His position was thus strengthened to such an extent that the president, with the agreement of the members of the cabinet, transferred executive powers to him in place of Geßler. . . .'[2]

In fact, Ebert proclaimed a state of emergency and transferred executive powers to Seeckt in the cabinet meeting held during the night of 8 to 9 November, and also the supreme command over the entire *Wehrmacht*, which was a prerogative

[1] Rabenau, *Seeckt*, p. 373.

[2] Hilmar Ritter von Mittelberger, 'Lebenserinnerungen', MS. in Bundesarchiv Koblenz; printed in *Vierteljahrshefte für Zeitgeschichte*, v, 1957, pp. 99–101. What Mittelberger does not explain is how he knew at that hour that Lossow was against the *Putsch* and that the Bavarian Reichswehr was *not* fraternizing with Hitler.

of the president; Seeckt was to take all measures required for the safety of the Reich.[1] Thus Seeckt's power was considerably greater than Geßler's had been. Geßler possessed no real power and depended on the support of the chief of the army command. Seeckt combined all the decisive functions in his hands, although the hated Stresemann was still chancellor. But the situation had also changed in a tactical sense. During the past weeks Seeckt had continuously played with the idea of a change in the constitution, of a dictatorship to be established 'by legal means', and had busily negotiated about it with the circles of the right. Now a dictatorship was established legally—on the basis of article 48 of the constitution—and Seeckt had to use his new powers to suppress the revolt in Munich and all attempts at revolution, 'at the behest and in the name of the republic and its constitution, which he repudiated . . .'.[2] It is true that Ebert transferred power to a declared enemy of the republic and of its constitution; but his was a masterly move, which frustrated all the plans directed against the constitution. Seeckt received power 'by legal means, as had always been his goal; but now he was no longer pleased with his success. In the way in which it had come about he certainly had not aspired to power'.[3]

Seeckt quickly liquidated the Munich *Putsch* and the conflict with the Bavarian Reichswehr. On 15 November the *Wehrkreiskommando* vii ordered the 'autumn manœuvres' and the training of members of the *vaterländische Verbände* to be stopped and forbade any recruiting for the Bavarian Reichswehr.[4] Short-term volunteers, however, were also required in northern Germany on account of the operations against Saxony and Thuringia. Hence 'reliable volunteers' were recruited, among whom there 'were naturally (!) also a large number of members of the nationalist *Verbände* . . .'.[5] When the second battalion of Infantry Regiment 12 was sent from Quedlinburg in central

[1] Rabenau, *Seeckt*, pp. 375–6.   [2] Hofmann, *Hitlerputsch*, p. 218.
[3] Rabenau *Seeckt*, p. 376.
[4] Notes of General Lieber on the Bavarian crisis, p. 64: Nachlaß Seeckt, box 19, no. 281, Militärgeschichtliches Forschungsamt.
[5] 'Vortragsnotizen betr. Verfahren wegen Landesverrat gegen Redakteur des Vorwärts auf Grund des Artikels 'Fort mit dem Ausnahmezustand' vom 25. Dezember 1923', Berlin, 4 June 1924: Nachlaß Schleicher, no. 32, Bundesarchiv Koblenz.

Germany to Saxony, its barracks were handed over to a unit which mainly consisted of *Stahlhelm* members, with whom 'considerable difficulties' developed later,[1] probably because they had joined the Reichswehr for their own political ends. Lieutenant-General Müller, the commanding officer in Saxony, expressed to a visitor his pride 'in the system of volunteers for four weeks and in the fact that *vaterländische* sports clubs kept lists of young men which allowed them to be called up!—Not only Severing has "political children"! . . .'. General Müller also mentioned his concern at the arduous duties imposed upon his troops; their discipline was bound to decline in the long run, and they could not bear the state of emergency much longer.[2]

In his new position Seeckt was more directly concerned with political questions than he had been prior to 8 November. On the 12th he wrote to one of his former chiefs: 'A crazy time, in which I am busy with all sorts of things, for which you did not train me at the time. . . . Today I am printing money and a newspaper. . . .'[3] One political problem remained of cardinal importance to Seeckt: to find a suitable successor to Stresemann, who was still chancellor. On 17 November Ebert suggested the name of Albert, another deputy of the German People's Party, and Seeckt had to give his opinion. Ebert favoured a termination of Seeckt's emergency powers as far as Prussia was concerned. 'This would have undermined Seeckt's position, particularly since he aimed at removing the Social Democratic government of Prussia.' On this issue a clash occurred on the following day between Ebert and Seeckt, who sharply contradicted the president; no agreement was reached. Albert refused the proffered chancellorship. Seeckt and Hasse then tried in vain to find another candidate; Hasse was in favour of Seeckt himself. Stresemann, to keep himself in office, wanted to abrogate the emergency powers altogether; but this Hasse believed to be 'impossible if Geßler and Seeckt remain firm'. On 22 November—the day of Stresemann's resignation— Seeckt again conferred with Ebert, but no settlement emerged.

[1] *Das 12. Infanterie-Regiment der Deutschen Reichswehr 1.1.1921 bis 1.10.1934*, Osterwieck/Harz, 1939, p. 53.

[2] Freiherr von Maltzahn to Count Westarp, Oberlößnitz-Radebeul, 1 Dec. 1923: Nachlaß Graf Westarp, Gärtringen.

[3] Seeckt to General von Kraewel, 12 Nov. 1923: Rabenau, *Seeckt*, p. 382.

Seeckt declined to comply with Ebert's wish that the executive powers should be handed to a minister responsible to parliament. Hasse hoped that a government would emerge 'as we desire it; without Seeckt this cannot be done'.[1] On the same day Seeckt wrote to his wife: 'I am just coming from the president, who is also working on the formation of the new cabinet. We did not part in peace: who knows whether you will perhaps find me unemployed when you come back. I have become too powerful for him, that is certain, and he wants to intercept me in good time, not to eliminate me, but to take me down a peg. Well—that we shall see about. . . .'[2]

About the smouldering conflict between the president and Seeckt his adjutant wrote at the end of November:

Does Seeckt prepare for the final struggle? Now I know that he does.—The struggle is: Seeckt *contra* Ebert.—During all these years of parliamentarianism, which Seeckt hates, and of the continuous cabinet crises, which Seeckt finds so undignified, he stood by Ebert out of well-conceived prudence, always with the one thought: one day my time will come. Thereby he undoubtedly strengthened Ebert's position, who needed a power behind him. This he found in the Reichswehr.—Thus the two, Ebert and Seeckt, pushed each other upwards.—For each needed the other. And the power of the Reichswehr grew too. . . . The president put the responsibility for the state on the shoulders of Seeckt, thus on the army. But therewith he delivered himself into the hands of the army, and so of Seeckt. Will he strike now? His goal is so near! . . .[3]

At the same time Hasse wrote that the right was beginning to lose confidence in Seeckt. 'They expected more activity from him, and without doubt it could be greater. I am not disappointed because I did not expect more.' Apparently Hasse knew Seeckt better than his adjutant. It is clear that the officers, who were Seeckt's closest collaborators, were getting depressed by his constant hesitations.[4]

---

[1] Notes of General Lieber on the Bavarian crisis, pp. 50–51, under 17, 18, 21, and 22 Nov. 1923, with quotations from Hasse's diary: Nachlaß Seeckt, box 19, no. 281, loc. cit.

[2] Seeckt to his wife, Berlin, 22 Nov. 1923: Nachlaß Seeckt, roll 28, microfilm in Institut für Zeitgeschichte.

[3] Diary of Seeckt's adjutant von Selchow, under 27 Nov. 1923: Nachlaß Seeckt, no. 289, p. 11, ibid.

[4] Notes of General Lieber on the Bavarian crisis, p. 51, under 29 Nov. 1923, with quotation from Hasse's diary: Nachlaß Seeckt, box 19, no. 281, loc. cit.

In the new government, which was formed by the chairman of the Catholic Centre Party, Wilhelm Marx, Seeckt—contrary to his own hopes—did not receive a post; nor was he consulted about the choice of the new chancellor.[1] Perhaps he hoped that the government of the 'good little chancellor'[2] would not last long and that then his own hour would come. It was in vain that the former General von Morgen addressed a passionate appeal to Seeckt: 'You have a power in your hands and such a chance of using it as hardly any German general before you has possessed. Seldom has a personality in German history stood before tasks of such magnitude, seldom before such enormous difficulties. But these you will overcome, of that I am convinced. And when the sacred hour arrives it will be as in 1813: "they all, all came". . . .' At the same time General von Morgen submitted to Seeckt a political programme which was, above all, directed against the government of Prussia—a problem which also occupied Seeckt: 'Therewith I come to the focal point of my letter: the national life can only revive if the administrative posts in the states, especially in Prussia, are occupied by men with national convictions. The international parasites (*Krippenfresser*) must disappear; then their influence on the masses will end; then the *Wehrmacht* will be reinforced by 150,000 reliable men of the militarized police. . . .'[3]

Only eight days later Seeckt received a memorandum on the situation in Prussia written by the deputy mayor of Königsberg, Goerdeler, who was a member of the German Nationalist Party; it probably advocated the amalgamation of the ministries of the Reich with those of Prussia.[4] At Seeckt's instruction Schleicher replied and advocated that the separate states and provinces should be transformed into autonomous administrative areas of the Reich, while the latter should confine itself to foreign policy, the preservation of a uniform administration

---

[1] Notes of General Lieber, p. 51, under 24 Nov. 1923; Gordon, op. cit., p. 355.

[2] Thus Seeckt to his wife on 13 Jan. 1924: Rabenau, *Seeckt*, p. 392.

[3] General von Morgen to Seeckt, Lübeck, 29 Nov. 1923: Nachlaß Seeckt, box 10, no. 72, Militärgeschichtliches Forschungsamt Freiburg; Rabenau, *Seeckt*, p. 388.

[4] See Gerhard Ritter, *Carl Goerdeler und die deutsche Widerstandsbewegung*, Stuttgart, 1954, p. 37.

in vital fields, and the handling of the necessary means of power. To Seeckt this was 'a question of the existence of the German nation and the only way of conducting power politics . . .'.[1] The ideas he had in mind emerged more clearly from a memorandum on 'Prussia and the Reich' that he wrote six weeks later. In it Seeckt demanded above all 'a strong Prussia which also exercised the powers of the Reich'. Most of the other German states should disappear, and only the south-German states should remain:

There are three kinds of states within the Reich; those which persevere and still have sufficient strength to continue their existence, but no prospect of a further development; those which have no right to exist; and one which contains the germs of growth. To the first kind belong Bavaria, Württemberg, Baden; to the second all other German states; the third is Prussia. The states, which possess no vitality and have no right to exist, must be absorbed by Prussia. . . . The two states, whose absorption by Prussia would be the biggest step forward and would cause least resistance, are Saxony and Thuringia. Both states have proved during the past year that they are unable to live. . . . At the head of the Reich stands the state president, who is elected by Prussia. . . . He appoints the prime minister of Prussia, who is also the chancellor. Under him are the two Reich ministries of foreign affairs and of defence. . . .[2]

What Seeckt aimed at was again not a federal, but a centralist solution, as Groener had advocated in 1919.[3] The smaller states would have disappeared, and Prussia would have become the dominating power in Germany; the majority of the Prussian offices would be combined with those of the Reich; the old dualism between them would be eliminated. Furthermore, the Social Democrats would be deprived of their positions in Prussia, Saxony, and Thuringia: the last two had 'proved that they were unable to live', apparently because radical left-wing governments had been formed there. Thus many of the political wishes of the army command would have been fulfilled at one stroke.

[1] Notes of General Lieber on the Bavarian crisis, p. 61, under 7 and 18 Dec. 1923: Nachlaß Seeckt, box 19, no. 281, loc. cit.

[2] Ibid., p. 4, under 5 Feb. *1924*; memorandum of 4 Feb. 1924: Rabenau, *Seeckt*, pp. 394–6. Very similar ideas were expressed in a memorandum written by Captain Marcks and printed in the defence ministry on 12 Aug. 1924: Schüddekopf, *Heer und Republik*, no. 83, pp. 201–3. For Seeckt's ideas on the subject in Oct. 1923, see above, p. 167.   [3] See above, pp. 34, 44.

Yet politics were to remain a prerogative of the army command itself, while the other generals were expressly warned not to engage in politics. At the same time Seeckt issued a decree to the divisional commanders who exercised—under him—the executive power in their areas of command. 'The exercise of executive powers has brought most of the senior leaders of the Reichswehr into close contact with politics. It is up to them to prove that this does not endanger the work of recent years, to transform the Reichswehr into an instrument of the policy of the Reich that stands above party and above the political conflicts. When he wields executive powers the Reichswehr leader does not become a politician, but he remains a soldier and acts . . . solely for the good of the whole state, the executive organ of which he is, favouring neither parties nor economic groups. . . .'[1]

The divisional commanders were in no way prepared for their new tasks and had little understanding of political questions. Their political ideals were those of the Hohenzollern Empire, while the new republican world was alien to them. Among the parties, the German Nationalist Party was closest to them; it was largely led by members of the nobility and former officers. When in November 1923 a representative of this party visited Lieutenant-General Müller, the commanding officer of *Wehrkreis* iv (Saxony), to put to him the wishes of his party with regard to ministerial and other appointments, he found the general very friendly and pleased about this approach.

I talked to him about the political situation and found to my surprise that he as well as his chief of staff, although men of national convictions, show a regrettable—and even in officers surprising—lack of understanding of political causalities and developments, in home as well as in foreign affairs. The commander gave the impression of a man who is very uncertain and undecided; with all the plenary powers he possesses he does not seem to have sufficient authority; he has to report all trifles to Berlin and get instructions from there; this probably explains his lack of initiative and his reluctance to take energetic measures on his own. It is the same mistake as made me suffer so often during the war: we were condemned to dependence on others, received orders from higher

[1] Der Chef der Heeresleitung, T 1 III, Berlin, 31 Jan. 1924: Wehrmacht-abteilung, Nachrichtenstelle, Geheim-Akten betr. Verschiedenes: Akten des Reichs-wehrministeriums, roll 52, microfilm in Institut für Zeitgeschichte.

quarters, at the receipt of which the situation had already changed, or the moment to act on one's own responsibility had passed. That was the system of Ludendorff which Seeckt seems to have inherited as a politician. . . .[1]

General Müller asked his visitor to come and see him frequently, but said he should always announce himself as 'general' so that nobody would suspect that he had political contacts.

At the end of 1923 Major von Schleicher summarized 'the successes hitherto achieved as follows: transfer of emergency powers to Seeckt, enterprises against Thuringia and Saxony, removal of the Social Democrats from the Reich government, beginning of an economic improvement and of a decline of prices. . . .'[2] Indeed, the position of the army was stronger than ever before. Seeckt stood at the pinnacle of his power. Yet Schleicher's last words indicated the change that was just starting. The inflation was virtually over, the economic crisis was abating. The separatist attempts in Bavaria and the Rhineland had failed, exactly as had the Communist uprising in Hamburg. In Saxony the Communists shrank from issuing the call to revolt. The whole political situation of Germany began to change: the struggle over the Ruhr was drawing to a close; a settlement of the Reparations question was in sight. An improvement set in which was to continue during the following years. But this also meant that the state of emergency and the transfer of executive powers to Seeckt were beginning to lose their justification. The question was how long they could be maintained without provoking new political difficulties; that question was to be decided during the following weeks.

'There can be no doubt that the Reichswehr was the cement which held the Reich intact during the dark days of 1923', an American historian has asserted recently.[3] But who threatened Germany's unity in 1923? In the first instance the separatists in Bavaria and in the Rhineland. But the Reichswehr was not used to defeat either movement. The Rhenish separatists were so

---

[1] Freiherr von Maltzahn, a former major-general, to Count Westarp, Oberlößnitz-Radebeul, 1 Dec. 1923: Nachlaß Graf Westarp, Gärtringen.

[2] Notes of General Lieber on the Bavarian crisis, p. 52, under 7 Dec. 1923: Nachlaß Seeckt, box 19, no. 281, loc. cit. On 23 Dec. 1923 Schleicher was prematurely promoted lieutenant-colonel: ibid., p. 55.

[3] Gordon, *Reichswehr and the German Republic*, p. 254, and similarly Rabenau, *Seeckt*, p. 400.

obviously a tool of French policy that they were repudiated by the large majority of the local population. With the collapse of Poincaré's policy, which aimed at a dismemberment of Germany, the separatists' short-lived rule also vanished. The Reichswehr could not contribute towards this as it was not allowed to enter the occupied area. The Bavarian separatists became a real danger through their co-operation with the Bavarian Reichswehr, which supplied them with arms and trained them. If both had unitedly marched north, as was expected for weeks, the non-Bavarian units would have had to show whether 'Reichswehr would fire on Reichswehr'. According to the experiences of the Kapp Putsch, it can hardly be assumed that Seeckt would have given such an order. The fraternization of units of the Fifth Division—and that was the division of Reinhardt—with the Bavarian nationalists[1] clearly indicated that the troops too would be unwilling to carry out such an order. It was Hitler who freed Seeckt from this quandary. But even the Hitler Putsch on 9 November was not suppressed by units of the Reichswehr, but by the Bavarian police, while enthusiastic young Reichswehr soldiers marched with Hitler.

The other threat to the unity of Germany came from the Communists, and against them the Reichswehr was used in Saxony, Thuringia, and Hamburg. Yet even if one puts the chances of a Communist revolution in Germany in 1923 high, it did not so much threaten Germany's unity as the existing constitution and social order. But the Communist rising in Hamburg remained isolated and was quickly suppressed. No attempt at revolution was made in either Saxony or Thuringia; the governments there, which were removed by the Reichswehr, were left-socialist led and did not threaten the Reich. When some years later National Socialist governments were formed in Thuringia and in Brunswick, nobody dreamt of using the Reichswehr against them, although they threatened law and order much more seriously than the left governments of 1923. The existing order was above all threatened by the vast inflation, which destroyed all bonds and caused chaotic conditions, and naturally the Reichswehr could not contribute anything to the fight against inflation.

[1] See above, p. 180.

The transfer of political power to General von Seeckt in November 1923 was perhaps a political necessity, and it certainly helped to calm the excitement and unrest reigning in Germany. As has been shown above, it was also a tactical master-stroke which deprived Seeckt of the chance to act against the constitution. But the unity of Germany was preserved by the decision of the three Bavarian generals to oppose Hitler and their own commanding general. From that moment the attempt was doomed to failure. The shots from the rifles of the Bavarian police at the Odeonsplatz in Munich sufficed to banish the spectre of civil war. To that outcome Seeckt contributed nothing. But his never-ending intrigues against Stresemann seriously weakened the position of the German government at a time when every patriotic German ought to have tried to strengthen it. It seems that Seeckt was more interested in gaining power himself; but it might perhaps be said in exculpation that to him the interests of Germany were identical with his own.

V

THE END OF THE SEECKT ERA

1. *Termination of the State of Emergency*

THE president was not the only man who wanted to terminate the state of emergency and the executive powers entrusted to Seeckt in November 1923; with the return of more normal conditions the senior officers too became disinclined to defend the republic in this way. In the defence ministry the Lieutenant-Colonels von Schleicher and von Stülpnagel were of the opinion that the emergency powers of article 48 could not be used indefinitely, 'and that the soldiers would make themselves ridiculous'.[1] On 1 February 1924 the commanding officer of *Wehrkreis* ii, General von Tschischwitz, also reported to Seeckt that the state of emergency was gradually wearing thin. Hasse suggested to Seeckt that he should discuss the question with Ebert: it was important that 'Seeckt and the president saw eye to eye on this'. On the following day Seeckt submitted his suggestions to Ebert: the state of emergency should only be continued in Bavaria, Saxony, and Thuringia. Ebert agreed and proposed that the army command should make a corresponding move about four weeks before the coming elections to the Reichstag.[2]

In fact this development took place much more quickly. The letter to the president about the rescinding of the state of emergency was dispatched as early as 13 February, stating: 'the authority of the state has been strengthened to such an extent that the recovery of our political and economic life, which has begun under the state of emergency, can continue without it. . . .' Accordingly, it was lifted as from 1 March 1924.[3] The right-wing parties severely criticized this decision. Crown

---

[1] Stülpnagel to Rabenau, 16 Apr. 1940: Nachlaß Seeckt, no. 287, p. 16, Militärgeschichtliches Forschungsamt Freiburg.

[2] Notes of General Lieber on the Bavarian crisis, p. 2, under 1–4 Feb. *1924*: Nachlaß Seeckt, no. 281, ibid. The Reichstag elections were held on 5 May 1924.

[3] Ibid., under 13 Feb. 1924; Rabenau, *Seeckt*, p. 397.

Prince Wilhelm wrote to General Reinhardt: 'I consider the termination of the state of emergency at the present time a somewhat daring experiment. I do not know the reasons which have induced His Excellency von Seeckt to take this decision, hence I cannot judge whether it is justified. . . .'[1] The German Nationalist newspaper, the *Kreuzzeitung*, attacked Seeckt so sharply on this issue that he requested the party leader, Count Westarp, to visit him. In their conversation Seeckt emphasized that he had proposed the lifting of the state of emergency on his own initiative, and to the surprise of the president and the chancellor; the Reichswehr had been unable to fulfil any longer the tasks imposed upon it by the state of emergency, particularly the prohibition of newspapers and meetings which it involved; this had imposed a political responsibility upon the army which it could not carry. If the need for public order made the reimposition of the state of emergency necessary, this should be envisaged. For the time being he believed it expedient to let the coming election campaign take place under normal conditions. He strongly denied the charge that he had retreated before the Social Democrats, to whom his step was 'very inconvenient'. Westarp replied that the German Nationalist Party was rather disappointed: they had expected that, if parliament by a majority decided to rescind the state of siege, he would refuse his consent, and bring about a conflict. Seeckt answered that this would have been possible; but in his opinion it was advisable that the elections should take place without a conflict.[2]

The hopes of the right that Seeckt would steer a course in its favour had once more been disappointed. Hasse thought 'that Seeckt was too soft towards Ebert. Perhaps he wanted to preserve his strength for the presidency. . . . On the other hand, Seeckt has made enemies of the ultra-right circles, even though he needs their support. There was always the danger that the influential position of the Reichswehr would suffer. . . .'[3] Thus Seeckt gave up the political power which he had wielded under the state of emergency, without rendering any serious opposition.

[1] Crown Prince Wilhelm to Reinhardt, Schloß Oels, 29 Feb. 1924: Nachlaß Reinhardt, Hauptstaatsarchiv Stuttgart.
[2] Count Westarp to von Brandenstein, Berlin, 22 Feb. 1924, and Westarp's notes of 23 Feb.: Nachlaß Graf Westarp, Gärtringen.
[3] Notes of General Lieber, p. 2, under 14 Feb. 1924: loc. cit.

He certainly did not do so out of devotion to the constitution or to the president, who desired a return to more normal forms of government; but perhaps Seeckt was unable to do anything with his power in the form in which he had received it.

When Seeckt was later asked, by someone close to him, whether it had not been a grave mistake to let power slip from his hands, he merely replied: 'Perhaps?'[1] In a memorandum about the state of emergency composed in February 1924 he wrote: 'It is not the function of the *Wehrmacht* to take on the responsibility for matters of day-to-day administration for a longer period. . . .'[2] That was certainly correct, but does not answer the above question. Some of his subordinates, too, were unconvinced that he had acted rightly. Six months later Lieutenant-Colonel Freiherr von Fritsch wrote to Stülpnagel: 'It will be very difficult for S. to put things right again now, since he has voluntarily relinquished the power which he held during the winter of 1923–24. . . .'[3] Probably Hasse, who knew Seeckt intimately, was right when he connected the lifting of the state of emergency with Seeckt's desire to become president when Ebert's term of office expired. Thus Seeckt's political ambitions again played a decisive part.

11. *The Army and the Great Political Issues*

The question which at this time became of central importance, also in discussions at the ministry of defence, was whether Germany should become a member of the League of Nations. 'Seeckt from the outset was not in favour. His reasons were difficult to understand. The most important probably was an indefinable feeling that it would be better for Germany not to join. When the question was being discussed, Seeckt very often did not speak against it, but listened quietly, and in the end would not give his consent. A further reason was perhaps that the Russians indicated that they would regard it as a violation of the Treaty of Rapallo if Germany joined the League of Nations. . . .'[4] To Seeckt, good political and military relations with Russia were of cardinal importance. Seeckt's closest

---

[1] Rabenau, *Seeckt*, p. 400.   [2] Ibid., p. 398, n. 2.

[3] Fritsch to Joachim von Stülpnagel, Königsberg, 24 Aug. 1924: Depot Stülpnagel, H 08–5/20, Bundesarchiv-Militärarchiv.

[4] Rabenau, *Seeckt*, p. 407, after his own contemporary notes.

collaborators were not united on this question. One of them, Lieutenant-Colonel von Stülpnagel, in February 1924 wrote a detailed memorandum, 'the security of France', in which he stated:

As Britain at the moment is neither able to wage war, nor willing to do so, she sees in the League of Nations the means of making France pliant. . . . To obtain for herself a dominating role in the League of Nations, she urges Russia and Germany to join it, and hopes to gain a majority, with the help of Russia, Germany, and Italy, against France with her satellites. . . . France aims and will always aim at the final destruction of Germany as a power. When France has become undisputedly the preponderant power on the Continent after the destruction of Germany, she will not hesitate any longer to fight Britain openly. . . . For both, Germany is merely an object. Britain wants to 'Austrianize' Germany under her influence, France wants to destroy Germany. . . .

In addition, it is the duty of the soldier as the guardian of the national conscience to see to it that a government which is influenced by economic and pacifist ideas does not betray the future of the nation for a dish of lentils of physical saturation. The same fears for the national future of Germany are aroused by the idea of a European corporation of the nations—a federal system of all European states—which is propagated today by the democratic side. This idea too can hinder a healthy national development and the military strengthening of the German nation. Germany must die if the pacifist and democratic ideology becomes stronger! Versailles was a wrong built on lies: this must be expunged one day by force through a military co-operation of all forces—unless France gives way first, rights the wrong, and reaches agreements with us which do not hinder our national development. This, however, cannot be expected and would be against the meaning of Franco-German history. Germany must exploit the conflicts between Britain and France, which in the long run cannot abate; she must not mitigate them by sacrificing her own interests, but must on the contrary sharpen them, so that the impression is created abroad that not Germany, but France, is responsible, if the British proposals for a League of Nations, disarmament, and economic pacification cannot be realized. If we succeed in this, Britain will in the long run only be able to obtain her aims vis-à-vis France by force of arms at the side of Germany. To work towards this should be the duty of German diplomacy, and is the task of the soldier.[1]

[1] Memorandum of Joachim von Stülpnagel of 20 Feb. 1924: Nachlaß Schleicher, no. 26, Bundesarchiv Koblenz. Stülpnagel then was the chief of the army department (T 1) within the *Truppenamt*.

In a lecture to the officers of the defence ministry, too, Stülpnagel spoke about the political, economic, and moral preconditions of the 'war of liberation' and criticized the lack of the will
to fight on the part of the government: it should be its task—
after the example of Prussia in 1813—to inculcate the nation
with the 'categorical imperative' of fighting and dying for the
fatherland.[1] The same ideas were expressed in a much more
primitive fashion by Lieutenant-General von Loßberg, the
commanding officer of *Wehrkreis* vi: 'One day the time will
come, the day of reckoning with those who torment us. I am
not a pacifist. If I as a general were a pacifist I ought to be
strung up. I am a resolute man who holds that we must show
our teeth to our tormentors, even if it should end in a war of
desperation. . . .'[2] In East Prussia it was the chief of staff of the
First Division, Lieutenant-Colonel Freiherr von Fritsch, who
openly preached the war of revenge against France; while
another officer of the *Wehrkreiskommando* attacked the 'Jewish
republic'.[3]

On the issue of whether Germany should join the League of
Nations a new clash developed between Seeckt and Stresemann,
who remained foreign minister when his government was overthrown. Seeckt opposed Germany's entry, above all because he
feared that the League would prevent Germany's rearmament.
In October 1924 he wrote a memorandum which pointed out
'that the military control by the League of Nations would
presumably, under the influence of France, be stricter than
hitherto, even if the Interallied Control Commission were
abolished. If Germany entered the League of Nations, it could
not reject its plan of control. . . .'[4] Such a control was particularly disagreeable to Seeckt at that time 'because of the aug-
mentation of the army which had taken place'—the volunteers
recruited during the state of emergency. On 26 August Seeckt
had a discussion lasting two and a half hours with the chancellor

[1] Sauer, 'Die Mobilmachung der Gewalt', in *Die nationalsozialistische Machtergreifung*, Cologne and Opladen, 1960, p. 774.

[2] Loßberg on 21 Jan. 1924: Schüddekopf, *Heer und Republik*, no. 84, p. 204.

[3] Memorandum of the ex-Major Riecker, late 1925: ibid., no. 87, p. 208. It
does not mention Fritsch's name, but only the Ia of the First Division: but that
was Fritsch, according to the *Rangliste des Deutschen Reichsheeres nach dem Stande vom
1. April 1924*, p. 9, and *vom 1. Mai 1925*, p. 9.

[4] Notes of General Lieber, p. 21, under 31 Oct. 1924: Nachlaß Seeckt, no. 281,
loc. cit.; ibid. the following quotation.

and the foreign minister about the military control; 'it was extremely difficult and at times very heated. The situation is very disagreeable and hard to judge. . . .'[1] The conflict between Seeckt and Stresemann became so bitter that once more Seeckt's resignation was considered likely.[2]

From Königsberg Fritsch wrote anxiously to Stülpnagel:

A few days ago I heard from a source which must be taken seriously that the position of Seeckt has been strongly undermined. Forces are at work (Stresemann etc.) which with all their strength are trying to eliminate him. He is to be replaced by a genuine democrat and pacifist. . . . In connexion with the negotiations in London and the creation of the *Reichsbanner Schwarz Rot Gold* by the Social Democrats I consider these things very remarkable. Independently of this news I have gained the impression that the left is planning a full-scale attack against the national spirit, so as to achieve the final victory of the international idea—capitalism, socialism, and pacifism. . . .[3]

At about the same time Seeckt and Schleicher were attempting to influence the right-wing parties in favour of moderation, in particular to persuade the German Nationalist Party to enter the government and to accept the Dawes Plan, which settled the German Reparations payments. At the end of May 1924 Seeckt had a conference with the leaders of the German Nationalist and the German People's parties, 'to influence them towards co-operation in the formation of the government. Schleicher has prepared everything behind the scenes, but the German Nationalists in the end declined. Hasse still hopes that they will enter a bourgeois government. . . .'[4] In August Seeckt again tried to persuade the German Nationalists to vote for the acceptance of the Dawes Plan. He reckoned that a section of them 'will become reasonable'; but on the following day he had to report that things looked less favourable—an opinion that was confirmed to him by the well-known historian and nationalist deputy, Professor Hoetzsch. On 29 August the

---

[1] Seeckt to his wife, Berlin, 26 Aug. 1924: Nachlaß Seeckt, roll 28, p. 279, microfilm in Institut für Zeitgeschichte.

[2] Rabenau, *Seeckt*, p. 407.

[3] Fritsch to Joachim von Stülpnagel, Königsberg, 24 Aug. 1924: Depot Stülpnagel, H 08–5/20, Bundesarchiv-Militärarchiv.

[4] Notes of General Lieber, p. 8, under 26 May 1924: Nachlaß Seeckt, no. 281, loc. cit.

Reichstag accepted the Dawes Plan: Seeckt considered that 'reason had triumphed'. The German Nationalists, however, were divided: only 48 of their deputies voted in favour, while 52, with the party's leaders, voted against—not a great success after Seeckt's efforts. Yet he believed that now there was 'the possibility of a further development. . . . The credit for this belongs mainly to Schleicher, who was on guard in the Reichstag today from 9 to 4.30. In the last resort it was a fight between two people who were not on the stage: on the one side Ebert, on the other someone whose name fortunately has not yet been mentioned by the newspapers. . . .' The result of a negative vote by the Reichstag would have been its dissolution—and that would have supplied the left with an excellent slogan for the elections; the outcome would have been bad in any case.[1]

Three months later this policy was still defended by Lieutenant-Colonel von Stülpnagel in a letter to his friend Fritsch, who had criticized it.

> With regard to the Dawes Plan and the entry of the German Nationalists into the government [Stülpnagel wrote], I defend the policy of Schleicher, for I agree with it. If the German Nationalists had unitedly voted for acceptance, in spite of all their reservations, and had not made themselves so ridiculous . . . they could have formed the government. As long as we must reckon with a parliament, this must be our aim. The rigid opposition of the German Nationalists during the past years has in my opinion not achieved anything. Their fear of the *völkische* wing drives people who think realistically towards the parties of the centre. The prospects for the elections are not rosy. . . . We must preach again and again to the right-wing parties: 'A national united front and personalities!' The party does not work sufficiently for either goal. . . .[2]

Yet in the elections of 7 December 1924 the German Nationalists gained half a million votes compared with the elections of May 1924. They now had 103 seats in parliament—more than ever before or after. Their split on the issue of the Dawes Plan had done no damage to the party. The Social Democrats, however, added 31 to their 100 seats and gained 1,800,000

---

[1] Seeckt to his wife, Berlin, 26, 27, 29, and 30 Aug. 1924: Nachlaß Seeckt, roll 28, pp. 279–80, 281–2, microfilm in Institut für Zeitgeschichte.

[2] Stülpnagel to Fritsch, Berlin, 21 Nov. 1924: Depot Stülpnagel, H 08–5/20, loc. cit.

votes. Both parties were helped by the growing economic and political stabilization, while the more extreme Communists and National Socialists lost heavily. Another aim of Seeckt was now achieved: for the first time German Nationalist ministers were appointed and took their seats in the cabinet.

Other officers, however, sharply criticized the policy of Seeckt and Schleicher, especially their compromises with the president and the chancellor. Fritsch wrote an outspoken letter to Stülpnagel:

I beg you not to hold it against me if I warn you against too great an optimism with regard to Ebert and Marx. In my opinion the first is a completely one-sided party leader of the Social Democrats and a cur (in spite of Schleicher). The second is perhaps honest, but too unimportant to play a decisive part; he is pushed by others, who are interested in having S. removed from his post. I have observed that, whenever the defence ministry has relied on the *bona fide* [*sic*] of Ebert, the matter has ended with their being cheated (*mit einem großen Hereinfall*). Schleicher perhaps still fondly believes that he can diddle Severing and company, but in fact unfortunately the opposite has always happened. . . . The ultimate consequence of S. refusing to resign is his dictatorship. I should like to hope that he is ready for this step, although it would be very difficult for him in connexion with this foreign political issue. Alternatively, suppose S. resigns: who shall become his successor? It should after all be a man who would continue the work in his spirit, and not a black, red and gold cur. . . . On the left, in my opinion, everything has been prepared for the attack during the past months. They will not hesitate if need be to ask the French for support. For months the propaganda of the Jewish papers has been directed to this end. . . . For in the last resort Ebert, pacifists, Jews, democrats, black, red and gold, and the French are all the same thing, namely the people who want to destroy Germany. There may be small differences, but in the end it all amounts to the same. . . .[1]

Stülpnagel attempted to calm Fritsch and explained that he too, as well as Seeckt, did not trust Ebert; but the president would not be so stupid as to remove Seeckt suddenly. In any case, it would be madness to adopt Fritsch's suggestion that the

---

[1] Fritsch to Stülpnagel, Königsberg, 16 Nov. 1924: ibid. It has to be remembered that black, red, and gold were the official German colours and Ebert the commander-in-chief of the Reichswehr.

Verbände or the army should be told, now, what Seeckt would do in such an eventuality.[1]

Other senior officers had a similar attitude towards the president and the members of the government. From Munich the new Bavarian commander-in-chief, Lieutenant-General Freiherr Kreß von Kressenstein, wrote to Seeckt, fearing that the Entente powers might demand his resignation:

> Whether it really comes to such a demand will depend on the result of the elections. The Entente will first look at the new German government before finally deciding whether or not to commit such an enormity. With all the confidence in the loyalty of the president and the defence minister towards Your Excellency which you may have, we must never forget that they are men of the revolution and influenced by their parties. I therefore think that we have to reckon with the possibility of a demand for the resignation of Your Excellency, and of a government inclined to fulfil this demand, and we must prepare ourselves for this eventuality. . . . I need not assure Your Excellency that you would have the whole united Reichswehr, as well as myself and the Seventh Division, behind you, if the government should not immediately reject the demand for your resignation with indignant protests. In my opinion nothing else would then remain but to proclaim a military dictatorship, to preserve the honour and dignity of our fatherland, and to protect the Reichswehr, threatened in its very existence. . . .

Such a step, however, required careful preparation, and it would probably be necessary to get in touch with the right-wing parties for this purpose.[2]

The German Nationalists themselves pointed out to the generals the dangers connected with the enforced resignation of Seeckt and suggested—as General Kreß had done in his letter to Seeckt—that they should take measures to meet such an eventuality. Thus a local party leader reported to Count Westarp about his contacts with Lieutenant-General von Loßberg, the commanding officer of *Wehrkreis* vi at Münster:

> I informed Loßberg about the clear intention of Ebert to remove Seeckt from his post, long before the publication of the French memorandum on the Reichswehr; I also pointed out to him the

---

[1] Stülpnagel to Fritsch, Berlin, 21 Nov. 1924: ibid. There follows the passage quoted on p. 202 about the policy of Schleicher and the German Nationalists.

[2] Lieutenant-General Kreß to Seeckt, Munich, 2 Dec. 1924: Nachlaß Seeckt, box 15, no. 39, Militärgeschichtliches Forschungsamt Freiburg.

danger of the *Reichsbanner Schwarz-rot-gelb* [*sic*] becoming the main recruiting depot for the Reichswehr, as well as commenting on several other military and political matters. I urgently advised that the leading generals should not let themselves be surprised. . . . Herr von Loßberg, whom I have known for about forty years . . . is a fervent patriot, a man who has sucked in the conservative convictions with his mother's milk, a staunch monarchist, and black, white and red to the very core—in a word, the model of a Prussian general. . . . With the open and honest Loßberg we can talk on a different footing than we can with Seeckt, on whom Loßberg as the stronger character exercises great influence. Loßberg is no *cunctator*; a promise given by him will never be withdrawn. . . .[1]

These almost simultaneous letters with their similar contents indicate that either the German Nationalists approached several leading officers, or that the latter were in contact with each other, to induce the Berlin *cunctator* to take action—at least if the government should try to remove him from his post. This situation did indeed occur in 1926—less than two years later—but then the dismissal of Seeckt took place with the approval, and was covered by the great authority, of the new president, Field-Marshal von Hindenburg. In 1924 Seeckt himself was approached by the former Great-Admiral von Tirpitz; he declared that the commanding officers of the *Wehrkreise* must support Seeckt if his position were endangered, and offered the help of the German Nationalist Party. But Seeckt refused: 'The army obeys, and I speak for it.' In his diary too he noted: 'Protest by the generals'.[2] It thus seems that he reckoned with the possibility of collective action by the generals in the event of his dismissal, with or without his consent.

At the end of February 1925 President Ebert died, and in May his successor, Field-Marshal von Hindenburg, was elected in the second ballot. Seeckt had been engaged in preparing his own candidature 'with passion'; but the campaign was not to start too early, because the chief of the army command was not to be drawn into the struggles of the political parties. Ebert's sudden death destroyed all the plans. In Seeckt's entourage the

---

[1] Freiherr von Maltzahn to Count Westarp, Oberlößnitz-Radebeul, 12 Dec. 1924: Nachlaß Graf Westarp, Gärtringen.
[2] Rabenau, *Seeckt*, p. 410.

idea was again ventilated that he should proclaim himself dictator, but he spurned the promptings. Yet he was bitterly disappointed, and wrongly considered Schleicher responsible for the failure.[1] Yet it was not Schleicher whom Seeckt moved from the defence ministry to the 'front', but Stülpnagel; his place as chief of the army department in the *Truppenamt* was taken by Lieutenant-Colonel Freiherr von Fritsch.[2]

Otto Hasse, too, was removed from the ministry, and became the commanding officer of the Third Division and of *Wehrkreis* iii (Berlin–Brandenburg). His place as chief of the *Truppenamt* went to an old associate of Seeckt, Major-General Wetzell.[3] The election of Hindenburg to the highest dignity brought with it a marked weakening of Seeckt's whole position. Under Ebert, Seeckt alone had represented the military sphere in the government; now this function was taken over by the president, who considered anything military to belong to his own field of competence.[4] Seeckt himself admitted to Count Westarp 'that his political influence had considerably declined. Ebert and his governments negotiated with him on general issues, especially in the field of foreign policy, as one power with another, so to speak; but the Field-Marshal consulted Seeckt almost exclusively on military questions. . . .'[5]

Yet Seeckt still participated in meetings of the cabinet and used his influence there to oppose Stresemann's foreign policy, which was to lead Germany to Geneva and Locarno. The old enmity between the two leading German politicians was as bitter as ever. No wonder, for Seeckt's recipe for the conduct of foreign policy was more than simple. At the end of June 1925 he informed the surprised cabinet that Germany must regain power, and as soon as that was achieved, reconquer all the territories lost in 1918.[6] About the same meeting Seeckt wrote to his wife:

[1] Rabenau, *Seeckt*, pp. 412–13, after his contemporary notes.
[2] *Rangliste des Deutschen Reichsheeres nach dem Stande vom 1. Mai 1926*, Berlin, 1926, pp. 3, 45.
[3] Ibid., p. 12. About Wetzell in Mar. 1920, see above, p. 89.
[4] General Marcks to Rabenau, 1 Aug. 1939: R. H. Phelps, 'Aus den Seeckt-Dokumenten', *Deutsche Rundschau*, lxxviii, Sept. 1952, p. 889.
[5] Count Westarp to Rabenau, Berlin, 8 June 1938: Nachlaß Seeckt, roll 26, no. 291, microfilm in Institut für Zeitgeschichte.
[6] Diary entry of Stresemann on 26 June 1925: H. A. Turner, *Stresemann and the Politics of the Weimar Republic*, Princeton, 1963, p. 203.

The council of ministers began at 7 and lasted until a quarter to one! . . . It was a hard struggle about the basis of our foreign policy, and I probably had the majority of those present on my side. In spite of this, they will probably paper over the cracks again; but perhaps it has been useful to speak one's mind openly and sharply for once. I would rather not entrust it all to paper. . . . [And a week later:] We have suddenly got into a cabinet crisis. . . . The issue, of course, is foreign policy; everybody is convinced that it has led us into a blind alley, and that the question is only how to get out of it. The ugly point . . . is, of course, Herr Str., who is unfortunately at the same time representative and leader of the People's Party. It is not really desirable to bring about a government crisis at this moment—one does not change horses in midstream—but the question arises whether it is not more important to push this man finally out and thus to make the road free for a different foreign policy. . . .[1]

At the beginning of October—after Stresemann's departure for Locarno—Seeckt was still of the same opinion: 'What will emerge at Locarno nobody really knows. A failure would still be best, but not an advantage either; an understanding would only be a success for our enemies. . . .' And to his sister: 'I can only expect bad things from Locarno. Relatively the best that could happen would be a foundering of the conference, the worst would be an understanding which could only bring us disadvantages. Nothing is more difficult than to make good a piece of stupidity. . . .'[2] In April 1926 Seeckt gave some of the reasons which induced him to adopt this attitude:

The situation has deteriorated considerably since last year. In foreign affairs I consider the Locarno-Geneva policy wrong because it ties us and brings no advantage. We are still too weak to give any direction, and are thus always led by others, never leading, at most a compliant ally whom one can drop when one gets reconciled or can find a better one. We could have waited and become internally stronger first, above all we could have kept an entirely free hand towards the east. This we no longer have. We have succumbed to British influence and are serving British interests. Our representatives are, after all, little men who are no match for British diplomacy and its kind condescension, like the chancellor, and ambitious

---

[1] Seeckt to his wife, Berlin, 26 June and 2 July 1925: Nachlaß Seeckt, roll 28, pp. 314, 324–5, microfilm in Institut für Zeitgeschichte.

[2] Seeckt to his wife and to his sister, Berlin, 4 Oct. 1925: Rabenau, *Seeckt*, p. 420.

busy-bodies who must have their fingers in every pie, like Stresemann, the man of general distrust; but it seems impossible to get rid of him. . . . My opposition to our foreign policy is generally known. . . .[1]

The close relations with Russia were clearly of cardinal importance to Seeckt. He did not see that Stresemann too wanted to continue them, and he was unable to appreciate the very real successes of Stresemann's foreign policy: it had already brought about a partial evacuation of the occupied Rhineland and a revolutionary change in Germany's relations with France and the western powers that would have seemed inconceivable in 1923. Seeckt's personal dislike of Stresemann blinded him, exactly as was the case in his relations with Brockdorff-Rantzau.

A further reason for Seeckt's opposition to Stresemann's foreign policy was that the Entente powers demanded a change in the position of the chief of the army command and the abolition of his powers of command. Seeckt feared—perhaps rightly—that Stresemann would make concessions on a question which to him was not vital, so as to achieve an earlier evacuation of the Rhineland. If he wanted to promote his principal aims he hardly had an alternative, as Germany's situation was still very difficult. In November 1925 the government indeed made a number of concessions to the Entente, and in the cabinet even Dr. Geßler sided with Stresemann and against Seeckt.[2] Perhaps Geßler was aiming at strengthening his own position, as he was entitled to exercise the power of command according to the *Wehrgesetz* of 1921; but in practice it was in the hands of Seeckt as far as the army was concerned. By a presidential decree of January 1926 the commanders-in-chief of the two *Gruppenkommandos* and the commanding officers of the ten divisions of the army were made directly subordinate to the minister of defence (the divisional commanders only in so far as they were not subject to the orders of the commanders-in-chief of the *Gruppen*). But this was not of any practical importance, for the two commanders-in-chief and the ten divisional commanders were still described as being 'under the chief of the army command'.[3] It was simply assumed that only his

[1] Seeckt to his sister, Berlin, 4 Apr. 1926: Rabenau, *Seeckt*, p. 430.
[2] Ibid., p. 421.
[3] The chief of the legal department in the defence ministry, Berlin, 12 Apr. 1928: Nachlaß Groener, box 22, no. 227, Bundesarchiv Koblenz.

authority to issue orders (*Befehlsgewalt*) was abolished, not his power of command (*Kommandogewalt*), and that the government had expressly sanctioned this distinction. 'In practice everything remained as it was. The units hardly heard of the change in Seeckt's position; and if they heard of it, they usually did not understand it, and Seeckt did not change anything whatsoever in his procedure. . . .'[1]

III. *Seeckt and the Officer Corps*

Seeckt attached the greatest importance to the education and training of the officer corps, especially of the general staff officers. Their selection, and the appointments of staff officers throughout the army, were among the tasks of the *Truppenamt*, which exercised the functions of the dissolved Great General Staff and the Prussian ministry of war. The chief of the *Truppenamt* himself conducted a general staff tour in the summer and a *kriegspiel* in the winter for the education of the staff officers. Responsibility for the training courses of the general staff officers belonged to the *Ausbildungsabteilung* (T 4), which stood directly under the chief of the army command.[2] As they were destined to occupy the leading positions in the army, the future staff officers were not only examined in military questions, but also in languages, history, political science, military economic problems, foreign affairs, and technical subjects. Seeckt demanded from them a good general knowledge apart from their professional training.[3]

As early as 1920 directives were issued for the training of the *Führergehilfen*, a name used to avoid that of general staff officer. As the military academy had also been dissolved, examinations were introduced for all the officers in the *Wehrkreise*. The papers were set and marked by the T 4. Those who passed with the highest marks were then ordered to attend the first *Führergehilfenlehrgang* in one of the *Wehrkreise*; in *Wehrkreis* vi these were only 20 out of 164 officers examined in 1922. At the end of this course the unsuitable officers were eliminated, and the others

---

[1] Rabenau, *Seeckt*, p. 422.

[2] The chief of T 4 was from 1925 to 1927, when he became chief of the *Truppenamt*, Colonel von Blomberg, the later war minister.

[3] Erfurth, *Geschichte des deutschen Generalstabes*, p. 124; Görlitz, *Der deutsche Generalstab*, p. 328.

were invited to a selection course arranged by the T 4. The best of them—again only a small percentage—were then commanded to attend a third course in Berlin under the auspices of the T 4. The participants numbered in general only about 12, and later at most 20 officers. The number of subjects taught there was considerably larger than in the first and second courses, and included naval and air operations, counter-espionage, foreign armies, supply and transport, as well as foreign and domestic politics.[1] A naval officer who in 1922 took part in the training of the staff officers in Berlin reported that the teaching concentrated above all on the daily needs of the general staff; military history was taught on the basis of the war of 1866 against Austria; three larger *kriegspiele* were arranged between January and April; every officer had to solve a tactical problem within three hours twice a month, and their solutions were discussed by the group in the presence of the teacher. The T 4 disposed of considerable sums to arrange and finance the courses. The naval officer also complained strongly about lack of understanding for the navy on the part of the staff officers and their contemptuous attitude towards it.[2]

The training of the general staff officers of course became known to the Interallied Military Control Commission, which was established in Germany under the terms of the Treaty of Versailles. At the end of 1924 it reported that the general staff still existed, that its personnel was selected according to the same principles as before the war—with the remarkable difference that now *all* officers were obliged to pass the entrance examination—and that the courses now lasted four years, compared with three at the former military academy in Berlin.[3] Again Stresemann was prepared to make concessions to the Entente: 'In any case it seems necessary to reorganize the *Truppenamt* in a form that entirely eliminates any suspicions of the Entente that it is a general staff. . .'; this applied also to the question of the so-called *Führergehilfen*. The ministry of defence

[1] Erfurth, op. cit., pp. 125-6; Görlitz, op. cit., p. 328.

[2] Lieutenant Mewis to chief of the naval command, Berlin, 18 Dec. 1922: Admiralität, Marine-Kommandoamt, Flotten-Abteilung, Allgemeines, 7895 A Ia I, Militärgeschichtliches Forschungsamt Freiburg.

[3] Report no. 45 of the I.M.C.C., Berlin, 20 Dec. 1924, p. 31: Schriftstücke aus dem Nachlaß Stresemann, vol. v, 3241 Pr. 13, D 706140 (German Foreign Office microfilms).

was asked to submit proposals for a different organization of their training 'so as to deprive the I.M.C.C. of any pretence for further reclamations . . .'.[1] But in this field, too, everything remained as it had been. Concessions on a point which was so central to him were out of the question for Seeckt; but such incidents further increased his intense dislike of Stresemann.

In other respects, too, Seeckt continuously endeavoured to promote the education of the officer corps, to strengthen its coherence, to improve its intellectual and moral level, and above all to enforce a clear separation between officers and other ranks. In May 1924 he expressed a criticism in a decree:

Officers and their ladies have engaged in slander, often without a shred of proper evidence. In several instances the chivalrous respect due to the honour of a woman has not been maintained, neither has the limit set by the authority of the superior officer and the comradely ties in the officer corps been respected. Officers have not shrunk from communicating rumours to outsiders, and these endanger most seriously the prestige of the individual and of the profession. Whoever spreads such rumours is as responsible as the author. The officer is naturally responsible for the actions of his wife. . . .

Another decree warned against immoderate drinking and transgressing the line separating officers and other ranks.[2]

Seeckt became even more indignant when an officer declared during an inquiry that several officers of his unit had, especially after festivities, taken non-commissioned officers and men home to have more drinks; therefore he had not hesitated to invite soldiers to his rooms to drink. Seeckt's comment was:

I can only express my sharpest displeasure about the indifference towards the educational principles clearly stated in my decrees which emerges from these depositions. I must demand from commanding officers the ruthless use of their authority, so that the first and most important principle of every usable army—unconditional obedience—is strictly enforced with respect to every officer. Unfortunately, towards the end of the war and in the subsequent disorders many lost their conviction that an order has to be carried out. I demand this period to be terminated for all members of the army.

[1] Note by Stresemann, n.d.: ibid., vol. viii, 3241 Pr. 16, D 707245–46.
[2] Decrees of 5 May and 30 Aug. 1924: Sammelheft zu Chef PA Nr. 675.33, pp. 3–5, Bundesarchiv-Militärarchiv.

In future I shall not only hold the individual responsible for the consequences of his actions, but also commanding officers if they neglect their educational duties in this way. . . .[1]

Any slighting of a superior officer was equally liable to punishment, even if the officer who had committed the offence held a senior rank. Thus a Bavarian colonel was informed that he was not considered suitable to be promoted general, in spite of his high qualifications, because in an officers' conference on the case of Lossow, held at Würzburg in October 1923, he had ridiculed his superior officers in Berlin.[2]

Yet it was in this field of personnel policy that Seeckt, during his last years of office, was sharply criticized by other high-ranking officers. After Seeckt's dismissal Colonel Freiherr von Falkenhausen wrote to Stülpnagel from Dresden that Seeckt 'did not really suffer any *personalities* next to him. And when I look at the *Rangliste*, I see in the highest places the results of this policy. And that worries me in view of recent events. . .'[3] Stülpnagel replied that Seeckt 'did not like to hear the truth, surrounded himself with stereotypes, and did not steer forward. You write yourself how hopeless the appointments have been. In addition, in questions of defence we have made no progress for years, only because S. could not be persuaded to discuss all these matters openly with the government. In too many things we have play-acted and have not educated characters, but yes-men. Have we learned nothing from the Wilhelminian period? After he relinquished emergency powers S's strength consisted only in his passivity. . . .'[4] Many years later Stülpnagel still thought that in the last years of Seeckt's command there had been the danger of the officer corps getting too old in its higher ranks: in his opinion, this was only remedied under Seeckt's successor, when Stülpnagel became the chief of the Personnel Office of the army.[5]

[1] Decree of 13 Oct. 1925: ibid., pp. 8–9.

[2] General Freiherr Kreß von Kressenstein to Reinhardt, Munich, 17 Dec. 1926: Nachlaß Reinhardt, Hauptstaatsarchiv Stuttgart.

[3] Colonel von Falkenhausen, commander of Infantry Regiment 10, to Colonel von Stülpnagel, Dresden, 13 Nov. 1926: Depot Stülpnagel, H 08–5/21, Bundesarchiv-Militärarchiv.

[4] Colonel von Stülpnagel, Infantry Regiment 17, to von Falkenhausen, Brunswick, 20 Nov. 1926: ibid.

[5] Joachim von Stülpnagel, '75 Jahre meines Lebens', pp. 241–2: copy in Bundesarchiv-Militärarchiv.

More bitter was the criticism of General Ritter von Möhl, commander-in-chief of *Gruppe* 2, who met Seeckt during the autumn manœuvres of 1924 without being told that he would soon be retired: 'I therefore state that we parted in the afternoon of 20 September at Biberach, and that on 24 September the letter stating that I should be replaced on 1 January (1925) was dispatched from Berlin. Even in General von Seeckt I would not have believed possible such a lack of sincerity, frankness, and comradeship, although my estimation of him as a character and soldier has always been very low. He cultivates Byzantinism and cliquism, the well-known main evils of the Prussian army since the "Wilhelminian period". . . .' And twelve months later, again to General Reinhardt, who had succeeded Möhl as commander-in-chief of *Gruppe* 2: 'I should very much like to wish you a "change of government" that either brings you to Berlin [as successor to Seeckt], or grants to the two commanders-in-chief [of the *Gruppen*] the position which has been their due on rational and legal grounds for several years. . . . With Geßler, Seeckt, and the whole clique connected with them nothing can be achieved; to appoint younger men I consider urgently necessary. . . .'[1]

Connected with Seeckt's disinclination to give senior posts to younger officers was his dislike of new military ideas. Colonel von Blomberg, who was then the chief of the T 4, recounts in his memoirs:

Our suggestions for new developments in the Reichswehr were not readily accepted by General von Seeckt. Three examples as an illustration: I suggested abandoning the use of lances of the cavalry soldiers, so as to increase the fire power of our three cavalry divisions. . . . Seeckt replied: 'For the same reason during the war I suggested relinquishing the lances. This was refused. Now the cavalry can retain the lances as far as I am concerned.' It is difficult to make sense of these words. We wanted to make a very modest attempt to open the road to motorization and proposed to put the companies of bicyclists on motor cycles. This would have been a beginning which promised further results. Seeckt replied literally: 'Dear Blomberg, if we want to remain friends, then you must refrain from such suggestions.' This too was difficult to understand. Finally,

---

[1] General von Möhl to General Reinhardt, Cassel, 20 Dec. 1924, and Munich, 4 Jan. 1926: Nachlaß Reinhardt, Hauptstaatsarchiv Stuttgart. Since the days of the Munich crisis there was a strong animosity between Möhl and Seeckt.

we had put our ideas about the required development of the Reichswehr into a longer memorandum, which above all proposed the
formation of an army of leaders, as the framework of a large-scale
rearmament. Every non-commissioned officer must be capable of
filling an officer's post, every man of taking over the duties of a non-
commissioned officer. The whole training and education of the
soldiers should be directed towards that end. . . . The memorandum
. . . was not well received by General v. S. His marginal notes were
very unfriendly and his final judgement devastating. Clearly,
General von Seeckt was under the impression that we younger ones
wanted to teach him. But we only intended to state something
soberly and realistically, and had only chosen to do so in writing
because it was impossible to do so by word of mouth. . . .[1]

Other officers held similar views. An officer, who served for
many years as adjutant to battalions and regiments, stated that
'new developments were hindered nearly everywhere by the
rather rigid ideas regarding tradition which often amounted
to an imitation of old forms'. The reception of new ideas was
too slow with regard to the treatment of the soldiers and their
education.[2] The young officers were trained in the spirit of this
tradition, the tradition above all of the glories of the past.
When the new infantry school was opened at Dresden in 1926
visitors found there pictures of 'Frederick William I as a young
prince' and 'Prince Leopold of Bavaria in command of his
battery', but no link whatsoever with the new state, not even a
picture of Friedrich Ebert. Many of the cadets—in the ninth
year of the republic—still wore the old Prussian sword-belt with
the crown because the new clasps were not yet ready.[3]

The officer cadets came from the social groups which for
generations had supplied the Prussian state with officers. In
1926 the fathers of more than 44 per cent. were serving or
former officers, and of more than 49 per cent. in 1927. Second
in place came the professions, higher officials, professors,
lawyers, doctors, and clergymen, with 41 and 34 per cent.
respectively. About 85 per cent. of the future officers came

---

[1] Werner von Blomberg, 'Erinnerungen bis 1933', iii. 95-6: MS. in Bundesarchiv-Militärarchiv.
[2] Quoted by H. Teske, 'Analyse eines Reichswehr-Regiments', *Wehrwissenschaftliche Rundschau*, 1962, p. 262.
[3] Major-General von Amsberg to Seeckt, Dresden, 20 Nov. 1926: Nachlaß
Seeckt, box 10, no. 72, Militärgeschichtliches Forschungsamt Freiburg.

from these two groups, and an additional 5 per cent. were the sons of owners of large estates. Only 6 to 7 per cent. were the sons of merchants and factory owners; all other social groups hardly counted. In 1920 21·7 per cent. of the officers of the army belonged to the nobility, in 1926 20·5 per cent., and on an average about 21 per cent., while the nobility comprised only 0·14 per cent. of the German population. The distribution of the noble officers among the different arms was, moreover, very uneven. In the cavalry 50 per cent. of the officers were noblemen in 1920, 45 per cent. in 1926, and nearly 50 per cent. in later years. Among the technical troops and the engineers, on the other hand, the figure was just over 5, or even less than 5 per cent.[1] In the Infantry Regiment 9 at Potsdam, which continued the tradition of the Prussian foot guards, more than half the officers were noblemen.[2] The senior officers of the army—but not of the navy—were mainly drawn from the nobility, the former guards regiments and the group which had commanded the army during the world war. In 1925 23 of the generals on the active list were noblemen. 'It was a relic of the privileged position of the noble officers at the time of the Emperor.'[3]

Nor did this change in later years, when the dismissal of Seeckt opened the possibility of effecting reforms. On the contrary, by 1932 the percentage of noble officers had increased from 20·5 to nearly 24. It had declined in the infantry, but increased in all other arms and almost doubled in the technical units and the engineers, where it had been particularly low. Among the officer cadets who were commissioned the percentage of noble officers was 17·4 on an average during the years 1923-9; but it grew to 30·4 in 1930, to 25·7 in 1931, and to 35·9 in 1932, more than double the original figure.[4] That the army command was conscious of the problem is shown by a note of Schleicher's adjutant, of 1930.[5] Frau von Schweinitz at

[1] Karl Demeter, *Das deutsche Offizierkorps*, Frankfurt, 1962, pp. 53–56; W. Sauer, in Bracher, *Die Auflösung der Weimarer Republik*, p. 258.

[2] Teske, loc. cit., p. 257.

[3] Erfurth, *Geschichte des deutschen Generalstabes*, p. 112; Gordon, *Reichswehr and the German Republic*, p. 201. Among the lieutenants and first lieutenants only 20·5 and 14·3 per cent were noblemen.

[4] Sauer, loc. cit., p. 258; Demeter, op. cit., pp. 55–56.

[5] Note by Captain Noeldechen, n.d., and letter by Frau von Schweinitz, Dresden, 4 Feb. 1930: Nachlaß Schleicher, no. 73, Bundesarchiv Koblenz.

Dresden asked that her youngest son be commissioned in the Saxon Cavalry Regiment 12; but the army's Personnel Office raised objections because of the high percentage of noble officers in this regiment, and on the other hand did not want to offend the applicant. In fact, the young Schweinitz was commissioned in the regiment in question on 1 April 1930.[1] As the regimental commanders could select the future officers, they naturally preferred the sons of the nobility and of former officers—the social groups which had supplied the Prussian army with officers for centuries. In 1930 95 per cent. of the officers came from social groups which had been considered eligible before the war. Only 5 per cent.—about 200 officers— came from the families of lower officials, farmers, artisans, and workmen, that is groups which had not been eligible before 1914.[2] At the end of 1929 Schleicher deprecated the fact that there was still reluctance to accept an officer cadet whose father was a miner or elementary school teacher: in his opinion, a young man from these circles who had successfully completed a secondary-school education should be particularly welcome.[3]

The importance of this factor, and in particular that of the prevalence of the nobility, should not be overestimated. The senior officers of middle-class origin—such as Seeckt's successor General Heye, the three Generals Hasse, and even General Reinhardt—were as conservative and 'national' in their views as the officers of noble origin. Both groups—from the cadet school to the general staff—had undergone the same system of education and training, and they formed a group that was extraordinarily homogeneous, politically as well as socially. It was indeed remarkable how completely officers with an entirely different social background became assimilated in the officer corps; men such as General Groener, who came from Swabia and whose father was a professional N.C.O. This was greatly facilitated by the strong *esprit de corps* which permeated the whole corps and the feeling of belonging to an *élite*. General Heye emphasized this in 1927 in a decree: 'An officer corps

---

[1] *Rangliste des Deutschen Reichsheeres nach dem Stande vom 1. Mai 1930*, Berlin, n.d., p. 61.

[2] H. Rosinski, *The German Army*, London, 1939, p. 186. In 1930 67 per cent. of the newly commissioned officers were the sons of officer families: ibid., p. 185.

[3] 'Notizen für die Kommandeurbesprechung', n.d., p. 4: Nachlaß Schleicher, no. 35, Bundesarchiv Koblenz.

must feel like a family or the community of an order, and must carefully watch that no member bring disrepute on the name of the regiment through talkativeness. This applies to all personal matters, which must not penetrate to outsiders from the circle of the regiment or battalion, and this equally applies to all larger questions within the framework of the entire officer corps. . . .'[1] He also declared that the officer must possess a *Herrenbewußtsein*, must be conscious of being a master and a gentleman.[2] In their attitude and behaviour there was no difference between the officers who were noblemen and those who were commoners. Above all, the officer corps was clearly separated from civilians as well as from other ranks, who came from entirely different social groups. This line of separation was time and again emphasized by Seeckt—undoubtedly with complete success. Only a small number of non-commissioned officers succeeded in gaining commissions. In 1928 there were 117 officers in the army who had been non-commissioned officers, about 3 per cent. of the strength of the officer corps.[3] Smaller still was the number of officers who had not attended a secondary school. Between 1924 and 1927 only eleven soldiers were commissioned who had only been to an elementary school; the large majority of those promoted officer had passed the leaving examination of a secondary school.[4]

The officer corps was equally homogeneous in its political views, especially as far as the older officers were concerned. They remained deeply hostile to the republic, parliamentarianism, the political parties and their 'squabbles', the new ministers and deputies. This new world was alien to the officers, and only a few tried to build a bridge to it. Weimar remained the 'system' that had destroyed the ideals of the officers' youth.[5] The forces which determined the political position of the officers had been destroyed in November 1918. 'What remained was merely a

[1] Decree of General Heye, Berlin, 22 Sept. 1927: Nachlaß Heye, H 08–18/7, Bundesarchiv-Militärarchiv.

[2] Decree of the same date: Hans Black, 'Die Grundzüge der Beförderungsordnungen', *Untersuchungen zur Geschichte des Offizierkorps*, Stuttgart, 1962, p. 144. This decree is not in Heye's Nachlaß.

[3] Joachim von Stülpnagel, '75 Jahre meines Lebens', p. 251: Bundesarchiv-Militärarchiv, H 08–5/27.

[4] Nachlaß Groener, box 21, no. 225, p. 4: ibid.

[5] Thus General Paul Mahlmann in a personal interview. Cf. Gordon, op. cit., p. 414: letter of General von Falkenhausen.

kind of monarchical idea which permeated the officer corps. This was preserved, not expressly as a political conception—at least not with the younger classes—but it sufficed to estrange the officer from party politics. He did not feel loyal to democracy, but to the fatherland or to the idea of the state, which he need not identify with democracy. . . .'[1] An officer, who was then a captain in the *Truppenamt* and stood close to Schleicher, wrote later:

> Therefore the *Wehrmacht* could only follow one slogan: to keep outside the political entanglements, have nothing to do with the parties, serve the state silently! Its idea of the state had to be different from that of the parties. . . . It was the idea of the state, standing powerfully and authoritatively above the parties and above bourgeois society, the idea of the old Prussian and German state, and at the same time the ideal of nation and fatherland, for which the armies of the wars of liberation and unification and of the world war had fought and bled. This ideal could only be realized by keeping aloof from the parties and by fighting against them. 'Above party' became the slogan of the Reichswehr. . . .[2]

Among the political parties, it was only the German Nationalist Party, with its strictly monarchical and 'black, white, and red' views, that attracted the sympathies of the officers. Hence Seeckt and Schleicher time and again attempted to make this party presentable, to wean it from its entirely negative attitude, and to persuade it to enter the government—with very little success because the extremist section of the party was unwilling to accept a policy of compromise. This attitude of the officers was even more marked in the provinces, where political realities counted far less than in Berlin. In 1927 a deputy of the conservative German People's Party, himself a director of a Silesian machine-tool factory, wrote to Stresemann apprehensively:

> It must be said that in the Reichswehr, or perhaps in some parts of it, there are in fact tendencies which we as members of the People's Party cannot silently accept. In general it is said, and reported from

---

[1] Gerhard Papke, 'Offizierkorps und Anciennität', *Untersuchungen zur Geschichte des Offizierkorps*, Stuttgart, 1962, p. 201.

[2] Lieutenant-Colonel Marcks, 'Das Reichsheer 1919 bis 1934', in Karl Linnebach, *Heeresgeschichte*, Hamburg, 1935, p. 20 (offprint). It has to be borne in mind that this was written after 1933, but the essay clearly pictures the basic attitude towards the parties and the state.

several quarters, that there are officers' messes of the Reichswehr in which only newspapers of the German Nationalists and of Hugenberg can be found. In the country one can equally clearly observe the very close connexions with the associations of the right and the extreme right, and the partiality of officers or whole officer corps for the purely monarchist form of state. As before the war, the military in official positions frequently have social contacts . . . only with the circles which possess the broad acres, and which are of course firmly German Nationalist. . . .[1]

The dislike of the republic extended to the official colours. As late as 1925 the minister of defence had to point out in a decree that the German colours were black, red, and gold. 'It is not permitted to use in official reports the term black-red-yellow.'[2] Even General Reinhardt urged in a letter to a democratic deputy that the black, red, and gold colours should be given up and thus the 'unity of flags' be restored.[3] Perhaps the reintroduction of black, white, and red would have reconciled certain officers to the existence of the republic. But the parties of the left and the trade unions would never have consented to such a step—and a change of the constitution required a majority of two-thirds in parliament. Such a retreat before the forces which every day proclaimed their hostility to the republic in the market place would also have been a grave tactical error. For the officers their loyalty to the colours of the Empire was natural and above any argument; but on this issue too they were separated from large sections of the people. This separation from the people was keenly felt by some younger officers, who demanded that the soldiers should go 'to the people' and to the workmen and recruit them for the army. But such ideas were refuted by the leaders of the army.[4]

Thus the officer corps neither served the government nor the republic, but the 'state' and the 'idea of the state', the 'nation'

[1] Deputy Max Schmidt to Stresemann, Hirschberg, 10 Jan. 1927: Nachlaß Stresemann, vol. 97, 7404 H, H 173403–04 (microfilm).

[2] Decree of 1 Apr. 1925: Reichskanzlei, Akten betr. Reichswehr, vol. v, R 43 I 686, Bundesarchiv Koblenz.

[3] Reinhardt to the deputy Dr. Haas, 11 Oct. 1924: Nachlaß Reinhardt, Hauptstaatsarchiv Stuttgart.

[4] An officer of the *Truppenamt*, Major von Rabenau (the later biographer of Seeckt), was instructed to write a pamphlet against the ideas put forward by Lieutenant Kurt Hesse in his *Von der nahen Ära der 'Jungen Armee'*, Berlin, 1925 (*Die alte Armee und die junge Generation*, Berlin, 1925).

and the 'fatherland': these, in contrast with changing governments and constitutional forms, possessed an eternal value.
The difference thus stressed also implied that the Reichswehr,
or its leaders, could one day reach the conclusion that the
republican form of state clashed with the interests of the 'nation',
that its interests demanded a change of the constitution. Was
the Reichswehr then justified in renouncing its obedience to the
president and the government? It looked as if the army
command reserved to itself 'the right to disobedience, but did
not exercise it for the time being and bided its time . . .'.[1] This
waiting attitude at the same time corresponded to Seeckt's
natural predilection for the role of a *cunctator*.

IV. *New Military Preparations*

The events of the year 1923 induced the Reichswehr to
accelerate its clandestine armaments and preparations for
mobilization, to recruit volunteers, to buy arms abroad, and to
prepare for an armed clash with France. While these steps were
understandable, seen against the turbulent background of that
year, the receding of the crisis and the improvement in Franco-
German relations after 1923 should have made it possible to
abandon the measures gradually. This, however, did not happen.
In 1925 'draft schemes were worked out in the *Truppenamt* to
increase and improve the *Wehrmacht* beyond the permitted
dimensions . . .'.[2] It was planned to treble the existing seven
infantry divisions, and a difference was made between the
preparations 'which can be made now without endangering
the secrecy', and those 'which can only be carried out at a time
of political tension, when the outbreak of a war is envisaged',
and when the restrictions imposed by the Treaty of Versailles
would no longer exist.[3] In addition to the 21 infantry divisions,
the army was to have 5 cavalry divisions (instead of the existing
3) and 39 frontier defence divisions (apparently to be recruited
from the older classes) as well as an air force. The greatest
difficulty expected was in the equipment and arming of these

---

[1] Sauer, 'Die Mobilmachung der Gewalt', in Bracher, *Die nationalsozialistische Machtergreifung*, p. 698.

[2] Rabenau, *Seeckt*, pp. 480–1.

[3] 'Rüstungsbestimmungen', Berlin, 19 May 1925: Akten des Heereswaffenamtes, WiIF 5/501, Bundesarchiv Koblenz.

units. It was even doubtful whether the existing stocks would be sufficient for an army of 21 divisions.[1] Yet the stocks were fairly large. At the beginning of 1927 General Heye informed the government that the clandestine depots contained about 350,000 rifles, 12,000 light and heavy machine guns, 400 trench mortars, 600 light and 75 heavy cannon, as well as vehicles and uniforms; the stocks of ammunition, however, were small and would only suffice for about one day of battle. But he claimed that something else was achieved—politically of great importance: 'the defence of the frontiers, which at first was in the hands of the para-military *Verbände*, had gradually been taken over by the army. Most of the weapons were now under the supervision of regular units and were looked after by special employees of the units. . . .'[2] Another grave problem was the lack of the most important raw materials, especially copper, tin, nickel, chromium, oil, and sulphur.[3] Detailed maps were therefore drawn up in the defence ministry to show the distribution of the various industries, stocks of raw materials, and sources of energy. General Heye stated further that another essential preparation consisted in the keeping of lists: the army command had to know how many men there were who had military training or were fit for army service; the number of those who had seen active service during the world war declined every year by 200,000, and would reach nil between 1930 and 1933.[2]

From 1924 onwards pilots and observers were systematically trained, partly under the cover of a civilian institution, partly on the German aerodrome at Lipetsk. At the beginning of 1924 the *Sportflug G.m.b.H.* was founded, with the support of the defence ministry; it soon maintained ten flying schools, where serving and former officers could use their flying experience and civilians were trained as pilots. After 1925 the flying groups of the army command had an annual budget of about ten million marks. Of this about half was spent on the flying schools, the maintenance of aeroplanes, and A.R.P. measures;

---

[1] Ibid.; Major Soldan of the Heereswaffenamt, 24 Sept. 1925: Akten des Heereswaffenamtes, WiIF 5/518, ibid.

[2] 'Auszug aus dem Protokoll der Ministerbesprechung vom 26. Februar 1927': Auswärtiges Amt, Büro des Staatssekretärs, Landesverteidigung, 4565 H, E 164073 (microfilm).

[3] The chief of the Heereswaffenamt, Major-General Ludwig, 12 Jan. 1927: Akten des Heereswaffenamtes, WiIF 5/896 and 5/2222, Bundesarchiv Koblenz.

about three millions went into research, development, and tests; and the remaining two millions was the cost of the establishment at Lipetsk.[1] Early in 1925 Seeckt created a special group within the army organization department of the *Truppenamt*— the T 2 III L—as the central office for all questions of flying and air warfare; but at the end of the year this group had to be dissolved again because of representations from the Entente powers.[2] In the navy, on the other hand, all questions concerning the air arm were distributed among four central departments of the naval command, one of them—the Sea Transport Division—being responsible for all contacts with the outside. The chief of the naval command, Admiral Zenker, enjoined all departments concerned to co-operate closely and to avoid all unnecessary written communications.[3] Apparently there was no contact on these issues between the army and the navy.

In 1924 short-term volunteers were trained in courses lasting several weeks. During a surprise visit to the Sennelager members of the Interallied Military Control Commission established that a training course for about a thousand young men had been held there between January and April, and that the next course was to start in January 1925. In the autumn of 1924 there was a course for non-commissioned officers, with many more participants than the commanding officer had admitted; apparently members of the *Jungdeutscher Orden* had taken part in it, as inscriptions made by its members were found in one of the barracks. Students of Marburg University were trained by the Infantry Regiment 15,[4] students from Tübingen by the Infantry Regiment 13 at Gmünd, and other short-term volunteers by the Artillery Regiment 5 at Ulm.[5] In April 1924 a former colonel gave a detailed report on the system of short-term volunteers to

---

[1] Völker, 'Die Entwicklung der militärischen Luftfahrt in Deutschland 1920–1933', *Beiträge zur Militär- und Kriegsgeschichte*, iii, Stuttgart, 1962, pp. 137, 144–5.

[2] Chef der Heeresleitung, Berlin, 22 Jan. 1925: Akten des Heereswaffenamtes, WiIF 5/509, Bundesarchiv Koblenz; Völker, op. cit., p. 146.

[3] Chef der Marineleitung, Berlin, 27 July 1925: Reichswehrministerium, Marineleitung, Verschiedenes, 7897 M I, Militärgeschichtliches Forschungsamt Freiburg.

[4] 'Bericht Nr. 45 über die Tätigkeit der I.M.K.K. während der Zeit vom 17. November–13. Dezember 1924', Berlin, 20 Dec. 1924, pp. 35–39: Auswärtiges Amt, Schriftstücke aus dem Nachlaß Stresemann, vol. v, 3241 Pr. 13, D 706144–8 (microfilm).

[5] Walter Bauer to Dr. Geßler, Tübingen, 1 May 1924: Nachlaß Geßler, no. 55, Bundesarchiv Koblenz; Scheringer, *Das große Los. . .* , p. 145.

the general meeting of the employers' association of Upper Hesse, as the costs were to be borne by voluntary contributions from industry and trade; for the district in question they were estimated at more than 800,000 marks for the first two years. A captain from the battalion at Gießen confirmed and supplemented the report and tried to disperse the doubts voiced in the meeting.[1] As short-term volunteers were trained by many units, the *Truppenamt* in July 1924 ordered that, if members of the Interallied Control Commission made inquiries, the answer was to be given 'that *during the state of emergency* men had been recruited for a short period to guard barracks. After the lifting of the state of emergency these men were slowly discharged. . . .'[2]

Stresemann, however, was convinced that this explanation was not sufficient, for time and again it was alleged that officers of the reserve were participating in manœuvres, that students were regularly trained, and that members of the *Verbände* received some military training, either by members of the Reichswehr or in close connexion with its units.[3] At the end of 1924 the Interallied Control Commission reported that it was still trying to investigate illegal recruiting, but that its investigations were impeded 'by obstacles which paralysed them and made it necessary to terminate them'.[4] The passive resistance of the German authorities had apparently become too strong; soon the activities of the Control Commission in Germany came to an end. One of Seeck's major objectives was achieved.[5] To disprove once and for all the allegations of the Entente powers about the military training of non-soldiers Stresemann considered it necessary to create legal prohibitions against any connexion of political or students' associations with the Reichswehr and any participation of Reichswehr officers as teachers or lecturers in such courses.[6] But this was not done; probably Seeckt's resistance could not be overcome.

[1] Schüddekopf, *Heer und Republik*, no. 88, pp. 209–10.
[2] Reichswehrministerium, Truppenamt, T 1, Berlin, 25 July 1924: Admiralität, Marine-Kommandoamt, Flottenabteilung, Allgemeines, 7895 A Ia I, Militärgeschichtliches Forschungsamt Freiburg.
[3] Notes of Stresemann, n.d.: Schriftstücke aus dem Nachlaß Stresemann, vol. viii, 3241 Pr. 16, D 707246 (microfilm).
[4] 'Bericht Nr. 45 über die Tätigkeit der I.M.K.K. . .', p. 40: ibid., vol. v, 3241 Pr. 13, D 706149 (microfilm). [5] Rabenau, *Seeckt*, p. 454.
[6] Notes of Stresemann, n.d. (end of 1924 or beginning of 1925): Schriftstücke aus dem Nachlaß Stresemann, vol. viii, 3241 Pr. 16, D 707246–47 (microfilm).

That the army continued these activities during the following years is proved by a report on the 'financial organization in *Wehrkreis* iii', which was circulated in the autumn of 1925 by the T 2 III, the department of the *Truppenamt* responsible for the defence of the frontiers. The means at the disposal of the Reichswehr were considered insufficient for its tasks, which included organization of reserves, military training outside the army, and guarding of the existing stocks of weapons. For these purposes very considerable sums were required, hence private sources had to be tapped in addition to the official ones—namely industry, banks, trade, agriculture, small enterprises, and retail trade. 'The separation into these groups makes it possible to work on them more intensively and to play off one group against the other. . . .' In the field of industry and trade the contributions were to be collected by the employers' associations of the provinces of Berlin, Brandenburg, Lower Lusatia, and Silesia (which together formed *Wehrkreis* iii); in the cases of agriculture and retail trade by local finance committees. At the head stood a steering committee formed by the presidents of the different employers' associations and influential personalities from agriculture, but the general direction remained with the *Wehrkreis*. The steering committee had to fix the amount of the contributions, which depended on the financial needs of the *Wehrkreis*: at that time industrial enterprises paid one mark a year for each employee, and agriculture graded contributions according to the tax returns and the size of the estates. The contributors had to undertake—'only morally!'—to pay for three years, otherwise a budget and orderly accounting would become impossible; every three months the *Wehrkreis* had to render accounts to the steering committee and to inform it about the progress of the work. This system was considered a great improvement on the earlier one, whereby the units had collected money on their own and had used the 'black' funds as they saw fit, with 'demoralizing' effects. Now the collection was in private hands, while the *Wehrkreis* and the units could remain in the background: 'for political reasons this is particularly important. . . .' The organiza- was 'the basis of the progress of material rearmament'.[1]

---

[1] 'Finanzorganisation beim W.K. III', 29 Oct. 1925: Akten des Heereswaffen-amtes, WiIF 5/2720, Bundesarchiv Koblenz.

Similar organizations came into being in other *Wehrkreise*. In December 1924 a dinner was held in the officers' mess at Rostock in Mecklenburg, which was attended by high officials, representatives of the university, of industry, and of agriculture; in all, some 60 to 70 people. The commanding officer of *Wehrkreis* ii (Pomerania, Mecklenburg, Schleswig-Holstein), General von Tschischwitz, addressed the gathering and informed them that as the district commands, the backbone of the old army, no longer existed something similar had to be created, and that made it necessary to have full-time employees, who had to be paid. He emphasized that in Pomerania there had been a good response to his plans, and that politics could only be conducted with the Reichswehr, not without it.[1] In Pomerania the *Kreis* officers of the frontier defence organization became employees of the Reichswehr. The *Wehrkreis* ii acquired some influence on the appointments of *Kreis* officers and on the use of and accounting for the money. The commanding officer of the Infantry Regiment 4 at Kolberg, Colonel Edwin von Stülpnagel, was entitled to issue orders in matters of frontier defence.[2] From Stettin a staff officer of the Second Division, Captain Count Brockdorff-Ahlefeldt, wrote to Schleicher that the Reichswehr had now taken the lead 'in the patriotic affairs'. The question, however, was whether its representatives had the qualifications required for the new tasks; in that respect he expressed serious doubts. Many of the local people were 'good soldiers, but bad politicians', and only too often did not want to understand; hence there was a danger, for the army as well as for the patriotic work in hand.[3]

About this work in four eastern Pomeranian *Kreise* the officer responsible for it reported later:

After I had completed five training courses a stop occurred, for internal political reasons. Radical circles at Hammerstein protested to the *republikanische Beschwerdestelle* in Berlin against the illegal military training of civilians on the military practice grounds. . . . From August 1924 onwards the courses were held without uniforms

---

[1] Anlage 3 to the letter of the deputies Hermann Müller and Otto Wels to Dr. Geßler, Berlin, 6 Dec. 1926: Reichskanzlei, Akten betr. Reichswehr, vol. v, R 43 I 686, ibid.

[2] Vogelsang, *Reichswehr, Staat und NSDAP*, pp. 45–46.

[3] Count Brockdorff-Ahlefeldt to Schleicher, Stettin, 1 Aug. 1925: Nachlaß Schleicher, no. 20, Bundesarchiv Koblenz.

and weapons and the number of participants was limited to thirty. . . . The training with the '98 rifle, the light and the heavy machine gun only took place indoors. . . . As the *Stahlhelm* was very strong and well organized in the *Kreise* of Schlochau, Neustettin, and Flatow, I co-operated closely with this organization. Here the symbiosis between the *Stahlhelm* and the frontier defence became effective. . . . It proved useful that I had been, since the beginning of 1924, the *Gaugeschäftsführer* of the *Stahlhelm* in the *Gau* Hammerstein. . . .

The leader of the *Gau*, Major Mackensen, and other owners of estates in the area were 'the heart and soul of the individual *Stahlhelm* and frontier defence sections . . .'.[1] Another former officer reported about the work in the neighbouring districts of Deutsch-Krone and Netzekreis: 'The main effort of all concerned consisted in the recruiting of volunteers, for which purpose groups of the *Stahlhelm* were founded in the localities'; the stocks of weapons and ammunition were distributed, controlled, and looked after; section leaders were trained in courses lasting eight days, and officers in courses lasting a little longer. From November 1924 the influence of the provincial leadership increased considerably, because it was instructed by the *Wehrkreis* ii at Stettin to see to a uniform control, also on the financial side. Early in 1926 the commandant of Hammerstein was charged with the uniform direction of all frontier defence matters, and at times whole companies of volunteers were assembled on the practice grounds for courses lasting eight days. In 1926 the frontier defence and all tasks connected with it were taken over by the Reichswehr, with the knowledge of both the Reich and the Prussian governments. In the *Wehrkreiskommando* at Stettin a staff officer was responsible for the frontier defence; under him stood former officers responsible for training, organization, weapons and equipment, and finance.[2]

The list of the district and *Kreis* officers of the frontier defence organization was known to the *Oberpräsident* of Pomerania; but he had strong reservations about them:

These officers administer the secret stores of weapons, move them hither and thither, function as contacts between the Reichswehr and

---

[1] Report of former Captain Franz Prail of 1955: Sammlung Oberst Dieter von Kleist, Zg. 244/57, Bundesarchiv-Militärarchiv. The *republikanische Beschwerdestelle* dealt with complaints about anti-republican and anti-constitutional activities.

[2] Report of the former Major-General von Nostitz-Wallwitz of 1954: ibid.

the *Verbände* of the extreme right etc., direct the continuous training courses of members of these *Verbände* . . . and give information on recruits for the Reichswehr. These confidential agents sit as civilian employees on all Reichswehr staffs: infantry commanders, artillery commanders, local commandants, cavalry divisions, and *Wehrkreise*. . . .

The accusations were sharply refuted by the *Wehrkreiskommando*:

The remaining weapons, which are scattered in the country and secured by the Reichswehr, are not continuously moved about, but are *gradually* collected in depots which belong to the Reichswehr. In conformity with the repeated strict instructions there are no contacts between the Reichswehr and the *Verbände* of the extreme right. Active soldiers do not participate in the training courses. The employees [of the army] are not consulted in matters of *replacement*. If units make inquiries about individuals, they give information if they can. . . .[1]

As will be seen, General Heye's assertion of February 1927 that 'most of the weapons were now under the supervision of regular units',[2] was much too optimistic for Pomerania; and the *Oberpräsident* was better informed about the close links between the frontier defence units and the *Stahlhelm* than the *Wehrkreiskommando*.

The developments in the province of Silesia were politically even more questionable. A report of the spring of 1924 maintained:

In the frontier *Kreise* near the Oder Reichswehr circles organized an *Oderschutz*. Its leaders were the heads of right-wing bands; nearly all the leading men of this organization were simultaneously leaders of political *Kampfverbände*. During the great strike of the Silesian agricultural workers, for example, the armed shock troops against the strikers were organized by Herr von Winterfeldt, who was also leader of the *Oderschutz*. . . . In addition, the supply of illegal weapons has become completely obscure through the contacts between the defence organizations and the Reichswehr, even for the Prussian civil authorities; they attempted to obtain from the Reichswehr lists of those arms depots which are Reichswehr

---

[1] Anlage 7a to the letter of the Wehrkreiskommando II, Abt. Ic, Stettin, 8 Apr. 1926 to the Oberpräsident of Pomerania, with a list of 36 district and Kreis officers: Geheim-Akten betr. Reichsheer vom Apr. 1926 bis Sept. 1937: Akten des Reichswehrministeriums, roll 34, Institut für Zeitgeschichte, Munich.

[2] See above, p. 221.

property. This has always been declined in principle in the provinces of Upper and Lower Silesia. Thus an arms depot confiscated
by the civil authorities is usually claimed by the Reichswehr as its
own property. . . .[1]

One of the officers responsible for the frontier defence organization, later described the political mood among the participants
in Silesia:

> For Silesia a sports school was created on the military practice
> grounds at Neuhammer under the direction of the former Captain
> von Winterfeldt, and courses were held there continuously. These
> courses soon became the meeting-place of youth leaders of many
> different associations and tendencies. . . . It was thus not surprising
> that, at first slowly and sporadically, later much more markedly,
> National Socialist ideas . . . were put forward in the discussions and
> defended passionately. . . As these young men of between 20 and
> 30 years were particularly well qualified, the Reichswehr did not
> want to forego their participation in the training programme. The
> course for 'guerrilla warfare behind the front' held in 1926 was very
> strongly attended by people with such leanings. . . .[2]

In Silesia too there existed in each *Kreis* a Kreis officer with his
own staff; there were more than forty such officers in the
province. 'It is particularly important to state that all these
Kreis officers of the Reichswehr are "accidentally" well-known
right-wing extremists. It is, however, true that a decree of the
defence ministry is observed in the sense that these gentlemen,
on taking over their functions, formally leave organizations
such as the *Stahlhelm*. . . .'[3] In Pomerania not even that seems
to have been done.

Later one of the leaders of the Pomeranian frontier defence
forces reported naïvely: 'Although the frontier defence was
absolutely non-political, it was always suspected. The efficient
organization, the contacts with the Reichswehr, which could
not be kept secret any longer, the "personal union" with the
Stahlhelm gave offence . . . to the Prussian government. The

[1] Report of 'a man who stands close to the Reichswehr': Schüddekopf, *Heer und
Republik*, no. 85, pp. 204–6.

[2] Report of the former Colonel Franz von Gaertner of 1952: Zeugenschrifttum,
no. 44, Institut für Zeitgeschichte, Munich.

[3] Anlage 6 to the letter of the deputies Hermann Müller and Otto Wels to
Dr. Geßler, Berlin, 6 Dec. 1926: Reichskanzlei, Akten betr. Reichswehr, vol. v,
R 43 I 686, Bundesarchiv Koblenz.

arms depots, chiefly in manor houses, seemed dangerous. . . .'[1] On 30 June 1923 a new agreement on frontier defence matters had been concluded between Dr. Geßler and the Prussian minister of the interior, Severing. This expressly forbade the training of volunteers in the use of weapons of any kind, and the participation of any organizations in the preparation or carrying out of the envisaged measures. These stipulations were clearly violated in Pomerania as well as in Silesia. It is true that the agreement also contained a clause which permitted the taking of special precautions in the eastern frontier districts.[2] But it was not stated that this clause invalidated the other provisions of the agreement. In any case, the Prussian minister of the interior, Grzesinski, strongly protested in November 1926 against these preparations:

All these organizations constitute . . . the form of the *secret system of mobilization* of the Reichswehr, which aims at the registration of the able-bodied men, as it was done in the old army by the district commands. In the directives of 30 June 1923, agreed upon by minister Severing and the defence ministry, nothing is stipulated about such measures of mobilization and their preparation; they were never envisaged and go far beyond the framework of the preparations permitted for the eastern frontier areas. The precondition even of these was that nothing was to be done without, and everything through, the civil authorities; while the Reichswehr has done the opposite and has undertaken virtually everything on its own. . . .

The organization is *politically completely one-sided*. It leans mainly on circles which are hostile to the republic. The nucleus of the organization is the *Kreis* officers, who are officers of the old army and stand, almost without exception, politically on the right. . . . The participants in the courses are recruited, as reports from the most different areas prove, almost entirely from members of associations and para-military organizations of the right or extreme right (*Stahlhelm*, *Wehrwolf*, etc.). . . . Thus the organization in practice amounts to a co-operation of the Reichswehr with the para-military *Verbände* of the right, the negative, if not openly hostile, attitude of which towards the republic is well known. In this way the prohibition of any links between the Reichswehr and these organizations,

[1] Report of H. Kreusler of 1954: Sammlung Oberst Dieter von Kleist, Zg. 244/57, Bundesarchiv-Militärarchiv.
[2] Schüddekopf, op. cit., no. 65, pp. 144–5; Reichskanzlei, Akten betr. Reichswehr, vol. v, R 43 I 686, loc. cit.

which has been promulgated by the defence ministry, remains on paper. . . .

In this connexion it should be mentioned that the contact men of the Reichswehr (*Kreis* officers) for frontier defence matters are at the same time officers reporting about the suitability of Reichswehr replacements, and that the participants in the training courses are considered in the first place as recruits. Thus in the end the *Wehrmacht* would be entirely recruited from members of the *Wehrverbände*. . . .

In view of the disadvantages, which have already appeared and are to be feared, I consider the existing system of frontier defence preparations untenable. . . . I therefore intend to renounce the agreement of 30 June 1923 and to replace it by new arrangements which make these defects impossible. . . .

The new regulations, Grzesinski demanded, should prohibit any training and officer courses, any army sports organization, the system of the *Kreis* officers, and the keeping of lists of able-bodied men.[1] Yet the Reichswehr could not possibly make concessions which would have destroyed all that had been achieved so far, under great difficulties. It was a Utopian programme.

In the army command these and similar incidents were bound to increase the old dislike of the Prussian government. Even before Grzesinski's letter was written Schleicher replied to a complaint of the Prussian government about the military training of non-soldiers with the words: 'The Reichswehr has had enough of the Prussian government's snooping.'[2] And another officer declared in the district office of Allenstein in East Prussia: 'What such a . . . minister as this Severing says leaves us of the Reichswehr quite cold.' His colonel declined to take any action against the officer.[3] Yet—in an effort, it seems, to meet the complaints of the Prussian government—the *Truppenamt* in March 1926 briefly pointed out that the following measures were forbidden: the support of *private* para-military organizations, the carrying out of preparations with regard to

---

[1] The Prussian minister of the interior to the prime minister of Prussia, Berlin, 6 Nov. 1926, pp. 4–5, 13–14, 16, 21–23: ibid. The above are only a few extracts from a letter which comprises 25 typed pages.

[2] Statement of the Prussian prime minister Otto Braun to Stresemann on 29 Oct. 1926: Nachlaß Stresemann, vol. 302, 7155 H, H 151925 (microfilm).

[3] Ibid., 7155 H, H 151924.

personnel (except in the eastern frontier areas), and practical military training with weapons. 'Only at the eastern frontier is it permitted to compile lists of the personnel required for the frontier defence units, and this must therefore be carried out. . . .' The officers working in this field were again enjoined to address themselves to the general population and not to co-operate only with the circles of the right. If that instruction were followed, there would be no objections to these measures, on grounds either of foreign or of domestic policy.[1] On the following day the chief of the *Truppenamt*, Major-General Wetzell,[2] once more emphasized the necessity of refusing any co-operation with the *Verbände*, orders, associations, &c. in the field of frontier defence. 'The importance of the army in the state rests in particular on the fact that we have succeeded, in six years of hard work, in detaching the soldiers from the struggle of political opinions and the conflict of interests; the same rule applies with equal force to our efforts in the realm of frontier defence. . . . I stress that the chief of the army command has instructed me to make this known to the chiefs of staff' of the *Gruppenkommandos* and of the infantry and cavalry divisions.[3]

At the same time Seeckt tried to achieve a more central direction in all matters of frontier defence. In a decree of January 1926 he declared that especially in this field 'the strictest central guidance' was indispensable, otherwise much time and effort would be wasted and the whole work might be endangered. Therefore all frontier defence questions came under the instructions of the chief of the *Truppenamt*, who received his directives from Seeckt. The latter also reserved to himself the decision in questions of principal importance.[4] Within the *Truppenamt* a special department, the T 2 III, was responsible for all frontier defence issues. Thus the army command attempted to assert its control in this controversial field, by taking measures against the many *Verbände* and para-military organizations of

[1] Truppenamt to Waffenamt, 31 Mar. 1926: Akten des Heereswaffenamtes, WilF 5/422, Bundesarchiv Koblenz.
[2] Wetzell had just succeeded General Hasse in the key position at the defence ministry.
[3] The Chef des Truppenamtes to the Chefs der Stäbe der Gruppenkommandos, Wehrkreiskommandos und Kavalleriedivisionen, Berlin, 1 Apr. 1926: ibid., WilF 5/509.
[4] Chef der Heeresleitung, Berlin, 15 Jan. 1926: ibid., WilF 5/1983.

the right, which continued to have their own political aims.[1]
Yet all local preparations in Brandenburg, Pomerania, and
Silesia depended upon the 'symbiosis' with the *Stahlhelm* and
similar associations. Their local leaders were usually the *Kreis*
officers, even if they had formally left the *Verband* in question.
And only in the eastern provinces of Prussia bordering on
Poland were the preparations at all in an advanced state.
All the decrees in the world could not change these basic facts;
and this meant also that the conflicts with the Prussian ministry
of the interior would continue. It was a problem that had
existed from the beginning and that could not be solved.

v. *Connexions with Russia*

During the years 1924 to 1926 the Russian enterprises remained of decisive importance for the Reichswehr. Slowly the
conflict between Seeckt and the German ambassador Count
Brockdorff-Rantzau abated, and the latter was gradually able
to assert greater political control over the military activities in
Russia. The two men saw eye to eye on the basic questions of
foreign policy. Both were in favour of an eastern orientation of
German policy and of friendly relations with Soviet Russia;
both were fervently opposed to the Treaty of Versailles and
therefore against Germany's entry into the League of Nations,
which in their opinion meant that Germany voluntarily sanctioned the treaty; both feared that this entry would block
Germany's free road to the east, to which they attached the
greatest value.[2]

Under the direction of one of Germany's leading flying
officers, Colonel Thomsen, a German military mission was
established in Moscow which became known as *Zentrale Moskau*.
It was responsible for the German military and armaments
enterprises in Russia and for the liaison with the Russian
military authorities; it could issue instructions to the German
officers working in Russia, for example as instructors of the
Red Air Force or in the German flying school at Lipetsk.
These officers—like Thomsen himself and his assistant, Major

---

[1] Vogelsang, *Reichswehr, Staat und NSDAP*, p. 43.
[2] Brockdorff-Rantzau to President Hindenburg in 1925: Nachlaß Brockdorff-
Rantzau, 9101 H/IV, H 224017–18 (microfilm).

von Niedermayer—were formally discharged from the Reichswehr before they went to Russia, but on their return to Germany
could once more become active officers.[1] While the relations
between Brockdorff-Rantzau and Niedermayer always remained bad because the count distrusted him and his irresponsible actions, Thomsen succeeded in establishing close and
friendly relations with the ambassador. In a birthday letter of
1926 the colonel wrote to him: 'Fate . . . has brought me into
the proximity of the greatest man Germany possesses. That I
gained the confidence of this man and was allowed to learn in
the school of his thought and his determination, was more than
I could have hoped for. . . .'[2] In view of such fulsome praise
Brockdorff-Rantzau's distrust of the military and their independent procedures began to disappear.

Early in 1924 Niedermayer informed the ambassador that
the *Gefu* sent its entire correspondence to Berlin through
Russian couriers, and not through German diplomatic channels.[3]
But this too was gradually changed. At the beginning of 1926
Seeckt ordered that the *Gefu* should be reorganized, and the
chief of the *Truppenamt* should exercise the decisive influence in
its affairs. He was to administer all the funds earmarked for
Russia; through him was to go the entire correspondence with
Russia, whether by letter or telegram, and the dispatch of personnel and supplies. In Moscow all *Gefu* matters were put under
the representative of the defence ministry there, Colonel
Thomsen, who was to co-ordinate all issues of military policy
in Russia; he was to receive all communications from the
defence ministry through a member of the staff of the *Truppenamt* (Major Fischer) and to address all his correspondence
to him. Fischer was equally made responsible for all contacts
with the Russian authorities in Berlin.[4] Officially, the *Gefu*,
which had lost much money through speculation, was then
dissolved and replaced by a new firm, *Wirtschaftskontor G.m.b.H.*

[1] Note signed Hencke, Berlin, 12 July 1926: Auswärtiges Amt, Büro von Staatssekretär v. Schubert: Akten betr. Militärische Angelegenheiten mit Rußland,
vol. iii, 4564/3, E 163630–1 (microfilm).
[2] Thomsen to Brockdorff-Rantzau, Moscow, 29 May 1926: Nachlaß Brockdorff-Rantzau, 9101 H/III, H 223703.
[3] Note of Brockdorff-Rantzau, Moscow, 4 Apr. 1924: ibid., 9101 H/XII,
H 226826.
[4] 'Ausführungsbestimmungen zur Umorganisation der Gefu', 11 Mar. 1926:
Nachlaß Niedermayer, Bundesarchiv-Militärarchiv.

This firm administered the remaining funds of the *Gefu* and regularly received large sums from the *Truppenamt*, to which it was subordinate.[1] The *Gefu* and its successor were also responsible for other foreign business transactions of the army, for example the production of cartridges in Sweden and Austria, and the sale of machines and guns to the Argentine, Chile, Sweden, Spain, and Turkey; but some of the officers clearly distrusted the commercial competence of the *Gefu* representatives.[2]

Of the *Gefu* enterprises in Russia, the production of shells for the Reichswehr, in particular, was carried out in different Russian works. In September 1926 three Russian boats brought 300,000 shells to Pillau and Stettin, together with the necessary fuses and gunpowder, but declared as pig-iron or aluminium. In Trotsk near Samara a Hamburg firm built a factory for the production of poison gas; but early in 1926 this work had to be interrupted for financial and other reasons.[3] The Junkers works at Fili, too, suffered from growing financial difficulties because—after the end of the inflation—the Reichswehr did not possess the large sums required and the Russians did not give enough orders to the factory.[4] The loss suffered at Fili, to September 1925, amounted to nearly 15 million marks, more than half of which was due to the fact that the Junkers works at Dessau had debited Fili with the interest charges and general costs of the whole Junkers firm. But the works at Fili too had suffered a loss of 50,000 marks for each aeroplane produced: a loss which the *Heereswaffenamt* considered 'almost grotesque'.[5]

---

[1] Lieutenant-Colonel von Senftleben to Lieutenant-Colonel Mentzel, Berlin, 20 Apr. 1926: Nachlaß Mentzel, no. 4, Bundesarchiv Koblenz; Hilger and Meyer, *The Incompatible Allies*, p. 194.

[2] 'Zu welchem Zweck benötigen wir die Gefu?', n.d.: Akten des Heereswaffenamtes, WiIF 5/1344, Bundesarchiv Koblenz.

[3] Anlagen 12 and 12a to the letter of the deputies Hermann Müller and Otto Wels to Dr. Geßler, Berlin, 6 Dec. 1926: Reichskanzlei, Akten betr. Reichswehr, vol. v, R 43 I 686, ibid.; von Senftleben to Mentzel, Berlin, 20 Apr. 1926: Nachlaß Mentzel, no. 4, Bundesarchiv Koblenz.

[4] Brockdorff-Rantzau to Maltzan, Moscow, 30 Apr. 1924: Nachlaß Brockdorff-Rantzau, 9101 H/IX, H 225908–9; and his report about a conversation with Trotsky in June 1924: H. W. Gatzke, *Stresemann and the Rearmament of Germany*, Baltimore, 1954, p. 81.

[5] 'Schlußbetrachtung des Heereswaffenamtes zum Status des Junkers-Flugzeugwerkes in Fili', Berlin, 15 June 1926: Nachlaß Geßler, no. 55, Bundesarchiv Koblenz.

On 30 January 1926 General von Seeckt and Major-General Hasse visited the Soviet embassy in Berlin. The conference lasted until 11.30 p.m. and was 'very interesting and perhaps not unimportant'. The Russians expressed their dissatisfaction with the *Gefu* and the financial obstacles, and complained about the slow progress and the difficulties with Junkers, with a poison gas and other factories. Agreement was reached that these difficulties should be resolved in discussions to be held in Berlin and that the work should be continued. The Russians asked for very considerable credits, about ten per cent. of which should be available for military purposes.[1] In the pursuance of these plans the Deputy People's Commissar for War, Unshlikht, came to Berlin two months later and negotiated with the ministry of defence. The Russian embassy gave a dinner in his honour, which was attended by the chancellor, Luther, the foreign minister, Stresemann, and the Generals von Seeckt and Wetzell (the chief of the *Truppenamt*). Unshlikht spoke about vast Russian plans for the production of heavy artillery, poison gas, and precision instruments, for which German support was required. If Germany was willing to co-operate, German officers could be trained in Russia: he had discussed these projects at the defence ministry, but what was the attitude of the German government? The surprised Stresemann declared in general terms his willingness to co-operate with Russia 'in all enterprises of peace', while Seeckt remained silent.[2]

Yet he was not always so taciturn towards the Russians. In January 1925 he attended a dinner in the Russian embassy, together with Hasse, who was then the chief of the *Truppenamt*. On the Russian side only the ambassador Krestinsky, Rosengolts from the Red Air Force, and the leader of the Russian trade delegation in Berlin, Stomonyakov, were present. The Russians expressed their doubts about Germany's foreign policy—at the time when Stresemann was preparing Germany's entry into the League—and about the possibilities of further military co-operation. Seeckt developed 'the directives for German policy. Impossible to lean either on France or Britain.

[1] Handwritten notes of Seeckt, 30 Jan. 1926: Nachlaß Seeckt, box 7, no. 53, Militärgeschichtliches Forschungsamt. Seeckt to his wife, Berlin, 31 Jan. 1926: Nachlaß Seeckt, roll 28, p. 352 (microfilm).

[2] Nachlaß Brockdorff-Rantzau, 9101 H/XII, H 226849–53; Helbig, op. cit., pp. 180–1; Hilger and Meyer, op. cit., p. 202.

Therefore on Russia. Wait and exploit an Anglo-French conflict. Goal in the east: frontiers of 1914!' When the Russians
asked whether Germany, if offered advantages, would not side
with Britain against Russia, Seeckt emphasized again: 'Germany cannot go against Russia.'[1] There is no doubt that Seeckt
and his listeners realized that the policy advocated by him was
in contrast with Stresemann's attempt at a *rapprochement* with
the western powers. Some weeks later the president of the
Council of People's Commissars, Rykov, told the German
ambassador that the Russians considered Seeckt 'one of the
firmest pillars of a sincere and cordial understanding between
Germany and Russia . . .'.[2]

The results of all these efforts were of great importance for
the Reichswehr. In 1926 25 German officers were sent to
Russia: 14 of them to attend training schools, 8 to participate
in manœuvres and exercises, one in experiments with poison
gas, and the others to learn Russian. Thirteen Russian officers
came to Germany, mainly to attend exercises and manœuvres;
but two of them were attached to the defence ministry, probably for training as general staff officers.[3] On 9 December 1926,
after negotiations lasting many months, a treaty was signed
about the establishment of a tank school at Kama near Kazan.
The Germans were to pay in the first instance 125,000 roubles
(about 250,000 marks); the school was to be opened in the
spring of 1927 if the buildings could be finished by then, and
the Russians were to be given 'as many places as possible' in
the first year. But they steadfastly declined to lend any tanks
to the school, and the Germans were for the time being unable
to supply them.[4] Hence the school could not be opened before
the spring of 1929.

Far more important was the aerodrome at Lipetsk, to the
north of Voronezh, where a beginning was made in 1924 with
the construction of a German flying base. This was entirely

[1] Handwritten notes of Seeckt, 15 Jan. 1925: Nachlaß Seeckt, box 7, no. 52,
Militärgeschichtliches Forschungsamt.
[2] Nachlaß Brockdorff-Rantzau, 9101 H/XII, H 226841; Helbig, op. cit., p. 169.
[3] Notes of 21 Feb. 1928: Auswärtiges Amt, Handakten von Dirksen, 9481 H,
H 276324 (microfilm).
[4] See the telegrams of Niedermayer, Moscow, 16 Sept. and 2 Oct. 1926, and of
Fischer, Berlin, 22 and 27 July, 23 and 27 Sept. 1926: Auswärtiges Amt, Büro von
Staatssekretär v. Schubert, 4564/2, E 162943-5, 162984, 163001, 163007, 163012,
163031.

financed by the Reichswehr. The first fighter aeroplanes were bought from the Fokker works in Holland with sums which came from the 'Ruhr fund' (to finance the passive resistance campaign in the Ruhr).

Around two runways there came into being a large complex of hangars, wharfs, production and repair shops. . . . There were administrative and living quarters, a hospital equipped with the most modern clinical apparatus, wireless and telephone installations, railway connexions, etc. The German flyers' colony was quartered in the wide area of the aerodrome, which was highly modern according to the standards of the time, camouflaged towards the outside as the 'fourth squadron' of a Russian flying unit. . . . The direction and management of the whole installation were exclusively German. The whole complex was carefully sealed off and guarded by Soviet militia. . . . The German personnel consisted of the permanent personnel, which remained at Lipetsk throughout the year . . . and numbered about 60 men; further, the personnel of the military training courses which were held during the summer months (about 50 men); finally, the personnel engaged in technical experiments (between 70 and 100 men); so that during the summer there were on an average about 200 Germans present. The Red Air Force was represented at Lipetsk by a fairly large number of soldiers, who were trained in special technical courses by German instructors (foremen and mechanics) in all technical branches. . . .

This is the description of a German flying officer who was trained at Lipetsk.[1] Thus the Reichswehr was enabled to train fighter pilots and observers, to test aeroplanes, to make technical experiments, and to collect experience which was to prove invaluable for the building up of a German air force.

Apart from Lipetsk, there is no evidence that the Reichswehr during these years reaped any substantial benefits from the agreements with Russia. It is true that the 300,000 'Soviet shells' were sent to Germany at the end of 1926; but that was not much of a return for the large sums spent in Russia. For Seeckt, however, the question of co-operation with Russia was, above all, a political issue: it was directed against France and Poland and was justified on account of Germany's political

---

[1] Helm Speidel, 'Reichswehr und Rote Armee', *Vierteljahrshefte für Zeitgeschichte*, i, 1953, especially pp. 24–26.

situation, independent of achievements in the practical field. To Seeckt the central issue was and remained the 'frontiers of 1914!' As a peaceful disintegration of Poland was out of the question, this goal naturally included the preparation for war in the unspecified future, whenever an opportune moment might arise.

vi. *The Navy*

After the experiences of the year 1923, when it emerged that the negotiator on the Russian side was in reality a Frenchman,[1] three years elapsed before the German navy re-established contacts with the Russians. Early in 1926 the Germans, using the occasion of a visit of the former chief of the naval command, Admiral Behncke, to Moscow, suggested tentatively that it might be possible to arrange an 'accidental meeting' with a prominent Russian naval officer. The Russians, however, declined because the German government had mentioned in parliament as a special reason for new German naval construction 'the growth of the Red Navy'. Thus Behncke had to confine himself to a declaration addressed to People's Commissar Chicherin during a dinner 'that the main task of the German navy lay in the secure control of the sea routes into the Baltic through Danish waters, to prevent a link between hostile powers and Poland; that a front against the east did not exist in German naval warfare, except against Poland, but only a front against the west, against the same powers as might also be Russia's enemies; thus the front of both Russia and Germany was in the same way directed against the west . . .'.[2]

Only a few weeks later the Russians—perhaps encouraged by these remarks—in their turn approached the German navy. A conference was held in Berlin which was attended by the Russian military attaché, Luniev, a Russian naval officer, Oras, four senior German naval officers, Colonel Thomsen from Moscow, and Major Fischer, who were responsible for the Russian contacts of the German army. The Russians desired a

---

[1] See above, pp. 146–7.

[2] Commander Saalwächter to chief of the naval command, at sea, near Matsushima, 18 Mar. 1926: Admiralität, Marine-Kommandoamt, Flotten-Abteilung, Marinepolitische Angelegenheiten: 7897 A Ic 1–1, Militärgeschichtliches Forschungsamt Freiburg.

co-operation with Germany to reorganize their navy: the German experiences in naval construction, especially of submarines, should be made accessible to the Russians, and in exchange the German navy should participate in the further development of German submarines and perhaps train personnel in Russia. The Russians had made designs for submarines and were invited to submit these to the naval command so that it could suggest modifications. The question of the training of German naval officers as pilots had been discussed together with that of German army officers; the Russian naval officer assured the Germans that in this respect too Germany would find Russia willing to support her.[1] One of the German naval officers present, Rear-Admiral Spindler, was then sent to Russia to inspect Russian naval installations at Kronstadt and elsewhere. The Russians submitted a number of requests to him, especially with regard to submarines. The Germans accepted these wishes with regard to the designs of certain submarines and evaluations of their types; but other Russian requests, for example that three experts in submarine construction should be sent to them, were left unanswered. The chief of the naval command, Admiral Zenker, decided that only submarine designs which could be classified as 'antiquated' should be given to the Russians, apart from Spindler's report about his journey. Another naval officer added to this note that, in his opinion, only some of the plans should be handed over; 'it remains important that we do not compromise ourselves, because the Russians cannot be trusted'.[2]

A conference was then held in the presence of Admiral Zenker 'about the directives and aims of German naval policy', at which the principal address was given by Captain von Loewenfeld, the former commander of the free corps which bore his name.[3] He discussed various European and non-European countries one after the other. Whoever supported his view

that Bolshevism in Russia does not attenuate, or only slowly, that Bolshevism is the greatest enemy of the culture of the Occident,

---

[1] 'Niederschrift über eine Besprechung am 25. III. 1926': Marineleitung, Akten betr. Rußland: I SKL. Ic—4, vol. i, PG/33617, Admiralty, London.
[2] Notes of various days in July 1926, ibid., and Marine-Kommandoamt, Flotten-Abteilung, Allgemeines, 7895 A Ia I, Militärgeschichtliches Forschungsamt Freiburg.   [3] See above, pp. 84–85, 98–99.

must see in Russia the greatest enemy Germany has at the moment.
. . . *Italy* tries to gain supremacy in the Mediterranean. Mussolini,
as a dictator and the destroyer of the Italian Social Democrats and
the Jewish freemasons, is an enemy of the German democrats, but
he is perhaps the man to fight France for supremacy in the Mediterranean. *France* . . . is for the time being unteachable in its marked
hostility to the Germans, with which it successfully infects the
Czechs, Poles, Danes, and Belgians. *Britain* is at the moment the
leader of western culture. If Britain is destroyed by Communism, or
the revolt of her colonies, the danger of the Bolshevization of Europe
becomes burningly acute. Britain has recognized the danger of
Bolshevism, hence the friends of the Bolsheviks are her enemies.
The *U.S.A.* is too far away and too little interested in the details of
Europe.

His suggestion was therefore, 'to seek, with caution, determina-
tion, and tact, an understanding with *Britain*, in the common
struggle against Bolshevism. Similarly a *rapprochement* with
Italy as a counterweight to France. . . . Only play with the
Russians: deceive them amicably, without their noticing it.' The
relations with the Russians should be used to put pressure on
Britain and to obtain a lessening of Bolshevik propaganda in
Germany.

Admiral Zenker agreed in general terms. He too was of the
opinion

that for the navy in the present situation a co-operation with *Britain*
was natural, and a military co-operation with Russia could only be
undertaken with great caution. *Poland* will disintegrate. The fourth
partition of Poland will come because that state is not viable, on
account of the maladministration reigning there. The chief [of the
naval command] does not believe in the possibility of a co-operation
with Italy against France, for we should have to pull the Italian
chestnuts out of the fire without receiving anything in return. . . .
Russia: utmost caution. No ties as the army command has established
them. In spite of this, the thread not to be cut, so as to be able to
put pressure on the Anglo-Saxons occasionally. *Italy* politely and
correctly. From the Italians we cannot expect much in the military
field. . . .[1]

---

[1] 'Niederschrift über die Besprechung beim Chef der Marineleitung am 22.7.26
über die Richtlinien und Ziele der deutschen Marinepolitik': Marine-Kommandoamt, Flotten-Abteilung, Marinepolitische Angelegenheiten: 7897 A Ic I–I,
Militärgeschichtliches Forschungsamt.

What clearly emerged was the open distrust of the army command and its 'ties' with the Russians; but also—in the case of Captain von Loewenfeld—a strong ideological bias, in his emphasis on the threats to the culture of the Occident, his sympathy with Italian Fascism, and his dislike of 'the Jewish freemasons'. But there is no evidence that Admiral Zenker shared these opinions.

A week later another naval officer summarized the reasons which forced the navy to adopt a cautious attitude towards the Russians: 'The advantages which such a co-operation may bring to Germany are in the first place in the economic field. The military benefits, which *may* accrue to us, will be relatively small. The Russians expect that we, full of confidence, give them everything that they desire, and meanwhile show the deepest distrust towards us. . . .' The greatest caution was necessary because of the many uncertain factors in Russia, in domestic and foreign politics as well as in economics, as any change in the system of government would have far-reaching consequences; this uncertainty forbade any close links in the military field; any co-operation should be limited to very restricted topics, for example submarines; even then the danger existed 'that we forge them a weapon which they will later use against us, that we commit military suicide. . . . We can wait until the Russians again approach us. . . . If they put forward any wishes, we can treat them at first in a dilatory fashion. . . . If our relations with the Russian navy became known, it would cause a strong reaction in Finland and would probably be considered a breach of trust. Above all, however, it would make very difficult, if not impossible, any *rapprochement* with the British navy. . . .'[1] When in the following month Rear-Admiral Spindler demanded a decision whether the navy should establish a group of experts in Moscow, as had the army, and whether Russians should be invited to attend naval exercises, Admiral Zenker declined both. His directive was: '*No further initiative from us.* Wait quietly to see what the Russians will do.' That was after a discussion with Seeckt, in which he informed the admiral in great detail 'about the plans of the army and his

[1] 'Stellungnahme von A II c zu dem Bericht des Konteradmirals a.D. Spindler über seine Rußlandreise', 29 July 1926: Marineleitung, Akten betr. Rußland: 1 SKL. Ic—4, vol. i, Admiralty, London.

opinion of the value of co-operation'.[1] During the following years the German navy maintained its independent and negative attitude towards Soviet Russia.

In other European countries, however, the navy was extremely active during these years. Like the army, it received, during the year of the struggle in the Ruhr, certain sums for which it did not have to render account.[2] The chief of the naval command, Admiral Behncke, entrusted the head of the Sea Transport Division, Captain Lohmann, with the administration of the money. As the captain later reported officially, it was the intention of the naval command to fill somehow the gaps created by the Treaty of Versailles in the defence of the country, 'outside the budget which was accessible to the Entente'. In the naval command discussions were held about the sum required, which was at first estimated at 200 to 250 million marks, but then reduced to 100 millions: what the navy finally received was 10 million marks. With the money Lohmann in the first instance bought speed-boats and paid for their maintenance. For this purpose the *Trayag* (*Travemünder Yachthafen A.G.*) was founded in 1924. Its main task was the development of speed-boats; the current costs came to between 150,000 and 200,000 marks a year, and the initial cost to 450,000 marks. The speed-boats were used for experiments in the firing of torpedoes—an activity prohibited by the Treaty of Versailles.[3]

Lieutenant-Commander Canaris—a former officer of the Loewenfeld brigade—drew the attention of Lohmann to the *Ingenieurskantoor voor Scheepsbouw*, which had been founded in 1922 in The Hague, and to the need of maintaining an efficient office for the construction and design of submarines. Lohmann then subsidized the Dutch office with almost a million marks. The *I.v.S.* could thus secure in 1925 an order for the construction of two submarines of 500 tons for the Turkish navy, which were built in a dock at Rotterdam.[4] At the beginning of the

[1] Note of 24 Aug. 1926, Marineleitung, Akten betr. Rußland: 1 SKL. Ic—4, vol. i, Admiralty, London.   [2] Cf. above, p. 155.
[3] Report by Lohmann, Berlin, 24 Sept. 1927, and Admiral Zenker to Dr. Geßler, Berlin, 9 Nov. 1927: Reichskanzlei, Akten betr. die von Kapitän z.S. Lohmann getätigten wirtschaftlichen Unternehmungen, vols. i–ii, R 43 I 603–04, Bundesarchiv Koblenz; Kapitän z.S. Lahs to the chief of staff, Berlin, 13 Feb. 1928: Marine-Leitung, Abteilung B, Verschiedenes, PG 34428 xi, Militärgeschichtliches Forschungsamt.
[4] Kapitän z.S. Schüssler, 'Der Kampf der Marine gegen Versailles 1919–1935':

same year Canaris travelled to Spain to canvass there for the
I.v.S. and to prevent the Spaniards from concluding an agreement with its rivals, Blohm & Voss of Hamburg. He emphasized
that the *I.v.S.* was closely connected with the only German
firm which had designed numerous submarines for Germany
and other countries, the Germaniawerft at Kiel, and that the
group represented by the *I.v.S.* was the only one with a special
office in a neutral country: therefore the German navy had
decided to support this group and no other. Under no circumstances must the naval command be by-passed as had been
done by Blohm & Voss. 'It must be achieved that the naval
command directly participates in the further development of
submarine construction and that the building and the running-
in of the boats in Spain is not done by Spanish personnel, but
by specially selected Germans who offer the guarantee that
their knowledge and experience will later benefit the German
navy. . . .'¹

At the end of February 1925 a group of interested Spaniards
visited Germany. Its attention was drawn once more to the
I.v.S., and it realized that through the *I.v.S.* the German war
experiences in the use of submarines and torpedoes could be
utilized. The Spanish industrialist Echevarrieta would visit
Germany to conclude the negotiations about the building of a
torpedo works at Cartagena. This visit took place soon after,
and the German naval officers succeeded in persuading him to
co-operate with the *I.v.S.*; the Spanish navy decided in favour
of the submarine type offered by the *I.v.S.* and rejected the
counter-offer made by Blohm & Voss; the German navy
throughout backed the *I.v.S.*—a factor which obviously influenced the Spaniards. The opinion in the naval command
was: 'The Spanish navy must be supported because a strengthening of Spain is a gain for Germany. Therefore interest in the
I.v.S. and its successes. . . .'² After another journey to Spain in

Trial of the Major War Criminals before the International Military Tribunal, xxxiv,
Nuremberg, 1949, pp. 566–7. Canaris later became an admiral and chief of
intelligence.
  ¹ 'Bericht des Korvettenkapitäns Canaris über seine Reise nach Spanien vom
28. Januar bis 17. Februar 1925', pp. 2, 12–15: Marineleitung, Akten betr.
Spanien: PG 48903 M (Sp), Militärgeschichtliches Forschungsamt.
  ² 'Entwicklung der spanischen Angelegenheit nach der Reise des Korvettenkapitäns Canaris nach Spanien im Februar 1925'; 'Stand der spanischen Angelegenheit'; 'Allgemeine Lage', n.d.: all ibid.

November 1927 Canaris reported: 'Echevarrieta has signed a contract with the Dutch firm in The Hague for the building of a submarine of 600 tons. The boat will be built at Cadiz, in the same way as the Turkish submarines have been built by the *I.v.S.* in the Dutch dockyard Fijnord. The boat represents a completely new type with fast-running engines supplied by the M.A.N. The main advantage is the considerable saving in weight. A boat of 600 tons achieves as much as a boat of 1,000 tons. The navy, through the *I.v.S.*, places at their disposal all its war experiences.' It was hoped that the Spanish navy would order another six submarines from Echevarrieta; he had already given an order for the building of eight speed-boats to the firm of Neesen at Travemünde, which were also to be built at Cadiz.[1]

In July 1926 the naval command noted with satisfaction that the *I.v.S.* had constructed several submarines for Japan, while two boats for the Turkish navy were being built. Other countries, such as Spain, the Argentine, Mexico, Russia, and Finland, also approached the *I.v.S.*; the negotiations with Spain and Finland were particularly promising, and the signing of further contracts was expected.[2] In November of the same year the chief of the naval command informed the German government that 'the construction of submarines at home and abroad was useless and would not be undertaken . . .'.[3] This was not a direct lie, nor was it the full truth. For the foundation and financing of the *I.v.S.* by the navy served the purposes of 'collecting practical experiences in submarine construction for the German naval command' and of enabling it to 'develop the building of men-of-war, especially submarines, by obtaining orders from foreign countries'.[4]

Another of the enterprises financed by Captain Lohmann was the *Severa G.m.b.H.* (*Seeflugzeug-Versuchsabteilung*), which was founded in co-operation with the German *Luft-Hansa* to promote the navy's air arm. The annual cost was estimated at

---

[1] 'Reise Spanien vom 8.11.–19.11.1927', Berlin, 21 Nov. 1927: Marineleitung, Akten betr. Spanien: PG 48903 M (Sp), Militärgeschichtliches Forschungsamt.

[2] 'Betr. Zusammenarbeit I.v.S. mit Abteilung K.', 16 July 1926: Marineleitung, Verschiedenes: PG 34 165/2 A I–III, Militärgeschichtliches Forschungsamt. About Finland cf. Raeder, *Mein Leben*, i. 231.

[3] 'Auszug aus dem Protokoll der Ministerbesprechung vom 29. November 1926': Reichskanzlei, Akten betr. Reichswehr, vol. v, R 43 I 686, Bundesarchiv Koblenz.

[4] 'Betr. Zusammenarbeit I.v.S. mit Abteilung K.', 16 July 1926: loc. cit.

1·2 million marks. From 1924 onwards the *Severa* organized refresher courses for war-time observer officers and training courses for young naval officers as observers. From 1925–6 it began to develop the types of seaplanes and aeroplanes that would be required in case of mobilization, and their equipment and armament—partly in co-operation with the army command. The *Severa* slowly acquired a number of aerodromes and bases for seaplanes and could thus expand its activities. Every year about six pilots and six observers were trained. Aeroplanes were built at Warnemünde by the Heinkel works, and in Scandinavia; in 1926 Captain Lohmann bought the Caspar works at Travemünde for the same purpose.[1] In February 1925 the Japanese military attaché, Captain Komaki, visited the naval command and informed it that the Interallied Control Commission was 'doubtless well informed about the construction of aeroplanes at Warnemünde and Copenhagen, especially since the British had an extensive espionage service in Germany . . .'.[2]

These extensive activities in Germany and other countries explain the lack of interest of the naval command in developing closer contacts with Russia, quite apart from its wish to establish better relations with the British navy. A Russian offer to train pilots at Odessa was refused, although the aerodrome there offered special geographical and climatic advantages.[3] If the same could be done in Germany, it was cheaper and would cause no difficulties with friendly countries, such as Finland. But probably ideological considerations, as put forward by Captain von Loewenfeld, contributed to this decision, which differed so strongly from the policy adopted by the army.

VII. *The Dismissal of Seeckt*

On 27 September 1926 a south-German local paper reported that the eldest son of the Crown Prince, Prince Wilhelm, had

---

[1] Report of Kapitän z.S. Lahs, Berlin, 13 Feb. 1928: Marineleitung, Abteilung B, Verschiedenes: PG 34 428 XI, Militärgeschichtliches Forschungsamt; Völker, *Die Entwicklung der militärischen Luftfahrt in Deutschland 1920–1933*, pp. 139, 156–7.

[2] Conversation with Captain Komaki on 6 Feb. 1925: Admiralität, Marine-Kommandoamt, Flotten-Abteilung, Attaché-Angelegenheiten: 1./SKL Ic—2–1, PG/33614, Admiralty, London.

[3] Speidel, 'Reichswehr und Rote Armee', *Vierteljahrshefte für Zeitgeschichte*, i. 18; Völker, op. cit., p. 135.

taken part, in uniform, in the exercises of the Infantry Regiment 9, which continued the tradition of the Prussian foot guards. A week later the same report appeared in the Berlin press. Thereupon a veritable storm broke out against Seeckt. On 1 October Seeckt had an interview with Dr. Geßler, during which he apparently denied that he knew anything about the matter.[1] Soon, however, he had to admit that this was not true. On 5 October Geßler wrote to Seeckt: 'You have declared that you will take the responsibility for the whole affair and will bear the consequences. To my greatest regret I am forced . . . to tell you now that, in view of the circumstances, I see no possibility of resolving the severe crisis which faces the government and the *Wehrmacht* without the resignation of the chief of the army command. For it is not correct that, as you said, only the well-known enemies of the army are hostile; the indignation about the affair is extremely strong, especially in the parties of the centre. . . . And the friends of the army in particular are annoyed that, time and again, its enemies are provided with ammunition for their machinations. . . .'[2]

Some weeks later Colonel von Stülpnagel wrote to a brother-officer: 'The affair of the prince only played a minor part, although it was the straw which broke the camel's back. If S. had talked it over quietly with G., G. would certainly have been willing to cover this, as he has covered so many other things. But Seeckt treated him harshly, and G. was not willing to stand that. . . .'[3] General von Rabenau too remarked: 'Geßler simply exploded about the way in which he was treated, or more correctly, believed that he was treated. He said quite openly that he no longer desired to be the puppet which can be moved by pulling the strings. . . .'[4] An officer who knew the conditions in the defence ministry intimately— he was then chief of staff of the Third Division and later became chief of the army command—General Freiherr von Hammerstein-Equord, added by hand to the words 'in which he was treated': 'and had been treated for years'; and some pages

[1] Report of the Minister Reinhold to Count Keßler at the beginning of 1927: Harry Graf Keßler, *Tagebücher 1918–1937*, Frankfurt, 1961, p. 502. Cf. Rabenau, *Seeckt*, pp. 533–4.   [2] Ibid., p. 535.

[3] Stülpnagel to Colonel von Falkenhausen, Brunswick, 20 Nov. 1926: Depot Stülpnagel, H 08–5/21, Bundesarchiv-Militärarchiv.

[4] Rabenau, *Seeckt*, pp. 552–3.

further on said that Geßler had 'always been treated *badly* by
Seeckt; that he did not deserve'.[1] Geßler's adjutant, Major
Schellbach, remembered 'that the resentment of the minister
increased every day, although Schleicher . . . tried to calm him.
. . . I am convinced that it was only then that he conceived the
idea that he could not, and would not, co-operate any longer
with the general. He announced this for the first time on
Saturday, 2 October; on that day he summoned Schleicher
and myself, and said he was facing the fact that he had probably
come to the parting of the ways with General von Seeckt; the
decision was extremely difficult for him, but he did not need
advice from anyone. . . .'[2]

At the end of October Geßler declared in a cabinet meeting
that 'until then he had had to face the dilemma that he ought
not to cause a conflict with Seeckt, because this might have had
bad consequences as long as the authority of the state was not
consolidated. . . . The worst of the past had been that it was
never possible to get a proper answer out of Seeckt. . . .'[3] In
Seeckt's own opinion the affair with the prince was merely the
occasion, not the cause, of his dismissal: 'What then was the
cause? The clash between the democratic, parliamentarian
system and a personality that was independent of it; and in the
last resort the unbridgeable gulf between the representative of
the old Germany and of the commanding position of its army,
and the power-consciousness of the republican and parliamentarian civil authorities. . . .'[4] Certainly, both factors were of
great importance: the personal clash between Seeckt and the
minister, who had had enough of being the puppet, and the
clash of principle between Seeckt and the parliamentary system.

Strangely enough, Seeckt left. When his wife spontaneously
exclaimed, 'The officers will form a Fronde', he merely replied,
'I have not educated them in that spirit.' 'But', Frau von Seeckt
continues, 'he did not believe that President von Hindenburg

---

[1] Pencilled marginals by Generaloberst von Hammerstein-Equord: ibid.,
pp. 553, 559: Verw. Buch Nr. 134, Bundesarchiv-Militärarchiv.

[2] Comments by Lieutenant-General Schellbach on Rabenau's book, fol. 14:
Nachlaß Geßler, no. 46, Bundesarchiv Koblenz. Ibid., fol. 3, a good example of
the treatment of Geßler by Seeckt.

[3] Notes of Stresemann, Berlin, 29 Oct. 1926: Nachlaß Stresemann, vol. 302,
7155 H, H 151924 (microfilm).

[4] Notes of 14 Oct. 1926: Rabenau, *Seeckt*, p. 558.

would consent to his dismissal. . . .' To his wife Seeckt also said: 'If this had been someone else I would have said [to the president], "*Herr Feldmarschall*, now we will fight". As it was my own case, I could naturally not propose this. . . .' Hindenburg merely offered Seeckt the post of ambassador.[1] According to another report, Seeckt suggested to Hindenburg that he should be publicly reprimanded and confined to his rooms for some days, but the president simply laughed about the proposal.[2] As Hindenburg rightly considered himself the commander-in-chief of the Reichswehr, and as it was very difficult to handle Seeckt, the aged president was apparently rather pleased to see Seeckt depart. When Dr. Geßler first reported to the president and expressed the opinion that Seeckt should go, Hindenburg's first reaction was: 'that man corrupts the character of the officer corps with his conceit'.[3] Indeed, there was a strong personal contrast between the highly intellectual Seeckt, with his many interests and plans, and the old field-marshal, who was personally and intellectually very simple and reserved, and who personified the Prussian weaknesses and virtues much more strongly than Seeckt.

As far as we know, only one officer of his entourage advised Seeckt to resist his dismissal, if need be by force of arms. That was Lieutenant-Colonel Freiherr von Fritsch, who was then the head of the Army Department in the *Truppenamt*, one of the most bitter enemies of the republic among the senior officers. Seeckt, however, was not willing to act against the president, although 'on the 5th and 6th October he still toyed with the plan of using the instrument of power that stood behind him, and even to employ force . . .'.[4] Yet he did not want a military *Putsch*—a repetition of the Kapp enterprise. That such an undertaking was hopeless from the start was much more obvious in 1926 than it had been in 1920; and hardly any officers would have supported a *Putsch* against the aged field-marshal.

An epoch in the history of the Reichswehr came to an end in 1926. It had brought to the army command great political

[1] Nachlaß Seeckt, roll 28, p. 371a: microfilm in Institut für Zeitgeschichte, Munich; Rabenau, *Seeckt*, pp. 553–4.

[2] Report of Minister Reinhold to Count Keßler: *Tagebücher 1918–1937*, p. 502.

[3] Gordon, *Reichswehr and the German Republic*, p. 325.

[4] Rabenau, *Seeckt*, p. 536.

power, and then a slow decline of that power. The republic was more firmly established, the economic situation had greatly improved, and Stresemann's foreign policy was gaining considerable successes. Would the army, under a new chief, recognize these facts? or would the Reichswehr and the republic continue to lead their separate lives? Seeckt within six years had implanted his own stamp upon the army; as he stated himself, it was the stamp 'of the old Germany'. On the other hand, Seeckt was a man of plans, but not of deeds, and even less, a reformer or a revolutionary, and that undoubtedly had certain advantages for the republic while it was still weak. The revolutionaries of the right had left the army; there remained the conservatives, who attempted to restore the old order and frowned on all experiments. Thus the Reichswehr became a royalist island within the republic, and Seeckt a substitute for the king, who shielded the army from the world outside.[1]

In the person of Field-Marshal von Hindenburg, however, the army and the state acquired a new head much better suited for that role. 'Hindenburg was still surrounded by the halo of the victor of Tannenberg. With that he had once overshadowed the Emperor and become the hero of the nation. His election to the presidency confirmed his popularity anew. Thus it was only natural that the Reichswehr looked up to him as the leader of the people and put its confidence in him in peace-time too.'[2] To the pronounced monarchists among the officers Hindenburg became a kind of regent of the House of Hohenzollern, who would one day vacate his place to the rightful ruler. To those officers, who were willing to make their peace with the republic, Hindenburg's election marked an important step in that direction. They were intensely loyal to the new commander-in-chief of the Reichswehr. While many officers had despised and looked down upon the first president, Ebert, they almost venerated his successor. But he also took over the part which had been played by General von Seeckt; he personified the 'royal shield' much more impressively and effectively than any general; he was the true 'substitute for the king'.[3] Thus no gap was created by

---

[1] Cf. above, pp. 103, 107.   [2] Groener-Geyer, *General Groener*, p. 246.
[3] For the navy, this has been emphasized by the former admiral Wilhelm Meisel: Zeugenschrifttum, no. 1739, Institut für Zeitgeschichte; Baum, 'Marine,

Seeckt's dismissal in the relations between the officer corps and the head of the state. On the contrary, as the Reichswehr could hardly be loyal to two 'royal substitutes' at the same time, Seeckt's disappearance was the logical outcome of the election of the new president. Seeckt's dismissal did not create an upheaval: it passed almost unnoticed.

Nationalsozialismus und Widerstand', *Vierteljahrshefte für Zeitgeschichte*, xi, 1963, p. 41. For the army, see Marcks, 'Das Reichsheer 1919 bis 1934', in Linnebach, *Heeresgeschichte*, Hamburg, 1935, p. 20; Gordon, op. cit., pp. 323–4, quoting the letters of several Reichswehr officers. In general, see Bracher, *Die Auflösung der Weimarer Republik*, Stuttgart and Düsseldorf, 1955, pp. 48–49.

PART THREE

FROM THE REPUBLIC
TO DICTATORSHIP

'Meeting with Hitler: sympathetic impression, modest, decent fellow who wants the best. . . . Hitler's intentions and aims are good, but he is an enthusiast, fiery, many-sided. The minister fully agreed with him to further his intentions for the good of the Reich. . . .'

(*Defence Minister Groener on his meeting with Hitler, speaking at the conference of military leaders on 11 January 1932*)

VI

MOVING TO THE LEFT?

1. *The New Army Command and the Republic*

T HE most obvious successor to Seeckt was one of the two senior generals, either General von Loßberg, commander-in-chief of the First Army Corps in Berlin, or General Reinhardt, commander-in-chief of the Second Army Corps at Cassel. Both were by-passed, Reinhardt presumably for political reasons, as strong opposition to his appointment was to be expected from the officer corps. Both generals were embittered by this and asked Dr. Geßler that they be retired. But he succeeded in persuading them to withdraw their requests. Among the divisional commanders, who had to be considered next as possible successors, the most suitable was perhaps the commander of *Wehrkreis* iii and the Third Division, Lieutenant-General Otto Hasse, because he had maintained the closest political contacts with Seeckt and been the chief of the *Truppenamt* during the critical years 1922–5. Hindenburg thus mentioned Hasse's name when he received Seeckt on 7 October 1926, but apparently Seeckt was not in favour. Instead, Seeckt, in a conversation with General Wetzell, the chief of the *Truppenamt*, expressed his preference for Lieutenant-General Heye, the commander of *Wehrkreis* i and the First Division in East Prussia. Heye was summoned to Berlin before General Reinhardt, who was in Switzerland, was able to return.[1] Heye had been a close associate of Seeckt for many years; when Seeckt in 1920 succeeded Reinhardt as chief of the army command, Heye became Seeckt's successor as chief of the *Truppenamt*. Thereafter he was the chief of the army's Personnel Office, and later commander in East Prussia, which—separated from Germany—was of great strategical importance in case of a war with Poland. Heye was only a few years younger than

---

[1] Rabenau, *Seeckt*, pp. 540, 547; Gordon, op. cit., p. 267.

Seeckt and was nearly 58 years old when he became his successor.

Perhaps Seeckt, in recommending Heye, wanted to make certain that his own course would be maintained and his achievements be preserved. Each of the other possible successors, Loßberg, Reinhardt, or Hasse—who were stronger personalities—would have steered a more independent course, be that for or against the republic. In the case of Heye, who was a much weaker man, this was not to be feared. 'Heye was an unconscious viceroy for an absent monarch.'[1] But it could be foreseen that under a weak chief of the army command his immediate entourage would exercise much greater influence than had been the case under Seeckt, and that the 'Chinese wall' which Seeckt had erected around the army might be breached at certain points.

Immediately after Seeckt's dismissal the largest German party, the Social Democrats, attempted to curtail the political autonomy of the army and to bring about political changes. The prime minister of Prussia, Otto Braun, approached Stresemann and Geßler and declared that he was not interested in what happened in 1923, but now a clean sweep must be made; near Küstrin on the Oder fortifications were being built, exclusively by members of the *Stahlhelm*. The son of a senior legal official had recently applied for admission to the army as an ensign, giving a number of very good referees; soon after this he was asked by a leader of the *Wehrwolf* whether it was true that he wanted to join the army, and when he questioned the *Wehrwolf* representative how he knew, he replied: 'the Reichswehr has asked us for information about you.' Braun further mentioned examples of the negative attitude of certain officers towards the republic. Geßler did not deny any of these incidents and merely stated 'that things must change now. . . . He would assemble the commanders of the *Wehrkreise* and, together with General Heye, who fully agreed with him, inform them that these things must stop. . . .'[2]

In a conference with the leaders of the Social Democrats,

[1] Gordon, op. cit., p. 268.

[2] Notes of Stresemann, Berlin, 29 Oct. 1926: Nachlaß Stresemann, vol. 302, 7155 H, H 151923–4 (microfilm). The *Wehrwolf* was a para-military organization of the extreme right.

which took place some weeks later, the minister of defence adopted the same attitude. The Social Democratic deputies complained in detail about the violation of the disarmament clauses by the army, its secret activities in Soviet Russia, the connexions between the army and the *Verbände*, their arms depots, the collaboration between the *Kreis* officers and right-wing organizations, and their role in providing recruits for the Reichswehr. Geßler declared that now, after Seeckt's dismissal, all this would be changed; he had already discussed it with Heye and the government in detail. He also asked the Social Democrats to send him the material which formed the basis of their complaints. On 6 December the deputies complied with his wish, emphasizing that the illegal relations between the army and the *Verbände* had been continuing 'until very recently', and that they were only sending 'a small selection from the mass of material' they possessed, to ensure the prompt investigation promised by Geßler.[1]

One of the points in this Social Democratic material concerned the 300,000 'Soviet shells', which had been shipped to Pillau and Stettin in September of that year. But three days before the letter to Dr. Geßler was dispatched, on 3 December, the *Manchester Guardian* published a well-informed article under the headlines 'Cargoes of Munitions from Russia to Germany' and 'Secret Plan between Reichswehr Officers and Soviet'. The article contained details about the production of aeroplanes and poison gas in Russia on Russian and German orders, and about the constant visits of German officers to Russia; it also mentioned the shipments of arms and ammunition from Russia to Stettin. On 5 December a translation of this article appeared in the Social Democratic *Vorwärts* under the headline 'Soviet shells for Reichswehr guns!'[2] On 16 December the Social Democratic deputy Scheidemann sharply attacked the Reichswehr and the German industrial concerns working in Russia, especially the Junkers works, which themselves had supplied

---

[1] Conference on 1 Dec. 1926: Schüddekopf, *Heer und Republik*, no. 93, pp. 214–17; the deputies Hermann Müller and Otto Wels to Dr. Geßler, Berlin, 6 Dec. 1926: Reichskanzlei, Akten betr. Reichswehr, vol. v, R 43 I 686, Bundesarchiv Koblenz.

[2] Both articles in Auswärtiges Amt, Büro von Staatssekretär v. Schubert, Akten betr. Militärische Angelegenheiten mit Rußland, vol. iii: 4564/2, E 163401 ff. (microfilm).

the Reichstag deputies with the necessary information in a confidential memorandum about their Russian enterprises.[1] Scheidemann's speech did not contain any sensational revelations—those had already been published in the press. But it showed how embittered many Social Democrats were about the independent policy of Seeckt; it gave public expression to an old resentment, which naturally was repaid in kind by the officers. They believed that 'what Scheidemann said was, in ordinary terms, mere treason . . .'.[2] Thus the relations between the Reichswehr and the Social Democrats deteriorated just at a time when Seeckt's dismissal and Heye's more conciliatory attitude indicated the possibility of an improvement. Even officers who did not stand on the extreme right expressed their 'deep inner disappointment about the unchecked preponderance of unfriendliness and indifference in military issues, and about the many utterances by left-wing circles which are regrettable from the point of view of the country's defence'. These, in General Reinhardt's opinion, made any co-operation with the left difficult, if not impossible.[3]

Even before this incident the relations between the Reichswehr and the Social Democrats became more strained for a different reason. After Seeckt's dismissal the president of the Reichstag (speaker), Paul Löbe, published an article on recruiting for the Reichswehr, which touched it on a very sore point. Löbe maintained that the *Stahlhelm, Wehrwolf*, and similar organizations exercised the decisive influence on the selection of recruits:

This state of affairs is untenable if the republic does not want the Reichswehr to lead it by the nose. Some legal stipulations, which may be introduced after the example of the Austrian army, can easily remedy this:

§ 1. Replacements take place according to the time of the applications, if the applicant is physically fit and fulfils the other conditions. No applicant can be rejected on other grounds.

§ 2. The carrying out of this provision is supervised by two civilian parliamentary commissioners at every recruiting office. . . .[4]

---

[1] Wheeler-Bennett, *Nemesis of Power*, p. 129. A copy of the memorandum in Nachlaß Mentzel, no. 5, fols. 1–177, Bundesarchiv Koblenz.

[2] Rabenau, *Seeckt*, p. 497.

[3] Reinhardt to the deputy Dr. Haas, Kufstein, 25 Jan. 1927: Schüddekopf, op. cit., no. 100, p. 228.   [4] *Breslauer Volkswacht*, 21 Oct. 1926.

According to the regulations in force at the time the selection of recruits was entirely in the hands of the commanding officer of the company or squadron in question. They could get in touch with non-political associations, labour exchanges, &c. to obtain information about potential recruits. Whether an association was political or non-political, could be ascertained from a list of 'political associations' issued by the ministry of the interior, which included the so-called *Verbände*. The ministry of defence strongly objected to the proposals of Löbe, which would deprive the company commanders of the responsibility for the spirit of their men: if anything undesirable happened, they could always disclaim any responsibility for men allocated to them from outside.[1] Dr. Geßler too opposed Löbe's plan in a right-wing paper, the *Berliner Lokalanzeiger*, and defended the existing system as 'absolutely non-political'.[2]

Geßler's defence of this system rested on a weak basis; for among the people of whom inquiries were made about recruits the *Kreis* officers figured prominently, and they were members of, or at least sympathizers with, the *Stahlhelm*. As the majority of the recruits came from the countryside, local political checks were possible without any difficulty. As the local officer corps had close links with the local landowners, all inquiries and recommendations could be made without any formalities. The existing system could only have been modified by a political control of these local influences—and that would have encountered enormous difficulties. The army command was alarmed and asked the commanding officers of the corps and divisions for their views. In their replies most of the generals 'rejected Löbe's plans with the usual arguments', but 'did not discuss the general problem'. Three generals, however—Hasse, Kreß von Kressenstein, and Reinhardt—although they too were opposed to Löbe's plans, wrote 'that his attack made it necessary to consider whether the army's attitude towards the present state and the parties supporting it was in the long run appropriate and defensible. This is particularly emphasized in the statement by General Hasse . . .', thus Schleicher was

[1] Reichskanzlei, Berlin, 23 Oct. 1926, 'betrifft Rekrutierung der Reichswehr': Reichskanzlei, Akten betr. Reichswehr, vol. v, R 43 I 686, Bundesarchiv Koblenz.
[2] Schüddekopf, op. cit., p. 218.

informed by Lieutenant-Colonel von Bonin, a senior officer of the *Truppenamt*.[1] Hasse wrote:

A vital nerve of our army is touched by the demand of Löbe and his political friends and of the majority of the Democrats that our recruiting system should be changed. If the demand is conceded the effects are incalculable. . . . The influences which would then be used would alone be able to destroy our *Wehrmacht* and to bring it down to the Austrian level—a wish that is openly expressed. The result would be that the men, and later the officer corps too, would be very quickly politicized. . . . The mass of our adversaries is among the burghers of the centre, or on the left, and among the Social Democrats. They distrust the *Wehrmacht*, which they believe to be reactionary and sharply monarchist. I should like to answer the question, whether we can do anything about it, in the affirmative. If the opinion of these groups were correct, their distrust would be justified. . . . But their opinion is incorrect; it is only that we have not yet proved this sufficiently clearly. . . . We have got a republic, we cannot change this for objective and for personal reasons, and we do not want to change it. Outside the army a large part of the reasonable people, even among the German Nationalists, certainly think the same way. . . . Such a declaration of the army in favour of the republic will not lead us into the arms of those groups which are the fanatical protagonists of the republican idea and believe that every republican must be decidedly on the left. On the contrary, we shall be able to preserve the traditional values of the monarchical period more openly and better than hitherto. . . . I do not fear a rift. I have not encountered any opposition to such ideas, either in my division, or in civilian circles, in recent months. . . .

Hasse finally recommended getting in touch with the German Nationalist Party and with monarchist circles in Bavaria before taking any steps in the direction he advocated.[2]

Other generals reacted much more sharply. From Dresden the commander of the Fourth Division, General Wöllwarth, wrote to Reinhardt that he had replied to the inquiry in no uncertain terms. 'In spite of this, we here have the feeling that they are not firm enough in Berlin. Instead of declaring that the whole plan is unacceptable to the army and refusing on

---

[1] Lieutenant-Colonel von Bonin, chief of the T 2 of the *Truppenamt*, to Schleicher, Berlin, 3 Dec. 1926: Nachlaß Schleicher, no. 35, Bundesarchiv Koblenz.

[2] Hasse to the chief of the army command, Berlin, 30 Nov. 1926: Nachlaß Seeckt, box 17, no. 130, Militärgeschichtliches Forschungsamt. Hasse's chief of staff was Colonel Freiherr von Hammerstein-Equord.

principle to enter any discussion, the defence ministry searches for rational arguments and other little remedies to impress Herr Löbe and comrades. . . . A comparison between the autumn of 1918 and the autumn of 1926 is obvious. After the elimination of the head [i.e. the Emperor and Seeckt respectively], the instrument has to be destroyed and the weapon be knocked from our hands. Can we passively await this, do we not have to raise our warning voices. . . ?'[1] Differences of opinion on this highly controversial question also existed within the defence ministry. Lieutenant-Colonel von Bonin was convinced that the ideas expressed by General Hasse would be sharply repudiated by Major-General Wetzell, the chief of the *Truppenamt*, and by Lieutenant-Colonel von Fritsch, the chief of the T 1, its most important department, while he apparently counted Colonel von Schleicher on the side of the reformers.[2] One of Seeckt's confidants, Major Köstring, wrote to his old chief that 'now they want to convert us finally and energetically to the republic. I fear that this will not work so quickly, for we officers of medium rank and the younger officers have been educated in the German way and do not bother about parties. . . .'[3]

In the field of foreign policy too, Colonel von Bonin was prepared to take account of the changed situation. In a memorandum he stated:

Locarno, with the arbitration treaties, has been concluded; Germany has joined the League; international economic combinations are in preparation; the Treaty of Versailles is observed in every point as far as our army is concerned; public opinion in Germany is to a large extent under the impression that the existing differences between the nations must be settled by means other than military; the great mass of the working population, which is politically organized, is further removed than ever from the idea of another war. The army too in the long run has to recognize the change that has taken place. The prospect of fighting another war in

---

[1] Wöllwarth to Reinhardt, Dresden, 10 Dec. 1926: Nachlaß Reinhardt, Hauptstaatsarchiv Stuttgart.

[2] von Bonin to Schleicher, Berlin, 3 Dec. 1926: Nachlaß Schleicher, no. 35, Bundesarchiv Koblenz.

[3] Köstring to Seeckt, Berlin, 30 Nov. 1926: Nachlaß Seeckt, box 15, no. 37, Militärgeschichtliches Forschungsamt. During the war, Köstring had been with Seeckt in Turkey.

the immediate future recedes. . . . We have clearly reached a turning-point. . . .[1]

That the army stood at the cross-roads, that it was time to clarify its position *vis-à-vis* the state and the nation, was also recognized by Colonel von Schleicher, the chief of the newly founded *Wehrmacht* department in the ministry of defence. Perhaps in reply to von Bonin, who suggested an agreement as to how the matter should be pursued, in any case only a few weeks later, Schleicher attempted to find an answer to these burning problems. Under the heading 'Attitude of the Reichswehr towards the State' he wrote:

It is a contradiction in itself if the armed guard of the state adopts an attitude of indifference, perhaps even of hostility, towards that state. The usual explanation, or better, excuse, is not valid; it runs: 'our attitude would be quite different if the conditions in the state were consolidated and improved, but this s . . . state is impossible.' Such criticism, however, is a gross overstatement and injustice. . . . No, let us not deceive ourselves, it does not depend on this, but above all on the attitude towards the issue: monarchy or republic? As things have developed meanwhile, this issue is no longer real. In Germany hardly a dozen serious and influential men consider the restoration of the monarchy useful in the foreseeable future, let alone possible and practicable. Basically, something else is decisive: a lack of moral courage. It is not considered 'right' to express such sober but unpopular truths. They fear a social boycott —the sharpest weapon of the circles which need a declaration of loyalty to the monarchy for political reasons. With all this, I have noticed during the past years that nothing makes the attempt at social ostracism so quickly ineffective as grasping the bull by the horns and telling the brutal truth to these people. . . . The real issue is not: republic or monarchy, but: what shall this republic look like? And it is absolutely clear that it can develop according to our wishes only if we participate in the work gladly and indefatigably. If we are willing to accept this idea, then we shall no longer avoid the word 'republic' so timidly, or look carefully over our shoulder whether anyone has heard it. . . . Things are very similar with regard to the issue of the colours. We certainly want our old, glorious flag restored. But to achieve that aim we cannot do anything more stupid than show a barely concealed aversion to the

---

[1] Memorandum of the T 2 of 6 Nov. 1926 (its chief was Colonel von Bonin): Rabenau, *Seeckt*, pp. 482–3.

colours of the Reich. The more sincerely and automatically we prove our respect for the colours of the Reich, the easier it will be to find a way to solve the problem. . . . For example, miracles can be worked if wreaths etc. show, apart from the black, white and red colours, a ribbon in black, red and gold. . . .

Schleicher's opinion with regard to the political parties was:

The best would be if the government veered towards the right, according to the good old principle that it is easiest to make concessions while winning. In general, I consider it the best policy, if the government's pendulum swings too strongly towards the right or left, to put the weight of the Reichswehr quite imperceptibly on the opposite side. . . .

Schleicher further suggested that offences and excesses in the political field should be ruthlessly punished and that Reichswehr members should be discharged, if they were unable to adopt the attitude towards the state, the government, and the people which was approved of by the chief of the army command.[1]

This lengthy memorandum was circulated 'from hand to hand' within the ministry of defence. But it seems that no replies to Schleicher's very outspoken suggestions have survived. According to the memoirs of von Bonin's successor as chief of the T 2 in the *Truppenamt*, Colonel Ritter von Mittelberger, General Heye went even further than Schleicher in an attempt to affect a *rapprochement* between the army and the representatives of the people. He thus hoped to promote an understanding of the interests of the Reichswehr and to obtain concessions in budgetary questions.

What Seeckt had achieved by his icy refusal of any negotiations with parliamentarians and the erection of a Chinese wall against the members of the government—a removal of the Reichswehr from all internal political influences—was endangered by a kind of palliness of the new chief of the army command, which encouraged unauthorized people to meddle with the internal affairs of the Reichswehr. A few days after I took over my new office, Heye informed me of his intention to invite parliamentary deputies of all political shades, with the exception of the Communists, to social

[1] Schleicher's memorandum, without heading or date, initialled by other officers between 30 Dec. 1926 and 4 Jan. 1927: Nachlaß Schleicher, no. 32, Bundesarchiv Koblenz; Vogelsang, *Reichswehr, Staat und NSDAP*, no. 3, pp. 409–13.

evenings to drink beer, and thus to arrange informal discussions and to disperse the distrust of the Reichswehr. I had to compile a list of those to be invited. . . .[1]

The minister of defence fully concurred with these plans and suggestions; he too realized that the demonstrative showing of the black, white, and red colours would increase the suspicions of republican circles. In 1927 he decreed:

Disagreeable discussions have taken place in public because members of the Reichswehr have shown only black, white and red colours from their private dwellings, and have laid down wreaths with black, white and red ribbons only. I have to state the following: in the present situation in Germany the use of the black, white and red colours without the simultaneous showing of the national colours of black, red and gold is a political demonstration and activity, and thus forbidden according to § 36 of the *Wehrgesetz*. In addition, such incidents will make more difficult my struggle to secure for the Reichswehr a position above party, serving only the state, and will provide ammunition for the enemies of the *Wehrmacht*. These circles try by every means to prove that the *Wehrmacht* has a completely one-sided attitude, and that its 'non-political' position is in truth only the cloak for an orientation towards the right. The greatest restraint is therefore essential on the question of the colours, which is the core of the political struggle. . . . I therefore give this order, especially so as to spare members of the *Wehrmacht* conflicts of conscience and to relieve them of responsibility in this question:

1. Members of the *Wehrmacht* are forbidden to show the black, white and red colours without the national colours of black, red and gold. . . .

Official Reichswehr buildings were to hoist the colours of the Reich together with the 'Reich war flag' (black, white, and red with a small black, red, and gold inset), unless the building in question had only one flag-staff—in that case the 'Reich war flag' alone was permissible.[2]

That a new wind was blowing in the defence ministry was also the opinion of Major-General Wetzell, the chief of the *Trup-*

[1] Hilmar Ritter von Mittelberger, 'Lebenserinnerungen', p. 241: MS. in Bundesarchiv Koblenz. He succeeded Colonel von Bonin as chief of the T 2 (army organization department) early in 1927.

[2] Decree of 15 Aug. 1927: Reichskanzlei, Akten betr. Reichswehr, vol. v, no. 5591, R 43 I 686, Bundesarchiv Koblenz.

penamt. He complained to Seeckt that his successor surrounded himself with new and younger men, who were 'more soft', that 'a new course' was steered in every sphere. Wetzell expressed his scepticism and belief that the innovations might be wrong.[1] He himself was replaced by Colonel von Blomberg, while Colonel von Stülpnagel took over the army's Personnel Office. In the German Nationalist Party the 'new course' caused 'grave dissatisfaction' with the ministry of defence, as a deputy of that party told one of Schleicher's subordinates. Such criticism, which he considered directed against himself, was sharply repudiated by Schleicher. He sent a letter to the deputy by registered mail: 'Unfortunately I do not know the matters which allegedly have caused displeasure or criticism. As I am accustomed, however, to get to the bottom of such remarks to clarify them, I should like to ask you . . . to let me know what has been said about the ministry of defence and about myself, and who felt obliged to take up a position against the ministry of defence.'[2] Apparently there was no reply. Obviously, the criticisms of the German Nationalist Party were directed against the new political line of the ministry as such.

Yet no real change was effected in the highly controversial question of Reichswehr recruiting. After lengthy discussions Dr. Geßler issued new regulations at the end of 1927, which left the selection of recruits in the hands of the commanding officers of companies and squadrons. All civilian influences remained excluded. It was forbidden, however, to make any inquiries from members of parties or organizations which were opposed to the state and its constitution; and admission to the Reichswehr was made dependent upon obtaining from the police a certificate of good conduct, which had to include information on the participation of the potential recruit in movements directed against the constitution.[3] Early in 1928 the new chief of the *Wehramt*, Colonel Freiherr von dem Bussche-Ippenburg, could state with satisfaction, in a conference of the departmental chiefs of the defence ministry, that the 'main attack', which had been directed against recruiting by the company commanders,

[1] Wetzell to Seeckt, Berlin, 7 Mar. 1927: Nachlaß Seeckt, box 15, no. 90/68, Militärgeschichtliches Forschungsamt.
[2] Schleicher to the deputy Schmidt-Hannover, Berlin, 23 Sept. 1927: Nachlaß Graf Westarp, Gärtringen.
[3] Caro and Oehme, *Schleichers Aufstieg*, p. 187.

had been 'warded off by the declaration that applications and acceptances had a ratio of 15 to 1, and that recruiting was entirely out of the question in view of such a vast supply (*Überangebot*)'. He expressly asked those present to use this explanation to meet inquiries from the outside. He also mentioned that the leaders of the Social Democrats and Democrats had declared their 'complete confidence' in the leaders of the Reichswehr and shown 'full understanding' of the issues of armament (*Rüstungsbelange*).[1] Apparently the leaders of the republican parties abandoned their opposition to the system of recruiting, as it had existed from the outset. The attack of Löbe petered out, as did so many other attempts at reform sponsored by the republican parties. On this issue the whole officer corps—including those who, like Schleicher and von dem Bussche-Ippenburg, belonged to the reforming party —was completely united and determined to ward off any criticism.

There remained the influence of the *Kreis* officers on the selection of recruits for the Reichswehr. As they were usually members of the *Stahlhelm*, or sympathized with this organization, it was only natural that they supported applications of its members and sent them with their approval to the regiment concerned.[2] Most of the recruits continued to be supplied by the *Stahlhelm* and other *vaterländische Verbände*. The majority of the commanding officers believed that recruits recommended by these organizations were the most suitable and were animated by the right spirit. As late as 1931 the minister of defence, Groener, stated: 'The commanders unfortunately still have the illusion that someone who is recommended by the bosses of the *vaterländische Verbände* must be a grand chap. . . .'[3] Influences such as these, exercised indirectly and personally, could not be eradicated by any parliament, or by any other civilian authority.

[1] 'Chefbesprechung am 5.3.28 unter Leitung Chef H.L. Einzelvorträge der Inspekteure und Amtschefs. Zusatzbemerkungen des Chefs H.L.', 5 Mar. 1928: Nachlaß Schleicher, no. 35, Bundesarchiv Koblenz.

[2] Görlitz, *Der deutsche Generalstab*, p. 361. Examples from the years 1927–28 in a memorandum of the Prussian ministry of the interior on 'Die sogen. Wehrsporttätigkeit des Stahlhelm in Rheinland und Westfalen' of 1929, Anlagen 43–45: Reichskanzlei, Akten betr. Stahlhelm Bund der Frontsoldaten, vol. ii, Bundesarchiv Koblenz.

[3] Groener to Gerold von Gleich, Berlin, 26 Apr. 1931: Nachlaß Groener, box 7, no. 27, Bundesarchiv-Militärarchiv; Groener-Geyer, op. cit., p. 280.

The opportunity to bring about reforms, which seemed to exist for a short time after Seeckt's dismissal, passed; the old system reasserted itself.

11. *Military Measures and the Government*

After Seeckt's dismissal the army command tried to bring about a closer co-operation with the Reich government and with the Prussian authorities in the field of frontier defence. In a cabinet meeting at the end of November 1926, which was also attended by the chiefs of the army and naval commands, Dr. Geßler declared that, for the security of Germany, he considered essential certain defence measures in the east which went beyond those permitted by the Treaty of Versailles; preparations had been made on the basis of an agreement with the Prussian minister of the interior, Severing; but in practice difficulties had arisen, because the lower military authorities went at times beyond the terms of the agreement, and the civil authorities were in certain cases too little accommodating; in the west General von Loßberg—the commanding officer of *Wehrkreis* vi—overstepped his instructions and was for that reason moved to Berlin, where his duties were more like those of an inspector; he would soon be retired; similar difficulties developed in the co-operation with the former chief of the army command; his successor and the minister agreed on the following procedure: together they would make a detailed estimate of what they considered necessary for the frontier defence forces; then the cabinet would have to decide to what extent it would take the responsibility for these measures; if it declined, they would be discontinued; agreement with Prussia should then be reached about the measures decided upon by the cabinet; under no circumstances must the Reichswehr transgress this programme. General Heye emphasized that the Reichswehr was 'non-political through and through' and urgently requested that no change should be made in the system of recruiting. He promised that detailed plans for the frontier defence would be submitted by 15 December, which could then be discussed by the cabinet. He declared that the Reichswehr did not want to have any links with the *Verbände* which should not occupy themselves with military matters.

Admiral Zenker explained that, while command of the North Sea could not be obtained, it was indispensable to gain command of the Baltic: this could be achieved and had to be prepared.[1]

Schleicher's ideas were very similar to those of Dr. Geßler. In the memorandum he wrote a few weeks later he explained that during the past years the army had been forced into an atmosphere of secretiveness and camouflage, which under the conditions of that time had to be accepted as the lesser evil; but in the long run the camouflage and the resulting haziness and confusion created considerable dangers to the existence, discipline, and morale of the army. In his opinion it was therefore essential to examine critically what existed or was being prepared, to preserve and further energetically what was vital, but ruthlessly to eliminate what was unnecessary and only a burden to the army. Above all, 'clarity and truth' must be created in all spheres: without them a fruitful continuation of the work was impossible. 'In the present discussions the question that has above all to be clarified is what the chief of the army command should demand as absolutely essential from the political authorities. . . . From this point of view I consider necessary a good preparation of the frontier defences in the east and all measures for a quick and complete mobilization of the military forces available in peace-time. . . . A curtailment of the defence work will in addition bring us a considerable relief in the political sphere and facilitate the financing of the work from *public* funds. . . .' It was essential to co-operate closely with the civil authorities; if a *Wehrkreiskommando* was still opposed to this, this was wrong and contrary to the orders of the army command; if the superfluous weapons were brought under the army's control, as had already been done in many cases, much friction could be eliminated. It remained forbidden to buy weapons, as the advantages to be gained were too small in comparison with the risks involved in these shady transactions.[2]

Early in 1927 Heye rendered to the government the

---

[1] 'Auszug aus dem Protokoll der Ministerbesprechung vom 29. November 1926': Reichskanzlei, Akten betr. Reichsmarine, vol. i, R 43 I 601; Akten betr. Reichswehr, vol. v, R 43 I 686, Bundesarchiv Koblenz.

[2] Nachlaß Schleicher, no. 32, ibid.; Vogelsang, op. cit., no. 3, pp. 410–13.

promised report about the frontier defence measures in the east of Germany, the secret arms depots of the army,[1] and the co-operation with the Prussian authorities, and requested the cabinet to consent to the measures taken; 'the co-operation with the civil authorities had been in part very satisfactory in *Prussia*. But the directives agreed upon between the ministers Geßler and Severing were not always observed; partly this was the fault of the Reichswehr, as its organs more than once transgressed the directives. Thereupon Prussia more or less terminated its co-operation and grave difficulties resulted. The co-operation in East Prussia had always been exemplary. Outside Prussia, the conditions were in general more difficult. . . .' The army command realized that this state of affairs could not continue; failure to inform the civil authorities about armaments time and again created difficulties at home and abroad; now the cabinet had to sanction the necessary measures and to accept the responsibility for them; the government also had to provide the necessary means; that the money was contributed by industry and agriculture, as was still in part the case, was 'unworthy of the state'. Chancellor Marx declared 'that the cabinet must assume the responsibility for these things, provided that it was informed in detail and that its consent was granted. . . . In his opinion, the military preparations must be continued. For the navy, too, everything must be done that was practical within the financial possibilities. . . .' Following Marx's suggestion the government then expressed its agreement with this policy.[2] Thus an important step was taken towards the control of the illegal military preparations by the German government. Heye's attitude was surprisingly conciliatory. He went out of his way to mention the 'good results' obtained in Prussia by co-operation with the civil authorities, in particular in East Prussia, where until a few months ago he had been the commanding officer. He even accepted part of the responsibility for the constant friction with the Prussian government. All this would have been unthinkable under Seeckt, who would never have admitted any fault of his own.

[1] See above, p. 221.
[2] 'Auszug aus dem Protokoll der Ministerbesprechung vom 26. Februar 1927': Auswärtiges Amt, Büro des Staatssekretärs, Landesverteidigung: 4565 H, E 164073–5, 164080–2 (microfilm).

Soon after this a conference was held between Heye and the Prussian prime minister Braun, who showed understanding for the organization of a frontier defence, but remained opposed to any preparations for mobilization in peace-time. They agreed on the following points: the 'civilian employees of the Reichswehr', who were active in the frontier defence organization, were not to be permitted to belong to any 'political' party or association (e.g. the *Stahlhelm*); the lists of the frontier defence forces were to be compiled and kept with the aid of the civil authorities, under the supervision of the Prussian ministry of the interior; and only people approved by them were to be in charge of arms and ammunition depots which could not be transferred into the custody of the army. The ministry of defence and the Prussian ministry of the interior further reached agreement about the 'theoretical and practical instruction of the frontier defence leaders and the required technical training with weapons'.[1] Early in 1928 the new chief of the *Truppenamt*, Colonel von Blomberg, reported that the lists of civilians liable to be called up in case of mobilization were being compiled with the aid of the civil authorities in East Prussia, but that in Pomerania, for example, little progress had been made; instruction of non-soldiers on machine-guns was to be introduced to a limited degree, and with great caution.[2]

During previous years arms caches of the frontier defence and similar forces, which were discovered and confiscated by the Prussian police, were often declared as Reichswehr property to prevent their seizure—a practice against which the Prussian authorities frequently protested. This was to be made impossible in future. All such depots had to be declared to the *Wehrkreiskommandos* by 15 June 1927, and the latter were to be responsible *vis-à-vis* the civil authorities; after that date, the army would not accept the responsibility for any undeclared weapons. If any were found, they could thus be confiscated by the police. The chief of the *Truppenamt* ordered that the army was only to protect those depots of the existence of which it had been informed prior to their discovery; any violations of this order would be

[1] Vogelsang, op. cit., pp. 52–53; 'Vortrag vor dem Herrn Reichsaußenminister über "Landesschutz"', Oct. 1927: Büro des Staatssekretärs, Landesverteidigung, 4565 H, E 164106 (microfilm).

[2] Notes of under-secretary of state von Schubert, Berlin, 6 Feb. 1928: ibid., 4565 H, E 164112.

punished by the chief of the army command.[1] All this indicated
that the army command was determined to co-operate more
closely with the civil administration and to establish better
relations with the Prussian authorities.

Yet the *Kreis* officers and the owners of landed estates, who
led the frontier defence organizations at the local level, were
bitterly hostile to the 'Marxist' Prussian government. The mere
fact that negotiations were taking place was bound to arouse
their distrust of the new policy and the new chief of the army
command. After a period of leave, spent in Western Pomerania
in the summer of 1927, Major von Bredow reported to his chief,
Colonel von Schleicher, the following remarks of former
officers and landowners about Heye: 'He is said to be very
timid.' 'He has not got the courage to continue what General
von Seeckt has started in frontier defence matters.' 'He dis-
continues things because he does not want to accept any
responsibility.' 'Now he intends to co-operate even with Severing and his clique in frontier defence affairs. That Seeckt has
never done. Thus it will be impossible to use the organization
to bring about internal changes.' Major von Bredow added:
'The military authorities, individual officers, etc. have not got
the courage to speak openly. They fear unpopularity, perhaps
even boycott. . . . If the entire officer corps defends its chief
without any reservation, those enemies will be silenced who
today are the loudest critics. But the precondition is that not
only the active officers do so, but also the inactive officers who
are employed by the army. These gentlemen too have certain
duties.'[2] It is clear that the *Kreis* officers especially, who were
to pursue the 'new course' in practice, were among its most
pronounced critics. Difficulties were also made by certain civil
authorities. When the commanding officer of *Wehrkreis* ii,
Lieutenant-General von Amsberg, visited the prime minister of
the state of Mecklenburg-Schwerin, to inform him about the
preparations for frontier defence and to enlist his support, the
latter declined, as this would entail a violation of the Treaty of
Versailles and he considered any such preparation superfluous.[3]

[1] Chef des Truppenamtes, Berlin, 20 May 1927: Akten des Heereswaffenamtes,
WiIF 5/2822, Bundesarchiv Koblenz.
[2] Notes by Major von Bredow, 22 July 1927: Nachlaß Schleicher, no. 35, ibid.
[3] Colonel Kaupisch to Schleicher, Stettin, 15 Mar. 1928: ibid., no. 32.

In the neighbouring *Wehrkreis* iii (Brandenburg and Silesia) there was similar opposition on the side of the district and *Kreis* officers. In December 1928 the commanding officer, General Hasse, addressed them and demanded that they should fulfil their tasks 'neutrally and in our spirit':

> We must not permit any political agitation against the state; I ask you to take measures against it. The idea which I propound, that a frontier defence, or, more correctly, an army, is only useful if it is supported by the mass of the people, is often objected to by gentlemen who support us. I know entirely loyal men who in their innermost hearts are of a completely different opinion and decline to be convinced. But I must carry my point. . . . With the exception of the radical extremists on both sides (it will never be possible to win over Communists who negate the state), I consider it perfectly possible to bring about, very cautiously, a widening of the circles from which the reservists are to be taken in case of war. . . . It is impossible to issue directives in this matter. According to our experience, circles belonging to the left are much easier won over to the cause of defence in the frontier areas, which are always threatened by the enemy, than in the interior of the country, further removed from the frontier. As soon as you cross the Oder, the danger is forgotten which unifies all . . . [in the areas further east].[1]

Ten years after the revolution the idea of a gradual expansion towards the left had to be put forward 'very cautiously' by one of the leading generals to the district officers responsible for two of the most important provinces of Prussia.

In practice the carrying out of these plans was violently opposed by the *Kreis* officers and their units. As one of the leaders in Pomerania reported later, the local formations were to be filled not only, as hitherto, by 'black, white and red nationalists', but also by 'black, red and gold Democrats and red Social Democrats'.

> This was very nicely thought out, but the execution in practice encountered unsurmountable obstacles. The *Pommerntreue* and the *Nationale Verbände*, which so far had been the only supporters of the frontier defence, were all nationalists who indignantly repudiated any co-operation with 'pacifists and socialists'. The *Pommerntreue*,

---

[1] 'Ansprache des Herrn Befehlshabers bei der Bezirksleiterbesprechung am 14.12.28.': Reichskanzlei, Akten betr. Landesverteidigung, vol. i, R 43 I 725, ibid.

not without justification, considered the arms caches their exclusive property, and they were proud of being the only bearers of arms in the country. . . . The Reichswehr authorities apparently did not see the situation clearly, for time and again they admonished us to see to it that Democrats and Social Democrats were finally admitted to our frontier defence formations; they probably also suspected us of passive resistance. . . . In fact we *Kreis* officers could not possibly make vigorous propaganda in these [republican] circles because then we should have lost the support of the *Nationale Verbände*, which alone were of any value to us. . . .[1]

Some senior officers, who had close connexions with the army command, intended to effect a change. Especially Colonel von Bonin—until 1926 chief of the T 2 department of the *Truppenamt*—tried, as the commanding officer of a battalion in East Prussia and later as the chief of staff of the First Division there, to gain the confidence of the republican parties and organizations and to recruit their members for the frontier defence units. He aimed at a democratization of the Reichswehr itself and realized that under modern conditions any military effort must be supported by the nation, not only by certain sections. His endeavours were backed by the ministry of defence and by other officers, but they aroused strong opposition, especially among prominent Junkers. Soon von Bonin was branded as a 'Red'. Although Schleicher defended him and declared that he had 'the special confidence of the minister of defence', he had to be recalled from East Prussia and resigned soon after.[2] The reform party in the Bendlerstraße was unable to overcome the deep distrust felt by the *Kreis* officers, the landowners, and also many active officers, against the republican organizations. This was expressed in the most drastic form in 1930 by a young lieutenant, who wrote to his fiancée: 'That we cannot organize a frontier defence force together with the *Reichsbanner*, because these scoundrels would betray everything, must be obvious to you. We alone are too weak and must have the support of

---

[1] 'Grenzschutz Ost' by Kurt Treuhaupt, written in 1955: Sammlung Oberst Dieter von Kleist, Zg. 244/57, Bundesarchiv-Militärarchiv. Even in 1955 the author used the contemptuous name of *Sozis* for the Social Democrats.

[2] Werner von Blomberg, 'Erinnerungen bis 1933', iii. 179, ibid.; 'Niederschrift über eine Chefbesprechung am 15. Oktober 1929': Reichskanzlei, Akten betr. Reichswehr, vol. vi, R 43 I 687, Bundesarchiv Koblenz; article in *Rote Fahne* of 24 Sept. 1929, ibid.

circles with military leanings. . . .'[1] To him, and to innumerable others, the members of the *Reichsbanner* (the mass organization of the republican parties) were traitors, or at least potential traitors. Thus all attempts at reform in matters of frontier defence were bound to be unsuccessful.

How strongly these illegal efforts were suspected by senior civil servants is shown by a memorandum written at the beginning of 1928. The new minister of defence, General Groener, visited Stresemann, together with General Heye and Colonel von Blomberg, and discussed among other issues the 'formation of a frontier defence'. After the officers had departed, the surprised foreign minister asked the senior official present why he had been so accommodating towards them during the conference. Thereupon he informed the minister that the measures, which were allegedly in preparation, were already completely carried out in East Prussia and Upper Silesia, and to a certain extent in Brandenburg and Pomerania. If the civil authorities did not participate in their further development it was to be feared that the Reichswehr would 'again engage in all kinds of careless activities with the *vaterländische Verbände*, which would be politically completely biased towards the right and thus include the danger of revelations from the left'. In his opinion, a remark of Heye was significant that even now the organizations of the right were agitated because of the recent reticence of the Reichswehr towards them; they spread the rumour that the work of Seeckt was being sabotaged by his successor; therefore there was no chance of preventing the whole enterprise, which undoubtedly was rather risky and objectionable.[2]

In the field of military planning the *Truppenamt* adhered to its programme of mobilizing 21 divisions in an emergency. In this case the military forces were to be organized in three 'waves'. The first one was to be formed by the reinforced divisions of the Reichswehr, with about 50 per cent. of its active personnel; the second 'wave' was to consist of field divisions with about 30 per cent. of its personnel, and the third of field divisions with about

[1] Lieutenant Helmuth Stieff to his fiancée, Jüterbog, 11 Oct. 1930: 1223/53, Institut für Zeitgeschichte. In the print in *Vierteljahrshefte für Zeitgeschichte*, ii, 1954, p. 296, the words 'because these scoundrels would betray everything' have been tactfully omitted by the editor.

[2] Memorandum by Ministerialdirektor Dr. Köpke of 23 Jan. 1928: Büro des Staatssekretärs, Landesverteidigung, 4565 H, E 164092–94 (microfilm).

10 per cent. of its personnel. The remaining ten per cent. of the active personnel was to be distributed among the reserves, training courses, schools, etc.[1] For this plan, large forces trained outside the official army were essential, to supplement the existing seven infantry divisions. Hence the frontier defence forces and the training provided by them remained of paramount importance to the army command.

Some progress was made during these years in equipping the army with certain weapons forbidden by the Treaty of Versailles. In 1928 the planning stage in the construction of a light tank was concluded and certain firms, Krupp, Daimler, and Rheinmetall, were each instructed to build two of these tanks. The first was shown by Krupp's to the officers of the *Waffenamt* in January 1930; it was to be completed by April, and the second, which was destined for Russia, by May 1930. The chief of the *Waffenamt*, Lieutenant-General von Vollard-Bockelberg, on that occasion expressed 'his special joy' about the speed and the accuracy of the tank and thanked Krupp's warmly for their 'good services'.[2] During the same period a new anti-aircraft gun with special apparatus was developed. The 9th battery of the Artillery Regiment 1 in East Prussia was designated the instruction battery for the others and was the first to be equipped with the new gun. The instruction of six other batteries in anti-aircraft practice began in 1929.[3] With regard to the air force, the chief of the army command in 1927 approved the plans for the equipment of an emergency army with a limited number of squadrons.[4] But comparatively little was achieved. As the *Waffenamt* reported at the end of 1928, it had been possible—because larger sums were now available for rearmament—to obtain new aeroplanes and to adapt older ones; but the preparations for large-scale production had not advanced because the types of the new equipment had not been agreed upon early

---

[1] 'Erfahrungen aus dem W. Kr. Sp. Isar 1927/28', 2 Mar. 1928: Marineleitung, Abteilung B, Chef des Stabes: PG 34 428 XI, Militärgeschichtliches Forschungsamt.

[2] Heeresleitung, Berlin, 19 July 1928; 'Protokoll über die Schußbesprechung über den Leichten Traktor', Berlin, 18 Jan. 1930: Akten des Heereswaffenamtes, WiIF 5/2544 and 5/2549, Bundesarchiv Koblenz.

[3] Wehramt, Feb. 1929: Marineleitung, Akten betr. Heeresangelegenheiten: 7895 A Ia XXV, Militärgeschichtliches Forschungsamt.

[4] Truppenamt, Berlin, 25 May 1927, to Waffenamt: Akten des Heereswaffenamtes, WiIF 5/2546, Bundesarchiv Koblenz.

enough and the designs were inaccurate and incomplete. With-in the *Truppenamt*, a special section—the T 2 V under Major Sperrle—was responsible for all air force matters.[1] The larger sums available came to a large extent from the budget of the Reich ministry of transport. From the amount allocated to the development of aeroplanes and engines a sum was diverted to projects of defence; in 1928–9 this sum amounted to 3,380,000 marks.[2] Apart from this, the Reichswehr disposed of large sums from its own budget, which were partly diverted to illegal purposes and administered by the chief of the *Wehramt*. Its chief at that time, Colonel Freiherr von dem Bussche-Ippenburg, described later how, for example, a certain sum for rifles was included in the official budget, which was several millions too high; this sum was then transferred to the 'black' budget. 'These measures were arranged during the budget discussions with the under-secretaries of state in the ministry of finance (Popitz and Schwerin-Krosigk) and the president of the audit office, and approved by them. The administration and expenditure of the black sums was checked by the audit office. . . .' All accounts were sent to the *Wehramt* and paid by it through a private bank.[3] In this field too the civil authorities were informed and gave their consent; the audit office checked all accounts—in contrast with the previous practice, under which the chief of the *Truppenamt* had administered the 'black' funds, and the accounts had been checked by him and a committee appointed by the army command, outside the sphere of the civil authorities.[4] Now not only the chancellor and the cabinet, but the two principal members of the budget committee of the Reichstag, were informed in detail by the *Wehramt*, so that no difficulties would arise in the committee. A supervisory committee, consisting of the under-secretaries of state of the ministries concerned and the president of the audit office,

---

[1] 'Bericht über die Tätigkeit der Wa. B. 6 im Dienstjahr 27/28', Berlin, 30 Nov. 1928, ibid.; T 2, 17 Oct. 1927, signed v. Mittelberger: Akten des Heereswaffen-amtes, WiIF 5/511, ibid.

[2] The minister of transport Dr. Schätzel to Chancellor Müller, Berlin, 11 Apr. 1929: Reichskanzlei, Akten betr. Landesverteidigung, vol. i, R 43 I 725, Bundes-archiv Koblenz.

[3] 'Äußerung über die schwarzen Mittel der Reichswehr' by General Erich Freiherr von dem Bussche-Ippenburg, 1952: Zeugenschrifttum no. 217, Institut für Zeitgeschichte.

[4] Directives of 1925: Nachlaß Schleicher, no. 37, Bundesarchiv Koblenz.

supervised the expenditure for illegal rearmament and controlled the 'black' funds.[1]

It was a curious form of 'legalizing' illegal actions; but it was preferable to the earlier state of affairs, when the civil authorities had not been informed and had no means of supervising these activities. Now they could be co-ordinated with the general policy of the government, and certain rash and incautious actions could be prevented or curtailed; even that possibility had not existed before. The contributions from industry and agriculture, which had been of paramount importance under Seeckt, diminished and were replaced by public funds. It is thus not surprising that the official army budget increased by over 50 per cent. within five years: from 459 million marks in 1924 to 642 millions in 1926, and to 728 millions in 1928.[2]

III. *Closer Relations with Russia*

After Seeckt's dismissal the German foreign ministry tried to obtain detailed information about the Russian enterprises of the Reichswehr, as it expected difficulties from the Entente powers after the article in the *Manchester Guardian* and the Reichstag speech of Scheidemann. Furthermore, the Russian ambassador Krestinsky visited Stresemann early in 1927 to inform him that the Soviet government was alarmed at the revelations. Krestinsky suggested that the German government should deny everything; but Stresemann declared this to be impossible because the Finnish government had already informed France and Britain that ships carrying war material from Leningrad to Stettin had made emergency landings in Finland.[3]

A few weeks later under-secretary of state von Schubert saw Major-General Wetzell, the chief of the *Truppenamt*, and Major Fischer, who was responsible in the defence ministry for the

[1] Dr. Schätzel to Chancellor Müller, Berlin, 11 Apr. 1929: Reichskanzlei, Akten betr. Landesverteidigung, vol. i, R 43 I 725, ibid.; General Freiherr von dem Bussche-Ippenburg in 1952: Zeugenschrifttum, no. 217, Institut für Zeitgeschichte; Raeder, op. cit., i. 233.

[2] Benoist-Méchin, *Histoire de l'Armée Allemande*, ii. 380. The figures given by Wheeler-Bennett, *Nemesis of Power*, p. 187, n. 2, are considerably higher: 490 millions in 1924, 704 millions in 1926, and 827 millions in 1928: the tendency is the same.

[3] Gatzke, *Stresemann and the Rearmament of Germany*, pp. 85–86.

military contacts with Russia. Schubert declared that the foreign ministry must now get a clear picture of the military co-operation: it could no longer be told as little as possible about these matters, so that it could always plead ignorance. General Wetzell then explained that, of current military matters, the Junkers enterprise was completed and the Reich had no further financial obligations; with regard to the poison gas factory, negotiations were still in progress about the German payments to Russia, which would presumably be between 2 and 5 million marks; the transport of shells to Germany was also concluded, and no more would be sent. Co-operation with Russia, he continued, only existed in four fields: the aerodrome at Lipetsk, the tank school at Kazan, experiments with poison gas, and exchange of military experience; the last two were 'entirely legal'; only the two schools 'undoubtedly did not entirely correspond with the stipulations of the peace treaty', but both were vital (*lebenswichtig*) to the German army; the aerodrome at Lipetsk was of cardinal importance, as Germany must have men trained in formation flying, as observers, photographers, etc. The whole enterprise was organized as a private flying school, the German mechanics and former officers working there were private employees; no active officers were permanently at Lipetsk; most of the pupils were private persons; there was no official connexion of the schools with the defence ministry; Germany was doing similar things in Turkey, to which no one had so far objected.[1]

The under-secretary of state remained doubtful whether the political risk entailed in the co-operation was justified. The decision was left to Stresemann, who agreed at the beginning of February 1927 that the two schools should continue. But it was stipulated that during the current year no active soldiers should be trained at Lipetsk. In the autumn their participation should again be discussed by the two ministries on the basis of the general political situation.[2] Clearly Stresemann wanted to await the reaction of the Entente powers to the revelations of

[1] Notes of Schubert, Berlin, 24 Jan. 1927: Büro von Staatssekretär v. Schubert, Akten betr. Militärische Angelegenheiten mit Rußland, 4564/3, E 163480–4 (microfilm).

[2] Note of 9 Feb. 1927: ibid., 4564/3, E 163486; notes by von Dirksen about a conversation with Colonel von Blomberg on 29 Dec. 1927: ibid., 4564/4, E 163921–2; Handakten Dirksen, 9481 H, H 276328–9.

December, and meanwhile curtail any direct participation of the Reichswehr in the Russian undertakings. Now, however, difficulties appeared on the Russian side. Major Fischer informed his old chief Seeckt:

They [the Russians] demanded from us that the schools etc. should be liquidated if no legal way could be found to continue them. They do not want to have another such surprise as the last 'revelations', with all their political repercussions. We made a corresponding suggestion and asked them for a speedy reply. Now we have heard that the Russian political authorities want to discuss the issue with our foreign ministry. It is obvious that the German Communist Party, which has been severely damaged by the last 'revelations' and their consistent denial, plays a part in this. Now the Russian Communist Party has taken control of the affair and drives! . . . It is clear that Britain is exercising pressure on our politicians to loosen our connexions with Russia. . . .[1]

Shortly after Fischer wrote to Seeckt that the Russian military authorities had not yet replied to the German proposals and were sheltering behind their political authorities, so that the Germans had to be more outspoken: strangely enough, this time the Russians were raising objections, while the German foreign ministry agreed to the continuation of the military activities.[2]

On 18 May 1927 a conference was held in the foreign ministry between the ministers Stresemann and Geßler, General Heye, and Colonel von Blomberg, the new chief of the *Truppenamt*, because the Russians demanded the express consent of the foreign ministry to the establishment of the tank school at Kazan. Stresemann declared that, in spite of certain reservations, he would agree to the Russian request. The German officers proposed in addition that near Orenburg experiments should be made with poison gas, but the Russians demanded full participation in the exercise and exchange of all the relevant material. Dr. Geßler voiced his doubts. He feared that the Russians, who one day might be Germany's enemies, would thus acquire very valuable material without giving much in return. He suggested holding the exercise on the practice

---

[1] Major Fischer to Seeckt, Berlin, 12 Mar. 1927: Nachlaß Seeckt, roll 18, no. 87, microfilm in Institut für Zeitgeschichte.

[2] Fischer to Seeckt, Berlin, 29 Mar. 1927: ibid.

grounds at Grafenwörth.[1] He overlooked the fact that the Russians had put at Germany's disposal the schools at Lipetsk and Kazan, and hence could claim something in return. At the beginning of June Seeckt was informed by Major Fischer that the Russian affairs were prospering, but that there was little prospect of the policy's being maintained by the defence ministry, while the foreign ministry was in favour.[2] Stresemann clearly accepted the Russian policy of the army command and continued to support it during the following years. Seeckt's dismissal smoothed the way. Fischer's fear that the defence ministry wanted to steer a different course was equally unjustified. Although General von Rabenau, Seeckt's biographer, stated that 'much that had been achieved by Seeckt could not be maintained' after his dismissal, no less a person than Heye's successor as chief of the army command, General Freiherr von Hammerstein-Equord, wrote in the margin of the book: 'Not correct. The Russian policy of Seeckt was continued *un*changed after his dismissal.'[3] But in this field too the civil authorities acquired a measure of control; an entirely independent military policy in the east was no longer possible.

Before the end of 1927 Colonel von Blomberg visited the foreign ministry again and requested a decision on the following two points: in spite of urgent Russian requests, the defence ministry had desisted from conducting experiments with poison gas near Orenburg, but the intention to make the experiments in Germany could not be carried out, and the Russians had renewed their request; hence the defence ministry asked for the consent of the foreign ministry. The other point concerned Lipetsk: it had been agreed that in 1927 no Reichswehr soldiers should be trained there, but if this continued to be so, the whole installation would be too expensive for the army and would have to be dissolved—an action that would arouse Russian suspicion. Therefore the defence ministry asked the foreign ministry to consent to the sending of active officers to Lipetsk; this was admittedly a violation of the peace treaty, but the vital

---

[1] Nachlaß Brockdorff-Rantzau: 9101 H/XII, H 226865–8 (microfilm).

[2] Seeckt's diary under 3 June 1927: Nachlaß Seeckt, no. 53, Militärgeschichtliches Forschungsamt.

[3] Rabenau, *Seeckt*, p. 320, annotated by von Hammerstein: Verw. Buch, no. 134, Bundesarchiv-Militärarchiv. Rabenau was misled by his violent indignation about Scheidemann's 'traitorous' revelations.

interests of the Reichswehr and of German defence were at stake.[1] Some weeks later Stresemann agreed to the experiments with poison gas near Orenburg. But he continued to voice strong objections to the sending of army officers to Lipetsk. At the beginning of February 1928 another conference was held between Stresemann, Geßler, and Blomberg. It was decided to adopt the expedient of sending young men to Lipetsk who had not yet joined the army and would only join it after their training at Lipetsk; 'to a very limited extent' active soldiers would be permitted to go there, but these had to be discharged from the army and should stay at the school for a minimum of two years; the greatest caution was to be used in sending them, and the number was not to exceed ten; of the other category twenty should attend in 1928.[2]

Ambassador Brockdorff-Rantzau protested against this strengthening of the military links with Russia in a letter to Stresemann. He reminded him that the late President Ebert had once spoken of them as 'puerile carelessness' and had wanted to terminate them; they should be allowed to peter out slowly 'on account of lack of the required means'.[3] How justified his warning was became clear only three months later. In June 1928 Colonel von Blomberg and another officer visited under-secretary of state von Schubert and told him that thirty officers had been discharged and sent to Lipetsk; no young men had been sent before they joined up because that would have been 'useless'; but thirty officers was insufficient, and the army intended to send another thirteen; that figure would be maintained during the coming years, 'as it was laid down in the earlier agreement'.[4] This, however, had stipulated that only ten officers were to go to Lipetsk and that they were to stay there for at least two years. It seems that Stresemann again demurred to the sending of officers to Lipetsk, perhaps because

---

[1] Notes by Ministerialdirektor von Dirksen, Berlin, 29 Dec. 1927: Büro von Staatssekretär v. Schubert, Akten betr. Militärische Angelegenheiten mit Rußland, 4564/4, E 163921–2.

[2] Notes by Staatssekretär von Schubert, Berlin, 6 Feb. 1928: ibid., 4564/4, E 163924–5.

[3] Brockdorff-Rantzau to Stresemann, Moscow, 12 Apr. 1928: Nachlaß Brockdorff-Rantzau, 9101 H/XII, H 226874–5.

[4] Notes by von Schubert, Berlin, 14 June 1928: Büro von Staatssekretär v. Schubert, Akten betr. Militärische Angelegenheiten mit Rußland, 4564/4, E 163932.

the earlier agreement had not been kept by the army command. In any case, he did not give his consent; but two weeks later the matter was submitted to the new chancellor, Hermann Müller, by the new minister of defence, General Groener. He informed the chancellor that thirty gentlemen had already left; now another thirteen were to be sent, a total of forty-three. To this the chancellor eventually agreed.[1]

Apart from this, fourteen German officers were sent to Russia, among them two to take part in experiments with poison gas, and six in exercises and manœuvres. The same number of Russian officers came to Germany, among them three to receive instruction in the work of the general staff: Eideman, the director of the Soviet military academy, Apoga, a teacher there, and Uborevich, the commander of the North Caucasian military area. Three German officers were to be seconded to the Red Army for the same purpose.[2] In 1929 it was intended to send many more German officers to Russia: sixteen to take part in exercises and manœuvres, one older staff officer to be attached to the Russian general staff, two flying officers to be seconded to individual Russian units, and four or five to learn Russian. Forty-two discharged officers were to go to Lipetsk, six as teachers and the others to be trained as pilots and observers, 'as in 1928'; there were also to be ten officer cadets, although Colonel von Blomberg had considered this 'useless' a few months earlier. Finally, eleven discharged officers were to be sent to the tank school at Kazan; but in the margin it was added: 'this seems to be the minimum'. In a conference between Stresemann, Groener, and Blomberg on 1 March 1929 it was agreed that most of these were to go to Russia; only the number of officers who were to attend manœuvres was reduced from sixteen to fourteen, and the two flying officers were apparently not sent. Instead, a few chemists, engineers, and fitters were dispatched to Russia to participate in experiments with poison gas.[3]

[1] Notes by von Schubert, Berlin, 29 June 1928: Büro von Staatssekretär v. Schubert: Akten betr. Militärische Angelegenheiten mit Rußland, 4564/4, E 163941–2.

[2] Notes by von Dirksen, Berlin, 14 Nov. 1927 and 21 Feb. 1928: Handakten von Ministerialdirektor von Dirksen, 9481 H, H 276324 and 276403; von Moltke to von Dirksen, 2 Jan. 1928: Dirksen, Russische Militärangelegenheiten, 9480 H, H 276175.

[3] 'Entsendung von aktiven und verabschiedeten Offizieren der Reichswehr nach R. im Jahre 1929', 21 Jan. 1929: Büro des Staatssekretärs v. Schubert, Akten

In the summer of 1928 the chief of the *Truppenamt* himself, now Major-General von Blomberg, visited Russia with several other German officers to attend manœuvres and to inspect the German schools. About the reception of the German officers he wrote: 'During the whole journey the Russians showed themselves most obliging. The War Commissar Voroshilov had given instructions to show everything and to meet all our wishes. . . . The reception of the German officers was everywhere friendly, often cordial and very hospitable. . . . The value of the co-operation for the Red Army was emphasized time and again, as was the wish to learn from the Reichswehr and to hear the verdict of the German officers, which is considered authoritative, about the achievements of the Red Army. . . .' Voroshilov inquired during the first conversation whether the Red Army could reckon on German support in case of a Polish attack; if Poland attacked Germany, Russia would give every help; could the Soviet Union rely upon German aid if she were attacked by Poland? Blomberg cautiously replied that this was a matter of high policy, for which the political authorities alone were competent. Voroshilov, however, declared that this was of crucial importance to Soviet Russia and repeated his question: the details of military aid need not be discussed; but significantly Blomberg refused to commit himself. Voroshilov also emphasized that the commanders of the Red Army attached great value to the study of the German Army and its training methods. He asked that the number of officers seconded be increased: five should take part for longer periods in the training of the German general staff officers, five be attached to technical units, and five participate in the winter training of the principal units. Voroshilov told Blomberg that he had encountered great difficulties in the Soviet government with regard to the German schools at Lipetsk and Kama; he considered it only fair that the army command in return should obtain the consent of the German government to the secondments. Again Blomberg declined to give any definite promise.

Blomberg was very favourably impressed with the German schools he visited, especially with the aerodrome at Lipetsk;

betr. Militärische Angelegenheiten mit Rußland, 4564/4, E 163947–9; notes by von Dirksen, Berlin, 1 Mar. 1929: Dirksen, Russische Militärangelegenheiten, 9480 H, H 276157.

during the exercises at Voronezh German aeroplanes closely co-operated with a Russian battery, and the Russians showed great understanding. The tank school at Kama near Kazan was nearly complete and well organized, but it was essential and urgent to finish the construction of the tanks, on which the school's work depended. The experiments with poison gas, too, were well organized and satisfactory, but had been retarded by the late opening of the plant at the beginning of the summer: they were to be continued until the late autumn and to be resumed early in 1929 on a larger scale. 'All three enterprises are in the best state and work very well, in so far as they are operating. Their great value for our armament cannot be doubted. . . .' The possibility of maintaining them should be preserved at any price. 'The Red Army attaches the greatest value to the co-operation with the Reichswehr. The instruction of Russian commanders in our training methods is a justified return for the facilities granted to us by the Russians for our schools etc. The strengthening of the Red Army connected with this is in the interest of Germany. . . .' During his journey Blomberg met the leading generals of the Red Army, its chief of staff, General Shaposhnikov, his successor Tukhachevsky, the chief of the Red Air Force Baranov, the Generals Blücher, Yakir, Uborevich, and the chief of the chemical warfare units, Fishman, and had discussions with them.[1] The connexions between the two general staffs were closer than they had ever been.

These close relations had political repercussions too. Thus the T 3 of the *Truppenamt*, which dealt with foreign armies, voiced its objections to the construction of the battle cruiser *A* by the navy, because the good relations with Russia might be affected.[2] Similarly, when difficulties arose at the beginning of 1930 about the conclusion of a contract between the Soviet government and the Rheinmetall concern providing for the establishment of a construction office for tanks and anti-tank vehicles in Russia, the then chief of the *Truppenamt*, Major-General Freiherr von

[1] 'Reise des Chefs des Truppenamts nach Rußland (August/September 1928)', Berlin, 17 Nov. 1928: ibid. 9480 H, H 276183–236. The report has 54 pages and is printed in the *Slavonic and East European Review*, xli, no. 96, Dec. 1962, pp. 218–41.

[2] Report by General Eugen Ott of 1952: Zeugenschrifttum no. 279, Institut für Zeitgeschichte. At that time he was a major in the *Wehrmachtsabteilung* of the ministry of defence.

Hammerstein-Equord, explained to under-secretary of state von Schubert: 'The Russians would now be very offended if we did not play; they expressed the opinion that then the friendship between the Russian and the German armies could not be maintained. They thus drew the conclusion that the entire German–Russian relations depended on the conclusion of the contract. . . .' Schubert replied that he was frightened by the idea that the Russian guns might one day fire on Germans. But General von Hammerstein was undeterred: 'he was of the opinion that the world-revolutionary plans would not be carried out if the Russians were "sated". It was essential to satisfy them by such contracts, etc. So far as a possible attack by the Russians was concerned, this would after all be directed in the first place against Poland, and that could only please us. Apart from this, the military had ascertained that for the time being the Russians were only planning for defence, and at the moment wanted to build only anti-tank vehicles. . . .'[1] These sentiments were echoed by the Russians. When the preliminary contract with Rheinmetall was concluded a grand dinner was given in Moscow; under the influence of much vodka, General Uborevich then exclaimed: 'Shall we not have got so far in two years that we can adjust the frontiers and kill the Poles? Poland must be partitioned once more.'[2]

About the same time the Russians approached the firm of Gebrüder Thiel at Ruhla, as they wanted to acquire the rights and designs of a time-fuse produced by that firm. The latter asked the defence ministry for its consent, which was to have been given. The T 3 was instructed to obtain also that of the naval command, but there difficulties developed. A senior naval officer wrote: 'The Russians are such uncertain customers that in my opinion we have no interest in giving them this valuable time-fuse. What are they going to give in return? . . . If we give them something, we want to have some advantage!' In his opinion, the army command was so 'intertwined with Russia' that it would simply give things away. General von Hammerstein, however, promised that, 'through his influence

[1] Notes by von Schubert, Berlin, 10 Feb. 1930: Büro von Staatssekretär v. Schubert, Akten betr. Militärische Angelegenheiten mit Rußland, 4564/4, E 164022–7.
[2] Notes by von Moltke, Berlin, 12 Feb. 1930: ibid., E 164052–4.

with the Russians', he would obtain services of equal value for the navy.[1]

A few months after these events General von Hammerstein succeeded General Heye as chief of the army command. Under his guidance the pro-Russian policy of the Reichswehr was continued. The common enmity towards Poland remained one of the decisive factors in the co-operation. At the end of 1930 the chief of the T 3 of the *Truppenamt*, Lieutenant-Colonel Fischer, explained to the critical naval officers: 'The army conducts an active military policy with *Russia, Finland*, and *Lithuania*. The last in spite of the Memel issue, because Lithuania is a potential ally against Poland. Lithuanian general staff officers participate in German general staff courses! Finland plays an important part because, if we could mediate between that country and Russia, Russia would not be compelled to keep eight divisions on the Finnish frontier in case of a war with Poland.—We are preparing an operational study to find out to what extent Russia and Lithuania can play their parts in our plans as allies against Poland.'[2] It is interesting that Fischer mentioned the Lithuanian staff officers who were trained by the army, but not the Russians to whom the same applied. Probably the army command did not want to enlighten the naval officers who were opposed to the military co-operation with Russia. And how many of them were able to distinguish between Russians and Lithuanians when meeting them?

IV. *The Lohmann Scandal and the New Naval Command*

During the years 1926 and 1927 the financial enterprises of Captain Lohmann, the head of the Sea Transport Division of the naval command, became more numerous and more involved. He endeavoured to invest the large sums at his disposal profitably to obtain more money for armament purposes, but the connexion with naval interests was often slight or non-existent. In Berlin Lohmann bought a house for 588,000 marks,

[1] The chief of the *Waffenamt* to the T 3, 5 Mar. 1930, with remarks by officers of the *Flottenabteilung*, Mar. to May 1930: Marineleitung, Akten betr. Rußland, 1 SKL. Ic–4, PG/33617: Admiralty, London.

[2] 'Einstellung des Heeres zum Auslande', Dec. 1930: Marine-Kommandoamt, Flottenabteilung, Marinepolitische Angelegenheiten, 1 SKL Ic 1–2, PG/33611, ibid.

and near the Tiergarten another one for as much as 1,895,000 marks; for this purpose a limited company, the *Tierga Berlin A.G.*, was founded. To the *Berlin Bacon A.G.* he contributed 50,000 marks 'to create certain essential links with Britain', and another 50,000 to a company engaged in ore mining. Another company financed by Lohmann engaged in experiments with ice-escapes, but in 1927 it went bankrupt, leaving a loss of 63,167 marks. Two oil transport companies received 180,000 marks, and a new tanker was built for 2,800,000 marks. The majority of the shares in a private bank in Berlin was bought with 1,650,000 marks 'for certain reasons within the framework of the whole enterprise'. A shipping firm at Copenhagen was given 500,000 marks 'to enable the navy, in a case of emergency, to establish certain things in hostile ports, through suitable agents'.[1]

Much larger sums were invested in the *Phöbus-Film-Gesellschaft*, which was 'to direct the interests of the German public to the questions of defence and maritime prestige (*Seegeltung*), and to enhance Germany's name abroad through sales to foreign countries'. In the first instance Lohmann bought shares in this film company to the value of 1,750,000 marks. In March 1926 the ministers of defence and of finance and the chief of the naval command signed a joint guarantee for a credit to the company of 3 million marks. In January 1927 another guarantee was signed for 3,500,000 marks, and in June a further one for 920,000 marks. All these were granted by well-known Berlin banking houses. The company also received loans of 1,057,770 and 270,000 marks.[2] Within two years it thus swallowed more than 10 million marks—more than the amount which the navy had received in 1923 from the 'Ruhr fund' for armament purposes. Through an indiscretion, this fact reached the German press in 1927 and caused a great scandal. Its victims were not

---

[1] 'Zusammenstellung der Lohmann'schen Unternehmungen', compiled in Feb. 1928 in the naval command, listing 26 'Lohmann' enterprises and the sums paid to them: Marineleitung, Abteilung B, Chef des Stabes (BZ), PG 34428 XI: Militärgeschichtliches Forschungsamt; 'Die Geldmittel des Kapitäns zur See Lohmann', by the former minister Saemisch, 11 Nov. 1927: Reichskanzlei, Akten betr. die von Kapitän z.S. Lohmann getätigten wirtschaftlichen Unternehmungen, vol. i, R 43 I 603, Bundesarchiv Koblenz.

[2] Admiral Zenker, the chief of the naval command, to Dr. Geßler, Berlin, 9 Nov. 1927, and report by Saemisch, Berlin, 11 Nov. 1927, ibid. In general, see Raeder, *Mein Leben*, i. 219.

only Lohmann himself, but also the chief of the naval command, and above all the minister of defence, Dr. Geßler, who since the Kapp Putsch had continuously covered the Reichswehr enterprises in parliament and in public, and had become a seemingly indispensable member of the changing governments. Geßler's signature under the guarantee of 3 million marks caused his downfall—only fourteen months after he had obtained the dismissal of Seeckt and thus gained a more independent position.

Geßler's successor was the last quartermaster-general of the Imperial army, Wilhelm Groener, who had played the decisive political part at the birth of the German republic and laid the foundations of the new military order. He had completely retired from political life and did not expect to re-enter it. But the army command desired to have a former general as the minister of defence, who would be better able to defend its interests. In the opinion of Schleicher no one was better suited for this post than his old chief, and he prevailed upon President von Hindenburg, whose second in command Groener had been, to call on Groener. He became minister of defence in January 1928; he was 'an invention of Schleicher'.[1] Groener energetically intervened in the naval command—urged on by pressure from the press and the public. Most of the 'Lohmann enterprises' were wound up; the total loss amounted to 26 million marks, more than double the sum which Lohmann had received.[2] Groener further demanded information about the enterprises in the field of defence which existed 'outside the Treaty of Versailles', including those outside Germany. The chief of the *Marinewaffenabteilung* replied cautiously that enterprises existing outside the Treaty of Versailles could not be listed on paper, but offered to inform the minister orally at a suitable moment. This the latter refused to accept and insisted on the speedy compilation of a written report. The order had to be carried out.[3]

[1] Thus Schleicher's former adjutant, the later General Ferdinand Noeldechen, in 1951: Zeugenschrifttum no. 276, Institut für Zeitgeschichte. Similarly, Wilhelm Heye, 'Mein Lebenslauf', p. 624: Nachlaß Heye, H 08–18/4, Bundesarchiv-Militärarchiv.

[2] The loss according to Geßler, *Reichswehrpolitik in der Weimarer Zeit*, p. 453; the sum received by Lohmann according to Saemisch's report of 11 Nov. 1927, loc. cit.

[3] The naval command to various departments, Berlin, 9 Feb. 1928; the

The report showed that the current costs of the *Severa G.m.b.H.*, which developed aeroplanes for the navy and trained its pilots and observers, amounted to 1,350,000 marks a year. The costs of the *Trayag* at Travemünde, which developed and maintained speed-boats, were from 150,000 to 200,000 marks, and those of the *Tebeg G.m.b.H.*, which had to prepare the development and production of weapons, ammunition, apparatus, and vehicles, to a maximum of 120,000 marks a year. The annual costs of the *Mentor Bilanz G.m.b.H.* were about 40,000 marks; this firm closely co-operated with the *Ingenieurskantoor voor Scheepsbouw* in The Hague and was responsible for the preservation and training of a skeleton staff of submarine designers and qualified personnel, as well as for experiments in this field. The naval command was obliged to pay the deficit of the Dutch firm up to 120,000 marks a year, and had given a guarantee of 250,000 marks for the two submarines built in Holland for the Turkish navy.[1] These firms, which served military purposes, were either not liquidated together with the other Lohmann enterprises, or were merely formally liquidated and replaced by new firms with the same tasks. Thus the *Severa* was to be renamed *Küstenflugabteilung* of the *Luft-Hansa*; but to this the Prussian government objected as it would saddle the German civil air lines with the responsibility, and therefore the name *Luftdienst G.m.b.H.* was chosen.[2] The close relations of the navy with the Spanish, Finnish, and Turkish navies also continued; so did the construction of submarines through the services of the office in The Hague.

The chief of the naval command, Admiral Zenker, was also retired as he was considered responsible for the Lohmann affair and had signed one of the guarantees for the Phöbus film company. Another reason seems to have been that he did not

---

Marinewaffenabteilung to the chief of staff, Berlin, 13 Feb., and the minister of defence to the naval command, Berlin, 12 Mar. 1928: Marineleitung, Verschiedenes, 7897 M I; Abteilung B, Chef des Stabes (BZ), PG 34428 XI, Militärgeschichtliches Forschungsamt.

[1] The chief of the *Seetransportabteilung*, Captain Lahs, to the chief of staff, Berlin, 13 Feb. 1928, ibid.

[2] For the *Mentor Bilanz G.m.b.H.*, see ibid. the conference of 27 Feb. 1928; for the *Severa*, documents of 12 and 26 Feb. 1929 in Reichskanzlei, Akten betr. Landesverteidigung, vol. i, R 43 I 725, Bundesarchiv Koblenz; Schleicher to Dr. Pünder, 22 Mar. 1929: Nachlaß Schleicher, no. 49, ibid.; Völker, op. cit., p. 139, n. 47.

favour the building of the battle cruiser *A*, on which the navy insisted for reasons of prestige. According to the description of a participant, the mood was 'icy' when Zenker handed over to his successor, Vice-Admiral Raeder, the two admirals addressing each other as 'Excellency' in the third person singular.[1] At the time of the Kapp Putsch, Raeder was the chief of staff of the central department under Admiral von Trotha. According to the *Berliner Tageblatt*, Raeder was 'the real *spiritus rector*' in the naval command, which sided with Kapp, and had suggested the arrest of sailors at Kiel who opposed the *Putsch*. In any case, he was so compromised that during the following two years he had to 'shelter' in the naval archives.[2] But he was soon reinstated. It was also held against Raeder that he had taken part in a birthday celebration in honour of the former Grand-Admiral Prince Henry of Prussia, that the latter visited the cruiser *Berlin* and addressed the ship's company while Raeder was the commanding officer of the Baltic station of the navy, and that he was present at the opening of the new house of the Imperial Yacht Club at Kiel when the health of its commodore, the former Emperor William II, was proposed.[3]

In view of these attacks Raeder claimed that time and again he had informed the sailors: 'We are the firmest support of the constitution and therefore have the responsibility of seeing to it that no attacks, justified or unjustified, upon the *Wehrmacht* are made on account of our attitude. I have educated the sailors and the officers of the Baltic station to be loyal to the constitution, so that they now hold uniformly the correct views. That was not the case at the outset. For the rest, I consider myself a prop of the republic a thousand times more valuable than all those noisy propagandists, who in reality only intend [*sic*] to make us loathe the republic. . . .' Raeder denied that he had had any

---

[1] Information given by Admiral Paul Zieb.

[2] Wheeler-Bennett, op. cit., p. 190, n. 1, and confirmed by a former admiral in his notes lent to the author by Dr. Baum. The article of the *Berliner Tageblatt*, of 26 Sept. 1928, in Archiv der Marine, Handakten Raeder, PG 33951 b, Militärgeschichtliches Forschungsamt.

[3] Raeder, *Mein Leben*, i. 208, 210. The attacks against Raeder in Archiv der Marine, Handakten Raeder, PG 33951 b, loc. cit., with the refutations of individual points by the naval command. There is no evidence that Raeder 'publicly proposed the health of the Kaiser at the first dinner given in honour of his appointment', as stated by Mr. Wheeler-Bennett, op. cit., p. 190, n. 1. This criticism was not even made by the republican newspapers at the time.

connexions with the *vaterländische Verbände* and maintained that he had instructed his staff in the same sense. But he considered himself entitled to participate in a celebration in honour of the absent Grand-Admiral on his birthday when another admiral proposed his health. But a colonel, apparently Schleicher, wrote in the margin: 'It was very inexpedient to do this on Prince Henry's birthday, and not to make certain that no political demonstration took place. . . . Why can the admirals not remember a former comrade *without* proposing his health?'[1]

In fact Raeder at the beginning of 1928 had given an address at Kiel in which he said:

The *Wehrmacht* . . . is a firm and reliable support, I should even like to say . . . the firmest and most reliable support of our German fatherland, the German Reich, the German Republic and its constitution, and we are proud of it. . . . The Reichswehr, army and navy, is today, in the hands of its leaders . . . and of the president of the Reich himself, an absolutely reliable instrument of power, which will do its duty, whether it is employed to defend the frontiers or to maintain law and order internally. Whoever holds this instrument in his hands possesses the power in the state. But if the state is to exist, this power must only be exercised by the constitutional authorities. No one else must be allowed to wield it, not even the political parties; the *Wehrmacht* must be entirely non-political, composed only of soldiers who decline to take part in any political activity in full consciousness that this is necessary. . . .[2]

When the attacks against Raeder began extracts from this speech were sent to the minister of defence. Interestingly enough, however, the sentence 'Whoever holds this instrument in his hands possesses the power in the state' and the preceding ones were omitted.[3] It was considered safer not to emphasize this point, above all as the chancellor was now a Social Democrat. Groener ordered an investigation of the attacks, which

[1] Raeder to Lieutenant-Commander Götting, the chief of the *Wehrmachtsabteilung* of the naval command, Kiel, 24 Sept. 1928, with a marginal note which seems to be Schleicher's: Archiv der Marine, Handakten Raeder, PG 33951 b, loc. cit.

[2] 'Rede für die geschichtliche Woche', Kiel, 23 Jan. 1928: Nachlaß Schleicher, no. 41, Bundesarchiv Koblenz. Extracts in 'Aufzeichnung des Reichskanzlers', Berlin, 27 Sept. 1928: Archiv der Marine, Handakten Raeder, PG 33951 b, loc. cit.

[3] Consequently the following sentence had to be slightly altered: 'Aufzeichnung des Reichskanzlers', Berlin, 27 Sept. 1928: Archiv der Marine, Handakten Raeder, PG 33951 b, loc. cit. In reality this seems to be a note *for* the chancellor; signed by Groener on 2 Oct. 1928.

produced no result. Raeder offered to resign, but this was not accepted.[1] He remained the chief of the naval command until 1943, a period of fifteen years, during which innumerable changes occurred in the army command; he was a real time-server.

Soon after his move to Berlin Raeder came into direct contact with the government, in which Social Democrats now occupied prominent positions. Groener wanted the government to assume responsibility for all rearmament projects of the army and navy which violated the Treaty of Versailles. Groener achieved his aim: 'the Chancellor, Müller, and the Minister of the Interior, Severing—the latter as he always did in military necessities—showed great understanding, while the Minister von Guérard, who belonged to the Centre Party, made difficulties . . .'. The same was reported by Raeder at the Nuremberg trials; he added that afterwards he and Heye had to inform Groener of all such undertakings, who discussed them with Severing, and that Severing showed much sympathy with the illegal enterprises of the Reichswehr.[2] As the army command often accused Severing of the opposite tendency, Raeder's statements are of special interest. But the explanation may have partly been that the Social Democrats had fewer political objections to the activities of the navy in Finland, Holland, Spain, and Turkey than to the understanding with the Red Army, which was not without political overtones, and was bound to arouse opposition from a strongly anti-Communist party. After the Lohmann scandal, the navy did not engage in any activities behind the government's back, either in the financial or in the political sphere. For Raeder was now convinced that any deception of the government, even with the best intention, could never have beneficial results.[3]

v. *The Politics of Groener*

The new minister of defence, who succeeded Geßler early in 1928 at the age of sixty, had played a decisive part in the early years of the republic. He concluded an alliance with Ebert and

[1] Archiv der Marine, Handakten Raeder, PG 33951 b, loc. cit.
[2] *Trial of the Major War Criminals before the International Military Tribunal*, xiii, Nuremberg, 1948, pp. 621–2. The cabinet meeting was held on 18 Oct. 1928.
[3] Raeder, op. cit., ii. 22.

the moderate Social Democrats, so as to re-establish law and order and to prevent 'chaos'. He organized the orderly return of the armies from the occupied countries to Germany, and a new army when the old army disintegrated. He decisively opted in favour of signing the Treaty of Versailles, because in his opinion Germany was unable to continue the war, and thus saddled the young republic with an almost intolerable burden. It has often been maintained that Groener was a south-German democrat;[1] but in reality, through his whole education and career he was moulded by Prussian ideas and by the traditions of the officer corps. Exactly as Seeckt and Schleicher, he was in favour of a unitary German state, for the combination of the Prussian with the Reich government; and he remained opposed to the Social Democrats because they were in his opinion hostile to the army. He had a high personal regard for President Ebert, who was 'a patriotic man', 'hated the revolution', and 'stood firmly on the side of the officers';[2] but this did not modify Groener's rejection of the party whose leader Ebert was. A German historian has written that Groener was willing 'to co-operate with all the republican forces which showed national feelings and gave to the army what it needed . . .'.[3] But it has to be remembered that the phrases 'national feelings' and 'what the army needed' could be interpreted differently and that the army command was apt to interpret them from its own point of view.

Groener's political opinions were clearly stated in a long letter to Hindenburg at the height of the Bavarian crisis of 1923, in reply to a letter in which Hindenburg expressed his hopes that the parliamentary system would soon be buried and the old order and discipline be restored. Groener too wanted to re-establish the authority of the state as a *rocher de bronce*, but he was convinced that

In the long run it will be impossible to abolish the parliamentary system. Britain owes the greatest achievements to parliamentarism, and France too has clearly not done so badly with it.

---

[1] Thus recently Helmut Häussler, *General William Groener and the Imperial German Army*, Madison, Wisconsin, 1962, *passim*.

[2] Groener to Oberstaatsanwalt Ernst, Potsdam, 5 Feb. 1936: Nachlaß Groener, box 8, no. 37, Bundesarchiv-Militärarchiv.

[3] Schüddekopf, *Heer und Republik*, p. 237.

The government labours to restore order and discipline; unfortunately its efforts are obstructed by the ultra-right circles, which time and again incite the left radicals to oppose the authority of the state. . . . As a result of the war the revolution broke out: I should consider it completely conquered if it were possible to reconcile the German nation to the Weimar Constitution, which should be amended in several respects. Constitutions are not made for eternity, they are capable of development, and this does not necessitate revolutionary upheavals. Marxism, which today is attacked so much for reasons of party politics, is finished. Its place has been taken by Communism; the fight against it is at the moment the most important task. . . . The fight against Communism is facilitated if it is undertaken in alliance with Socialism, because basically there are—as in Russia—no more bitter enemies than Socialists and Communists. . . . The working class in its mass will never be converted to 'capitalism', but it is inspired by strong national sentiments, in spite of the slogan of the international proletariat. It would be a mistake to do harm to these national feelings because the representatives of capitalism are still haunted by the ghost of so-called Marxism; very few people know what this means. . . .[1]

These sentences show political understanding and moderation; they also prove that Groener remained loyal to the ideas which inspired him in 1918.

In practice, however, things looked very different, and soon Groener clashed with prominent Social Democrats. When the budget for 1930 was prepared at the end of 1929, after the beginning of the great economic crisis which was to undermine the foundations of the republic, Groener demanded for the Reichswehr—army and navy—a total of 761 million marks: 110 millions more than parliament had granted for 1929. After a discussion with the Social Democratic minister of finance, Hilferding, Groener declared his willingness to reduce his demand to 723 millions, still 73 millions more than the budget of the current year. Hilferding and the Social Democrats particularly objected to the inclusion of the first instalment for the construction of the battle cruiser B, amounting to more than 10 millions, which was to be completed by 1934. Already the

[1] Groener to Hindenburg, Berlin, 1 Nov. 1923: Nachlaß Groener, box 7, no. 28, Bundesarchiv-Militärarchiv. The phrase that he intended to 'make the crown as firm as a *rocher de bronce*' was used by Frederick William I: *Acta Borussica, Behördenorganisation*, ii, Berlin, 1898, no. 175, p. 352: royal order of 24 Apr. 1716.

construction of the first battle cruiser had caused strong resistance among the Social Democrats and a violent Communist agitation against them. It was inevitable that the demand for the building of the second cruiser at this time would meet with strong opposition. Hilferding therefore wrote to Groener that he could not give his consent to the demands; as the first instalment for the new battle cruiser accounted for over one-third of the additional naval requests, the matter, in his opinion, need hardly be emphasized. Groener reacted sharply:

It lies in the nature of the matter that my way of seeing the general political effects is basically different from yours. It must be said once and for all that above all the still strongly anti-militarist attitude of the Social Democratic Party—quite apart from that of a small group of incurable pacifists—creates difficulties for the most modest demands of the *Wehrmacht*, only because the agitation against the *Wehrmacht* belongs to the ancient armoury of this party. This applies in particular to the planned battle cruiser B. . . . I am convinced that a large section of the German people not only fully understands my point of view on the whole issue of defence, but passionately desires the preservation of the *Wehrmacht*. These very circles have reproached me on several occasions because of my concessions in defence matters. I therefore do not intend to capitulate again this year before the doctrinaire attitude of the Social Democratic Party, and I would not be willing to accept a majority decision of the cabinet. . . .[1]

Groener's tactics were entirely successful, as they had been successful a year before in the case of the battle cruiser A.[2] It was not he, but Hilferding, who had to resign at the end of 1929.

Groener, however, was not always equally successful, in particular when he resumed the old struggle with the Prussian civil authorities. When a pacifist exhibition, 'War and Peace', was opened at Breslau by the *Oberpräsident* of Silesia, Lüdemann, with a speech, Groener protested that it was 'intolerable that a private exhibition, which in its exhibits is directed against the government's policy and attacks ministries, is aided with an opening speech from a high-ranking official. . .'. Lüdemann replied that the tendency of the exhibition

[1] Hilferding to Groener, Berlin, 12 Nov. 1929, and Groener to Hilferding, Berlin, 13 Nov.: Nachlaß Dietrich, no. 356, Bundesarchiv Koblenz.
[2] In Nov. 1928 Groener threatened to resign if the building of the battle cruiser A was further delayed: Wheeler-Bennett, op. cit., p. 192.

conformed with the government's policy, which aimed at the preservation of peace. This was denied by Groener, who also objected to the supposition that he had misjudged the tendency of the exhibition. When the Prussian minister of the interior, Severing, defended the criticized *Oberpräsident*, Groener complained to the chancellor, who by this time was no longer a Social Democrat but a Catholic, Brüning, and sharply demanded that measures should be taken by the Reich against Prussia:

In my opinion the action of the *Oberpräsident* Lüdemann and its approval by his superior minister mean a furthering of Bolshevist disintegration by high Prussian authorities. . . . While all sensible leaders and parties, as well as the Holy See and the central organs of other denominations, have entered the fight against the systematic poisoning of the souls of youth and nation (*die systematische Vergiftung der Jugend- und Volksseele*), certain Prussian authorities support this cultural Bolshevism. . . . I do not believe it possible to change the intellectual disposition of certain Prussian authorities. The more necessary is it in my opinion that the Reich should create guarantees that, in future, men in official positions can no longer make propaganda for the destruction of the foundations of our state and nation. . . .[1]

In the spring of 1930—after the overthrow of the government of Hermann Müller—a new wind was blowing from the Bendlerstraße, and even the name of the Pope was invoked to impress the chancellor.

Some months earlier Groener protested in a similar vein against a series of articles published in the journal of the *Reichsbanner Schwarz-Rot-Gold*, in which the Reichswehr had been criticized, but by no means opposed on principle. On this occasion, too, Groener wrote to the chancellor, at that time still a Social Democrat: 'It transgresses the measure of what is tolerable', Müller was told, 'if the officer corps of the *Wehrmacht* of the Republic is made suspect in this shocking fashion . . . and overwhelmed with unjustified reproaches. . . . One cannot criticize the commanding officers if, after such stylistic exercises,

---

[1] The minister of defence to the minister of the interior, Berlin, 11 Nov. 1929 and 11 Apr. 1930, and to the chancellor, Berlin, 19 May 1930: Reichskanzlei, Akten betr. Reichswehr, vol. vi, R 43 I 687, Bundesarchiv Koblenz. The letters were written by the W III b of the *Wehrmachtsabteilung*, which was the department of Schleicher.

they reject any contacts with the *Reichsbanner Schwarz-Rot-Gold*, inclusive of friendly and social ones. These undignified articles . . . also make it impossible for me to instruct an officer of the defence ministry to give the lecture at the conference of youth leaders in the Harz, which the leaders of the *Reichsbanner* desire. . . .'[1] Instead of welcoming the opportunity to explain the position of the army to the leaders of the great mass organization of the republicans, the articles were used as an excuse to break off all contacts. It is true that Groener about the same time issued an instruction that the local officer corps were to establish social contacts with prominent Social Democrats; but there was little enthusiasm to obey it, nor much willingness to accept such invitations. When the Infantry Regiment 16 at Bremen invited, among other guests, several Social Democrats, only one of them accepted. And when an officer had an animated discussion with the guest, a leading member of the city council, there was much indignation among the other guests.[2]

In his public speeches Groener used very clear words in favour of the republic and its colours, and equally against the *Verbände* of the extreme right and their political pretensions. When he visited the naval school at Mürwik, which was a centre of right-wing extremism,[3] he declared:

When today we see above this building the new German flag, black, red and gold, side by side with the war flag of black, white and red, this means that the two belong together, that there is no conflict, that the conclusion cannot be drawn that the *Wehrmacht* is something different from the Reich, or a state within the state. The *Wehrmacht* is nothing but a part, an important part, of the whole nation; it is the instrument of the power of the German Republic, which nobody is permitted to attack. When above us the flags flutter peacefully together, this symbolizes the links between past and present, the past not solely of 1914 and the preceding years, or the past since 1870, but the links with a much earlier past; for the colours black, red and gold go back to a very much older time than do the black, white and red. . . .

[1] The minister of defence to the chancellor, Berlin, 24 June 1929: Reichskanzlei, Akten betr. Reichsbanner Schwarz-Rot-Gold, vol. i, R 43 I 767, Bundesarchiv Koblenz. This letter, too, came from Schleicher's department.
[2] Information given to the author by Lieutenant-General Mahlmann.
[3] See above, pp. 98, 133–4.

In his notes for this address Groener also emphasized 'loyalty to the new state'.[1]

Again, Groener's notes for an address to the infantry school at Dresden stressed the non-political character of the Reichswehr and rejected the *Verbände* and their political aims, which might curtail or eliminate the Reichswehr as an instrument of power. 'Relation of the *Wehrmacht* to the parties and para-military associations [is] strictly above party, obedient to the law and the constitutional government, not influenced by any party-political tendencies. Only power—Reichswehr. The pretensions of the para-military associations [are] intolerable. . . . Greatest danger: political inclinations. Enormous strength of the *Wehrmacht* if united from top to bottom, firm internally, forming an instrument of power within the state which no one can push aside. . . .'[2] But here the minister of defence was subjected to censorship: neither the *Militär-Wochenblatt* nor the *Marine-Rundschau* printed his remarks against the *Verbände*, but only the sentence: 'The *Wehrmacht* must stand absolutely above all the parties, obedient to the law and to the constitutional government.'[3] Clearly, the editors of the two military journals did not subscribe to all the ideas of Groener. Striking, in particular, was his emphasis on loyalty to the republic and its colours, and the attempt to establish a link between the old Germany and the new.

VI. *The Rise of Schleicher*

The indispensable adviser of Groener in political affairs was the much younger Kurt von Schleicher, who had closely co-operated with the quartermaster-general during the years of the World War and the revolution. Under Seeckt, Schleicher acquired wide political experience and multifarious connexions with parliamentary deputies and the political parties and pressure groups. This was recognized by removing Schleicher's department from the jurisdiction of the *Truppenamt* and subordinating it directly to the defence minister as a separate

---

[1] Speech of 3 July 1929 and notes of Groener: Nachlaß Groener, box 22, no. 229, Bundesarchiv-Militärarchiv.

[2] Groener's notes for a speech at Dresden on 17 Dec. 1929: ibid.

[3] *Militär-Wochenblatt*, no. 25, 4 Jan. 1930; *Marine-Rundschau*, no 1, 1930: ibid. In 1930 Groener declared that it was the task of the Reichswehr, 'abseits aller Parteipolitik nur der Idee des Staates zu dienen': Schüddekopf, op. cit., p. 238.

Wehrmachtsabteilung. Schleicher as its chief had in his hands all the political threads, but his ambition was not yet satisfied. Early in 1929 he achieved not only his preferential promotion to the rank of major-general, but also the establishment of a new office, the *Ministeramt*, which in practice gave him the position of the under-secretary of state in the defence ministry. This office combined all organs and departments of the ministry that stood directly under the minister, with the exception of the army and navy budget sections. The chief of the *Ministeramt* had to represent the minister of defence in 'all questions which the chiefs of the army and naval commands do not themselves want to represent', above all in parliament and the cabinet; furthermore, it was stipulated some months later, 'in all questions which have no connexion with military matters' and 'in military matters of a purely political nature'.[1] Thus Schleicher became Groener's *'cardinal in politicis'* who 'performed excellent work behind the scenes', and whom Groener trusted blindly in all political affairs.[2] Soon the new general exercised a political influence stronger than that of any other person in Germany.

Schleicher's new office and his far-reaching influence meant that the position of the chief of the army command correspondingly lost in importance, as Schleicher's power grew. Heye was very much weaker than Seeckt, who never suffered any rival influence, and Groener was much stronger than the feeble Geßler, who had served as Seeckt's office-boy. Heye himself felt strongly about this undermining of his whole position. He complained to Groener that, if not in name then in fact, an under-secretary now stood between the minister and the chief of the army command, who was junior to the chief; that members of the *Ministeramt* increasingly forgot his existence, and sent new instructions directly to subordinate offices; and that great uncertainty was created within the ministry, which he was unable to overcome.[3] Groener's reply, which was based on Schleicher's notes, was more than outspoken:

I saw and I see in the chief of the army command not the political, but the technical adviser of the minister, and in the first place the

[1] Decrees of 21 Feb. and 8 Oct. 1929: Nachlaß Schleicher, no. 36, Bundesarchiv Koblenz.

[2] Groener to Gerold von Gleich, Berlin, 4 Jan. 1930: Groener-Geyer, *General Groener*, p. 262. Cf. Geßler, op. cit., p. 399.

[3] Heye to Groener, Berlin, 23 Nov. 1929: Nachlaß Schleicher, no. 36, loc. cit.

military teacher and leader of the army, the first and highest *soldier*. Precisely these considerations have caused me to create and to expand the *Ministeramt*. I admit, of course, that this development had to lead to a certain change in the position of the chief of the army command, and I should fully understand, dear Heye, if you hesitated to take part in this development. Under these circumstances, I do not want to press you to consent to my request that you should continue at your post at least until the autumn of 1930, and I would fulfil your often expressed wish to be relieved of your duties, albeit with a heavy heart. . . .

This letter, however, was not sent; the matter was settled verbally.[1]

Several other officers have testified that Heye's impression was quite correct and that the matter was openly discussed in the officer corps. Thus the chief of the Army Organization Department wrote later that Heye was easily influenced and was guided by men who enjoyed his confidence.

Thus a clique came into being which governed. The trio of Stülpnagel, Schleicher, and von dem Bussche was considered all-powerful in the defence ministry. . . . Heye had a markedly conciliatory and kind-hearted disposition and lacked self-confidence, inner firmness, and consistency. He was not a fighter; in complete contrast with Seeckt, he tended to draw back if there was strong resistance. . . . Heye was more and more by-passed and cold-shouldered, and he indicated this to me on the occasion of a report on a matter in which the decision rested with him, not with the minister. . . .[2]

Lieutenant-General Wöllwarth wrote much more drastically to Reinhardt:

Seeckt, Reinhardt, and Wetzell had to be eliminated, so that the clique could entirely dominate the weak Heye and Groener, who was called back by them. I particularly regret this, for I hoped that the clever Groener would see through the intrigues of the clique; but I had to learn during a long conversation that he is infatuated with these people. Quite significant is his remark: 'The army has

---

[1] Groener to Heye, Berlin, Dec. 1929 (draft with notes in Schleicher's hand), ibid. 'Ist *nicht* abgesandt worden!'

[2] Hilmar Ritter von Mittelberger, 'Lebenserinnerungen', pp. 242–3: MS. in Bundesarchiv Koblenz. Not only Schleicher, but the Colonels von Stülpnagel and von dem Bussche-Ippenburg too had meanwhile been promoted major-generals.

to put up with the next chief of the army command remaining in
his position for ten years.' Whom he means by 'the next chief of the
army command' is obvious. . . .

In the writer's opinion, it was the last High Command of the
Imperial army which now ruled the roost, the people 'who once
before had steered the ship onto the rocks'.[1] The man to whom
Wöllwarth alluded as the next chief of the army command was
clearly Joachim von Stülpnagel, who was closely linked with
Schleicher from the Seeckt period; at that time he was the
chief of the army's Personnel Office.

Still more concerned about this development was Heye's son,
a naval officer who about this time was posted to the ministry
of defence. He reported to Schleicher a conversation which
he had unintentionally overheard and thus summarized:

> How will things continue in the *Wehrmacht*? Well, the chief of the
> army command is a good chap, a puppet that dances to the tune of
> the chief of the *Ministeramt*, of Stülp[nagel] and v.d.B[ussche].
> That ring dominates everything. They promote each other. . . .
> In two years we shall have achieved it; then the chief of the army
> command will be allowed to parade with his guard regiment—all
> the rest will have been swallowed by the minister and the 'secretary
> of state'. . . . The power instrument of the *Ministeramt* dominates and
> usurps everything, and what will happen if one day ministers and
> under-secretaries of state come and exploit this? That briefly was
> the content of the conversation. I only quote it because it is not
> isolated but reflects prevalent opinions. . . . In the navy the same
> opinions are held, carried there by army officers (in one instance
> even ensigns, who ridiculed the chief of the army command while
> attending an alcoholic party in a naval garrison!). . . .[2]

From the practice grounds at Munsterlager a captain who had
been one of Schleicher's underlings wrote to him as early as
1928:

> In general, *Herr Oberst* [i.e. Schleicher] is believed to be a very
> ambitious man, without any strength of character, who uses his
> intellectual gifts . . . to get for himself gradually the position of an

---

[1] Wöllwarth to Reinhardt, Dresden, 24 Mar. 1929: Nachlaß Reinhardt,
Hauptstaatsarchiv Stuttgart. This indeed was a prophetic remark.

[2] Kapitänleutnant Heye to Schleicher, Flensburg, 30 Oct. 1929: Nachlaß
Schleicher, no. 35, Bundesarchiv Koblenz. Heye, thirty-five years later, was to
show the same outspokenness in his critical remarks on the Bundeswehr of the
German Federal Republic.

under-secretary of state. . . . I am convinced that the mass of the younger and even the staff officers arrive at such views because the personality and the work of *Herr Oberst* are totally unknown to them. They only know that *Herr Oberst* is the political adviser of the minister, and thus all political decrees (about the flags, etc.), which are considered concessions to the left, are attributed to the influence of *Herr Oberst*. With the senior officers, or those who have worked in the defence ministry (for example, Major von Rabenau!), other reasons must be decisive. . . .

A major of an artillery regiment had told the writer that he heard nothing but negative comments on Schleicher and that this view equally predominated in the navy.[1]

Because he did not belong to the Schleicher 'clique' in the defence ministry, the chief of the *Truppenamt*, Major-General von Blomberg, was often exposed to unfriendly interference from their side.[2] In 1929 Groener and Schleicher succeeded in effecting a change in this key position. Blomberg's successor was an old friend of Schleicher from the Third Foot Guards, Major-General Freiherr von Hammerstein-Equord, so that the most important posts were now filled by Schleicher and his friends. A new conflict with the Prussian government on matters of frontier defence offered the opportunity to remove Blomberg from his post. During the Ruhr crisis of 1923 a secret organization was formed, the *Feldjäger*, who were trained for guerrilla warfare behind the enemy front. At the end of 1928 the Prussian police received information that the *Feldjäger* had not been disbanded, but were still holding exercises, and that in the province of Hesse-Nassau even National Socialists belonged to them. In a meeting on 9 November 1928 Groener, Heye, and Blomberg told the indignant Prussian ministers that officially the *Feldjäger* no longer existed and were being 'withdrawn'. As Blomberg wrote in his memoirs, this corresponded to 'our general line of camouflage, namely, to deny everything. . .'. But the Prussian ministers were not satisfied and declared that they did not think much of 'playing at soldiers'. In December 1928 the defence ministry expressly forbade 'any

[1] Captain Burdach to Schleicher, Munster, 18 Nov. 1928: Nachlaß Schleicher, no. 3, ibid.   For Geßler's decree about the flags, see above, p. 262.

[2] Hilmar Ritter von Mittelberger, 'Lebenserinnerungen', p. 242: MS. in Bundesarchiv Koblenz.

practical frontier defence measures in the west and any military activity in the demilitarized zone' of the Rhineland.[1] In practice this meant that the Reichswehr officially retired from these activities, which were then continued by the *Stahlhelm* and similar organizations.

The official denial, however, had a disagreeable aftermath as far as Blomberg was concerned. Either there was a new denunciation from the Rhineland in the spring of 1929, or it was found out that he himself had watched one of the exercises which were now officially forbidden. In any case, Blomberg was recalled to Berlin by telegram from a general staff tour. When he saw him Schleicher described the situation to Blomberg as 'very bad'; the government was convinced that the denunciation of the 'guerrilla war' was correct. When Blomberg reminded Schleicher of their usual practice of denying everything, Schleicher interjected that Blomberg had watched these exercises even after the official prohibition; the government felt that it had been deceived and not told the truth, and Blomberg would have to bear the consequences and resign. 'My surprise', he wrote later, 'was as great as my indignation; but this was not directed against the Social Democratic ministers, but against the minister of defence, Groener, or, more correctly, against the real wire-puller, Schleicher. They themselves had denied in front of the cabinet what they knew about in outline, and now they had arranged matters apparently in such a way that I was to be thrown to the wolves. . . . On the next day I heard that the cabinet was to discuss my case, but I was not to be heard. After several hours Schleicher telephoned to me and informed me . . . that General Heye had saved me. . . .' Heye accepted the responsibility himself and demanded his own retirement; this crisis, however, the ministers wanted to avoid and declared themselves satisfied with a promise that Blomberg would be sent away from Berlin.[2] In the autumn of 1929 he was sent to East Prussia as the commanding officer of the First Division and of *Wehrkreis* 1.

After the removal of Blomberg from his post as chief of the

[1] 'Von General von Schleicher zur vertraulichen Kenntnis übersandt', 31 Oct. 1929: Reichskanzlei, Akten betr. Stahlhelm, vol. i, K 2307, Bundesarchiv Koblenz; Vogelsang, op. cit., pp. 57–58; Werner von Blomberg, 'Erinnerungen bis 1933', iii. 172: Bundesarchiv Koblenz.

[2] Ibid., iii. 171–4.

Truppenamt and his replacement by Schleicher's friend Hammerstein, the question became increasingly important who was to succeed Heye as chief of the army command. As Stülpnagel wrote later, there was 'no confidence in Heye'. 'Heye's personality did not command the respect Seeckt had commanded. His great zeal and his strong emphasis on comradeship, which he expressed even to non-commissioned officers when inspecting their messes, showed a lack of the true master feeling (*Herrengefühl*), and did not impress the officer corps. I warned Heye often, but he did not understand me. . . .'[1] It was generally expected that Stülpnagel would be the next chief of the army command, as he was considered a much stronger personality than Heye.[2] The final decision rested with President von Hindenburg, but there can be no doubt that Groener and Schleicher exercised the real influence. In June 1930 Stülpnagel wrote apprehensively to Schleicher that it was essential to choose the successor soon if it was true that Heye would be retired on 1 October. 'As you know there are more and more groups inside the ministry which discuss the pros and cons of the persons in question and engage in feuds with each other, cliques which are neither in the general interest, nor in that of the successor. The situation in the whole army is similar. Rumours are spread, distrust is growing, words are misinterpreted, etc.—a constant subject of discussion in the officer corps! . . .' Stülpnagel added that if the decision went in favour of Blomberg or Hammerstein he would welcome it and leave the army without any feeling of bitterness or hurt pride. He also denied that he intended to become 'a political general'—some remarks of his made in a conversation with landowners of Brandenburg had been misunderstood; he would support the policy of Groener and Schleicher, as he had done during the past ten years in close co-operation with Schleicher; the existence of 'a political general' was only justified in war and revolution, otherwise it became 'ridiculous'.[3]

---

[1] Joachim von Stülpnagel to Dr. Geßler, n.d.: Nachlaß Geßler, no. 46, p. 45, Bundesarchiv Koblenz. Cf. ibid., no. 18, the letter of Kapitänleutnant Heye to Dr. Geßler, complaining about the strong animosity against his father, especially in circles of the right and officers' associations.

[2] Notes by Schleicher's adjutant, Captain Noeldechen, n.d.: Nachlaß Schleicher, no. 34 ii, ibid.

[3] Stülpnagel to Schleicher, Berlin, 4 June 1930: Nachlaß Schleicher, no. 69, ibid.

Yet this letter, with its emphasis on their old friendship and on Stülpnagel's support for Schleicher's policy, apparently did not impress Schleicher. A few weeks later he informed Stülpnagel that Groener had decided in favour of Hammerstein. To others he remarked that he would have preferred Stülpnagel, but was unable to oppose his friend and old companion Hammerstein. In Stülpnagel's opinion, Groener and Schleicher had for many years thought of him for this post, but on account of his independent tendencies they feared that he would be less accommodating and might curtail their political influence; Groener in all his decisions depended upon Schleicher. 'He now played his political game alone and wanted to have for the future a chief of the army command who was bound to him and easy-going. That Hammerstein promised to be, in his indolent way. . . .'[1] Colonel Freiherr von Fritsch tried to persuade Stülpnagel not to leave the army: if he left, there would be no-one to counteract 'the pernicious influence of Groener and Schleicher'; their methods in dealing with the units, their indifference towards the officer corps, were bound to cause much damage, especially in the officer corps, and he was looking to the future full of apprehension.[2] Outside the army, too, it was known to whom Hammerstein owed his rapid promotion to the highest post. A deputy of the German Nationalist Party, who had served with them in the Third Foot Guards, congratulated Schleicher heartily and expressed the hope that his appointee would bring him joy; the Third Foot Guards were trumps, not only in the old time, but also in the new.[3] The British military attaché commented: 'The Army Command is now passing into the control of a group of the younger and more pushful generals who tolerate the Weimar Constitution and all that it stands for only so long as the field-marshal remains as the representative Head of the State.'[4] In the 'system' of Schleicher the connexions with the House of Hindenburg

[1] Stülpnagel, '75 Jahre meines Lebens', pp. 278–9: Bundesarchiv-Militärarchiv H 08–5/27.

[2] Fritsch to Stülpnagel, Stettin, 27 July 1930: ibid., H 08–5/23.

[3] The deputy von Plehwe to Schleicher, Dwarischken near Schirwindt, 22 Sept. 1930: Nachlaß Schleicher, no. 69, Bundesarchiv Koblenz.

[4] Colonel J. H. Marshall-Cornwall in Sept. 1930: *Documents on British Foreign Policy 1919–1939*, ed. by E. L. Woodward and R. Butler, 2nd series, vol. i, London, 1946, p. 512, no. 2.

were of decisive importance—father and son Hindenburg had also served in the Third Foot Guards.

Many senior officers believed that Schleicher's only motive was personal ambition, that he only strengthened the position of the minister of defence because he wanted to occupy it himself after Groener, and that he weakened the power of the chief of the army command for reasons of personal aggrandisement.[1] But there was a second motive: Schleicher sincerely believed that he was acting in the interests of the Reichswehr; in his scale of values they always occupied the first place. Yet the interests of the Reichswehr could assume strange forms in his mind. In 1929 he addressed the cabinet for two hours to achieve a direct intervention by Stresemann with the French foreign minister Briand, requesting that the Reichswehr officers competing at the international equestrian tournament at Aachen (which was in the demilitarized zone) should be allowed to wear uniform.[2]

Schleicher's policy during the years 1928–9 was to a large extent identical with that of Groener; it is virtually certain that Groener's policy of affecting a *rapprochement* with the republic was inspired by Schleicher who already under Seeckt had pursued the same objective. He was one of the very few senior officers who had an eye for political reality and adopted a pragmatic attitude towards parliament, parties, trade unions, and other forms of political life. In this field he reaped considerable successes, especially in the parliamentary committees; it was due to his efforts that the representatives of the two large republican parties, the Centre and the Social Democrats, adopted a positive attitude to the aims and demands of the Reichswehr, and often supported them in the committees.[3] These successes, however, did not assuage Schleicher's dislike of the Social Democrats, especially the Prussian government, as the friction with it on the issue of frontier defence continued throughout the period. In the autumn of 1928 Schleicher gleefully informed Groener that 'the strong man of Prussia' continued to make the life of the chancellor difficult in all military questions, and that Prussia was as oppositional towards a cabinet under Social Democratic leadership as previously towards a conservative government.[1]

In 1929 Schleicher made notes for a conference of senior officers in which he again stressed the 'non-political attitude of the Reichswehr'. Decisive in this respect was the attitude of the officer corps, and particularly important the education of the officer cadets; all attempts at influencing the army in the direction of an extremist party must be opposed; he considered the 'National Socialists much more dangerous than the Communists because they hide their revolutionary tendencies under a national cloak'; two officer cadets had been misled by them. In words very similar to those used by Groener in his speech to the infantry school, Schleicher declared that all para-military *Verbände* were bad, that their existence, and even more so any recognition of their activities, meant an 'intolerable degradation of the *Wehrmacht*'; any participation of soldiers in meetings which had a party-political character must be declined, for example celebrations in honour of the constitution organized by the *Reichsbanner Schwarz-Rot-Gold*; thus 'the special position of the *Wehrmacht* in the state' was to be preserved. At the same time Schleicher stressed that orders had to be carried out. It was quite incomprehensible that the defence ministry had been asked whether the prohibition of all frontier defence measures in the demilitarized zone could be circumvented and the civil authorities hoodwinked: 'such dishonesties are the reason, and at least a wonderful pretext, for the distrust and the anti-militarist attitude of certain Prussian authorities. . . .'[2] According to new directives of the government, adopted in April 1929, active military preparations for the frontier defence were only permitted in the Prussian provinces to the east of the Oder and prohibited in the Rhineland and on the western frontiers.[3] When the Prussian minister of the interior objected to the continuation of these measures in the Rhineland by members of the *Stahlhelm*, contrary to the directives of the year 1923,[4]

[1] Schleicher to Groener, Berlin, 3 Sept. 1928: Nachlaß Groener, box 21, no. 224, Bundesarchiv-Militärarchiv.
[2] 'Notizen für die Kommandeurbesprechung', n.d.: Nachlaß Schleicher, no. 35, Bundesarchiv Koblenz (autumn of 1929).
[3] Notes of 20 Feb. 1930: Vogelsang, op. cit., no. 4, p. 413.
[4] See above, p. 229.

Groener indignantly attributed this to the failure of the Prussian government to effect an appropriate development of the directives: its attitude time and again had frustrated the efforts of his ministry to include larger circles of the population in the preparations for frontier defence.[1] Here too, the tone used against the Prussian government had become noticeably sharper by the beginning of 1930.

Above all, Groener and Schleicher now believed that the time had come to bring about a change of government in the interests of the Reichswehr. Until the beginning of 1930 the government of Germany was formed by the parties of the 'great coalition', from the People's Party to the Social Democrats, with their leader Hermann Müller as the chancellor. The difficulties of this government grew in the course of 1929 on account of the incipient world economic crisis, the lack of funds, the Reparations problem, the increasing unemployment figures, and the suffering of large sections of the nation. In December Schleicher had a number of discussions about these problems and came to the conclusion that the government could not last much longer.[2] His contacts with the moderate right-wing parties—the Centre, the People's Party, and the moderate German Nationalists—were to prepare the ground for the formation of a government further to the right. At the beginning of the new year Groener proudly informed a personal friend: 'During my official absence my *"cardinal in politicis"* has done excellent work behind the scenes. I hold the best trumps in my hands. Thus we await quietly what 1930 will bring. In any case, Schleicher will not be duped. How little you know Schleicher! . . . Remain loyal to the German Nationalists, with whom I have got the best contacts, in so far as they are not the blind followers of Hugenberg (*blöde Hugenbergianer*). This party must again be made fit to conclude alliances and join the government. . . .'[3] As it was impossible to remove the Social Democrats from their Prussian stronghold, they should at least

---

[1] The Prussian minister of the interior, Berlin, 24 Oct. 1929 and 5 Apr. 1930: Reichskanzlei, Akten betr. Stahlhelm, vols. i and ii, K 2307/K 647487 and 647740, Bundesarchiv Koblenz; the minister of defence to the Prussian minister of the interior, Berlin, 15 Jan. 1930: ibid., K 2307/K 647713.

[2] Vogelsang, op. cit., p. 69.

[3] Groener to Gerold von Gleich, Berlin, 4 Jan. 1930: Groener-Geyer, *General Groener*, p. 262.

be excluded from the central government; the Chancellor Müller should not be given powers by the president to dissolve parliament and hold new elections, nor be granted emergency powers on the basis of article 48 of the constitution.[1]

Early in 1930—unfortunately the date cannot be ascertained —Schleicher's adjutant wrote notes on the political situation which contained the following suggestions: 'No power of dissolution to this government or to a government of the Weimar coalition. . . . No dissolution of parliament, but *formation of a new government on a non-party basis.*' The new chancellor was to be the leader of the Centre Party, Brüning, or if he refused, the leader of the People's Party, Scholz; he would be entrusted with the task of 'forming a government of personalities, prepared to carry out the work of economic and financial restoration without consulting the parties and without any coalition ties'. The advantages of this solution, in the writer's opinion, were that the entire right—excluding a few followers of Hugenberg—, the agrarians, and the representatives of industry, banks, and trade would support the government; Hugenberg would be isolated and the sterile opposition of the German Nationalists would be ended; the *Stahlhelm*, which the president desired to be included, would come out in favour of the government and with a declaration of loyalty to Hindenburg; confidence and optimism would be restored, 'which could not be revived with the old firm'. Groener was to complain about the 'sabotage of the frontier defence by Prussia', the 'underground struggle of Prussia against the *Wehrmacht*', the 'attack of the Social Democratic Party against the naval construction programme', and other points.[2] The remark about the wishes of the president, and a note later added to the name of Brüning—'he will certainly do it and carry it through'—prove that the whole scheme was not merely a plan, but that very concrete steps had been taken to

---

[1] According to Rabenau, *Seeckt*, p. 651, Hindenburg was willing in 1930 to grant dictatorial powers under article 48 to the leader of the Social Democrats as the chancellor. But Groener declared through Schleicher that this was 'impossible' for him as the minister of defence.

[2] Notes by Captain Noeldechen, n.d. (written probably in Jan. 1930, in any case before 10 Mar. 1930): Nachlaß Schleicher, no. 23, Bundesarchiv Koblenz. Partly printed by Vogelsang, op. cit., no. 5, pp. 414–15. Probably the notes were written before 17 Febr., the date of Groener's letter to Hermann Müller, quoted below, p. 355.

carry out the programme. It was directed above all against the Social Democrats and the Prussian government.

If the Reichswehr, after the dismissal of Seeckt, moved slightly towards the left and towards a recognition of the republic, this move was abruptly halted by the onset of the great economic crisis. From that time onwards the Reichswehr, under Schleicher's guidance, moved steadily towards the right. At the end of 1926 he declared: 'It would be best if the government veered towards the right.'[1] He was to act according to this principle during the following years. When Schleicher's candidate, Brüning, became chancellor in March 1930 the under-secretary of state, Dr. Pünder, wrote in his diary: 'Behind the scenes they have worked at this coalition for weeks, especially Treviranus and General von Schleicher. What we have found out has not all been pleasant.'[2]

[1] See above, p. 261.
[2] H. Pünder, *Politik in der Reichskanzlei*, p. 46, under 30 Mar. 1930. Treviranus was the leader of the 'volkskonservative Partei' and a confidant of Schleicher.

VII

THE REICHSWEHR DURING THE CRISIS

1. *Officers and National Socialists*

FROM 1929 onwards the Reichswehr leaders not only had to face the problems of the severe economic crisis and of the political measures necessitated by it, but also the quickly growing extremist movements of the left and right. It was only during these years that Hitler's National Socialists acquired an ever-growing mass following in northern Germany, above all in circles from which many of the recruits of the Reichswehr were drawn. But after the experiences of the year 1923, and Hitler's attempts to undermine the discipline of the army, the army command almost automatically adopted a negative attitude towards the new wave of extremism which threatened the very foundations of society. From the outset the army command had attempted to prevent the army from being influenced by party politics and political extremism. This was easily achieved with regard to Communist propaganda. All its efforts at winning over Reichswehr soldiers were defeated by their patriotic and nationalist convictions, which were the antithesis of Communist ideas. Occasionally there were a few Communists among the soldiers, but they could quickly be isolated and discharged. Various gifts, special leave, and even promotion, were promised as rewards for the discovery of Communist propaganda in the Reichswehr.[1] But even without these, Communism was unable to find an echo in its ranks, as the soldiers were not recruited from radical working-class circles and the world of international Communism was alien to them.

It was entirely different with regard to the ideas of National

---

[1] 'Belohnungen an Soldaten für Abwehr von Spionage- und Zersetzungs-versuchen in der Wehrmacht', sent by General von Schleicher on 17 Nov. 1930: Büro des Reichspräsidenten, vol. 763, pp. 234–8, Deutsches Zentralarchiv, Potsdam.

Socialism. They made little impression on the older officers, as many observers and witnesses of the time have testified. The older officers had grown up in the world of the German Empire and remained loyal to it, in spite of war and revolution, or perhaps because of them. Their opinions were strictly conservative and 'black, white and red'; they were opposed to all revolutionary experiments and slightly shocked by the crude propaganda of this 'proletarian movement'. Many of them did not take the 'Bohemian lance-corporal' seriously and did not believe in his success. Their attitude was like that of conservative officials. They maintained good relations with the circles of the German Nationalist Party, with the *Stahlhelm*, the associations of former officers, and the members of regimental clubs, who were their 'comrades', but not with the unemployed and ne'er-do-wells who were so prominent in Hitler's *S.A.* (Storm-troopers). Many soldiers found the *S.A.* and its playing at soldiers 'ridiculous'.[1] It is true that the leaders of the *S.A.* were often former officers; but these were the revolutionary adventurers of the free corps, whom Seeckt had removed from the Reichswehr, or doubtful characters, such as Göring or Röhm, who were looked down upon by the older officers. For professional reasons too they were opposed to Hitler's private army, which was not destined—as were the *Stahlhelm* and other paramilitary *Verbände*—to swell the ranks of the army in an emergency. It was above all a social cleavage, which separated those who had found a place within the existing order from those who had not.

In September 1930 Hitler gained his first great electoral success, and the National Socialists' parliamentary representation jumped from 12 to 107. This frightened many officers, but also created a fatalistic attitude. 'It is the *Jugendbewegung*,' they told the British military attaché; 'it can't be stopped.'[2] But some senior officers, such as Colonel Ludwig Beck, the commanding officer of the Artillery Regiment 5, sharply criticized Schleicher's cautious attitude towards the National Socialists and hoped

[1] Leo Freiherr Geyr von Schweppenburg, *Gebrochenes Schwert*, Berlin, 1952, p. 54; Hermann Foertsch, *Schuld und Verhängnis*, Stuttgart, 1951, pp. 22–23; confirmed in personal conversations in May 1961 by Major-General Curt Ulrich von Gersdorff and Lieutenant-General Paul Mahlmann.

[2] Report of Colonel J. H. Marshall-Cornwall of Sept. 1930: *Documents on British Foreign Policy 1919–1939*, 2nd series, i. 512, n. 2.

much from Hitler and his 'movement'; the election result of 14 September was celebrated by Beck in the officers' mess.[1] Yet at that time he was certainly an exception among the senior officers. It was different with many young officers, who had been schoolboys during the world war, and for whom the Empire was a mere shadow of the past. The National Socialists' revolutionary *élan*, their repudiation of Versailles and the Weimar 'system', their exaggerated nationalism were extremely attractive to young men who came from the same social groups as many young National Socialists and had the same basic ideas. 'They saw and heard the national tunes to which the ears of the soldiers are particularly attuned in all nations and at all times', wrote an officer later, who at that time was a captain.[2]

In the opinion of a colonel of the *Truppenamt*, who himself considered National Socialism completely destructive and akin to Bolshevism, for many young officers the movement offered 'a means of escape from Germany's financial and political troubles'.[3] As early as 1929 Lieutenant Henning von Tresckow from the Infantry Regiment 9, which continued the traditions of the Prussian foot guards, lectured on the *Brechung der Zins-knechtschaft* (breaking of the shackles of interest—a popular Nazi slogan) in the officers' mess at Potsdam.[4] In the Cavalry Regiment 4 at Potsdam, the regiment preserving the traditions of the Prussian horse guards, the lieutenants declared that only Hitler could save Germany, and could not be shaken in this conviction by any counter-arguments.[5] Curiously enough, it was at Potsdam, with its strong Prussian and Hohenzollern traditions, and among young officers from the oldest noble families, that Hitler found enthusiastic followers. But in other

[1] Report of General Eugen Ott of 1952: Zeugenschrifttum, no. 279, Institut für Zeitgeschichte.

[2] Foertsch, op. cit., pp. 21–22.

[3] Note by Colonel Marshall-Cornwall, Berlin, 8 May 1930, on a conversation with Colonel Kühlenthal: *Documents on British Foreign Policy 1919–1939*, 2nd series, i. 478.

[4] H. Teske, *Die silbernen Spiegel*, Heidelberg, 1952, p. 31; 'Analyse eines Reichswehr-Regiments', *Wehrwissenschaftliche Rundschau*, xii, 1962, p. 260. Tresckow later became one of the leaders of the military opposition to Hitler, and committed suicide after the failure of the plot of 20 July 1944.

[5] Moriz von Faber du Faur, *Macht und Ohnmacht*, Stuttgart, 1953, p. 127. Among the lieutenants of the Cavalry Regiment 4, 13 out of 23 were noblemen according to the *Rangliste des Deutschen Reichsheeres nach dem Stande vom 1. Mai 1930*, Berlin, n.d., pp. 54–55.

regiments too there were some enthusiastic young National Socialists who made propaganda for Hitler's ideas among their comrades.[1] Many more were instinctively opposed to the republic and its constitution, and to the cautious attitude adopted by the 'office generals' of the Bendlerstraße.

At the beginning of 1930 the son of the chief of the army command, Naval Lieutenant Heye, apprehensively wrote to Schleicher that the

> younger officers who had still greater ideals than the mere struggle for existence . . . are not pro-Nazi because of the Nazi programme, but because they believe they discover there a force which fights the decline of the Reich, which does what they perhaps expect from the Reichswehr; because with us, on account of lack of information, and in certain cases one-sided influences, they do not see a goal— naturally apart from the goal in foreign policy; because what is demanded from them is always obedience, but seldom co-operation. . . . I realize that one cannot go to everybody and give reasons for all orders. But I am certain that more must be done than hitherto. . . .[2]

Even more pessimistically a captain, who commanded a battery of the Artillery Regiment 3 in Silesia, wrote to Schleicher in the spring of 1931:

> My second and more lasting impression of the 'front' is less favourable. It concerns the young officers. I have only found this out in the course of the second winter [I have been here], during several long evenings in the officers' mess. In the first place the quickness of their judgement on all issues of home and foreign policy, without any knowledge of the subject, is astonishing. I believe that, in spite of all his *insouciance*, the pre-war lieutenant was much more cautious in difficult questions. Certainly, the turbulence of our time must be taken into account when we look at our new generation; but precisely those with intellectual interests are the most prominent in their sharp criticisms, although they are certainly more cautious towards me on account of my past service in the W department: this is simply a lack of intellectual modesty, a lack of perception that higher offices demand more vision and more reflection.

[1] Thus General Geyr von Schweppenburg about the Cavalry Regiment 14 in Mecklenburg: Zeugenschrifttum, no. 680, Institut für Zeitgeschichte. The same was the case in the Cavalry Regiment 11 in Silesia and in the Infantry Regiment 16 at Bremen, according to the recollections of Generals von Gersdorff and Mahlmann.

[2] Kapitänleutnant Heye to Schleicher, Berlin, 17 Jan. 1930: Nachlaß Schleicher, no. 34 ii, Bundesarchiv Koblenz.

Criticism is trumps. We have here a fanatical defender of Nazi sentiments with whom it is hardly possible to argue. We hear critical remarks which should never be tolerated from the point of view of discipline. I do not believe either that these impressions are limited to Sprottau, for similar things are reported from other places. . . .[1]

A gulf began to open between the young officers and their seniors which was deeper than the differences usually separating the generations.[2]

Groener and Schleicher were well aware of this problem. Groener himself visited the officers' mess of the Potsdam cavalry regiment to try and influence the lieutenants in favour of moderation.[3] The ministry of defence sent lecturers to the units who were to enlighten them on political problems. One of these 'itinerant lecturers' later reported that he encountered open opposition only from the officer cadets at the Infantry School at Dresden—which was in itself highly significant and an echo of the events of 1923.[4] In general, however, the lecturers had little success with their efforts to abate the tension which existed between the ministry and the 'front' of the Reichswehr. The majority of the officers, who received their information exclusively from the right-wing press, simply did not understand the policy of the army command.[5] In contrast with Seeckt, who relied on straightforward military obedience, Schleicher wooed the officers, but their distrust was not assuaged. In October 1930 he had to acknowledge that the majority of the commanding officers of the divisions had declined to make use of the 'itinerant lecturers'.[6] If the ministry expected the commanding officers of the units to argue with the lieutenants, it overtaxed

[1] Captain Lindemann to Schleicher, Sprottau, 7 Apr. 1931: ibid. Until 1929 L. had served under Schleicher in the *Wehrmachtsabteilung*, and was therefore '*vorbelastet*' as a '*W-Mann*'.   [2] Geyr von Schweppenburg, op. cit., p. 54.
[3] von Faber du Faur, op. cit., p. 128. At that time he was a major in the Potsdam cavalry regiment.
[4] Report of General Eugen Ott (at that time a major): Zeugenschrifttum, no. 279, Institut für Zeitgeschichte. The Infantry School was at that time under Major-General Freiherr von Falkenhausen who was then retired, probably for political reasons, and went to China.
[5] Report of General Hermann Foertsch: Zeugenschrifttum, no. 37, p. 12, Institut für Zeitgeschichte; Sauer, 'Die Reichswehr', in Bracher, *Die Auflösung der Weimarer Republik*, p. 283.
[6] 'Neue Dokumente zur Geschichte der Reichswehr', *Vierteljahrshefte für Zeitgeschichte*, ii, 1954, no. 1, p. 402.

them, for their whole tradition was 'non-political', in the sense of despising all party politics and all party-political discussions. They were by tradition conservatives and monarchists, but unable to make any impression on their juniors at a time of growing political extremism.

In the navy the situation was more straightforward. Since the mutiny of November 1918 and the events of the Kapp Putsch, its officer corps was strongly 'anti-Marxist'. Many of the younger officers had belonged to the naval brigades of Ehrhardt and von Loewenfeld; their revolutionary ideology was in many ways similar to that of National Socialism. The sympathy with its ideas was noticeable as early as 1929–30. Many naval officers were impressed by its 'national' and 'social' demands and its violent repudiation of Communism and 'Marxism'.[1] The officer appointed in the autumn of 1931 to command the Third Torpedo-Boat Flotilla discovered that 'a large part of his men sympathized with the National Socialists'. When he mentioned this to the commanding officer of the Fourth Flotilla he refused to believe him. He arranged a party with his officers and, to his great surprise, found out that the same was true there. But— as in the army—the older officers were on the whole more cautious and more conservative.[2] The opposition offered by the Social Democrats to the construction of the two battle cruisers *A* and *B* was an additional factor influencing the navy against 'Marxism' and in favour of a party which promised a vast programme of naval construction.[3] The naval command, however, sharply rejected any extremist propaganda in the navy, and in particular the speeches of the naval chaplain, Ronneberger, at Wilhelmshaven.[4] Yet the situation in the same port at the beginning of the 1930's was characterized by a naval officer with the words: 'All the sailors at that time were Nazi.'[5]

[1] Baum, 'Marine, Nationalsozialismus und Widerstand', *Vierteljahrshefte für Zeitgeschichte*, xi, 1963, p. 45; Abshagen, *Canaris*, Stuttgart, 1949, p. 86; Sauer, in *Die nationalsozialistische Machtergreifung*, Cologne and Opladen, 1960, p. 740.

[2] Recollections of Admiral Leopold Bürkner: Zeugenschrifttum, no. 364, Institut für Zeitgeschichte.

[3] Baum, loc. cit., p. 43; Abshagen, op. cit., pp. 87, 92.

[4] The minister of defence, signed Schleicher, Berlin, 16 Mar. 1931: Marineleitung, Zusammenstellung von Reichstagsbeschwerden, 7814; Vorträge Chef W bei Chef M.L., 21 Mar. 1932, 7813, Militärgeschichtliches Forschungsamt Freiburg.   [5] Abshagen, op. cit., p. 86.

11. *The Case of Scheringer and Ludin*

The situation in the junior ranks of the officer corps was illuminated by a famous case which was tried in 1930 in the highest German court, the *Reichsgericht* at Leipzig. Some lieutenants of the Artillery Regiment 5 at Ulm—one of them had fought aginst the Rhenish separatists as a schoolboy and later joined the 'Black' Reichswehr—remained faithful to the spirit of a 'national uprising', an uprising that was to be directed against both the internal and the foreign foe. During their period of training in the years after 1924 there was much abuse of the republic: 'The republic must go. With the republic nothing can be done. . . . Or are you perhaps here to defend the republic? Great hilarity. . . .' Through the barrack rooms at Ulm there roared in the evenings the Ehrhardt song: 'Swastika on the steel helmet, black, white and red ribbon. We are called the storm brigade of Ehrhardt!' The officers and non-commissioned officers closed their eyes to these happenings, and similarly when some recruits did not repeat certain phrases of the oath to the constitution. 'I assume', the lieutenant in charge declared, 'that these men have swallowed something. The official ceremony is thus concluded.'[1]

The young revolutionaries were soon bitterly disappointed with the Reichswehr and its leaders, the 'office generals', for in the years after 1926 Heye and Schleicher followed a course of *rapprochement* with the republic. At the beginning of 1929 the three Lieutenants Ludin, Scheringer, and Wendt decided to establish contacts with officers in other units. They wrote and duplicated a leaflet which began with the apodictic words: 'The spirit of the Reichswehr is dead.' All the officers who favoured a national revolution must combine and make sure 'that the Reichswehr does not fire on a national uprising of the people, but joins the revolt and becomes the nucleus of the people's army of the future and of the national liberation'. The officers were divided into four groups: the adherents of the 'national revolution', the mass of the decent ones who had not yet understood the issues, the aspirants to pensions who had no

---

[1] Scheringer, *Das große Los*, pp. 151–3. On 15 May 1924 Dr. Geßler forbade the singing of the Ehrhardt song and of another song '*Blau Äuglein*' which had the same tune: Reichskanzlei, Akten betr. Reichswehr, vol. v, R 43 I 686, Bundesarchiv Koblenz. Thus the singing must have occurred in several instances.

political interests, and the staff officers and office generals
hostile to the national movement. The recipients of the leaflet
were asked to distribute it and to send in their opinions to Ulm.
'The echo is not unfavourable.'[1]

This programme was not specifically National Socialist, but
rather national revolutionary, derived from the ideology of the
free corps and other extreme nationalist formations. It also
reflected the ideas of Scharnhorst and the radical soldiers of
the War of Liberation against Napoleon, assuming that Germany in 1929 faced the same situation. Thus the young lieutenants, through an older captain of another regiment, first
established contacts with Seldte, the leader of the *Stahlhelm*.
The captain, who was less radically inclined, was above all
embittered about the bad chances of promotion in the Reichswehr 'and about the many incapable staff officers of pre-war
times who occupy the posts of command'—this too an echo of
the old friction between the 'front' and the Bendlerstraße. But
in the autumn of 1929 Ludin and Scheringer visited the *Reichs-
leitung* of the National Socialists at Munich. There they met two
former officers, the Captains Pfeffer von Salomon and Wagner
—the first a famous free corps leader, a participant in the Kapp
Putsch and the sabotage actions in the Ruhr, the second dismissed from the army as a ringleader of the mutiny in the
Munich Infantry School of November 1923. In the eyes of the
young lieutenants both were heroes, surrounded by the halo of
revolutionary deeds. Scheringer informed them that it could
be achieved within a short time that the 'Reichswehr does not
fire when the National Socialists use force against the Young
Plan or seize power in Germany'; certain units would support
the movement. Ludin added: 'We are determined to revolu-
tionize the officer corps in so far as it is not yet senile, even if we
are sent to prison. . . .'[2]

At the end of 1929 the ministry of defence received informa-
tion about the contacts between the lieutenants and the National
Socialists and about their efforts at winning over other officers.
Two of the lieutenants were arrested at the Ulm barracks.
They were to be tried for treason, after attempts to settle the

---

[1] Scheringer, op. cit., pp. 179–80.
[2] Ibid., pp. 184–5, 194–5. For the past history of the *S.A.* leaders, see Sauer,
op. cit., p. 699, n. 33, p. 839.

matter by disciplinary measures had failed. Their arrest as well as their public trial were severely criticized in the officer corps, even by officers who did not sympathize with Hitler. While many of the younger officers took their side, the majority of the older ones were against them; in their opinion, 'such a thing was simply not done'.[1] As early as November 1929— before the plans were discovered—Groener issued a sharp decree against the machinations of the National Socialists:

> There can be no doubt that the *N.S.D.A.P.* aims at the disintegration of the *Wehrmacht*. Under the cloak of 'nationalism' the party works consciously against the state and its government and tries to undermine its instrument of power, the *Wehrmacht*, so as to be able to carry out its treasonable plans the more easily at an opportune moment. . . . Hitler describes the loyal carrying out of its duty by the Reichswehr, above party and within the framework of the constitution, as showing lack of character. . . . It is incompatible with the oath, which the members of the Reichswehr have sworn to the constitution, if they sympathize with a party which aims at the destruction of this constitution. For such soldiers there is no room in the ranks of the *Wehrmacht*! Whoever thinks that he cannot remain above party . . . has to ask for his discharge, which has to be granted. . . .

Groener urged the commanding officers to pay close attention to the education of their officers and officer cadets: upon this depended the existence of a solid army. He had intended to discharge two ensigns because of their political convictions, and only pardoned them on account of their youth and their good military records.[2]

Two months later, in January 1930, Groener in the same vein issued a 'pastoral letter' to the Reichswehr because of the case of the three lieutenants:

> The Communists believe that the time is approaching when they can overthrow the state and the society of today. . . . The aim of the National Socialists too, however vaguely it is formulated, is the same.

[1] Foertsch, op. cit., p. 22; Major-General von Gersdorff and Lieutenant-General Mahlmann in personal conversations with the author.

[2] The minister of defence, Berlin, 19 Nov. 1929: Kommando Kreuzer 'Königsberg', Innerpolitische Angelegenheiten, PG/34427, Admiralty, London. The case of the two officer cadets is the same as the one mentioned by Schleicher to the senior officers, above, p. 305. They were commissioned on 1 Mar. 1931, i.e. rather belatedly.

They too want the violent destruction of the state of today and the dictatorship of their party. They differ from the Communists only in that they have a national basis. They pretend that they intend to liberate Germany from the chains of Versailles by tearing up the treaties, but they admit themselves that we do not possess the power to do so. In the first place they therefore aim at civil war, and thus woo the *Wehrmacht*. In order to use it for their party-political aims, they pretend that they alone represent the truly national idea. National Socialists as well as Communists aim at the destruction of the existing system by means of violence. That means civil war, civil war in a country surrounded by hostile neighbours and connected as no other country is with the world economy. . . .

The Reichswehr has to find its way free from these extremes. It cannot entertain fantastic plans, vague hopes, high-sounding slogans. It carries an enormous responsibility for the continuance of the national state. It knows that its attitude in the hour of peril will decide the fate of the nation. . . . It is the sacred task of the *Wehrmacht* to prevent the cleavage between classes and parties from ever widening into suicidal civil war. At all times of national emergency there exists one unshakeable rock in stormy seas: the idea of the state. The *Wehrmacht* is its necessary and most visible expression. It has no other interest and no other task but to serve the state. Therein lies the pride of the soldier and the best tradition of old times. The *Wehrmacht* would destroy its essence and itself if it descended into the arena of party conflicts and itself took sides. Our only goal is to serve the state, far from all party politics, to save it and to maintain it, against the enormous pressure from without and the insane strife within. . . .[1]

The trial of the three lieutenants took place at Leipzig from 23 September to 4 October 1930—after the elections of 14 September which brought Hitler his first great success. The accused charged Groener and the army command with steering a 'course to the left' and with a 'lack of national sentiment'. Scheringer declared in the spirit of his revolutionary idealism: 'The Reichswehr is not a police force to preserve law and order in the state. The war of liberation always remains the last goal. The Reichswehr can agree only with those sections of the people that profess a military spirit and are for the war of liberation, never with the pacifists. . . .' It must be prevented

---

[1] The minister of defence, Berlin, 22 Jan. 1930: Groener-Geyer, *General Groener*, pp. 266–7; Schüddekopf, *Heer und Republik*, no. 108 b, pp. 260–2; partly quoted in G. A. Craig, *The Politics of The Prussian Army*, Oxford, 1955, p. 433.

at all costs that 'the last national movement is stifled or suppressed through the use of the Reichswehr by the government'.
The accused officers were convinced that there was a gulf
between the army command and the 'front' of the army, that
the bureaucratic leadership could not be trusted, and that it
was therefore essential to act without it. The officer corps was
no longer united. What Seeckt had achieved with such great
efforts was endangered.[1] After a trial which lasted nearly two
weeks, and in which numerous officers and even Adolf Hitler
were heard as witnesses, the accused were found guilty of the
preparation of a treasonable enterprise and were sentenced to
eighteen months' 'honourable' imprisonment. While they were
serving their sentences Scheringer was converted to Communism
by fellow-prisoners, while Wendt joined the revolutionary
National Socialists of Otto Strasser; only Ludin remained
loyal to Hitler and later became a high-ranking *S.A.* leader
and the German ambassador to Slovakia.[2] Their ideological
world was revolutionary, and at the same time that of an
extreme and romantic nationalism.

The trial created a sensation not only among the general
public but especially in the officer corps. How deep was the
split in its ranks is proved by the letters of a lieutenant of the
Artillery Regiment 3 to his fiancée. Two days after the opening
of the trial he asked her to follow the press reports closely.

With most of what they [the accused] say we can unfortunately
only agree, and you will read many things which only too often have
also aroused my indignation. Perhaps the good side of the whole
affair is that the eyes of the fellows on top (*den Leutchen da oben*) will
be opened to the colossal dissatisfaction in the officer corps. . . .

A few days after the end of the trial he wrote:

The trial has proved beyond doubt that the ministry of defence,
with its General von Schleicher, who in these questions calls the
tune, has caused a severe crisis of confidence in the army. . . . Without doubt the accused have acted wrongly and have violated the
rules of military discipline. But are not their troubles also ours?

---

[1] Caro and Oehme, *Schleichers Aufstieg*, pp. 200–1; Schüddekopf, op. cit.,
pp. 268, 270, 289; Sauer, 'Die Reichswehr', in Bracher, *Die Auflösung der Weimarer
Republik*, p. 282.
[2] Caro and Oehme, op. cit., p. 203; Schüddekopf, op. cit., p. 268, n. 685;
Scheringer, op. cit., discusses these events in great detail.

All this I have told you often enough, and at least 90 per cent. of the officer corps think the same way. That the grievances are justified must be recognized by all. If this is not done, we are put on a par with soulless mercenaries; but this we are not and do not want to be. Yet our highest superiors believe that they can do so because they too are infected with parliamentarianism and can no longer juggle with the heart [*sic*], but only with figures and 'reason'. As the climax of the whole affair Groener, two days ago, in an address to the officers of the defence ministry, treads on our feelings with his spiteful words about 'the Utopias of the two young chaps at Leipzig'. If we did not hope that this whole clique of Schleicher and Co., for whom we are mere pawns in their own advancement, will be swept away one day by the true national movement which nobody can stop, we should resign our commissions right away. In any case, the indignation here is enormous. . . .[1]

Some days later the same officer wrote that the sole responsibility for the regrettable events rested with the parties which supported 'this system of vexation'. But the army leaders had to be criticized sharply because in their indolence they did not find a remedy and identified themselves with the views of 'the men of November' 1918 (*Novemberlinge*), 'to whom honour as we know it is unknown', and dragged the whole case before a public court. It should have been dealt with by a court of honour, and the officers in question should have been quietly dismissed the service, without much ado. 'But thus the whole dirty linen has been washed in public and has brought us into a false position on all sides. . . .' The political and the military leaders must take into account 'the elixir of life of the soldier, his unselfish love of the fatherland. If that is touched he resists, if he still has enough spirit in him. . . .'[2] On many points—the criticisms of the army command and its policy, the negation of the parliamentary system and the political parties, the repudiation of 'the men of November', the fervent hope in the victory of the national movement—these ideas were the same as those of Ludin and Scheringer; 'and at least 90 per cent. of the officer

---

[1] Lieutenant Helmuth Stieff to his fiancée, Jüterbog, 25 Sept. and 7 Oct. 1930: 1223/53, Institut für Zeitgeschichte; the second printed by Vogelsang, op. cit., no. 8, p. 419. Stieff was executed after the failure of the plot of 20 July 1944.

[2] To the same, Jüterbog, 11 Oct. 1930: printed in *Vierteljahrshefte für Zeitgeschichte*, ii, 1954, pp. 295–6, with the omission of the remark about 'the men of November'.

corps think the same way'. The letters prove how strongly even young officers, who disapproved of the steps taken by the three lieutenants and who were not National Socialists, were influenced by the slogans of the extreme right, by its propaganda against the 'system' of Weimar and the 'office generals'.

The anti-parliamentarian ideas were even shared by an officer of more moderate views who was very familiar with the conditions in the defence ministry, Naval Lieutenant Heye. He wrote to his father on the occasion of the Leipzig trial that there was a lack of confidence in the leadership of the Reichswehr, which was believed to be in the hands of parliament. 'What outsiders and these officers reproach *you* with, is that you have offered no resistance to these doings of parliament. They make this reproach because they do *not* know the legal powers and the constitutional rights of the minister, and because they believe that the chiefs of the army and the naval commands are the true commanders-in-chief. . . .' General Heye ought to demand that the army should not suffer for the mistakes of the political authorities, which must bear the responsibility for the effects of their actions. The only two possibilities were a *Putsch*, which was 'nonsense', or a change of the constitution that eliminated all parliamentary supervision of the army; Heye should establish personal contacts with right-wing leaders, such as Hugenberg of the German Nationalist Party, or Duesterberg and Seldte, the leaders of the *Stahlhelm*, to inaugurate the necessary changes.[1]

That there was a 'crisis of confidence' in the Reichswehr was also recognized by Groener; but to his military way of thinking it appeared that the crisis could have been avoided

if all commanding officers had paid more attention to the spirit and the views of the officer corps. But unfortunately (this must be stated clearly) some commanding officers evade all political conversations with their subordinates because of inner uncertainty or even lack of moral courage, or perhaps because they are afraid that they would not be considered sufficiently national, or that they might make themselves unpopular with their officer corps. . . . Even a simple briefing of the officers with the views propounded by me during the past year . . . would have been sufficient to instruct the young men

---

[1] Hellmuth Heye to his father, 8 Oct. 1930: Nachlaß Heye, H 08–18/7, Bundesarchiv-Militärarchiv.

and to convince them of the foolishness and mistakenness of their opinions. . . .[1] [Groener considered it] an arrogance without parallel and a regrettable lack of respect for authority, if young officers, whose only legitimation is their youth, criticize their highest superiors for their lack of national sentiment . . . and presume that they alone know what is national. . . .[2]

As Lieutenant Heye saw quite clearly, these orders neglected the central issue: there could be no obedience without confidence, and confidence in the political leadership was missing.[3] It was politically naïve to believe that 'a simple briefing of the officers' would counter the ever-growing radicalism among Germany's youth, or that rational arguments would avail against emotion and enthusiasm. The orders also showed how badly informed Groener and Schleicher were about the mood among the young officers and how helpless they were in coping with it.

A few weeks later, in a conference with the divisional commanders, Groener declared: 'I am indignant that there are officers who doubt my national convictions and my fervent military determination (*Wehrwille*), and who dare to reproach me with steering a "course to the left". . . . For exactly the opposite is true. Since I became minister of defence all my thoughts and efforts have been directed towards one goal, the liberation of our country. . . .' This goal, however, could not be gained by storm, but only in the long run and by much patience, not by the romantic fire of youth, but by 'the most fervent glow of the ripe man'. The whole *Wehrmacht* ought to have known how strongly he defended its interests in severe parliamentary battles and kept it free from all political influences, especially those of the left. The *Wehrmacht* could only be used if it was united and firm, and that it could be only if there existed within it 'but one discipline, one obedience, one authority, and that complete. . . . The developments which have led to the trial at Leipzig destroy your work and mine.' Groener also spoke about the problems of Germany's youth, the reasons why it was attracted to National Socialism, and about the

[1] The minister of defence, Berlin, 6 Oct. 1930: Groener-Geyer, op. cit., pp. 271–2; Demeter, op. cit., pp. 305–6.
[2] The minister of defence, Berlin, 6 Oct. 1930: Groener-Geyer, op. cit., p. 270.
[3] Hellmuth Heye to his father, 8 Oct. 1930, loc. cit.

infantry school, where this influence was particularly notice-able; even the Reparations problem and Italian Fascism were discussed.[1]

During the same conference Schleicher spoke at length about the National Socialists and their programme. Three kinds of people voted for them: the idealists who in their patriotic enthusiasm saw the war of liberation as the first demand of the day; secondly, those who were 'deprived of their rights', especially the landowners and the middle classes who had lost everything or were going to lose everything, and 'the circles which are close to us', which had to stand by and watch how all that used to be sacred—religion, church, school, theatre, princely houses—was pulled down and treated with contempt; thirdly, those who in their innermost hearts belonged to the Communists. What surprises most in this analysis is Schleicher's strong sympathy with the views of those 'deprived of their rights' and their attacks upon the state and the prevalent intellectual tendencies. Schleicher's remarks about the National Socialist programme were made in a similar vein:

> Almost everybody can subscribe to the *national part* of the pro-gramme, even if one considers demands, such as the 'renunciation of the peace treaties', as a goal, but not as something that can be carried out now. More important than such demands . . . is the wave of indignation brought forth by the National Socialist move-ment against Bolshevism, treason, filth, etc. Here the National Socialist agitation undoubtedly has extremely stirring effects. . . . With regard to the *social part* of the programme any optimism would be mistaken! The opinion must be opposed that the socialist demands of the Nazis are 'not meant seriously'. They are meant seriously, and their nucleus is hardly different from 'pure Communism'. . . .

In the military field, Hitler intended to make the *Wehrmacht* a 'party army of the National Socialists'; if he succeeded in winning over the younger officers, the army would disintegrate, as the example of the Ehrhardt brigade during the Kapp Putsch showed. At the first signs that the army no longer obeyed its leaders the radicals would know that their hour had come and the country would be in flames. The attacks of the right-wing

---

[1] Groener's notes for a conference on 25 Oct. 1930: Nachlaß Groener, box 22, no. 229, Bundesarchiv-Militärarchiv.

papers—mainly those of Hugenberg—upon the army command on the occasion of the Leipzig trial were, in Schleicher's opinion, so dangerous 'because the soldiers—especially the younger sections of the officer corps—believe that what comes from this side must be correct'. The line taken by the right-wing papers was that those ministers should go who were an obstacle to the participation of the National Socialists in the government, i.e. Brüning, the chancellor, and also Groener, because the Nazis were claiming his post too The situation was similar to that of 1923 when Seeckt repudiated the endeavours of the right to establish a dictatorship and was called an 'ambitious place-hunter', a 'friend of the Jews', 'not a national man'.[1]

The new chief of the army command, General von Hammer-stein-Equord, at a hunting party also sharply attacked the attitude of the right-wing press and that of former generals who had written articles against the army, without trying to find out the truth, on the occasion of the Leipzig trial. His own political attitude he described to Schleicher as follows:

I have expressly emphasized that we took these defamations and reproaches by the right so seriously because they came from the quarter to which we ourselves belong. Then I pointed out how unsuitable the present time was to force the right wing and the army apart. . . . I have further declared that in the last resort the security of the Reich rested solely on the authority of the president and the machine-guns of the army, and that we would not allow madmen to provoke unrest and civil war in Germany. The establishment of a dictatorship was not mentioned, only the support of the legitimate government by the army in a case of emergency. The allegation that I envisaged a dictatorship with the *Reichsbanner* against the right is nonsense and ridiculous.[2]

Worries about the results of the Leipzig trial were also expressed by General Heye when he left the army: 'That I as the most senior active officer and military leader regret that this trial took place, that its effects fill me with apprehension, that I find it particularly difficult to leave the army just at this

---

[1] 'Neue Dokumente zur Geschichte der Reichswehr', *Vierteljahrshefte für Zeit-geschichte*, ii, 1954, no. 1, pp. 403–7. The notes were written by one of the partici-pants, Major-General Liebmann.

[2] Schleicher to the adjutant of the Crown Prince, Berlin, 1 Dec. 1930: Nachlaß Schleicher, no. 48, Bundesarchiv Koblenz.

moment, without being able to help in eliminating the after-effects—these things I need not emphasize. . . .'[1] In truly prophetic words Heye also expressed his fears that one day, owing to the swift political changes, the influence in military affairs might fall into the wrong hands.

III. *The Policy of the Army Command*

The man who at the end of 1930 succeeded Heye as chief of the army command was only partly suited to steer the army through the storms of the crisis engulfing Germany. General Kurt Freiherr von Hammerstein-Equord was one of the younger officers—at that time he was only 52 years old—who had risen quickly in the Reichswehr. At the time of the Kapp Putsch he was only a major and had sided strongly against his father-in-law, General von Lüttwitz. He had close personal links with Groener and Schleicher, going back over many years. In 1929 he became Blomberg's successor as the chief of the *Truppenamt*—the key position in the defence ministry. He thus undoubtedly belonged to the small circle of senior officers who were the potential successors of Heye. Yet another general who was directly subordinate to Hammerstein later wrote: 'Hammerstein was a political rather than a military general. His interest in the army and its affairs was remarkably small. He neither sought nor found the close contacts with the units which were so vital in his position. His political gifts were marked. He looked at political matters with a sober and cool judgement. He had no understanding whatsoever for right-wing extremism and brusquely rejected the National Socialist movement. . . .'[2]

Probably it was this disposition of Hammerstein which induced Groener and Schleicher to prefer him to Stülpnagel, who had been their first choice. At the end of 1930 Groener wrote to a close friend: 'I am very satisfied with my new chief of the army command; in the political arena he has already earned his spurs. I am really glad that I was not duped by Stülpnagel, who more and more proves himself a weakling and would apparently like to desert to the Nazis. He believes that

[1] 'Abschied!', n.d.: Nachlaß Heye, H 08–18/7, Bundesarchiv-Militärarchiv.
[2] Hilmar Ritter von Mittelberger, 'Lebenserinnerungen', p. 270: MS. in Bundesarchiv Koblenz. At that time Major-General von Mittelberger was the 'Inspekteur der Waffenschulen'.

he is Scharnhorst and Gneisenau combined and wants to be a great man perforce. . . .'[1] Four months later Groener compared Hammerstein favourably with his predecessors Seeckt and Heye: Seeckt issued orders against the *vaterländische Verbände* which nobody took seriously; 'under Heye things did not improve because the good uncle . . . allowed the lieutenants to do as they pleased. That will be quite different under Hammerstein. I trust in his influence upon people, which is far above normal. Hardly anyone can escape his authority, myself included. . . .'[2]

Like Blomberg and other officers who had personal know-ledge of the Red Army, Hammerstein was influenced by its example, above all by its close links with the masses of the population. For the Reichswehr he aimed at bringing about closer connexions with the workers and at overcoming its political isolation, especially from the republican mass organiza-tions. These views earned him the name of a 'red general' in the defence ministry.[3] But only his three daughters, who were active members of the Communist Party, were 'red'. Hammerstein himself was far too much an aristocrat and a nobleman to move to the left. Addressing the senior officers in February 1932 he declared expressly: 'We all stand on the right by conviction. . . .'[4] As an aristocrat he considered it beneath his dignity to bother about day-to-day moves and countermoves; all who knew him agree that this disinclination developed into an 'unusual dislike of normal work', which had its effects even on his military duties.[5] This, however, made him unsuitable for the post of chief of the army command at a time of severe crisis. Further-more, he had little support in the defence ministry and in the officer corps where he was considered a protégé of his friend Schleicher. To him he left the guidance and initiative in all political affairs. In 1932 Groener remarked sarcastically: 'Hammerstein, the non-political soldier and huntsman, follows his friend Schleicher like a well-trained hound. . . .'[6] Yet

---

[1] Groener to Gerold von Gleich, Berlin, 28 Dec. 1930: Nachlaß Groener, box 7, no. 27, Bundesarchiv-Militärarchiv.

[2] Groener to the same, Berlin, 26 Apr. 1931: ibid.

[3] Erfurth, *Geschichte des deutschen Generalstabes*, p. 119.

[4] Hammerstein on 27 Feb. 1932: *Vierteljahrshefte für Zeitgeschichte*, ii, 1954, no. 4, p. 421. Cf. above, p. 324, his remark to Schleicher.

[5] Sauer, in *Die nationalsozialistische Machtergreifung*, p. 733.

[6] Groener to von Gleich, Berlin, 22 May 1932: Groener-Geyer, op. cit., p. 326.

Hammerstein had strong political interests and often took sides on political issues; but he did not combine with them the readiness to act energetically that was so essential during these years.

In April 1931 Hammerstein explained his political views to the officers of the *Gruppenkommando* 2 at Cassel. There was, he said, a strong national and a strong Communist wave; the army had to stand above party, but at the same time to confront these strong currents. The national wave was to be welcomed, but not if it became revolutionary; the National Socialists had been left in no doubt that they would be fought by the sharpest methods if they used illegal means. Hammerstein believed that this warning induced Hitler to adopt strictly legal methods; 'he really wants this, not only ostensibly!' There were indications that the national wave had passed its peak, and that many of the discontented were returning to the Communists. 'We who saved Germany from chaos are more national than the extremists of all shades.' The army must sharply reject the pretensions of the right, while those of the left were of no interest; all enemies of the army must be fought, especially the grumblers on the right; attacks upon the minister and the army command were attacks upon the army as such, which must be refuted publicly, at any suitable opportunity, and without any consideration for the social or other position of the attacker. 'Things are going very well at the moment: we have the field-marshal as president; an excellent man as *chancellor*, who apart from his other qualifications has all military matters at heart (during the war commanding officer of a machine-gun company); a *minister* who is particularly good at representing our interests in parliament. No one else could have achieved so much for the army, and in addition a thoroughly decent man! . . .'[1] Hammerstein's optimism with regard to the political developments was not justified by events, as the economic and political crisis was becoming ever more acute; but perhaps he was alluding to the great political influence of the Reichswehr and its close co-operation with the Brüning government. Indeed, the political weight of the army grew parallel with the increasing severity of the crisis.

[1] 'Besprechung des Ch. H. L. am 24.4.31 in Kassel': notes by Major-General Liebmann: *Vierteljahrshefte für Zeitgeschichte*, ii, 1954, no. 2, pp. 410–11.

It is remarkable that Hammerstein went out of his way to recommend the chancellor as well as the minister to the officers, as if he feared criticisms from their side. The chancellor had military matters at heart—his war record was specifically mentioned—and Groener had achieved so much for the army during the budget discussions. Even more surprising is the reference to Groener's honest character, which indicates that officers had criticized him—because of his attitude on 9 November 1918, on account of the Scheringer trial, or because of his private life: in the autumn of 1930 Groener married a second time, and soon after, his wife gave birth to a child. This was an infringement of the code of honour of the officer corps, which Hindenburg did not forgive Groener, and which seriously damaged his authority in the officer corps.[1] Even under Hitler any young officer was refused permission to marry when he applied for consent on the grounds that his fiancée was expecting a baby. Hammerstein's recommendation of Brüning and Groener to the officers was a sign of uncertainty in the highest quarters, which was to show itself time and again during the following years. Already in October 1930 Hammerstein had sharply condemned the gossip in the army, especially about the minister and the last chief of the army command, and declared that whoever criticized the minister also attacked the person of the new chief.[2]

At the end of 1930 Groener wrote to his friend: 'It is extremely easy to work with the chancellor. . . . I have concluded a firm pact with him, and as long as the president goes with us, we shall cope with parliament one way or the other. . . .' Groener expressed his increased self-confidence and pride after the autumn manœuvres of 1930 in these words: 'In the political developments in Germany not a stone must be moved any longer without the word of the Reichswehr being thrown decisively into the balance [sic]. . . .'[3] With this claim the Reichswehr became the final arbiter in all issues of internal policy—a claim which even Seeckt would hardly have made in 1923.

[1] Eschenburg, 'Die Rolle der Persönlichkeit in der Krise der Weimarer Republik', Vierteljahrshefte für Zeitgeschichte, ix, 1961, p. 14.
[2] 'Neue Dokumente zur Geschichte der Reichswehr', ibid. ii, 1954, no. 1, p. 408.
[3] Groener to Gerold von Gleich, 28 Dec. 1930: ibid., p. 409, n. 38; ibid., n. 39, the words used in a speech after the autumn manœuvres of 1930.

With it the Reichswehr truly descended into the arena of political conflicts. In practical politics Groener largely depended upon Schleicher. He informed Groener about everything that was of interest to him, and the other matters were left to Schleicher; their discussions took place every day, often several times on the same day. As Groener put it: 'Schleicher makes my policy.' But Schleicher also became the adviser of President von Hindenburg, especially when the old gentleman became alienated from Groener, his close associate over many years, on account of Groener's matrimonial affairs. Thus Schleicher gradually assumed the position of an independent member of the government.[1]

At this time Schleicher was occupied with plans and negotiations which aimed at a strengthening of the Brüning government and its powers, which were based on article 48 of the constitution. As the elections of September 1930 had deprived the government of a parliamentary majority—it now depended on the 'toleration' of the Social Democrats—Schleicher envisaged a policy which, if need be, could be carried through against parliament. A programme should be drawn up with 'a strong emphasis on national interests', apart from the necessary economic and financial measures; the government should stress that it hoped to find a majority approving of it, but also its determination to carry it out, even with a minority. In the present Reichstag it was anyhow impossible to form a majority government, so that in Schleicher's opinion the initiative passed to the president and the government nominated by him; it would then depend on further developments whether the Reichstag would be dissolved again or would commit hara-kiri by adjourning itself for an indefinite period.[2] Schleicher clearly welcomed the formation of a government which depended upon the confidence of the president but not of parliament: the crisis made it unnecessary to observe the democratic procedures, and parliament could be dispensed with.

For a considerable time Schleicher had attacked 'the hostile attitude of certain Prussian authorities to the army', the 'underground struggle of Prussia against the *Wehrmacht*', and the

---

[1] Eschenburg, op. cit., pp. 11, 14.
[2] Schleicher to Lieutenant-General Count von der Schulenburg, Berlin, 26 Sept. 1930: Vogelsang, op. cit., no. 6, p. 415.

'sabotage of the frontier defence by Prussia'.[1] In the course of 1930 these views crystallized into a definite plan. After the Social Democrats had been eliminated from the central government, they were to be deprived of their positions in Prussia; Seeckt's old plans to alter radically the federal structure of Germany, by depriving the states of important powers, were revived.[2] In July 1930 a right-wing deputy of the Prussian Diet, Count Garnier, wrote to Schleicher that he had given much thought to their conversation about the 'red Prussia'; he too had the strongest aversion to taking part in the Diet under 'this radical left government'; but Schleicher should not forget that the government of Otto Braun had only a very weak majority behind it, which would not last for ever; the extremely serious crisis would not be overcome more easily if Prussia, Bavaria, and Saxony were deprived of their independent existence; such matters would have to be handled with the utmost caution, before arriving at any decisions on which the very existence of Germany might depend.[3] Schleicher, however, was undeterred by such considerations, even if they came from a quarter which was as strongly opposed to 'red' Prussia as he was himself. He therefore replied to Count Garnier that, on the basis of his experience during the last ten years, he was in principle of a different opinion on the issue Reich versus member states. 'According to my firm conviction, this governing next to each other and against each other, which entails an intolerable waste of energy and money in all fields, will not be altered basically by a change of government in the states, above all not in Prussia. . . .'[4] Schleicher was blind to the dangers inherent in his course, especially at a time when it was essential to unite all moderate forces against the wave of extremism which threatened the existence of state and society. The weakening of the Social Democrats, caused by the political crisis, provided a heaven-sent opportunity to weaken them still further: exactly two years later Schleicher's aim was achieved and the Prussian government was overthrown by a *coup d'état*.

---

[1] 'Notizen für die Kommandeurbesprechung', n.d., and notes by Captain Noeldechen, n.d.: Nachlaß Schleicher, nos. 23, 35, Bundesarchiv Koblenz.

[2] See above, pp. 190–1.

[3] Count Garnier to Schleicher, Turawa near Oppeln, 10 July 1930: Nachlaß Schleicher, no. 44 i, ibid.

[4] Schleicher to Count Garnier, Berlin, 25 July 1930, ibid.

Before the end of 1930 Schleicher was equally busy with plans to reshuffle the Reich government. In December he visited the under-secretary of state in the chancellor's office to discuss with him 'the possible developments', if the foreign minister, Curtius, was forced to resign. In Schleicher's opinion, this would provide a good opportunity to replace the minister of the interior, Wirth, who 'in his opinion was also redundant' (and too left for his liking), by the minister of defence, Groener, while Brüning should also become the foreign minister.[1] Ten months later—after the resignation of Curtius—the government was reformed exactly as Schleicher had suggested. In October 1931 Schleicher still supported Groener without any reservation; as his adjutant wrote later, 'Schleicher not only supported the idea, but for obvious reasons the suggestion was his' that Groener should combine the two key posts on the internal side.[2] Yet during the same month Schleicher, in a conversation with one of the *Stahlhelm* leaders, openly criticized Brüning: intellectually and in foreign affairs he was an important personality, but in home affairs he was not sufficiently energetic. Schleicher's visitor had the impression that he wanted to keep Brüning as foreign minister, but was searching 'for a strong man with a military spirit for home affairs'—an aim with which his visitor fully agreed.[3]

It seems likely that Groener was the 'strong man with a military spirit', and that Schleicher intended to make him chancellor in place of Brüning. In any case, that was the impression of two other *Stahlhelm* leaders, Seldte and Duesterberg, who met Groener and Schleicher in December 1931. They reported afterwards that Brüning's position was considered very weak inside the cabinet, and that his replacement by Groener was under discussion; Brüning should remain the foreign minister; the ministry of defence was apparently aiming at a military dictatorship.[4] These schemes were to be carried

---

[1] Pünder, *Politik in der Reichskanzlei*, p. 80, under 8 Dec. 1930. For Schleicher's attacks on Curtius and Wirth, see Caro and Oehme, op. cit., pp. 211–12.

[2] Notes by the later general Noeldechen, Feb. 1951: W. Conze, 'Dokumentation zum Sturz Brünings', *Vierteljahrshefte für Zeitgeschichte*, i, 1953, no. 5, p. 273.

[3] Report by the *Stahlhelm* 'chancellor' Wagner, Berlin, 29 Oct. 1931: 61 Stahlhelm I, vol. 264, pp. 286–7, Deutsches Zentralarchiv Potsdam.

[4] 'Vertraulicher Rundbrief', Berlin, 18 Dec. 1931: Stahlhelm-Akten, vol. 78 i, Kriegsarchiv Munich.

out through the support of the president, whose 'political adviser' Schleicher had become. Hardly a day passed, during times of political tension, Schleicher's adjutant reported later, when the president's son, Oskar von Hindenburg, did not appear, or when they did not telephone and ask for advice from the presidential palace.[1] Like Schleicher, Oskar von Hindenburg was an officer on the active list, and they had served together as junior officers in the Third Foot Guards. Neither the one nor the other was 'provided for in the constitution'.

The issue which became of cardinal importance during these months was the attitude to be adopted towards Hitler and the National Socialists. In October 1930 Schleicher maintained that the formation of a government ranging from the Centre Party to the National Socialists was Utopian, as neither party was in favour of a coalition.[2] Yet in the course of the following year he changed his mind. At the end of 1930 Hitler recalled the former captain Ernst Röhm from Bolivia and before long appointed him commander of the S.A. Soon Röhm visited the ministry of defence where he had old friends and was received by Schleicher. He repeated the assurances given by Hitler at the Scheringer trial that he was opposed to revolution and did not aim at the disintegration of the Reichswehr. The revolutionary S.A. leaders, men like Captain Stennes in Berlin and Röhm's predecessor, Captain Pfeffer von Salomon, were expelled in 1930; thus an obstacle to a *rapprochement* was removed. What Schleicher and Röhm had in common was their burning wish to see Germany strong and rearmed. A question they discussed was the admission of National Socialists and S.A. men to the frontier defence units, where they would receive military training. In March 1931 Schleicher wrote to Röhm, after one of their meetings, that in principle it was the right and duty of every German to serve in the defence of his country; excluding only those who did *not* reject a violent uprising against the constitutional form of the state and its institutions. Whoever participated in measures of defence should not suffer any per-

[1] Notes by Noeldechen, Feb. 1951, loc. cit.
[2] Schleicher addressing the senior officers on 25 Oct. 1930: 'Neue Dokumente zur Geschichte der Reichswehr', *Vierteljahrshefte für Zeitgeschichte*, ii, 1954, no. 1, p. 407.

secution by the authorities of the Reich or a member state.[1] In fact National Socialists were allowed to join the frontier defence units.

One of Schleicher's collaborators during these years wrote later that Schleicher looked at the development of the National Socialist Party with more realistic eyes than Groener. He thought

that it was a healthy reaction of the body politic and in addition the only party which could gain votes from the radical left and had already won them. . . . As long as the party remained in the comfortable state of opposition, it was bound to grow further. . . . Schleicher saw the only effective means of countering this in freeing the *N.S.D.A.P.* as soon as possible from sterile opposition and admitting it to a share in the unpopular responsibility. In his drastic fashion he said: 'Industry knows exactly why it elects the least accommodating and most vociferous shareholders to the board of directors.' He saw a certain parallel in the development in England. There the slogan 'Let Labour try' prevailed against misgivings of the older parties about the first Labour government that had not been justified. . . .[2]

In the summer of 1931 Schleicher's aim was a *rapprochement* with the parties of the extreme right and the formation of a strong right-wing government—ideas he expressed on several occasions to his confidants. In September General von Hammerstein met Hitler in a private flat; Schleicher did not appear. After a discussion which lasted four hours Hammerstein declared that, 'apart from the speed', Hitler wanted really the same things as the Reichswehr. Schleicher met Hitler at the end of the following month.[3] A few days later he wrote to Röhm: 'Many thanks for the material sent to me, from which I could convince myself that the leadership of the *N.S.D.A.P.* does everything to keep the party on the line of the strictest legality, advocated by the party chief. Part of the material belongs to the sphere of the ministry of the interior where I have no influence whatsoever, in contrast with the vicious and lying allegations of

---

[1] Vogelsang, op. cit., 118, 129; Sauer, in *Die nationalsozialistische Machtergreifung*, pp. 848–51; Wheeler-Bennett, op. cit., pp. 226–7.
[2] Memorandum of Major-General von Holtzendorff of 1946: *Vierteljahrshefte für Zeitgeschichte*, i, 1953, no. 2, pp. 268–9.
[3] Vogelsang, op. cit., pp. 124, 127.

the Mosse Communists. . . .'[1] Not only in accepting at its face value the material sent by Röhm, but even in the jargon used by him—'Mosse Communists' for the staff of the republican newspapers published by the Mosse publishing house—Schleicher approximated to the ideas of the addressee.

At that time Groener believed that Hitler was 'doubly and trebly tied to the stake of legality'; his intention was 'to catch the Nazis without pushing the Sozis into opposition'.[2] In addressing the commanding officers of the divisions and corps at the beginning of 1932 Schleicher points out that the National Socialists had shown themselves 'loyal'; therefore the army command had changed its attitude towards them; while National Socialists were still not allowed to join the army—that too would come in the foreseeable future—they were now admitted to the frontier defence units and as employees in the army workshops and enterprises. There were, he continued, two groups among the National Socialists: collaborators and revolutionaries; the expelled *S.A.* leader Stennes represented the latter tendency, and it was a great feat of Hitler that he coped so quickly with the Stennes 'revolt' in Berlin. The implication clearly was that the 'revolutionary' elements among the *S.A.* had been eliminated. Groener supplemented Schleicher's remarks. He even declared that Hitler was 'determined to eradicate the revolutionary ideas', an impression gained by him when he received Hitler.[3] According to an official account of the same conference Groener said:

Meeting with Hitler: sympathetic impression, modest, decent fellow who wants the best. In his demeanour, type of the earnest autodidact. The minister has clearly stated that he will support the legal efforts of Hitler by all means, but that Nazi fomenters of unrest will be opposed as before. . . .

Hitler's intentions and aims are good, but he is an enthusiast, fiery, many-sided. The minister fully agreed with him to further his intentions for the good of the Reich. The minister has also instructed the [governments of the] states, in the sharpest form, to

[1] Schleicher to Röhm, Berlin, 4 Nov. 1931: Schüddekopf, op. cit., no. 133, p. 328.
[2] Groener to Gerold von Gleich, Berlin, 1 Nov. 1931: Vogelsang, op. cit., pp. 138–9.
[3] Schleicher and Groener on 11 Jan. 1932: *Vierteljahrshefte für Zeitgeschichte*, ii, 1954, no. 3, pp. 416–17.

be fair towards the Nazis: only excesses should be opposed, not the movement as such. . . .[1]

A few weeks later National Socialists were permitted to join the Reichswehr, and Reichswehr soldiers to attend meetings where the swastika was displayed.[2]

Yet only a fortnight later Groener wrote to his friend von Gleich:

The Nazis must be prevented by all means from obtaining the posts of president and chancellor. . . . I do not believe that they will use force because Hitler knows full well that any such attempt would result in the most energetic use of the means of power of the state. The Reichswehr is so completely in our hands that in *that* case it would certainly function. Hammerstein is a man who would use brute force, quite different from Seeckt in 1923–4. But if the wolf dons the sheep's clothing of loyalty, he is much more dangerous to the Reichswehr. The Nazis more and more show themselves as most unreliable people. . . .

Groener further informed his friend that Schleicher was engaged, 'behind the scenes . . . quite secretly', in a new operation of reforming the government: Brüning was considerably weakened, but he hoped to prop him up again. In other respects too Groener was still rather optimistic: he thought that his relations to Hindenburg were still very good and that all intrigues against him personally had failed to make any impression on the president.[3] To the historian Friedrich Meinecke Groener remarked in an equally optimistic vein: 'It is quite wrong to ask where the Reichswehr stands. The Reichswehr does what it is ordered to do, and that's the end of it.'[4] These words were very similar to those used by Seeckt on similar occasions; but the precondition then was that the army and its leaders were completely united, and that was no longer the case in 1932.

Schleicher's 'top secret operation' apparently concerned

---

[1] 'Führerbesprechung beim Reichswehrminister am 11. Januar 1932': Nachlaß Groener, box 22, no. 231: Bundesarchiv-Militärarchiv. The text published in Groener-Geyer, op. cit., pp. 285–6, is incomplete.

[2] Decrees of 29 Jan. 1932: *Vierteljahrshefte für Zeitgeschichte*, ii, 1954, p. 416, n. 62.

[3] Groener to von Gleich, Berlin, 24 Jan. 1932: Groener-Geyer, op. cit., pp. 288–9.

[4] Meinecke, *Die deutsche Katastrophe*, p. 69.

negotiations aiming at the formation of a new government, which was to be orientated much more strongly to the right. This was to ensure at the same time the support of the right-wing parties for an extension of Hindenburg's period of office as president, which was coming to an end in 1932. Early in February Schleicher thought of Freiherr von Lüninck, who stood close to the German Nationalist Party, as the new chancellor; Hugenberg, their leader, was to become vice-chancellor, and two more German Nationalists ministers. A few days later, however, Schleicher informed the two *Stahlhelm* leaders, Seldte and Duesterberg, that Hindenburg was willing to appoint Seldte chancellor, again with Hugenberg as the vice-chancellor; 'a soldier' was to become the minister of defence.[1] No name was mentioned, but it seems that Schleicher already at this stage thought of a new defence minister, as Groener was no longer an active 'soldier'. It is also uncertain to what extent Brüning was informed of these moves. In the conversation between Schleicher and Hugenberg Brüning's name was apparently not mentioned any more. But the negotiations were shipwrecked by the immoderate demands of the National Socialists, who demanded the post of defence minister,[2] and of the German Nationalists, whose leader Hugenberg wanted to be the chancellor as well as the prime minister of Prussia. As Hammerstein informed the divisional and corps commanders at the end of February, everybody put forward his party's demands and desired 'political power for himself alone', without allowing a share in power even to a neighbouring group; but it could not be justified to hand power over to the Nazis as a payment in advance.[3] A re-election of Hindenburg by an agreement between the parties thus became impossible.

Not without justification Hammerstein spoke about a 'heap of ruins in internal politics' and attributed the responsibility to the leaders of the right-wing parties. As Hindenburg and Hitler would be rival candidates in the coming presidential elections, the obvious outcome was, in his opinion, a front of Hindenburg

---

[1] The *Stahlhelm* 'chancellor' Wagner to the *Stahlhelm* leaders, Berlin, 14 Apr. 1932; the *Stahlhelm* leader Marklowski to the *Stahlhelmgaue*, Berlin, 22 Mar. 1932: 61 Sta 1, vol. 296, p. 182, vol. 297, p. 57, Deutsches Zentralarchiv Potsdam.

[2] Notes by Wagner, 13 Feb. 1932: ibid., vol. 296, pp. 134–5.

[3] Hammerstein on 27 Feb. 1932: *Vierteljahrshefte für Zeitgeschichte*, ii, 1954, no. 4, p. 420 (notes of Major-General Liebmann).

versus Hitler: the basest defamations of Hindenburg were already being circulated. Thus the army command, always loyal to the field-marshal, now became more critical of Hitler. As Hammerstein pointed out on the same occasion, the army would put a clear 'No' to demands that it should give up its idealistic position above party, that party officers (*Parteibuch-Offiziere*) should be commissioned, that the *S.A.* should be armed, that a Fascist militia should be created as in Italy. Such demands would be bitterly opposed, for every rifle was needed against the foreign enemy; a change in the plans of mobilization for internal ends would make the army useless against the enemy for two years; there would be no civil war![1] During the preceding months Groener and Schleicher had tried to bring about a *rapprochement* with Hitler, with the aim of 'taming' him and his followers and granting them a share in the government. It was clear that the attempt had failed, that the National Socialists did not desire a share in power, but the entire power. Yet this was not the last time that the attempt was made; Schleicher in particular remained faithful to the concept of 'taming' Hitler.

If one bears in mind that Groener, Hammerstein, and Schleicher were intelligent and experienced men, who after the Scheringer trial had ample reason to distrust Hitler, their attitude during the winter of 1931–2 is almost incomprehensible. Certainly, many people inside and outside Germany did not recognize the true nature of National Socialism. But Groener's idea of Hitler as a 'modest, decent fellow who wants the best', whose 'intentions and aims are good', was grotesque. Schleicher's relations with Röhm and the exchange of letters were incompatible with his official position, and the expressions used in them were grist to Hitler's mill. Were the eyes of the generals blinded by their dislike of the republic and its institutions, by the 'military' character of National Socialism, by the loudly advertised 'nationalism' of Hitler and Röhm? Did the generals hope to achieve with Hitler's help the desired goal of German rearmament? Did they vaguely feel that the Reichswehr by its very structure was isolated from the nation, and hope that National Socialism would provide the longed-for bridge to the people? These are questions which no one can answer for

---

[1] Hammerstein on 27 Feb. 1932: ibid., pp. 421–2.

certain, but it seems likely that a combination of several of these factors led to the total misjudgement of Hitler and his aims by the leaders of the Reichswehr.

When Hitler became the official National Socialist candidate against Hindenburg in the presidential elections, Schleicher's attitude too became more critical. When personal acquaintances inquired for whom they should vote in the first ballot, he replied: 'Hindenburg is the only candidate able to defeat Hitler. As I am convinced that Hitler is as suited to become president as the hedgehog to serve as a towel, and as I fear that his presidency would lead to civil war and finally to Bolshevism, the decision for whom to vote is in this case really not difficult. . . .' Hindenburg, he continued, was not inclined towards the left, nor was Brüning an obstacle to the formation of a right-wing government: this had been made impossible by the disunity in the right-wing camp and 'the megalomania of the Nazis, who were demanding that the entire state apparatus should be handed over to them', and who were declared Socialists. Thus Schleicher could not understand how so many people could expect an anti-socialist course from them.[1] Unfortunately, however, he did not remain true to these convictions during the following months; for how could the National Socialists be 'tamed' if they demanded 'that the entire state apparatus should be handed over to them'? Schleicher's former chief, on the other hand, the retired General von Seeckt, advocated the election of Hitler to the presidency, and thus took sides against Hindenburg, the commander-in-chief of the Reichswehr.[2]

iv. *The Fall of Groener*

In spite of their more pronounced criticisms of the National Socialists in the course of the election campaign, the attitude of Groener and Schleicher towards them in the spring of 1932 was

---

[1] Drafts of Schleicher's letters of 23 and 27 Feb. 1932: Nachlaß Schleicher, no. 24, Bundesarchiv Koblenz. In the first ballot there were several other candidates, the *Stahlhelm* leader Duesterberg as well as a Communist.

[2] Seeckt to his sister, n.d.: Rabenau, *Seeckt*, p. 665. After his dismissal Seeckt became a member of the Reichstag for the conservative German People's Party, but did not play a prominent part in politics. He later left Germany and became the military adviser to General Chiang Kai-shek.

by no means entirely negative. At the beginning of April Groener wrote to his friend von Gleich that there were difficult weeks ahead in the political game, until the elections to the different Diets had been held.

Then we shall have to start to make the Nazis capable of governing (*die Nazis regierungsfähig zu machen*), as it is no longer possible to suppress the movement, which is certain to grow further, by force. Naturally, the Nazis must nowhere be allowed to form the government alone, above all not in the Reich. But in the states the attempt must be made here and there to let the Nazis take part in a coalition and to wean them from their Utopias by positive governmental work. I cannot see a better way, for I would consider it a very ill-starred enterprise to try and destroy the party by an anti-Nazi law similar to the old law against the Socialists. That would merely give the party a new impetus, as happened with the Socialists in the past. It is different with the *S.A.*, which must be eliminated in any case, and the so-called Iron Front at the same time; that would be the best. . . .[1]

These sentiments, directed not only against the National Socialists, but equally or even more so against the republican organizations of the left, were echoed by Schleicher in a more pronounced form. At about the same time he wrote to Groener that, for the coming elections to the Prussian Diet, the left wing planned to mark him as an ally of the Social Democrats and to win him over to fight the right-wing parties; to achieve this aim they were using any means, such as the threats of the Social Democratic leaders and the Prussian ministry of the interior that they would not vote for Hindenburg on 10 April 1932 if Groener did not dissolve the *S.A.*; they were also trying to picture the well-meaning Groener as the victim of the devilish Schleicher, but this lie was so obvious and ancient that it no longer made an impression. 'I am really looking forward to 11 April—then it will be possible to talk to this lying brood with no holds barred (*mit diesem Lügengesindel einmal offen Fraktur reden können!*). . . . After the events of the last days I am really glad that there is a counter-weight [to the Social Democrats] in the

---

[1] Groener to Gerold von Gleich, Blankenburg, 2 Apr. 1932: Vogelsang op. cit., no. 20, pp. 444–5. The 'Iron Front' was an alliance of the republican mass organizations—the *Reichsbanner*, the trade unions, the workers' sports and gymnastics clubs, &c.—against the National Socialists.

form of the Nazis, who are not very decent chaps either and must be stomached with the greatest caution. If they did not exist, we should virtually have to invent them.' In these circumstances, Groener's course, Schleicher thought, was the only correct one: 'not in favour of anyone, not against anyone'; the question of the *S.A.* could only be solved by subtle methods, not by the ministers of the states, who did not possess the necessary finesse.[1] It had been in vain that the Social Democrats voted for Hindenburg and thus made his re-election possible— a step which had not been easy for them and which exposed them to violent Communist attacks. The day after the election Schleicher hoped to show them who was the real master.

Yet it was not only Severing, the Prussian minister of the interior, but the ministers of all the larger German states who now demanded a dissolution of the *S.A.* in the form of an ultimatum.[2] They constituted a serious danger to law and order, organized riots and brawls, and were preparing for civil war and 'the night of the long knives'. Their dissolution was a matter of great urgency if the state was to survive. As the Brüning government depended on the toleration of the Social Democrats, and as Groener wanted to avoid measures against the *S.A.* by individual states, he informed the ministers of the interior on 5 April that he intended to propose to Hindenburg in the following week that the *S.A.* and *S.S.* should be dissolved by an emergency decree. At the same time he declared that not all members of the *S.A.* were dangerous to the community; among them were many thousands 'with the best sentiments', who should not be repudiated by the state; the impression made by them was 'definitely good'; they should be brought closer to the state and weaned from their negative views.[3] What alienated the members of the *S.A.* from state and society was in fact the severe economic crisis and the disintegration noticeable in many fields; especially in the large towns the membership consisted largely of unemployed youngsters, rowdies, and the riff-raff of society. It would be virtually impossible to bring these 'closer to the state' and to inculcate them with 'positive'

---

[1] Schleicher to Groener, Berlin 25 Mar. 1932: Nachlaß Groener, box 21, no. 224; Bundesarchiv-Militärarchiv; Groener-Geyer, op. cit., p. 304.

[2] Bracher, *Auflösung der Weimarer Republik*, p. 486.

[3] Vogelsang, op. cit., no. 21, p. 448.

ideas, as Groener planned. The very unattractiveness of the Weimar Republic militated against this.

Three days later, on 8 April, Groener informed the chiefs of the army and naval commands of his intentions with regard to the *S.A.* After Groener had spoken, Schleicher, in the strongest form, gave the reasons for the dissolution. General von Hammerstein agreed without hesitation and with crude expressions. Admiral Raeder asked whether it would not be possible to dissolve the *Reichsbanner* simultaneously, to avoid making a bad impression on the Reichswehr. Schleicher declined: this was out of the question at the present time. Raeder did not repeat his question; as he told Groener later, because he considered it useless on account of Schleicher's firm refusal. In Groener's opinion, the result of the discussion was a complete agreement between him and the generals. In the evening Schleicher telephoned the under-secretary of state in the chancellor's office and told him that the psychological moment for the dissolution of the *S.A.* had come; he had always said that the right moment must be awaited, and was glad that the government had waited with patience: now it was time to hit hard.[1]

Yet this unanimity lasted less than 24 hours. On the next day, 9 April, the day before the presidential election, one of Schleicher's collaborators, Major Marcks, the head of the press section in the defence ministry, remarked to Groener that he was against the dissolution of the *S.A.* He had informed Schleicher of his objections, and now it was Schleicher's task to speak to Groener. When Schleicher came he said that he had spent a sleepless night on account of the impending dissolution and thought that it would have an unfavourable influence on the elections to the Prussian Diet; the leaders of the German People's Party and the Peasant Party had visited him to point out that their parties would suffer severely if there were a dissolution. Groener replied that these small parties were not viable and would lose many votes whether the *S.A.* were dissolved or not, as the voters were turning towards the large

---

[1] Groener's 'Chronologische Darstellung der Vorkommnisse, die zu meinem Rücktritt als Reichswehr- und als Reichsinnenminister geführt haben' under 8 Apr.; Groener to von Gleich, Berlin, 18 June 1932: Nachlaß Groener, box 21, no. 224, box 7, no. 27, Bundesarchiv-Militärarchiv; Vogelsang, op. cit., no. 22, p. 450.

parties. Schleicher proposed to adopt different tactics and to impose a number of conditions upon Hitler, which he would have to fulfil within a given time; if not, the moment for the dissolution would have come; if he accepted the conditions, he would undermine his own position. Groener did not have the impression that Schleicher had changed his opinion on any grounds of principle, but saw in it a tactical move such as Schleicher was accustomed to make.[1] But Schleicher, without even informing the minister, telephoned on the same day to the chancellor's office that the decree dissolving the *S.A.* would probably not be issued right away, but that first a kind of ultimatum would be put to the National Socialists, which was clearly contrary to Groener's plan.[2]

During a conference of the ministers and under-secretaries of state with Brüning on the evening of 10 April the under-secretary of state Meißner, as the representative of the president, took up Schleicher's idea of an ultimatum to Hitler with a time limit. Schleicher seconded Meißner—his close connexions to the House of Hindenburg had clearly brought about this proposal; but in the end Schleicher agreed to an immediate dissolution. When the conference was continued on the next day both Schleicher and Meißner were absent. At breakfast Meißner told another under-secretary that the president, influenced by Schleicher through Hindenburg's son, had changed his mind. According to the diary of yet another under-secretary, Schleicher induced Hindenburg's son to counsel his father that he should refuse to sign the decree, in the writer's opinion 'a colossal breach of confidence towards his [Schleicher's] chief, His Excellency Groener!'[3] Brüning, however, succeeded in overcoming Hindenburg's hesitations, and the decree was signed by the president, although General von Hammerstein and the commanding officer of the Second Division at Stettin, General von Bock, reported to him their objections to the dissolution of the *S.A.* Schleicher also tried to induce Raeder and his officers in the naval command to make representations

---

[1] Groener's 'Chronologische Darstellung' under 9 Apr.: loc. cit.

[2] Memorandum by Staatssekretär Pünder under 9 Apr.: Bracher, op. cit., p. 487.

[3] Memorandum by Pünder under 10 Apr., ibid., p. 488; Groener's 'Chronologische Darstellung' under 11 Apr., loc. cit.; Pünder, *Politik in der Reichskanzlei*, p. 118, under 11 Apr. 1932.

to the president, but Raeder refused.[1] It thus seems very likely that Hammerstein and Bock acted on Schleicher's prompting.

In the following month Hammerstein, in an address to senior army officers, gave two reasons for his opposition to Groener's policy. In the first place, the time chosen for the dissolution was wrong because a date so soon after Hindenburg's election compromised the field-marshal and looked like a payment to the left wing for its electoral support; secondly, the dissolution violated the army's position 'above party', as the minister too had to be above party. When the generals had been informed of the intended dissolution they had, Hammerstein maintained, 'in good time fought strongly with Groener about the dissolution' and for the first time had not succeeded.[2] This allegation is contradicted by Groener's account, according to which only Raeder voiced doubts, but Hammerstein agreed vociferously.[3] Nor is there any evidence to confirm Hammerstein's version. Hammerstein's new interpretation of the minister's position 'above party' in practice condemned him to inactivity if he did not balance any step against the law-breakers of the extreme right by a simultaneous step against the republican organizations, which upheld the constitution and supported the government. A strange doctrine, which illustrates how 'non-party' the leaders of the Reichswehr were.

The situation had become so confused that on 12 April Brüning and Groener once more deliberated on the measures to be taken, this time together with the Prussian ministers Braun and Severing. These—both Social Democrats—again demanded the issue of the emergency decree against the *S.A.*: otherwise the states would act independently. This argument seems to have been decisive. On the same day Brüning and Groener informed the president of their reasons for taking action, and Hindenburg signed the decree dissolving the *S.A.*, albeit with hesitation.[4] Groener's plan had apparently succeeded in spite of all opposition. But, as Admiral Raeder reports, it became quickly known in the defence ministry that the divisional commanders disapproved of the dissolution;

[1] Eschenburg, 'Die Rolle der Persönlichkeit in der Krise der Weimarer Republik', *Vierteljahrshefte für Zeitgeschichte*, ix, p. 19.

[2] Hammerstein at Berchtesgaden on 21 May 1932: *Vierteljahrshefte für Zeitgeschichte*, ii, 1954, no. 5, pp. 423-4 (notes by Major-General Liebmann).

[3] See above, p. 341.   [4] Bracher, op. cit., p. 489.

Schleicher remarked to a naval officer that he only realized now how disastrous the effect would be on the army; he had now told Groener that he was 'a dead man' and that the cabinet would fall. Schleicher's department, the *Ministeramt*, informed the chiefs of staff of the divisions that it strongly disapproved of the decree; but the naval command declined to issue a corresponding statement, for Raeder considered it a 'military impossibility' that the minister's own office should renounce its loyalty to him and confuse the subordinate officers by making the fact known.[1] It is thus not surprising that immediately after the publication of the decree the chiefs of staff of the divisions telephoned rather worriedly and asked the reasons for this one-sided measure.[2] On 15 April Schleicher was able to report to Groener 'that there was a storm brewing in the house of the president and in the defence ministry against the emergency decree. According to his cautious remarks those participating in the campaign were the former commander of the Third Division, von Stülpnagel, . . . General von Horn of the *Kyff-häuserbund*, and the commanding officer of the Second Division, von Bock. Other names General von Schleicher did not mention. . . . I demurred that the Reichswehr had to obey, but this he did not accept. . . .'[3]

From outside, especially from the extreme right, the 'storm' was fanned and Groener was attacked violently. From Potsdam the Crown Prince wrote to him in person and pointed out that ever since November 1918, when Groener had brought about the abdication of the Emperor,[4] the 'national circles' had attacked him frequently and sharply and distrusted him deeply. Because the Crown Prince had often defended Groener on such occasions, he felt all the more hurt when Groener signed the decree dissolving the *S.A.* 'I can only consider the decree a grave mistake and a very serious danger to internal peace. It is incomprehensible to me how you as the minister of defence can help to destroy the wonderful material that is united in the *S.A.* and *S.S.* and receives there a valuable educa-

[1] Raeder, *Mein Leben*, i. 270.
[2] Report of General Ott, who was then one of Schleicher's subordinates in the ministry, of 1952: Zeugenschrifttum, no. 279, Institut für Zeitgeschichte.
[3] Groener's 'Chronologische Darstellung' under 15 Apr.: Vogelsang, op. cit., no. 22, p. 454.
[4] See above, p. 6.

tion. . . . The dissolution of the *S.A.* and *S.S.* must shatter the confidence of the national circles in the ministry of defence', a confidence which the writer of the letter had always tried to maintain.[1]

The right-wing press demanded loudly—as Raeder had done first on 8 April—that the *Reichsbanner*, the republican organization, should equally be dissolved. As early as January 1932 Schleicher had informed the divisional and corps commanders that it was 'intolerable' that the *Reichsbanner* everywhere usurped public authority (*Gerechtsame*).[2] Two departments of the defence ministry were instructed to collect material against the *Reichsbanner*; but, according to one of the officers concerned, this 'was very thin'; it consisted almost entirely of newspaper clippings of recent dates.[3] In the course of his campaign against his own minister Schleicher mentioned to Oskar von Hindenburg the existence of this material; but he added that he could do nothing behind Groener's back, while the president was free to consult the chief of the army command. Thus Hammerstein was called to Hindenburg and ordered to hand over the material against the *Reichsbanner*.[4] On 15 April Hindenburg wrote to Groener that he had received evidence that organizations similar to the *S.A.* and *S.S.* also existed in other parties; if this were correct, he must demand their dissolution and requested the material to be checked. This letter was handed to the press, although it made it public that the government was no longer united, and contained a clear indication that the president disagreed with the policy of the defence minister.[5] On the following day the *Wehrmachtsabteilung*, which was under Schleicher, rearranged the material against the *Reichsbanner* and added a covering note: 'The demeanour of the *Reichsbanner* furnishes sufficient proofs of activity parallel with that of the now dissolved *S.A.*'; allegedly it was proved that its activities in three fields—usurpation of police and military functions,

---

[1] Crown Prince Wilhelm to Groener, Potsdam, 14 Apr. 1932: Nachlaß Groener, box 22, no. 231, Bundesarchiv-Militärarchiv.

[2] Schleicher on 11 Jan. 1932: *Vierteljahrshefte für Zeitgeschichte*, ii, 1954, no. 3, p. 416.

[3] Report of Schleicher's adjutant, Captain Noeldechen, of 1951: Zeugenschrifttum, no. 276, Institut für Zeitgeschichte; Vogelsang, op. cit., p. 177.

[4] Ibid., p. 178.

[5] Bracher, op. cit., p. 492; Eschenburg, op. cit., pp. 19–20; Caro and Oehme, *Schleichers Aufstieg*, p. 230.

and preparation of a revolt—were in conflict with the law.[1] But the evidence submitted did not support these allegations.

In fact there was a cabinet crisis, for the government depended upon the confidence of the president and the army command, and these no longer had any confidence in the minister of defence. This soon became publicly known. An old friend and former free corps leader wrote to Schleicher from Hanover that he had heard that there was a conflict between Schleicher and Groener and that the latter would resign. If this were true he wanted to offer his congratulations and he hoped that Schleicher would co-operate ever more closely with Hitler. According to the writer's information, the Reichswehr up to the rank of captain was almost 100 per cent. Nazi; only from that of major upwards was there a democratic 'softening of the spinal cord'. He believed that Groener was 'Germany's bad spirit', always siding with the big battalions, hence he would welcome his removal most heartily.[2] At a dinner at the end of April the under-secretary of state Meißner informed his neighbour that he had strongly opposed the dissolution of the S.A., together with Hammerstein and Schleicher, but they had been unable to prevail against Groener, who had been the *spiritus rector*.[3]

On 10 May the matter was debated by the Reichstag, where Groener defended the dissolution with the fully justified words: 'Without the S.A. peace and order would have existed for years.' But his attacks on the 'state within the state' formed by the National Socialists went unheard in the tumultuous scenes created by their deputies.[4] An official who attended the meeting, and who sympathized with Groener, noted: 'In the afternoon . . . Groener spoke very unfortunately. There was no manuscript. The unpractised speaker was unable to cope with the constant interruptions, but nevertheless tried continuously to take them into account and to reply. At the end of the speech, which lasted 45 minutes, the impression was catastrophic.'[5] Seeckt, who was present as a deputy, informed his wife:

    [1] Vogelsang, op. cit., p. 177.
    [2] Major von Stephani to Schleicher, Hanover, 19 Apr. 1932: Nachlaß Schleicher, no. 17 iii, Bundesarchiv Koblenz.
    [3] Vogelsang, op. cit., no. 16, p. 440.
    [4] Bracher, op. cit., p. 494; Groener-Geyer, op. cit., p. 316.
    [5] Pünder, op. cit., p. 120.

'Groener's speech was a catastrophe! He is seriously ill, worked quite helplessly with pieces of paper, did not finish a sentence. . . . Finally every sentence was drowned by laughter. Very painful for every decent man. . . . In any case, a serious reverse for the government, which will perhaps change everything quickly. . . .'[1] A leading conservative politician, Count Westarp, immediately after the speech had a conversation with the chancellor, in which he informed the latter that, according to everybody's impression, Groener was 'unequal to his task on medical and political grounds; for the Reichswehr, which was strongly influenced by National Socialism, it could be fatal if it became known that it stood under a man who was exhausted . . .'. Westarp advised Brüning that Groener should immediately resign for reasons of health, otherwise the Reichswehr might split.[2]

Schleicher recalled Hammerstein from manœuvres and asked the chief of the naval command to report to Hindenburg that the interests of the Reichswehr demanded Groener's resignation, but Raeder declined.[3] On 11 May Schleicher telephoned very early to his confidant in the chancellor's office, Planck, and told him that if Groener did not resign he and the leading generals of the defence ministry would immediately ask to be retired. This threat he repeated to the under-secretary of state when he appeared in his office. As Hammerstein had apparently not yet returned to Berlin and Raeder had declined to join in, it does not seem that Schleicher had any authority for this ultimatum. Then Schleicher went to the Reichstag, where he took his seat next to Groener on the ministerial bench; 'both discussed the situation apparently in a very friendly way'. Schleicher later told the under-secretary that Groener declined to take 'political leave' and would only resign if he received a vote of no confidence or was no longer supported by the president or the chancellor.[4] Yet on 12 May Groener resigned as minister of defence. Schleicher and Hammerstein had achieved their aim. Some days later a strongly conservative friend of Hindenburg remarked: 'The state of affairs in the defence

---

[1] Seeckt to his wife, Berlin, 10 May 1932: Nachlaß Seeckt, roll 28, microfilm in Institut für Zeitgeschichte.

[2] Memorandum of Westarp, 1 June 1932: *Vierteljahrshefte für Zeitgeschichte*, i, 1953, no. 13, p. 282.

[3] Raeder, op. cit., i. 271.   [4] Pünder, op. cit., pp. 120–1.

ministry, with the generals politicizing this time against their own chief, is a novel development which is disagreeable to me, although I think that Groener has deserved this unhappy end to his career. . . .'[1]

Already before Groener fell Schleicher had met Hitler twice. Goebbels's comment on their first conversation was that it 'took a good course'. The second, 'decisive conversation' took place on 8 May and was also attended 'by certain gentlemen close to the president'. Goebbels noted: 'Brüning will allegedly fall within the next few days. The president will withdraw his confidence from him. The plan is to form a cabinet dependent upon the confidence of the president; the Reichstag will be dissolved. . . .'[2] In contrast with Groener, Schleicher remained faithful to his concept of 'taming' the National Socialists by giving them ministerial posts after a general election. This is confirmed by an utterance of Hammerstein at the end of May: 'We [sic] then take Westarp so that he can prepare the transition to a participation of the Nazis after a general election.' In particular, Colonel von Reichenau, the chief of staff of the First Division in East Prussia, strongly advocated this solution: 'he could not restrain the Reichswehr and the population of East Prussia if the Nazis were not admitted to the government. . . .'[3] These plans of Schleicher clearly influenced his reply to Brüning, who offered him the succession to Groener as defence minister. On 13 May he urged the chancellor not to rush matters, and to believe his assurance that he had not discussed the issue with anyone. He put himself entirely at Brüning's disposal and promised 'that he would do everything that the *Herr Reichskanzler* ordered: Brüning was the only man who could master affairs in Germany in the foreseeable future.'[4] But this did not prevent him from negotiating busily with Hitler behind Brüning's back. In Groener's opinion, Schleicher did not intend to help the National Socialists into power, but aimed at power for himself, through his influence with Hinden-

[1] von Oldenburg-Januschau to Freiherr von Gayl, Biegen, 21 May 1932: *Vierteljahrshefte für Zeitgeschichte*, i, 1953, no. 5, p. 424.
[2] Joseph Goebbels, *Vom Kaiserhof zur Reichskanzlei*, Munich, 1934, pp. 89, 93, under 28 Apr. and 8 May 1932.
[3] Notes by Count Westarp on a conversation with Treviranus on 29 May: *Vierteljahrshefte für Zeitgeschichte*, i, 1953, no. 13, p. 284.
[4] Pünder, op. cit., pp. 122–3.

burg. 'Schleicher trusts to his own skill to lead the Nazis by the nose. He also hopes to get the better of Hugenberg. The man takes on rather a lot, but he dares to do so because he has Hindenburg in his pocket. . . . Schleicher's idea for a long time has been to govern without the Reichstag with the help of the Reichswehr. . . .'[1]

The crisis which led to Groener's resignation fatally weakened the Brüning government. The internal conflicts had become generally known and given a new impetus to the National Socialists. They had also proved the weakness of this type of government: it rested on the confidence of the president, and he was an old man of 84 who did not possess any political training and was easily influenced. His confidence in Brüning, who declared his solidarity with Groener, was badly shaken; only a few weeks later it disappeared altogether. If Schleicher in May 1932 wanted to support Brüning, he could easily have done so by accepting his offer of the post of minister of defence. His adjutant, Captain Noeldechen, remarked later: 'Schleicher did not want to spend himself as defence minister in a Brüning cabinet because he considered its span of life limited. Brüning was overthrown by the opposition from the right, but Schleicher did not aid him. . . . But Schleicher had to find a solution which took account of the enormous growth of the *N.S.D.A.P.* This seemed no longer possible with Brüning as the chancellor. . . .'[2] One question Noeldechen did not ask himself: by what right did Schleicher attempt 'to find a solution which took account of the enormous growth' of the National Socialists? This was, after all, not the function of the army command, but of the government, and to support it was the duty of the Reichswehr. The chief of the naval command wrote later about the time of Groener's resignation: 'In these days began the efforts of General von Schleicher to form a new government, which—after the resignation of Brüning on 30 May—resulted in the formation of the von Papen Cabinet, with Schleicher as minister of defence. . . .'[3] It is impossible to ascertain Schleicher's exact role in the overthrow of the Brüning government. But even the

---

[1] Groener to von Gleich, Berlin, 22 May 1932: Nachlaß Groener, box 7, no. 27, Bundesarchiv-Militärarchiv.
[2] Thus Noeldechen in 1951: *Vierteljahrshefte für Zeitgeschichte*, i, 1953, p. 274.
[3] Raeder, op. cit., i. 271.

cautious interpretation of his adjutant shows that Schleicher was not a passive onlooker. Groener's fall, which was engineered by Schleicher, undermined the position of Brüning. If Schleicher in this situation did nothing to help Brüning, if he at the same time exercised pressure upon the chancellor—as Brüning reported to another member of the cabinet[1]—and used his strong influence on the president to the same effect, then he must bear at least a large part of the responsibility for the end of the last constitutional government of the Weimar Republic.

Schleicher's basic ideas had not changed: the National Socialists must be given a share in political responsibility. If Brüning could not manage to work this miracle, he had to go. Schleicher broke with Groener at the moment when he gave up the concept of 'taming' and took sharp measures against the *S.A.* as the situation demanded. But how the National Socialists were to be brought to co-operate with the state, that question Schleicher could not answer either; even he could not square the circle. Hitler himself had never given any cause to assume that he would be content with less than complete power, and his followers were even more radical and hungry for power than their 'leader'. The new government, under Franz von Papen, which Schleicher inaugurated, also encountered the determined opposition of the National Socialists. But the Brüning government was still supported by wide circles of the population and 'tolerated' by a majority in parliament: neither was true of the Papen government. It relied solely on the confidence of the old president and on the support of the Reichswehr.

v. *The Frontier Defence and Reichswehr Expansion*

In a memorandum on the resignation of the Brüning government drawn up in the office of the president in June 1932 it was stated:

By the reception which the dissolution of the *S.A.* had in public ... the position of the minister of defence with the president was seriously shaken, the more so because the president, as the commander-in-chief of the Reichswehr, established that the soldiers

---

[1] Information given by the Minister Treviranus to Count Westarp on 28 May 1932: *Vierteljahrshefte für Zeitgeschichte*, i, p. 282 (memorandum written by Westarp on 1 June 1932). On 29 May Treviranus told Westarp that Brüning's fall was engineered by Schleicher, and probably also by Hammerstein: ibid., p. 284.

could not understand the one-sided procedure of the defence minister and thus criticized it strongly. These criticisms of the *Wehrmacht* were not only directed against his favouring of the left, but also resulted from the consideration . . . that the frontier defence units were very much weakened by the exclusion of the young National Socialists who formed their main strength (*Hauptkontingent*).

Therefore the president considered it best that Groener should resign as minister of defence, for Schleicher, Hammerstein, and Raeder confirmed to the president 'that there was no longer any confidence in him among the officer corps and the other ranks of the Reichswehr. . .'.[1] This meant a curious transmission of parliamentary ideas to the army—at a time when the government no longer depended on the confidence of the Reichstag; it was also a consideration contrary to any conception of military discipline that officers and other ranks were entitled to pass a vote of no-confidence in their leaders. Above all, the memorandum was contrary to the truth on one very important point: the National Socialists hardly anywhere formed the 'main strength' of the frontier defence units; if Schleicher or Hammerstein had informed Hindenburg to this effect, they had misinformed their commander-in-chief for tactical reasons.

In the Prussian provinces to the west of the Polish Corridor—eastern Pomerania, eastern Brandenburg and the Grenzmark Posen—the situation was clear. In Pomerania the National Socialists from early on adopted a negative attitude to the issues of frontier defence. In eastern Brandenburg too, the leaders of the *Stahlhelm* predominated as leaders and helpers. Attempts of the *S.A.* at a *rapprochement* were ignored.[2] One of the local leaders reported later: 'In Pomerania the National Socialist movement was hardly noticeable. Before the "seizure of power" men joined it who partly pursued quite different goals and were morally defective. Because of lack of members the *S.A.* in Pomerania accepted dubious elements which had been rejected by the *Stahlhelm* and the frontier defence. Thus there was a sharp conflict between the *Stahlhelm* and the *S.A.* . . . This was also transmitted to the officers who were active in the

[1] Memorandum of 10 June 1932: Vogelsang, op. cit., no. 25, p. 462.
[2] Ibid., p. 158.

frontier defence. . . .', and to Major von Briesen, the acknow-
ledged leader and organizer of the frontier defence units of
Pomerania and the Grenzmark; the National Socialists continued to object to the 'personal union' between the *Stahlhelm*
and the frontier defence.[1] This was probably the reason why
local *S.A.* leaders in Pomerania refused to serve in the frontier
defence units, as Hammerstein reported in May 1932.[2] The
training of the formations was the task of former officers and
non-commissioned officers; but from about 1932 active officers
were also employed for this purpose.[3]

In East Prussia, which was isolated and would be particularly
endangered in case of a war, comparatively large sections of the
population participated in the frontier defence preparations.
There too the leaders of the *Stahlhelm* and the *Jungstahlhelm*
played an important part, but even the *Reichsbanner*, local
authorities, and offices of posts and telegraphs participated
actively.[4] During Reichswehr exercises and manœuvres volunteers were incorporated into the units in considerable numbers,
either former soldiers who wanted to refresh their military
knowledge, or younger men who were trained for a few weeks.
There were special courses for leaders and section leaders, and
others for practice with machine-guns, trench-mortars, and
artillery. There were six frontier defence units, each consisting
of one regiment with artillery and engineer groups.[5] The
National Socialists did not preponderate in these units, although
they participated in them.

In Silesia it was different. Here, as elsewhere, the former
officers, who were trained by the army, were 'politically conservative. It can be assumed that all the officers who attended
the courses voted for the German Nationalists. Quite different
was the composition of the volunteers in the countryside. Here
a very high percentage belonged to the *N.S.D.A.P.*', one of the

[1] Report by H. Kreusler of 1954: Sammlung Oberst Dieter von Kleist, Zg.
244/57, Bundesarchiv-Militärarchiv. Cf. Walter Görlitz, *Generalfeldmarschall
Keitel*, Göttingen, 1961, p. 63.
[2] Hammerstein at Berchtesgaden on 21 May 1932: *Vierteljahrshefte für Zeitgeschichte*, ii, 1954, no. 5, p. 423.
[3] Information given by General Paul Mahlmann from his experience in the
years 1932–3.
[4] Vogelsang, op. cit., p. 157.
[5] Werner von Blomberg, 'Erinnerungen bis 1933', iii. 183–4: MS. in Bundesarchiv-Militärarchiv; Vogelsang, op. cit., p. 158.

leading officers reported later.[1] In 1932 there were difficulties because the party suddenly declared that its members could only belong to the frontier defence units if they were commanded by National Socialists. This amounted to a demand that the *S.A.* formations should be trained and equipped by the army. Further south, in Saxony, on the Czech frontier, the district officers and their helpers largely belonged to the *Stahlhelm*; young farmers and farmhands were trained by officer cadets during weekends, and the trainees too were mostly members of the *Stahlhelm* or the *Jungstahlhelm*. In Dresden older pupils of the secondary schools—mainly the sons of former officers and senior civil servants—were selected and received their military training at the Dresden Infantry School.[2]

The Reichswehr preferred to co-operate with the *Stahlhelm*, rather than any others among the para-military *Verbände*, partly because it had the best discipline from a military point of view, partly because its ideology and politics were closest to those of the army. Thus the flying groups of the *Stahlhelm* were used in 1932 to launch a *Wehrflugorganisation*, which combined all the trained flying personnel outside the army and was led by the commanding officer of Breslau, Colonel Wilberg.[3] The *Jungstahlhelm*, which included the younger generation of the 'front soldiers', received considerable sums from the defence ministry 'for the physical training of youngsters'. Between December 1930 and December 1931 Schleicher paid to its leader, a former officer, 40,000 marks;[4] but the total amount was probably much higher. The *Stahlhelm* in its turn desired even closer links with the army. At the beginning of 1933 the Crown Prince wrote to his friend Schleicher, referring to earlier complaints, that leaders of the *Stahlhelm* had again complained to him that the confidential co-operation was not as good as it might be; he attributed this to the lack of interest and understanding shown by Hammerstein, and advised Schleicher to talk to the *Stahlhelm* leaders about it.[5] There is no doubt that

---

[1] Report by Colonel Franz von Gaertner of 1952: Zeugenschrifttum, no. 44, Institut für Zeitgeschichte.
[2] Vogelsang, op. cit., p. 159; Kurt Schützle, *Reichswehr wider die Nation*, Berlin, 1963, pp. 69–70.
[3] Görlitz, *Der deutsche Generalstab*, p. 366.   [4] Vogelsang, op. cit., p. 231.
[5] Crown Prince Wilhelm to Schleicher, Berlin, 19 Jan. 1933: Nachlaß Schleicher, no. 17 v, Bundesarchiv Koblenz.

the large majority of the officer corps sympathized with the *Stahlhelm*, which was strongly militarist and Prussian, and loyal to the black, white, and red colours.

The attitude towards the large republican organization of the *Reichsbanner* remained negative. A lieutenant-colonel, who then served in the *Truppenamt*, wrote later that the *Reichsbanner*, while professing to defend the republic, might cause serious disturbances by its attitude during internal political conflicts.[1] One of Schleicher's closest collaborators, Major Ott, remarked later that the distrust of the *Reichsbanner* was particularly strong in the frontier provinces of Silesia, East and West Prussia, and that the efforts of the defence ministry to counter this tendency proved in vain. As Ott's explanations to the cabinet in December 1932 were to show, he fully shared the views of the officer corps on this point.[2] In these circumstances it did not help much that the leader of the *Reichsbanner*, Höltermann, repeatedly visited the defence ministry in the summer of 1932 and expressed the wish that his men should not be excluded from the frontier defence units; he expressly approved of an 'expansion' of the army and the measures of frontier defence; 'don't ask many questions', he declared, 'but act'. He and his friends, he explained, would have no objections to a 'reconstruction' of the Reichswehr.[3]

Groener planned an even closer co-operation between the army and the *Stahlhelm*. The pre-military training of the younger generation was to be transferred to it under state supervision, and taken out of the hands of the other para-military organizations, such as the *S.A.* For this purpose a *Reichskuratorium für Jugendertüchtigung* was founded, with the former General Edwin von Stülpnagel as its president. Thus the *Verbände* should be weaned from politics and made useful in a military sense.[4] With a first budget of 1,500,000 marks 18 military sports schools were founded. In the courses arranged by them in November 1932

---

[1] von Manstein, *Aus einem Soldatenleben*, p. 169.

[2] Report by General Ott of 1952: Zeugenschrifttum, no. 279; Institut für Zeitgeschichte. For his views in Dec. 1932, see below, p. 380.

[3] Bredow's notes of 15 June, 3 and 6 Aug., 5 Sept. 1932: Vogelsang, op. cit. pp. 286, 303; Nachlaß Ferdinand von Bredow, no. 1, fos. 8, 137, Bundesarchiv-Militärarchiv.

[4] Meinecke, op. cit., pp. 100–1; *Vierteljahrshefte für Zeitgeschichte*, ii, 1954, no. 3, p. 416.

the large majority of the participants came from right-wing organizations: exactly one-third from the *S.A.* and Hitler Youth, and more than one-quarter from the *Stahlhelm*; at Dresden all the participants were National Socialists, which was considered an exception, and at Magdeburg none, which was to be rectified during the next course in December. At Munich only 16 per cent. of the participants were National Socialists and 10 per cent. belonged to the *Reichsbanner*, the only school where its members were admitted.[1] Even in this field the strong bias against the *Reichsbanner* prevailed.

As the *Stahlhelm* and other right-wing organizations continued to form the 'backbone' of the frontier defence units in eastern Germany,[2] and as their arms depots were only imperfectly controlled by the army, the Prussian civil authorities remained highly suspicious of these activities, and the friction between them and the ministry of defence continued. At the beginning of 1930 Groener complained to the chancellor in strong terms about the 'more or less negative attitude' of the Prussian authorities.

In my opinion it is incompatible with the authority of the Reich if the largest German state . . . more or less adopts an attitude of passive resistance to a clear decision of the cabinet and tries to avoid an official and responsible co-operation. . . . For reasons of internal and foreign policy the Reich cannot permit that a state government as important as that of Prussia should at best merely suffer the measures ordered by the Reich government to be carried out, but in certain cases even render passive resistance to them. Sometimes it is difficult not to speak of sabotage of these measures. . . .[3]

Groener's cue was supplied by Schleicher, who about the same time mentioned, among the complaints of the defence minister, the 'sabotage of the frontier defence by Prussia' and the 'underground struggle of Prussia against the *Wehrmacht*'.[4]

Yet, surprisingly enough, during the following months there occurred a *rapprochement* between the defence minister and the

[1] Schützle, op. cit., appendix, pp. 5–7, with detailed figures.
[2] von Manstein, op. cit., p. 169.
[3] Groener to Chancellor Hermann Müller, Berlin, 17 Feb. 1930: Reichswehrministerium, Marineleitung, M I, PG 48896, Militärgeschichtliches Forschungsamt Freiburg.
[4] Notes of Captain Noeldechen, n.d. (before Mar. 1930): Nachlaß Schleicher, no. 23, Bundesarchiv Koblenz.

Prussian minister of the interior—perhaps connected with the fact that now Severing again occupied that post. In November 1930 Groener informed Wirth, the German minister of the interior, that during the past months the 'directives' on frontier defence (approved by the government in April 1929) had been sent to the *Oberpräsidenten* of the Prussian provinces and that they had been instructed to discuss the matter with the military and to report on the results; thus Prussia 'after an obstruction lasting more than 18 months' had accepted the policy of the government. In December Severing informed Groener that he had sent the 'directives' on frontier defence to the *Oberpräsidenten* and had instructed them to carry them out in co-operation with the responsible military authorities.[1] It was a considerable success for Groener and the policy of the army command. This, however, did not mean the end of the friction with the Prussian authorities. At the beginning of 1932 Schleicher declared to the divisional and corps commanders that, if the Social Democrats resigned in Prussia, they could not deny that they had taken part in frontier defence measures; but they were already alleging that much was done contrary to the agreement reached.[2]

In June 1932 Schleicher drew up a memorandum for the German Foreign Office containing the minimum demands Germany was to put forward should there be an international convention on disarmament. In Schleicher's opinion, such a convention must incorporate the figures to which Germany had a 'legal claim', namely parity either with France, or with Poland and Czechoslovakia; Germany must claim all the weapons not forbidden by such a convention, and demand a period of military service varying from three to twelve years, a reinforcement of certain units, a few units to be armed with heavy artillery, tanks, flak, and aeroplanes, a small militia with a period of service of three months, and no limitation of the military budget. If these minimum demands were not accepted, the interests of the Reichswehr demanded that the negotiations should be broken off: this would inevitably result in an expan-

[1] Groener to Dr. Wirth, Berlin, 8 Nov. 1930; Severing to Groener, Berlin, 23 Dec. 1930: Reichskanzlei, Akten betr. Landesverteidigung, vol. i, R 43 I 725, Bundesarchiv Koblenz.
[2] Schleicher in Berlin on 11 Jan. 1932: *Vierteljahrshefte für Zeitgeschichte*, ii, 1954, no. 3, p. 417 (notes by Major-General Liebmann).

sion of the army within the framework of these demands.[1]
That this was not a theoretical programme, which was still in
the planning stage, but that very concrete steps had been taken
in this direction, was shown during a conference of the commanding officers of the Fifth Division in August of the same year.
Under the heading 'expansion of the *Wehrmacht*' the chief of
staff reported that the seven infantry divisions would be increased 'to an absolutely serviceable state'; service in the form
of a militia was to begin with the new recruits; but the soldiers
already enlisted had to serve their full twelve years. A representative of the *Truppenamt* supplemented the information: every
infantry company was to be increased by about twenty men
from 1 April 1933; additional units of the engineers, the intelligence, and motorized formations would be set up from the
same date; the division would receive one battery of heavy and
one of anti-aircraft guns; in the autumn 200 more officers
would be enlisted, and in the spring of 1933 another 300—an
increase of the officer corps by about 13 per cent. The necessary
legal measures would be taken, but all rumours should be
scotched.[2] The envisaged 'expansion' was already a fact.

Yet the equipment of the army with weapons, which Germany
was forbidden to possess by the Treaty of Versailles, had not
progressed very far. In the spring of 1931 the army had a total
of six medium and four light tanks, which had been produced
by Daimler, Krupp, and Rheinmetall. The medium tanks had
one 7·5 cm. gun and three heavy machine-guns, and the light
tanks one 3·7 cm. gun and one heavy machine-gun. A still
smaller tank was under construction. The units were being
equipped with a 3·7 cm. anti-tank gun; it was envisaged that
in the period 1933–8 each infantry regiment would receive six,
and each cavalry regiment three of these guns, and that in
every division a separate anti-tank company would be formed,
which was to be armed with the same gun.[3] Even less progress
had been made in the development of poison gases, in spite of
the experiments in Russia. In the spring of 1931 a discussion

[1] W. Deist, 'Schleicher und die deutsche Abrüstungspolitik im Juni/Juli 1932':
ibid. vii, 1959, pp. 167–8.
[2] Notes by Colonel Hahn on a 'Kommandeurbesprechung am 20.8.32':
Nachlaß Eugen Hahn, no. 52, Heeresarchiv Stuttgart.
[3] 'Kurze Denkschrift über die Kampfwagenwaffe', 12 Mar. 1931: Akten des
Heereswaffenamtes, WiIF 5/2720, Bundesarchiv Koblenz.

took place in the *Truppenamt* on the question whether Germany should in future forgo poison gases, and what the programme in this field should be for the years 1933-8. Apparently there had been serious differences of opinion on this issue between the *Truppenamt* and the *Waffenamt*.[1]

In the field of military aviation the progress was much greater. Until the end of 1930 there were no air-force formations; the training of pilots was still undertaken on a civilian basis in Germany or at Lipetsk in Russia. Then, however, a ministerial conference attended by the ministers of defence, transport, and foreign affairs waived the clause of the Treaty of Versailles prohibiting Germany from possessing any stocks of aeronautical material, so that a secret store of aeroplanes could be created. From 1931 onwards three of the seven *Wehrkreise* possessed flying units which consisted of four light aeroplanes each. Their personnel had largely been trained at Lipetsk.[2] During the period 1927-32 the first equipment for a total of 173 aeroplanes was to be made available, and during the period 1933-7 for a total of 31 echelons with 229 aeroplanes; but the echelons in Germany were only to be formed with regard to their personnel. In fact, by the autumn of 1931 there were only available 29 reconnaissance planes, 15 fighter planes, and 26 night bombers; others were under construction. The development of a long-distance reconnaissance and of a fighter plane was to be concluded in 1931 after the necessary tests; and a night bomber was to be tested in 1932. From 1933 onwards a planned rearmament would become possible, with the larger sums which would then become available.[3] Apart from aeroplanes, suitable weapons, bombs, wireless, and photographic apparatus, etc. were being developed and tested.[4] In the opinion of the *Truppenamt*, the envisaged number of echelons would be insufficient for an army of 21 divisions; another 18 echelons should therefore be formed in the years 1933-7, consisting of bombers,

---

[1] 'Besprechung mit General Adam, T. A.', Berlin, 14 Sept. 1931: ibid., WiIF 5/2526.
[2] Völker, *Die Entwicklung der militärischen Luftfahrt in Deutschland 1920-1933*, pp. 159, 171.
[3] 'Protokoll über die am 26. und 27.2.31 vor dem Herrn Amtschef gehaltenen Vorträge über das Arbeitsgebiet der Wa. Prw. 8', Berlin, Oct. 1931: Akten des Heereswaffenamtes, WiIF 5/3179, Bundesarchiv Koblenz.
[4] Chef des Truppenamtes, Berlin, 12 Nov. 1930: ibid., WiIF 5/507.

reconnaissance, and fighter planes.[1] As to the personnel for these aeroplanes, at Lipetsk alone about 120 fighter pilots were trained in the years until 1933, and about 100 observers up to 1930; then this activity was transferred to Brunswick, where another 80 observers were trained. A list of the flying officers of the army, compiled in November 1930, included 167 names, among them many who later became leading officers of the *Luftwaffe*.[2]

It may be asked why the western powers did not take steps against the many violations of the Treaty of Versailles which must have come to their notice. During earlier years it was the *rapprochement* between France and Germany, inaugurated by Briand and Stresemann, that enabled the Reichswehr to continue the activities which began in 1923. This also brought about the withdrawal of the Interallied Control Commission, which had collected a considerable amount of material on the violations of the Treaty by the army. The lack of unity in the allied camp, and differences of opinion between their political and military leaders, helped the Reichswehr and were well known to it. In 1930 the head of the counter-intelligence department, Lieutenant-Colonel von Bredow, informed the military authorities that the French possessed detailed information about the four departments of the German general staff, and about the inspectorate of the flying school. In a personal conversation with a senior officer of the British War Office he had been told that the War Office did not worry about the military developments in Germany, nor about an increase in the strength of the army and navy, but that it followed with the greatest interest the developments in the air and the work done at Brunswick, Warnemünde, Staaken, and other aerodromes and in aircraft factories. The British, French, and Belgians were exchanging information about flying matters in Russia and in Germany; but the British did not give other reports to the French about German activities in violation of the Treaty, because they did not wish to enable France to prevent a reconciliation with Germany. The French, on the other hand, gave nearly everything to the British, but complained that the

---

[1] Völker, op. cit., p. 169. This would have meant a total strength of about 300 aeroplanes for the army of 21 divisions.

[2] Speidel, 'Reichswehr und Rote Armee', *Vierteljahrshefte für Zeitgeschichte*, i, 1953, pp. 29–30; Völker, op. cit., pp. 224, 255–9: Chef der Heeresleitung, Berlin, 6 Nov. 1930, signed by Major-General Ritter von Mittelberger.

latter did not use it; the War Office was willing to do so, but the Foreign Office was against any steps being taken, and the advent of the Labour government enhanced this discrepancy.[1]

In these circumstances the activities in Russia could be pursued unhindered. The aerodrome at Lipetsk and the tank school at Kama continued to be of vital importance to the army. This was pointed out unequivocally in 1931 by Colonel Fischer, who had meanwhile become the head of the department of the *Truppenamt* dealing with foreign armies, the T 3. The question had been asked, he wrote, what concessions Chancellor Brüning could make to the British ministers MacDonald and Henderson if they broached the subject of the German activities in Russia. Fischer emphatically pointed out 'that any concession with regard to the co-operation with the Russians in the German experimental stations must be avoided. All that can be done therefore is to deny all such allegations in the future, as we have successfully done for the past ten years....' If the Russians heard of any German concessions to Britain they would be justified in accusing the Germans of disloyalty.[2] The successors to von Blomberg as chief of the *Truppenamt*, General von Hammerstein and General Adam, also visited Soviet Russia as the guests of the Red Army, which showed itself anxious to show the guests as much as possible. They saw the Russian war academy as well as the air academy with its modern research centre.[3] In addition German officers were attached to Russian units for longer periods, and Russian officers continued to be trained in the German general staff courses in Berlin.[4] In 1932 a large group of Russian officers, led by Marshal Tukhachevsky, attended the German manœuvres and were even received by President von Hindenburg.[5] The relations clearly were as close as they had ever been.

[1] Abwehrabteilung, Berlin, 8 Jan. 1930, signed von Bredow: Marine-Kommandoamt, Flottenabteilung, Marinepolitische Angelegenheiten, 1 SKL IC 1–2, PG 33611: Admiralty, London.

[2] T 3, Berlin, 13 July 1931, signed Fischer: Nachlaß Schleicher, no. 28, Bundesarchiv Koblenz.

[3] von Manstein, op. cit., p. 139; ibid., pp. 146–57, about his second visit to Russia in the autumn of 1932.

[4] 'Vortrag', 30 Apr. 1931: Wehrmachtabteilung, Nachrichtenstelle, Geheim-Akten betr. Verschiedenes: microfilm, roll 52, Institut für Zeitgeschichte.

[5] Hilger and Meyer, *The Incompatible Allies*, p. 251.

That the army command had an 'overwhelming interest in the Russian army' was also recognized by the naval command; at the beginning of 1931 it expressly declared that it shared these views 'from the point of view of land warfare'. But this did not modify the navy's negative attitude towards Soviet Russia. As a naval officer informed the chief of the *Truppenamt*, this was due to the navy's dependence upon the two great naval powers, Britain and the U.S.A., which forced Germany to maintain closer relations with them; additional factors were her special interest in Finland, which permitted Germany to undertake there certain military developments; and the backwardness of the Red Navy, which had recently been confirmed by a visit of senior German naval officers to the Baltic and Black Sea fleets. They had convinced themselves that the Red Navy was still 'in the first primitive stages of a possible later development', so that Germany had nothing to receive and nothing to learn from it.[1] These ideas were repeated almost verbatim in a letter from the naval command to the *Truppenamt* a few months later. It emphasized once more the special interest of the navy in Finland, where Germany could develop submarines: as Finland felt continuously threatened by the Soviet Union, closer links with the Red Navy would deprive Germany of this possibility. A new point concerned the 'serious doubts' of the naval command about closer relations on grounds of discipline: naval visits, partly in German, partly in Russian ports, would become inevitable and bring the German sailors into the closest contacts with Russian sailors; this was 'highly undesirable' and had to be avoided at any price.[2]

In a lecture on problems of counter-intelligence Lieutenant-Commander Lietzmann of the naval command repeated this and alleged that the Red Navy was even more strongly influenced by political training and Communist ideology than the Red Army; the pre-condition of a successful co-operation in war-time was closer contact in peace-time, and this would mean reciprocal naval visits, which were undesirable. In the draft the following significant sentence followed: 'It would be

---

[1] Lecture of Lieutenant-Commander Lietzmann to the chief of the *Truppenamt* on 9 Jan. 1931: Marine-Kommandoamt, Flottenabteilung, Marinepolitische Angelegenheiten, 1 SKL IC 1–2, PG 33611: Admiralty, London.

[2] The chief of the naval command to the *Truppenamt*, Berlin, 2 May 1931: Marineleitung, Akten betr. Rußland, 1 SKL Ic–4, PG 33617, ibid.

irresponsible to expose our excellent personnel, which comes from the most valuable sections of the nation, in their thousands to personal contacts with the Soviet sailors, even for a limited time.' For that reason alone the idea of a co-operation with the Red Navy had to be abandoned, attractive as it might be from the point of view of power politics. In the same lecture Lietzmann pointed to the permanent state of uncertainty which existed in Poland; a smouldering fire was burning there which 'in connexion with the intolerable issue of the Corridor, can set afire the ever-growing combustible material and become a bright flame at any time'. With its few modern destroyers, submarines of French origin, and other out-of-date vessels, the Polish navy, he admitted, was of small importance; but with its bases in the Bay of Danzig and close to East Prussia it could always endanger the German lines of communication and had therefore to be taken into account.[1] Eight months earlier the same naval officer had made another point with regard to Poland, which was to have a strong influence on the political thought of the army command in the years to come. He claimed that Poland aimed at the conquest of Danzig and East Prussia, that a boundless nationalism permeated the Polish nation, and that in the pursuit of its imperialist goals it would be the last to adhere to considerations of international law. Thus, if internal conflicts broke out in Germany, during which the Reichswehr had to be used to restore order, Poland might seize the chance to realize its imperialist plans against Germany; in that case, it was more than likely that Russia would let the Poles pursue these aims without intervening herself.[2] These considerations, and especially the last one, were highly theoretical: all German military planning since the days of Seeckt was based on a common front with Russia against Poland.

The aeroplanes required by the navy were developed in two Baltic ports, by the Heinkel works at Warnemünde and by the Caspar works at Travemünde. As early as the summer of 1930 the navy was able to show officers of the Spanish navy several new aeroplanes at Warnemünde, among them a fighter plane

---

[1] Lecture by Lieutenant-Commander Lietzmann on 4 June 1931: Marine-Kommandoamt, Flottenabteilung, Marinepolitische Angelegenheiten, 1 SKL IC 1-2, PG 3361: Admiralty, London.

[2] 'Außenpolitischer Beitrag zum Vortrag bei der Frontvertreter-Besprechung', Berlin, 29 Oct. 1930: ibid.

which could be catapulted, a fighter plane which could be used on the high seas, a reconnaissance plane which could be catapulted from aboard ship, and a catapult for men-of-war. Two aeroplanes of the same type and a catapult could be built and shown at Cadiz if required. A torpedo plane could not yet be shown, but its construction by Heinkel had started and it would perhaps be ready by the summer of 1931.[1] Within the naval command there was a special section, comprising about twenty officers, which was responsible for the preparations and planning—training, military deployment, and technical development—in all air force matters.[2] Close relations existed in particular with the Finnish, Spanish, and Turkish navies which employed German advisers and built submarines and other ships according to German specifications and with the help of German deliveries.[3] On the basis of these manifold connexions the naval command could without difficulty abstain from the activities in Russia that were so vital to the army command. This, apart from any ideological differences, explains their entirely different approach to the issue of co-operation with Soviet Russia.

[1] 'Protokoll der Besprechung beim Chef der Marineleitung i. V. am 5. August 1930': Marineleitung, Spanien, PG 48903 M (Sp), Militärgeschichtliches Forschungsamt Freiburg.

[2] Chef der Marineleitung, Berlin, 4 Oct. 1930: Marineleitung, M I, PG 48896, ibid. Cf. Völker, op. cit., appendix 9, p. 249.

[3] 'Unternehmungen im Auslande', memorandum by Lieutenant-Commander Suadicani, 14 Sept. 1931: Marineleitung, Auslandsberichte, M II-1, PG 48898: Admiralty, London; notes by the same officer of 1 Dec. 1930: Marineleitung, Spanien, PG 48903 M (Sp), Militärgeschichtliches Forschungsamt Freiburg.

VIII

THE ESTABLISHMENT OF DICTATORSHIP

1. *Schleicher and the Papen Government*

THE new chancellor, Franz von Papen, who succeeded Brüning at the end of May 1932, was the candidate of Schleicher. Politically he was hardly known: Papen belonged to the extreme right of the Catholic Centre Party—the party to which Brüning too belonged—and was a deputy to the Prussian Diet, but not a member of the Reichstag. He had old, friendly relations with Schleicher; at one time they had been members of the same general staff course, together with Hammerstein. In the Prussian Diet Papen was the protagonist of a decisive change of front: the Centre Party must move to the right and leave the Prussian government, which for many years had been formed by a coalition of the Centre with the Social Democrats; thus the government of Otto Braun would have fallen—an old aim of Schleicher's.[1] Two days after the publication of the decree which dissolved the *S.A.* ad *S.S.*, on 16 April, Papen published an article which advocated that 'the valuable elements which are to be found in the great reservoir of the right' should be brought closer to the state. 'The Centre Party has very often proudly pointed out that its historical mission after the revolution had consisted in moving the Social Democrats towards the state and making them "bourgeois". Should it not have the same historical duty towards the movement which is flooding the German lands from the right?'[2] This was exactly the idea of Schleicher, who thought that the dissolution of the *S.A.* made it impossible to bring 'the valuable elements' among them to a closer co-operation with the state. As he himself told

---

[1] Bracher, *Auflösung der Weimarer Republik*, p. 518, n. 172, pp. 519, 525.
[2] Papen in *Der Ring*, no. 16, 16 Apr. 1932: ibid., p. 519; Caro and Oehme, *Schleichers Aufstieg*, p. 260.

Papen at the end of May, the fall of Brüning was necessary precisely because the dissolution prevented treatment of the National Socialist issue in a manner 'acceptable' to the Reichs-wehr, and merely drove their followers into a more extremist attitude.[1] On this crucial issue Papen and Schleicher were in full agreement.

In the eyes of Hammerstein the new government was only a government of 'transition to a co-operation with the Nazis after a general election'.[2] Schleicher too aimed at preparing the way for a participation in the government by the National Socialists. Schleicher's collaborators considered that after the events of the past weeks a Schleicher government would have been logical; but he was disinclined 'to take on an office which which would have forced him to appear frequently in parlia-ment and in public'.[3] As in his opinion the government was in any case only transitional, a weak minister who was easy to manage was good enough to fill the post of chancellor at a most critical time; while Schleicher could remain in the back-ground and need not 'spend himself'. When worried members of the Pomeranian *Landbund* (Agrarian League) pointed out to Schleicher before Papen was appointed that 'Papen is no head', Schleicher replied calmly: 'that he is not supposed to be. But he is a hat'.[4] Schleicher seems to have been equally disinclined to become Groener's successor as the minister of defence, for as such he would have to appear far more in public. Seeckt informed his wife that to his surprise General Hasse was a can-didate for the post of defence minister; 'the idea is not his, but naturally that of Schl., who believes that he can guide him completely, and that is probably correct. . . . All depends on whether they can win over the Old Man to it. . . .'[5] Perhaps, however, Hindenburg was not in favour of this scheme, or the pressure from other quarters was too strong; in any case, Schleicher himself became the minister of defence and thus the 'strong man' in the cabinet. He therefore had to resign from

[1] Bracher, op. cit., p. 520.   [2] See above, p. 348.
[3] Report of Major-General von Holtzendorff of 1946: *Vierteljahrshefte für Zeit-geschichte*, i, 1953, no. 2, p. 270.
[4] Information given by F. K. von Zitzewitz-Muttrin in 1951: Bracher, op. cit., p. 519, n. 179.
[5] Seeckt to his wife, Berlin, 25 May 1932: Nachlaß Seeckt, roll 28, microfilm in Institut für Zeitgeschichte. Wrongly quoted by Rabenau, *Seeckt*, p. 673.

the Reichswehr as an active officer. His successor as the chief of
the *Ministeramt* within the defence ministry was his close collaborator Colonel von Bredow, hitherto the head of the counter-
intelligence department.[1]

Immediately after the formation of the new government
Schleicher again negotiated with Hitler, to settle the lines of
'the co-operation between the Papen government and the
N.S.D.A.P.' Hitler was promised that the dissolution of the
S.A. would be revoked and the Reichstag be dissolved, while
he undertook that his party would tolerate the new government
—until the elections, after which the National Socialists would
enter the government. 'Until the summer the co-operation
continueds moothly. . . .'[2] This did not mean that Schleicher no
longer had any reservations about the National Socialists. He
certainly did not want to hand over the Reichswehr to them
and deeply distrusted the activities of the *S.A.* and *S.S.*, which
quickly resumed their semi-military tasks and clearly regarded
themselves as the army of the future. Even General von Blomberg, who soon became a loyal follower of Hitler, voiced his
objections to a National Socialist 'army'.[3] The focal point of
a speech made by Schleicher in June before the officers at the
army camp of Döberitz 'was his declaration that under no
circumstances would he hand over the army to a party'. The
change of government, he declared, had been 'necessary so as
not to bring the army into a position where it would have to
fire on a majority of *Volksgenossen* who particularly excelled in
furthering the military spirit (*Wehrwille*) and thus were close
to us in their goal . . .'.[4] Not only the last allegation was remarkable, for the National Socialists' professed goal was the establishment of a dictatorship and the abolition of the parliamentary
system—aims to which Schleicher apparently subscribed. Even
more surprising was the assertion that a majority of *Volksgenossen* (the term used by Hitler when addressing mass rallies)

[1] Vogelsang, op. cit., p. 210.
[2] Report of Major-General von Holtzendorff of 1946: *Vierteljahrshefte für Zeitgeschichte*, i, 1953, no. 2, p. 270. In general see Bracher, op. cit., pp. 546–8; Caro
and Oehme, op. cit., p. 261.
[3] Notes of Colonel von Bredow, 27 June 1932: Nachlaß Bredow, no. 1, fo. 20,
Bundesarchiv-Militärarchiv.
[4] Lieutenant Stieff to his fiancée, Döberitz, 17 June 1932: Vogelsang, op. cit.,
no. 28, p. 472.

stood on his side. In fact the National Socialists in 1930 had polled 18 per cent. of the votes cast, and on 31 July 1932 this increased to 37 per cent.—but that was six weeks after Schleicher's speech. Only in the elections to the Diet of Mecklenburg-Schwerin did the National Socialists, a few days before Schleicher's speech, gain an absolute majority; hence, probably, his assertion which was in complete contrast with the facts. At the beginning of July Colonel von Bredow too declared: 'we . . . have no cause to push the Nazis away. . . .'[1]

That Schleicher's policy was entirely compatible with a critical attitude towards the National Socialists is also shown by the letter addressed to him by one of his followers, who had been the adjutant of the chief of the army command and was now a staff officer in the Bavarian division. He wrote that he was extremely curious how Schleicher would take account of the mass hysteria of National Socialism after the elections to the Prussian Diet. In Bavaria, 'the leading simpletons' were well enough known, hence there was a very sober attitude towards the party.

However, if the National Socialist movement were judged only by its nebulous aims, its dubious programme, and its inferior leaders, a devastating judgement would have to be reached. But even so, the fact cannot be denied that eleven million German voters demonstrate in their dark longing a strong national will to live, and for this end seek new forms. To me it appears the most important task of future statecraft to find these forms and to capture the ideas of the movement for the state. Only a personality with complete intellectual freedom will be able to achieve this. Hence I am convinced that you, *Herr General*, whom I admire so much, will master this difficult task with a firm hand. . . .[2]

These words corresponded completely with Schleicher's plans and ideas, and there can be no doubt that he too was convinced that he would be able to master the formidable task. Another former collaborator of Schleicher believed as late as February 1933 'that what has been achieved now, the combination of all national forces towards a common effort of construction, has

---

[1] *Ministeramt*, 2 July 1932: ibid., p. 229.
[2] Major von Fumetti to Schleicher, Munich 5 Apr. 1932: Nachlaß Schleicher, no. 63, Bundesarchiv Koblenz.

been the aim and work' of Schleicher, referring expressly to his remarks during the summer of 1932.[1]

Before the elections to the Reichstag of July 1932 another goal of Schleicher and the army command was achieved: the 'co-ordination' of the Prussian government with that of the Reich. Even before Brüning's fall Hammerstein announced to the senior officers that the political situation was such that the future of the cabinet depended upon Prussia; 'both governments *must* be put on a par, that is the meaning of the Prussian elections and of Hindenburg's election . . .'.[2] For weeks the 'national' movement had demanded in the sharpest terms that a Reich Commissioner should be appointed for Prussia and that the Reich government should take measures against the Prussian government on the basis of article 48 of the constitution. This permitted the use of armed force against the government of a state which did not fulfil its legal or constitutional obligations, or in which law and order were seriously threatened: neither was the case in Prussia. Again the Crown Prince made himself the spokesman of the extreme right wing, and advised Schleicher in a letter to take energetic measures and to force the states to obedience, either by the issue of emergency decrees or by the appointment of a Reich Commissioner, if they persisted in their opposition to the lifting of the ban on party uniforms.[3] For the Brüning government, in addition to dissolving the *S.A.*, had also prohibited the wearing of any party uniforms—a measure about which the *Stahlhelm* and similar organizations complained vociferously, although it equally affected the organizations of the left, and was clearly intended to diminish political unrest and agitation.

Now the army command felt strong enough to carry out its programme. On 20 July 1932 the leading ministers of Prussia were informed by Papen that he had been appointed Reich Commissioner for Prussia by the president on the basis of article 48. A state of siege was proclaimed for Berlin and Brandenburg; the commanding officer of *Wehrkreis* iii, Lieutenant-

---

[1] The commander of the *Hessen*, Captain Carls, to Schleicher, at sea, 9 Feb. 1933: Nachlaß Schleicher, no. 64.

[2] Hammerstein at Berchtesgaden on 21 May 1932: *Vierteljahrshefte für Zeitgeschichte*, ii, 1954, no. 5, p. 424.

[3] Crown Prince Wilhelm to Schleicher, 24 June 1932: quoted by Bracher, op. cit., p. 577, n. 97.

General von Rundstedt, was entrusted by Schleicher with executive powers. All strategical points of the capital were occupied by armed soldiers. With the memories of the Kapp Putsch only twelve years earlier, the army reckoned with the possibility of armed resistance, be that by the Prussian police or by the organizations of the left.[1] Only six days before the *coup* the *Truppenamt* replied to a request of the *Wehrkreiskommando* iii dating from January and permitted it to use certain cavalry units of the *Wehrkreis* ii, if 'internal unrest in Berlin' should make it necessary 'to seal the whole periphery of the city and to control all traffic'. The *Wehrkreiskommando* iii was empowered to get in touch with squadrons in Mecklenburg and Pomerania for the planning of the necessary military measures, but the defence ministry had to give its consent if they were to be used.[2] But there was no resistance; the Prussian ministers gave way to a mere show of force. On the evening of 20 July even the 'red' working-class quarters of Berlin were completely peaceful: the picture was in no way different from that of any other day.[3] The 'red Prussia' had ceased to exist.

In addition, the *coup d'état* in Prussia created the pre-condition for a reform of the constitution at which Seeckt and Schleicher had aimed for many years. In future the offices of chancellor and prime minister of Prussia could be combined; the largest German state had lost its autonomy. In the *Wehrmachtsabteilung* it was stated a few weeks later that the 'Reich–Prussia solution' and an 'independent presidential cabinet' (a cabinet appointed by the president but independent of parliament) must be maintained at any price; 'any step backwards intolerable'.[4] The *coup* had been carried out with the full approval of the army command, which bore a large part of the responsibility for it, and it dragged the army even more strongly into party politics. It meant military intervention against a constitutional government and the parties supporting it—from the Centre to the Social

[1] Ibid., pp. 583–6.
[2] The chief of staff of *Wehrkreiskommando* iii to the defence ministry, Berlin, 18 Jan. 1932, and reply of the *Truppenamt*, Berlin, 14 July 1932, signed Adam: Truppenamt, T I, Akten betr. Innere Unruhen I, II H 611, Militärgeschichtliches Forschungsamt Freiburg.
[3] Recollections of the author, who visited the Berlin working-class quarters on the evening of 20 July together with a friend.
[4] *Wehrmachtsabteilung*, 29 Aug. 1932: Vogelsang, op. cit., no. 35, p. 480.

Democrats—and in favour of a government which in the elections of 31 July was supported by a mere 6 per cent. of the voters.[1] Above all, the *coup* facilitated greatly the seizure of power by the National Socialists six months later; for it eliminated the influence of the republican organizations in the largest German state and completely paralysed their will to offer resistance to the establishment of a dictatorship—a will which was not particularly strong in any case. By furthering the *coup* the Reichswehr finally and irrevocably joined the anti-democratic front.

The lifting of the ban on the *S.A.* and the elimination of the 'Marxist' government of Prussia merely whetted the appetite of the National Socialists. In the army command the suspicion grew that the *S.A.* units intended to acquire Reichswehr weapons and planned deeds of violence against their political enemies. Therefore Colonel von Bredow, a few days before the elections of 31 July, invited the *S.A.* leaders Röhm and Göring to visit him and warned them against taking any illegal measures. He was coolly informed by the two ex-officers that they claimed the right to take vengeance, that the *S.A.* had for years been trained to do so, and that 'Marxism' must be totally destroyed: 'You can impose the greatest hardships upon us, you can let us starve, but no one—not even our *Führer*—will be able to deprive us of the right of taking revenge!' Bredow's warnings were disregarded.[2] The *S.A.* leaders followed their own revolutionary course.

The general election of 31 July 1932, which was to prepare the way for the National Socialists to join the government, brought them the expected electoral success: they polled almost 14 million votes, and the number of their deputies increased from 107 to 230. They became by far the largest party in a parliament of 608 members, followed by the Social Democrats with 133 and the Communists with 89 deputies. But this very victory destroyed in Hitler and his followers any readiness to make concessions that might have existed before. They now demanded nothing less than the posts of chancellor and Prussian

[1] The German Nationalists, the only party supporting the government, polled 5·9 per cent. of the votes cast.
[2] Bredow's notes of 26 July 1932: Nachlaß Ferdinand von Bredow, no. 1, fos. 47–48, Bundesarchiv-Militärarchiv.

prime minister, minister of the interior of the Reich and Prussia (and thus control of the police), the ministers of justice, agriculture, air transport, and 'popular education', the last two being new creations. These demands, which would have given him all key positions, Hitler made in a meeting with Schleicher which apparently took place on 5 August outside Berlin. During or soon after this meeting Schleicher gained the impression that it was necessary to risk a strong participation of the National Socialists in the government. To one of his collaborators Schleicher remarked after his return that he must now try and win over Hindenburg to the idea of making Hitler chancellor. Hitler had succeeded in convincing Schleicher by the following argument: if some National Socialists received ministerial posts, but he himself remained outside the cabinet, the 'leadership principle' which dominated his party would require automatically that his consent be obtained for every decision; thus the cabinet would in practice be paralysed.[1]

A few days later Schleicher's successor in the *Ministeramt*, Colonel von Bredow, noted for a conference of departmental chiefs with the chief of the army command: 'Hitler did not want any position but that of chancellor. Meanwhile he has increased his demands. . . . Situation not good. Defence minister *in favour* of Hitler's chancellorship. . . . Hitler would thus have been forced to show whether he can govern. The movement would have been dragged from its unproductive opposition to positive work. . . .' If it remained in the cold, it would become more extreme, and there might be an 'explosion. The valuable movement—the good stock—would be lost. . . .'[2] The decisive argument of Schleicher still was that the 'valuable' and 'good' followers of Hitler would be lost (to the Communists?) if he remained in opposition. At about the same time Groener mockingly remarked to the historian Meinecke: 'as if there were not many valuable youngsters in the other camp too'.[3] In fact the S.A., especially in the large cities, consisted largely of toughs, semi-criminal types, and hoodlums who proved their value

---

[1] Th. Vogelsang, 'Zur Politik Schleichers gegenüber der NSDAP 1932', *Vierteljahrshefte für Zeitgeschichte*, vi, 1958, p. 92 and n. 15; Vogelsang, *Reichswehr, Staat und NSDAP*, pp. 257–8.

[2] Notes by Colonel von Bredow, Berlin, 15 Aug. 1932: *Vierteljahrshefte für Zeitgeschichte*, vi, 1958, no. 4, p. 100.

[3] Meinecke, *Die deutsche Katastrophe*, p. 71.

above all in fights with their political adversaries, in breaking up their political meetings, and in provoking riots.

In a cabinet meeting on 10 August Schleicher declared that he saw two possibilities of a development: either the present government remained in office without a change, in the hope of winning a majority by its achievements in the long run, or it negotiated with the National Socialists about their joining the government in some form; the simplest solution would be to give ministerial posts to some National Socialists; but with that one would probably not get very far, because it was essential that Hitler himself participated in the responsibility; while he, in the interests of his movement, was bound to attribute decisive importance to his gaining the highest post. The other solution too entailed great difficulties, Schleicher emphasized; but there was no longer a danger that the means of power did not fully support the government, and the *Wehrmacht* in particular was willing, if need be, to take on anyone who resisted the government's authority. In the course of the meeting Schleicher supplemented his explanations and maintained 'that the entry of National Socialists into the government was bound to lead to conflicts between those who joined the government and the *S.A.* and *S.S.* formations. If National Socialists joined the government, they were bound to aim at getting rid of these formations. Otherwise these formations would be petted as before. . . .'[1] As far as the *S.A.*—but not the *S.S.*—was concerned these were indeed prophetic words that were to come true in the 'night of the long knives' of 30 June 1934, when the *S.A.* leaders were massacred by the *S.S.* But it was an illusion to believe that Hitler's demands and aims would become more moderate as a result.

In general, Schleicher's conception had been modified to a certain extent, probably because of Hindenburg's refusal to appoint the 'Bohemian lance-corporal' chancellor. The idea of the 'taming' of the National Socialists still played a part— Schleicher's 'simplest solution'—but he now had to admit that with this method 'one would probably not get very far'. Therefore there was now added the idea of 'getting rid of the *S.A.*', of the inevitable conflict between the 'moderate' and the 'radi-

[1] Minutes of a cabinet meeting, Berlin, 10 Aug. 1932: *Vierteljahrshefte für Zeitgeschichte*, vi, 1958, no. 3, pp. 94–95, 97.

cal' National Socialists if the former entered the government—
an aim that thus became still more desirable. In reality this was
wishful thinking, for there were no 'moderate' National
Socialists. In the negotiations which took place during the
following days Papen and Schleicher did not succeed in persuading Hitler to join the Papen government, in which he was
offered the posts of vice-chancellor and Prussian prime minister,
and his followers several ministerial seats. The negotiations
broke down because this offer remained far below Hitler's
demands. The result was a growing alienation between the
government and the National Socialists. The conclusions drawn
in the defence ministry was that it was 'impossible for the president and the defence minister to resign. The defence minister
will put his stamp on every cabinet. He does not require 51 per
cent.'[1] A few days after the breakdown of the negotiations, the
new under-secretary of state in the chancellor's office, Dr.
Planck, one of Schleicher's confidants, told the retired under-
secretary: 'Schleicher is now on top and full of beans.'[2] He was
clearly eager to govern with less than 51 per cent., in fact with
considerably less, for among all the political parties only the
German Nationalists supported the government, and they had
no mass support.

In the Reichswehr, too, the consequence of these events was
that the relations with the National Socialists became considerably cooler, and that the army command once more spoke out
strongly against the *S.A.*—for the first time since the fall of
Groener and Brüning. At the beginning of August Colonel von
Bredow had informed the chiefs of staff:

A co-operation between the army and the S.A. etc. in the case of internal
unrest is not envisaged. The *Wehrmacht* does not require any support
by *Verbände* of any kind to maintain order.

. . . As experience shows, we must reckon with the fact that our
attitude of being completely above party will not at the outset
encounter the necessary understanding in all circles of the *N.S.D.A.P.*
. . . On the other hand, the attempts of the *N.S.D.A.P.* to establish
contacts with the Reichswehr and to achieve a relationship of

[1] Wehrmachtsabteilung, Berlin, 29 Aug. 1932: Vogelsang, *Reichswehr, Staat und NSDAP*, no. 35, p. 481.
[2] Planck to Dr. Pünder on 17 Aug. 1932: Pünder, *Politik in der Reichskanzlei*, p. 141; ibid., the details of the government's offer to Hitler according to Planck's information.

greater trust are to be welcomed as such; everything must be avoided that could be felt as a rebuff or could cause offence. The required discretion of the Reichswehr must not create the impression that the *Wehrmacht* is devoid of understanding the patriotic and military spirit permeating the National Socialist movement. . . .

Apart from this I shall try and obtain a promise from the leaders of the *N.S.D.A.P.* that in future no party uniforms are worn when they are in official contacts with Reichswehr authorities.[1]

This meant that such official contacts were not repudiated by the army, as its famed non-partisan attitude would have required, but were welcomed, provided that the National Socialists did not wear uniforms on such occasions. If the chiefs of staff were instructed to avoid anything that the National Socialists could construe as a rebuff, they had virtually no option but to co-operate with them.

After the negotiations between the Papen government and Hitler had broken down Hammerstein remarked 'that now he could again sleep peacefully because he knew that he could again, if need be, order the soldiers to fire on the Nazis'; since Saturday, 13 August, there had been a violent feeling against them in the army.[2] At the autumn manœuvres of the Second Infantry Division in Mecklenburg Hammerstein spoke to the assembled officers 'with such a sullen and threatening sharpness against any kind of National Socialist violence, as I have never experienced from any other quarter', one of those present wrote later.[3]

On 20 August a representative of the *Truppenamt* declared at a meeting of commanding officers in southern Germany: 'Unjustified demands of the *S.A.* and *S.S.* leaders to army. Finally demand made that soldiers must salute them! Hitler unreliable, no longer independent, nor master of the movement. Repeatedly he did not keep promises. Strong tension between ministry of defence and *S.A.* Not impossible that they will act against constitution.' The commanding officer of the Fifth Division, Lieutenant-General Liebmann, added: 'Whoever lifts his hand against

---

[1] The chief of the *Ministeramt* to the chiefs of staff, Berlin, 5 Aug. 1932: Vogelsang, op. cit., no. 32, pp. 477–8.

[2] Remark to under-secretary of state Planck on 15 Aug. 1932: Pünder, op. cit., p. 140.

[3] Report by General Freiherr Geyr von Schweppenburg of 1956: Zeugenschrifttum, no. 680, Institut für Zeitgeschichte.

the Reichswehr will have it cut off. Riots will be suppressed quickly by the use of troops and with brutal force. No firing into the air. If there is firing we shall aim and hit!'[1] The commanding officer of the Cavalry Regiment 14 in Mecklenburg replied to an inquiry of the defence ministry about the mood among his soldiers: 'I guarantee that my regiment will fire in the direction I order it to fire', although among his officers there were several faithful National Socialists.[2] Another commanding officer, Colonel Blaskowitz, emphasized in addressing his officers: 'If the Nazis commit any stupidities they will be opposed with all our force, and we shall not recoil from the most bloody conflicts. In particular it is believed that the army and police are absolutely in the position to cope alone with these fellows. . . .'[3] All these declarations of August 1932 are of special interest because it has often been said that the army command hesitated to use the army against the National Socialists because it was infected with Nazi ideas and thus no longer reliable. In reality there can hardly be a doubt that the army would have obeyed an order to fire on National Socialist rioters and that, together with the militarized police, it was strong enough to cope with any threat to internal peace.

At the same time Colonel Blaskowitz explained the general political situation to his officers in the following terms:

The parties are Germany's misfortune. By their selfishness (*Eigenbrötelei*) they prevent any stable and useful work of the government, which today is more essential than ever to lead us out of this misery. Therefore the government must be freed from the chains of parliamentarianism, to be able to work independently, supported by the confidence of the president and the power of the Reichswehr. Both instruments of power symbolize most clearly the idea of German unity and are particularly suitable, on account of their position above party, working solely for the good of the state, to have a steadying effect; they thus form the only basis for a government such as we need now. Brüning was not able to follow the president completely on this road that he intended to take for a long time, and in the end Brüning became again more or less depen-

---

[1] Notes by Colonel Hahn on 'Kommandeurbesprechung am 20.8.32': Nachlaß Eugen Hahn, Heft 52, Heeresarchiv Stuttgart.

[2] Report by General Freiherr Geyr von Schweppenburg of 1956, cf. n. 3, p. 374.

[3] Lieutenant Stieff to his wife, 21 Aug. 1932: *Vierteljahrshefte für Zeitgeschichte*, ii, 1954, p. 297.

dent upon the parties. Therefore he had to go. Undoubtedly the
N.S.D.A.P. has smoothed the path of Schleicher's policy in many
ways. But its demand to exercise complete power is contradicted by
the need of having a government above party. Therefore it will be
treated now exactly like the other parties. . . .[1]

Here the policy of Schleicher was developed into an ideology,
the ideology of the Reichswehr, 'freed from the chains of parliamentarianism' and those of the political parties. If a chancellor became dependent upon them, 'he had to go'.

By the middle of August Schleicher too had accepted the
general political line of the Papen government and supported
it during the following weeks. The 'independent presidential
cabinet' had to be maintained at any price; 'any step backwards is intolerable'.[2] At the beginning of October Schleicher
remarked to the former under-secretary of state Pünder that
the work of the government was progressing very well; its 'main
task', that of bringing the Nazis into the government, had not
been achieved, but a 'complete "disenchantment"' with the
Nazis' had occurred; the Prussian government had 'of course'
not been removed because it endangered law and order, but
only so as 'to terminate the intolerable dualism between the
Reich and Prussia'; someone only had to find the courage to
act, reasons could always be invented afterwards.[3] The important point, however, was that the 'main task' of the government
had not been fulfilled, and therefore Schleicher continued to
maintain his contacts with leading National Socialists. He
clearly was still convinced that he would one day succeed in
persuading them to join the government. In addition he began
to fear that the 'reactionary' course of the cabinet would drive
more and more people into opposition, that perhaps one day
all the radical elements would combine in their resistance to
the government. In case Papen planned to alter the constitution, if need be, and to establish a dictatorship supported by the
president and the army, the soldiers might have to be used to
defend a government and a policy which was repudiated by the
overwhelming majority of the nation. Leading officers began

[1] Lieutenant Stieff to his wife, 21 Aug. 1932, *Vierteljahrshefte für Zeitgeschichte*,
ii, 1954, p. 297. Blaskowitz was the later Colonel-General who during the war
became an outspoken critic of Hitler's policy in occupied Poland and Russia.

[2] *Wehrmachtsabteilung*, 29 Aug. 1932: Vogelsang, op. cit., no. 35, p. 480.

[3] Schleicher on 6 Oct. 1932: Pünder, op. cit., p. 149: notes of 8 Oct. 1932.

to worry that in such an eventuality the army would have to fight 'not against an illegal revolutionary movement, but solely in defence of too narrow a political basis'.[1] Thus Schleicher and the army command gradually diverged more and more from the policy of Papen, whom they had elevated to the leading position.

On 12 September the Reichstag was once more dissolved. The elections of 6 November 1932 resulted in a serious decline of the National Socialists: they lost two million votes and dropped from 37·2 to 33·1 per cent. of the votes cast, while the German Nationalists, who supported Papen, increased their share from 5·9 to 8·3 per cent. Only three days before the election an event occurred which seemed to confirm the fears entertained in the defence ministry. The National Socialists and the Communists combined to proclaim a strike of the Berlin transport workers, which took place against the advice of the trade unions, because a poll of their members failed to produce the majority of three-quarters required by their by-laws. The opportunity of the strike was used by the members of the para-military formations of the two extremist parties to commit sabotage on a large scale, to pour concrete into tramway points, to pull down high tension cables, to beat up workmen unwilling to strike, and to attack the police who protected them. Even radical students of Berlin University proudly recounted the deeds they had perpetrated in these 'battles'. For some days the police found it extremely difficult to restore law and order and to protect the transport system. A 'united front' of the most radical sections of the population was established. The losses suffered by the National Socialists in the elections of 6 November are partly explained by these events, for many, who believed that Hitler would save Germany from Bolshevism, now realized that the danger had come closer through the united front of his 'brown' battalions and the 'red 'ones. The likelihood that one day the army might have to be used in the defence of an unpopular government had also increased; and nine-tenths of the electors still voted against this government. What would the military situation be like if the army and the police had to fight against the combined National Socialists and Communists? And what would be the political consequences of such an action?

[1] Vogelsang, op. cit., p. 316; Bracher, op. cit., pp. 661–2.

ii. *The Fall of Papen*

Under the impact of the Berlin transport workers' strike, and the election results of 6 November, the head of the *Wehrmachts-abteilung*, Lieutenant-Colonel Ott, was permitted by Schleicher to investigate the question in a *kriegspiel* whether the Reichs-wehr could cope with a possible state of emergency directed against the terror of the right and the left. The possibility of internal unrest and the use of the armed forces had existed since 1930, as it did in 1923; but hitherto the planning on the military side envisaged an attempt at a *Putsch* by the National Socialists or the Communists, but not by both together. The Berlin strike seemed to create a novel situation, although the bloody encounters between National Socialists and Communists continued all over Germany. An officer, who then served in the defence ministry, testified many years later how strongly the thoughts of his fellow-officers were affected by the events of the Berlin transport strike.[1] It was not recognized that this fleeting alliance with the common purpose of creating 'chaos' could not possibly last, that the mutual hatred separating Communists from National Socialists was as great as their contempt of the 'system' of Weimar. The fears of all those who believed that the National Socialists were in reality disguised Bolsheviks seemed to come true.

Thus there assembled in November—the date is unfortunately not known—in the defence ministry the representatives of the seven infantry divisions, of the navy, the ministry of the interior, the Prussian government and police, and of other authorities concerned with the effects of a state of emergency. In a study lasting three days every area of Germany was investigated according to the situation which was likely to develop there.[2] As Schleicher told the leading officers a few weeks later, in this study 'the *worst* case' was assumed, namely that a general strike had broken out all over Germany.[3] The memories of the Kapp Putsch and the helplessness of the army confronted by a general strike became alive. In Hamburg a general strike of the dockers

---

[1] Foertsch, *Schuld und Verhängnis*, p. 19; cf. Bracher, op. cit., p. 674, n. 88.

[2] Report by Eugen Ott of Nov. 1946: Zeugenschrifttum, no. 279, Institut für Zeitgeschichte.

[3] Schleicher in mid-December 1932: *Vierteljahrshefte für Zeitgeschichte*, ii, 1954, no. 6, p. 427 (notes by General Liebmann).

was envisaged; this would cripple the vital functions of the port, namely the import of essential foodstuffs and most of Germany's overseas exports; the available forces of the police, army, and navy were small; the *Technische Nothilfe*—an organization formed to maintain vital services during a strike—would have to bear the main burden in fighting the strike. But its leader declared this to be impossible because it was not equipped for such demands, and most of its members were National Socialists who would not function in such a situation.[1]

For the Rhine–Ruhr area three questions were investigated: the closing down of the mines and heavy industry, the stopping of traffic on the Rhine, and the revival of separatist tendencies. The situation was considered especially critical because the Reichswehr could not be used in the demilitarized zone; hence the police alone would have to maintain order, though during earlier rioting in the Ruhr its forces had proved much too weak. After recent experiences it was also considered doubtful whether the police would take measures against the Communist terror expected in the Ruhr; 'thus in the centre of Germany's economic life the maintenance of order could not be guaranteed. . .'. In East Prussia the situation was worse, because here it was assumed

that radical Polish elements would try and use the tension inside Germany to seize East Prussia. The East Prussian division—in case of a conflict cut off from the Reich and thrown back upon its own resources—had to rely on large sections of the population with military inclinations to assemble even a weak frontier defence force. The overwhelming majority of these reinforcements had to come from the ranks of the *N.S.D.A.P.* because it had acquired a dominating position especially among the youth of . . . East Prussia. In case of a state of emergency against the National Socialists these forces had to be counted out. . . . In addition, there was the serious danger of an internal conflict in the army, for in isolated East Prussia we had succeeded least in keeping it away from National Socialist influence. The result for East Prussia was that the army would have to fight on two fronts with entirely insufficient forces. To reinforce them from the Reich was out of the question. . . .[2]

The same was the result of the *kriegspiel* for the other parts of Germany. It proved that it would be impossible anywhere to

[1] Ott's report of Nov. 1946, loc. cit.; most of the report in Schüddekopf, *Heer und Republik*, no. 151, pp. 374–5.   [2] Ibid.

save forces which might then be concentrated at the most critical points. Ott therefore reported to Schleicher

> that the forces of order in the Reich and the states were in no way sufficient to maintain the constitutional order against the National Socialists and the Communists and to protect the frontiers. Thus it was the duty of the defence minister to prevent the proclamation of a military state of emergency by the government. After me the representatives of the seven divisions expressed the same opinion and asked me to inform the minister emphatically that the tension in the Reich had to be relieved without making use of the *Wehrmacht*. General von Schleicher was much impressed and sided with us. . . .

Thus far Ott's report written many years later. At that time Schleicher himself told the senior officers that riots could be suppressed, 'but how could we cope with sabotage and passive resistance? These ideas had their effect on me. . . .'[1] Thus the lessons of the *kriegspiel* assumed historical importance.

The army command was of course entitled to presume 'the worst case' for a study of this kind. But even that did not justify disregarding any positive factors: Ott's report does not contain a single word about the forces which would have co-operated with the Reichswehr and the police had the National Socialists and Communists made a common attack upon the constitutional order. These forces would have been, in particular, the republican mass organizations of the *Reichsbanner*, the free trade unions, and the workers' sports and gymnastic associations, and also the Christian trade unions. As National Socialists and Communists had not much influence among the factory workers, for their followers were largely recruited among the unemployed and other victims of the crisis, only a comparatively small proportion of the workers would have gone on strike if the extremists had proclaimed it—the situation would have been entirely different from that of the Kapp Putsch, when the trade unions proclaimed and led the strike movement. No doubt, Communists and National Socialists—as during the Berlin transport strike—would have committed sabotage and tried to prevent the workers from entering the factories; but such tactics, like similar Communist attempts earlier, would have been met

---

[1] Schleicher addressing the divisional and corps commanders in mid-December 1932: *Vierteljahrshefte für Zeitgeschichte*, ii, 1954, no. 6, p. 427.

by the determined resistance of the trade unionists. Equally unjustified was the doubt voiced about the reliability of the Prussian police, which was always ready to suppress riots caused by the extremist parties. This view reflected the old conflicts with the Prussian government and the Social Democratic leaders of the Prussian police, who had, however, been removed meanwhile from their posts. Nor was it correct that 'the overwhelming majority of the reinforcements' for the defence of East Prussia 'had to come from the ranks of the *N.S.D.A.P.*', for there the *Stahlhelm* as well as the *Reichsbanner* strongly participated in the frontier defence units.[1] The fear of a Polish attack upon East Prussia in the case of internal unrest in Germany was even more speculative. It was made extremely unlikely by the military understanding between the Reichswehr and the Red Army; as recently as 1928 Voroshilov had assured Blomberg that in the case of a Polish attack upon Germany Russia was ready to render any help.[2] In fact, all Polish military planning was directed against Soviet Russia, and it was only in 1936, after the occupation of the Rhineland by Hitler, that Marshal Rydz-Śmigły ordered the preparation of plans directed against Germany.[3]

Even more surprising is the fact that this Polish attitude was known in the defence ministry. In July 1932—only four months before the *kriegspiel*—Colonel von Bredow reported to Schleicher, on the basis of 'two interesting reports about Poland . . . that the responsible authorities do not want any conflicts in the east'.[4] The one-sided allegations and explanations of Ott and Schleicher make it seem probable that the *kriegspiel* was meant to prove a thesis: a continuation of the Papen government would not only lead to the outbreak of riots, but would endanger the work of Seeckt and Schleicher, the allegedly nonpolitical role of the Reichswehr. Schleicher declared only a few weeks later: 'Papen would have brought the *Wehrmacht* on to the streets within a few days. Prospects for the *Wehrmacht* then extremely poor: worry that within a few days we should stand in the streets with machine-guns against nine-tenths of the

---

[1] See above, p. 352.   [2] See above, p. 281.

[3] *Polskie Siły Zbrojne w Drugiej Wojnie Światowej*, i. 1, London, 1950, pp. 116 ff.

[4] Bredow's notes for Schleicher of 27 July 1932, signed by Ott and Schleicher on the same day: Nachlaß Ferdinand von Bredow, no. 1, fo. 54, Bundesarchiv-Militärarchiv.

nation. . . .'[1] Again a most curious account, for on 6 November the National Socialists and Communists together polled exactly 50 per cent. of the votes cast; it was out of the question that the Reichswehr might have to fight simultaneously against the followers of the other parties, such as the Centre, the Social Democrats, or the German Nationalists. In June Schleicher had mentioned that the Reichswehr must not be brought into a position where it would have to fire on a majority of the people; now this majority, in Schleicher's arithmetic, by adding the Communists, became 90 per cent.—that there were other forces in Germany he deliberately overlooked. And this happened at a time when the contacts with the *Reichsbanner* had become considerably closer.[2]

As early as 23 November Schleicher inquired from Hitler whether he was willing to support a Schleicher government. But Hitler refused brusquely, and the president too was by no means delighted by the prospect of making Schleicher chancellor.[3] Hindenburg was determined to keep Papen as his chancellor; and the latter planned, if need be, to govern indefinitely without the Reichstag, to dissolve the political parties and the *Verbände*, and to modify the constitution—plans which met with the approval of the president, who intended to support his chancellor in case of a conflict with parliament. Schleicher privately discussed the situation with the other ministers and told them that Papen's continuation in office brought with it the danger of civil war, and that the Reichswehr must not be worn out in such a war—independently of the issue whether it would gain the upper hand.[4] In a meeting of the cabinet on 2 December Lieutenant-Colonel Ott reported on the preparations for a military state of emergency and the 'serious dangers' connected with it. He informed the ministers that 'peace and order in Germany could not be maintained by the military against the *S.A.* and *S.S.*, possibly also against the *Reichsbanner Schwarz-Rot-Gold*. As one of the ministers present remembered later, he found this opinion all

---

[1] Schleicher addressing the divisional and corps commanders in mid-December 1932: *Vierteljahrshefte für Zeitgeschichte*, ii, 1954, no. 6, p. 427.
[2] Vogelsang, 'Zur Politik Schleichers gegenüber der NSDAP 1932': ibid., vi, 1958, p. 105.   [3] Notes by Colonel von Bredow of 26 Nov. 1932, ibid.
[4] Notes by under-secretary of state Meißner of 2 Dec. 1932: ibid., no. 6, p. 106; Bracher, op. cit., p. 673.

the more convincing because 'very many soldiers of all ranks were strongly influenced by the Nazis' discipline, their enthusiasm, and their proclaimed readiness to make sacrifices—in contrast with the parliamentary democracy of the time', and strong inner resistance was to be expected from the soldiers if it came to a conflict.[1] Papen also remembered that Ott's report led to the decision of the cabinet to avoid at all costs the civil war which Schleicher feared.[2] It is true that he does not mention the fantastic allegation about the *Reichsbanner*; but it fits completely with the report written by Ott himself after the war. It also fits with the whole attitude to the *Reichsbanner* which the *Wehrmachtsabteilung* adopted at the time of the *S.A.* dissolution, when it alleged that it was proven that the *Reichsbanner* was preparing a revolt.[3]

On the same day, 2 December, Ott wrote a memorandum for Schleicher about the situation in case of a general strike. In such an eventuality, reinforcements for the army, the police, etc., could at best be obtained from the *Stahlhelm*; in his opinion, 'all others, including Christian and free trade unions, would probably be unreliable'. Although here Ott cautiously inserted the world 'probably', this also reflects his deep distrust of the republican forces, in particular the trade unionists. Then, he continued, the psychological situation for the army and the police would be very difficult, for the other side would use the argument that they were being used, not to maintain law and order, but in the interests of the upper class against the people.[4] The reproach that the Reichswehr was acting 'against the people' in favour of the old upper class, from which so many officers came, was bound to touch it on a very sensitive spot. In such a case, too, difficulties might arise within its own ranks. It is almost certain that Schleicher also spoke at the cabinet meeting to the same effect.[5]

At the meeting nearly all the ministers supported Schleicher and opposed Papen's plans to effect changes in the constitution and to rule without parliament. Hence Papen was forced to resign. The new chancellor appointed by the president was

[1] Freiherr von Braun to Papen, 5 July 1957: Vogelsang, op. cit., p. 111, n. 65.
[2] Papen's notes of 12 Nov. 1957: ibid., p. 113.   [3] See above, pp. 345–6.
[4] Vogelsang, *Reichswehr Staat und NSDAP*, no. 38, pp. 484–5.
[5] There are no minutes of this cabinet meeting in the files of the Reichskanzlei.

Kurt von Schleicher, who also became Reich Commissioner for Prussia and remained minister of defence. Probably Schleicher would have preferred to remain in the background; but it was Papen who suggested his name to the president, and there was virtually no other choice.[1] The republic now had a general as its chancellor and a field-marshal of 85 years as its president. Its fate depended upon the co-operation between its two highest dignitaries, for Schleicher could reckon as little as Papen upon finding a majority in parliament to support his policy. He too depended upon the confidence of Hindenburg; but his predecessors had already found out that this confidence might become a broken reed.

On the previous day, 1 December, Schleicher had resumed his contacts with Hitler, again through Lieutenant-Colonel Ott. He offered Hitler in the name of Schleicher the post of vice-chancellor in the new government; the allocation of further posts would be discussed later. In Schleicher's opinion it was the duty of the National Socialists to co-operate with the state in a positive sense—it was his old aim of granting to them a share in the political responsibility. Hitler, however, declined with the argument that his movement must be given the entire power. But then Göring explained to Ott that Hitler's refusal was not final: a compromise might be possible on the basis that Göring was nominated prime minister of Prussia and minister of aviation.[2] With this meagre result Ott returned to Berlin. Among Hitler's lieutenants only one, the head of the party's organization, Gregor Strasser, was in favour of genuine negotiations with Schleicher. In November Schleicher had been informed by Strasser that he was willing to act independently if the approaches to Hitler brought no result.[3] Schleicher's plans for the future were based on this promise from one of the most important National Socialist leaders.

III. *Schleicher as Chancellor*

On 2 December 1932 Kurt von Schleicher stood at the zenith of his power—a power which he had not sought in this form.

---

[1] Notes by Meißner of 2 Dec. 1932: *Vierteljahrshefte für Zeitgeschichte*, vi, 1958, no. 6, pp. 106–7.

[2] Bracher, op. cit., pp. 671–2; Vogelsang, op. cit., p. 330.

[3] *Ministeramt*, 23 Nov. 1932: *Vierteljahrshefte für Zeitgeschichte*, vi, 1958, p. 105, n. 44.

Exactly as six months before when he wanted another general to become minister of defence, he would now have preferred another politican as chancellor, for example the president of the Reichsbank, Dr. Schacht.[1] Schleicher loved power, but he liked to wield it behind the scenes and disliked the glare of publicity. His manifold activities during the past years, his many contacts and endeavours had made him well known; but he had few friends, and there was little confidence in him. Too many people had been offended by him, or had become the victims of his intrigues. Warningly his old friend Groener wrote to him at the end of November:

You desire a meeting with me to learn the reasons for the 'estrange-ment' that has taken place between us. My dear Schleicher, the expression 'estrangement' is much too mild. I will be open and honest. Wrath and fury boil within me because I have been disap-pointed by you, my old friend, pupil, adopted son, my hope for the nation and fatherland. . . . Who has 'confidence' in you now? hardly anyone; you are considered exceptionally intelligent, clever, and cunning and one expects you to become chancellor because of your cleverness. You are welcome to it. But do not work with alacrity, but with wisdom; no more light-cavalry charges, one thing must be solved after the other. . . . The attempt to eliminate the dualism between the Reich and Prussia by brutality is stupid because of the effects on the other states. Stop using the horsewhip. That Hitler can do, too; for that you are not needed. . . .[2]

Schleicher's power corresponded to that of his old chief Seeckt when the exercise of executive power was entrusted to him in 1923. Then, too, civil war was threatening; political extremism had increased dangerously; and article 48 of the constitution provided the legal basis for the actions of the government, which ruled by issuing emergency decrees. But in 1923 the Stresemann government was supported by a parliamentary majority, and the Reichswehr stood behind Seeckt. The basis on which Schleicher's power rested was much smaller; he had little support in parliament, and many officers disliked and dis-trusted him. It is true that many key positions in the defence ministry were occupied by his followers; but many of the younger officers and other ranks sympathized with National

[1] Bracher, op. cit., p. 676, n. 99.
[2] Groener to Schleicher, Bad Schandau, 27 Nov. 1932: Groener-Geyer, *General Groener*, pp. 330-2.

Socialism. The army would have followed Seeckt without asking any questions. But since his dismissal 'the authority and the influence of the chief of the army command had declined. . . . General von Hammerstein did not possess the authority which permitted a decision of far-reaching importance. . . .'[1] The chief of the army command not only lacked firm support, he equally lacked the will for decisive action. Neither Schleicher nor Hammerstein had the stature of a Yorck who in 1812 defied the orders of his king. The Prussian army was educated to render obedience, and this it owed to the ancient field-marshal who held the highest rank in the state. His orders it would have carried out, but it could not act without them.

Even after the unsuccessful negotiations with Hitler of 1 December Schleicher had not given up hope that the National Socialists would tolerate his government; but at the same time he pursued his plans of co-operation with Gregor Strasser and other 'moderate' National Socialists. He hoped that not only Strasser, but also the trade-union leaders Leipart and Stegerwald (the leaders of the Free and the Christian trade unions) would join the government. But these plans failed. After some initial hesitation the attitude of Hitler hardened and became as hostile as it had been towards the Papen government. The ranks of his party remained closed; Schleicher did not succeed in effecting a split, but the attempt increased Hitler's enmity. On 8 December Gregor Strasser resigned his party offices and his seat in parliament, and soon after went abroad; there was no repercussion. Another plan of Schleicher, to gain the support of the Social Democrats, equally failed. About the middle of December Major-General von Bredow, the chief of the *Ministeramt*, submitted to their leaders suggestions for a co-operation: the *N.S.D.A.P.* was to be dissolved, parliament was to be adjourned for an indefinite period, the *Reichsbanner* and the *Stahlhelm* were to be amalgamated into a veterans' association, and the other *Verbände* were to be wound up. The Social Democrats were offered seats in the government, but they declined to support Schleicher in any form.[2]

[1] Hilmar Ritter von Mittelberger, 'Lebenserinnerungen', p. 270: MS. in Bundesarchiv Koblenz. At that time he was a major-general, directly subordinate to Hammerstein.

[2] Bracher, op. cit., pp. 677–84; Papen's notes of 12 Nov. 1957: *Vierteljahrshefte für Zeitgeschichte*, vi, 1958, no. 7, p. 113.

Schleicher, however, was not discouraged and was still occupied with plans to ensure the co-operation of the National Socialists, while at the same time considering the possibility of a conflict with them. In mid-December he explained to the senior officers that, in the course of January 1933, the question had to be resolved whether the government had a firm majority; as soon as parliament assembled the National Socialists would be asked whether they co-operated or not; if not, the battle would be joined and parliament would be dissolved; in that battle the moral right was on the side of the government; it would not be fought with flea-bites—prohibitions for three days—but measures were to be taken such as the Nazis them-selves would take when in power; the reins would not be slackened, and no pardon would be given; the Nazis had no chance, but it was not in the interest of the state to destroy them; the aim remained to bring them to co-operation under Strasser, with Hitler's blessing; new attempts must be made to make them share in the responsibility.[1] These words were surprisingly opti-mistic, considering that all previous attempts had failed, and that Strasser had resigned and ceased to count as a political factor.

At the same conference Lieutenant-Colonel Ott spoke about the pre-military training and the reconciliation of the youth with the state. In this field 'very good progress' had been made, and the various *Verbände* were competing for the money given by the defence ministry for promoting the fitness of youngsters. The ideas and plans of Schleicher emerged clearly from Ott's further remarks: the educational policy of the German states must be 'redirected' towards the homeland and the state; in Prussia in particular there was an 'incredible' alienation of the youth from the state, and all 'heroism' was missing; a change of textbooks and lectures to 'inculcate the military spirit' were essential. It was also planned to introduce a voluntary work-service of six months—later to be extended to twelve—after which the participants should join labour units or undergo pre-military training. Farmers who could not afford paid labour should be aided by voluntary helpers. Unemployed youngsters should be grouped together in units and be given hot meals from public funds. Thus social measures would be combined with the

---

[1] Schleicher addressing the divisional and corps commanders, 13–15 Dec. 1932: ibid., ii, 1954, no. 6, p. 428 (notes by General Liebmann).

plans to promote the pre-military training and the labour service of Germany's youth. As no minister had yet been appointed for these tasks, Ott functioned as the 'chief of staff'. Other officers were active in the field of pre-military training, and Schleicher's special thanks were expressed to them.[1] All these were highly political tasks and aims; they show the great influence wielded by the army during Schleicher's chancellorship, an influence for which it would be difficult to find a parallel.

Schleicher realized that he had to find support for his government among the parties or trade unions; until he succeeded in doing so he would play them off against each other and thus paralyse their influence. The National Socialists in particular were suffering from grave financial difficulties, and were hardly able to restrain their followers. But one thing Schleicher did not envisage: that his enemies too—and there were many of them —could play the same game against him. Among these enemies one of the most prominent since 2 December was Franz von Papen—called 'Fränzchen' contemptuously by Schleicher. Papen sought his way back to power, and the only possible way was an alliance with Hitler. Thus Hitler and Papen met on 4 January 1933 in the house of the banker Kurt Freiherr von Schröder at Cologne. Papen proposed to Hitler an alliance between National Socialists, Conservatives, and German Nationalists, and a government that was to be led jointly by himself and Hitler. Hitler renewed his claim to the chancellorship: Papen's followers could join his government if they were willing to support his policy. On this basis agreement was reached. The next step was to overcome the opposition of Hindenburg to Hitler's becoming chancellor. On 22 January another meeting took place, this time in the house of Joachim von Ribbentrop at Dahlem near Berlin; Papen was accompanied by Colonel Oskar von Hindenburg and the president's under-secretary of state, Dr. Meißner. Three days later Oskar von Hindenburg again appeared in Dahlem and indicated that the chancellorship of Hitler within the framework of a 'new national front was not entirely hopeless'.[2] A *rapprochement* be-

---

[1] Ott addressing the divisional and corps commanders on 13–15 Dec. 1932: *Vierteljahrshefte für Zeitgeschichte*, ii, 1954, no. 6, pp. 429–30.

[2] Bracher, op. cit., pp. 692, 708–9, with quotations from notes by Kurt von Schröder and Joachim von Ribbentrop.

tween the House of Hindenburg and Hitler had begun, with Papen as the go-between.

These negotiations did not remain unknown to Schleicher. On 23 January he reported to Hindenburg; he admitted the failure of his plans to divide the National Socialists, and requested powers to dissolve parliament; no election was to be held for the time being, and the two extremist parties were to be dissolved. When the president reminded Schleicher of the events of 2 December and the fear of a general strike, Schleicher replied that meanwhile the situation had improved considerably: no general strike would take place, the Social Democrats and trade unions would tolerate a state of emergency, the Reichswehr could be augmented by volunteers and would thus be able to defeat the National Socialists—no opposition was to be expected from the western powers.[1] These conclusions were largely justified; but they came rather belatedly, for they equally applied to the situation at the beginning of December. Hindenburg, however, refused to grant the requested powers to Schleicher. He well remembered the means used to achieve the fall of Papen, and his sympathies were still with the chancellor whom Schleicher had overthrown. Papen had never evacuated the premises of the chancellor and thus had unlimited access to the old president whose palace was adjoining the chancellery.

If he had not gained any significant support among the parties and trade unions, Schleicher believed that at least he could rely completely on the army. Yet even this was no longer true. The group surrounding him was called by the younger officers the 'commendation club'; its members had promoted each other and were largely former guards officers.[2] But not all senior officers belonged to this club, and some of them were bitter enemies of Schleicher. One of them, Werner von Blomberg, the commanding officer of the First Division in East Prussia, was received by Hindenburg during the decisive days of January without Schleicher's knowledge. Through his close contacts with the Red Army Blomberg was strongly influenced by its example and sought for the Reichswehr, too, close links with the masses of the people. Two officers on his staff—Colonel von Reichenau and the divisional chaplain Müller—were enthusiastic followers of Hitler and influenced their general in

[1] Ibid., p. 710.   [2] Walter Görlitz in *Die Welt*, 26 Jan. 1963.

this direction. It is thus not surprising that Blomberg now strongly opposed Schleicher's plans and advocated a government of 'the national front' under Hitler as the solution most welcome to the army. In his opinion, the officer corps and the army would disintegrate in an armed clash with the *S.A.* and *S.S.* because the younger generation strongly sympathized with their 'national convictions'.[1]

Schleicher believed that his only possible successor as defence minister was Seeckt, who for a considerable time had pronounced in favour of Hitler, but who was disliked by Hindenburg. Now, however, Hitler and Papen found in Blomberg an active high-ranking officer who could be used for their plans and to whom not even Hindenburg could object. Thus Schleicher's position was not only threatened from outside—a danger against which he could take precautions—but also from inside his own bastion. The rift between the 'office generals' and the 'front' reappeared, with fatal consequences not only for Schleicher but also for the army. It can at least be doubted whether the president would have accepted the solution advocated by Papen, if Blomberg had not supported these plans and had not put himself at Hitler's disposal.[2] The incident also proved how weak the position of the chief of the army command had become. In earlier years it would have been impossible for the commanding officer of a division and his chief of staff[3] to follow their political schemes in Berlin without informing their chief. Above all, these schemes were directed not only against the policy of the chancellor and defence minister, but indirectly also against the policy of the chief of the army command, who was closely associated with Schleicher. Now it was not only the lieutenants who differed from the policy of the army command, but also some very senior officers.

IV. *The Reichswehr and the Seizure of Power*

On 26 January Schleicher once more approached Hindenburg and requested him to grant the desired emergency powers —but Hindenburg again refused to do so. On the same day the

---

[1] Bracher, op. cit., pp. 712–14; Vogelsang, op. cit., p. 375. For the causes of the enmity between Blomberg and Schleicher, see above, p. 301.

[2] Cf. Blomberg's remark of 3 Feb. 1933, below p. 394.

[3] Colonel von Reichenau: Bracher, op. cit., p. 713.

chief of the army's Personnel Office, Lieutenant-General Freiherr von dem Bussche-Ippenburg, made his weekly report to the president, and he was on this occasion accompanied by General Freiherr von Hammerstein. When the two generals entered the chamber the old field-marshal exclaimed: 'If the generals do not obey orders I shall dismiss the whole lot.' Hammerstein smilingly reassured Hindenburg that the Reichswehr stood unquestioningly behind him. But later Hammerstein mentioned his political worries, caused by the impending resignation of Schleicher as chancellor, for he naturally knew that Hindenburg refused to grant Schleicher any emergency powers.[1] What Hammerstein and Schleicher feared was a new Papen cabinet, which would again be opposed by all the political parties, with the sole exception of the German Nationalists, and hence would have a minute basis: 'the army then would have to defend this basis of 7 per cent. against 93 per cent. of the German nation', and this would be more than grave.[2] At the same time Hammerstein warned the president strongly against Hitler, for he feared that the army might become subject to the influence of the National Socialists and be induced to disobedience.[3] Again he thought of the danger that the army might be used to defend an unpopular government; otherwise the remark about inducing it to disobedience would not be understandable. Hindenburg reacted sharply and rejected any attempt at influencing him. At the end, however—perhaps to dispel Hammerstein's anxiety—he declared: 'You will not think it possible, gentlemen, that I should appoint this Austrian lance-corporal chancellor.'[4] It seems as if Hindenburg had not quite followed Hammerstein's arguments and reacted in this form to the mentioning of Hitler's name; for Hammerstein did not intend to prevent the appointment of Hitler, but that of Papen.[5] Apparently the generals knew very little about the real

---

[1] Notes by General Erich Freiherr von dem Bussche-Ippenburg of 1951: Zeugenschrifttum, no. 217, Institut für Zeitgeschichte (with the date of 27 Jan. 1933 for the report to Hindenburg).

[2] Notes by Hammerstein of 28 Jan. 1935: Bracher, op. cit., p. 733.

[3] von dem Bussche-Ippenburg to Kunrat von Hammerstein, 17 Feb. 1953: quoted by Bracher, op. cit., p. 717, n. 137.

[4] This remark of Hindenburg is reported by Hammerstein (notes of 28 Jan. 1935, ibid., p. 733) as well as Bussche-Ippenburg (letter of 17 Feb. 1953, ibid., p. 717, n. 137).

[5] Hammerstein's notes of 28 Jan. 1935, ibid., p. 733.

situation, the agreement between Hitler and Papen, and the participation of Oskar von Hindenburg and Dr. Meißner. The president's remark about the Austrian lance-corporal was not likely to dispel their anxiety.

A few days later, on the morning of 29 January, a discussion took place between Hammerstein and Schleicher, who had meanwhile resigned as chancellor but continued to function as such until the appointment of a successor.

We were both convinced [Hammerstein wrote later] that only Hitler was possible as the future chancellor. Any other choice would lead to a general strike, if not to civil war, and thus to a totally undesirable use of the army against the National Socialists as well as against the left. We considered whether we knew of any way to influence the situation to avoid this misfortune. The result of our considerations was negative. We saw no possibility of exercising any influence upon the president. Finally, I decided, in agreement with Schleicher, to seek a meeting with Hitler. . . .[1]

General von dem Bussche-Ippenburg also reports from memory that the generals discussed the situation, and what the army could do:

the danger of Hitler's nomination existed in spite of the declaration of the president two days before. Schleicher was very resigned and saw no alternative to a 'loyal' attitude towards the president. One of the generals (I do not remember whether Hammerstein or Adam) made the suggestion: 'truly, one ought to take measures against Hindenburg'. But this idea was rejected after a brief and quiet deliberation. All the generals present considered it out of the question to employ the Reichswehr in any form against its commander-in-chief. . . .[2]

That the idea of a possible resistance was discussed and rejected by the generals on the morning of 29 January seems certain. What is doubtful is whether this resistance was to be directed against the plan of reappointing Papen, which they considered likely, or against the appointment of Hitler. It seems probable that the former was the case, as Hammerstein reported only two years after the event. For months the army command

---

[1] Bracher, op. cit., p. 733.

[2] Notes by von dem Bussche-Ippenburg of 1951: Zeugenschrifttum, no. 217, Institut für Zeitgeschichte.

had tried to avoid a situation in which the army would have to defend a government which had no popular backing. On the other hand, it desired a participation of the National Socialists in the government. In August Schleicher had been willing to accept Hitler as chancellor and leading National Socialists as ministers. Certainly, he intended to remain minister of defence. But on 29 January he knew nothing of the possibility of being replaced by Blomberg. In general, it is surprising how badly the army command was informed during the decisive days. Therefore Hammerstein visited Hitler in the afternoon and asked him whether he believed that the negotiations between him and the presidential palace were serious or fictitious: if the latter were the case, he would once more try and influence the course of events, so as to prevent a serious misfortune.[1] This too indicates that the army command was far removed from considering resistance to the appointment of Hitler.

In spite of this, during the night of 29 to 20 January the wildest rumours began to circulate: the Potsdam garrison was marching on Berlin, Hindenburg and his closest advisers were to be arrested, the Reichswehr was intending to establish a military dictatorship. They were probably caused by the remark made to Hitler by a go-between of Schleicher and the National Socialists, Werner von Alvensleben: if the people of the Wilhelmstraße (the entourage of Hindenburg) were not negotiating seriously with him, the defence minister and the chief of the army command ought to alarm the Potsdam garrison and make a clean sweep in the Wilhelmstraße.[2] The element of truth in this was that in the evening of the 29th Alvensleben had visited Schleicher, and that he and Hammerstein had again mentioned their apprehensions that the negotiations were not meant seriously. The front of the army command was still directed against the possibility that the negotiations might *not* succeed; but even in that case resistance was not contemplated.

In the early morning of 30 January 1933 General von Blomberg arrived in Berlin from Geneva, where he had attended the Disarmament Conference. On the platform he was met by Oskar von Hindenburg and by Major Kuntzen, Hammerstein's adjutant. The latter instructed him in the name of the chief of the army command to report to the Bendlerstraße, while

[1] Hammerstein's notes of 28 Jan. 1935, Bracher, op. cit., p. 734.   [2] Ibid.

Oskar von Hindenburg brought an order from the president that he should come to see him. Blomberg chose to disregard the order of his military superior and went to the president—probably because of his old dislike of Schleicher and his plans, and a strong attachment to the field-marshal.[1] Apparently Blomberg and Hitler immediately reached an agreement—according to Blomberg's own remark as early as 8 a.m.—and that decided the issue of the formation of the new government. Only four days later Blomberg informed the senior officers: 'At the *formation of the cabinet* the question of the defence minister was the main issue. The entry of the Nazis into the government was decided when a general on the active list was willing to co-operate with Hitler (the other solution considered possible by Hitler, that a leading Nazi should become defence minister, seemed unacceptable to the president). After the Hitler–Blomberg agreement—Monday at 8 o'clock—the issue was decided and the oath was rendered at 11.30. . . .'[2] In fact Blomberg took the oath as defence minister earlier—even before Hitler and the other ministers; this indeed was for Hindenburg the most important point. In the new government of Hitler there were only two other National Socialists—Frick and Göring—'surrounded' by as many as nine Conservatives and German Nationalists.

Four days later Blomberg mentioned to the senior officers the 'frenzy of enthusiasm' (*Begeisterungsrausch*) which now engulfed Germany. In his opinion, the cabinet was an 'expression of the broad national will and the realization of what many of the best have aimed at for years. Admittedly, it only represents a minority of the nation, but a firmly formed minority counting millions, who are determined to live and, if need be, to die for their idea. Great possibilities result from this if the leading men possess a firm heart and a happy hand. . . .' About the policy of Schleicher Blomberg said that he had intended to prevent the use of the army against a general strike of the right and the left, to effect a conciliation between the National Socialists and the government, and to admit them to political responsibility; while Schleicher had succeeded in the first, he had failed in the

---

[1] Wheeler-Bennett, *Nemesis of Power*, p. 284; Bracher, op. cit., p. 726.

[2] Blomberg addressing the divisional and corps commanders on 3 Feb. 1933: *Vierteljahrshefte für Zeitgeschichte*, ii, 1954, no. 7, p. 433 (notes by General Liebmann).

second through no fault of his own, but now his aim had suddenly been achieved.[1] Blomberg was not the only senior officer who thought along these lines. The commander of the battleship *Hessen*, Captain Carls, wrote to Schleicher: '. . . what has been achieved now, the combination of all national forces towards a common effort of construction, has been the aim and work of *Herr General*. I believe that in the ever-changing game of politics there is no happier end than handing over to others the completed work. . . .'[2] General Hasse wrote much more sceptically: he could not form a picture of the ideas animating the president when he dismissed Schleicher, but he could not explain the events other than by 'vicious personal intrigues'; his conviction that Schleicher in the future would still remain 'the saviour of Germany from deep distress' was unshaken.[3]

A few weeks later, on 1 March, Blomberg went much further and informed the senior officers that there was '*one* party on the march. Consequently the attitude of remaining "above party" loses its meaning and there remains only one course: support without any reservation!' Colonel von Reichenau, who had succeeded Bredow as chief of the *Ministeramt*, was even more outspoken and declared on the same occasion: 'It is essential to recognize that we stand in the midst of a revolution. What is decayed in the state must fall, and this can only be done by using terror. The party wants to proceed mercilessly against Marxism. The task of the *Wehrmacht* is to stand at attention. . . .'[4] Reichenau was one of the few senior officers who recognized the revolutionary character of National Socialism and fully agreed with it; Hitler's 'seizure of power' was heartily welcomed by him, as he knew Hitler personally and succumbed to his personality.[5] Blomberg was strongly influenced by the younger Reichenau, who had been his chief of staff in East Prussia. Another senior officer who saluted the 'seizure of power' was

---

[1] Blomberg on 3 Feb. 1933: ibid., p. 432.

[2] Captain Carls to Schleicher, at sea, 9 Feb. 1933: Nachlaß Schleicher, no. 64, Bundesarchiv Koblenz.

[3] General Hasse to Schleicher, Berlin, 31 Jan. 1933: ibid.

[4] Blomberg and Reichenau on 1 Mar. 1933: H. Mommsen, 'Der Reichstagsbrand und seine politischen Folgen', *Vierteljahrshefte für Zeitgeschichte*, xii, 1964, p. 406, n. 222; Vogelsang, 'Hitlers Brief an Reichenau vom 4. Dezember 1932', ibid., vii, 1959, p. 433 (notes by General Ott, Zeugenschrifttum, no. 279, fo. 19).

[5] Foertsch, *Schuld und Verhängnis*, pp. 24, 32.

Colonel Ludwig Beck, who was to succeed General Adam as chief of the general staff and later became one of Hitler's most determined opponents.[1] Another officer of the general staff who fell under Hitler's spell was Colonel Keitel; in July he returned 'much impressed' from the meeting of *S.A.* leaders at Reichenhall; 'he had a conversation with Hitler . . . and was truly enthusiastic about him. His eyes were marvellous and how the man could talk. . . .'[2] Among the senior officers, however, Beck, Keitel, and Reichenau were the exceptions rather than the rule, at least for the time being.

It was different with the junior officers, where enthusiasm for Hitler was much more widespread. When on the evening of 30 January 1933 an enthusiastic crowd celebrated the victory of the 'national revolution' in the streets of Bamberg, a lieutenant of the Bavarian Cavalry Regiment 17 in full uniform put himself at the head of the procession. When his military superiors reprimanded him he submitted to their reproaches with composure, and told his comrades 'that the great soldiers of the time of the Wars of Liberation would have shown more sympathy with such a genuine rising of the people . . .'.[3] The name of the lieutenant was Claus Schenk Count von Stauffenberg, who, eleven years later, by his attempt on Hitler's life attempted to rid Germany of the tyrant. Among the pupils of the revived war academy, too, there were in 1933 many enthusiastic National Socialists, especially from Bavaria; the majority were sympathizers or indifferent, and only a small group was critical of Hitler.[4] In the navy too the 'seizure of power' was enthusiastically welcomed; in the autumn of 1933 a visitor found the mood there 'rather primitive and uncritical of Hitler'.[5] On 3 April Goebbels paid a visit to the officers' mess at Potsdam and addressed the officers. After the visit Hammerstein remarked resignedly 'that the lieutenants had accepted him [Goebbels] completely'.[6]

[1] Sauer, in *Die nationalsozialistische Machtergreifung*, p. 737.

[2] Frau Keitel to her mother, Helmscherode, 5 July 1933: Görlitz, *Generalfeldmarschall Keitel*, p. 53.

[3] Foertsch, op. cit., p. 22, on the basis of a report by Colonel Sauerbruch who served in the same regiment.

[4] Sauer, op. cit., p. 738, on the basis of a report by General Blumentritt.

[5] Ibid., p. 740; report of General Ott, Zeugenschrifttum, no. 279, Institut für Zeitgeschichte.

[6] Sauer, op. cit., p. 738.

At the beginning of June 1933 General von Blomberg once more emphasized the distance separating the army from the Weimar Republic and his devotion to the National Socialist movement. In his opinion, the fact that the army was not *gleichgeschaltet* was due to its having been 'non-political. Our being non-political never meant that we were in agreement with the system of the former governments; but it was a means to prevent our getting too involved in this system. . . . Now this being non-political is finished, and there remains only one thing: to serve the National Socialist movement with complete devotion. . . .'[1] The obvious warmth of these words was in striking contrast to the coldness with which the leading officers of the Reichswehr had always regarded the Weimar Republic. The vast possibilities of rearmament which now opened before their eyes were to win many more hearts for Hitler. One of those who remained sceptical was Schleicher, who at the end of of 1933 sent his Christmas greetings to Groener, with the remark that during the past year the name of the town of Potsdam 'had been used rather a lot because no breath of its spirit has been noticed . . .'.[2] The 'spirit of Potsdam' to which Hitler liked to refer so often was very different from the spirit which had permeated the Prussian army. When the murdered Schleicher was carried to his grave six months later, only two officers dared to follow the coffin: General von Hammerstein and an unknown lieutenant.

v. *The Reichswehr and Politics*

In the German Empire of 1871 the army and its officer corps enjoyed a prestige and an influence unparalleled in the other countries of that time. The officers clearly were the first Estate and had a particularly close relationship with the bearer of the crown. But in spite of their strongly conservative and loyalist views they were not directly concerned with politics. Politics played no part in their discussions, in their regimental training, and in the courses at the war academy. 'Only a very few gave any thought' to political matters, and this applied equally to

[1] Blomberg addressing the divisional and corps commanders on 1 June 1933: ibid., p. 730. Cf. Sauer's comment.

[2] Schleicher to Groener, Potsdam, 23 Dec. 1933: Nachlaß Groener, box 21, no. 224, Bundesarchiv-Militärarchiv.

the senior officers. They too, in the opinion of General Groener, 'were kept like blind men in a world which was inevitably political . . .'.[1] Even during the world war this did not change fundamentally, although Ludendorff, Groener, and a few other officers occupied highly political positions.

The events of 9 November 1918, however, brought a sudden and fundamental change. The military and political collapse and the outbreak of revolution undermined the foundations on which the existence and the corporate feeling of the officers rested. Not only the High Command, but every single officer was forced to take up a position towards the revolt of the sailors, the new Socialist government, the workers' and soldiers' councils, the decline of discipline in the army and navy, and the activities and propaganda of the radical left. The danger threatening from the extreme left and the necessity of organizing the return of the units from the front induced the High Command to con-clude an alliance with Friedrich Ebert, the chairman of the new government, which became the basis of its later policy and of the new state. This situation also brought about within the officer corps a strong *penchant* towards politics, as appeared in the conferences of staff officers as early as 16 and 20 December 1918. This was an inevitable development, as the officers were suddenly confronted with surroundings hostile to them, by attacks on everything that they held sacred. This enmity found its symbolical expression in tearing off the officers' epaulettes. The officer corps was bound to consider the revolution and its consequences as an attack upon itself and its whole world. It could only react to the revolution and the new order with strong opposition. That the officers in spite of this put themselves at the disposal of the new government was an event which had far-reaching consequences.

The revolutionary events also destroyed the unity of the officer corps. The strength of its position in the Empire rested above all on the fact that in all important questions it always acted in unison. On the fundamental issue—the attitude to be adopted to the new government and the new state—strong differences of opinion soon appeared among the officers, which led to the formation of groups and factions. The clearest example of these was the conflict between the leaders and

[1] Groener, *Lebenserinnerungen*, pp. 51, 59-60.

officers of the free corps and those of the army command, which finally erupted in the Kapp Putsch. Then it became evident that the Reichswehr was split from top to bottom: the chief of the *Gruppenkommando* 1, the commanding officer of the First Division, the chief of the naval command, and many other senior officers sided with the mutinous free corps. Groups of officers hostile to each other came into being earlier on the issue whether the Treaty of Versailles should be accepted or not, whether resistance to it would be possible at least in the east of Germany. A gulf opened between the new Prussian minister of war and later chief of the army command, General Reinhardt, who was willing to make concessions to the new state and its leaders, and other generals, such as Groener and Seeckt, who declined to make such concessions and aimed at securing the autonomy of the Reichswehr, its independence from all civilian influences and from parliamentary control. The result of the Kapp Putsch, and the election of Seeckt as the new head of the army by the assembled officers, was that the latter tendency triumphed. The officers, who during the Kapp Putsch adopted an attitude of *attentism* and declined to be drawn into the conflict between the free corps and the government, became the leading group that put its imprint on the Reichswehr. During the following period too it pursued a policy of *attentism*.

Yet this victory of Seeckt and his followers did not mean the end of politics in the army and of political groupings, nor did it terminate the constant interventions of the army command in political questions. Seeckt was a loyal follower of Groener, who in July 1919 coined the phrase: 'politics must be conducted by a few only—tenaciously and silently'. Seeckt was a highly political general, himself aimed at the highest political offices in the state, developed and pursued his own political line in foreign policy, negotiated independently with the emissaries of Soviet Russia, and rendered in the years after 1923 determined resistance to the official German foreign policy. Under Seeckt several senior officers—especially Hasse, Schleicher, and Stülpnagel—were active as his political advisers and executive organs. Seeckt stood at the height of his political influence when in 1923 the president transferred to him the exercise of executive powers, and when his political aim—the fall of the Stresemann government—was finally achieved. His steady undermining of the position of the chancellor during a most serious political crisis shows to what length he was willing to go in order to achieve his goal. When General von Lossow at Munich supported the separatist plans of the Bavarian government and attacked the Weimar Republic, he in truth followed the example set by his chief. That no civil war broke out in 1923 was the merit neither of Seeckt nor of the Reichswehr: it was due to the independent action taken by Hitler. At the decisive moment neither Seeckt nor Lossow was willing 'to take the plunge'; but this was certainly not on account of their loyalty to the republic and to the constitution which they had sworn to defend.

The negative attitude of Seeckt to the republic and parliamentarianism also applied to the Reichswehr as such. It remained loyal to the monarchy and its symbol, the black, white, and red colours, which it preserved in the form of the 'war flag'. It repudiated the black, red, and gold colours of the republic and its symbol, the German eagle. Service to the republic was replaced by service to the state, which became an abstract term. The officer felt bound to the fatherland and to the state as an idea, but he did not identify these with the existing democratic order.[1] Seeckt himself formulated this identity of Reichswehr and state in the sharpest and most arrogant form: 'The army shall not become a state within the state, but in serving the state merge with it and become the purest image of the state. . . . The army serves the state, and only the state, for it *is* the state.'[2] A much younger officer expressed this idea proudly: 'In *our* hands lies the state. We affirm that it has been linked to the life of our nation for thousands of years and has developed with it. Its face is our face. We are the bearers of the state!'[3] And another officer wrote later that it was the task of the soldier to preserve the *Reich*, 'a mythical term which embraced everything that has been called "the eternal Germany": nation, country, and state . . .'.[4] This fiction absolved the Reichswehr from clarifying its relations with the existing republic and its institutions, and

[1] Papke, 'Offizierkorps und Anciennität', *Beiträge zur Militär- und Kriegsgeschichte*, iv. 201.

[2] Hans von Seeckt, *Gedanken eines Soldaten*, Berlin, 1929, pp. 113, 116.

[3] Kurt Hesse, *Von der nahen Ära der 'Jungen Armee'*, Berlin, 1925, p. 40.

[4] von Manstein, *Aus einem Soldatenleben*, p. 55.

it included the claim that the army could renounce its services
to the republic if it should clash with the eternal values of the
nation as defined by the Reichswehr. But Seeckt erred when he
maintained that the army was not a state within the state. The
result of his building a 'Chinese wall' round the army, of the
rigid separation from all new ideas and from the political
parties, combined with its great political influence, was that
the Reichswehr did form a state within the state. General
Foertsch, who was then a junior officer, wrote that the views
animating the army were neither hostile nor friendly towards
democracy and parliamentarianism; 'they were impersonal,
operating in a vacuum, and turned the Reichswehr into a state
within the state, a state outside the existing state . . .'.[1] Groener
as minister of defence declared in 1929 that the Reichswehr
was the 'only power' and an 'element of power within the state
that no one can disregard'.[2]

Seeckt's policy was continued by his successors, especially by
Groener and Schleicher. This was accomplished easily because
Groener and Seeckt from 1919 shared the same political views,
and because Schleicher was already, under Seeckt, partly
responsible for the drafting and the carrying out of political
directives. It is true that Seeckt's successors—Heye as well as
Schleicher—steered a course of *rapprochement* with the republic
and its governments during the years of economic and political
stabilization up to 1929. But this did not cause a departure
from the basic political principles of Seeckt. There remained
the strong dislike of the Prussian government, which was led by
Social Democrats, the opposition to the Social Democrats who
were considered hostile to the interests of the army, and the
close collaboration with the *vaterländische Verbände*, above all the
Stahlhelm, in questions of frontier defence. It was precisely the
continuation of this co-operation which made it impossible to
improve relations with the Prussian authorities, in spite of all
official declarations; for the Social Democrats too considered it
necessary to take preventive measures to defend the frontiers
in case of a Polish attack, but they were naturally opposed to

[1] Foertsch, *Schuld und Verhängnis*, p. 15.
[2] Groener's notes for a speech to the Infantry School at Dresden on 17 Dec.
1929: Nachlaß Groener, no. 229, Bundesarchiv-Militärarchiv. Cf. Groener's
statement about the power of the Reichswehr in the autumn of 1930, above,
p. 328.

the arming and training of men who wanted to destroy the 'red Prussia'.

There was no solution for this problem. Since the German-Polish frontier battles of the years 1919–21, during which the army command had to rely on the free corps and other irregular formations, the protection of the eastern frontier remained one of the main problems facing the army, and its own forces were considered insufficient for the purpose. Thus the army command had to co-operate with the *Verbände* of the political right; the *Kreis* officers—who also played an important part in vetting recruits—were largely identical with the local leaders of the *Stahlhelm*, the *Pommerntreue*, and similar organizations which were hostile to the republic. It is true that the army command, after the dismissal of Seeckt, tried to get members of the *Reichsbanner* and other republican organizations admitted to the frontier defence units, but these attempts met with more or less open opposition from the local army officers and the leaders of these units. It proved impossible to separate the Reichswehr from the *Verbände*, whatever the army command might order. In addition, the officer corps fully agreed with the nationalist ideas and aims of the *Verbände* and was convinced that truly national views were only to be found on the political right. Equally, only these circles supported without any reservation Groener's and Schleicher's struggle against pacifism and 'cultural Bolshevism'. It is thus not surprising that the slight move towards the left of the years 1926–9 was followed by a much more determined move towards the right, as soon as the great economic crisis affected Germany.

The close military understanding with Soviet Russia was a further inheritance from the period of Seeckt; the German military schools there enabled the Reichswehr to train officers and to develop weapons which were considered 'vital' to its interests. In Germany, too, secret measures of rearmament were continued and led to a slow 'expansion' of the Reichswehr. Also continued was the system of political contacts, especially with 'national' and conservative groups and parties, which Schleicher had built up under Seeckt, the system of constant negotiations with their leaders and of intrigues behind the government's back. Just as, after the Kapp Putsch, the Fronde of the officers was directed against the minister of defence, Noske, to whom they owed so much, so Groener later attacked the minister of finance, Hilferding, and senior Prussian civil servants in the sharpest terms, because in his opinion they disregarded the 'interests' of the army and navy. In this field Schleicher, with his genius for political intrigue, was far more successful than Seeckt. Seeckt only promoted the fall of one government—that of Stresemann—but in later years failed to obtain the dismissal of Stresemann from the post of foreign minister. Schleicher, however, was the prime mover in the fall of three governments—those of Hermann Müller, Heinrich Brüning, and Franz von Papen—and in the appointment of their successors, not to mention the overthrow of the Prussian government of Otto Braun. The 'puerile carelessness' with which he selected Papen as the successor to Brüning[1] clearly indicates Schleicher's qualification for this role—as does the faulty arithmetic with which he attempted to prove his case.

The *kriegspiel*, which led to the fall of Papen only six months after his appointment, had a certain basis in reality: the old fear of the army command that the soldiers would one day have to fight against the majority of the nation: a repetition of the situation of the Kapp Putsch must be avoided at any price. Thus the officer corps became the prisoner of its own ideology. By their deep distrust of the *Reichsbanner* and the trade unions the officers were induced to reckon these organizations automatically among their enemies and to add the republican forces to the 'united front' of National Socialists and Communists. Its old enmity with Poland also induced the army command to assume the danger of a Polish attack upon East Prussia in the case of internal unrest in Germany, although the good understanding with Soviet Russia was to protect Germany against precisely this danger. Yet only a few weeks after the *kriegspiel* Schleicher was convinced that the *Reichsbanner* and the trade unions would support him if it came to a conflict with the National Socialists.

It has recently been said in defence of Schleicher that he was the only one among the leading politicians of the time who possessed a conception which offered a chance of success in opposing the National Socialists.[2] But in reality his conception

---

[1] Eschenburg, in *Vierteljahrshefte für Zeitgeschichte*, ix, 1961, p. 26.
[2] Paul Sethe, in *Die Zeit*, 3 Jan. 1964, p. 5. Eschenburg, op. cit., pp. 26–27, holds a different opinion.

only consisted in the often repeated idea that they should be 'tamed' and brought closer to the state and to political responsibility; the 'valuable youth' in the *S.A.* and *S.S.* should be weaned from their extremism. These ideas rested upon an illusion and showed a fundamental misunderstanding of the nature of National Socialism. In this respect too the officer corps became the prisoner of its own ideology. The nationalism so loudly proclaimed by Hitler induced the officers to believe that his nationalism was closely akin to their own, that—as Hammerstein put it—'apart from the speed' Hitler really had the same aims as the Reichswehr.[1] In addition, the officer corps, at least in its younger classes, was permeated with National Socialist ideas. If the army took strong measures against Hitler there was the danger of a new split. Thus Schleicher deserted his old friend and mentor Groener when he dissolved the *S.A.* and *S.S.*, and soon after, he forced Groener to resign as the minister of defence.

At the moment when Hitler threatened to seize power the army command still feared that Papen would be reappointed chancellor and, above all, that a gulf would then separate the army from the large majority of the nation. Hitler's chancellorship, on the other hand, brought with it the close links, if not with the whole nation, then at least with a very large part of it, the backing by the masses which was so important to the army. For this reason, General von Blomberg and Colonel von Reichenau opted for Hitler—against their own superior officers. As the factions in the army now not only separated the older from the younger officers, but also affected the highest ranks, the army command would have been unable to act even if it had wanted to. The Reichswehr stood behind Seeckt; it stood no longer behind Hammerstein and Schleicher. Not only the army command could engage in political intrigue, but other officers could do the same.

The actions of Groener, Seeckt, and Schleicher demonstrated the grave dangers which threatened the young and weak republic from political generals. The republic needed the army against attempts at revolution from within and attacks by Polish irregular forces from without, and the army was led by the officer corps of the Imperial army. This original defect could

[1] See above, p. 333.

not be eliminated later. No one could expect the officers to welcome the new order or to become converts to it. But, as the example of General Reinhardt showed, there were officers willing to co-operate loyally with the new government and to form a republican army. It was the tragedy of the Weimar Republic that this attempt broke down so quickly and that the restorative forces triumphed so completely in the army and navy. If the republic after 1930 had possessed an army entirely loyal to it, the great crisis would have taken a different course. A Reichswehr which in the hour of peril would have co-operated with the Prussian police and the republican organizations, instead of intriguing against them, could have been the rock on which the waves broke. But the policy of the army command prevented such a co-operation and led to a weakening of the republic and of the organizations willing to defend it. In so doing, however, the army command also undermined the foundations of its own power. The position it had acquired could only be held while the government remained weak. If a really strong government supplanted it, the autonomy of the Reichswehr would come to an end, and with it the strong influence which it wielded in the political sphere.

BIBLIOGRAPHY

A. UNPUBLISHED SOURCES

Admiralty, London

Admiralität, Marine-Kommandoamt, Flotten-Abteilung, Marinepolitische Angelegenheiten, November 1929–June 1940: PG 33 611.

Reichswehrministerium, Marineleitung, Auslandsberichte: PG 48 898.

Reichswehrministerium, Marineleitung, Akten betr. Rußland: 1 SKL Ic–4, Band 1: PG 33 617.

Kommando Kreuzer '*Königsberg*', Innerpolitische Angelegenheiten: PG 34 427.

Auswärtiges Amt (microfilms)

Büro des Staatssekretärs von Schubert, 58/4, 'Landesverteidigung': 4565 H.

Büro des Staatssekretärs von Schubert, Akten betr. Militärische Angelegenheiten mit Rußland: 4564/1–4564/4 (5 vols.).

VON DIRKSEN, Russische Militärangelegenheiten, ab 17.XI.1928: 9480 H.

Handakten von Herrn Min.-Dir. von Dirksen: 9481 H.

Nachlaß Ulrich Graf von Brockdorff-Rantzau: 9101 H/I—H/XII.

Nachlaß Stresemann, vol. 97 and 302: 7404 H and 7155 H.

Akten betr. Politische Schriftstücke aus dem Nachlaß des Reichskanzlers bzw. Reichsministers Gustav Stresemann, vols. 1, 5, and 8: 3241 Pr. 9, 13, and 16.

Bundesarchiv Koblenz

Reichskanzlei, Akten betr. Landesverteidigung, vol. 1: R 43 I 725.

Akten betr. Oberste Heeresleitung und Heerführer: R 43 I 702.

Akten betr. Organisation Escherich (Orgesch), Organisation Consul, Wehrwolf, Stahlhelm u. a. Rechtsverbände, vols. 1–3: 2731–2733.

Akten betr. Reichsbanner Schwarz-Rot-Gold, vol. 1: R 43 I 767.

Akten betr. Reichsmarine, vol. 1: R 43 I 601.

Akten betr. Reichswehr, Volkswehr und Wehrpflicht, vols. 1–7: R 43 I 682–688.

Akten betr. Reichswehrgesetz, vol. 1: R 43 I 609.

Akten betr. Stahlhelm Bund der Frontsoldaten, vols. 1–2: K 2307/ K 647375–647956.

Akten betr. die Untersuchung der von Kapitän z. S. Lohmann getätigten wirtschaftlichen Unternehmungen, vol. 1: R 43 I 603.

Nachlaß Hermann Dietrich, no. 356, 'Wehrmachtangelegenheiten'.

Nachlaß Otto Geßler, nos. 17, 18, 19, 46, 55.

Nachlaß Wolfgang Mentzel, nos. 3, 4, 5, 9.

Nachlaß Hilmar Ritter von Mittelberger, 'Lebenserinnerungen'.

Nachlaß Kurt von Schleicher.

Bundesarchiv-Militärarchiv

Akten des Heereswaffenamtes: WiIF 5/126, 422, 499, 501, 507, 509, 511, 512, 518, 1344, 1983, 2222, 2235, 2526, 2544, 2546, 2549, 2720, 2822, 3179.

Sammelheft zu Chef PA Nr. 675.33 PA (2) vom 30.3.33.

Verwaltungsbuch Nr. 134: Rabenau, *Seeckt — Aus seinem Leben*, with marginal notes by General von Hammerstein.

WERNER VON BLOMBERG, 'Erinnerungen bis 1933. III' (written in 1943).

Sammlung Oberst Dieter von Kleist, with reports on *Grenzschutz Ost*.

Nachlaß Generalmajor Ferdinand von Bredow.

Nachlaß Wolfgang Fleck.

Nachlaß Generaloberst Werner Freiherr von Fritsch: H 08–33/1.

Nachlaß Wilhelm Groener.

Nachlaß Wilhelm Heye: H 08-18/4 and 7.

Nachlaß Friedrich Hoßbach: H 08-24/4.

Nachlaß Generalleutnant Arnold Lequis.

Nachlaß Oskar Ritter von Niedermayer.

Nachlaß Joachim von Stülpnagel: H 08-5/20—H 08-5/26.

JOACHIM VON STÜLPNAGEL, '75 Jahre meines Lebens', Düsseldorf, 1960: H 08-5/27.

Deutsches Zentralarchiv, Potsdam

Büro des Reichspräsidenten, vols. 761–3, Reichswehr, Politische Angelegenheiten.

61 Stahlhelm 1, vols. 98, 112, 264, 276, 296, 297.

Gärtringen

Nachlaß Graf Kuno Westarp.

Hauptstaatsarchiv Stuttgart

Nachlaß des Generalleutnants Eugen Hahn, nos. 27 and 52.

Nachlaß Walther Reinhardt.

Institut für Zeitgeschichte, Munich

Akten des Reichswehrministeriums, rolls 28, 34, 52 (microfilms).

Briefe des Generalmajors Helmuth Stieff: 1223/53.

Nachlaß Seeckt, rolls 18, 19, 20, 21, 24, 26, 28 i–iii (microfilms).

Zeugenschrifttum, no. 37: General a. D. Hermann Foertsch.

Zeugenschrifttum, no. 44: Oberst i. G. Franz von Gaertner.

Zeugenschrifttum, no. 217: General a. D. Erich Freiherr von dem Bussche-Ippenburg.

Zeugenschrifttum, no. 276: General a. D. Ferdinand Noeldechen.

Zeugenschrifttum, no. 279: Generalmajor a. D. Eugen Ott.

Zeugenschrifttum, no. 364: Admiral a. D. Leopold Bürkner.

Zeugenschrifttum, no. 680: General a. D. Leo Freiherr Geyr von Schweppenburg.

Zeugenschrifttum, no. 1739: Admiral a. D. Wilhelm Meisel.

Zeugenschrifttum, no. 1785: Konteradmiral a. D. Siegfried Sorge.

Kriegsarchiv, Munich

Akten des Gruppenkommandos 4, Bund 1, 2, 7, 11, 13, 14, 16.
Akten der Bayerischen Landespolizei Bamberg, Bund 12, Akt 3.
Stahlhelm-Akten, vol. 78 i.

Marine

Reports by several senior naval officers in the possession of Dr. Walter Baum.

Militärgeschichtliches Forschungsamt, Freiburg

Nachlaß Hans von Seeckt.
Admiralität, Marine-Kommandoamt, Flotten-Abteilung, Allgemeines: 7895 A Ia I.
Admiralität, Marine-Kommandoamt, Flotten-Abteilung, Belagerungszustand: 7896 A IIa 236.
Admiralität, Marine-Kommandoamt, Flotten-Abteilung, Marinepolitische Angelegenheiten: 7897 A Ic 1–1.
Admiralität, Marine-Kommandoamt, Flotten-Abteilung, Organisatorische Fragen: PG 34 057 A Ia–V.
Archiv der Marine, Handakten 'Raeder', Paket 7813: PG 33 951 b.
Flottenkommando, Akten betr. Innenpolitisches: PG 34 464 G 9b.
Reichswehrministerium, Marineleitung, M I: PG 48 896.
Reichswehrministerium, Marineleitung, Akten betr. Heeresangelegenheiten: 7895 A Ia XXV.
Reichswehrministerium, Marineleitung, Akten betr. Spanien: PG 48 903 M (Sp).
Reichswehrministerium, Marineleitung, Verschiedenes: 7897 M I.
Reichswehrministerium, Marineleitung, Verschiedenes: PG 34 165/2 A I–III.
Reichswehrministerium, Marineleitung, Vorträge Chef W bei Chef M. L.: 7813.
Reichswehrministerium, Marineleitung, Zusammenstellung von Reichstagsbeschwerden: 7814.
Reichswehrministerium, Marineleitung, Abteilung B, Chef des Stabes (BZ), Verschiedenes: PG 34 427 X, PG 34 428 XI.
Reichswehrministerium (Heer), Jn 1 Geh. Kdos. Allgemein 1930: II H 226.
Reichswehrministerium (Heer), Truppenamt, Akten betr. Innere Unruhen I, Hauptakte: II H 611.

B. PUBLISHED SOURCES

BRAMMER, KARL, *Verfassungsgrundlagen und Hochverrat*, Berlin, 1922.
CARSTEN, F. L., 'Reports by two German Officers on the Red Army', *The Slavonic and East European Review*, xli, 1962, pp. 217–44.
CONZE, WERNER, 'Dokumentation zum Sturz Brünings', *Vierteljahrshefte für Zeitgeschichte*, i, 1953, pp. 261–88.
DEUERLEIN, ERNST, *Der Hitler-Putsch*, Stuttgart, 1962.

EPSTEIN, JULIUS, 'Der Seeckt-Plan', *Der Monat*, no. 2, Nov. 1948.

ERNST, FRITZ, *Aus dem Nachlaß des Generals Walther Reinhardt*, Stuttgart, 1958.

FOERSTER, WOLFGANG, *Ein General kämpft gegen den Krieg—Aus nachgelassenen Papieren des Generalstabchefs Ludwig Beck*, Munich, 1949.

GÖRLITZ, WALTER, *Generalfeldmarschall Keitel—Verbrecher oder Offizier?* Göttingen, 1961.

KESSLER, HARRY GRAF, *Tagebücher 1918–1937*, Frankfurt, 1961.

PHELPS, REGINALD H., 'Aus den Seeckt-Dokumenten', *Deutsche Rundschau*, lxxviii, nos. 9–10, Sept.–Oct. 1952, pp. 881–91, 1013–23.

PÜNDER, HERMANN, *Politik in der Reichskanzlei*, Stuttgart, 1961.

ROTHFELS, HANS, 'Ausgewählte Briefe von Generalmajor Helmuth Stieff', *Vierteljahrshefte für Zeitgeschichte*, ii, 1954, pp. 291–305.

SCHÜDDEKOPF, OTTO-ERNST, *Das Heer und die Republik—Quellen zur Politik der Reichswehrführung 1918 bis 1933*, Hanover and Frankfurt, 1955.

STRESEMANN, GUSTAV, *Vermächtnis*, ed. Henry Bernhard, i, Berlin, 1932.

Trial of the Major War Criminals before the International Military Tribunal, xiii, xiv, xxxiv, Nuremberg, 1948–9.

VOGELSANG, THILO, 'Neue Dokumente zur Geschichte der Reichswehr 1930–1933', *Vierteljahrshefte für Zeitgeschichte*, ii, 1954, pp. 397–436.

—— 'Die Reichswehr in Bayern und der Münchner Putsch 1923', ibid. v, 1957, pp. 91–101.

—— 'Zur Politik Schleichers gegenüber der NSDAP 1932', ibid. vi, 1958, pp. 86–118.

—— 'Hitlers Brief an Reichenau vom 4. Dezember 1932', ibid. vii, 1959, pp. 429–37.

WOODWARD, E. L., and BUTLER, ROHAN, *Documents on British Foreign Policy 1919–1939*, Second Series, i, London, 1946.

C. MEMOIRS

D'ABERNON, Lord, *An Ambassador of Peace*, ii, London, 1929.

FABER DU FAUR, MORIZ VON, *Macht und Ohnmacht*, Stuttgart, 1953.

GESSLER, OTTO, *Reichswehrpolitik in der Weimarer Zeit*, ed. Kurt Sendtner, Stuttgart, 1958.

GEYR VON SCHWEPPENBURG, LEO FREIHERR VON, *Gebrochenes Schwert*, 2nd ed., Berlin, 1952.

GROENER, WILHELM, *Lebenserinnerungen*, ed. Friedrich Freiherr Hiller von Gaertringen, Göttingen, 1957.

LÜTTWITZ, WALTHER FREIHERR VON, *Im Kampf gegen die November-Revolution*, Berlin, 1934.

MAERCKER, GEORG, *Vom Kaiserheer zur Reichswehr*, Leipzig, 1921.

MANSTEIN, ERICH VON, *Aus einem Soldatenleben 1887–1939*, Bonn, 1958.

MEINECKE, FRIEDRICH, *Die deutsche Katastrophe*, Wiesbaden, 1946.

NOSKE, GUSTAV, *Von Kiel bis Kapp*, Berlin, 1920.

—— *Aufstieg und Niedergang der deutschen Sozialdemokratie*, Zürich, 1947.

RAEDER, ERICH, *Mein Leben*, i, Tübingen, 1956; ii, Tübingen, 1957.

SCHERINGER, RICHARD, *Das große Los unter Soldaten, Bauern und Rebellen*, Hamburg, 1959.

SEECKT, HANS VON, *Aus meinem Leben 1866–1917*, Leipzig, 1938.
SEVERING, CARL, *1919/1920 im Wetter- und Watterwinkel*, Bielefeld, 1927.
TESKE, HERMANN, *Die silbernen Spiegel*, Heidelberg, 1952.
WINNIG, AUGUST, *Heimkehr*, Hamburg, 1935.

D. SECONDARY AUTHORITIES

ABSHAGEN, KARL HEINZ, *Canaris—Patriot und Weltbürger*, Stuttgart, 1949.
BAUM, WALTER, 'Marine, Nationalsozialismus und Widerstand', *Vierteljahrshefte für Zeitgeschichte*, xi, 1963, pp. 16–48.
BENOIST-MÉCHIN, *Histoire de l'armée allemande*, i, Paris, 1936; ii, Paris, 1938.
BLACK, HANS, 'Die Grundzüge der Beförderungsordnungen', *Beiträge zur Militär- und Kriegsgeschichte*, iv, Stuttgart, 1962, pp. 65 ff.
BRACHER, KARL DIETRICH, *Die Auflösung der Weimarer Republik*, Stuttgart and Düsseldorf, 1955.
CARO, KURT, and OEHME, WALTER, *Schleichers Aufstieg*, Berlin, 1933.
CARR, EDWARD HALLETT, *The Bolshevik Revolution 1917–1923*, iii, London, 1953.
—— *German-Soviet Relations between the two World Wars*, Baltimore, 1951.
CRAIG, GORDON A., 'Reichswehr and National Socialism—The Policy of Wilhelm Groener', *Political Science Quarterly*, lxiii, 1948, pp. 194–229.
DEIST, WILHELM, 'Schleicher und die deutsche Abrüstungspolitik im Juni/Juli 1932', *Vierteljahrshefte für Zeitgeschichte*, vii, 1959, pp, 163–76.
DEMETER, KARL, *Das deutsche Offizierkorps in Gesellschaft und Staat 1650–1945*, Frankfurt, 1962.
Die Wirren in der Reichshauptstadt und im nördlichen Deutschland 1918–1920, Darstellungen aus den Nachkriegskämpfen deutscher Truppen und Freikorps, vi, Berlin, 1940.
ERFURTH, WALDEMAR, *Die Geschichte des deutschen Generalstabes von 1918 bis 1945*, Göttingen, 1957.
ESCHENBURG, THEODOR, 'Die Rolle der Persönlichkeit in der Krise der Weimarer Republik—Hindenburg, Brüning, Groener, Schleicher', *Vierteljahrshefte für Zeitgeschichte*, ix, 1961, pp. 1–29.
FOERTSCH, HERMANN, *Schuld und Verhängnis*, Stuttgart, 1951.
GATZKE, HANS W., *Stresemann and the Rearmament of Germany*, Baltimore, 1954.
—— 'Russo-German Military Collaboration during the Weimar Republic', *American Historical Review*, lxiii, 1958, pp. 565–97.
GORDON, HAROLD J., *The Reichswehr and the German Republic 1919–1926*, Princeton, 1957.
GÖRLITZ, WALTER, *Der deutsche Generalstab 1657–1945*, Frankfurt, 1950.
—— 'Griff in die Geschichte', *Die Welt*, 26 Jan. 1963.
GROENER-GEYER, DOROTHEA, *General Groener, Soldat und Staatsmann*, Frankfurt, 1955.
HAAS, LUDWIG, 'Der Kampf um die Reichswehr', *Deutsche Republik*, i, 1926–7.
HALLGARTEN, GEORGE W. F., 'General Hans von Seeckt and Russia 1920–1922', *Journal of Modern History*, xxi, 1949, pp. 28–34.
HELBIG, HERBERT, *Die Träger der Rapallo-Politik*, Göttingen, 1958.

HERZFELD, HANS, *Das Problem des deutschen Heeres 1919–1945*, Schloß Laupheim, Württemberg, s.a.

HESSE, KURT, *Von der nahen Ära der 'Jungen Armee'*, Berlin, 1925.

HILGER, GUSTAV, and MEYER, ALFRED G., *The Incompatible Allies*, New York, 1953.

HOFMANN, HANNS HUBERT, *Der Hitlerputsch*, Munich, 1961.

MARCKS, ERICH, 'Das Reichsheer 1919 bis 1934', in Linnebach, Karl, *Heeresgeschichte*, Hamburg, 1935.

MEIER-WELCKER, HANS, 'Die Stellung des Chefs der Heeresleitung in den Anfängen der Republik', *Vierteljahrshefte für Zeitgeschichte*, iv, 1956, pp. 145–60.

MOMMSEN, HANS, 'Der Reichstagsbrand und seine politischen Folgen', *Vierteljahrshefte für Zeitgeschichte*, xii, 1964, pp. 352–413.

MÜLLER, RICHARD, *Vom Kaiserreich zur Republik*, ii, Vienna, 1925.

PAPKE, GERHARD, 'Offizierkorps und Anciennität', *Beiträge zur Militär- und Kriegsgeschichte*, iv, Stuttgart, 1962, pp. 177 ff.

RABENAU, FRIEDRICH VON, *Seeckt—Aus seinem Leben 1918–1936*, Leipzig, 1940.

REINHARDT, WALTHER, *Wehrkraft und Wehrwille*, Berlin, 1932.

ROSENBERG, ARTHUR, *Geschichte der Deutschen Republik*, Karlsbad, 1935.

ROSINSKI, HERBERT, *The German Army*, London, 1939.

SAUER, WOLFGANG, 'Das Bündnis Ebers-Groener', unpublished Ph.D. thesis, Berlin, 1956.

—— 'Die Reichswehr', in Bracher, *Die Auflösung der Weimarer Republik*, Stuttgart and Düsseldorf, 1955, pp. 229–84.

—— 'Die Mobilmachung der Gewalt', in *Die nationalsozialistische Machtergreifung*, Cologne and Opladen, 1960, pp. 683 ff.

SCHMIDT-RICHBERG, WIEGAND, 'Die Generalstäbe in Deutschland 1871–1945', *Beiträge zur Militär- und Kriegsgeschichte*, iii, Stuttgart, 1962, pp. 11 ff.

SCHÜDDEKOPF, OTTO-ERNST, 'Karl Radek in Berlin', *Archiv für Sozialgeschichte*, ii, 1962, pp. 87–166.

SCHÜTZLE, KURT, *Reichswehr wider die Nation (1929–1933)*, Berlin, 1963.

SEECKT, HANS VON, *Gedanken eines Soldaten*, Berlin, 1929.

SPEIDEL, HELM, 'Reichswehr und Rote Armee', *Vierteljahrshefte für Zeitgeschichte*, i, 1953, pp. 9–45.

STRÖBEL, HEINRICH, *Die deutsche Revolution*, Berlin, 1920.

TESKE, HERMANN, 'Analyse eines Reichswehr-Regiments', *Wehrwissenschaftliche Rundschau*, xii, 1962, pp. 252–69.

TURNER, HENRY ASHBY, *Stresemann and the Politics of the Weimar Republic*, Princeton, 1963.

VOGELSANG, *Reichswehr, Staat und NSDAP*, Stuttgart, 1962.

VÖLKER, KARL-HEINZ, 'Die Entwicklung der militärischen Luftfahrt in Deutschland 1920–1933', *Beiträge zur Militär- und Kriegsgeschichte*, iii, Stuttgart, 1962, pp. 121 ff.

VOLKMANN, E. O., *Revolution über Deutschland*, Oldenburg, 1930.

WHEELER-BENNETT, JOHN W., *The Nemesis of Power—The German Army in Politics, 1918–1945*, London, 1954.

INDEX

Adam, Wilhelm, lieutenant-general, 360, 392, 396.

Aeroplanes, 51, 155, 237, 273, 282, 287, 356.

— manufacture of, 50, 135–8, 141, 143, 146, 234, 245, 255, 358–9, 362–3.

Agrarian League (*Landbund*), 150–1, 172, 365.

Ahrens, colonel of police, 78.

Air Academy, Russian, 360.

Air force, nucleus of, 148–9, 220–2, 237, 244–5, 273–4, 276, 358–9, 363.

Albatros works, 135, 138.

Albert (German People's Party), 188.

Alvensleben, Werner von, 393.

Amsberg, Joachim von, lieutenant-general, 269.

Annaberg, battle of, 149.

Anti-aircraft batteries, 273.

— guns, 273, 356–7.

Anti-Semitism, 31, 85, 98, 131–2, 176, 203, 240–1, 324.

Anti-Socialist laws, 339.

Anti-tank gun, anti-tank vehicle, 282–3, 357.

Apoga, teacher at the Russian War Academy, 280.

Arbeitsgemeinschaften, Arbeitskommandos (of the dissolved free corps), 148, 150, 158–9, 168.

Argentine, 234, 244.

Armistice, November 1918, 5–6, 62, 63.

Army budget, 275, 292, 356.

Audit Office (*Rechnungshof*), 274–5.

Austria, 4, 125, 199, 210, 234.

— army of, 256, 258.

Auswärtiges Amt, 356.

— and Russian policy of Reichswehr, 275–9.

— Seeckt and, 104, 115–16.

Baden, state, 191.

Baltic area, 23, 66, 147.

— evacuation of, 64.

— ports, 143, 361, 362.

— sea, 238, 266, 362.

— states, 64, 67, 147.

— station of the navy, 63, 288.

Baranov, P. I., Russian general, 282.

Battle cruisers, building of, 282, 288, 292–3, and n. 2, 307, 314.

Bauer, Gustav (Social Democrat), 43, 78, 81, 89.

Bauer, Max, colonel, 77.

Bavaria, state, 38, 40, 49 n. 1, 130, 180, 191, 196, 258, 330, 367, 396.

— government of, 130, 153–4, 160–1, 166, 174–7, 179, 182, 400.

Bavarian police, 177, 194–5.

— Reichswehr, 38, 97, 109–10, 124–8, 129–30, 174–9, 182, 185–7, 194.

— Separatists, 153, 177, 186, 193, 400.

Bayern und Reich (para-military organization), 178.

Beck, Ludwig, major, later colonel, 9, 310–11, 396.

Behncke, Paul, admiral, 119, 238, 242.

Belgium, 154, 240, 359.

Below, Otto von, general, 39–41, 43.

Berendt, Richard von, general, 170, 172, 175.

Bergmann, Walter von, general, 86.

Berliner Lokalanzeiger (right-wing newspaper), 257.

Berliner Tageblatt (democratic newspaper), 31, 288.

Bermondt-Avalov, prince, 64, 67.

Bernstorff, Count Johann Heinrich, 31, 115.

Bernuth, Robert von, general, 91.

Bersol (German-Russian company), 143.

Bethmann Hollweg, Theobald von, 106.

Bismarck, Otto von, 67.

'Black' funds of army, 224, 274–5.

'Black Reichswehr', 159, 168–9, 315.

Black, red, and gold colours (flag), 58–60, 124–5, 128, 203, 219, 261–2, 295–6, 400.

Black, white, and red colours (flag), 59–61, 63, 98, 124–5, 128, 178, 205, 218–19, 260–2, 295, 354, 400.

Blaskowitz, Johannes, colonel, 375.

Blohm & Voß, Hamburg, 135, 243.

Blomberg, Werner von, colonel, later general, 106, 213–14.

— chief of the *Truppenamt*, 263, 268,

Blomberg (cont.)
272, 277–80, 300–1, 325–6, 360.
— in Russia, 281–2, 381, 389.
— in East Prussia, 301–2, 366, 389–90, 404.
— minister of defence, 393–5, 397.
Blücher, W. K., Russian general, 282.
Blücher (para-military organization), 178.
Bock, Fedor von, major, later colonel, general, 79, 158, 168–9, 172, 342–4.
Bohemia, 3.
Bolshevism, see Soviet Russia.
— cultural, 294, 402.
— danger in Germany, 45, 60, 73, 85, 88, 91, 124, 311, 323, 377.
Bonin, von, lieutenant-colonel, 258–9, 260, 271.
Borne, von dem, general, 45.
Braun, Johann Ritter und Edler von, general, 29, 56.
Braun, Magnus Freiherr von, 382–3.
Braun, Otto (Social Democrat), 119, 254, 268, 330, 343, 364, 403.
Bredow, Ferdinand von, major, later colonel, 269, 359, 366–7, 370–1, 373, 381, 386, 395.
Breslauer Volkswacht (Social Democratic newspaper), 256.
Brest-Litovsk, Treaty of, 4.
Briand, Aristide, 304, 359.
Briesen, von, major, 352.
Britain, 67, 69, 136, 275, 291.
— and Germany, 138, 199, 207, 235–6, 240, 360.
— policy of, 66–68, 199, 240, 277, 359.
— espionage, 245, 359.
— Foreign Office, 360.
— War Office, 359–60.
British army, 3.
— navy, 241, 245, 361.
Brockdorff-Ahlefeldt, Count Erich, captain, 225.
Brockdorff-Rantzau, Count Ulrich, 71, 115, 139, 141–2, 208.
— at Versailles 1919, 37–38.
— ambassador in Moscow, 115, 138, 144–7, 232–3, 279.
Brüning, Dr. Heinrich (Centre), 294, 324, 327–9, 340, 342–5, 347–8, 360.
— Schleicher and, 307–8, 329, 331, 335, 338, 365, 403.
— fall of, 348–50, 364, 368, 373–6, 403.
Brunswick, state, 194.

Buchrucker, Ernst, major, 150, 158–9, 168.
Budget, of army and navy, 275, 292, 356.
Bulgaria, 5.
Bussche-Ippenburg, Erich Freiherr von dem, colonel, later general, 263–4, 274, 298–9, 391–2.

Cadet schools, 50, 104.
Canaris, Walther Wilhelm, naval lieutenant, later captain, 83, 242.
Carls, Rolf, naval captain, 367–8, 395.
Caspar works, Travemünde, 245, 362.
Centre Party, 43, 124, 154, 190, 258, 290, 304, 306–7, 332, 364, 369, 382.
Chicherin, Georgi V., 137, 139, 144, 238.
Chief of the army command, creation of office, 53–55.
— influence of, 66, 206, 297–9, 386, 390, 404.
— position of, 58, 92, 108, 111, 123–4, 208–9, 297–8.
Chile, 234.
Claß, Justizrat Heinrich (Pan-German), 166.
Coat of Arms of German Republic, 125, 128, 400.
Cockade, black, white, and red, 60, 125–6, 128, 176.
— new, 125–8, 183.
— white and blue, 128.
Communism, 181, 292, 309, 314, 319, 323, 361; see also, Soviet Russia.
Communist International, 71, 147.
— Party of Germany (K.P.D.), 42, 61, 139, 203, 261, 270, 277, 293, 305, 309, 317–19, 323, 326–7, 370–1.
— activities in 1921, 132.
— activities in 1923, 147, 153, 163, 180, 193–4.
— activities in 1932, 340, 377–80, 382, 403.
— Party of the Soviet Union, 277.
Constitution of 11 August 1919, 48–49, 58–59, 84, 124, 162, 219–20, 312, 321, 343, 400.
— Article 48 of, 158, 166, 187, 196, 307, 329, 368, 385.
— celebration of, 59, 120.
— Groener and, 34–35, 37, 44, 191, 291–2, 317.
— protection of, 95, 96, 108, 164, 288–9.

Constitution (*cont.*)
— Schleicher and, 37, 190, 369, 376.
— Seeckt and, 95, 117, 120, 167, 181, 187, 198, 369.
Control Commission, Inter-Allied Military, 51, 148, 200, 210–11, 222–3, 245, 359.
Cuno, Wilhelm, 144–5, 154, 156, 158, 163.
Curtius, Julius (German People's Party), 331.
Czechoslovakia, 137, 240, 353, 356.

d'Abernon, Viscount Edgar Vincent, 103–4, 115.
Daimler works, building of tanks by, 273, 357.
Danner, Jakob Ritter von, colonel, later general, 126, 183.
Danzig, Polish plans against, 362.
Dassel, Johannes von, general, 91, 93–94.
Dawes Plan, 201–2.
Democratic Party (D.D.P.), 258, 264, 270–1.
de Neufville, captain, 63.
Denikin, A., White Russian general, 67–68.
Denmark, 3, 238.
Dernburg, Bernhard, 31.
Deutschvölkische Freiheitspartei, 156; see also *Völkisch*.
Disarmament, 130, 199.
— negotiations, 356, 393.
Dualism between Reich and Prussia, 37, 44, 167, 191, 330, 369, 376, 385.
Duesterberg, Theodor (*Stahlhelm* leader), 321, 331, 336, 338 n. 1.
Düppel, battle of, 3.

East Prussia, 27, 38, 43, 62, 84, 93, 149, 200, 253, 271, 348, 389, 395.
— defence of, 147, 149, 267–8, 271–2, 352, 362, 379, 381, 403.
Ebert Friedrich (Social Democrat), 7, 10, 26, 71, 214, 249, 291.
— alliance with Groener, 11–15, 19–23, 290, 398.
— and Groener, 27, 34, 44, 47, 52, 54, 56–57.
— and Seeckt, 31, 95, 104, 115, 151, 170, 181, 188–9, 197–8, 206.
— commander-in-chief of the Reichswehr, 32, 49, 111, 115, 142, 181, 206.
— and army officers, 46, 61, 76–77.

Ebert Friedrich (*cont.*)
— during Kapp Putsch, 82–83, 86, 92, 99.
— and Soviet Russia, 139–42, 145, 279.
— during crisis of 1923, 163, 166, 170–2, 185–9, 196–7.
— in 1924–5, 202–3, 204–5.
Ecchevarrieta, Spanish industrialist, 243–4.
Ehrhardt, Hermann, lieutenant-commander, 79, 83, 89, 119, 133–5, 169.
Ehrhardt Brigade, 60, 76–80, 83, 89, 92, 98, 133–4, 159, 314, 323.
Ehrhardt song, 98, 133, 176, 315 and n. 1.
Eichhorn, Emil (Independent Socialist), 22.
Eideman, R. P., director of Russian War Academy, 280.
Einwohnerwehren (citizens' defence units), 113.
Entente, forces of, 5, 41, 67, 111, 113, 115, 149, 210.
— policy of, 38, 43, 64–65, 69, 75, 76, 113, 130, 136, 145, 204, 208, 222–3, 275–6.
— deliveries to, 51.
Enver Pasha, 70–71.
Epaulettes, abolition of, 18, 25, 27, 398.
— reintroduction of, 75.
Epp, Franz Ritter von, colonel, later general, 59, 97, 130, 160.
Erzberger, Matthias (Centre), 5, 45, 62–64.
— murder of, 134.
Escherich, Georg (leader of *Orgesch*), 156.
Estorff, Otto von, general, 84, 91, 94.

Falkenhausen, Alexander Freiherr von, colonel, 36, 212, 313 n. 4.
Fascism, Fascists, 241, 323, 337.
Feldjäger (guerilla units), 155, 300.
Feldmann, Hans von, colonel, 81.
Finland, 241, 244–5, 275, 284, 290, 361.
Finnish navy, 287, 361, 363.
Fischer, captain, later major, colonel, 75, 138, 142, 233, 238, 275, 277–8, 284, 360.
Fishman, Y. M., Russian general, 282.
Fleck, Wolfgang, major, later colonel, 90, 129.
Fliegerzentrale (in defence ministry), 148, 222, 274, 359.

Flying officers, training of, 143, 237, 359.
— schools, 221–2, 232, 236–7, 281–2, 358–9.
Foertsch, Hermann, lieutenant, later captain, 378, 401.
Foreign Office, see *Auswärtiges Amt*.
France, 3, 69, 105, 138, 140, 147, 208, 235, 275, 291, 356, 359.
— fight against, 30, 155, 164, 200, 220, 237.
— policy of, 41, 68, 119, 137, 142, 145, 153–5, 181, 194, 199–200, 203, 240.
— power of, 140, 163, 199.
— Ruhr occupation by, 153–5, 164.
— espionage, 359.
Frankenland (para-military organization), 178.
Frederick William I, king of Prussia, 3, 34, 214, 292 n. 1.
Free Corps, formation of, 21–22, 56, 72, 147, 178–9.
— military actions by, 23, 64, 402.
— reduction and dissolution, 38, 51, 75–76, 148–50.
— members taken over into Reichswehr, 32, 75, 133–4.
— fighting in Upper Silesia, 118, 131, 149, 402.
— continuation of, 118, 150–2, 159, 168–9.
— ideology of, 74–75, 169, 314, 316.
— *See also* Ehrhardt Brigade, Gardekavallerieschützendivision, *and* Loewenfeld Brigade.
Free Corps Roßbach, 151, 159.
Free Masons, 240–1.
Frick, Wilhelm, 394.
Fridericus Rex (clandestine military organization), 150.
— films, 121.
Friedrichs, colonel (leader of Berlin para-military units), 172.
Fritsch, Werner von, major, later colonel, 35, 64, 198, 200–3, 206, 248, 259, 303.
Frontier defence measures, 122, 147–52, 155, 221, 224, 230–2, 265–73, 305–6, 332–3, 351–6, 401–2.
— in Brandenburg, 158–9, 224, 232, 269, 272, 351, 379, 381.
— in East Prussia, 149, 268, 271–2, 352, 354.
— in Grenzmark Posen, 351–2.

Frontier defence (*cont.*)
— in Lower Lusatia, 150, 224.
— in Pomerania, 150–1, 225–8, 232, 268, 270, 272, 351–2.
— in Rhineland, 300–1, 305.
— in Saxony, 353.
— in Silesia, 151, 224, 227–8, 232, 269, 352–3, 354.
— in Upper Silesia, 118, 152, 228, 272.

Gardekavallerieschützendivision, 22–23.
Garnier-Turawa, Count (German Nationalist), 330.
Gefu (*Gesellschaft zur Förderung gewerblicher Unternehmungen*), 143, 233–5.
Generalkommandos (of Imperial German army), 26, 32, 35–36, 52, 84–85.
General staff, of Imperial German army, 4, 6–9, 16–17, 19, 50, 56, 108, 209.
— and formation of the Reichswehr, 23–24, 28, 45, 55–56.
— of the Reichswehr, 9, 53, 138, 280–1, 359, 396.
— of the Red Army, 137–8, 236, 280, 360.
— officers of, in Reichswehr, 149, 316.
— training of, 209–11, 281, 284, 301, 360.
General strike, danger of, 378–80, 383, 389, 392, 394.
— in March 1920, 85–86, 88, 91, 380.
Genoa, conference at (1922), 139, 142.
German Empire, founded 1871, 3–5, 7, 12, 35, 127, 192, 310–11, 397–8.
— traditions of, 8, 30, 126, 249, 258.
German Nationalist Party, 77, 79, 93, 165–6, 192, 197, 201–5, 218–19, 258, 263, 310, 336, 373, 377, 382, 391.
— members of, 190, 303, 306–7, 321, 388, 394.
German People's Party, 93, 121–2, 154, 163, 201, 207, 306–7, 338 n. 2.
— members of, 120, 171, 188, 218, 341.
Germaniawerft, Kiel, 243.
Geßler, Dr. Otto (Democrat), minister of defence, 92, 97, 104, 109, 112, 119–20, 122–3, 129, 158, 161–3, 165–6, 170–5, 186–8, 204, 208, 213, 229, 246–8, 253–5, 262–3, 265–7, 277–9, 285, 297.
— fall of, 286, 290.
Geyr von Schweppenburg, Leo Freiherr, lieutenant-colonel, 374–5.
Gilsa, Erich von, major, 57, 79, 82, 90, 93.

Gleich, Gerold von, general, 306, 335, 339.

Gleichschaltung, 368, 397.

Gneisenau, Neidhardt von, 326.

Goebbels, Joseph (National Socialist), 348, 396.

Goerdeler, Carl (German Nationalist), 190.

Goltz, Count Rüdiger von der, major-general, 64–67, 69.

Göring, Hermann (National Socialist), 169, 310, 370, 384, 394,

Gorlice, battle of, 65.

Graefe, Albrecht von (*Deutschvölkisch*), 157.

Groddeck, von, general, 87.

Groener, Wilhelm, general, 4, 38, 46, 104, 147, 216, 325, 398, 404.

— quartermaster-general, 5–8, 10, 286, 398.

— alliance with Ebert, 11–12, 15, 290–1.

— and the government, 16, 19–24, 33–35, 37.

— against workers' and soldiers' councils, 27–29, 34–35, 47.

— against Reinhardt, 27–29, 52–58, 92.

— and Versailles, 37, 39–44, 291.

— and Noske, 44, 54.

— and politics in the army, 44, 47–48, 58, 72–73, 162, 399.

— and Ebert, 44, 47, 54, 57, 115 and n. 3, 291.

— and formation of the Reichswehr, 44–45, 286, 291, 399.

— resignation from army, 52, 58.

— minister of defence, 264, 272, 280, 286, 289–98, 301–4, 306–7, 327–47, 354–6, 401.

— political views of, 291–5, 317–18, 320–2, 402–4.

— and Nazi Party, 313, 317–18, 324, 333–46, 371.

— fall of, 346–51, 365, 373, 404.

— in retirement, 326, 371, 385, 397.

Grzesinski, Albert (Social Democrat), 229–30.

Gudowius, Erich, colonel, 26 n. 3, 168.

Guérard, Theodor von (Centre), 290.

Habsburg Empire, 5.

Hagenberg, major-general, 84.

Hahn, Eugen, captain, later colonel, 82, 84.

Hahnke, Hans von, co onel, 87, 9

Hamburg, Communist revolt in (1923), 193–4.

Hamburg–America shipping line, 154.

'Hamburg points', December 1918, 18–20, 25.

Hammerstein-Equord, Kurt Freiherr von, major, later colonel, general, 364.

— in 1919, 46, 53.

— during Kapp Putsch, 46, 77, 79–80, 325.

— and Seeckt, 246–7.

— in 1923, 175.

— and Soviet Russia, political views, 278, 283–4, 325–8.

— chief of the *Truppenamt*, 282–3, 300, 302, 325, 360.

— chief of the army command, 284, 303, 324–6, 345–7, 351–3, 368, 386, 391–3, 396–7, 404.

— personality, 325–6.

— and National Socialists, 325, 327, 333, 335–7, 341–3, 348, 365, 374, 404.

Harbou, Christian von, major, 14–16.

Hasse, Otto, lieutenant-colonel, later colonel, general, 58, 69, 82, 111, 149, 399.

— and Seeckt, 54, 58, 104, 106–7, 119–21, 161, 188–9, 198.

— chief of the *Truppenamt*, 121, 136, 143, 146.

— and Soviet Russia, 136–9, 142–5, 235.

— and Kapp Putsch, 78, 82–83.

— and Bavarian officers, 161.

— political views, 158, 164–6, 201, 216.

— during 1923 crisis, 155, 158, 161, 164, 169, 188–9, 196–7.

— as commanding general, 206, 253–4, 257–9, 270, 365.

— and fall of Schleicher, 395.

Hasse, Paul, lieutenant-general, 216.

Heereskammer, 121, 126.

Heinkel works, Warnemünde, 155, 245, 362–3.

Helfritz, major-general, 158.

Henderson, Arthur, 360.

Henry, Prince of Prussia, grand-admiral, 288–9.

Hergt, Oskar (German Nationalist), 166.

Hermannsbund (para-military organization), 178.

Hertling, Count Georg, 105, 106 n. 1.

Hesse, Kurt, lieutenant, 219, 400.
Hesterberg, major, 85, 98.
Heye, Hellmuth, naval lieutenant, 299, 312, 321–2.
Heye, Wilhelm, colonel, later general, 216.
— in 1919, 40, 57.
— during Kapp Putsch, 80–82, 89.
— chief of the *Truppenamt*, 143, 253.
— chief of the army command, 221, 227, 253–6, 261–3, 265–9, 272, 290, 299–302, 315, 321, 324–6, 401.
— and Soviet Russia, 277.
Hierl, Constantin, colonel, 160.
High Command of Imperial Army (*Oberste Heeresleitung*), 4–6, 9–15, 19–30, 33–34, 37, 39, 44, 52, 58, 73, 147, 299, 398.
Hilferding, Rudolf (Social Democrat), 164, 292–3, 403.
Hindenburg, Oskar von, lieutenant-colonel, 304, 332, 342, 345, 388, 392–4.
Hindenburg, Paul von, field-marshal, 4, 9, 11–14, 18–20, 33, 52, 62, 72, 147, 291, 327.
— and Versailles, 39, 42–44.
— President of the German Republic, 205–6, 247–50, 253, 286, 302–3, 307, 328–9, 332, 335–40, 342–51, 360, 365, 368, 371, 375, 382, 384, 388–95.
— the Reichswehr and, 249–50, 327, 337, 386.
Hindenburg Battalion, 156.
Hirsch, Paul (Social Democrat), 31.
Hitler, Adolf, 9, 160, 169, 173, 178–9, 182–3, 186, 194–5, 309–12, 317–19, 323, 327, 332–4, 337–8, 342, 346, 348, 350, 366, 370–4, 377, 381–2, 384–93, 400, 404.
— chancellor, 394–7.
Hitler Putsch in Munich, 182–7, 194.
Hitler Youth, 355.
Hoetzsch, Otto, Professor (German Nationalist), 201.
Hofmann, Hans Georg, lieutenant-colonel, 183.
Hohenzollern, House of, 8, 17, 105, 129, 133, 249, 311.
Holland, 155, 242, 287, 290.
Höltermann, Karl (*Reichsbanner* leader), 354.
Holtzendorff, Hans Henning von, major-general, 333.

Horn, Rudolf von, general, 169–70, 344.
Hugenberg, Alfred (German Nationalist), 219, 306–7, 321, 336.
Hugenberg press, 219, 323–4, 349.
Hülsen, Bernhard von, general, 80.

Imperial German army, 4–6, 10, 71, 397, 404.
— German navy, 7–8.
— war flag, 59, 61, 84, 125, 262, 400.
— Yacht Club, Kiel, 288.
Independent Social Democrats (U.S.P.D.), 10–11, 16, 21–22, 45, 61, 121.
Infantry School at Dresden, 184, 214, 296, 305, 313, 323, 353.
— School at Munich, 143, 175–6, 179, 183–5, 316.
Inflation of the Mark, 143, 153, 163–4, 194, 234.
Ingenieurskantoor voor Scheepsbouw (*I.v.S.*), The Hague, 242–4, 287.
'Iron Front' (Republican defence organization), 339.
Italy, 199, 240.
— Fascism in, 241, 323, 337.

Jagow trial, 88, 94.
Japan, 245.
Japanese navy, 244.
Jarosch, major, 9.
Jewish question, *see* Anti-Semitism.
Jungdeutscher Orden, 151, 156, 222.
Jungstahlhelm, 352–3.
Junkers works, Dessau, 136–8, 234, 255–6.
— works at Fili, 138, 143, 234–5, 276.

Kahr, Dr. Gustav Ritter von, 117, 166, 173–5, 180–2.
Kama, German tank school at, 236, 276–82, 360.
Kapp, Dr. Wolfgang (German Nationalist), 77, 80, 82–89, 92–93, 95–98.
Kapp Putsch, March 1920, 17, 43, 66, 74, 77–89, 91–99, 103, 107–10, 115, 117, 123–4, 135, 149, 155–7, 174, 182, 194, 248, 314, 316, 323, 369, 378, 380, 399, 402–3.
— general strike against, 85–86, 88, 91, 380.
— committee investigating the, 94–95, 97–98.

Kapp Putsch (cont.)
— amnesty after, 97.
Keitel, Wilhelm, colonel, 396.
Kessel, von, general, 36, 62.
Kiel, naval mutiny at, 7, 21, 88, 314, 398.
— unrest during Kapp Putsch at, 88, 98, 288.
Kolchak, A., White Russian general, 67–68.
Kopf, Hinrich (Social Democrat), 72.
Kopp, Victor, 135–6, 141.
Köster, Roland (Social Democrat), 118.
Köstring, Ernst, major, 259.
Krasin, Leonid, 136, 143.
Kreis officers (in frontier defence), 147–8, 150–1, 225–30, 232, 255, 257, 264, 268–71, 402.
Kreß von Kressenstein, Friedrich Freiherr von, general, 174, 177, 183, 185, 204, 257.
Krestinsky, Nicolai, 142, 147, 235, 275.
Kreuzzeitung (German Nationalist newspaper), 197.
Kriegspiel, November 1932, 378–81, 403,
Krupp, Essen, 135–6, 141.
— building of tanks by, 273, 357.
Kuntzen, Adolf, major, 393.
Küstrin, Putsch at, 1923, 168–9, 172.
Kuttner, Erich (Social Democrat), 23 n. 1, 72–73.
Kyffhäuserbund (ex-service men's organization), 344.

Labour Party, 333, 360.
Labour Service, 387–8.
Landbund, 150–1, 172, 365.
Landesjägerkorps, Freiwilliges, 22–23, 35.
Landsberg, Otto (Social Democrat), 19.
Latvia, 64, 68.
League of Nations, Germany and, 167, 198–201, 232, 235, 259.
— Russia and, 198.
Lebedev, P. (Russian chief of staff), 137, 144.
Leipart, Theodor (Social Democrat), 386.
Leipzig trial of Scheringer and Ludin, 315, 317–22, 324, 328, 332, 337.
Lenin, V. I., 64, 135, 136 n. 1.
Lequis, Arnold, lieutenant-general, 14, 17, 21, 85.
Lersner, Kurt Freiherr von (German People's Party), 171.
Lettow-Vorbeck, Paul von, general, 84.

Leuna works, 132.
Leupold, Ludwig, lieutenant-colonel, 127–8, 160, 176.
Liebknecht, Karl (Communist), 7, 18, 23.
Liebmann, Curt, lieutenant-general, 374–5.
Lietzmann, lieutenant-commander, 361–2.
Lindemann, Fritz, captain, 312–13.
Lipetsk, German flying school at, 155, 221–2, 232, 236–7, 276, 278–82, 358–9, 360.
Lippmann, Oberpräsident of Pomerania, 35–36.
Lithuania, 68, 105, 284.
Lithuanian general staff officers, 284.
Löbe, Paul (Social Democrat), 256–9, 264.
Locarno, Treaty of, 206–7, 259.
Loewenfeld, Wilfried von, naval lieutenant, later captain, 83, 85, 98–99, and n. 2, 134–5, 239–41, 245.
Loewenfeld Brigade, 76, 83–85, 98, 133–4, 159, 239, 242, 314.
Lohmann, naval captain, 242, 244–5, 284–6.
Lohmann scandal, 285–7, 290.
Loßberg, Friedrich von, general, 40, 42, 61, 86, 155, 200, 204–5, 253–4, 265.
Lossow, Otto Hermann von, general, 160–1, 173–5, 177–86, 212, 400.
Lüdemann, Hermann, Oberpräsident of Silesia, 293–4.
Ludendorff, Erich, general, 4, 48, 104, 154 n. 1, 157, 179, 182–4, 186, 193, 398.
Ludin, Hanns, lieutenant, 315–20.
Luft-Hansa, 244, 287..
Luniev, Russian military attaché, 238.
Lüninck, Hermann Freiherr von, 336.
Luther, Hans (German People's Party), 235.
Lüttwitz, Walther Freiherr von, general, 38, 40, 45–47, 60–61, 72, 76–77, 80–89, 90, 92–93, 96, 103, 325.
Luxemburg, Rosa (Communist), 7, 18, 23.

MacDonald, Ramsay, 360.
Mackensen, von, major, 226.
Maercker, Georg, major-general, 35, 85–87, 93.
Maltzan, Ago Freiherr von, 144–5, 147.

Manchester Guardian, 255, 275.

Manstein, Erich von Lewinski von, lieutenant-colonel, 8–9, 354, 400.

Marcks, Erich, captain, later major, 218, 341.

Marine-Rundschau, 296.

Marshall-Cornwall, J. H., British military attaché, 303, 310.

Marx, Wilhelm (Centre), 190, 203, 267.

'Marxism', 64, 176, 178, 292, 314, 370.

'Marxists', 269, 370.

Mecklenburg-Schwerin, state, 225, 269, 367, 369, 374–5,

Mediterranean, 240.

Meinecke, Friedrich, historian, 335, 371.

Meißner, Dr. Otto, 342, 346, 388, 392.

Memel issue, 284.

Mentzel, Wolfgang, lieutenant-colonel, 144–5.

Meurer, rear-admiral, 63.

Mexico, 244.

Militär-Wochenblatt, 296.

Military Academy, Berlin, 4, 50, 209, 396–7.

— in Russia, 280, 360.

Military dictatorship, plans of establishing a, 74, 154, 170, 203–5, 324, 376, 382, 393.

Militia, 19.

Minister of defence, competence of, 32.

— power of command over Reichswehr, 49, 52, 54, 57, 108, 111–12, 122–4, 208.

Minister of finance, 136, 164, 285, 292, 403.

Minister of transport, 58.

Ministry of defence, foundation of, 53–54.

— budget of, 275, 292.

— organization of, 297.

— 'black' funds of, 224, 274–5.

— *Ministeramt* in, 297–9, 344, 366, 371, 386, 396.

Mittelberger, Hilmar Ritter von, lieutenant-colonel, later colonel, general, 177, 186, 261, 298.

Mobilization, preparation of, 50, 148–9, 155–9, 220–1, 229, 266, 268, 272–3, 337.

Möhl, Arnold Ritter von, general, 38, 40, 59, 86, 97, 109, 124–9, 160, 172, 175, 213.

Moltke, Helmuth von, 4, 70.

Morgen, von, general, 190.

Mosse, Rudolf, publishing house, 334.

Müller, Alfred, lieutenant-general, 180 188, 192–3.

Müller, Hermann (Social Democrat), 64, 280, 289–90, 294, 304.

— fall of, 294, 306–7 and n. 1, 403.

Müller, Ludwig, army chaplain, 389.

Munich Soviet Republic, April 1919, 35.

Mussolini, Benito, 240.

Napoleon, 3, 50, 70, 316.

National Assembly, demand for calling of, 13, 15, 18, 20.

— elections to, 18, 25.

— and peace treaty, 38, 40, 42–43, 49.

— and German colours, 58–59, 125.

'National Revolution', 183, 315, 318–19, 394–6.

National Socialist Party (N.S.D.A.P.), 203, 316–17, 333, 349, 352, 366, 370–1, 373–4, 376, 379, 381, 386.

National Socialists, 72, 156, 160, 172, 178, 228, 300, 305, 309–55, 365–7, 370–82, 384, 386–9, 392–7, 403–4.

Nationale Verbände, see *Vaterländische Verbände*.

Naval Brigades, *see* Ehrhardt Brigade and Loewenfeld Brigade.

— Mutiny, *see* Kiel, mutiny at.

— School at Mürwik, 98, 133–4, 295.

Navy, officer corps of, 8, 98, 133–5.

— and Kapp Putsch, 83–84, 98, 288, 399.

— and Noske, 83.

— and Soviet Russia, 146–7, 238–42, 245, 283, 361–3.

— air arm of, 155, 222, 244–5, 287, 362–3.

— and National Socialists, 314, 396.

— and Poland, 238, 362.

Neesen, firm at Travemünde, 244.

Niederdeutscher Heimatbund (para-military organization), 158.

Niedermayer, Oskar Ritter von, major, 135–8, 141, 145–6, 233.

Niemann, Alfred, major, 36.

Nobility, abolition of, 18.

— in officer corps, 215–16.

— of Prussia, 3, 104.

Noeldechen, Ferdinand, captain, 215, 307, 331–2, 349.

Noske, Gustav, People's Commissar, 21, 24, 26, 28.
— *Oberbefehlshaber in den Marken*, 21–22, 53.
— minister of defence, 22, 32, 45–46, 52–57, 60–62, 71–79, 85, 91, 97, 103, 109, 122, 403.
— and Versailles, 41–44.
— resignation of, 91–92.
— Seeckt and, 91, 109–10, 115.

Oath to German Constitution, 59–60, 81, 87, 93, 94, 117, 119, 133, 175–7, 315, 317, 400.
— to Bavarian state, 175–6, 179, 185.
Oberland (Bavarian para-military organization), 178.
Oberste Heeresleitung, see High Command.
Occident, culture of, 239–41.
Oderschutz (Silesian frontier defence organization), 151, 227.
Officer corps, general traits of, 3–4, 8, 29–30, 216–17, 397–8.
— education of, 55, 114, 184, 209–11, 216, 259, 305, 317.
— code of honour of, 114, 174, 211–12, 328.
— new badges of rank of, 25, 27.
— political views of, 44, 87, 216–20, 319–20, 398, 402, 404.
— social origins of, 3, 214–16.
— numbers of, 50.
— increase of, 357.
— selection of, 33, 56, 73, 97, 216.
Officers' associations, 110–11, 310.
Officers' councils, 40–42, 89, 113.
Oldenburg, state, 133.
Oldershausen, Freiherr von, general, 78–80.
Oras, Russian naval officer, 238.
Organisation Consul (O.C.), 119, 134.
Organisation Escherich (Orgesch), 156.
Ott, Eugen, major, later lieutenant-colonel, 354, 378, 380–4, 387–8.
Oven, Burghard von, general, 60, 78–79, 89, 92, 155–7.

Pabst, Waldemar, captain, 77.
Pacifism, pacifists, 109, 199, 200–1, 203, 270, 293–4, 318, 402.
Papen, Franz von, 168, 349–50, 364–6, 368, 373–7, 386, 388–92, 403–4.
— fall of, 381–4, 389, 403.

People's Commissars, government of, 10–12, 19–23, 25, 398.
Personnel Office (of German army), 29, 55–56, 108, 148, 212, 216, 263, 391.
Petrov, Russian military attaché, 146–7.
Pfeffer von Salomon, Franz, captain, later *S.A.* leader, 169, 316, 332.
Phöbus-Film-Gesellschaft, 285, 287.
Planck, Erwin, 347, 373.
Plehwe, Karl von (German Nationalist), 303.
Pleitegeier, 127–8.
Pöhner, Ernst, 180.
Poincaré, Raymond, 194.
Poison gas, production of, 50, 143, 234–5, 255, 357–8.
— experiments with, 236, 276–9, 280, 282, 357.
— factory, in Russia, 234–5, 276.
Poland, 38, 67–69, 140, 149, 164, 167, 232, 237–8, 240, 253, 356, 362.
— ceding of territory to, 38, 40.
— fighting with, 16, 23, 30, 35, 118, 147, 402.
— fourth partition of? 68–69, 139–40, 236, 238, 240.
— plans of attack against, 39–42, 137–9, 143, 281, 283–4.
— aggressive plans of, 145, 281, 362, 379, 381, 401, 403.
Police, 33, 115, 371, 375, 383.
— Bavarian, 177, 194–5.
— Prussian, 24, 78–79, 84, 118, 121, 132, 148, 158, 162, 190, 369, 378–81, 405.
— army functioning as, 33, 118–19, 132–3, 318.
Polish army, 16, 17.
— Corridor, 351, 362.
— insurgents, 118, 130–1, 149, 404.
— navy, 361.
Pommerntreue (frontier defence organization), 270–1, 402.
Popitz, Dr. Johannes, 274.
Potsdam, spirit of, 397.
— traditions of, 311.
Poznań, 39, 41, 68.
Prussia, kingdom of, 3–4, 6, 12, 69–70, 214, 218, 311.
— state, 34, 36–37, 40, 44, 49 n. 1, 68, 190–1, 330, 336, 355, 368, 370–1, 384, 387, 402.
— government of, 22, 36, 53, 118, 121, 158, 167, 188, 190, 226–8, 230, 287,

Prussia, government of (*cont.*)
304, 308, 330, 355, 364, 368–9, 376, 378, 381, 401, 403.
— and frontier defence measures, 151–2, 229–30, 265–9, 300, 305–7, 330, 355–6.
— Diet of, 105, 330, 339, 341, 364, 367.
— and the Reich, *see* Dualism.
Prussian army, 3–4, 8, 42, 50, 57, 76, 104, 168, 213, 216, 386, 397.
— war minister, ministry, 11, 14–15, 21–22, 24–25, 28–29, 32, 52, 62, 108, 209, 399.
— police, *see* Police.
Pünder, Dr. Hermann, 308, 342, 346–8, 373, 376.
Putsch, danger of, 49, 132, 168–9, 248, 321, 378; *see also* Hitler Putsch *and* Kapp Putsch.

Rabenau, Friedrich von, captain, later major, later general, 91, 112, 125, 127, 132, 166, 170, 219 n. 1, 246, 278, 300.
Radek, Karl, 70, 138, 142–3.
Raeder, Erich, naval captain, later admiral, 83, 135, 288–90, 341–5, 347, 349, 351.
Rapallo, Treaty of, 139, 198.
Rathenau, Walther (Democrat), 115–16.
— murder of, 119, 134.
Rausch, Bernhard (Social Democrat), 95.
Recruiting, for Reichswehr, 227, 230, 255–9, 263–4.
Red Air Force, 144–5, 232, 235, 237, 282, 360.
— Army, 64, 146, 149, 280–3, 290, 326, 360–1, 381, 389.
— general staff of, 137, 144, 282.
— Navy, 146, 238–9, 241, 361–2.
Reform of Constitution, 369, 382.
— Groener and, 34–35, 37, 44, 191, 291–2.
— Schleicher and, 34, 37, 190, 291, 369.
— Seeckt and, 167–8, 190–1, 291, 369.
Regiment Reichstag (Social Democratic free corps), 23.
Reichenau, Walther von, lieutenant-colonel, later colonel, 348, 389–90, 395–6, 404.
Reichsbanner Schwarz-Rot-Gold, 201, 205, 271–2, 294–5, 305, 324, 341, 345, 352,

354–5, 380–3, 386, 402–3.
Reichsflagge (Bavarian para-military organization), 178.
Reichskommissar, for Prussia, 368, 384.
Reichskriegsflagge, 125, 262, 400.
Reichskuratorium für Jugendertüchtigung, 354–5.
Reichsverband deutscher Berufssoldaten, 110–11.
Reinhard, Wilhelm, colonel, 60.
Reinhardt, Walther, colonel, later general, 21 n. 2, 93, 104, 216, 298, 405.
— Prussian war minister, 21–22, 24–32, 36, 52–57, 62, 399.
— against Versailles, 39–42.
— chief of the army command, 22, 53–54, 58, 63, 65–81, 89–92, 103, 112, 399.
— general at Döberitz, 131–2.
— — at Stuttgart, 103, 107, 110, 159, 164, 194, 197, 219.
— — at Cassel, 103, 213, 253–4, 256–8.
Reparations, 193, 201, 306, 323.
Republikanischer Führerbund, 72–74.
Reventlow, Count Ernst zu (*Deutsch-völkisch*), 121.
Revolution, of November 1918, 7–10, 12, 17, 107, 127, 217, 291, 310, 398.
— fight against, 75–76, 84, 133, 320, 398.
Rheinmetall A. G., 282.
— building of tanks by, 273, 282–3, 357.
Rhineland, 208, 381.
— Separatists in, 153, 193–4, 315, 379.
— demilitarized zone of, 194, 301, 304–5, 379.
Ribbentrop, Joachim von (National Socialist), 388.
Röhm, Ernst, captain, later S.A. leader, 97, 160, 169, 310, 332–4, 337, 370.
'Röhm Putsch', June 1934, 372.
Ronneberger, naval chaplain, 314.
Roon, Albrecht von, 4.
Rosenblatt, Russian agent, 142.
Rosengolts, Arkadi P., 144–5, 235.
Roßbach, Gerhard, lieutenant, 157, 161, 169, 183, 185 n. 1.
Rote Fahne (Communist newspaper), 152.
Ruhr industry, 142, 379.
— occupation of, 1923, 153–5, 193.
— rising in, 1920, 88, 109 and n. 1.
— sabotage in, 1923, 155, 157, 316.

Ruhr (*cont.*)
— passive resistance in, 1923, 153–4, 156, 164, 168, 237.
'Ruhr fund', 155, 237, 242, 285.
Ruith, Adolf Ritter von, major-general, 183.
Rundstedt, Gerd von, lieutenant-general, 368–9.
Russia, 4, 66–69, 105.
Russo-Polish war, 68–70, 137, 149.
Rydz-Śmigły, Edward, Polish general, 381.
Rykov, Alexei, 236.

S.A. (*Sturmabteilungen*), 169, 310, 319, 334, 340, 351–5, 366, 370–4, 382, 390, 396, 404,
— dissolution of, 1932, 339–50, 364, 366, 370, 383, 404.
— chief of staff of, 332.
Saemisch, Dr. Friedrich, president of audit office, 274.
Saxony, state, 40, 49 n. 1, 191, 196, 330.
— during Kapp Putsch, 85–86, 88.
— 'red' government of, 153, 180, 191, 193.
— employment of Reichswehr against, 156, 180–2, 187–8, 194.
Schacht, Hjalmar, 385.
Scharnhorst, Gerhard Johann David, 50, 70, 316, 326.
Scheidemann, Philipp (Social Democrat), 7, 37, 43, 64, 255–6, 275.
Schellbach, major, 247.
Scheringer, Richard, lieutenant, 315–20.
— trial at Leipzig, 315, 317–20, 328, 332, 337.
Scheüch, Heinrich, general, 11, 14–15.
Schiffer, Dr. Eugen (Democrat), 89–90.
Schleicher, Kurt von, major, later colonel, general, 40, 96, 385.
— and formation of free corps, 16–17, 21.
— and Groener, 16, 19, 57, 58, 286, 296–8, 304, 329, 336, 339, 341–51, 385, 404.
— and economic recovery, 17.
— and unitary state, 34, 37, 330.
— and politics, 48, 122, 158, 166, 193, 196, 201–3, 218, 260–1, 305–8, 315, 399, 401–4.
— and negotiations with Russians, 136, 142.
— and Seeckt, 118, 120–2, 209, 186, 190, 206, 247, 296, 401–3.

Schleicher (*cont.*)
— and frontier defence, 122, 225, 230, 266, 269, 301, 305, 355–6.
— chief of *Wehrmachtsabteilung*, 257, 259, 263–4, 271, 289, 296–7.
— chief of *Ministeramt*, 216, 297–9, 302–8, 312, 326, 329–32, 335–6, 353–6.
— and National Socialists, 305, 310, 313, 322–4, 332–4, 337–44, 348–50, 364–7, 371–3, 384, 386–7, 394, 403–4.
— minister of defence, 349, 364–73, 376–8, 380–4.
— chancellor, 383–93.
— fall of, 392–5, 404.
— and 'Spirit of Potsdam', 397.
— murder of, 397.
— criticisms of, 298–301, 303–4, 319–20.
Schmettow, Count, general, 84–85.
Schmidt, Max (German People's Party), 218–19.
Schoeler, Roderich von, general 86, 88.
Scholz, Ernst (German People's Party), 307.
Schöpflin, Georg (Social Democrat), 59.
Schröder, Kurt Freiherr von, banker, 388.
Schubert, Carl von, 275–6, 279, 283.
Schulenburg, Count Friedrich von der, lieutenant-general, 6, 156.
Schulz, Paul, lieutenant, 150, 158–9.
Schweinitz, von, lieutenant, 216.
Schwerin von Krosigk, Count Lutz, 274.
Sedan, battle of, 3, 125.
Seeckt, Hans von, general, 30, 103–7, 256, 259, 263, 298, 330, 338 n. 2, 365.
— political views in First World War, 105.
— and Germany's collapse, 17.
— and the new government, 17, 31–32.
— and politics, 31–32, 48, 66, 70, 73, 92, 104, 115–22, 127, 132, 162, 192.
— aiming at the presidency, 197–8, 205–6.
— in eastern Germany, 31, 35, 64, 147.
— at Versailles, 37–38.
— and Treaty of Versailles, 40, 42–43, 152, 206, 232.
— and Reinhardt, 53–58, 90, 92, 399.
— and formation of the Reichswehr, 53–57, 75–76, 148, 310, 399.
— and Soviet Russia, 67–71, 115–16, 136, 139–43, 198, 208, 232, 235–8, 241–2, 277–8, 362, 399, 402.

Seeckt (cont.)
— and Poland, 67–69, 137, 139–40, 236–8.
— and frontier defence, 148, 150–2, 231, 265, 267, 269, 272.
— and Kapp Putsch, 78–80, 83, 86–92, 94, 99, 155, 194, 399.
— chief of the army command, 92, 95, 97, 103, 108–16, 160–1, 208–9, 211–14, 223, 261, 275, 296, 302, 319, 326, 381, 386, 400–1, 404.
— 'royal substitute', 107, 249.
— and Dr. Geßler, 109, 122–4, 163, 208, 246–8.
— during crisis of 1923, 117, 153–8, 161–3, 165–75, 179–95, 324, 328, 335, 385, 399–400.
— and Stresemann, 163–5, 169–72, 181, 187–8, 195, 200–1, 206–8, 211, 399–400, 403.
— and foreign policy, 1924–6, 198–201, 206–8, 235, 399.
— and domestic policy, 1924–6, 196–8, 201–6, 218, 248.
— dismissal of, 205, 246–50, 253–5, 265, 275, 278, 286, 308, 402.
— succession to, 253–4.
— and Hitler, 338, 390.
— and Groener as defence minister, 346–7.
— criticisms of Seeckt, 212–14, 246–7.
Seisser, Hans von, colonel of Bavarian police, 172, 180, 182.
Selchow, Hans Harald von, captain, 120–1, 156, 166, 189.
Seldte, Franz (Stahlhelm leader), 316, 321, 331, 336.
Separatists, in Bavaria, 153, 177, 186, 193, 400.
— in Rhineland, 153, 193–4, 315.
Severa (Seeflugzeug-Versuchsabteilung) G.m.b.H., 244–5, 287.
Severing, Carl (Social Democrat), 119, 122, 151–2, 158, 188, 203, 229–30, 265, 267, 269, 290, 294, 340, 343, 356.
Shaposhnikov, B. M. (chief of Russian general staff), 144, 282.
Simons, Dr. Walter (President of Reichsgericht), 116.
Sklyansky, E. (Deputy People's Commissar for War), 70–71.
Social Democratic Party (S.P.D.), 31, 43, 46, 71, 74, 97, 99, 117, 119, 122, 154, 156, 202–3, 254, 293, 306–7.

Social Democrats, 10–11, 16–21, 23, 55, 64, 72, 74, 93, 96, 163–4, 166, 180, 191, 193, 197, 201, 254–6, 264, 270–1, 289–95, 301, 304, 308, 314, 329–30, 334, 339–40, 343, 356, 364, 369–70, 382, 386, 389, 401.
Soldiers' Councils, 7, 9–10, 13, 16, 18, 20, 24–29, 33.
— opposition to, in army, 27–29, 34 and n. 1, 37, 113.
Solf, Dr. Wilhelm (Democrat), 31.
Soviet Republics (in Germany), 35.
Soviet Russia, 67–69, 115, 149, 198–9, 232, 360–2.
— revolution in, 7, 10, 105.
— civil war in, 23, 67, 147.
— Bolshevism, 7, 10–11, 64, 66–70, 71, 239–40.
— anti-Bolsheviks, 64–67, 147.
— alliance with? 69–71, 139, 167, 236, 362, 381, 399, 402–3.
— government of, 71, 135, 140, 275, 277, 281–2.
— treaties with, 142, 145, 236.
— German military installations in, 143, 164, 232–3, 236–7, 255, 276–82, 360, 402.
— German factories in, 138, 142–3, 234–5, 255–6, 282–3.
— See also Kama and Lipetsk.
'Soviet shells', 234, 237, 255.
Spa, negotiations at, 113.
Spain, 234, 243–4, 290.
Spanish navy, 243–4, 287, 362–3.
Spartacists (later Communists), 7, 16, 18, 23 and n. 1, 176.
Spartacus rising, January 1919, 22, 25, 72.
Speed-boats, 242, 244, 287.
Sperrle, Hugo, major, 274.
Spindler, Arno, rear-admiral, 239, 241.
Sportflug G.m.b.H., 221.
S.S. (Schutzstaffel), 344–5, 366, 372, 374, 382, 390, 404.
Stab-in-the-back, 9.
Stahlhelm, Bund der Frontsoldaten, 151, 156, 158, 178, 188, 256–7, 264, 307, 310, 316, 321, 331, 336, 353–4, 368, 381, 383, 386, 401–2.
— and frontier defence, 151, 226–9, 232, 254, 268, 301, 305, 351–5, 401–2.
— Jungstahlhelm, 352–3.
— flying organization of, 353.
State of siege, 34, 36, 368, 380, 382.

Stauffenberg, Count Claus Schenk von, lieutenant, 396.
Stegerwald, Adam (Centre), 386.
Stennes, Walter, captain, later *S.A.* leader, 168-9, 332, 334.
Stieff, Helmuth, lieutenant, 271, 319-20.
Stinnes, Hugo, industrialist, 136.
Stockhausen, Karl von, major, 46, 57, 79.
Stomonyakov, B. (Russian diplomat), 235.
Strasser, Gregor (National Socialist), 384, 386-7.
Strasser, Otto, 72, 319.
Stresemann, Gustav (German People's Party), 115-16, 122, 162.
— chancellor, 117, 145-6, 163-6, 170-2, 173, 180, 186-8, 195, 385.
— fall of, 170-1, 188, 195, 403.
— foreign minister, 200-1, 206-8, 210-11, 218, 223, 235-6, 249, 254, 272, 275, 304, 359.
— and Russian enterprises of Reichswehr, 145, 276-80.
Stülpnagel, Edwin von, colonel, later general, 225, 354.
Stülpnagel, Joachim von, major, later colonel, general, 30, 39-40, 42, 198, 206.
— during crisis of 1923, 154-5, 164, 169-70, 186.
— and politics, 164, 166, 196, 199-203, 399.
— and Seeckt, 104, 122, 169-70, 212, 246,
— chief of army's Personnel Office, 212, 263.
— general commanding Third Division, 298-9, 344.
— chief of the army command? 299, 302-3, 325-6.
Submarines, construction of, 50, 135, 146, 239, 242-4, 287, 361, 363.
— plans and designs, 239, 242-3, 287.
Swastika flag, emblem, 80, 98, 183, 335.
'Swastika on the Steel Helmet' (Ehrhardt song), 98, 133, 176, 315.
Sweden, 234.
Switzerland, 19, 147, 253.

Tanks, 236, 356.
— construction of, 273, 282.

Tanks (*cont.*)
— tank school at Kama, 236, 276-82, 360.
Tannenberg, battle of, 249.
Tantzen, Theodor (prime minister of Oldenburg), 133.
Tebeg G.m.b.H., Berlin, 287.
Technische Nothilfe, 379.
Teichmann, lieutenant, 176.
Thaer, von, colonel, 26 n. 3, 93, 108.
Thaysen, von, colonel, 78.
Thiel, Gebrüder, firm at Ruhla, 283.
Thomsen–von der Lieth, colonel, 145, 232-3, 238.
Thuringia, state, 191, 194, 196.
— 'red' government of, 153, 180, 191, 193.
— employment of Reichswehr against, 156, 181-2, 187, 194.
Tieschowitz von Tieschowa, Hans, major-general, 175-6, 179, 183-4.
Tillessen, Heinrich, former naval officer, 134 n. 2.
Tillessen, Werner, naval captain, 134 and n. 2.
Tirpitz, Alfred von, former admiral, 205.
Torpedo boats, 51, 314.
Torpedo plane, 363.
Torpedo works, 243.
Torpedoes, 242-3.
Toruń, 39, 68.
Trade unions, Christian, 380, 383, 386.
— Free, 380, 383, 386.
Trayag (*Travemünder Yachthafen A.G.*), 242, 287.
Tresckow, Henning von, lieutenant, 311.
Treviranus, Gottfried (German Nationalist), 308.
Trotha, Adolf von, vice-admiral, 40, 78, 83, 98, 288.
Trotsky, Leo, 70-71, 135, 137, 144.
Truppenamt (general staff), 53, 57-58, 63, 69, 80, 82-83, 106, 108, 136, 143, 149, 206, 220, 223, 272, 282-4, 296, 325, 354, 357-8, 361, 369, 374.
— tasks of, 55, 148, 209-10, 222, 224, 230-1, 233-4, 274.
— *Sondergruppe R.*, 138, 233.
Tschischwitz, Erich von, general, 26 n. 3, 170, 196, 225.
Tschunke, Fritz, captain, later major, 136 n. 1, 137 n. 3.

Tukhachevsky, M. N. (Russian chief of staff), 282, 360.
Turkey, 5, 71, 234, 276, 290.
Turkish navy, 242, 244, 287, 363.

Uborevich, I. P., Russian general, 280, 282-3.
Ukraine, 67.
Ulmannis, Kárlis (Latvian prime minister), 64.
Unification, wars of (1864-71), 3-4, 8, 218.
United States of America, 5, 39, 240, 361.
Unity of Germany, 6-7, 35, 39, 42, 45, 153, 166, 177, 193-5.
Unshlikht, I. S. (Deputy People's Commissar for War), 235.
Unterland (Bavarian para-military organization), 183.
Upper Silesia, disputes about, 130-1, 136.
— fighting in, 118, 130-1, 149-50.
— frontier defence of, 152, 228, 272.

Vaterländische Verbände, 118, 151-2, 155-69, 171-2, 177-80, 183, 187, 204, 221, 223, 227, 229-32, 255, 257, 264-5, 270-2, 289, 295-6, 305, 310, 326, 353-4, 373, 382, 386-7, 401-2.
— in Bavaria, 153, 177-80, 183, 187.
— See also Jungdeutscher Orden, Stahlhelm, Wehrwolf, and Wiking.
Verbände, see Vaterländische Verbände.
Versailles, Treaty of, 69, 140, 199, 232, 259.
— preparation of, 33, 37.
— acceptance of, 38, 49, 291, 399.
— provisions of, 37, 50-52, 73, 76, 111, 113, 146, 148, 167, 210, 220.
— actions against, 148, 150, 155, 210, 220-32, 242, 255, 265, 269, 273, 276, 278, 286, 290, 357-9.
— liberation from, 65-67, 132, 311, 318.
Vertrauensleute, Vertrauensräte, in the army, 10, 13, 16, 20, 24, 28, 33, 62, 96, 113, 127.
Völkisch, 130, 157, 176-7, 202.
Völkischer Beobachter (National Socialist newspaper), 173.
Volksmarinedivision (red sailors' unit), 20.
Vollard-Bockelberg, Alfred von, lieutenant-general, 273.

Voroshilov, K. J., (People's Commissar for War), 281, 381.
Vorwärts (Social Democratic newspaper), 46, 72-73, 255.

Waffenamt (in defence ministry), 108, 234, 273, 358.
— tasks of, 55.
Wagner, Robert, captain (National Socialist), 316.
Wagner, Siegfried ('chancellor' of the Stahlhelm), 331.
Wangenheim, Adolf von, colonel, 84.
War Academy, Berlin, 4, 50, 209, 396-7.
— in Russia, 280, 360.
War Criminals, extradition of, 41-43, 45, 62, 63, 75.
War Guilt issue, 35, 41-43, 62.
Warsaw, battle of, 70, 149.
Wars of Liberation (1813-14), 3, 70, 190, 200, 218, 316, 396.
Watter, Oskar Freiherr von, general, 86.
Wehramt (in defence ministry), 108, 263, 274.
Wehrgesetz of 23 March 1921, 49, 110-13, 161, 208, 262.
Wehrmachtsabteilung (in defence ministry), 260, 296-7, 312, 345, 369, 378, 383.
Wehrwolf (para-military organization), 229, 254, 256.
Weimar Constitution, see Constitution.
Wels, Otto (Social Democrat), 11, 21.
Wendt, Hans Friedrich, lieutenant, 315, 319.
Westarp, Count Kuno von (German Nationalist), 166, 197, 204, 206, 347-8.
Wetzell, Wilhelm, lieutenant-colonel, later colonel, general, 78, 89.
— chief of the Truppenamt, 206, 231, 235, 253, 259, 262-3, 275-6, 298.
White Russians, 64, 66-67, 147.
Wiking (para-military organization), 151, 178.
Wilberg, colonel, 353.
Wilhelm, Crown Prince, 197, 245, 344, 353, 368.
Wilhelm, Prince of Prussia, 245-6.
Wilhelmshaven, naval mutiny at, 7, 88, 314.
— unrest during Kapp Putsch at, 88.
— politics at, 314.
William I, King and Emperor, 8.

William II, King and Emperor, 8, 47, 114, 129, 212–13, 215, 249, 288.
— abdication of, 6–8, 107, 344.
— extradition to Entente? 41, 45, 62.
— birthday of, 129, 133.
— pictures of, 128, 133.
— 'Supreme War Lord', 3, 8, 81.
Winnig, August (Social Democrat), 39 and n. 1.
Winterfeld, von captain, 227–8.
Wirth, Josef (Centre), 71, 118, 121, 124, 136–42, 154, 331, 356.
Wirtschaftskontor G.m.b.H., Berlin, 233–4.
Wolff, Theodor (Democrat), 31.
Wöllwarth, Erich, general, 258–9, 298–9.
Workers' Councils, 28, 34, 37, 47.
Workers' and Soldiers' Councils, 7, 10, 13–20, 23, 34–37, 398.
— first congress of, 18, 20.
— Executive Council of, 14–15, 18–19.

World War (1914–18), 4–7, 48, 62, 105, 154 n. 1, 296, 398.
Wrisberg, Ernst von, general 77, 81.
Württemberg, state, 22, 40, 49, n. 1, 191.
Württembergers, 6, 22, 29, 40.
Wurtzbacher, general, 137.

Yakir, I. E., Russian general, 282.
Yorck, Count, 156.
Yorck, Hans David Ludwig von, 386.
Young Plan, 316.

Zeitfreiwillige (short-term volunteers), in 1923, 155, 158–60, 178–9, 183, 187–8, 200.
— in 1924, 222–3.
— after 1929, 357.
— students as, 159, 222–3.
Zenker, Hans, admiral, 222, 239–41, 244, 266, 286–8.
Zentrale Moskau (German military centre in Moscow), 232.
Zinsknechtschaft, Brechung der, 311.

PRINTED IN GREAT BRITAIN
AT THE UNIVERSITY PRESS, OXFORD
BY VIVIAN RIDLER
PRINTER TO THE UNIVERSITY